For
Bessie and Hardin Doyle
Mom and Dad

Contents

Editor's Foreword

Let us now praise the necrologist. The work of film historians, film scholars, and even film buffs is fairly well known, but when was the last time anyone wrote about a film necrologist—that devoted individual who spends his life recording the birth and death dates of members of the motion picture industry. The attention of such individuals to detail is quite extraordinary— indeed, their entire task is detail-oriented. They do not deal in generalizations, but seek only the ultimate truth. When was a person born and when did they die. The dean of American film necrologists is Billy H. Doyle, who is possessed not only of encyclopedic knowledge but also is willing, and happy, to share his findings with anyone. Through the years, I have called on Billy on countless occasions for information on one obscure film personality or another, and he has never let me down. His help is evident in a number of my books, including *Great Radio Personalities, The Vaudevillians,* and *Silent Portraits.* (The scope of those volumes should make it apparent that Billy does not just concern himself with the film industry, but with all areas of popular entertainment.)

I was pleased when Billy responded with alacrity to my suggestion that he compile the ultimate silent screen actor necrology. There has long been a desperate need for definitive listings of birth and death dates for those many thousands who appeared in American silent films in one capacity or another. It might be relatively easy to find such documentation on Gloria Swanson or Blanche Sweet, but in the myriad of film encyclopedias that have been published in recent years, where does one look for such information on comedienne Teddy Sampson or character actor Charles Stevens? The answer lies in Billy H. Doyle's book.

A further problem confronting the film researcher is the matter of factual accuracy. Anyone can write down a date, but is it the correct one? With Billy H. Doyle, the answer is always yes. When he provides a date, one knows he has studied not only the obituary notices in trade papers such as *The Billboard* and *Variety*, but also he has examined social security records, birth certificates, death certificates, and other official documentation. He is an avid researcher into the birth and the death of a film personality. To paraphrase William Blake, he will not rest from mortal toil until he is certain that the data is correct. As government bureaucracies find new means to be unhelpful, Billy H. Doyle discovers new methods to thwart their efforts to prevent his gaining access to the truth. Many state agencies will only provide birth certificates to the next-of-kin, and so Billy H. Doyle has become an "honorary" relative to countless film personalities.

I can understand an individual's desire to hide a correct date of birth, but there are those in the industry who have attempted to obscure their passing. Recently there was the strange case of Vilma Banky, a silent star brought over from her native Hungary by Samuel Goldwyn. She played opposite Ronald Colman and Rudolph Valentino and enjoyed a relatively successful career in the mid to late 1920s. At her death, she instructed her lawyer not to divulge her passing. As Billy H. Doyle records here, she died on March 18, 1991. The *New York Times* published her obituary on December 12, 1992, almost two years after her death, possibly the longest period of time between a celebrity's death and a newspaper's record of it.

To complement his necrology, Billy H. Doyle has written short essays on fifty "lost players" of the silent film era, major figures in their day who are completely forgotten, and whose deaths went unnoticed. Mary Fuller was a pioneering actress with the Edison Company and the star of the first serial, *What Happened to Mary?*, in 1912. For decades film historians have been asking the same question—what *did* happen to Mary Fuller? Billy H. Doyle reveals her sad ending. Another actress from the early silent period, comedienne Fay Tincher, has been another major puzzle, solved here for the first time.

Billy H. Doyle first began working on his film necrology while still at college in the 1950s. It has been worth the wait. Recorded here are not only complete birth and death dates, but also the places where these events occurred, for more than 7,000 silent film performers. Who would have thought that there were so many actors and actresses in American silent films?

Librarians will particularly welcome this necrology. Film buffs and students may perhaps be initially drawn to the supporting essays. But everyone will thank Billy H. Doyle for his tremendous achievement.

Anthony Slide

Acknowledgments

My thanks to the following who helped to make it a reality: Q. David Bowers, Alan Brock, the late Barry Brown, Bill Cappello, the late Chauncey Carr, Nina de Raverne, Geoffrey Donaldson, the Editors of "Classic Images," the late Bob Evans, the late Tommy Fulbright, Lee Fuller, Russell Green, Luther Hathcock, John Holdstrom, Dale Forning, Ken D. Jones, Jim Lacy, the staff of the Louisville Free Public Library, Donald Lee Nelson, Barrie Roberts, Hanns-Georg Rodek, David J. Shaw, Mrs. Sheila F. Shay, Anthony Slide, William T. Stewart, the late John Thayer, Evelyn Mack Truitt, Roi Uselton, and Hans Wollstein.

My thanks to Sam Grossman and Donald Lee Nelson for the use of their photographs found in this book.

Billy H. Doyle
Valley Station, KY

The Lost Players

What became of those once well-known film actors whose fame did not survive their time? Many faded into the haze of film history, some died on the threshold of stardom and many saw their careers decline into bit and extra roles.

When one researches the silent era of film history, the periodicals of the time reveal the careers of numerous prominent actors, now forgotten, whose fame rivaled many of the well-known legendary stars. Neglected over the years these players have become "Lost Players."

I hope that these "Lost Players" essays will once again let these actors take their place in film history and will reacquaint the reader with former stars who briefly soared to stardom's heights and then quickly descended into film history's realm of anonymity.

Leah Baird

Leah Baird has become one of the early film stars whose fame lies buried in the pages of long-forgotten film magazines. A talented actress, she later became a noted scenarist whose career ended appearing in atmospheric and bit roles among stars who had never heard of her.

Leah Baird was born of German parentage in Chicago, Illinois, on June 20, 1883 and was educated at the Sacred Heart Convent. She later attended a business school and trained for secretarial work, but her interest in local stock companies afforded her the opportunity to try her hand at acting and within a short time she had made a name for herself as a "heavy" in Toronto and Buffalo stock companies. Several successful seasons followed in stock with the Morton Snow Stock Company in Troy, New York and the Arthur Byron Stock Company before her work in *The Mummy and the Humming Bird* (1907) attracted the attention of William A. Brady. Brady then cast her in a featured role opposite Douglas Fairbanks, Sr., in *The Gentleman from Mississippi* (1908-1910). Her beauty and success as a

Brady actress soon attracted the attention of film producers, who persuaded her to forsake the stage for the fledgling film industry.

In 1911, Miss Baird signed with the Vitagraph Company and made her film debut opposite Maurice Costello in *Wooing of Winifred.* As a member of Vitagraph's stock company of players, she was schooled in the company's comedies opposite their leading comedians. Between 1912-1913, in a wide variety of roles in films usually about 1000 feet in length, she appeared in *Chumps, The Adventures of the Italian Model, All for a Girl, The Black Sheep, The Dawning, Days of Terror, Adam and Eve, Lord Browning and Cinderella, The Old Silver Watch, Sue Simpkins' Ambition, The Diamond Mystery, The College Life, The Tiger Lily, Two Sets of Furs,* and *The Vampire of the Desert.*

In 1913, the actress left the Vitagraph Company and joined the Universal-IMP Company as star and leading lady. There, under the direction of Herbert Brenon, she appeared in a series of films opposite King Baggot, including the lavishly made four-reel film version of *Ivanhoe*, which was filmed at Chepstow Castle in Wales, *Absinthe*, with many scenes filmed in France, and opposite William E. Shay and Herbert Brenon in *Time Is Money,* filmed in Germany. Her other IMP films (1914) included Brenon's major fantasy production filmed in Bermuda, *Neptune's Daughter*, in support of Annette Kellermann; and *Love and a Lottery Ticket, An Old Rag Doll, Out of the Far East, The Silver Loving Cup, The Watch Dog of the Deep,* and *His Last Chance.*

Lured back to the Vitagraph Company in mid-1914, Miss Baird starred in a series of two-reel domestic dramas including *An Affair for the Police, His Wedded Wife, The Man That Might Have Been, Hearts to Let, The Return of Maurice Donnelly, Saints and Sinners, The Slightly Worn Gown, The Primal Instinct, The Bond of Blood,* and the feature *The Lights of New York* between 1914-1916, The success of her short dramas had other studios clamoring for her services and in late 1916 she appeared under the direction of Lois Weber in the Universal drama *The People vs. John Doe.* In 1917, she starred in Bluebird's *The Devil's Pay Day,* supported Ruth Roland in George Backer's *The Fringe of Society,* supported Rita Jolivet in Ivan's *One Law for Both*, and she starred with James Morrison in Ivan's *Sins of Ambition.*

The actress's career peaked between 1918-1920 with starring roles in the successful 15-episode Pathé serial *Wolves of Kultur,* Ivan's *Life or Honor?*, Graphic's *Moral Suicide* and *The Echo of Youth*, Arco's *As a Man Thinks, The Capitol,* and *The Volcano* and at her own Cliffside, New Jersey, studio she wrote and starred in *Cynthia-of-the Minute.* Between

1921-1925, Miss Baird involved herself in several facets of filmmaking (writing and producing) as well as appearing in Pathé's *The Heart Line,* Artcraft's *Don't Doubt Your Wife,* Graham's *The Bride's Confessions,* Associated Exhibitors' *When Husband's Deceive, Destroying Angel* and *Is Divorce a Failure?* and Arrow's *The Unnamed Woman.*

By 1925, Miss Baird had abandoned acting to devote her time to script writing which had begun in her early Vitagraph days (*The Dawning, The Kiss of Retribution, A Soul of Bondage,* and *The Stronger Sex*) and had continued throughout her career (*Destroying Angel* and *Is Divorce a Failure*). As a scenario writer between 1925-1933, she authored *Barriers Burned Away, The Primrose Path, The Shadow of the Law* (also coproduced), *Devil's Island, The False Alarm, Spangles, Stolen Pleasures,* and *The Return of Boston Blackie* before retiring in 1934. In 1941, she became a bit actress (*Bullets for O'Hara, Lady Gangster, Yankee Doodle Dandy, Air Force* and *My Reputation*) for Warner Bros. and for United Artists in *Around the World In 80 Days* (1956) she had one of her last roles.

The professional career of Miss Baird is well documented in early film magazines, but little was published on her private life. *Photoplay Magazine* (December 1915) reported that the actress had married the manager of a middle western film exchange, Arthur F. Beck, the producer of several of her films. When Miss Baird died after a long illness on October 3, 1971, in Los Angeles, Beck was listed as her only survivor.

Mabel Ballin

Mabel Ballin became a star under the auspices of her husband Hugo Ballin, the well-known artist, art director, scenarist, director, and producer. In the early 1920s, Mr. and Mrs. Ballin were one of several husband-and-wife filmmakers whose adaptations of the literary classics—starring Mrs. Ballin—were found outmoded and outdated by the *Jazz Singer* era of movie-going public and critics.

Born Mabel Croft in Philadelphia, Pennsylvania in 1885, Mabel Ballin, upon the death of her mother, became a ward of her grandparents at the age of two. Reared by a strict disciplinary grandmother whose life was devoted to missionary work in the city's tenements, Miss Croft made her first public appearance as a performer upon the platform of a Salvation Army hall playing the tambourine at the age of six. She was educated in the neighborhood public schools and lived in the tenements. The early life of the future actress was harsh and abounded in poverty; she was taught the skills of a seamstress by her grandmother and she later became an apprentice to a dressmaker. A wealthy customer, impressed by her dressmaking skills, became fond of the young girl and paid her tuition to a school of industrial art where she learned the art of illustrating. At the age of seventeen she became a surreptitious theatre attendant, which brought an end to her art career. Against her grandparents' wishes, Miss Croft secretly sought theatrical work. When an advertisement appeared in a New York newspaper for prospective stage aspirants, she, unbeknownst to her grandparents, left Philadelphia for a life upon the stage.

In New York City, a bit role in the musical comedy *Bankers and Brokers* opened the door to the theatrical world—where soon after the close of the play she met the young artist, Hugo Ballin. After a tour with the Frank Daniels' Company (1905-1910), appearing in *Sergeant Brue, The Tattooed Man*, and *The Hoyden*, writer Robert W. Chambers played the matchmaker and Miss Croft became Mrs. Hugo Ballin at his Connecticut home before outbreak of World War I.

The outbreak of war in Europe limited the sale of Ballin's paintings. Limited for funds, the couple turned to the film industry for a livelihood. In 1917, Ballin joined the Goldwyn Pictures Corporation as an art director and Mrs. Ballin (known throughout her career as Mabel Ballin or Mrs. Hugo Ballin) became an actress for the Vitagraph Company with her first film credits in the company's one-reel *Bobby* series in support of the popular child star Bobby Connelly. Her tenure at Vitagraph was brief and, after appearing in support of Richard Barthelmess and Winifred Allen in Triangle's World War I drama *For Valour* (1917), she joined her husband at the Goldwyn Studio (1917-1918) and appeared in supporting roles in *The Spreading Dawn, The Danger Game, The Glorious Adventure, The Service Star, The Turn of the Wheel*, and *Laughing Bill Hyde*.

In 1919, Mrs. Ballin played leading roles in World's *The Quickening Flame*, Maurice Tourneur's *The White Heather*, Goldwyn's *Lord and Lady Algy*, Haworth's *The Illustrious Prince* and in 1920, under the direction of Rex Ingram, she appeared in Universal's *Under Crimson Skies*. After the formation of the Ballin Independent Company in 1919, Mrs. Ballin became the company's star with her husband as the director, producer, scenarist, and art director.

The Ballins' first production was *Pagan Love* (1920), which the critics stated was "tediously slow moving." Undaunted by the lack of success of their first feature, in 1921 the Ballins filmed *East Lynne, Journey's End*, and *Jane Eyre*, which the critics described as "artistic." After starring in her husband's 1922 films *Other Women's Clothes* and *Married People*, the

Ballins (1923) found their company in financial trouble and returned to the fold of the Goldwyn Company where they appeared in cameo roles with the company's stars in the comedy-drama *Souls for Sale.* With Goldwyn's help, Hugo Ballin reactivated his company in 1923 and filmed Thackeray's novel *Vanity Fair*, which a *Photoplay* reviewer stated was "easily Hugo Ballin's most-workmanlike effort," but Mrs. Ballin's role of "Becky" did not find favor with the public and doomed the film at the box office and the Ballins' film company.

Absent from the screen in 1924, Mrs. Ballin starred in Encore's *Barriers Burned Away* (1925) before returning to supporting roles in Westerns (*Beauty and the Bad Man, Code of the West* and *Riders of the Purple Sage*). In 1925, Mrs. Ballin was again directed by her husband in the Madeline Brandeis production of *The Shining Adventure.* When the film failed to revive their careers she retired from the screen and after serving as art director on Gloria Swanson's *The Love of Sunya* he retired from active film work.

After years of anonymity *Variety* reported Hugo Ballin's death on November 27, 1956—Mrs. Ballin was listed as his survivor. When she died in Santa Monica on July 24, 1958, there was only a brief death announcement in the trade papers for the once prominent actress.

Nigel Barrie

The tall handsome muscular British import Nigel Barrie epitomized the leading man of the late teens and early twenties. Eagerly sought after by the major film femme stars, his popularity was an added asset to the success of the star's film as his potential star power filled the theatres throughout the 1920's with adoring fans.

Born with the very British name of Roynon Cholmondeley Nigel-Jones, the son of W. C. Nigel-Jones, in Calcutta, India on February 5, 1889, Nigel Barrie received his education at Haileybury College in England with additional college work completed in Heidelberg, Germany. Educated no doubt for a diplomatic career he found the theatre more to his liking and began his stage career as a juvenile in the companies of Sir Frank Benson, Sir Herbert Beerbohm Tree, and Fred Terry. He appeared in the chorus and understudied the lead in the musical comedy *The Count of Luxemberg* before he came to the United States with Grace George in *Half and Half.* After stage engagements in *Gypsy Love* and *The Laughing Husband* and a vaudeville tour with Joan Sawyer as a professional dancer, he exited the stage for the screen.

When film serials became the popular rage, Barrie accepted a guest appearance role in the Wharton Brothers 15-episode serial *Beatrice Fairfax* (1916). His work in the serial resulted in the Famous Players Company signing him as Marguerite Clark's leading man in the *Babs* series (*Bab's Diary* and *Bab's Matinee Idol).* Following his work in the Bab's series he was signed by Clara Kimball Young as the leading man in her company's production of *The Marionettes* (1918); upon the completion of the film he joined and served with the 78th squadron of the RAF in Canada in World War I.

When the war ended, Barrie resumed his film work and again appeared opposite Clara Kimball Young in her company's production of *The Better Wife* (1919), a British drawing room drama. In the years 1919-1920, he was without a doubt the busiest of the British leading men, appearing opposite Marion Davies in Cosmopolitan's *The Cinema Murder,* Alma Rubens in Robertson-Cole's *Diane of the Green Van,* Bessie Barriscale in B. B. Features' *Josselyn's Wife* and *Tangled Threads,* Marguerite Clark in Famous Players' *Widow by Proxy,* Blanche Sweet in Hampton's *The Girl in the Web,* Katherine MacDonald in her company's productions of *The Notorious Miss Lisle* and *The Turning Point,* Pauline Frederick in Roberston-Cole's *A Slave of Vanity,* and Margarita Fischer in Hampton's *Their Mutual Child.* Few actors could compete with Barrie's success at this time as he was at the peak of his career and was one of the screen's most enduring leading men.

In 1921, to help stave off the decline of Clara Kimball Young's flagging career, Barrie again appeared opposite her in Equity's *Charge It,* but the film did little to revitalize Miss Young's career and as her popularity declined her leading man's successes mounted. Throughout the 1920s (1921-1927), Barrie appeared in numerous films (*The Little Minister, Peg o' My Heart, Hogan's Alley, The Bolted Door, The Desert Sheik, The Amateur Gentleman, The Love Thief,* and *The Climbers*). Returning frequently throughout his career to England for film roles when his Hollywood career declined, Barrie returned to England in 1927 and for the next decade appeared in British films before ending his career around 1937.

Married twice, first to Helen Lee (1919-1925), Barrie's second marriage to Gertrude Pocklington apparently ended with his death. When the actor retired, he quickly faded from the film scene and was rarely mentioned by film historians. What had become of the former matinee idol?

A British film researcher made a search for the actor and was unable to uncover anything. He did find in a film directory biography that he had attended Haileybury College, the same college as the researcher. In the Haileybury Registry, he found what he had sought: "Roynon Cholmondeley Nigel-Jones (name changed to Nigel Barrie) born 5 February 1889; died 8 October 1971."

Vedah Bertram

When Vedah Bertram, a film starlet being groomed as "Broncho Billy" Anderson's leading lady, died unexpectedly she became the first noted film player to be mourned by the movie-going public. When her death was reported in the trade papers and film magazines, the public for the first time suffered the loss of someone created on film, the first of many that would follow in the years to come.

A wide gap separated staid old scholarly aristocratic Boston from the early film studios of Los Angeles, but Miss Bertram bridged the gap when she joined "Broncho Billy" Anderson at the Western Essanay Company in Lakeside, California. There she became the actor's first leading lady in his popular outdoor western melodramas that pulled patrons into those early store-front theatres.

The daughter of newspaperman, Jerome Buck, Vedah Bertram was born Adele Buck in Boston, Massachusetts on December 4, 1891. Educated in the proper Bostonian manner she attended boarding schools and later Wellesley College. As a young socialite she was never on the stage, not even vaguely interested in drama in her college days. But "Broncho Billy" Anderson, in search of an actress for his westerns, saw a photograph of the young social leader in the newspaper and offered her a film contract. Against her parents wishes she accepted his offer and to protect the family name she took the pseudonym of Vedah Bertram.

Entering films in 1911 Miss Bertram adapted easily to the rugged western life of the Anderson one-reelers, whose titles told the story (*Broncho Billy and the Indian Maid, The Road Agent's Love, A Moonshiner's Heart, The Bandit's Child, The Ranch Girl's Mistake, The Deputy's Love Affair, Broncho Billy's Last Holdup, The Foreman's Cousin*, and *Broncho Billy's Narrow Escape*).

So successful had Miss Bertram become as Anderson's leading lady that fans eagerly wanted to know more about her. Articles on the aspiring actress began appearing in film magazines extolling her beauty and her bright future. Success seemed assured when suddenly stricken with stomach pains the actress was admitted to an Oakland, California hospital. She left word that her father and her brother were to be notified if she died but not otherwise. After undergoing surgery for appendicitis the actress died on August 26, 1912. Her death did not go unnoticed by the news media. Her obituary appeared in the major trade journals and film magazines.

Francelia Billington

Versatility was the primary requisite for the early screen heroine. An actress' skills in horseback riding, swimming, rowing, diving and driving an automobile often took precedent over her dramatic skills. The early film actress Francelia Billington, an expert in these skills, learned how to ride a horse in Texas, how to swim, row, and dive in New Orleans, and how to drive an automobile in Los Angeles. Her expertise as an outdoor heroine made her one of the most sought-after leading ladies for the masculine heroes in the first decade of filmmaking.

Born the daughter of musician Adelaide Bueter and James Billington in Dallas, Texas, on February 1, 1895, Miss Billington was educated at the Sacred Heart Convent after the family settled in Los Angeles in 1905. Growing up in Los Angeles and under her mother's tutelage she developed an excellent soprano voice which helped to enhance the plays that the convent presented.

Miss Billington, without any formal stage training, made her film debut under the direction of George Melford for the Kalem Company (1912) when the director needed a leading lady to replace Alice Joyce who had been transferred to the company's New York studio. As Carlyle Blackwell's leading lady in *The Mayor's Crusade* and *The Usurer*, she spent only six months with Kalem before she became a member of the West Coast Company of Thanhouser where she appeared in minor roles (*Carmen* and *The Widow's Stratagem*). Her minor role in *Carmen* won her an excellent review by Louis R. Harrison in *The Moving Picture World*, who stated that Miss Billington acted superbly if even for just an instant on the screen.

Harrison's comment caught the attention of film executive Charles J. Hite who signed Miss Billington to a Reliance-Majestic Company contract in April 1913. Over the next two years (1913-1914) she was starred by the company in a series of short dramas and comedies (*The Banker's Son, Dora, The Fraternity Pin, Hearts and Hoofs, The Message of the*

Flowers, The Blotted Page, and *Broken Nose Bailey*) before the company cast her in feature films in 1915 with leading roles in *A Child of God* and *Strathmore.* In 1916, the actress joined the Universal Company where under the brand names of Red Feather, Bluebird, and Gold Seal, she successfully appeared in a wide variety of roles, including *Bettina Loved a Soldier, The Black Sheep of the Family, The Evil Women Do, The Mainspring, The Naked Hearts,* and *The Right to Be Happy.* Her Universal successes resulted in William Russell's signing Miss Billington as his leading lady in the action-packed, comedy-dramas *The Frame Up, High Play, The Masked Heart, The Fighting Gentleman, New York Luck, Pride and the Man, Sands of Sacrifice, The Sea Master, In Bad, The Shackles of Truth, Snap Judgement,* and *The Midnight Trail,* a series of films that Russell made for the American Film Company.

In 1919, at the height of her popularity, Erich von Stroheim cast Miss Billington in her most memorable role, Mrs. Armstrong, in *Blind Husbands,* which won the actress accolades from the film critics. Not destined for the great dramatic roles, the actress returned to the popular action-packed melodramas as the leading lady of the ill-fated daredevil stunt pilot Omer Locklear in *The Great Air Mystery* before returning to the Western film genre for the remainder of her career. In 1920, as Tom Mix's leading lady, she appeared in Fox's *Desert Love* and *The Terror* with Lester Cuneo as the villain. The heroic Mix won the actress's hand in marriage on film but it was the villainous Cuneo who in real life married the actress in 1920. Throughout the early 1920s, Miss Billington appeared as the heroine opposite the villainous Cuneo in *The Ranger and the Law, Blazing Arrows,* and *Blue Blazes.* The husband-wife costarring team and marriage ended tragically in 1925 when the actress divorced Cuneo and he killed himself two days after the divorce became final. Thereafter Miss Billington's career steadily declined and after roles in *Tex* (1926), *A Rough Shod Fighter* (1927), and a supporting role in Hoot Gibson's *The Mounted Stranger,* she ended her film career.

Suffering from tuberculosis Miss Billington died on November 24, 1934, in Glendale, California. A brief obituary, appeared in the Glendale paper but there were no obituaries in the trade papers. The actress' death went unnoticed by the film industry and the public.

Lily Branscombe

The fame of Lily Branscombe lies in those long ago pioneer days when, for the Essanay Company, she starred opposite Francis X. Bushman, Bryant Washburn, and John Steppling in those ancient one- and two-reelers that the early companies ground out to satisfy the public's demand. Her career was brief (1911-1912); she apparently preferred the stage to the screen as shown by the brevity of her career.

Lily was born the daughter of Arthur Rodman (mother's name unknown) somewhere in New Zealand on February 28, 1876. After receiving her education in New South Wales, Miss Branscombe began her stage career in 1894 playing the role of "Little Eva." While playing in Australian stock she met and married actor Herbert Ashton in New Zealand. When the couple came to the United States is unknown but they were residing in San Francisco when their son, Herbert Ashton, Jr., was born in 1902 (he later became an actor, director, and author).

When the petite, dark-haired actress joined the Essanay Company of Chicago in 1911, Francis X. Bushman and Bryant Washburn were the reigning male stars and, as Bushman's leading lady, she appeared in *Her Hour of Triumph, The Melody of Love,* and *Out of the Depths* and with Washburn in *The Letter.* Equally adapted to comedy, Miss Branscombe was teamed with John Steppling in *Pals, Billy Changes His Mind, Bringing Father Around, Down Jayville, In Quarantine, A Little Louder, Miss Simkin's Boarder, A Mistaken Calling,* and *Mr. Tibb's Cinderella.*

The company's stable of players (in 1912) included E. H. Calvert, Frank Dayton, Eleanor Blanchard, Billy Mason, Dolores Cassinelli, Beverly Bayne, Gertrude Scott, and Whitney Raymond. Miss Branscombe starred opposite them in a wide variety of comedic and emotional roles (*Well Matched, Alkali Ike in Jayville, The Warning Hand, The Clue, Three to Once, Back to the Old Farm, The Snare, Her Adopted Father, The Scheme, The Road to Transgression, The Moving Finger, Mr. Up's Trip Tripped Us, Mr. Hubby's Wife, The Love Test, The Listener's Lesson, Legacy of Happiness,* and *Alias Billy Sargent*) before abruptly ending her film career.

The actress left the silent drama and returned to the stage with her husband where she combined her stage career with motherhood. After leaving the screen Miss Branscombe never tried for any film comebacks. With the passing of years her name faded into those early pioneer days of filmmaking and when Ashton died in New York City on January 31, 1930, his surviving wife was listed as Lily Granstone. The actress made her home in San Francisco to be near her son and it was there she died on September 26, 1970 from a heart attack brought on by pneumonia.

Pauline Bush

"She is daintier than you would think from her pictures—a woman of extreme refinement and unusually high ideals. She is unduly modest when it comes to talking about herself, anyone who has the impression that she is egotistical is very much mistaken," was how a *Motion Picture Magazine* writer described Pauline Bush in a 1916 interview. Miss Bush developed and excelled at creating just such an image in her film roles in the early days when she appeared as a leading lady and star in numerous one- and two-reelers.

Pauline Elvira Bush, the daughter of Charlotte Garfield and Russell Bush, was born in Wahoo, a suburb of Lincoln, Nebraska on May 22, 1886. Educated in a private school in Virginia, she later attended the University of Nebraska before going to Los Angeles for her health, where she studied for a stage career at the Cumnock School.

Miss Bush's first stage engagement was in support of Julia Sanderson in *Kitty Gray* (1907). After a successful season in musical comedy, she toured in stock before she journeyed west and joined the Liberty Stock Company in Oakland, California. While appearing at the Liberty Theatre in 1911 she was offered and accepted a film contract with the American Film Company in Los Angeles. At the American Company she met Allan Dwan who directed her films and whom she married in 1915.

In the days when the short film reigned supreme, Miss Bush and Dwan were among the elite of the film world, filming numerous Western and outdoor comedy-dramas. Under Dwan's direction, Miss Bush became J. Warren Kerrigan's leading lady between 1911-1912 in American's *Cattle Gold and Oil, The Poisoned Flume, The Sheriff's Sisters, The Coward, Driftwood, The Haters, The Land of Death, The Outlaw Colony,* and *The Thread of Life,* only a few of the many short films Miss Bush, Kerrigan, and Dwan filmed.

In 1913, Miss Bush followed Dwan to the Universal Company, where she became an actress who not only excelled in Westerns but in a wide range of roles from comedy to drama. At Universal between 1913-1915, she appeared successfully for the company's subsidiary branches under the brand names of Rex (*The Harvest of Flame, Her Bounty, Jewels of*

Sacrifice, Lights and Shadows, A Mountain Melody, Outside the Gates, and *A Small Town Girl),* Bison *(The Forbidden Room, The Gratitude of Wanda, The Higher Law,* and *In Love and War*), Gold Seal (*Bloodhounds of the North, Honor of the Mounted* and *The Lie*), Powers (*Mental Suicide*) and Victor (*Back to Life, Remember Mary Magdalen* and *The Restless Spirit*). In 1914, Dwan directed Miss Bush in *Richelieu,* her only feature film (4 reels) prior to the 1920s, a historical drama of Seventeenth-century France with Murdock MacQuarrie in the role of Cardinal Richelieu. In these early days of the two-reelers Miss Bush appeared opposite two legendary stars who began their careers under Dwan's direction. With Lon Chaney she appeared in *Discord and Harmony, Her Life's Story, Honor of the Mounted,* and *Idyl of the Hills*, and with Wallace Reid in *The Animal, In Love and War, Man's Duty, The Picket Guard, The Wall of Money*, and *Women and War.*

By 1916, Miss Bush had retired and was content to leave the filmmaking to her husband, who went on and became one of the screen's leading directors. When the actress' marriage to the director ended in divorce around 1919, the one- and two-reeler days that had made Miss Bush a star were now in film history's distant past; when she tried for a film comeback in 1924 in support of Betty Compson in *The Enemy Sex,* she found the film world so changed that she never again made any comeback attempts. When she died of pneumonia on November 1, 1969, in San Diego, California under the name of Pauline E. Dwan, she had for been out of the limelight for so long that no obituaries appeared for the once-famous actress in any of the trade papers.

June Caprice

When William Fox announced in 1916 that "within six months June Caprice would be the best known woman on the screen," he believed that he had found his Mary Pickford heroine. In the pre-World War I era, the film producers were eagerly searching for a Pickford heroine whose qualifications included youth, beauty, and innocence. Marguerite Clark and Mary Miles Minter were successful prototypes of the role, as were June Caprice, Gladys Leslie, and Marguerite Courtot, but the careers of the second-string Pickfords were usually short, as the fairy-tale ingenue role did not provide longevity for an actress once the look of innocence faded. The meteoric rise to stardom for these stars quickly set, as did the role they portrayed—for the flapper of the 1920s was waiting in the wings and would forever bring to an end the screen's age of innocence.

June Caprice was born Betty Lawson on November 19, 1899, in Arlington, Massachusetts. Educated in Boston, she began her film career when she won a Mary Pickford look-alike contest held by a Boston theatre. Abandoning her education, she went to New York City, and it was there in the summer of 1916 that she was discovered by William Fox, who immediately publicized her as Fox's Mary Pickford. Making her film debut in *Caprice of the Mountains* (1916), she was one of the first stars to take her screen name from the role she played (Caprice) with June coming from the sixth month.

The film made her a Fox star with the critic of the *New York Times* writing of her debut, "The new Fox star is young, pretty, graceful, petite, with eloquence of gesture augurs a bright future in the movies." Under the direction of John Adolfi and other directors her film titles usually synopsized her role in the film. At Fox under Adolfi's direction, she starred in 1916-1917 in *Little Miss Happiness, The Mischief Maker, The Ragged Princess, A Child of the Wild, A Modern Cinderella, Patsy,* and *The Smalltown Girl.*

Fox's prophetic statement of making Miss Caprice the best-known woman on the screen proved he knew what be was talking about. Quickly the film magazines began publishing numerous articles on her, her portraits abounded on the cover and in the magazines, and her fans eagerly sought information from the "Answer Man" about the star. In 1917, when Fox assigned Harry Millarde as the director of her films, a romance developed between the star and director which later culminated in marriage. Under Millarde's direction, her star shone brightly in Fox's 1917-1918 productions of *The Sunshine Maid, Unknown 274, Blue Eyed Mary, A Camouflage Kiss, Every Girl's Dream, The Heart of Romance, Miss U.S.A.,* and *Miss Innocence.* By 1919 the actress had outgrown her fairy tale heroine roles and she left Fox and joined Albert Capellani's company where in more mature roles she appeared in the P. G. Wodehouse *Saturday Evening Post* story *A Damsel In Distress,* the society comedy-drama *The Love Cheat,* the film version of the musical comedy *Oh Boy!* and the drama *In Walked Mary.* In 1920, she left Capellani's company to star with George B. Seitz in his first feature film, *Rogues and Romance.* Seitz also produced, directed, and wrote the scenario. After playing the female lead opposite Seitz in his 1921 fifteen-episode serial *The Sky Ranger*, Miss Caprice ended her film career.

Happily married, the former actress found marriage, motherhood, and the role of one of Hollywood's society leaders more rewarding than stardom on the screen. Her marriage to Millarde ended with his death in New York City on November 2, 1931. Miss Caprice's death came five years later on November 9, 1936, in Los Angeles following a lingering illness. She was survived by her daughter, June Elizabeth Millarde.

Dolores Cassinelli

The *Motion Picture Classic* (April-May 1920) described its cover portrait of Dolores Cassinelli as

> An appropriate Easter cover girl is Dolores Cassinelli, who comes from Italy, the land of sunshine and flowers. Although she was born in Italy, Miss Cassinelli was brought to this country at an early age and she is really a typical American girl.
>
> A singer of no mean ability and an accomplished musician, Miss Cassinelli is a screen star of unusual attainments. She has been popular in films since the days of Essanay.

The quote, typical of film magazine prose at that time, teased the reader by printing meaningless biographical information. Apparently Dolores Cassinelli kept her private life from the public, because there is scarcely any information on the actress' life outside of the film studio.

Elvere Dolores Cassinelli (who appeared in early films as E. Dolores Cassinelli but dropped the "E" after leaving Essanay) was born in Italy (as reported in film magazines), in New York City (as reported in the film directories), and in Chicago, Illinois (as stated on her death certificate) on July 4, 1893, with her parents' names unknown. *Who's Who 1920* printed that she was born in New York City, early in life moved to Chicago with her parents, and was educated at the Holy Name Convent, where it was assumed that she would become a nun. Her interest in drama resulted in the mother superior's suggesting that she be allowed to pursue an acting career.

Reported to have been an accomplished singer and musician there is nothing in the film magazines or film biographies of a stage career for Miss Cassinelli. What with the close proximity of the Essanay film studio the aspiring actress probably began her professional career there when she joined the company in 1911. The actress' earliest film credit is a one-reel comedy *Bill Bumper's Bargain* opposite Francis X. Bushman. As one of the company's contract players between 1912-1913, she appeared in a wide variety of roles in numerous one-reelers such as *Billy the Butler, Do Dreams Come True, From the Submerged, The Laurel Wreath of Fame, The Price of Gold, The Tale of a Cat, The Broken Heart, Cinderella's Gloves, Mr. Dippy Dipped, A Successful Failure,* and *A Wolf Among Lambs.*

After the termination of her Essanay contract, Miss Cassinelli joined the Emerald Company and appeared in *The Voice of Freedom* (1915) and the *Tom and Jerry* series (1915-1916) before stardom came in independent productions. In 1918, opposite George Larkin, she starred in the Bernarr Macfadden Culture Photoplay *Zongar*, but it was for the Leonce Perret Production Company that she became known as the screen's popular "Cameo Girl," with starring roles in *The Million Dollar Dollies* (1918), *Lafayette, We Come!* (1918), *Stars and Glory* (1919), *The Unknown Love* (1919), and *Tarnished Reputation* (1920). For producer Albert Capellani in 1919 she starred in the dramas *The Right to Life, Virtuous Model*, and for Edwin Carewe in *The Web of Deceit* (1920). One of Miss Cassinelli's last starring roles was in *The Hidden Light* (1921), a Schomer-Ross production. Had Miss Cassinelli been affiliated with a major film studio rather than independent studios she might have become one of the legendary silent film stars.

When the independent producers no longer offered Miss Cassinelli starring roles, the actress' decline began. She was only offered supporting roles in *Forever* (1921), *Anne of Little Smoky* (1921), *The Secrets of Paris* (1922), *The Challenge* (1923), *Jamestown* (1923), *Dangerous Money* (1924), and *The Unguarded Hour* (1925). Retirement came in the mid-1920s when the actress no longer saw a future in pursuing a film career. Never married, Miss Cassinelli made her home in one of New York City's theatrical hotels until age forced her into a nursing home in New Brunswick, New Jersey, where she remained until her death on April 26, 1984. There were no obituaries for the "Cameo Girl of the Movies."

Marjorie Daw

The nursery rhyme name of Marjorie Daw labeled her, but the name and her ingenuish beauty made her one of the most sought-after leading ladies of Hollywood's legendary actors. The actress' meteoric fame catapulted her to the pinnacle of Hollywood society; she served as Mary Pickford's maid of honor when she married Douglas Fairbanks, Sr., and she married the son of a prominent film mogul, but when the marriage failed, she ended her film career and faded into obscurity.

Margaret House, the daughter of Ella Chandler and John House, was born in Colorado Springs, Colorado on January 19, 1902. An early film biography related that Miss House found herself without a father or mother and with a newly born brother, Chandler, upon her hands when but a teenager. When most girls were going to high school she was compelled to seek employment. What brought the sister and brother to Los Angeles is unknown but as youngsters growing up in Los Angeles they became bit players for the Universal Company (her brother Chandler House later appeared in child roles in several well-known films).

The bit roles led to Miss House joining the Lasky Company in 1915 where, in a series of small roles, she appeared as Marguerite House before changing her name to Marjorie Daw. Early fan magazines credited Geraldine Farrar as her discoverer when she was given a small part in *Joan the Woman* (1916). This film provided the young actress with some much needed publicity. Miss Daw in an interview in the British film magazine *Picturegoer* (1924) said that her first big part was in Cecil B. DeMille's *The Warrens of Virginia* (1915) as Blanche Sweet's younger sister "Betty Warren" but previously she had appeared in Lasky's *The Chorus Lady, Out of the Darkness, The Puppet Crown, Secret Orchard, The Unafraid,* and *The House of the Golden Windows* before *Joan the Woman.*

The wholesomeness previously exemplified by Miss Daw's roles in 1917 led to ingenue parts in Lasky's *Jaguar's Claw* and the role of "Emma Jane Perkins" in Mary Pickford's *Rebecca of Sunnybrook Farm.* Probably her association with Mary Pickford led to Miss Daw being signed by Douglas Fairbanks, Sr., as his leading lady in *A Modern Musketeer* (1917). Fairbanks, seeking a leading lady, found her in Marjorie Daw, as she appeared in more Fairbanks films than any other actress (*Arizona, He Comes Up Smiling, Bound in Morocco, Mr. Fix-It,* and *Say! Young Fellow*).

In 1920, one of the screen's most sought-after leading ladies, she appeared in the Maurice Tourneur production of *The Great Redeemer* opposite House Peters, and under Marshall Neilan's direction appeared successfully in *Don't Ever Marry, The River's End,* and *Dinty.* Throughout the 1920s (1921-1927) for the major film companies she appeared in Paramount's *Experience, The Pride of Palomar* and *The Call of the Canyon,* First National's *Bob Hampton of Placer, Penrod, The Dangerous Maid,* and *Wandering Daughters,* Selznick's *Love Is an Awful Thing* and *Rupert of Hentzau,* Fox's *Patsy, A Fool There Was, East Lynne,* and *Outlaws of Red River,* FBO's *Mary of the Movies,* Universal's *Cheated*

Hearts, Arrow's *In Borrowed Plumes*, Metro-Goldwyn-Mayer's *Spoilers of the West*, and United Artist's *Topsy and Eva*. Always the leading lady and never the star the actress did not pursue her career with the coming of sound.

After a brief marriage to director Albert Edward Sutherland ended in divorce in 1925, she married Myron Selznick, the son of Lewis J. Selznick and brother to David O. Selznick, in 1925. A daughter, Joan, was born to the union. The marriage, a stormy one, ended in the divorce in 1942 and she later married a man by the name of Myers. After her divorce from Selznick, she disappeared from Hollywood and from her daughter's life. When Miss Daw died in Huntington Beach, California, on March 18, 1979, an investigator, hired by daughter Joan, was trying to locate her. Joan had not seen her mother in twenty years. When death came to the former actress, there were no obituaries for her in any of the trade journals. Perhaps she wanted it that way.

S. Rankin Drew

Sidney Rankin Drew, a youthful film actor and director who went to war and never came back, was a member of the Drew-Rankin-Barrymore theatrical families. His father was the son of Louisa Lane Drew (grandmother of Ethel, Lionel, and John Barrymore), his mother a prominent stage actress and playwright, his grandfather the noted actor and stage manager McKee Rankin, and his uncle the stage great John Drew. In his distinguished relatives footsteps the young actor was carrying on the family tradition of making a name for himself, not in the theater but the film industry, when World War I abruptly ended his career and his life.

A native of New York City, S. Rankin Drew was born in 1892, the son of actress-playwright Gladys Rankin (who used Georgie Cameron as her pen name) and stage comedian Sidney Drew. The family's theatrical background resulted in his making his stage debut at an early age in the Culter School's production of *The Private Secretary*, but much of his stage training came by touring the vaudeville circuits extensively throughout the States and Canada with his father. His first legitimate stage appearance was in the Shubert farce *Billie* written by his mother, and he later toured in vaudeville in his mother's one-act sketch *The Still Voice*.

Tired of the constant traveling a stage career necessitated, the young actor was encouraged by his cousin Lionel Barrymore to join the infant film industry. In 1913, when his father joined the Vitagraph Company, he, too, joined . To avoid name confusion, he was known as S. Rankin Drew. Vitagraph immediately put the young actor to work in numerous short dramas: *His Tired Uncle, The Penalties of Reputation, The Glove, An Infernal Tangle, An Unwritten Chapter, The Snare of Fate,* supporting his father in *The Still Voice, A Game of Cards, The Idler, Marrying Sue, The Tattoo Mark,* and *Maria's Sacrifice.* His first feature film was in support of Maurice Costello in *Mr. Barnes of New York* (1914). In 1915, recognized by the company as an actor with star potential, he supported Norma Talmadge in *Janet of the Chorus,* Edith Storey in *O'Garry of the Royal Mounted* and *The Island of Regeneration,* James Morrison in *The Third Party,* Antonio Moreno in *The Quality of Mercy* and not only costarred but directed Virginia Pearson in *Thou Art the Man.* Drew's talent as a director equaled his acting talent and Vitagraph kept the company's youngest director busy in 1916 directing and starring with Virginia Pearson in *The Vital Question* and *The Hunted Women,* starring in *Who Killed Joe Merrion?,* and directing Charles Kent in *Kennedy Square,* but it was his work with Anita Stewart as writer, director and actor that made him a star. He directed and starred with Miss Stewart in *The Daring of Diana* and *The Suspect* (he also wrote the scenario). In 1916, when the company turned over to him the directorship of their yearly prestigious production of Robert W. Chamber's novel *The Girl Philippa* with Drew as director and Miss Stewart as costar, he did not disappoint the Vitagraph executives. When the film was released in January 1917, it broke all previous records for box-office receipts in a single day when it took in $3,471 at the Rialto Theatre in New York, and the film continued its box-office success throughout the country. Critics commented on the film's unusual effect with the use of two projectors simultaneously, projecting both a proclamation of war and scenes of mobilization, to create an effect similar to that of double exposure.

In 1916, for the Master Drama Features, Inc., Drew wrote and directed Christine Mayo in the controversial Willard Mack story *Who's Your Neighbor?,* a film trimmed from seven to five reels in order to obtain the acceptance of the National Board of Review before its release in 1918. Also, in late 1916, the director made his last film, *The Belle of the Season,* for the Metro Pictures Corporation (rereleased in 1919).

By the time Drew completed *The Belle of the Season,* the United States had joined the European conflict. Eager to join up, the young director and actor became one of the first film stars to enter military service. To get to Europe, Drew joined the American Ambulance Corps as a driver, but once abroad, he became a pilot with the Lafayette Esquadrille. In the skies over

France on May 19, 1918, he encountered the enemy and his plane was shot down, killing the young pilot. His death shocked the stage and film world and the tragedy hastened the death of his father in 1919. After the war ended, his stepmother, Lucille McVey, visited France, where she found the grave of her stepson with the words "Sidney Rankin Drew, Hero" engraved on a cross.

Bessie Eyton

The early photographs of Bessie Eyton reveal an extraordinarily beautiful young woman whose face in another time could have been found on a da Vinci canvas. One of the screen's pioneers, her beauty brought the fans into the theatres but it was the stunts she performed in the melodramas that kept the viewers in their seats. Under contract to the Selig Company's Los Angeles branch from 1910 until the company's demise in 1918, she was one of its busiest and most popular players.

Miss Eyton was born Bessie Harrison, the daughter of Clarabell and Edgar Harrison, in Santa Barbara, California, on July 5, 1890. Her early years are shrouded in anonymity and fail to reveal much about her early life. She was educated in the Santa Barbara schools and at the age of fifteen married theatre manager and later prominent film executive Charles Eyton whom she probably met through her musician father. When the marriage ended in divorce in 1915 the actress continued using Eyton as her professional name and writers referred to her as Miss rather than Mrs. Eyton.

Who's Who in the Film World 1914 stated that, unlike many other photoplayers who made their mark in the silent drama, Miss Eyton had no experience on the legitimate stage. Within a short time after joining Selig her talent and devotion to her work made her one of the company's most sought-after young ingenues. Teamed with the company's leading actors Hobart Bosworth, Thomas Santschi, and Wheeler Oakman in numerous melodramas (usually anywhere from 696 feet to 2000 feet in length), she appeared (1911-1913) in *Carmen of the Isles, The Coming of Columbus, The Last of Her Tribe, Monte Cristo, An Old Actor, The Story of Lavania,* (in this film she performed the stunt of falling backward from a second-story window of a burning house without suffering any injuries, a daring stunt for that time), *Terrors of the Jungle, A Western Romance,* and *A Wild Ride*. However it was the success of the classic nine-reel film version of the Rex Beach novel *The Spoilers* (1914) and *In the Days of the Thundering Herd* (1914) that made her one of Selig's most popular leading ladies. Throughout 1914-1915, the two- and three-reelers continued (*The Abyss, The Fire Juggler, Playing with Fire, The Fork in the Road, The Primitive Way,* and *A Studio Escapade*), as did leading roles (1916-1917) opposite Tom Mix in *Twisted Trails* and *The Heart of Texas Ryan;* but it was the role of "Virginia Carvel" in the twelve-reel version of the Winston Churchill novel *The Crisis* (1916) that won her plaudits from the critics as an emotional actress. At the peak of her success as a leading lady she appeared (1916-1917) in *The Cycle of Life, The Prince Chap, Beware of the Strangers* and *Little Lost Sister.* With Selig to the very end, Miss Eyton appeared in leading roles in *The Still Alarm, Who Shall Take My Life?* and *The City of Purple Dreams* before the company ceased operation in 1918.

After her Selig days, Miss Eyton was never again to enjoy the popularity she had once known. After appearing opposite Harold Lockwood in *Lend Me Your Name* (1918), the former leading roles became supporting roles in *Way of a Man with a Maid* (1918), *Children of Banishment* (1919), *The Usurper* (1919), *Cheap Kisses* (1924), and *The Girl of Gold* (1925).

With the decline of her film career, Miss Eyton's marriage to Clarke Brewer Coffey ended in divorce on July 3, 1923 (Miss Eyton had married Coffey in Santa Barbara, California on September 29, 1916) and soon after she retired from films. She later returned in the late twenties as a bit player and extra until 1935. After 1935, the actress's life became a tragic scenario reminiscent of one of her early melodramas with the last reel lost somewhere in the passing years. From an interview with Miss Eyton's half-brother's former wife, the tragic and mysterious events of the actress' life can now be written. After a horrendous argument with her mother, Miss Eyton walked out of the home and was never seen or heard from again. Her family spent years searching for her, without success. What happened to Bessie Eyton after she walked out of the house? Did she change her identity? Did she leave California? Or was she one of those nameless streetpersons found dead with her identity unknown?

Margarita Fischer

The scenario for the film career of Margarita Fischer lacks the glamour that surrounded many early film players. In the pre-World War I period she was one of the screen's most popular and revered stars, having appeared in a wide range of comedic and tragic roles. Miss Fischer's career prospered and spanned the silent film era primarily under the direction of her husband, Harry A. Pollard. For an actress whose name once emblazoned the movie marquees, she, today, has been forgotten by historians.

The daughter of Katherine Hagney and John Ficher (the "s" was later added to the name), Margarita Fischer was born on February 12, 1886, in Missouri Valley, Iowa. Her parents were traveling actors and Miss Fischer made her stage debut at the age of eight in her father's company. Known on the stage as "Babe Fischer" she trouped in stock (at the age of twelve she starred in her own Pacific Coast company), repertoire, grand opera, and vaudeville. By 1910, she was a well-known vaudeville actress and appeared at the American Music Hall in Chicago as a headliner in the Joseph M. Patterson sketch *By Products.*

As with many of her contemporaries, Miss Fischer was induced to desert the stage when the offer of a film contract promised more than the continuous hardships encountered on the road. She made her film debut for the Selig Polyscope Company in Chicago (1910) but her tenure there was brief. In 1911, she joined the IMP Company and appeared as King Baggot's leading lady in *The Girl and the Half-Back, A Lesson to Husbands, Over the Hills,* and *The Trinity.* Moving on to the Bison Company (1912- 1913), she costarred opposite Robert Z. Leonard in *The Old Folks' Christmas* and *Robinson Crusoe* and Wallace Reid in *The Tribal Law,* as well as other one- and two-reelers made by the studio.

In 1912, before IMP merged with the Universal Company, Miss Fischer appeared in a series of short films (about 1000 feet in length) with Harry A. Pollard as her leading man. The reel screen romance of the stars became a real romance off the screen and culminated in marriage (at the time of Pollard's death, a source said they had been married for seventeen years, but it could have been longer). After their marriage, Pollard took control of his wife's career and she appeared with him or was directed almost exclusively by him until 1918.

With Pollard as her leading man, Miss Fischer appeared (1912) in numerous one- and two-reelers (*Better Than Gold, Big Hearted Slim, The Call of the Drums, The Dove and the Serpent, The Exchange of Labels, Melodrama of Yesterday,* and *The Worth of Man*) for the IMP Company, before appearing with her husband under the direction of Otis Turner in the company's 1913 film version of *Uncle Tom's Cabin* (a film version they, too, would film later). For the Rex Company (1913) she costarred with Robert Z. Leonard in a series of short films (*The Boob's Dream Girl,*

In Slavery Days, Like Darby and Joan, The Stolen Idol, The Turn of the Tide, and *The Wayward Sister*) that promoted her status as a leading lady.

Miss Fischer and Pollard joined the American Film Company (1914) and under the company's Beauty brand name she starred and he wrote, directed, and appeared in numerous two-reelers (*Bess the Outcast, Closed at Ten, A Flurry of Hats, The Man Who Came Back, Modern Othello, Sally's Elopement, Sweet Land of Liberty,* and *The Tale of a Tailor*). With the decline of the short film, Miss Fischer moved into the feature film (1915) and under Pollard's direction appeared in American's *The Girl from His Town, Infatuation, The Miracle of Life, Nancy's Husband,* and *The Quest* before Pollard formed his own company and starred his wife (1916-1917) in *Miss Jackie of the Navy, The Pearl of Paradise, The Butterfly Girl, The Devil's Assistant,* and *The Girl Who Couldn't Grow Up*. When the Pollard Company disbanded in 1918, Miss Fischer returned to the American Company and appeared (1918-1920) in a string of comedy-dramas including *Ann's Finish, Fair Enough, Impossible Susan, Jilted Janet, The Mantle of Charity, The Primitive Woman, The Square Deal, Molly of the Follies, The Tiger Lily, Trixie from Broadway, Their Mutual Child,* and *The Thirtieth Piece of Silver.*

The changing decade of the 1920s found Miss Fischer's career in decline with limited appearances in Pathé's *The Weekend* (1920) and *The Payment Guaranteed* (1921), under Pollard's direction in Universal's *K—the Unknown* (1924) and Paramount's *Any Woman* (1925). The actress had hopes of reestablishing herself as a star when in 1925 Pollard began the remake of *Uncle Tom's Cabin* for Universal, with James Lowe as "Tom," Miss Fischer in the role of "Eliza," and Virginia Gray as "Little Eva." The film in production for two years was to be Universal's prestigious production of 1927. The highly publicized and expensive remake failed miserably at the box office, much to the chagrin of the Universal executives. Critics found Lowe's performance only adequate, Miss Fischer miscast, and Pollard's direction a throwback to the two-reeler era. The film's failure ended Miss Fischer's career as a leading actress and Pollard's aspiration of greatness as a director.

With the days of the silent era numbered, Miss Fischer retired and Pollard became a contract director for Metro-Goldwyn-Mayer, where he remained until his death on July 6, 1934, in Pasadena, California. After her husband's death, Miss Fischer possibly returned as a "bit" actress, as her death certificate gave her last employment as an actress with the Universal Company. After years of anonymity, the actress died of a cerebral thrombosis on March 11, 1975, in Encinitas, California.

Mary Fuller

The forerunner for all the countless serials produced by the film companies was *What Happened to Mary?* starring Mary Fuller. The popular serial became Miss Fuller's contribution to film history. When historians write of the pioneer days of filmmaking, the serial is often mentioned in connection with the historical aspects of the film series, but as the years passed the serial ironically became Miss Fuller's epitaph.

What happened to Mary Fuller has plagued researchers for decades. It was inconceivable how one of the screen's first major stars could vanish without a trace—but it happened to her, and for years the actress' whereabouts remained suspended in anonymity. It was only when noted film researcher Bill Cappello took up the task of solving the mystery that the life of Mary Fuller unfolded. Extensive research by Cappello only deepened the mystery with three major questions emerging from his research: why did the actress' film career end so abruptly, why was she not interred in the family cemetery with the other members of her family, and what had happened to her? To answer these questions he researched newspapers, city directories, and files in libraries, located relatives, and studied cemetery files. All of the aforementioned aided in solving the mystery and what Cappello uncovered could easily have been the scenario for one of her *What Happened to Mary?* episodes.

Mary Claire Fuller, the second of four daughters of Nora Swing and Miles Fuller, was born into a well-to-do Washington, D. C., family on October 5, 1888. (Her father was an attorney and the principal of the business college "The Drillery.") Educated locally, she excelled in language, fluently speaking French and German. Described by a sister as "headstrong and unmanageable," she quit in the first year of high school. As a child she studied the piano and the art of mimicry, and when she left school, her love for mimicry enabled her to embark upon a stage career.

How extensive was Mary Fuller's stage career? Little can be found on this chapter of her life, as the actress rarely spoke or wrote of it. By late 1906, she had left home and had probably joined a touring stock company. The *Toledo Times* (Nov. 2, 1914) wrote after she became a film star, "Wonder how many of the moving picture fans in Toledo, who 'just dote on Mary Fuller,' the famous star of the movies, associate her with little Claire Fuller, the sprightly little ingenue of the old Lyceum Stock Company, which so delighted Toledoans several years ago?" An old *Fulton Theatre Magazine Program* (Oct. 11. 1915) stated that when she completed her education she went to New York City and secured a minor part with an unimportant stock company. Discouraged by the hardships of touring in stock she decided to apply for a position as an extra with one of the moving picture studios.

Terry Ramsey, in *A Million and One Nights*, wrote that Mary Fuller's film career began in 1907 when director Fred Thompson took her from the stage to appear for the Vitagraph Company in *The Ugly Duckling*. With the Vitagraph Company (1906-1909) she learned the rudiments of filmmaking, appearing in the one-reelers *Leah the Forsaken, The Stage Struck Daughter, The Foundling, The Flower Girl of Paris, Jessie the Stolen Child, King Lear*, and *Elektra*. After only a brief stay with Vitagraph, Miss Fuller, in late 1909, joined the Edison Company where, under the direction of Edwin S. Porter, J. Searle Dawley, and Bannister Merwin (1909-1911), she appeared in a wide variety of roles in numerous short films (*Fuss and Feathers, Hansel and Gretel, The House of Cards, The Engineer's Romance, Frankenstein, The House of Seven Gables, Michael Strogoff, Aida, A Modern Cinderella, A Stage Romance, The Three Musketeers*, and *The Professor and the New Hat*). So popular had the young actress become with the public that the company decided to star her in her own film series.

With the release of the film series *What Happened to Mary?* on July 20, 1912, the film serial was conceived. The first serial differed from later serials as each of the twelve one-reels was made-up of a complete episode that did not leave the heroine in some dire strait. In conjunction with the *McClure's Ladies World Magazine* the stories were published prior to their screening. The public eagerly awaited each issue of the magazine to read and then view the episode on the screen. So successful was the film series that the circulation of the magazine increased, it made the Edison Company a major studio, made Mary Fuller one of the screen's first superstars, and made the serial genre a part of film history.

The Edison Company's chief asset between 1912-1913, Miss Fuller was kept busy starring in numerous one- and two-reelers: *The Little Wooden Shoe, Treasure Island, The Cub Reporter, Treasure Island, More Precious Than Gold, A Daughter of the Wilderness, Kathleen Mavourneen, Mary Stuart, The Pied Piper of Hamelin, A Woodland Paradise* (also wrote the scenario), and starred in the *What Happened to Mary?* sequel, the six-episode serial *Who Will Marry Me?*

Miss Fuller's film series and short film dramas (1912-1915) made her one of the screen's renown stars with the monthly film magazines clamoring for interviews. *Motion Picture Magazine* ran excerpts from her diary for several months, her portraits appeared on the cover regularly or in the photo gallery section of all the major film magazines, and her fans could buy Mary Fuller pillows, spoons, dishes, playing cards, and hats. By 1914, she had become Mary Pickford's first rival, with *Motion Picture Magazine* picking Miss Fuller, Miss Pickford, Clara Kimball Young, Earle Williams, and J. Warren Kerrigan as the screen's most popular stars.

At the peak of her popularity the Edison Company kept Miss Fuller busy as the star of the two-reelers: *An Affair of the Dress, The Chinese Fan, Comedy and Tragedy, Frederick the Great, A Lonely Road, The Necklace of Rameses, The Princess of the Desert* and the last of her film series, *The Active Life of Dolly of the Dailies.* Tired from overwork and disappointed when the Edison Company failed to promote the *Dolly* series, Miss Fuller left Edison when Universal offered her a lucrative film contract in the spring of 1914.

As a Universal star under the company's various brand names (Victor, Gold Seal, Laemmle and Red Feather), Miss Fuller's 1914-1915 two-reelers included *A Girl of the People, Heart of the Hills, The Witch Girl, The Bribe, A Daughter of the Nile, Jeanne of the Woods, The Laugh That Died, The Taming of Mary, A Witch of Salem Town,* and *My Lady High and Mighty.* With the decline of the one- and two-reelers, Miss Fuller made her feature debut in the Civil War drama *Under Southern Skies* (1915) followed by *The Woman Who Lied.* In 1916, the starring roles continued in *A Huntress of Men, The Strength of the Weak, Thrown to the Lions,* and the film shorts *The Little Fraud, The Limousine Mystery, Love's Masquerade,* and *Three Wishes.* With the completion in 1917 of *The Public Be Damned* and *The Long Trail,* Mary Fuller abruptly ended her film career, to the dismay of her many fans.

Baffled by her disappearance from the film studios, Cal York in *Photoplay* (October 1920) asked

> Where is Mary Fuller? Nobody knows—but a lot of people seem to care. The Answer Man's mail contains at least a dozen letters a month asking what has happened to Mary, but even the Answer Man is up against it. Mary Fuller has disappeared. Her actor friends from Edison have tried to find traces of her, without success. A lawyer who formerly handled her affairs has failed to locate her. No doubt she prefers to remain in seclusion—but, why? An intelligent woman, a splendid actress, still young—why should she wish to hide from the world? It is a question no one seems able to answer.

What Miss Fuller's public and friends from the film world did not know was that in 1917 she suffered a nervous breakdown over a failed romance with a married Metropolitan Opera singer. When the man's wife refused to divorce him, the actress was so devastated that it resulted in a complete nervous collapse. The breakdown necessitated lengthy treatment so she ended her film career, returned to her mother's home in Washington, D.C., and severed all association with her actor friends and her public in 1917.

Under the care of her mother, Mary Fuller occupied the second floor of the house where she spent her days playing her piano and painting. By the mid-1920s, the wealth she had accumulated as a film star had been depleted and she reemerged from her seclusion in 1926 to try for a film comeback. She returned to Hollywood, where for the next three years she tried unsuccessfully to reenter films. (*Photoplay* reported in "Studio News East and West" that "Mary Fuller is having a gorgeous time on her first trip to Hollywood.")

When the Hollywood producers showed no interest in the once famous star, Miss Fuller's only recourse was to return to her mother's home. Intensely depressed over her financial situation, she returned to the reclusive life on the second floor and with the passing years, under the care of her mother, there she remained. The death of her mother in 1940 brought on another breakdown and for the next six years her oldest sister cared for her until her mental deterioration necessitated her being placed in St. Elizabeth Hospital on July 1, 1947. There she remained for the next twenty-five years, hearing and talking to voices only she heard until her death on December 9, 1973. The hospital, apparently unable to locate any family members, buried the former star in an unmarked grave in the Congressional Cemetery—miles from the family cemetery. There were no obituaries for the former actress; she had long been forgotten by her public and actor friends.

William Garwood

With his matinee idol good looks, William Garwood was the epitome of the early screen hero. In the days prior to the feature films, he was one of the most sought-after leading men. With his immaculate grooming, no actor looked better in a tuxedo. Somewhat vain, he subtly used the trait in a humorous manner that his feminine fans found irresistible. The leading actresses of the day eagerly wanted him as a costar because they knew a "Garwood film" would pull-in his feminine fans and would be successful at the box office.

William Davis Garwood, Jr., (the "Jr." was dropped but he often stressed the "junior" in interviews) was born on April 28, 1884, in Springfield, Missouri (mistakenly on his death certificate Mississippi is listed as place of birth). He attended the Springfield public schools and at the age of fifteen spent several years in New Mexico before returning to Springfield to attend Drury College, where he excelled as an outstanding athlete (track and football) and actor noted for his literary readings. When he decided to pursue a theatrical rather than a business career, his father, who vehemently opposed his choice, allowed him the chance to get the theatre out of his system before settling down to the security of a profession with a future.

The aspiring actor began his theatrical career with the Elitch's Gardens in Denver, Colorado, where for two seasons in stock with Bruce McRae, Jack Gilmore, May Buckley, Maude Fealy, and Douglas Fairbanks he did "utility" work (any type of work on and off the stage) gradually advancing to better roles before leaving the company. His Denver experience led him to New York, where he secured a position with Virginia Harsned, followed by engagements in Charles Frohman's original production of *Mizpah* and *Just Out of College*. Later he was with Kyrle Bellow in *Brigadier Girard*, Miller Kent in *Raffles*, and on the road with Dustin Farnum in *Cameo Kirby*. In between these engagements he appeared in stock in Columbus, Ohio, at the Alcazar in San Francisco, and at the Auditorium in Los Angeles before idleness in the theatre forced him, as it did others, to turn to motion pictures.

In December 1909, Garwood joined the Thanhouser Company, making his film debut in 1910; after a brief return to the theatre he came back to Thanhouser, where he rapidly became one of the company's leading players in numerous one- , two- , and three-reelers (*Jane Eyre, The Vicar of Wakefield, The Lady from the Sea, David Copperfield, The Woman in White, The Merchant of Venice, Under Two Flags, Vengeance Is Mine, Aurora Floyd, Little Dorrit, Robin Hood, Carmen,* and *Cymbeline*) opposite such Thanhouser stars as Florence La Badie, Marguerite Snow, Maude Fealy, and Mignon Anderson. When the Thanhouser players returned from their winter sojourn in Los Angeles to New Rochelle on April 30, 1913, Garwood remained in Los Angeles and joined the Majestic Company, where he starred in numerous shorts (*Dora, The Body in the Trunk, Fate's Decree, Hearts and Hoofs, The Ingrate, The Van Warden Rubies,* and *The Green-Eyed Devil*) before making his feature debut in the Majestic drama *Imar the Servitor* (1914).

After leaving Majestic in 1914, the actor joined the American Company, where he was successfully teamed with Vivian Rich in a series of two-reel dramas *(The Girl in Question, In the Candlelight, The Painted Lady's Child, The Taming of Sunnybrook Nell, Their Worldly Goods, The Aftermath,* and *Cameo of Yellowstone).* After leaving American he briefly appeared for the IMP Company opposite the popular ingenue Violet Mersereau in a series of two- and three-reelers *(Driven by Fate, Larry O'Neill, On Dangerous Ground, The Stake, The Supreme Impulse, Thou Shalt Not Lie,* and *Uncle's New Blazer),* as well as directing Miss Mersereau in *Wild Blood* and *You Can't Always Tell.* When Universal offered him a contract as actor and director he signed with them in 1915 and appeared opposite Violet Mersereau in *The Wolf of Debt* and Stella Razetto in *Lord John in New York* (this was the first episode in the serial *Lord John's Journal*). In 1916, as an actor, he again appeared opposite Miss Mersereau in *Broken Fetters* and for Universal he directed and appeared in *He Wrote a Book, A Society Sherlock,* and *Soul at Stake.* In late 1916, he signed with Thomas H. Ince and appeared in Kay-Bee's *The Little Brother* (1917) and Famous Players-Lasky's *The Guilty Man* (1918); he also appeared at this time in Rolfe's *A Magdalene of the Hills* (1917), Author's Photo-Plays' *Her Moment* (1918) and opposite Mary Miles Minter in American's *Wives and Other Wives* (1918). In 1918, Garwood ended his film career; some film directories mention his directing a film in 1919 but no such film credit can be found. It was said that through wise investments he had amassed a fortune so he retired and completely disappeared into film history.

What happened in the years after Garwood left the screen is unknown, his name rarely if ever appeared in print. Only through his death certificate was his demise uncovered. The once popular actor died from a coronary occlusion and cirrhosis of the liver due to chronic alcoholism on December 28, 1950 in Los Angeles. There were no survivors nor were there any obituaries for the former star in the trade papers.

Maude George

Maude George is remembered today for her portrayals in four of Erich von Stroheim's films but throughout the teens she appeared in leading and character roles and in the 1920s she was one of the screen's busiest character actresses, noted for appearing in roles older than her years. An actress who never fell into the "movie star" mold, she was one of the silent screen's sophisticates, a role no other actress could play as well as Miss George.

Born the daughter of Della Stimpson and Miles George (a brother to actress Grace George) on August 15, 1888 in Riverside, California, Miss George was educated at the Cumnock's Girl's School in Los Angeles. It was there she embarked on a stage career in stock at the old Burbank Theatre, spent two seasons with Conrad Le Marie over the Orpheum circuit, touring the United States, Canada, and Australia playing in *The Sultan's Favorite,* returned to Los Angeles and was appearing in stock at the Los Angeles Morosco Theatre when she forsook the stage for a film career.

The actress entered films for the Universal Company (1915) and under Otis Turner's direction quickly won recognition for her dramatic work in *Business in Business, The Frame-Up,* and *A Little Brother to the Rich.* In 1916, after appearing in several J. Warren Kerrigan films *(The Beckoning Trail, The Gay Lord Waring, Langdon's Legacy, The Pool of Flame, The Silent Battle, The Social Buccaneer,* and *A Son of the Immortals),* her stature as an actress under the capable hands of Lois Weber rose to leading lady status from her work in Weber's *Idle Wives* (Miss Weber starred) and in Mr. and Mrs. Carter De Haven's comedy *A Youth of Fortune.* In 1917, she appeared in leading roles in *Even As You and I, Heart Strings, The Piper's Price,* and as a scenario writer wrote the script for *The Fighting Gringo.*

Miss George's Universal work attracted the attention of Thomas H. Ince and under his supervision she was cast as William S. Hart's leading lady in his popular version of *Blue Blazes Rawden* (1918), which was highly praised by the critics, and under Fred Niblo's direction supported Enid Bennett in Ince's *The Marriage Ring.* In 1919, after a series of routine comedy-dramas *(The Lamb and the Lion, The Midnight Stage,* and *A Rogue's Romance)* for various film companies, Miss George supported Pauline Frederick in Goldwyn's *Madame X* (1920) before Erich von Stroheim made her a member of his stock company of players.

Von Stroheim did not want "movie stars" or recognized dramatic actors in his stock company, he wanted players whom he could develop into the characters they were to portray under his directorship. Under his direction, Miss George expertly played the despicable greedy Parisian modiste "Madame Mallot" in *The Devil's Passkey* (1920), the fake "Princess Olga" in *Foolish Wives* (1922), the brothel madame "Elvira" in *Merry-Go-Round* (1923), and the cigar-smoking mother "Princess Maria" in *The Wedding March* (1928). Miss George became those characters under von

Stroheim's direction, and while the actress Maude George has long been forgotten, the characterizations have become a part of silent film lore.

Throughout the 1920s, Miss George appeared in a wide variety of character roles in support of the era's great stars including Pauline Frederick in *Roads of Destiny* (1921), John Gilbert in *Monte Cristo* (1922), Corinne Griffith in *Six Days* (1923), and *The Garden of Eden* (1928), Vivian Martin in *Soiled* (1924), Lowell Sherman in *The Love Toy* (1926), and Mae Murray in *Altars of Desire* (1927) before making her film exit in *The Veiled Woman* (1929).

As with so many of her contemporaries, after leaving the screen, little was heard of the actress. After her marriage to Arthur Forde ended in divorce in 1918, she married businessman Frank Passmore on June 10, 1927. The Passmores lived quietly and obscurely in Sepulveda, California, and the former actress died there on October, 10, 1963. She was survived by her husband.

Myrtle Gonzalez

The Spanish influenza epidemic was extensively reported in the theatrical trade papers in the fall and winter of 1918-1919 with the ominous headlines—"Boston Theatres Closed by Health Authorities" and "Influenza Assumes a Threatening Aspect." Week after week the trade journal *The Billboard* published pages listing victims from the entertainment industry; the film-going public was shocked to learn that within days the deadly disease took the lives of two of the screen's most popular players—the heroic idol Harold Lockwood (October 19, 1918) and one of the screen's best-known leading ladies, Myrtle Gonzalez. A member of one of California's oldest families of Spanish descent, Myrtle Gonzalez was born in Los Angeles, the daughter of Lillian Cook and Manuel G. Gonzalez, on September 28, 1891. Educated in the Los Angeles schools, at an early age she showed remarkable dramatic talent as a singer; the aspiring singer appeared in many local concerts and benefits before embarking on a stage career in Los Angeles with Fanny Davenport and Florence Stone in juvenile roles.

The emergence of the film studios in Los Angeles provided the young stage actress with a means of performing her craft without those strenuous on-the-road tours her frail health could not endure. When the Vitagraph Company in 1912 offered her a film contract Miss Gonzalez accepted and became a member of the company's troupe of players. With her dark

Spanish beauty she soon became one of the company's most sought-after players, appearing in numerous one- and two-reelers primarily of the out-of-door genre *(The White Feather, Anne of the Mines, The Man from the Desert, The Legend of the Lone Tree,* and *The Offending Kiss).*

In 1914, Miss Gonzalez supported Edith Storey and the ill-fated William Desmond Taylor in Vitagraph's six-reel drama *Captain Alvarez* and was William Duncan's leading lady in *The Chalice of Courage* (1915). Sometime in 1915 the actress severed her contract with Vitagraph and signed with the Universal Company. Her work at Universal under the direction of Lynn F. Reynolds earned her the title of "the Virgin Lily of the Screen" for her dramatic roles in *The End of the Rainbow, The Girl of the Lost Lake, A Romance of Billy Goat Hill, The Secret of the Swamp God's Crucible, The Greater Law, Mutiny, The Show Down,* and *Southern Justice* between 1916-1917. Pleased with the actress' work and popularity with the public Universal planned to make her one of the company's stars in 1918.

Known to her fans as a robust out-of-door heroine on the screen she, in reality, had always been frail and suffered from a heart disease. When stricken with Spanish influenza her condition quickly deteriorated from her weakened heart. On October 22, 1918, in her Los Angeles home the young actress succumbed to the disease. Survivors included her son James, from an earlier marriage to James P. Jones, and her husband, Allen Watt, formerly a Universal assistant director, whom she married on December 1, 1917.

Evelyn Greeley

Evelyn Greeley, one of the great beauties of the silent screen, was reported by some magazines as the granddaughter of the famous journalist Horace Greeley. Truth or fiction, such publicity was eagerly read by the fans and accepted as the truth, whereas the facts uncovered about the actress lack the validity of truth as does other pertinent biographical information printed in early film directories about her.

The film directories gave Evelyn Greeley's birthplace as Lexington, Kentucky, but her death certificate states that she was born the daughter of Frances Marko and Stephen Huber in Austria on November 3, 1888. Educated at the Frances Shimer Academy and the University School for Girls (could have been any school anywhere and read well in her studio biography), she began her stage career in stock and toured with the Poli Players Stock Company before abandoning the stage for films.

The actress's entrance in films occurred in 1914 as a "bit" actress in Chicago for the Essanay Company, with her earliest film credit being in a supporting role opposite Francis X. Bushman and Marguerite Snow in the Quality Picture Corporation's *The Second in Command* (1915). Her beauty attracted the attention of the executives of the obscure Dixie Film Company, who starred her in 1916 in *Just a Song at Twilight* and *Tempest and Sunshine.* In 1917, she signed with the World Film Corporation, which cast her opposite Carlyle Blackwell between 1917-1919 in a series of comedy-dramas: *The Burglar, The Good-for-Nothing, The Price of Pride, The Social Leper, The Beautiful Mrs. Reynolds, The Beloved Blackmailer, By Hook or Crook, The Golden Wall, His Royal Highness, Leap to Fame, The Road to France* (listed in some directories as *The Allies), Courage for Two, Three Green Eyes,* and *Hit or Miss.* Miss Greeley's other World films included *The Brand of Satan* (1917), *The Volunteer* (a 1917 World War I drama which starred Madge Evans as herself with most of the other World Company's stars appearing as themselves) and she was starred in 1919 in *Bringing Up Betty* and *The Oakdale Affair* with Reginald Denny, *Me and Captain Kid* with Raymond McKee, and *Phil-for-Short* with Hugh Thompson.

Miss Greeley's World contract was terminated in 1920 and thereafter she was unable to find the success she had known at World. In 1921, she was seen in *Diana of Star Hollow* for Producers Security and in Fox's *His Greatest Sacrifice.* In 1922, her early film *Just a Song at Twilight* was reissued and after appearing in Pathé's *Pasteboard Crown* she was re-united with her former World costar in a British production of *Bulldog Drummond* (1922). British directories also list her and Carlyle Blackwell appearing in 1923 in their 1917 hit *Good-for-Nothing* (possibly a remake or a reissue of the film), whatever it was it was Miss Greeley's last film credit.

An actress who never tried for any film comebacks, her 1922 marriage to actor John Smiley ended in divorce, as did her marriage to wealthy businessman James H. Rand in 1960. When she died on March 25, 1975, in West Palm Beach, Florida, Miss Greeley's husband, Morgan Laity, survived her.

Winifred Greenwood

Winifred Greenwood enjoyed leading lady and star status at two early pioneer film companies—Selig Polyscope Company in Chicago and the American Flying A Company in Santa Barbara. At the Flying A Company she teamed with Edward Coxen and George Field in numerous two- and three-reelers and they were among the company's most popular players. After moving to other studios and with the decline of the short film, she became a character actress with her career ending as it did with so many of the pioneer film stars in bit and extra roles.

Miss Greenwood was born in Geneseo, New York, on January 1, 1885. Her father died when she was eight years old and her mother, a Virginian, raised and educated her to be a school teacher. She studied at the New York State Normal School but abandoned the teaching profession for the "wicked life upon the stage," making her debut in vaudeville with the King's Carnival Company touring the United States and Canada. Her first speaking part was as the ingenue lead in the musical *Zig-Zag Alley.* From musical comedy to melodrama she starred with J. J. Kennedy in *The Midnight Express.* Successes followed in *Sapho* and *Camille* with various well-known stock companies and at one time she had her own stock company. Always partial to the boards, she continued to return to the stage throughout and after her film career.

Miss Greenwood's extensive stage background made her a natural for films, and she made her debut for the Selig Company in 1910 with one of her earliest film credits being a 1000-foot film version of *The Wizard of Oz.* Along with Kathlyn Williams she became one of the company's leading stars who helped the company open its million-dollar studio. Between 1911-1913, Miss Greenwood starred in numerous one- and two-reelers, scoring a success with Kathlyn Williams in the first film version of *The Two Orphans* (reissued in 1916) and other films including *Tempted by Necessity, Under Suspicion, His Chance to Make Good, An International Romance, The Last Dance, A Detective's Strategy, The Prosecuting Attorney, Dixieland, Belle Boyd-A Confederate Spy, Pauline Cushman-the Federal Spy, The Understudy,* and *The Millionaire Cowboy.*

Leaving the Selig Company in 1913, Miss Greenwood joined the American Flying A Company where she was successfully starred with Edward Coxen (as the hero) and George Field (as the villain). After seven months of being saved by the hero, reel life took an ironic twist when in real life Miss Greenwood married not the hero but the villain of her films (the marriage to George Field ended in divorce five years later).

The 1913-1915 short film output for Flying A was substantial and too many to name, but a sampling of the Greenwood-Coxen-Field films included *The Drummer's Honeymoon, The Shriner's Daughter, What Her Diary Told, The Broken Barrier, The Derelict, Down by the Sea, The Little House in the Valley, The Lure of the Sawdust, The Silent Way, A Slice of Life, Alice of Hudson Bay, The Guiding Light, High Cost of Flirting, Key to the Past, Out of the Ashes, The Water Carrier of San Juan,* and *The Zaca Lake Mystery.* Miss Greenwood also starred in many other films with other Flying A players *(The Wishing Stone, When a Woman Waits, The Truth of Fiction,* and *The Clear-Up)* before moving into feature films.

With the decline of the short film, Miss Greenwood made the transition to feature films in 1916, appearing in leading roles in *Dust, The Inner Struggle, Lying Lips, Reclamation, The Voice of Love,* and *A Woman's Daring.*

After leaving Flying A, she found her leading roles slipping to character roles and between 1917-1920 she appeared in Balboa's *The Alien Blood* and *The Inspiration of Harry Larrabee,* Marine's *Lorelie of the Sea,* Bluebird's *Danger Within* and *The Deciding Kiss,* Jesse D. Hampton's *Come Again Smith,* Metro's *Are All Men Alike?,* Lasky's *The Crystal Gazer* and *The Life of the Party,* and Famous Players-Lasky's *Believe Me 'Zantippe, The Goat, Too Many Millions, M'liss, Maggie Pepper, Men, Women and Money, Putting It Over, An Adventure in Hearts,* and *Young Mrs. Winthrop.*

Throughout the 1920s, when Miss Greenwood was not appearing on the stage she would return to films, and she had small roles in *The Faith Healer, The Dollar-a-Year Man, Don't Call Me Little Girl, Love Never Dies, Sacred and Profane Love, To the Last Man, The Flame of the Yukon,* and a bit part with several other film pioneers in DeMille's *King of Kings.*

With no film credits after 1927 she perhaps continued in films as an extra or bit player. There was another marriage for the actress but it was apparently unsuccessful. Age and poor health necessitated her entrance to the Motion Picture Country House. The last two years of the actress' life was spent in and out of the hospital. The actress died in Woodland Hills, California on November 23, 1961. Her Los Angeles *Times* death announcement did not list any survivors.

Lillian Hall

As the ill-fated "Beth March" in *Little Women* and as "Alice Munro" in Maurice Tourneur's *The Last of the Mohicans,* Lillian Hall proved herself to be one of the most promising leading ingenues of the early 1920s and perhaps would have reached stardom had she not abandoned her career for matrimony. When she left the screen little was ever heard of her and with the passing years some historians have confused her with the well-known British film player Lillian Hall-Davis (died October 25, 1933) probably due to the similarity in their professional names.

A Brooklynite, Miss Hall was born the daughter of Kate I. Johnson and Frederick Hall on March 15, 1896. Educated in her native city, she attended a business college but, enamored with the stage, she forsook the business world when she was offered a role with a Philadelphia stock company. Soon after, she entered films.

Miss Hall began her film career around 1917 with her first film credit for the Norma Talmadge Company in support of Miss Talmadge in *The Safety Curtain* (1918). Between 1918-1919, the aspiring actress supported Elaine Hammerstein in the World War I drama *Wanted for Murder,* June Elvidge in World's *Coax Me,* Evelyn Nesbit in Fox's *My Little Sister,* Taylor Holmes in Triangle's comedy *Taxi,* and Dorothy Bernard (role of "Jo March") in William Brady's *Little Women* with Miss Hall as the tragic "Beth March" for which the critics praised her portrayal.

In 1920, Miss Hall's status as one of the rising young ingenues continued to climb with her appearing as Pat O'Malley's leading lady in Edgar Lewis' *Sherry,* opposite Johnny Dooley in the Radin Company's production of *Skinning Skinners,* opposite Cullen Landis as the ingenue lead in Eminent Authors Pictures' production of Rex Beach's *Going Home,* opposite Sessue Hayakawa in Haworth's comedy-drama *An Arabian Knight,* the ingenue lead opposite David Butler in the D. N. Schwab Production of *Fickle Women* before appearing in the role that would forever secure a place for her in silent film history.

Without a doubt, Maurice Tourneur's film version of *The Last of the Mohicans* (1920) is the best of the many versions and under Tourneur's direction the players stepped out of the James Fenimore Cooper pages as the characters came to life on the screen—Wallace Beery as the villain "Magua," Barbara Bedford as the ill-fated "Cora," Albert Roscoe as "Uncas," and Miss Hall as "Alice Munro." Miss Hall did her best work in the film and, thereafter, only appeared in routine features between

1921-1922 *(Hearts of Youth, Oliver Twist, Jr., The Secret of the Hills, A Shocking Night,* and *The Forest King)* before she retired from the screen.

When Miss Hall met, fell in love, and married the popular young actor Glenn Tryon on October 19, 1924, he wanted a stay-at-home wife and she relinquished her career for matrimony. With her retirement she gradually became known only as Mrs. Glenn Tryon with her days as one of the screen's popular ingenues slipping farther and farther into the past with each passing year. When the marriage later ended in divorce, the former actress never remarried. When she died as Lillian Tryon by hcr own hand from barbiturate intoxication on March 18, 1959 in Los Angeles, there were no obituaries for the former leading lady in the trade journals.

Gloria Hope

With her auburn hair and blue eyes, Gloria Hope was the epitome of the silent screen ingenue who on a film lot met a dashing young screen hero, married him, and lived happily ever after. The storybook marriage of Miss Hope to Lloyd Hughes was the romantic venture portrayed in countless screen scenarios but real romances were not reel romances, the off-screen romances of the stars seldom had a happy ending. When Miss Hope's marriage to Hughes succeeded, it was highly publicized in film magazines with reams of pages written on their private and professional lives as successful film players who found happiness in Hollywood.

Born Olive Francis (Thomas Ince changed her name to Gloria Hope), the daughter of Nellie Beech and William W. Francis on November 9, 1899, Miss Hope was educated in the Newark, New Jersey, schools. Before beginning her training as a school teacher, on a visit to her aunt in Los Angeles, she had an opportunity to visit the Thomas H. Ince Studio. It happened that the studio was looking for a girl to complete the cast for a film Roy W. Neill was directing, so they took a test and engaged her for the part that very day. According to fan magazines, several players entered films by visiting a studio and accidentally being signed to a film contract. More than likely, their visit to the studio was due to knowing one of the studio's executives whose power at the studio resulted in a contract.

Under Roy W. Neill's direction, Miss Hope made her film debut in *Free and Equal*, filmed in the summer of 1917 but not released until later because it was not complimentary to blacks. The public first saw her in Ince's crime drama *Time Locks and Diamonds* (1917) opposite William Desmond. Impressed by Miss Hope's talents Ince cast her as the ingenue

(1918) in *The Guilty Man, The Law of the North,* and *Naughty, Naughty;* to gain additional experience she supported Bessie Barriscale in her production of *The Heart of Rachael,* was Franklyn Farnum's leading lady in *$5,000 Reward* and supported Lillian Gish in D. W. Griffith's World War I drama *The Great Love.* One of the screen's busiest ingenues by 1919, she was Jack Pickford 's costar in his productions of *Bill Apperson's Boy* and *Burglar by Proxy,* played opposite Tom Moore in Goldwyn's *The Lord Quex,* and appeared in Harry Garson's production *The Hushed Hour* and in Universal's *The Outcasts of Poker Flat* and *The Rider of the Law.*

The popularity of Miss Hope with the public made her in demand by the studios and in 1920 she appeared in leading roles in Selznick's *The Desperate Hero,* Fox's *Prairie Trails* and *The Texan,* Robertson-Cole's *The Third Woman,* Famous Players-Lasky's *Too Much Johnson,* and Select's *Seeds of Vengeance.* In 1921, after appearing in Universal's *Colorado* opposite Frank Mayo, a far more important event took place in Miss Hope's life.

Miss Hope met Lloyd Hughes on the Ince lot and a romance developed between the two young players. When Miss Hope married Hughes on June 30, 1921, she became one of the most-written-about brides of the year. Fan magazine writers clamored for interviews and wrote of the ideal Hollywood marriage. After all the publicity, it is amazing the marriage survived, but it did, with Miss Hope limiting her film work thereafter. In 1921, after appearing in *Courage* and *The Grim Comedian,* she made only two appearances in 1922 (*Trouble* and supported Mary Pickford and her husband in *Tess of the Storm Country*). After roles in *That Devil Quemado* (1925) and *Sandy* (1926) she retired from the screen to devote her time to the role of wife and motherhood.

As Mrs. Lloyd Hughes, little was heard of the actress after her retirement. Her ideal marriage to Hughes ended with his death on June 6, 1958. His obituary said that he was survived by his wife, the former actress Gloria Hope, a son, and a daughter. When Gloria Hope died in Pasadena, California, on October 29, 1976, from cardiac arrest, her death went unreported.

Clara Horton

At the age of fourteen, Clara Horton was the personification of youth. Her storybook beauty made her an ideal leading lady for the youthful Jack Pickford, Charles Ray, and Cullen Landis. *Motion Picture Classic* (February 1921) described the young ingenue as, "She looks much like a doll with her lovely golden curls, exquisite coloring, soft curves, and the daintiest hands imaginable. Her eyes are a puzzle. At first glance they are blue, a deep dark blue, but within a few minutes you are willing to wager all your possessions that they are black."

Clara Marie Horton, the daughter of Gertrude Wilcox and Leroy Horton, was born in Brooklyn, New York, on July 29, 1904. Educated by private tutors, she began posing for New York artists at the age of three and was discovered for films when Pat Powers saw her standing on a Brooklyn street with her mother. She was invited to the studio and within an hour she had played a scene before the camera.

The young model began her professional career at the age of eight when she joined the Eclair Company, soon becoming the company's leading child actress. Publicized as the "Eclair Kid" her popularity in a series of short films (*Because of Bobbie, The Darling of the Mounted, Dolls, Clara's Mysterious Toys, A Friend in Need, Filial Love, Making Uncle Jealous*, and *The Spectre Bridegroom)* lured the public into the theatres, much to the delight of the film producers. Between 1915-1917 for Ideal, Powers, Universal, and Bison companies, Miss Horton's successes in *The Long Shift, Shadows of the Harbor, A Soul's Tragedy, Us Kids, The Vengeance of Guido, Nadine of Nowhere*, and *Under the Paw* brought her stardom as a leading lady. As Jack Pickford's leading lady, she appeared in the role of "Becky Thatcher" in *Tom Sawyer* (1917), *Huck and Tom: Or the Further Adventures of Tom Sawyer* (1918), as "Dolly Sheldon" in *In Wrong* (1919), and as "Margaret" in *The Little Shepherd of Kingdom Come* (1920). Miss Horton's success resulted in Charles Ray's wanting her as his leading lady for his production of *Nineteen and Phyllis* (1920). In 1919, for the first film produced by Eminent Authors Pictures Incorporation, she starred opposite Cullen Landis in the Northwest drama *The Girl from the Outside;* the success of the film brought a reteaming of the pair in the comedy *It's a Great Life* (1920). Other films for her between 1917-1920 were *The Plow Woman, The Yellow Dog, Everywoman, The Winning Girl, Blind Youth*, and *The Servant in the House*.

Continuously kept busy by the various studios in 1921 *(Action, The Light in the Clearing*, and *Prisoners of Love)* Miss Horton limited her film appearances between 1922-1924 *(Penrod, Mind Over Motor*, and *Wrongs Righted)* probably due to the awkward age and wornout from her busy schedule of filmmaking. The actress was quoted at this time as saying, "I had been on the screen since my childhood and I was tired of all the make-believe. I wanted to live a real ordinary life."

Married to Hyman Brand in 1925, Miss Horton returned to films, having cast off the childish roles of her past for flapper roles (1925-1927) in *All Around the Frying Pan, Makers of Men, Speed Madness, The Wheel, Beyond the Trail, The Broadway Gallants, Winning the Futurity, The Fightin' Comeback, The Fortune Hunter,* and *Sailor Izzy Murphy.* The actress' flapper roles did little to advance her career and, after a series of Radio Pictures opposite George O'Hara, she retired from the screen.

After her marriage to Brand ended, Miss Horton married Edwin H. Laufer and the couple made their home in Whittier, California. With the passing of years the actress faded into the past and few fans knew that the saleslady in a lady's dress shop was once the famous ingenue they idolized on the silent screen. When Miss Horton died from a heart disease on December 4, 1976, in Whittier, there were no obituaries for the former actress in the trade papers. She was survived by her husband.

Mae Hotely

Film historians often write of the great early film comedians but seldom do they mention the early comediennes, who were just as popular in those pioneer days: Alice Washburn, Gale Henry, Alice Howell, Margaret Joslin, and Mae Hotely. They were once stars whose comedic antics filled theatres with laughter but who today have been relegated to footnotes in film history.

Mae Hotely, one of the earliest of the film comediennes, was born in Maryland on October 7, 1872 (place of birth and name of parents are unknown). Nothing can be found on her early years; when and where she met actor and director Arthur Douglas Hotaling is also unknown. Since Hotaling was well-known in vaudeville, more than likely it was there that they met and married.

Mrs. Hotaling's (shortened to Hotely) career was the result of Hotaling's association with Siegmund Lubin, the founder of the Lubin Company. Lubin hired Hotaling in 1896 as a writer and cinematographer. Later, when he was put in charge of a film unit in Jacksonville, Florida, his wife served as his leading lady and his brother, Gerry, was the cameraman. In those early Jacksonville days, Miss Hotely stated that she appeared in a wide variety of parts from ingenue to old woman but it was her ability for the absurd that delighted the movie-going public and made her a star.

By 1915, Miss Hotely's "Sis Hopkins" type of role resulted in her being voted one of the most popular players of the year. From 1909 to 1916, when the husband-and-wife team severed their contract with Lubin, the comedienne appeared in numerous short films *(A Hot Time in Atlantic City, Man Wanted, A Gay Time in New York City, The Actress and Her Jewels, Nora the Cook, Fixing Aunty Up, A Stage Door Flirtation, Kate the Cop, Training a Tightwad, She Must Elope, The Detective, Minnie the Widow, Her Wooden-Leg, and An Awful Artist)* usually with Billy Reeves or the up-and-coming comedian Oliver "Babe" Hardy caught up in the hilarious antics of her comedies. Equally adept at drama, critics praised her performance in *A Mountain Mother* (1913) but it was the slovenly "Sis Hopkins of the kitchen" roles that typed her throughout her career.

When Hollywood became the center of the film industry, Mr. and Mrs. Hotaling settled there, where he remained active in the film industry, primarily as an actor and she (with her brand of comedy now outdated) retired after appearing in *Girls Who Dare* (1929). At the time of Hotaling's death (July 13, 1938), his *Variety* obituary listed no survivors. Miss Hotely became virtually a forgotten star of the past and when she died on April 6, 1954, in Coronado, California, her obituary did not appear in any of the leading trade journals.

Justine Johnstone

Justine Johnstone was without a doubt one of the most beautiful stars to ever grace the stage and screen. She is remembered mostly for her beauty, but she also had a brilliant mind, and it was her intelligence that provided her with a meaningful vocation far from the entertainment world. When the time came for her to turn her back on the bright lights of Broadway and the glamour of Hollywood, she did so, never looking back.

Born the daughter of Sophy and Gustave Johnstone in Englewood, New Jersey, on January 31, 1895, Miss Johnstone, after leaving the Englewood public schools, attended the Manor School at Larchmont, New York. The blonde beauty of the teenager attracted the attention of photographers and she won a beauty contest sponsored by the First International Exposition of Photographic Arts. Her work as a photographer's model attracted the attention of stage and film producers.

When the Famous Players Company offered the young model the role of the spiteful and selfish "Amelia" in support of Marguerite Clark, she accepted and made her film debut in *The Crucible* (1914). With Vernon and Irene Castle, Miss Johnstone began her stage career in *Watch Your Step*. Within a short time the beauty of the actress won her a role in Gaby Deslys' play *Stop! Look! Listen!* When Florenz Ziegfeld cast her in the *Follies* of 1915-1916, he made her one of Broadway's brightest musical comedy stars eagerly sought after by the producers. In support of Raymond Hitchcock in *Betty* (1916), Ed Wynn in *Over the Top* (1917), and Tom Powers in *Oh, Boy* (1917), she became the epitome of the Broadway musical comedy star.

In 1917, after several well-known artists called her "America's loveliest woman" and known as the "most beautiful blonde on Broadway," Miss Johnstone realized that musical comedy actresses were never taken seriously as actresses. She abandoned the musical comedy stage and joined the Poli Stock Company in Waterbury, Connecticut where for the next seven months she appeared in stock to gain additional stage experience. While appearing in stock her romance with Broadway producer Walter Wanger resulted in marriage in 1919.

As Taylor Holmes' leading lady in his comedy *Nothing But Lies* Miss Johnstone began her brief film career. With the film's success she signed with the Realart Company where she was one of the company's stars (1920-1921) in *Blackbirds, A Heart to Let, Sheltered Daughters*, and *The Plaything of Broadway.* In 1921, she told interviewer Grace Lamb that she didn't want to play bobbed-hair ingenues nor impossible maidens with languishing eyes. When Realart failed to provide her the challenging roles she sought, she ended her contract.

In 1923, Mr. and Mrs. Walter Wanger went to England and while there Miss Johnstone appeared on the London stage in *Polly Preferred.* After returning to New York City in 1925 Miss Johnstone ended her film career after appearing opposite Anita Stewart in Metro's *Never the Twain Shall Meet.*

As the wife of a noted producer, the mother of a son, Oliver Wanger, and tiring of the life of a social leader, Miss Johnstone became interested in medicine and, with no medical or scientific background, she entered the College of Physicians and Surgeons in New York City to study medicine. In 1931, she became an associate of Dr. H. H. Thomas and Dr. Samuel Hirschfield in the field of pathological research. When her marriage to Wanger ended in divorce in 1938, the former actress, now a noted pathologist, devoted the remainder of her life to medical research. When, as Justine Wanger, she died of congestive heart failure in Santa Monica, California, on September 3, 1982, the once "most beautiful blonde on

Broadway" had been out of the limelight for so long that there were no obituaries published in the trade papers.

Lamar Johnstone

The virile handsomeness of Lamar Johnstone made him one of the screen's romantic heroes of the early two-reel melodramas, who by his own choice successfully became the screen's most handsome villain.

Johnstone was born in Fairfax, Virginia, in 1886 and educated in New York City, but the early years of the actor's life are a mystery. Film biographies stated that his first theatrical experience was in summer stock in Rome, Georgia (1908). He then toured the South, playing juvenile roles for two years with the Harrington Players in repertoire and ended his stage career when he toured the Orpheum circuit for a season in a vaudeville musical comedy sketch (1910).

The actor's stage work and his good looks resulted in his being signed briefly by the Kalem Company, for whom he made his film debut. Lured away by the Eclair Company, Johnstone was signed for romantic leads opposite Barbara Tennant in a series of film shorts *(Because of Bobbie, Robin Hood, Silent Jim, Foiling a Fortune Hunter*, and *Filial Love)*. When the Majestic Company signed him in 1913, he appeared in leading roles in numerous two-reelers opposite the company's leading ladies (Vera Sisson, Francelia Billington, Marguerite Loveridge, and Ann Drew) in a wide variety of heroic roles *(A Trade Secret, The Tie That Binds, The Reformed Candidate, The Banker's Son*, and *The Message of the Flowers)*. The following year (1914) the actor joined the Selig Company at Edendale where as the handsome hero he was seen in *The Lady and the Tiger, The Face in the Window, The Lady Killer, A Tragedy of Panama*, and *Unfinished Portrait.*

When the American Company offered him the role of the villain in the company's 1916 fifteen-episode serial thriller *The Secret of the Submarine* opposite Juanita Hansen, the actor gladly switched from hero to villain, a role he thoroughly enjoyed playing. He was quoted in *Motion Picture Magazine* (October 1916) as saying of his part in the serial, "Mine is a role without a single redeeming trait. I'm bad, morally, at the beginning of the serial, and I get worse with every chapter. Every chance I get, I pick on some defenseless girl. I try to double-cross the woman I'm working with. Realizing this fact, I expect no sympathy whatever from the audience—and if I get any, I'll be bitterly disappointed, for I want them to admit I am acting as if I really were that sort of man."

With the success of *The Secret Submarine* and the movie-going public's acceptance of the feature film, a new phase began in Johnstone's career. The former two-reeler hero became one of the screen's most popular villains, only occasionally playing the hero. Between 1916-1919 he was seen with William Farnum in *Ben Blair, The Last of the Duanes, The Lone Star Ranger* (as the killer), and *Wolves of the Night.* He tried to rid Alma Rubens of her inheritance in *Diane of the Green Van,* was a fake hypnotist in Dustin Farnum's *A Man in the Open,* Tyrone Power's pampered son in *The Planter.* He supported Kathlyn Williams in *The Ne'er-Do-Well,* Juliette Day in *The Calender Girl,* Billie Rhodes in *The Girl of My Dreams,* Constance Collier in *Tongues of Men,* Monroe Salisbury in *That Devil Bateese,* Olive Thomas in *The Spite Bride,* and Charles Ray in *The Sheriff's Son* for the various studios (Selig, Pallas, Morosco, American, Bluebird, Fox, Ince, and Selznick).

On May 21, 1919, while he was on location with the William Farnum company in Palm Springs, California, the film colony was shocked to learn of the handsome villain's sudden death. A brief obituary appeared in the trade journal *The Billboard,* but *Variety* failed to report his death.

Mollie King

The life of Mollie King in the waning days of the second decade of the new century was a Lepape *Vogue* cover. A stunning blonde beauty, she epitomized the successful musical comedy star before the flapper of the 1920s forever changed the role of women. Envied not only for her success on the stage but also as a member of the theatrical smart set, she had the best the times offered—swathed in furs as she emerged from long limousines, dressed in the latest designer gowns on her way to and from the theatre, and living in an apartment in the exclusive Ansonia Hotel where her living room windows looked down upon Broadway, the street that was home to her.

A New York City native, Mollie King was born the daughter of Mary Costigan and Thomas King on April 16, 1898, the youngest of three children (brother Charles became a Broadway star and well-known film player and sister Nellie became a well-known musical and comic opera star). Born into a theatrical family, she made her debut in vaudeville at the age of eight months and her first stage part of consequence was at the age of seven in Maxine Elliott's *Her Own Way,* a hit both in New York and London. As a child actress she also appeared in *A Royal Family, The Little Princess,* and *Joshua Whitcomb* before touring the Orpheum Circuit with her sister (she had earlier toured the vaudeville circuits with her brother and sister as *The Three Kings).* On her return to New York City, she appeared at the Winter Garden in the *Passing Show of 1913* and *Ziegfeld Follies* before graduating from Wadleigh High School.

Truly a product of her theatrical environment, Miss King was a seasoned performer by the time of her graduation from high school. With her schooling behind her, the popular actress understudied Elizabeth Brice in *The Winsome Widow* and was supporting Sam Bernard in *The Belle of Bond Street* (1914) when executives of the World Company lured her away from the Broadway musical comedy stage to star in films. Miss King made her film debut in *A Woman's Power* (1916), the film version of the Charles Neville Buck novel *The Code of the Mountains.* As a World star, successes followed in *Fate's Boomerang, The Summer Girl,* and *All Men* in 1916 before signing with the Astra-Pathé Company for starring roles (1917-1918) in *Kick In, Blind Man's Luck,* and *The On-the-Square-Girl.* The success of these dramas led to her starring in two of the company's popular serials *The Mystery of the Double Cross* and *Seven Pearls.* After starring in Ivan's *Human Clay* Miss King was tired of film drama and returned to the stage.

In 1919, when offered one of the leading roles opposite her brother in *Good Morning Judge,* she returned to the Broadway stage for a successful run and also found time to appear in the film version of Isabel Ostrander's mystery drama *Suspense,* but the year's big event for the actress was her marriage to wealthy Kenneth D. Alexander. Marriage limited her stage and film work and after appearing on the screen in *Greater Than Love* (1920), *Women Men Forget* (1920), *Suspicious Wives* (1921), *Her Majesty* (1922), and on the stage in *Blue Eyes* (1921) "Mollie of Manhattan" turned her back on her theatrical and film career.

A life literally spent in the theatre, the actress ended her professional career and became a member of New York's social set who followed the society seasons between New York and Florida. Thereafter when her name appeared in print it was as Mrs. Alexander attending some social function. When the "crash of 29" and the depression left many of the former wealthy with financial difficulties, the Alexanders found themselves among them. In 1935, when Miss King's sister died, *Variety* printed that her husband was gravely ill but that she planed to Palm Beach with a surgeon in an effort to save her sister. When the marriage to Alexander ended (by death or divorce is unknown) the former actress married Thomas Claffey. The couple lived quietly in Fort Lauderdale, Florida, until December 28, 1981, when Miss King died from a stroke. She was survived by her husband.

Kathleen Kirkham

When "The End" flashed upon the screen in those pre-World War I film dramas, the virginal ingenue and hero embraced and lived happily ever after with the heavy (male or female) paying for his or her dastardly deeds. The female heavy was known as a vampire as she had the power (sexual) to vamp the hero away from the hearth of home, and it was she who usually had the best role. Theda Bara epitomized the vampire but throughout the teens and twenties the studios had a bevy of female heavies for luring the hero away from the heroine and luring the movie-going public to the theatres. One of those long forgotten ladies of sin was Kathleen Kirkham who, for the most part, played the role throughout her film career.

Born the daughter of Caroline Leisen and Richard Kirkham, Kathleen Kirkham was born in Menominee, Michigan, on April 15, 1895, and was educated primarily at the Cummock School in her native state. As with so many young school girls at this time, the enticing lure of the stage led her to join a stock company in Lakeside, Wisconsin. Traveling the stock circuits later led her to Los Angeles where she appeared opposite Dustin Farnum in stage productions of *The Virginian* and *The Squaw Man.*

Miss Kirkham attended a couple of dramatic schools before making her film debut in a small role in the Fine Arts production *Strathmore* (1915) but the heavy role in *The Eyes of the World* (1917) labeled her with the type of parts she was destined to play. Primarily a free-lance player between 1916-1920, the actress appeared for Douglas Fairbanks' company in *A Modern Musketeer, Arizona*, and *He Comes Up Smiling*, played Tarzan's mother (Lady Greystoke) in Elmo Lincoln's *Tarzan of the Apes,* loses out for her treachery to Colleen Moore in *When Dawn Came,* was the frustrated wife in *Parlor, Bedroom and Bath,* blackmailed Frank Keenan in *Dollar for Dollar,* is tried for murder in *The Master Mind,* and Nigel Barrie fell prey to his flirting stepmother (Miss Kirkham) in *Josselyn's Wife;* the actress also played mother roles and scheming ladies who made life miserable for the heroine *(The Gay Lord Quex, The Seal of Silence, The Married Virgin, The Third Kiss,* and *The Beloved Cheater).* In a 1920 interview the actress said, "I've been married to almost every character man on the screen, and I've been the mother of many a young girl who was really older than myself, or anyway, just one or two years younger."

The 1920s found Miss Kirkham in demand by the various studios for her ability to play the heavy you loved to hate. The actress's roles, usually the second lead, varied little *(Beau Revel, The Innocent Cheat, Back to Yellow Jacket, A Homespun Vamp, The Lonely Road, The White Moth, The Isle of Retribution,* and *The King of the Turf)* between 1921 and 1926. With the film industry in a period of change, Miss Kirkham, now happily married to H. N. Woodruff and tired of the vampish roles, ended her film career. Her marriage ended with the death of Woodruff and when Miss Kirkham died on November 7, 1961, her occupation was listed as a cook in a Santa Barbara private residence. Burial for the actress was in Hollywood Cemetery.

Virginia Kirtley

Of all Charlie Chaplin's leading ladies, Virginia Kirtley has the distinction of being the first and the least remembered. In those long-ago early days of filmmaking, the film magazines and trade journals reveal a popular starlet whose career as leading lady to the slapstick comedians promised her stardom, but she preferred marriage and when tragedy ended the happy union, it was too late to recoup her former popularity.

Born the daughter of Virginia Kirtley and Tom Saffell in Bowling Green, Missouri, on November 11, 1883, Miss Kirtley attended Culter Academy and Colorado College before embarking on a stage career in 1910 with the Burbank Theatre in Los Angeles and briefly in stock with Florence Stone before entering films.

In 1912, when the IMP Company offered the actress a film contract, she accepted but her IMP stay was brief. In 1913, she joined Mack Sennett's Keystone Company and became Chaplin's leading lady in his film debut, the one-reeler *Making a Living* (1914). While appearing in only three of Chaplin's comedies (the others were *A Film Johnnie* and *Tango Tangles),* she appeared in Sennett's *The Woman Haters, Chicken Chaser, A Flirt's Mistake, Too Many Brides,* and *A Bathing Beauty* before joining the American Company (1915). She became the leading lady for Irving Cummings *(The Doctor's Strategy, The First Stone, The Haunting Memory, In the Mansion of Loneliness,* and *When the Fire Bell Rang),* Joseph Harris *(The Constable's Daughter* and *Mrs. Cook's Cooking),* and Webster Campbell *(Dreams Realized, Oh, Daddy,* and *Persistence Wins).*

In mid-1915, she joined the Selig Company and for next three years—appearing primarily opposite Robyn Adair—starred in a series of one-, two- and three-reelers *(Her Careers, Mother's Birthday, Polishing Up Polly, The Voice of Eva, The Framed Miniature, The Girl Detective, The Grinning Skull, Only a Rose, The Last of the Clan, The Purchase Price,* and *The Road to Fame).* On loan to the Centuar Film Company she was seen in the feature Western drama *A Law Unto Himself* (1916). After appearing in the social drama *Who Shall Take My Life?* (1918), Miss Kirtley abandoned her acting career.

In 1917, when Miss Kirtley married the popular Nestor comedian Eddie Lyons, she was at the peak of her popularity. After her marriage she gradually ended her acting career and collaborated with her husband on writing scenarios *(The Nightcap)* for the Eddie Lyons and Lee Moran comedies. After the birth of her daughter, Frankie, she retired from the screen for the role of housewife and mother. Tragedy struck on August 30, 1926, when Lyons died from a brain tumor. In 1928, Miss Kirtley tried to resume her acting career but her comeback was unsuccessful—too many years and too many changes had occurred in the film industry. The former actress retired and lived in obscurity until her death on August 19, 1956 in Sherman Oaks, California.

Fred Mace

Fred Mace, an early film comedian and charter member of the Keystone Company, appeared in numerous comedies in the company's early days. Had he not "gone Hollywood" and stayed with Keystone throughout his career he would perhaps be remembered as one of the legendary Keystone star comedians, but his determination to be a major star made it easy for film producers to persuade him to leave Keystone and head his own company as star, director, producer, and writer. Mack Sennett did not prevent the comedian from striking out on his own and, when he failed to make it, Sennett allowed him to return to the Keystone fold where with his teammates he found success. What Fred Mace failed to understand was that stardom for him came with the madcap Keystoners and not as a star of his own films.

Fred Mace was born in Philadelphia, Pennsylvania, on August 22, 1878. Educated in the city's public schools, he studied dentistry but dentistry lacked the allure of the stage and when an opportunity came to join the Wilbur Opera Company (1899) he abandoned it for the life of a roving actor. After years on the road in musical comedy *(The Chinese Honeymoon, Piff! Paff! Pouff, The Chocolate Soldier,* and *The Time, the Place and the Girl)* the constant traveling lost its appeal and he sought a more stable livelihood. Through his acquaintance with Mack Sennett he joined, in 1910, the comedy branch of the Biograph Company. Under Sennett's supervision he won a modicum of popularity as the actor who poked fun at Sherlock Holmes as "Algy" the blundering watchman and as "One Round O'Brien" the "Don Quixote" of the boxing ring in early Biograph comedies *(A Lucky Toothache, A Village Hero, The Lucky Horseshoe, Mr. Peck Goes Calling, Caught with the Goods,* and *The Wonderful Eye).*

With the success of the film parodies, Sennett teamed him in 1912 with Mabel Normand in *Brave and Bold, The Leading Man, The Close Call, His Own Fault, The First Kidnapping Case, The Brave Hunter,* and *The Fickle Spaniard.* So successful had he become as a Biograph comedian that when the IMP Company offered him a contract to star in his own comedies he departed from Biograph and Mack Sennett. The two comedies Mace made for IMP *(A Widow's Wiles* and *Lie Not to Your Wife)* failed to find favor with the public and his contract was canceled.

When Mack Sennett left Biograph in 1912 and formed his own Keystone Company, he took Mabel Normand, Ford Sterling, and Fred Mace with him to Los Angeles. When the newly formed company began production, Mace, under the direction of Sennett, George Nicholls, and Henry Lehrman, was teamed with Miss Normand and Sterling in numerous successful comedies. The success of the one-reelers made him one of Keystone's most recognizable clowns and his success attracted the attention of other companies who offered him lucrative contracts to star in his own films. The actor's departure from Keystone (1913) for Majestic, Gem, University, and Apollo companies led to a series of forgettable comedies several of which were based upon characters he and Sennett had developed at Biograph and Keystone. At this time (1913-1915) his most productive output was for the Apollo Company usually opposite Marguerite Loveridge (Marguerite Marsh) in *One Round O'Brien Comes East, His Nobs the Plumber, His Turkish Bath, Village School Days, Apollo Fred Sees the Point,* and *Up and Down.*

When his comedies failed at the box office and his career as a solo star was in decline, Mack Sennett again offered his friend the safety of Keystone—teamed once again with Mabel Normand *(Mabel at the Wheel, Mabel's Heroes* and *My Valet)* and Anna Luther *(Crooked to the End).* In *Motion Picture Magazine* (November 1915) he wrote a poignant article titled "Say His Head Has Been Reduced" about his opinionated self-centeredness as star who deserved more than what Keystone offered him. He went on and stated that the mistake of his life was leaving Keystone and striking out on his own and when he was offered a chance to return he gladly accepted. When he returned, he found other and more popular comedians and after appearing (1916) in *Love Will Conquer, Village Vampire, Bath Tub Perils, A Lover's Might, An Old Scoundrel,* and *His Last Scent* Mace terminated his contract with Keystone and his association with Mack Sennett; there would not be another opportunity for the comedian to return.

In 1917, with his film career virtually over in Los Angeles, he returned to New York City, seeking film or stage roles. The roles failed to materialize. Distress over his unemployment brought on a stroke and he was found dead on February 21, 1917, in his suite at the Hotel Astor. He was survived by his widow and parents.

Martha Mansfield

Martha Mansfield was one of several musical comedy actresses whom artists and photographers labeled "the most beautiful girl in New York City" at the end of World War I. The beauty of these actresses attracted the attention of film moguls who made film stardom a reality for the former Broadway beauties. Miss Mansfield's entrance into films followed this route but tragedy prevented the actress from obtaining her goal as one the greats of the silent era.

The daughter of Harriett Gibson and Morris Ehrlich was born in Mansfield, Ohio (or New York City) on July 14, 1899. The place of birth is questionable. Mansfield listed in film directories; her death certificate gives New York City; and she at times said New York City in interviews. But it was in Mansfield, Ohio, that she lived for the first fourteen years of her life. Following her education, which she received in her native city, the aspiring actress began her stage career in a stock company. When the stock engagement ended a few weeks later she and her mother left Mansfield to launch a stage career in New York City.

As with countless other hopefuls the rounds were made to theatrical producers without any success. When not making the rounds she also did modeling for artists and photographers to make ends meet. Finally the break came when she was offered a part (probably in the chorus) in DeWolf Hopper's 1913 musical *Hop O' My Thumb,* followed by an engagement in one of the Winter Garden's spectacular revues. Her showgirl ability brought her to the attention of Florenz Ziegfeld and Charles Dillingham who cast her in their production of *The Century Girl* (1916). After appearing in a production of A. H. Woods' *On with the Dance* (probably a touring company) Miss Ehrlich signed a film contract.

With a great deal of fanfare the French film comedian Max Linder was signed by the Essanay Company in December 1916 for a series of *Max* two-reel comedies. Essanay signed Martha Ehrlich (early fan magazines listed her under her real name) as Linder's leading lady in the series (by the time the series ended she had dropped Ehrlich for Mansfield). The 1917 series was not a success for Linder but the beauty of the talented Miss Mansfield attracted the attention of the Metro Film Corporation who signed her as Harold Lockwood's leading lady in *Broadway Bill* (1918).

As a Ziegfeld Girl Miss Mansfield appeared in *Midnight Frolic* (1919) before abandoning the stage for the screen. As one of the screen's promising young players of 1919 she appeared in supporting roles in World's social drama *The Hand Invisible*, Selznick's drama *The Perfect Lover* opposite Eugene O'Brien, and Fox's *Should a Husband Forgive?*

The 1920 Famous Players-Lasky film version of Robert Louis Stevenson's *Dr. Jekyll and Mr. Hyde* advanced the actress from supporting to leading lady. The star John Barrymore and the director John S. Robertson wanted an actress who was beautiful the way a young girl should be—sweet, vivid, and wholesome. They found that Miss Mansfield had the qualifications and cast her in the role of "Millicent Carew," a role that rewarded her forever with her moment in film history.

The success of *Dr. Jekyll and Mr. Hyde* made Miss Mansfield an actress in demand by other studios and her career continued its rise with leading roles in 1920 in *Civilian Clothes, Mothers of Men, Women Men Love*, and *The Wonderful Chance*. In 1921, she became one of the Selznick Company's leading players in *Gilded Lies, The Last Doon*, and *The Man of Stone*. A star on the rise in 1922-1923 she was seen in a wide range of roles *(Queen of the Moulin Rouge, Till We Meet Again, Fog Bound, Is Money Everything, The Leavenworth Case, The Little Red Schoolhouse, Potash and Perlmutter, The Silent Command, The Women in Chains*, and *Youthful Cheaters)* before signing with the Fox Company in 1923.

As one of the stars of Fox's film version of the popular David Belasco play *The Warrens of Virginia*, Miss Mansfield was sent with the other players on location to San Antonio, Texas. In the role of "Agatha Warren," the actress had just finished filming a scene and returned to her automobile in her Civil War costume when her clothing suddenly burst into flames from a recklessly dropped match. Miss Mansfield jumped from the car consumed in flames, her costar Wilfred Lytell threw his overcoat over her, saving her face and neck, The fire was quickly extinguished ,but she had received severe burns about the body. The actress was rushed to a local hospital where she died less than twenty-four hours later on November 30, 1923. Miss Mansfield was returned to New York City for burial.

Vivian Martin

Once known as the youngest star on the Broadway stage, Vivian Martin entered films in the industry's infancy, became a star, and headed her own film company. When the public and the film producers failed to let her grow into the adult roles of the 1920s, she returned to the stage and became a success in roles she was unable to play on the screen.

A daughter of a traveling actor, Vivian Martin was born in Sparta near Grand Rapids, Michigan, on July 2, 1893. As a child actress she was educated while traveling with her parents on the road. By accident she made her stage debut when one of the children appearing in the Richard Mansfield production of *Cyrano de Bergerac* (1899) became ill and her father, an actor in the company, suggested his daughter take over the role. As a child actress she quickly won recognition in children's parts with Andrew Mack, appeared in the title role opposite Crystal Herne in the Shubert production of *Little Lord Fauntleroy* (1905). Recommended to Charles Frohman by Maude Adams she toured for a year in the title role of *Peter Pan* and by 1908 she was appearing with William H. Crane in *Father and the Boys*. She became a Broadway star between 1911-1914 in *The Spendthrift, My Only Son, Officer 666, Stop Thief!, The Marriage Game*, and *The High Cost of Living*.

The Broadway successes of the young actress resulted in her signing a film contract in 1914 with the World Picture Corporation and making her film debut in the drama *The Wishing Ring: An Idyll of Old England*. Film stardom came quickly for the actress who Lillian Montanye described as a "Dresden china figurine with the happy mischief-laden eyes" who survived countless rags to riches misfortunes to live happily ever after in the arms of Harrison Ford or Douglas MacLean or Jack Pickford or Niles Welch or Tom Moore. Between 1915-1916, for the World Company, she starred in a wide range of comedy-dramas including *Butterfly on the Wheel, Old Dutch, Little Miss Brown, Little Mademoiselle, Merely Mary*

Ann, Over Night, The Little Dutch Girl, Her Father's Son, A Modern Thelma, The Right Direction, and *The Stronger Love*.

In 1917, Miss Martin joined the Famous Players-Lasky Film Corporation and starred as she said in the "scrubby and raggedy" roles that varied little between 1917-1919 when her career peaked in *The Fair Barbarians, Forbidden Paths, The Girl at Home, Little Miss Optimist, Molly Entangled, The Trouble Buster, A Kiss for Susie, Giving Becky a Chance, The Spirit of Romance, The Sunset Trail, The Wax Model, Her Country First, Mirandy Smiles, The Home Town Girl, His Official Fiancee, Jane Goes A-Wooing, Little Comrade, Louisiana, The Third Kiss*, and *You Never Saw Such a Girl*. So popular was she in 1920 that when she left the Lasky Company, she starred in the first feature made by the British Gaumont Company in the United States, *Husbands and Wives*, and briefly formed the Vivian Martin Production Company starring in *The Song of the Soul*. When she formed her own company a *Motion Picture Magazine* article (1921) described her as, "A business woman with an artistic temperament and is clever enough to combine the two to her very great advantage. She has studied every side and every angle of the picture business. She is a past mistress of screen technique."

By 1920, with the fairy tale heroine of innocence in the past, Miss Martin after appearing in Graham's *Mother Eternal* (1921) and Goldwyn's *Pardon My French* (1921) and *Soiled* (1924) ended her film career. Realizing the storybook ingenue image had typecast her in films she returned to the stage successfully in *Just Married* (1921) in the role of "Roberta Adams," a role she played for the next two years. In 1923, after appearing in *The Wild Westcotts*, she took *Just Married* (1924) for a successful run to London. On her return to the United States she and Donald Brian toured the Keith vaudeville circuit in a version of *Just Married* (1925). Returning to the Broadway stage in 1926, she appeared between 1926-1929 in *Puppy Love, Hearts Are Trumps, Half-a-Widow, Caste, Mrs. Dane's Defense, Sherlock Holmes*, and *Marry the Man* before retiring.

With the passing years Miss Martin gradually faded from the limelight with little thereafter found in print about her. Her private life she always guarded. Her 1913 marriage to William Winter Jefferson, the son of actor Joseph Jefferson, ended in divorce but her successful marriage in 1926 to Arthur W. Samuels paved the way for her to enjoy a way of life she had never known as an actress. In later years her only connection with the theatre was as a benefactress of the New York Professional Children's School, which she supported until her death. When the once star of the

Mary Fuller (*Courtesy Donald Lee Nelson Collection*)

Fay Tincher (*Courtesy Donald Lee Nelson Collection*)

Maude George (*Courtesy Donald Lee Nelson Collection*)

Margarita Fisher (*Courtesy Donald Lee Nelson Collection*)

Dorothy Phillips (*Courtesy Donald Lee Nelson Collection*)

Bessie Eyton (*Courtesy Donald Lee Nelson Collection*)

Martha Mansfield (*Courtesy Donald Lee Nelson Collection*)

Lucille Ricksen (*Courtesy Donald Lee Nelson Collection*)

Marjorie Daw (*Courtesy Donald Lee Nelson Collection*)

Allene Ray (*Courtesy Sam Grossman Collection*)

Dolores Cassinelli (*Courtesy Sam Grossman Collection*)

Myrtle Gonzalez (*Courtesy Donald Lee Nelson Collection*)

Violet Mersereau (*Courtesy Donald Lee Nelson Collection*)

William Garwood (*Courtesy Sam Grossman Collection*)

Fred Mace (*Courtesy Sam Grossman Collection*)

David Powell (*Courtesy Sam Grossman Collection*)

stage and screen died on March 16, 1987, in New York City, her passing only warranted a brief death announcement in the *New York Times*.

Violet Mersereau

An actress of incredible beauty, Violet Mersereau was the epitome of the silent screen ingenue; so successful was she in the role that her career began and ended as an ingenue. When she gave the hero that defenseless "please help me" look she not only won his heart but the hearts of the audience as well. Truly one of the most popular of the early-day stars, her career ended in the mid-1920s and with the cessation of her career she faded into obscurity never to be heard from again.

Miss Mersereau was born in New York City on October 2, 1897. Her mother was a French actress know as Mme. Luzanzie. At the death of her father when she was nine her mother, in order to make a living, turned to the stage for herself and daughters (sister Claire Mersereau also became a stage and film actress). In 1906, Violet Mersereau began her stage career when Margaret Anglin engaged her for a season. Her success as a child actress led to the role of "Flora" in the original company of *The Clansman* and starring in the road company of *Rebecca of Sunnybrook Farm.*

Allen Douglas wrote in *Motion Picture Magazine* (November 1915), "Violet Mersereau does not like to speak about herself—I could see that the very minute I began to talk to her." She had an intense desire for privacy. Very little was published about her, and what can be found in the early film magazines often conflicts with the known facts.

The early magazines reported that Miss Mersereau made her film debut in 1911 with David Horsley's Nestor Company, but there are film credits for her as early as 1908. Perhaps this can be explained by her statement, "After leaving Miss Anglin's company I made a beginning in motion pictures, at an awkward age, dressed to look as old as possible before I returned to the stage during the theatrical season and where in the summer I would sign up with some film concern." No doubt the actress was talking about her American Biograph days when between 1908-1911 she appeared under the direction of D. W. Griffith in numerous short films *(The Feud and the Turkey, The Test of Friendship, A Gold Necklace, Her Terrible Ordeal, Sunshine Sue*, and *The Cricket on the Hearth).*

When the actress joined the Nestor Company she was told by a director that as long as she could ride and swim she would be all right for ingenue leads. The early two-reelers of the Nestor Company *(Alias Yellowstone*

Joe and *The New Clerk)*, the IMP Company *(The Shot That Failed* and *The Big Sister)* and the Bison Company *(A Western Girl's Dream* and *An Even Break)* demonstrated to the actress that the director knew exactly what he was talking about.

After she was loaned to Famous Players for the title role in *The Spitfire* (1914) opposite Carlyle Blackwell, Miss Mersereau under Carl Laemmle's capable hands was groomed for stardom and she became IMP's leading ingenue in a series of films opposite the popular William Garwood *(The Tenth Commandment, When the Heart Calls, The Blank Page, The Broken Toy,* and *Driven by Fate).* Between 1916-1919 the actress's Universal career peaked with the ingenue leads in *The Wolf of Debt*, the Northwest drama *Autumn, Broken Fetters, The Great Problem, The Honor of Mary Blake, The Narrow Paths, The Path of Happiness, The Boy Girl, The Girl by the Roadside, Little Miss Nobody, The Little Terror, The Raggedy Queen, Susan's Gentleman, Morgan's Raiders, Together*, and *The Nature Girl.*

When the actress terminated her contract in 1919, her films for other companies *(Finders Keepers, Out of the Depths, Luck*, and *Thunderclap)* lacked the success of her Universal films. Her Fox films *Nero* (1922) and *The Shepherd King* (1923) met with some success but the film mores were changing and Miss Mersereau's ingenue roles had become relics from an earlier day of filmmaking. After appearing in the forgettable Lee-Bradford film *The Wives of the Prophet*, the actress ended her film career.

With the passing of the years the whereabouts of the once popular actress are clouded in unfounded rumors. One source stated that she died in Italy, another rumor is of her death in 1961, but no one has been able to verify her death with substantiated proof. In the early 1940s, Miss Mersereau and her sister were living in New York City, but her whereabouts since is unknown.

Corliss Palmer

In late 1918, the Eugene V. Brewster Publications *(Motion Picture Classic, Motion Picture Magazine*, and *Shadowland)* announced the "Fame and Fortune Contest" for aspiring young actresses and actors (a few men did submit photographs). The rules required two photographs accompanied by a fact sheet (name, age, address, and experience) that would allow the judges (Mary Pickford, Olga Petrova, Howard Chandler Christy, Thomas Ince, J. Stuart Blackton, Maurice Tourneur, Samuel

Lumiere, Carl Laemmle, Jesse Lasky, David Belasco, Blanche Bates, and Eugene V. Brewster) to pick "Monthly Honor Roll" winners with the photographs appearing in the magazines. At the end of the year about twenty-five "Honor Roll" girls were invited to New York City for a series of screen tests from which the winners would be picked. They received two years of publicity in the magazines and roles in films by the various companies. The "Fame and Fortune Contest" ran monthly in the Brewster magazines from 1919 until its demise in July 1923. The contest was an immediate success as thousands and thousands of photographs were submitted to the magazines. From the girls who entered, only two won lasting film stardom—Clara Bow and Mary Astor; other winners (Blanche McGarrity, Virginia Brown Faire, Corliss Palmer, Helen Lee Worthing, Allene Ray, and Hazel Keener) won a modicum of fame as leading ladies in the 1920s.

One of the 1920 contest winners was Corliss Palmer of Macon, Georgia, a Southern teenager whose beauty promised her an opportunity for stardom; however, when she became romantically involved with her mentor, the once favorable publicity became unfavorable and within a short time she found herself on a downward slide that led to alcoholism and confinement in a state hospital for the mentally insane.

Corliss Palmer was born the daughter of Julia Farrell and Luther Martin near Macon, Georgia (probably the small town of Edison, Georgia) on July 25, 1902 (her death certificate gives 1909 as year of birth). Educated in Macon she attended the Lanier High School and as did so many other high school girls she submitted her photographs to the "Fame and Fortune" contest. When the judges picked her as one of the finalists, she was invited to New York for screen tests. *Motion Picture Magazine* (February 1921) reported, "Corliss Palmer, of Macon, Georgia, came North without an atom of dramatic training, or an iota of theatrical or motion picture experience. To her great surprise, it was found that she possessed greater beauty and screen possibilities than the thousands who had entered the contest and she was accordingly made the winner."

Her mentor, Eugene V. Brewster, enamored with Miss Palmer's beauty and talent quickly used his influence as a publisher to provide the publicity needed for stardom. He flooded the magazines with photographs and articles about her. He had the Wilton Chemical Company of Brooklyn develop and manufacture the "Corliss Palmer Face Powder" and she became a featured writer in *Motion Picture Magazine* on her beauty secrets. Brewster's film company cast her in starring roles in a series of forgettable films which included *Ramon, The Sailmaker* (her film debut),

From Farm to Fame, In the Blood, Flaming Virtue, The Man Disturber, and *The Thistle and the Rose* between 1921-1922.

Brewster's publicity campaigns had made Miss Palmer a recognized star in the printed pages of his magazines but her films were rejected by the public. In 1926 the divorce of Mrs. Brewster from her husband and the marriage of Miss Palmer to Brewster provided lots of negative publicity for the actress. As the wife of an influential publisher and a member of Hollywood's social life, the actress in the mid and late 1920s appeared prominently for various studios in *Her Second Chance, Honeymoon Hate, A Man's Past, Polly of the Movies, The Return of Boston Blackie, Clothes Make the Woman, George Washington Cohen. Into the Night, The Night Bird, The Noose, Scarlet Youth, Trial Marriage, Broadway Fever,* and *Sex Madness.* After appearing in Paramount's *Honeymoon Lane* (1931) her film career and marriage to Brewster ended. From then on the fast lane of life was a downward spiral for the actress. A later marriage to stuntman and rodeo performer William Taylor removed her from Hollywood's social life. With her husband she traveled the rodeo circuits and over the years heavy drinking took its toll. Miss Palmer was later admitted to the Carmarillo State Hospital where on August 27, 1952, she died. At the time of her death her occupation was listed as seamstress. The former "Fame and Fortune Contest" winner who had been out of the limelight for so long died without any reported obituaries in the trade papers.

Virginia Pearson

When film historians write of the early film vamps they usually refer to Theda Bara, Nita Naldi, and Barbara La Marr. These women were exotically gifted at driving their victims to ruin before the gods of fate made them pay for their evil deeds. Virginia Pearson, an actress historians often omit from the genre, once ranked as one of the screen's leading vampires. While the vamps of the pre-WWI era lived lives dedicated by their studios to enhance their screen images, Miss Pearson differed from her sister vamps in that when the cameras stopped she cast off the vampish accoutrements for the role of a homemaker and wife of a well-known film actor.

Virginia Pearson was born the daughter of Alice Galloway and Joseph R. Pearson in Louisville, Kentucky, on March 7. 1888. Educated in the Louisville public schools, she became interested in the arts and, at the age of fifteen, sold sketches to Kentucky newspapers. After the completion of her education she briefly became a reporter on *The Courier Journal* and *The Louisville Times* before joining a stock company under Henry W. Savage's management. She later told a magazine writer that "as a stage actress I had no early struggles that many actresses encountered, the stage roles came easy to me from the start." Success in stock eventually led her to Broadway where in 1909 she appeared opposite Robert Hilliard in Porter Emerson Brown's play (inspired by Rudyard Kipling's poem "The Vampire") *A Fool There Was*. Miss Pearson's success as the vampire typecast the actress thereafter as to the roles she would play throughout her starring days on the stage and screen. Other stage successes included *Nearly Married* (1913) and in support of William Faversham in *The Hawk* (1914). The actress' dark exotic beauty and acting skills brought her to the attention of film producers and her film debut came about as she said, "Tired and bored of the idleness between stage engagements I embarked upon a film career."

When exactly Miss Pearson entered films is in question; one source stated that she entered films in 1910 but other sources list her first film credits as *Aftermath* and *The Stain* in 1914. The actress joined the Vitagraph Company in 1915 and became one of the company's brightest stars in *The Turn of the Road, The Reward, The Hunted Woman, The Vital Question, The Writing on the Wall,* and *Thou Art the Man.* Lured away from Vitagaph by William Fox she became one of the company's leading vamps along with Theda Bara and Valeaka Suratt in 1916, with the company's publicizing her as "The beautiful Dixie photoplayer," "the modern Cleopatra of the movies," "the screen's heretic," "the statuesque William Fox Star," and "the screen' s most versatile beauty." As a Fox star between 1916-1919, the actress's film titles synopsized the worldly vampish roles she played in *Blazing Love, Daredevil Kate, Hypocrisy, A Tortured Heart, The War Bride's Secret, All for a Husband, The Biting Truth, Royal Romances, Sister Against Sisters, Thou Shalt Not Steal, When False Tongues Speak, Wrath of Love, Buchanan's Wife, A Daughter of France, The Firebrand, Her Price, The Liar, The Queen of Hearts, The Love Auction,* and *Stolen Honor.*

In 1919, Miss Pearson with her husband, the well-known screen villain Sheldon Lewis (the marriage probably occurred while they were appearing on the stage), formed the Virginia Pearson Photoplay Company with the actress as the star and Lewis as the treasurer and the leading villain. The company's two productions were *The Bishop's Emeralds* and *Impossible Catherine* (a modern day version of Shakespeare's *The Taming of the Shrew*).

With the coming of the "Jazz Age," the former film vamps became past icons with the actresses retiring from the screen as did Theda Bara or switching to character roles as did Miss Pearson. Throughout the 1920s Miss Pearson appeared prominently in *Wildness of Youth* (1922), *A Prince of a King* (1923), and in 1925 supported Lon Chaney in *The Phantom of the Opera,* Priscilla Bonner in *The Red Kimono* and Larry Semon in *The Wizard of Oz.*

After a vaudeville tour (1925-1926) with Lewis she returned to the screen in 1926 in *Atta Boy!, The Taxi Mystery,* and the serial *Lightning Hutch* and to the stage in the title role of the highly praised Henry Sundermann production of *Magda.* Between 1927-1929 she remained in demand at the various studios appearing in Chadwick's *Driven from Home,* Metro-Goldwyn-Mayer's *The Actress, Big City,* and *Trelawney of the Wells,* Pathé's *What Price Beauty,* and Universal's *Smilin' Guns* and *Silks and Satins.* The early 1930s brought an end to her career; after minor roles in *Danger Man* (1930), *Primrose Path* (1931), and *Back Street* (1932), Miss Pearson retired permanently from the screen.

The former actress spent her retirement living with her husband in obscurity in the Los Angeles area until the news media reported the death of Lewis on May 7, 1958. Death only briefly separated them; a month later, on June 6, 1958, Miss Pearson died from uremic poisoning.

Dorothy Phillips

By the early 1920s fate had bestowed upon Dorothy Phillips stardom on the silent screen, a storybook marriage to Allen J. Holubar, a prominent director and producer, and motherhood with the birth of daughter, Gwendolyn. The actress at the peak of success easily merged her professional and private life into one of wife, mother, and actress. The success of her films under Holubar's directorship made her one of the most sought-after stars whom the film magazine writers courted for interviews. The writers, anticipating interviewing a glamorous film star, came away with a story on a happily married woman who preferred discussing her life as a housewife and mother rather than the life of an actress. Miss Phillips' success and happiness suddenly ended with the untimely death of her husband.

Dorothy Phillips was born Dorothy Gwendolyn Strieble on Aisquith Street in Baltimore, Maryland, on October 30, 1889. Her education began at St. John's Convent and later she attended the Eastern Female High School and Shaftesbury College before making her stage debut.

The stage career of the aspiring actress began in her native city with the George Fawcett Stock Company, where she first faced the footlights at the Albaugh Theatre on North Charles Street under the name of Dorothy Phillips. After success with the Fawcett Stock Company she soon headed for the bright lights of Broadway, where for Henry W. Savage she was the star's understudy in *Mary Jane's Pa* and created the title role in *Pilate's Daughter.*

With no scheduled stage work in the summer of 1911, Miss Phillips made her film debut as Francis X. Bushman's leading lady in Essanay's *The Rosary, The New Manager, The Gordian Knot, Fate's Frolics*, and starred in *Love in the Hills* before returning to the stage in the fall in the Savage production of *Everywoman* opposite Allen J. Holubar. By the end of the play's run Miss Phillips had married her leading man.

Unable to find stage roles together the newlyweds decided to cast their fates with the fledgling film industry and in 1913 joined the Essanay Company. At Essanay Miss Phillips appeared in *The Final Judgment, The Price of Gold*, and opposite her husband in *The Prophecy* and *The Social Calls*. Carl Laemmle, impressed with the husband-and-wife's work on the stage, signed them to an IMP Company contract and Miss Phillips appeared in a series of two-reelers between 1914-1915 *(The Skull, Three Men Who Knew*, and *A Photoplay Without A Name).* In 1915, when the Rex Company merged with Universal, Miss Phillips appeared as Ben Wilson's leading lady in numerous two- and three-reelers *(The Cad, A Happy Pair, The Mystery of the Locked Room*, and *The Valley of Silent Men).*

By 1916, with the one- and two-reelers giving way to the feature film (five or more reels), Miss Phillips and Holubar were two of the screen's most prominent figures—she as a star and he as a director and producer. After the birth of her daughter (1916), Miss Phillips starred in Universal's *My Country Calls Me, The Mark of Cain, The Place Beyond the Winds, A Doll's House, Fires of Rebellion, The Girl in the Checkered Coat, Hell Morgan's Girl*, and *The Piper's Price* (Lon Chaney usually had the role of the villain in Miss Phillips' films). In 1917 under her husband's direction Miss Phillips scored a success in the society drama *A Soul for Sale*. In 1918-1919 after starring in *Broadway Love, The Grand Passion*, and *Destiny*, she starred exclusively under her husband's direction in the Universal hits *The Mortgaged Wife, The Risky Road, The Talk of the Town, The Heart of Humanity, Paid in Advance*, and *The Right to Happiness.*

After *Once to Every Woman* (1920) the husband-and-wife team left Universal and formed their own company with Miss Phillips as the star and Holubar as the producer and director.

Now at the pinnacle of success and counted as among the elite of Hollywood's professional and social life Miss Phillips starred in her husband's productions of *Man Woman Marriage* (1920), *Hurricane's Gal* (1922), and in Principal's *The World's a Stage* and Truart's *The Unknown Purple*.

The Hollywood hierarchy pointed with pride. at the image the Holubar family gave the world of life in Hollywood. The future never looked brighter for the actress when her husband starred her in *Slander the Woman* (1923). Soon after the completion of the film Holubar was stricken with a series of debilitating illnesses and the young executive died on November 20, 1923 in Los Angeles from pneumonia at the age of thirty-three.

Devastated by her husband's death Miss Phillips did not resume her film career until 1925 in Fox's *Every Man's Wife*, Truart's *The Sporting Chance*, and PDC's *Without Mercy*. In 1926, in one of her last starring roles, she appeared in the serial *The Bar-C Mystery*. Thereafter (1926-1930) the once starring roles became supporting roles *(Upstages, The Gay Deceiver, Cradle Snatchers, Broken Gates, Women Love Diamonds*, and *Jazz Cinderella)*. After 1930 she, as did other contemporaries, gradually faded into the film scenery as a bit and extra player (last seen in *Violent Saturday*, 1955 and *The Man Who Shot Liberty Valance*, 1962). When the former star died March 1, 1980, in Woodland Hills, California, only the local papers reported her death. She was survived by her daughter and four grandchildren.

David Powell

The Bluebook of the Screen (1924) wrote, "If a biography came under the title of 'Women I Have Kissed' David Powell would be one of the first to qualify, for his caresses have been showered upon the most famous queens of the screen—in pictures of course." Powell was indeed one of the handsomest of the leading men of the silent screen whose career was cut short by a early death.

The actor, who on the screen became the epitome of the British army officer (*Photoplay* writer Julian Johnson called him "the military heart burglar") was born in Glasgow, Scotland, on December 17, 1894. Educated in Glasgow, he began his stage career playing Shakespearian roles in one of Sir Herbert Beerbohm Tree's companies. Powell came to the United States in 1907 with Ellen Terry in *The Good Hope* and *Captain Brassbound's Conversion.* For three seasons with Forbes-Robertson he was in *The Passing of the Third Floor Back.* He next scored a success in a series of one-act plays at New York's Princess Theatre and was seen in *The Yellow Jacket* and *Outcast,* the latter with Elsie Ferguson in 1914.

Soon after the completion of the run of *Outcast* he was seen on the screen romancing Fania Marinoff in Famous Players' *One of the Girls* (1914). After making his film debut the handsome actor was quickly in demand by the female stars who clamored for him as their leading man—Mary Pickford *(The Dawn of a Tomorrow* and *Less Than Dust),* Hazel Dawn *(The Fatal Card),* Billie Burke (serial *Gloria's Romance* as the engaging villain), Ann Murdock *(The Beautiful Adventure),* Alice Brady *(Maternity, The Better Half,* and *Her Great Chance),* Elsie Ferguson *(The Lie),* Edna Goodrich *(Her Husband's Honor),* Clara Kimball Young *(The Price She Paid),* and other stars of the 1920s.

Powell became Famous Players best-known leading man; his good looks in a military uniform (and there were few films in which he did not appear in a uniform) pulled the female fans into the theaters which helped greatly in the success of the films of the company's female stars. In 1920, he appeared successfully with Mae Murray in *Idols of Clay, On with the Dance,* and *The Right to Love* and with Elsie Ferguson in *Lady Rose's Daughter* before he was sent to England in 1921 by Famous Players for a series of films *(Appearance, Dangerous Lies, The Mystery Road,* and *The Princess of New York).*

By 1922, Powell should have been starred in his own films. Why did Famous-Lasky not star him? A quote by Julian Johnson in 1917 of the actor's screen persona probably explained the reason, "He is a faultless photoplay leading man and an adorable villain, and in the last two years has caused as much palpitation of the heart in the dark showshops as any celluloid gentleman you might summon to the bar." Famous Players found him more profitable as a leading man rather than a star.

The leading man roles in 1922-1923 continued with the "Boston Blackie" drama *Missing Millions* with Alice Brady, a Northwest action drama *The Siren Call* with Dorothy Dalton, and the matrimonial drama *The Glimpses of the Moon.* In 1923, Powell left Famous Players and appeared in George Arliss' *The Green Goddess,* but the films made after leaving Famous Players-Lasky failed to measure up to his previous successes *(The Hero, Virtuous Liars, Lend Me Your Husband,* and *The Man Without a Heart).*

The strenuous work on his last two films *(The Lost Chord* and *Back to Life)* impaired the actor's health and Powell suffered a nervous breakdown. The news of his death from pneumonia in New York on April 16, 1925, shocked the film colony after his recovery had been reported by the news media. He was survived by his wife and child.

Allene Ray

Allene Ray, one of the 1920 "Fame and Fortune Contest" winners, was a silent serial star the Pathé Company nurtured and developed as a replacement for Pearl White. The company made her a star but never of the magnitude of Miss White, due primarily to the decline in popularity of the serials by the mid-1920s. The upheaval in the industry in 1926 with the coming of sound films and the changing attitudes of the film-going public brought an end to Miss Ray's career.

Born the daughter of Willie Ray Mullins and John Burch on a ranch near San Antonio, Texas on January 2, 1901, Miss Ray attended schools in San Antonio and Devine, Texas. Like most Texas-born children she learned to ride a horse as early as she learned to walk. Her reputation as a rider who could take one of the meanest broncos and turn it into a mild, well-mannered animal won her recognition as an expert equestrian. Her love for the outdoor life made her equally well-known in all outdoor sports (in the sport of swimming she would take a thirty-foot dive without the slightest hesitation). Little did she realize that these skills developed in her early years would one day make her a popular serial star.

Her blond beauty attracted the attention of a San Antonio theatrical manager who persuaded Miss Ray to make her stage debut in one of his local musical comedies. Impressed with her stage work, Tex O'Reilly, the O. Henry of the plains, with Bert Lubin engaged her for the ingenue lead in the first of the Tex O'Reilly film series *Honeymoon Ranch* (1920), opposite aviator and actor Harry "Tex" McLaughlin. McLaughlin died soon after the completion of the film from injuries he received when slashed by an airplane propeller as he was changing from one plane to another in mid-air.

The aspiring actress, while making *Honeymoon Ranch,* submitted photographs to the "Fame and Fortune Contest" and much to her surprise the judges picked her as one of the finalists. In September 1920, Miss Ray traveled to New York City for screen tests. When picked as the second-place winner (Corliss Palmer was the winner), she was given a role in the Eugene V. Brewster film *Ramon the Sailmaker.* Still under contract for the O'Reilly film series Miss Ray returned to San Antonio and for O'Reilly and Lubin appeared (1920-1922) in *West of the Rio Grande, The High Card,* and *Partners of the Sunset.* With the completion of the O'Reilly and Lubin films she returned to the film studios of the East and West, where as a contest winner she was given supporting roles in Metro's *Your Friend and Mine* (1923) and in Fox's *Times Have Changed* (1923).

When Pearl White announced her retirement from films in 1924, the Pathé Company desperately needed a replacement. Director George B. Seitz, because of the "Fame and Fortune Contest" publicity, felt that the beautiful Miss Ray with her Texas background would make an ideal heroine for the company's upcoming serial. He cast Miss Ray opposite Harold Miller *In The Way of a Man* (a 10-episode serial also released as a seven-reel feature film); so popular was the serial with the public that the company again under Seitz's direction cast her as the star of *The Fortieth Door* (1924) and *Galloping Hoofs* (1924), two popular serials that proved Seitz had indeed had found a replacement for Pearl White. Under the direction of William Parke she again had a box-office winner in the exciting *Ten Scars Make a Man,* a serial of complicated plots and subplots. In 1925, when Seitz teamed her with Walter Miller in *Sunken Silver,* their success in the film made them a box-office winning team whose serials gave the declining genre a reprieve for a few years.

When Seitz joined the Paramount Company (1925), the team of Miller and Ray was put into the capable hands of Spencer G. Bennet, who starred them in a series of serials *(Play Ball, The Green Archer, Snowed In, House Without a Key, Hawk of the Hills, The Man Without a Face,* and *The Black Book)* that kept the public anxiously coming back week after week for the most popular serials filmed between 1925-1929. Miss Ray left Pathé to become Tim McCoy's leading lady in her last successful serial *The Indians Are Coming* (1930). Tired of the hazardous life of the serial queen, Miss Ray's career ended after a series of low-budget films *(Overland Bound, Westward Bound, The Phantom,* and *Gun Cargo).*

In 1925, Miss Ray married Larry Wheeler and after her retirement from the screen the couple made their home in Temple City, California. There she remained living in obscurity but not forgotten by the serial aficionados and film researchers who often wondered of her whereabouts. Apparently Miss Ray felt that her film career was in the past and there she wanted it to remain. When the actress died on May 5, 1979, in Temple City of cancer, there were no obituaries in the trade papers for this once popular and beautiful serial star.

Kittens Reichert

"Six years old and in the phone book"' so read the 1917 *Photoplay* article on the popular child film player Kittens Reichert. The article stated that she was the only six-year-old in the United States with her own name in the telephone directory. Known as one of the most beautiful and talented children in filmland she was never the star in her films but won stardom for the juvenile roles she played in support of the major stars between 1915-1919. When she retired from the screen at the age of sixteen she was never again remotely associated with the film industry. When death came, she had been away from films for so long that her obituary went unreported in the trade papers.

Born Catherine Alma Reichert on March 3, 1910, in Yonkers, New York, she was given the nickname of Kittens early, which she used throughout her film career. Her education took place in the film studios and magazine articles wrote of her priorities over the films—they were gum drops, comic supplements, and dolls of any kind, with her film work somewhere down the list.

Film history sources tend to disagree as to at which studio she made her film debut, but these sources agree that she first attracted the public's attention opposite William Farnum as Mavis Duval in Fox's *A Soldier's Oath* (1915). Her other 1915 releases included Famous Player's *The Eternal City* in support of Pauline Frederick, *Ivan's Forbidden Fruit* (re-released as *Who's to Blame* in 1920), and Metro's *The Song of the Wage Slave,* the northwest drama inspired by a Robert W. Service poem. By 1916 her popularity afforded her prominent roles in support of Theda Bara in *The Eternal Sapho,* Bertha Kalich in *Ambition,* and Stuart Holmes in *Sins of Men.* For Universal, she supported Violet Mersereau in *The Great Problem* and *Broken Fetters* and for Ivan she supported Mignon Anderson in *Her Husband's Wife* and Maude Fealy in *The Immortal Flame.*

In 1917, at the peak of her popularity, the juvenile actress found herself among the screen's busiest actresses with roles for Fox opposite June Caprice in *Every Girl's Dream* and *Unknown 274,* Theda Bara in *Heart and Soul* and *Tiger Woman,* Mary Martin (not the musical comedy star) in the role of "Pearl" in *The Scarlet Letter,* for Vitagraph opposite Alice

Joyce in *Her Secret* and for the U. S. Amusement Company opposite Catherine Calvert in *The Peddler* and *House of Cards.* In 1918, Miss Reichert appeared for Fox in Frank Lloyd's successful film version of *Les Miserables* in the role of young "Cosette." After appearing in James Vincent's production of *The Spirit of Lafayette* (1919), her film career ended when she failed to follow the film studios to the West Coast.

The Reichert family chose to remain in the cast and allow Miss Reichert to attend schools locally and enjoy what was left of her childhood. Little was heard of the former actress until she tried for a comeback in W. C. Fields' *So's Your Old Man* (1926) filmed at Paramount's Long Island studio. When the film failed to revitalize her film career, she permanently retired from the screen.

In the intervening years Miss Reichert married a man by the name of Lundy but the marriage did not last. When her father's work took him to Fort Knox, Kentucky, in 1959, she moved with the family to Valley Station, where she made her home. The former actress resided there until her death on January 11, 1990, in Louisville, Kentucky. She was survived by two sons. Interment for the former child actress was in a military cemetery in Fort Knox.

Lucille Ricksen

Lucille Ricksen stepped from a fairy-tale book illustration in the early 1920s to become one of the screen's leading ingenues. When in 1924 she was selected as a Wampas "Baby Star," stardom seemed assured for the young actress. But all hopes of lasting fame ended when she was stricken with tuberculosis which ended her film career and life at the age of fifteen.

Lucille Ricksen, the daughter of Ingeborg and Samuel Ericksen (the "E" was dropped when she entered films), was born on August 22, 1909, in Chicago, Illinois. With a sporadic education in Chicago she began her film career there with the Essanay Company at the age of four. Her early years as a film actress are obscure and it was not until the Goldwyn Company cast her opposite Johnny Jones (Edward Peil, Jr.) in the two-reel film version of Booth Tarkington's Edgar stories *(Edgar and the Teacher's Pet, Edgar Camps Out, Edgar's Little Saw,* and *Edgar Takes the Cake)* in 1920 that she came to the public's attention.

The popularity of the *Edgar* series led to children roles in Goldwyn's *The Old Nest* (1921), *Remembrance* (1922), and her first adult role in *The Rendezvous* (1923). The popularity of the flapper roles in the early 1920s made her, with her youth and beauty, a candidate as one of the screen's youngest flappers (1922-1923) in Universal's *Forsaking All Others* (supporting Colleen Moore), *The Girl Who Ran Wild, The Married Flapper,* and *Trimmed in Scarlet*; but it was as the flapper in Marshall Neilan's melodrama *The Stranger's Banquet* (1922) in support of Claire Windsor that she scored as a dramatic actress. Dramatic roles followed with supporting roles in Thomas Ince's *Human Wreckage* (1923) and in the Universal Jack Mulhall serial *The Social Buccaneer* (1923).

From the actress's previous work, in 1924 the Western Associated Motion Picture Advertisers (Wampas) selected her (along with Clara Bow, Marion Nixon, Dorothy Mackaill, and Alberta Vaughn) as one of the year's "Baby Stars," a chosen group of young actresses Wampas predicted for future stardom. While many of the Wampas "Baby Stars" failed to reach stardom, Miss Ricksen, with her beauty and talent, was truly headed for stardom in 1924 with supporting roles in First National's *Idle Tongues, The Galloping Fish,* and *Those Who Dance,* Fox's *The Painted Lady,* FBO's *Vanity Price* and *Judgment of the Storm,* and Universal's *Behind the Curtain* and *Young Ideas,* when she signed a contract that offered her leading and starring roles in the coming year.

With a Metro-Goldwyn contract (1925) Miss Ricksen was cast as Claire Windsor's daughter, the ingenue lead, in the drama *The Denial.* It was the actress's last role. Overworked from a busy film schedule the actress, in frail health, collapsed suffering from tuberculosis and diagnosed by her physician as seriously ill with her recovery in doubt. The news of the young ingenue's illness shocked the film colony with many friends coming to her aid. As her illness progressed the actress was nursed and watched over by her mother whose health had also begun to fail. While tending to her daughter's needs she collapsed across Miss Ricksen's bed and died within minutes. The shock of her mother's death complicated by her illness hastened the actress' death on March 13, 1925, in Los Angeles. She was survived by her brother Marshall Ricksen.

William Sherwood

World War I, the last of the Romantic Wars, found film actors eager to answer their country's call to serve. William Sherwood, a promising young actor on the threshold of stardom was one of those handsome young youths who answered his country's call, but a freak accident prevented him from carrying out his duty as a soldier.

William Sherwood, usually known as Billy, was born in New Orleans, Louisiana, in 1896. Educated in New Orleans' public schools, he later attended Tulane University where he was bitten by the acting bug. Making his stage debut locally in a stock company he joined other stock companies and ventured north playing juvenile roles in a wide variety of well-known plays.

Sherwood began his film career as an assistant director and a bit player. After appearing in supporting roles in one- and two-reelers, the actor's first feature film credit was as John Davidson's son in the George Kleine production *The Danger Signal* (1915); the following year he appeared as the juvenile lead who romanced and won the hand of Evelyn Brent in *The Spell of the Yukon*. In *Broken Chains* (1916) as the brother of Ethel Clayton he is killed and the hero Carlyle Blackwell is accused of his murder.

The popularity of the youthful actor with the public resulted in his being voted one of the most promising newcomers in the *Motion Picture Magazine* "Popular Players Contest" in late 1916. As an up-and-coming young juvenile in 1917, he appeared in support of stage greats Kitty Gordon in *The Beloved Adventuress*, Mabel Taliaffero in *The Jury of Fate*, Lew Fields in *The Corner Grocer*, the controversial S. Rankin Drew's *Who's Your Neighbor* (a film originally condemned by the National Board of Review due to the prostitution theme and passed only when it was trimmed from seven to five reels), and supported Carlyle Blackwell in *The Good for Nothing*.

After starring as the sculptor in the fantasy film *The Triumph of Venus* (1918), the actor enlisted in the army. He was sent to Washington, D.C., for training. Several weeks after his arrival, while playing around with several companions, he lost his balance and fell over a railing three stories to a concrete floor. He was rushed to Walter Reed Hospital, where after a few days he seemed to be recovering when suddenly on May 24, 1918, he took a turn for the worse and died within hours. The body of the actor and soldier was returned to New Orleans for burial.

Lucille Lee Stewart

The film career of Lucille Lee Stewart was overshadowed by that of her sister Anita Stewart. Anita Stewart was a major star of the silent screen and sister Lucille's career paralleled that of Anita's but she never became a big star. She did become a well-known leading and supporting player, as well as the wife of her sister's one-time director, Ralph Ince.

Born the daughter of Martha Lee and William H. Stewart in Brooklyn, New York, on December 25, 1889, Lucille Lee Stewart was educated in Brooklyn schools and later appeared briefly in vaudeville. She became one of the early members of Vitagraph's Flatbush Studio after her marriage to director Ralph Ince, whom she met while singing in the choir of the Sheepshead Bay Episcopal Church and soon after married.

With the close proximity of the film studios, practically in the Stewart's backyard, Lucille Stewart's earliest film credit is the short American Biograph film *The New Lid* (1910) opposite her brother-in-law Thomas H. Ince. In 1912, when her husband signed with the Vitagraph Company as Anita Stewart's director she, too, joined the company. While at Vitagraph opposite her sister and under her husband's direction, Miss Stewart appeared in the early film shorts *The Godmother, Wife Wanted, The Right and the Wrong of it, Diana's Dress Reform, The Classmate's Frolic,* and *The Song of the Shell* (1912-1914) and the five-reel feature *The Sins of the Mothers.* In 1916, Vitagraph starred her under Ince's direction in *The Conflict, The Destroyers, His Wife's Good Name,* and *The Ninety and Nine,* but the Ince's days at Vitagraph were numbered. They left in November 1916 and did not work together again until 1918 when, for Advanced Motion Picture Corporation, she starred in and he wrote and directed *The Eleventh Commandment.* Then they joined the Metro Company and Miss Stewart starred under her husband's direction in *Five Thousand an Hour* and supported Ethel Barrymore in *Our Mrs. McChesney.* In 1919, the Inces ended the husband-wife team after making *The Perfect Lover* and *Sealed Hearts* for Selznick. In the fall of 1919, under the direction of Emmett J. Flynn, she appeared as William Russell's leading lady in the Fox Western drama *Westward Ho!* Thereafter Miss Stewart's roles were as supporting actress in *The Woman Gives* (1920) opposite Norma Talmadge, *A Woman's Business* (1920) opposite Olive Tell, and in *Shams of Society* (1921) opposite Barbara Castleton, after which she temporarily left the screen.

After her divorce from Ince in 1925, she made a film comeback as a character actress in *Bad Company, Friendly Enemies, Fifth Avenue,* and *Sunshine of Paradise Alley* (1925-1926) but the actress found the industry in turmoil and with the coming of sound Lucille Lee Stewart ended her film career and later opened a bookstore.

As the years passed her name primarily appeared in print as a survivor. She was listed as the former wife of Ralph Ince when he was killed in an automobile accident on April 11, 1937, and as her sister's survivor when she died from acute barbiturate intoxication on May 4, 1961. When Lucille

Lee Stewart died on January 8, 1982, in Hemet, California, there were no survivors.

Edith Storey

From the early Western melodramas filmed in the prairies of the West, Edith Storey graduated to roles in Shakespearian dramas that elevated her to the ranks of one of the screen's first tragediennes. Critics showered her with accolades for her brilliant work in Vitagraph's 1914 production of *The Christian,* writing that the actress would always be remembered for her portrayal of "Glory Quayle." Today, the once reigning star is virtually forgotten.

Born in New York City on March 18, 1892, the daughter of Minnie L. Thorne and William C. Storey, Miss Storey attended the city's public schools when not appearing on the stage as a child actress. At the age of eight she appeared in support of Eleanor Robson in *Audrey,* toured in the 1903 road production of *The Little Princess,* journeyed to Australia in the original production of *Mrs. Wiggs of the Cabbage Patch,* and was to have begun a second season in the play when she abandoned the stage for a film contract.

Miss Storey joined the fledgling Vitagraph Company in 1908 and was cast in a wide variety of roles—riding the range in the morning and playing the heroine in one of the classics in the afternoon. The hardships of those early years (1908-1910) provided a training ground for the actress with roles in *Barbara Fritchie* (supporting Julia Arthur), *Les Miserables, The Life of Moses, A Brave Irish Lass, The Way of the Cross, King Lear, Twelfth Night*, and *Saved by the Flag.* In 1911, Vitagraph loaned her to the Méliès Company for a series of Western melodramas filmed in Texas *(Bessie's Ride, A Spanish Love,* and *The Kiss of Mary Jane).* The Texas filming experience turned the actress into an expert horsewoman. A friend said that Miss Storey could ride anything that had hair and four legs, could throw a rope, and shoot with the best of the cowpunchers; these skills no doubt were valuable assets to the actress in the early Vitagraph melodramas.

Recalled to the Vitagraph's Brooklyn studio in late 1911, the actress appeared in numerous one- and two-reelers over the next three years *(A Tale of Two Cities, The Lady of the Lake, The Victoria Cross, Coronets and Hearts, The Vengeance of Durand, A Homespun Tragedy, 'Mid Kentucky Hills,* and *The Still Voice).* By 1914 Miss Storey had become one of Vitagraph's busiest stars and by 1916 was one of the company's most popular stars in *Captain Alvarez* (1914), *The Christian* (1914), *A Florida Enchantment* (1914), *The Dust of Egypt* (1915), *The Island of Regeneration* (1915), *On Her Wedding Night* (1915), *An Enemy of the King* (1916), and *The Tarantula* (1916). In 1917 Miss Storey, now one of the screen's superstars, after the completion of *Aladdin of Broadway* terminated her Vitagraph contract and joined the Metro Company. The actress' Metro films *(The Claim, The Demon, The Eyes of Mystery, The Legion of Death, Revenge, The Silent Woman, Treasure of the Sea,* and *As the Sun Went Down)* in 1918-1919 failed to measure up to her Vitagraph successes and after appearances in Haworth's *Moon Madness* (1920) and Robertson's Cole's 1921 features *Beach of Dreams, The Golden Hope*, and *Greater Profit* the actress retired from the screen.

When the U.S. entered World War I, Miss Storey volunteered her services and for several months drove an ambulance before resuming her film work. When she retired from the screen she made her home at Eaton's Neck on Long Island where she lived for many years. With the passing of years, Miss Storey became a former star whose fame failed to survive the test of time; she was rewarded with a star on "The Hollywood Walk of Fame" (1501 Vine). When death came to the actress there were no obituaries published in the trade journals and consequently several incorrect dates for her demise have been published by film researchers. It was only with the help of the Social Security files that the date of death was uncovered. The actress, having never married, died on October 9, 1967, in Northport, New York. Her occupation was listed as a retired actress of the silent screen.

Jerome Storm

Jerome Storm began his film career as an actor, became a well-known supporting player, but soon realized that his aspirations were not in front of but behind the camera. When given the opportunity to switch from acting to directing he did so and within a short time he became a promising director noted for the realism of smalltown life in his films. But the small-town vogue so popular in the early 1920s films was short-lived and by the end of the decade Mr. Storm had moved to the poverty-row companies. Within a short time, he disappeared from the industry and was virtually forgotten.

Born the son of Althea Reno and Francis D. Storm on November 11, 1890, in Denver, Colorado, Jerome Storm was educated locally and commenced his stage career in stock at the Elitch's Gardens. He appeared for several seasons before going on the road in juvenile roles in the productions of James O'Neill, Olga Nethersole, and Robert Edeson. His stage work provided the means of his entrance into films as an actor with the Broncho Company. His earliest film credit was in the film short *Romance of Sunshine Alley* (1914) opposite Mildred Harris, soon followed by KB's *The Squire's Son* where he met and formed a friendship with Charles Ray. In 1915 for the Domino Company, he appeared in the two-reelers *In the Land of the Otters, The Bride of Guadeloupe,* and under the supervision of Thomas H. Ince he supported Bessie Barriscale in his first feature film *The Cup of Life,* followed by KB's two-reeler *The Pathway from the Past* and Domino's *The Lighthouse Keeper's Son.*

The actor's friendship with Thomas H. Ince made him a member of the Ince Company and on the Ince lot he appeared in juvenile roles in 1916 in *The Honorable Algy, Civilization, The Primal Lure,* and *Somewhere in France.*

By 1917, he was one of Ince's leading players. He supported Frank Keenan in the historical drama *The Bride of Hate,* William Desmond in the mystery comedy *The Iced Bullet,* and Charles Ray in *His Mother's Boy, A Corner in Coleens,* and *The Pinch Hitter*; but when Thomas Ince offered Storm a chance to direct Enid Bennett in *The Keys of the Righteous* (1918), he accepted the challenge. The success of the film led to Storm directing Miss Bennett in *Naughty, Naughty, The Biggest Show on Earth, A Desert Wooing,* and *The Vamp,* thus terminating his acting career.

In 1919, when Ince assigned him as the director of the Charles Ray films, Storm, who highly regarded Ray for his naturalness, reached his peak as a director and made Charles Ray a major star in his small-town dramas (which he believed were successful due to naturalness being a greater asset than the so-called "screen technique"). Between 1919-1920, he directed Ray in *The Busher, Crooked Straight, The Egg Crate Wallop, The Girl Dodger, Hay Foot, Straw Foot, Greased Lightning, Bill Henry, Homer Comes Home, Red Hot Dollars, Alarm Clock Andy, A Village Sleuth, An Old Fashioned Boy, Paris Green,* and *Peaceful Valley.* In 1920, the Ray-Storm partnership was broken to permit the formation of Jerome Storm Productions with his first film starring Lillian Gish. The film apparently did not materialize nor did his company. In 1921 he directed Katherine MacDonald in First National's *Her Social Value.* Throughout the 1920s he directed numerous films, the most notable being Fox's

Arabian Love (1922), *St. Elmo* (1923), and *The Brass Bowl* (1924), Paramount's *Children of Jazz* (1923), First National's *The Goldfish* (1924), and Chadwick's *Some Pun'kins* (1925) and *Sweet Adeline* (1926).

After a series of forgettable films in the late 1920s *(Ranger of the North, Dog Justice, Fangs of the Wild,* and *Courtin' Wildcats)* for the poverty-row studios, Storm directed a few low-budget Westerns in the early 1930s before severing all ties with the film industry.

On July 10, 1958, a realtor by the name of Jerome V. Storm died in Desert Hot Springs, California, but was this man the once popular juvenile film actor and later prominent silent film director? There was nothing on the death certificate that would connect him to the film industry. In 1950 the trade paper *The Billboard* published the death of Jerome Griffith Storm, the son of Mildred Richter and director Jerome Storm, but it was only after the discovery of the death of the director's mother, Althea Storm, in 1934 that at last verification could be made. The death certificate of Althea Storm verified the realtor who died in 1958 was indeed the once well-known actor and director.

William Stowell

Big and rugged outdoorsman William H. Stowell was one of the screen's busiest leading men from the very earliest days of filmmaking. For a career that spanned only a decade his film output opposite some of the screen's major stars readily shows his popularity among his peers and the public. He perhaps would have become one of the legendary silent film stars had fate not stepped in and brought his career to a tragic end far away from the film capitol.

William H. Stowell's existence can be found only in early film magazines and film directories with little on his private life reported, and it is from these early publications that his life unfolds. Born on March 13, 1885, in Boston, Massachusetts, he was educated in the Boston schools. Upon the completion of his education he began his stage career in musical comedy in Chicago, became a leading man at the Whitney Opera House, and spent three seasons appearing in leads for road companies touring the East. As with so many of the pioneer film players, he turned to the fledgling film industry when the stage roles were few and far between.

In the early days of the one- and two-reelers, the actor, while in Chicago, was offered a film contract with the Selig Company in 1909. He stated in an interview that when he applied for a position with the studio they did not ask if he could act but could he ride a horse and swim. Fortunately he had these requirements and from 1909 to 1915 these skills were constantly used by the company in numerous short dramas *(Sons of the Northwoods, The Two Orphans, As the Fates Decree, The Devil and Tom Walker, In Tune with the Wild, The Mystery of the Seven Chests, The Redemption of Greek Joe,* and *A Wartime Romance).* In 1915 after leaving Selig he went to Hollywood with the American Company where the short films *(The Great Question* and *The Tragic Circle)* gave way to features *(The Buzzard's Shadow* and *The End of the Road)* in support of Harold Lockwood and May Allison. In 1916, the actor found himself one of the American Company's busiest actors and was starred in *The Man from Manhattan* and *Overalls,* costarred opposite Audrey Munson in *The Girl O'Dreams* and Rhea Mitchell in *The Overcoat* and supported Harold Lockwood and May Allison in *The Other Side of the Door,* Frank Borzage in *Immediate Lee,* William Russell in *The Love Hermit,* and E. Forrest Taylor in *The White Rosette* before leaving the American Company in 1917 when Universal offered him a contract.

After joining Universal Mr. Stowell was teamed and found success costarring with Dorothy Phillips in *Bondage, A Doll's House, Fires of Rebellion, The Flashlight, The Girl in the Checkered Coat, Hell Morgan's Girl, The Piper's Price, The Rescue, Pay Me,* and *Triumph* and starred in the western drama *Fighting Mad.* So successful had the Phillips-Stowell team become that Universal (1918-1919) starred them in a series of successful dramas *(Broadway Love, The Grand Passion, The Mortgaged Wife, The Risky Road, The Talk of the Town, Destiny, The Heart of Humanity, Paid in Advance,* and *The Right to Happiness)* and when not working with Miss Phillips he was kept busy by the company as costar of Mildred Harris in Lois Weber's *When a Girl Loves* and in support of Monroe Salisbury and Colleen Moore in *The Man in the Moonlight.*

At the peak of his popularity in 1919, Universal sent a company on location to film a Universal Smithsonian Expedition film in the Belgian Congo with Stowell as the star. On the way to the location site on November 24, 1919, the train had stopped in Elizabethville to take on water when suddenly and without warning a loaded oil tanker crashed into the rear car of the train, killing most of the occupants, including William Stowell. The actor, a bachelor, left no immediate survivors.

Rosemary Theby

The film career of Rosemary Theby spanned the silent era from its beginning to its end as star, leading lady, and character actress before her career climaxed as an atmosphere and bit actress after the advent of sound. Married to one of the screen's early comic actors, she and her husband were members of the Hollywood elite throughout the silent era but their careers declined when the films found a voice and today Rosemary Theby is a forgotten player from the past.

Born the daughter of Katherine and George Masing on April 8, 1885, in St. Louis, Missouri, Rosemary Theby was educated in private schools in St. Louis and studied drama at the Sargent Dramatic School in New York City. After briefly appearing on the New York stage in 1910, she joined the Vitagraph Company where she quickly became one of the company's most promising newcomers with roles in numerous Vitagraph short films including *A Geranium, As You Like It, The Fortune in the Teacup, The Hand Bag, The Lights of St. Bernard, The Mills of the Gods, The Reincarnation of Karma, Rock of Ages, Out of the Storm, The Master Painter, His Silver Bachelorhood, A Husband's Trick, The Classmates, Frolic, The Little Minister*, and *The Web.*

When offered leading roles by the Reliance Company in 1913, Miss Theby left Vitagraph and successfully appeared in *The Fight for Right Ashes, The Glow Worm, The Heart of a Rose, Her Rosary, Maria Roma, The Missing Ring, The Tangled Web, Targets of Fate*, and *The Wager.* In 1914 she joined the Lubin Company and under the direction of Harry C. Myers she costarred with him in a series of one- and two-reel comedies (*The Attorney's Decision, The Comedienne's Strategy, The Double Life, The Hopeless Game*, and *The Price of a Ruby*) which proved successful and made stars of Miss Theby and Myers.

By the time the couple joined the Universal Company, Miss Theby had married Myers and it was as husband and wife that they starred in Universal-Victor's 1914-1916 short comedies *The Little Grey Home, The Bride of Marble Road, Cards Never Lie, Father's Child, He Was Only a Bathing Suit Salesman, Tomboy Girl, Saved by a Dream, The Latest in Vampires, Love Spasms, A Model Husband, The Pipe Dream,* and co-starred with Lawrence D'Orsay in the five-reel film version of his stage success *The Earl of Pawtucket.*

In 1916, lured to the Vim Company for a series of one- and two-reelers, they starred in *Gertie's Garters, The Good Stenographer, Green Eyes,*

Hubby's Relatives, His Wedding Promise, Honeymoon Car, Marked No Funds, A Persistent Wooing, Their Dream House, The Lemon in Their Garden of Love, The Tormented Husband, and *A Financial Frenzy.* In 1917 after appearances in Pathé's *Police Protection, Jumping Jealousy,* and *Rusticating* the screen team of Theby and Myers ended and thereafter only infrequently did they appear together.

The decline of the short film thrust Miss Theby into the most productive period of her career as star and leading lady in a wide variety of roles in feature films. For Bluebird Photoplays she was Franklyn Farmum's leading lady in *The Winged Mystery* (1917), opposite Bert Lytell (1918-1919) in Metro's *Boston Blackie's Little Pal, Unexpected Places,* and *Faith,* supported Lillian Gish in Artcraft's *The Great Love* (1918), starred with Francis Ford in the Louis Burston serial *The Silver Mystery* (1916), starred in Ince's *The Midnight Patrol* and Triangle's *Love's Pay Day.* The years 1919-1920 for various film companies (Metro, Elk Photoplays, Pioneer, Selznick, and Fox) she was seen in *The Amateur Adventuress, Are You Legally Married? Upstairs and Down, When a Woman Strikes, Yvonne from Paris, The Mystery 13* (serial), *Peggy Does Her Darndest, Tangled Threads, The Butterfly Man, The Hushed Hour, The Little Grey Mouse, Rio Grande, A Splendid Hazard, Terror Island, Whispering Devils,* and *The Dice of Destiny.*

Between 1921-1930 Miss Theby was one of the screen's busiest actresses, appearing in numerous films with important roles in *A Connecticut Yankee in King Arthur's Court* (supporting her husband in his best known film) (1921), *The External Flame* (1922), *The Girl of the Golden West* (1923). *Behold the Woman* (1924), *The Red Lily* (1924), *So Big* (1924) *As Man Desires* (1925), *Fifth Avenue Models* (1925), *The Truthful Sex* (1926), *A Bowery Cinderella* (1927), *The Port of Missing Girls* (1928), *Trial Marriage* (1929), and *Midnight Daddies.* By the mid 1920s with her starring days over, Miss Theby's name had slipped to supporting and character roles but throughout the decade she continued to appear in one film after another. After appearing in the early 1930s in *10 Nights in a Bar Room, Fatal Glass of Beer,* and *The Man on the Flying Trapeze,* her career had virtually ended with only bit parts to follow *(San Francisco)* after 1935.

When Harry C. Myers died in Beverly Hills on December 25, 1938, one of Hollywood's successful marriages ended. Miss Theby was listed as his only survivor. After her husband's death the actress faded into obscurity and as the years passed, her whereabouts became a mystery—did she leave the state of California, did she remarry? No one knows. It is inconceivable how the death of an actress of her magnitude would not be reported in the newspapers and the trade papers but it happened with Rosemary Theby. When, where, and what happened to the once famous star is unknown.

Mary Thurman

To her fans the gamin-like antics of Mary Thurman were straight out of the John Held, Jr., cartoons. A flapper of the 1920s she had a varied film career that ran the gamut of Mack Sennett comedy to the drama of Allan Dwan, which made her among the most talented of the young stars of the silent screen. When Maude Cheatham described Miss Thurman in a *Motion Picture Classic* article as "straight, slim and very much alive with eyes of deep blue with a lurking mischievousness in their depths that flashes at unexpecting moments, with her dark hair bobbed and banged and with her marked sincerity and frankness she brings a certain suggestion of boyishness despite her potent feminine charms," they were the identical characteristics epitomized by the Held flapper and Miss Thurman truly epitomized the Held flapper of the "roaring twenties."

Born on April 27, 1894, in Richfield, Utah, Miss Thurman's education took place there and after graduating from the University of Utah she turned to teaching school as a vocation. She probably would have made teaching a career had she not visited Los Angeles in 1916. While having tea at the Alexander Hotel one afternoon, a director from the D. W. Griffith studio asked her if she had ever thought of going into motion pictures. He asked her to visit the studio, she did, was signed at once, and within an hour she was working in a cafe scene. After making several two-reelers for Griffith and appearing in DeWolf Hopper's *Sunshine Dad* (1916), playing the leading feminine roles with Douglas Fairbanks in his first two starring films *(Double Trouble* and *The Lamb*), she signed with Mack Sennett.

As a Mack Sennett bathing beauty she encountered the slapstick antics of the Keystone comedians and her comedic talents soon ranked her as a comedienne equal to any on the Sennett lot . She had feature roles usually opposite Charlie Murray in Keystone's (1916-1918) two-reelers *His Last Laugh, His First False Step, Pinched in the Finish, The Betrayal of Maggie, A Bedroom Blunder, Watch Your Neighbor,* and others. When tiring of the art of slapstick she went to Sennett and asked him to release her from her contract so that she could see what she could do in drama.

He released her and told her there would always be a place for her at Keystone if she ever wanted to return.

Before branching out into drama Miss Thurman appeared for various companies (Goldwyn, Hampton, Famous Players, and Mayflower) in a series of comedy feature films *(The Poor Boob, The Prince and Betty, Spotlight Sadie,* and *This Hero Stuff)* before appearing in the Western drama *Sand* as William S. Hart's leading lady. Miss Thurman found drama and melodrama challenging, and under Allan Dwan's direction (1920-1921) she appeared in leading roles in *In the Heart of a Fool, The Scoffer, A Broken Doll,* and *The Sin of Martha Queed* and as William Russell's leading lady in *The Valley of Tomorrow, Bare Knuckles,* and *The Lady from Longacre.*

One of the screen's busiest actresses in the golden age of the silent era, Miss Thurman, between 1921-1923, appeared in leading roles opposite Dustin Farnum in *The Primal Law,* Richard Barthelmess in *The Bond Boy,* Henry Hull in *A Pride for a Knight,* Monte Blue in *The Tents of Allah,* Gloria Swanson in *Zaza,* and starred in *Wife in Name Only.* In 1924-1925 her leading roles had become supporting roles *(For Another Woman, The Law and the Lady, Love of Women, Playthings of Desire, Trouping With Ellen, Back to Life, The Fool, Little Girl in a Big City, The Mad Marriage,* and *The Necessary Evil)* and with her career in decline the actress, after a role in *The Wives of the Prophet* (1925), due to an intermittent illness contracted when making a film in Florida, was under treatment in a New York City hospital when she suddenly collapsed and died on December 22, 1925, from pneumonia.

Having had no theatrical training, it is doubtful that Mary Thurman could have made the transition from the silent to the sound media. It is somewhat ironic that the film career and life of one of the silent screen's most popular and talented flappers paralleled that of the silent screen and the demise of the two within months of each other brought an end to an age—the age of the silent screen.

Fay Tincher

Once described by writers as the "feminine Charlie Chaplin," Fay Tincher began her film career as a D. W. Griffith vamp but later, with her spit curl, became the screen's stereotype of the "not so bright" secretary parodied so often in the slapstick comedies. In a career that spanned the silent era, she became one of the screen's leading comediennes who occasionally appeared in drama, but it was her comedic roles that made her famous. When the silent slapstick comedies gave way to Mickey Mouse and the art of animation, the former comedian became a has-been whose future lay in bit and atmospheric roles. Miss Tincher chose to end her career and leave the Hollywood scene. When she did, the once famous comedienne was never heard from again.

Fay Tincher, the oldest of four daughters of Mary Elizabeth Hartley and prominent businessman George W. Tincher, was born on April 17, 1884, in Topeka, Kansas. The prominence of her parents in the city enabled her to receive a well-rounded education—elocution lessons at the age of five, attending the Powin Elementary School, and graduating from one of the Topeka high schools. Always interested in the theatre, after high school she left Topeka and enrolled in the Chicago Musical College in 1898. While there she appeared in the school's production of *The Prince of Pilsen* before leaving to tour with the Shogun Stock Company. She joined the Weber Music Hall in 1901 in New York City as a chorus girl which led to a role as one of the music maidens in the Henry W. Savage production of the comic opera *Tomorrow Land* (1905).

As a Broadway chorus girl of note Miss Tincher abandoned her stage career at the death of her father (1906) and with her sister lived abroad for the next three years where she took the grand tour. After her return to New York she joined the Keith two-a-day vaudeville circuit making a name for herself in the Arthur Hopkins sketch *The Dance Dream* and musical comedy before she met a strange man who asked her, "How would you like to get into Moving Pictures?"

Sitting with a friend in a New York cafe, the strange man, a D. W. Griffith representative, felt that due to her resemblance to Mabel Normand, Mr. Griffith could use her. The next day after meeting the director he signed her at once for the vampire role in his next film. The film was *The Battle of the Sexes* (1914) in which as the siren Cleo she made life miserable for Lillian Gish. Delighted with her humorous portrayal of the siren, Griffith cast her as the worldly woman in the prologue of *Home, Sweet Home* and as an adventuress in *The Escape*. By the time she arrived in Hollywood in 1914 Griffith felt Miss Tincher's forté was comedy and not drama. She agreed with him and launched her career as a comedienne.

For the Komic Company (1914-1915) Miss Tincher appeared in numerous slapstick comedies opposite Elmer Booth and Max Davidson under Edward Dillon's direction with Anita Loos writing some of the scripts, As Ethel in the *Ethel and Bill Series* her comedic talents as the gum-chewing secretary in her black-and-white, striped costume made the comedienne famous. When she signed with Fine Arts for the highly publicized role of Dulcinea in DeWolf Hopper's *Don Quixote* (1916) she successfully molded her talents to the role which made her an ideal Hopper foil. The success of the film led to her being teamed with Hopper in *A Rough Knight, Sunshine Dad,* and *Mr. Goode, the Samaritan.* At the peak of success the comedienne was in demand by the film magazine writers who often compared her to Chaplin. The Fine Arts' successes led to her being signed by Triangle as the star of their Keystone comedies *(The French Milliner, The Two O'Clock Train, Bedelia's Bluff, The Lady Drummer*, and *Laundry Liz).* In 1917, the World Company offered her the chance to form her own company but when the venture failed to materialize she joined the Christie Company (1918-1921) and starred in the short comedies *Rowdy Ann, Go West Young Woman, Dining Room, Kitchen and Sink*, and *Striking Models.*

In 1923, the Universal Company decided to turn the well-known comic strip *The Gumps* into a comedy film series and as Min, the wife of Andy Gump, Miss Tincher was starred with Joe Murphy in the two-reel series for the next five years (also while at Universal in 1924 she supported Laura La Plante in the comedy melodrama *Excitement).* The end of the *Gump* series brought an end to the leading roles for the comedienne. After a supporting role in Helen Kane's musical *Dangerous Nan McGrew* (1930), she ended her film career and left Hollywood.

The former comedienne returned to Los Angeles in 1932 when her sister died of acute alcoholism. The informant on the death certificate was listed as Fay Tincher of Chicago. The sister was buried in Forest Lawn by her mother (died 1931); her other two sisters were buried with her father in Topeka. After the death of her sister, Fay Tincher virtually disappeared. What had become of the once famous comedienne? Where had she gone after leaving Hollywood for the last time? These were questions which seemed unanswerable to the film researcher.

Over the years as a film researcher I searched and questioned others about the comedienne's whereabouts. I searched newspapers and trade papers for a marriage or an obituary, I wrote libraries seeking any information on file for the actress. My research was in vain, there just wasn't anything to be found. As the years passed I came to believe that her whereabouts would forever be unknown. After discovering in 1991 that Social Security information had been made accessible to the public, I wrote the Cambridge Statistical Research Association requesting a search in the department's death file. A search was made and the department found only one Fay Tincher on file. The printout sent to me stated that a Fay Tincher born on April 17, 1884, had died in Brooklyn, New York, in October 1983. At last, I believed I had found the actress, but I needed additional proof. With the information uncovered I was able to view her death certificate which stated she had died in Brooklyn on October 11, 1983 but the place of birth, parent's name, and occupation was unknown. The certificate stated that she had never married. This was without a doubt the former comedienne but I wanted additional verification. From the Social Security Administration I applied and received a copy of her application for a social security number. There I found the needed proof as her parents were listed as Mary E. Hartley and George W. Tincher and the place of birth was Topeka, Kansas. On further investigation I found that Fay Tincher was interred in an unmarked grave at Silver Mount Cemetery on Staten Island in New York City. At long last the elusive once famous film comedienne had been found.

Mabel Trunnelle

"Miss Mabel Trunnelle will need no introduction, for she will readily be recognized as one of the leading stars in the Motion Picture world," so said the *Motion Picture Story Magazine* (April 1911). The popular brunette Edison star appeared in numerous comedies and melodramas in the very earliest days of the film industry, and Miss Trunnelle's gracious lady roles typed her in sophisticated roles later exemplified by Elsie Ferguson, Norma Shearer, and Greer Garson.

The actress was born the daughter of Margaret McGonigle and Louis Trunnelle in Dwight, Illinois, on November 8, 1879, and it was in Dwight that she received her education. In interviews in the early film magazines she refused to comment on her early years. From the articles one can glean only the mention of her days on the stage as she spoke of appearing in a production of *Polly of the Circus* and touring in stock in New Orleans, Syracuse, and Philadelphia. While touring in stock Miss Trunnelle met and married Herbert Prior, a well-known stage actor.

Miss Trunnelle and Prior became members of the Edison Stock Company sometime between 1907-1910; the actress stated that she entered films in 1909 but records show that she and Prior, along with Charles Ogle and Frank McGlynn, were members of the company as early as 1907. Within a span of two years (1909-1911) Miss Trunnelle starred in numerous short films usually with Prior as her leading man *(The Doomed Ship, The Prince and the Pauper, Three of a Kind, Silver Threads Among the*

Gold, The Battle of Bunker Hill, The Big Dam, and *In the Days of Chivalry).*

Briefly, in 1911, Miss Trunnelle and her husband left Edison for the Majestic Company where they appeared in a series of comedy-dramas *(The Silent Call, A Game for Two, Hazel Kirke, Thorns of Success,* and *Willie's Dog)* before they returned to the Edison fold in 1912. Between 1912-1915 as the star of the *Olive* series and literally hundreds of one- and two-reelers *(How Washington Crossed the Delaware, The Duke's Dilemma, Janet of the Dunes, The Phantom Ship,* and *Young Mrs. Winthrop)* she became one of Edison's major stars.

With the short film giving way to the feature film, Miss Trunnelle was starred by Edison in *The Destroying Angel* (1915), the historical drama *Eugene Aram* (1915), the Western drama *Ranson's Folly* (1915), *The Heart of the Hills* (1916), the war drama *A Message to Garcia* (1916), the supernatural drama *The Ghost of Old Morro* (1917), and the social drama *The Master Passion* (1917). In decline by 1916 these films were among the company's last with Miss Trunnelle and Prior remaining with Edison almost to the very end before joining the Vitagraph Company. After a feature role with Earle Williams in *The Grell Mystery* (1917), Miss Trunnelle roles were less frequent; semiretired, she appeared in Paramount's *Singed Wings* (1922) and Asher's *The Love Trap* (1923) before permanently retiring from the screen.

The pioneer film couple made their home in the Hollywood suburb of Glendale and Prior continued as one of the busiest character actors on the screen throughout the 1920s and later an atmospheric extra in many films until his death on October 3, 1954. Miss Trunnelle continued living in her Glendale home until death claimed her on April 29, 1981, at the age of 101.

Marie Walcamp

Melodramatic serials—once so popular—made stars of Pearl White, Ruth Roland, Helen Holmes, and Marie Walcamp. Of the four, only Pearl White is remembered, but in the early days of filmmaking the others were equally famous for their countless daring and perilous adventures. Marie Walcamp, known as the "daredevil of the movies," won stardom by jumping from careening automobiles, leaping from ships in mid-ocean and fearlessly appearing with wild jungle animals (attacked by a lion in one of her serials she bore a scar from the encounter for the rest of her life). Her action-oriented films made her a star but her reputation as a "daring do" heroine limited her to the type of film roles offered her by the producers.

Born in Dennison, Ohio, on July 27, 1894, little is known of Miss Walcamp's early years. In early film magazine interviews she revealed that she appeared with several stock companies in the East and on the Pacific Coast and later appeared in musical comedy opposite Kolb and Dill, Weber and Fields, DeWolf Hopper, Anna Held, and Frank Daniels. When introduced to film director Henry McRae, who offered her a film contract, she gladly abandoned the stage to try her luck as a film performer.

Miss Walcamp's film career began in late 1912 or early 1913 when she joined the Universal Company making her debut in early comedies (the actress was an exception as she spent most of her film career at Universal whereas most actors in those early days moved from one studio to another frequently). In 1914, under Henry McRae's direction, she was teamed with William Clifford in a series of two-reel melodramas with western and jungle backgrounds that were the locales of the majority of her films throughout her film career *(Olana of the South Seas, Our Enemy Spy, Rescued by the Wireless, The Trail Breakers, The Brand of His Tribe, From the Lion's Jaw, Jungle Master, The Law of the Lumberjack,* and *The Law of the Range).* The popularity of the Walcamp-Clifford team *(The Blood of the Children, Custer's Last Scout,* and *The Terrors of the Jungle)* resulted in the company also teaming her with Wellington Player in more action-packed melodramas *(The Circus Girl's Romance, A Daughter of the Jungle, The Jungle Queen, The Toll of the Sea,* and *Coral)* which undoubtedly made her the company's busiest player in 1915.

In 1916 Miss Walcamp briefly escaped from the west and the jungles for a series of Lois Weber and Phillips Smalley's sophisticated social dramas *(Hop, The Devil's Brew, The Flirt, Where Are My Children,* and *John Needham's Double)* before the company quickly returned her to the outdoor action genre. Lacking the beauty of a drawing-room heroine, Miss Walcamp's stamina and athletic abilities were the chief assets the company used to turn her into a serial star. Her serial work began in 1916 when she appeared in chapters 10-13 of the Wharton propaganda serial *Patria* opposite Irene Castle, but her own starring Western serial *Liberty, A Daughter of the U.S.A.* was released first. The success of the serial made her a star and over the next few years (1917-1920) she became Universal's answer to Pearl White and Ruth Roland with successes in *The Red Ace, The Lion's Claw* (while making this serial her shoulder was badly mangled when a lion attacked her), *The Red Glove* and for her last serial the company sent her to the Orient to film *The Dragon Net*. Her costar in the serial was Harland Tucker and while on location the stars became romantically involved and were married before the company returned to the States.

The active life of a serial queen did not keep Miss Walcamp from appearing in the Western feature *Tongues of Flame* (1918) and Universal's two-reel series *Spurs and Saddles* (1919). In 1921, under the direction of Lois Weber, the actress again tried to charge her serial queen image when she appeared in *The Blot*; when the drama failed to rekindle her film career she was absent from the screen until 1924 when she appeared in *A Desperate Adventure*, *Treasure Canyon*, and *Western Vengeance*. With her career having peaked Miss Walcamp retired permanently after *In a Moment of Temptation* (1927).

As with many of her contemporaries, Miss Walcamp faded into film history with little heard of her thereafter. The former star's *New York Times* obituary reported that her husband found his wife dead on November 17, 1936, in their gas-filled Los Angeles home after returning from a business trip. Mr. Tucker said that his wife had been ill and despondent for several months and he believed her suicide was due to ill health.

Eleanor Woodruff

The photograph of Eleanor Woodruff in Daniel Blum's *A Pictorial History of the Silent Screen* long puzzled the film researcher as to what became of the once prominent leading lady after her exit from films. Lesser players of Miss Woodruff's time can easily be found in film lore, but there was never anything in print on her life after her last curtain call or the director's last "that's a wrap." Did she live happily ever after or were her years filled with tragedy?

The later events in the life of Miss Woodruff do not fall easily into place for the researcher who finds himself hampered with so many years of the actress's anonymity. The reemergence of the actress began with an article discovered while perusing old issues of the trade paper *The Billboard*. The article reported the announcement of actress Eleanor Stark Woodruff's marriage to stock broker Dorsey Richardson on April 4, 1931.

Born into an old distinguished Pennsylvania family in Towanda on September 12, 1891, Miss Woodruff was educated in public schools and the National School of Oratory. Against parental opposition she joined the Orpheum Stock Company in Philadelphia in 1909 and within a year she became the company's leading lady in *Beverly of Graustark, The Spendthrift*, and *The Gamblers,* before making her Broadway debut in *The Five Frankfurters.*

After the run of *The Five Frankfurters,* the actress made her film debut in 1912 for the Pathé Company, where she quickly distinguished herself in dramatic roles. Miss Woodruff became a star (1913-1914) in the two- and three-reelers *The Two Mothers* (reputed to be the first two-reel film ever made in the United States), *All Love Excelling, The Bomb Boy, The Finger of Fate, In the Mesh of Her Hair, The Ticket-of-Leave Man, A Leech of Industry, The Second Generation, Rods of Wrath, The Sword of Damocles,* and *The Winning Hand.* She costarred with Pearl White in the legendary serial *The Perils of Pauline* and starred in the war drama *The Last Volunteer* and *Big Jim Garrity,* (a drama about drugs not released until 1916) before leaving the Pathé Company.

On January 2, 1915 Miss Woodruff joined the Vitagraph Company where, over the next two years in the company's two- and three-reelers and feature films, she appeared in leading roles in *His Rinkie, The West Wind, From the Dregs,* costarred opposite Charles Richman in *The Heights of Hazard,* William Courtenay in the company's prestigious film *The Island of Surprise* (the film opened the Vitagraph Theater in New York on January 16, 1916), Darwin Karr in the historical drama *Britton of the Seventh,* and Charles Richman and James Morrison in the WWI drama *The Hero of Submarine D-2.* In 1916 the actress joined the World Film Company and starred opposite Holbrook Blinn in *The Weakness of Man* (the film version of Leo Tolstoy's play *The Living Corpse)* and, after starring in William Randolph Hearst's first feature release *Jaffery* (1916), Miss Woodruff ended her film career.

The actress had no qualms about forsaking the silent drama when Otis Skinner prevailed upon her to return to the Broadway stage as his leading lady in Booth Tarkington's *Mister Antonio* (1916). Throughout the following decade (1921-1931) she became one of the stage's busiest leading ladies in *Nemesis, Honors Are Even, Back to Methuselah,* in Pirandello's original production of *Six Characters in Search of an Author,* the London production of George M. Cohan's *So This Is London,* and other well-known plays before her final Broadway appearance in Somerset Maugham's *The Breadwinner* (1931).

With Miss Woodruff's marriage to Richardson in 1931, her theatrical career ended, but what of the years after 1931? The *New York Times Obituary Indices* failed to include an obituary for the actress but did include one for Richardson. His obituary (died November 8, 1961) stated the prominent investment banker was a former State Department official and economic adviser to Presidents John F. Kennedy and Lyndon B. Johnson and had died in Princeton, New Jersey. Survivors included daughter Rosalie and granddaughter. Memorial services had been held at Trinity Episcopal Church in Princeton. Richardson's obituary made no mention of his wife. Had they divorced or had she died? The answer to the question was found in the Princeton newspapers.

After her marriage, Miss Woodruff relinquished her role of actress for the roles of wife, mother, businesswoman, teacher, and socialite. As Richardson climbed the ladder of success in the business world, his wife complemented his rise by her work in social, political, and club work. She volunteered many hours to the USO during World War II and was active in the Republican Party. (Miss Woodruff was a lifelong honorary member of the Women's Republican Club in New York.) As a businesswoman, she became a well-known interior decorator and taught speech and diction in one of the Princeton schools.

Eleanor Woodruff died on October 7, 1980, in Princeton, New Jersey. Her obituaries reported the death of the former prominent social figure and distinguished stage actress who appeared in a few movies. Her obituary also revealed a former star who did indeed live happily after the final fade-out on the screen and the last curtain-call on the stage. Her enriched life as actress, wife, mother, and businesswoman contradicts the tragic lives encountered by so many of her peers.

Silent Screen Necrology

Explanation of Entry Format

A complete silent screen necrology is virtually impossible to compile—many early film actors' deaths went unreported in the trade journals. Regrettably there are some omissions in this necrology due to the lack of published birth, professional, and death information.

Actors: The necrology includes actors (foreign and U.S.) who appeared in silent films. Also included are film directors, producers, authors, politicians, and sports figures who appeared in extra, cameo, and feature roles.

Time: The necrology's time span is from the late 1800s to 1928. Also the actors from the transitional period (silent to sound) are included.

Name: Professional name listed. Included in parenthesis are other professional names used. Also in parenthesis are professional nicknames and full names of actors who were professionally known by initials.

Place of Birth: b. (born) followed by place of birth if known. Abbreviations are used for states and countries but the country is spelled when it makes place of birth more identifiable.

Date of Birth: Known birth data included. Question marks are used when the century is unknown and c. (circa) and year used when around the time of birth.

Place of Death: d. (died) followed by place of death if known. Same criterion used for place of death as for place of birth with the exception that Co (county) is listed when the California city is unknown.

Date of Death: Known death data included. Question marks are used when year of death is unknown for a deceased actor and c. (circa) and years used for around the time of death.

A

Aasen, John: b. Minnesota, 1887; d. Mendocino, CA, 1 Aug 1938.

Abbas, Hector: b. Amsterdam, Holland, 9 Nov 1884; d. London, Eng, 11 Nov 1942.

Abbe, Charles S.: b. Windhan, CT, 23 May 1860; d. Darien, CT, 16 Jun 1932.

Abbe, Jack Yutaka: b. Japan, 1895; d. Tokyo, Japan 3 Jan 1977.

Abbe, James: b. Alfred, ME, 17 Jul 1883; d. San Francisco, CA, 11 Nov 1973.

Abbey, May: b. Hartford, CT, 1872; d. New York, NY, 20 Aug 1952.

Abbott, Frank: b. California, 16 Jul 1878; d. Los Angeles, CA, 2 Feb 1957.

Abbott, Gypsy: b. Atlanta, GA, 31 Jan 1897; d. Los Angeles, CA, 25 Jul 1952.

Abbott, Marion: b. Danville, KY, 27 Jan 1867; d. Philadelphia, PA, 15 Jan 1937.

Abel, Alfred: b. Leipzig, Ger, 12 Mar 1865; d. Berlin, Ger, 12 Dec 1937.

Abel, Walter: b. St. Paul, MN, 6 Jun 1898; d. Esset, CT, 26 Mar 1987.

Abeles, Edward S.: b. St. Louis, MO, 4 Nov 1869; d. New York, NY, 10 Jul 1919.

Abingdon, William L.: b. Tewcester, Eng, 2 May 1859; d. New York, NY, 17 May 1918.

Abramson, Lizzie Einhorn: b. Rumania, 1857; d. New York, NY, 14 Jan 1945.

Abril, Dorothy: b. Paterson, NJ, 10 Jun 1897; d. Los Angeles, CA, 28 Apr 1977.

Achterberg, Fritz: b. Berlin, Ger, 2 Nov 1880; d. 12 Oct 1971.

Acker, Eugene: b. Stockholm, Sweden, 13 May 1889; d. San Francisco, CA, 26 Jun 1971.

Acker, Jean: b. Trenton, NJ, 23 Oct 1893; d. Los Angeles, CA, 16 Aug 1978.

Ackerman, Walter: b. New York, NY, 28 Jun 1881; d. Los Angeles, CA, 12 Dec 1938.

Acord, Art: b. Glenwood, UT, 17 Apr 1890; d. Chihuahua, Mex, 4 Jan 1931.

Acosta, Enrique: b. Mexico, 26 Feb 1870; d. Los Angeles, CA, 22 May 1949.

Adair, Janice: b. Morpeth, Eng, 1904; d. 13 Jul 1948.

Adair, Jean: b, Hamilton, Ont, Can, 13 Jun 1873; d, New York, NY, 11 May 1953.

Adair, Robyn: b. Miles City, MT, 1885; d. 19??.

Adalbert, Max: b. Danzig, Ger, 19 Nov 1874; d. Munich, Ger, 7 Sep 1933.

Adams, Allen: b. 18??; d. 1918.

Adams, Barton: b. 1900; d, Los Angeles, CA, 9 Jul 1970.

Adams, Blake: b. Scotland, 18??; d. London, Eng, 17 Aug 1913.

Adams, Claire: b. Winnipeg, Can, 24 Sep 1898; d. Melbourne, Austral, 25 Sep 1978.

Adams, Constance (Mrs. Cecil B. DeMille); b. Orange, NJ, 27 Apr 1874; d. Los Angeles, CA, 17 Jul 1960.

Adams, Edith: b. 1879; d. New York, NY, 10 Jan 1957.

Adams, Ernie: b. San Francisco, CA, 18 Jun 1885; d, Los Angeles, CA, 26 Nov 1974.

Adams, James B. (Jimmy): b. Paterson, NJ, 4 Oct 1888; d. Glendale, CA, 19 Dec 1933.

Adams, John Wolcott: b. Worcester, MA, 1874; d. New York, NY, 3 Jan 1925.

Adams, Kathryn: b. St. Louis, MO, 25 May 1895; d. Los Angeles, CA, 17 Feb 1959.

Adams, Lionel: b. New Orleans, LA, 1866; d. New York, NY, 10 Aug 1952.

Adams, Stella: b. Sherman, TX, 24 Apr 1883; d. Woodland Hills, CA, 17 Sep 1961.

Adams, Victoria: b. Missouri, 17 Jun 1897; d. Los Angeles, CA, 13 May 1961.

Adams, William P.: b. Tiffin, OH, 1887; d. New York, NY, 29 Sep 1972.

Adamson, Evelyn: b. 1901; d. 29 Oct 1958.

Adler, Jacob P.: b. Odessa, Russ, 1855; d. New York, NY, 1 Apr 1926.

Adler, Sarah: b. Odessa, Russ, 1865; d. New York, NY, 28 Apr 1953.

Adolfi, John G.: b. New York, NY, 19 Feb 1888; d. Canoe River, Bri. Col., 11 May 1933.

Adoree, Renee: b. Lille, Fr, 30 Sep 1898; d. Tunjunga, CA, 5 Oct 1933.

Agar, Jane: b. Sharon Township, OH, 2 Mar 1889; d. Lakewood, OH, 10 Jun 1948.

Agnew, Robert: b. Dayton, KY, 4 Jun 1899; d. Palm Springs, CA, 8 Nov 1983.

Aguglia, Mimi: b. Catania, Sicily, 21 Dec 1884; d. Woodland Hills, CA, 30 Jul 1970.

Aherne, Brian: b. King's Norton, Worcs, Eng, 2 May 1902; d. Venice, FL, 10 Feb 1986.

Aherne, Patrick: b. King's Norton, Worcs, Eng, 6 Jan 1901; d. Woodland Hills, CA, 30 Sep 1970.

Aicken, Elinor: b. England, 1834; d. 5 May 1914.

Aimoso, Raymond: b. La Fere, Fr, 1889; d. Paris, Fr, 22 Aug 1944.

Ainley, Henry: b. Leeds, Eng, 21 Aug 1879; d. London, Eng, 31 Oct 1945.

Ainsworth, Sidney: b. Manchester, Eng, 21 Dec 1872; d. Madison, WI, 21 May 1922.

Aitken, Spottiswoode: b. Edinburgh, Scot, 16 Apr 1868; d, Los Angeles, CA, 24 Feb 1933.

Aked, Muriel: b. Bingley, Yorks, Eng, 9 Nov 1887; d. Settle, Yorks, Eng, 21 Mar 1955.

Albanesi, Meggie: b. London, Eng, 8 Oct 1899; d. Broadstairs, Kent, Eng, 9 Dec 1923.

Alberni, Luis: b. Barcelona, Spain, 4 Oct 1886; d. Woodland Hills, CA, 23 Dec 1962.

Albers, Hans: b. Hamburg, Ger, 22 Sep 1893 ; d. Munich, Ger, 24 Jul 1960.

Albert, Dan: b. Nashville, TN, 1890; d. Nashville, TN, ? Aug 1919.

Albert, Elsie: b. North Caldwell, NJ, 20 Nov 1888; d. Oregon, 7 Oct 1981.

Albert, Katherine: b. 1902; d. Santa Monica, CA, 26 Jul 1970.

Alberti, Fritz: b. Hanau, Ger, 22 Oct 1877; d. ? Sep 1954.

Alberti, Viola: b. Lewiston, PA, 1874; d. 19??.

Albertson, Arthur W.: b. Waycross, GA, 6 Jan 1891; d. New York, NY, 19 Oct 1926.

Albertson, E. Coit: b. Reading, PA, 14 Oct 1880; d. Los Angeles, CA, 13 Dec 1953.

Albertson, Frank: b. Fergus Falls, MN, 2 Feb 1909; d. Santa Monica, CA, 29 Feb 1964.

Albes, Emil F.: b. Pyrmont, Ger, 30 Oct 1861; d. 22 Mar 1923.

Alcovar, Pierre: b. France, 14 Mar 1893; d. 1954.

Alden, Mary: b. New York, NY, 18 Jun 1883; d. Woodland Hills, CA, 2 Jul 1946.

Alderson, Erville: b. Kansas City, MO, 11 Sep 1882; d. Glendale, CA, 4 Aug 1957.

Aldine, James: b. Pearl River, NY, 17 Nov 1902; d. Long Beach, CA, 27 Jan 1985.

Aldor, Bernd: b. Constantinople, Turkey, 23 Mar 1887; d. 19??.

Aldridge, Alfred: b. New Orleans, LA, 1876; d. Los Angeles, CA, 4 May 1934.

Alexander, Ben: b. Goldfield, NV, 26 May 1911; d. Los Angeles, CA, 5 Jul 1969.

Alexander, Claire: b. New York, NY, 1897; d. Alhambra, CA, 16 Nov 1927.

Alexander, Clifford: b. San Jose, CA, 17 Jan 1891; d. San Francisco, CA, 2 Mar 1965.

Alexander, Edward: b. Ogdensburg, NY, 2 May 1886; d. Dearborn, MI, 15 Aug 1964.

Alexander, Frank (Fatty): b. Olympia, WA, 25 May 1879; d. Los Angeles, CA, 8 Sep 1937.

Alexander, Georg: b. Hanover, Ger, 3 Apr 1889; d. Berlin, Ger, 30 Oct 1945.

Alexander, Sir George: b. Reading, Eng, 19 Jun 1858; d. London, Eng, 15 Mar 1918.

Alexander, Gerard: b. 1877; d. Los Angeles, CA, 8 Apr 1962.

Alexander, Janet: b. Ewell, Surrey, Eng, 18??; d. 28 Jun 1961.

Alexander, Muriel: b. Cape Town, So Africa, 1884; d. Johannesburg, So Africa, ? Mar 1975.

Alexander, Richard: b. Dallas, TX, 18 Nov 1902; d. Woodland Hills, CA, 9 Aug 1989.

Alexander, Sara: b. Wheeling, WV, 1839; d. New York, NY, 24 Dec 1926.

Alexandre, Rene: b. 18??; d. France, ? Dec 1914.

Alexis, Demetrius: b. Alexandria, Egypt, 1 Dec 1899; d. Los Angeles, CA, 12 Mar 1973.

Algier, Sidney H.: b. Shamokin, PA, 5 Dec 1885; d. West Los Angeles, CA, 24 Apr 1945.

Ali, George: b. 1866; d. Freeport, NY, 26 Apr 1947.

Alison, George: b. London, Eng, 1865; d. Norwalk, CT, 14 Jan 1936.

Allaire, Josiah: b. 1865; d. 8 Oct 1935.

Allan, Maud: b. Toronto, Can, 27 Aug 1880; d. Los Angeles, CA, 7 Oct 1956.

Allardt, Arthur: b. New York, 7 Apr 1883; d. 19??.

Allen, Alfred: b. Alfred, NY, 8 Apr 1866; d. Los Angeles, CA, 18 Jun 1947.

Allen, Christopher: b. 1869; d. Los Angeles Co., CA, 7 Nov 1955.

Allen, Dave: b. Albany, NY, 15 Aug 1885; d. Los Angeles, CA, 3 Jan 1955.

Allen, Dorothy: b. Houston, TX, 1896; d. New York, NY, 30 Sep 1970.

Allen, E. H. (Edwin Hampton Allen): b. 15 Nov 1885; d. Los Angeles Co, CA, 13 Aug 1942.

Allen, Estelle: b. Portland, OR, 5 Jan 1892; d. Los Angeles, CA, 14 Jul 1970.

Allen, Harry R.: b. Sydney, Austral, 10 Jul 1883; d. Los Angeles Co, CA, 4 Dec 1951.

Allen, Joseph: b. Bristol, Eng, 2 Jan 1840; d. Chicago, IL, 12 Jan 1917.

Allen, Joseph: b. Boston, MA, 1872; d. Newton, MA, 9 Sep 1952.

Allen, Kenneth: b. 1903; d. Alameda, CA, 15 Jan 1976.

Allen, Maud: b. 18??; d. Washington, DC, 7 Oct. 1956.

Allen, Phyllis: b. Staten Island, NY, 25 Nov 1861; d. Los Angeles, CA, 26 Mar 1938.

Allen, Ricca: b. Victoria, Can, 9 Jun 1863; d. Los Angeles, CA, 13 Sep 1949.

Allen, Richard (Frank Barnes); b. 1875; d. Bronx, NY, 1 Nov 1940.

Allen, Rose (Carrie Doran); b. 31 Mar 1885; d. Los Angeles, CA, 3 May 1977.

Allen, Sam: b. Baltimore, MD, 25 Dec 1861; d. Los Angeles, CA, 13 Sep 1934.

Allen, Viola: b. Huntsville, AL, 27 Oct 1869; d. New York, NY, 9 May 1948.

Allenby, Thomas: b. Australia, 1861; d. Los Angeles, CA, 19 Dec 1933.

Allerton, Helen (Helen Kilduff): b. 1888; d. Golf, IL, 4 Nov 1959.

Allgood, Sarah: b. Dublin, Ire, 15 Oct 1879; d. Los Angeles, CA, 13 Sep 1950.

Allison, May: b. Rising Farm, GA, 14 Jun 1890; d. Bratenahl, OH, 27 Mar 1989.

Allworth, Frank: b. 1900; d, Philadelphia, PA, 2 Sep 1935.

Allyn, Lilly: b. 1886; d. Philadelphia, PA, 5 May 1944.

Alstrup, Carl: b. Copenhagen, Den, 11 Apr 1877; d. 2 Oct 1942.

Alter, Lottie: b. La Crosse, WI, 16 Jan 1879; d. Beecherst, NY, 25 Dec 1924.

Althouse, Earl F.: b. 1893; d. Gladwyne, PA, 6 Feb 1971.

Alvardo, Don: b. Albuquerque, NM, 4 Nov 1904; d. Los Angeles, CA, 31 Mar 1967.

Amador, Charles Edward: b. Mexico, 5 Mar 1896; d. Chula Vista, CA, 7 Apr 1974.

Ames, Gerald: b. Blackheath, Eng, 12 Sep 1881; d. London, Eng, 2 Jul 1933.

Ames, Percy: b. Brighton, Eng, 1874; d. New York, NY, 28 Mar 1936.

Ames, Robert: b. Hartford, CT, 23 Mar 1889; d. New York, NY, 27 Nov 1931.

Ander, Charlotte: b. Berlin, Ger, 14 Aug 1902; d. 5 Aug 1969.

Anderson, Capt. C. E.: b. Sweden, 27 Oct 1882; d. Los Angeles Co, CA, 24 Mar 1956.

Anderson, Claire: b. Detroit, MI, 8 May 1895; d. Venice, CA, 23 Mar 1964.

Anderson, Dallas: b. Grieff, Scot, 12 Jul 1874; d. Richmond, VA, 16 Nov 1934.

Anderson, Florence: b. 1882; d. New York, NY, 25 Nov 1962.

Anderson, G. M. (Broncho Billy): b. Little Rock, AR, 21 Mar 1884; d. Los Angeles, CA, 20 Jan 1971.

Anderson, James: b. Scotland, 1872; d. Glasgow, Scot, 22 Mar 1953.

Anderson, Lawrence: b. Hampstead, Eng, 1893; d. London, Eng, 28 Mar 1939.

Anderson, Leona: b. Philadelphia, PA, 1897; d. Columbus, OH, 29 Mar 1985.

Anderson, Margaret: b. New York, NY, 1884; d. New York, NY, 22 Apr 1922.

Anderson, Mignon: b. Baltimore, MD, 31 Mar 1892; d. Burbank, CA, 25 Feb 1983.

Anderson, Nellie (Helen Relyea Anderson): b. Brooklyn, NY, ? Jun 1874; d. 19??.

Anderson, Robert: b. Denmark, 1890; d. 19??.

Andor, Paul (Wolfgang Zilzer): b. Cincinnati, OH, 20 Jan 1901; d. Berlin, Ger, 26 Jun 1991.

Andra, Fern: b. Chicago, IL, 24 Nov 1893; d. Aiken, SC, 8 Feb 1974.

Andrada, David DeCosta: b. Brooklyn, NY, 27 Dec 1865; d. Long Branch, NJ, 3 Jan 1941.

Andre, Monya: b. 12 Apr 1897; d. Los Angeles, CA, 5 Jan 1981.

Andrew, Sylvia: b. London, Eng, 1895; d. Santa Monica, CA, 31 Mar 1959.

Andrews, Ann: b. Los Angeles, CA, 13 Oct 1890; d. New York, NY, 23 Jan 1986.

Andrews, Bobbie: b. England, 20 Feb 1896; d. 11 Nov 1976.

Andreyor, Yvette: b. 1892; d. 1962.

Andriot, Poupee: b. 1899; d. Northridge, CA, 13 Nov 1988.

Angelo, Jean: b. Paris, Fr, 17 May 1875; d. Paris, Fr, 26 Nov 1933.

Anker, William: b. France, 1860; d. 19??.

Annerley, Frederick: b. England, 18 Oct 1887; d. 13 Nov 1967.

Anry, Barat: b. 1871; d. Versailles, Fr, 4 Jan 1929.

Anson, George W.: b. Montrose, Scot, 25 Nov 1847; d. London, Eng, 2 Aug 1920.

Anson, James (Yakima Jim): b. 1883; d. Los Angeles, CA, ? Aug 1925.

Anson, Laura: b. Omaha, NE, 2 Jan 1892; d. Woodland Hills, CA, 15 Jul 1968.

Anthony, Jack: b. Pennistown, Scot, 1900; d. Dunbar, Scot, 28 Feb 1962.

Antonov, Aleksandr P.: b. Russia, 13 Feb 1898; d. 26 Nov 1962.

Aoki, Tsura: b. Tokyo, Japan, 9 Sep 1892; d. Tokyo, Japan,18 Oct 1961.

Aoyama, Yukio: b. Nagoya City, Japan, 1888; d. 19??

Apfel, Oscar: b. Cleveland, OH, 17 Jan 1879; d. Los Angeles, CA, 21 Mar 1938.

Appel, Anna: b. Bucharest, Romania, 1 May 1888; d. New York, NY, 19 Nov 1963.

Appel Sam: b. Magdalina, Mex, 8 Aug 1871; d. Los Angeles Co, CA, 18 Jun 1947.

Appleby, Dorothy: b. Portland, ME, 6 Jan 1908; d. Long Island, NY, 9 Aug 1990.

Applegate, Hazel: b. 1886; d. Chicago, IL, 30 Oct 1959.

Appling, Bert: b. Madera, CA, 6 Dec 1871; d. Downey, CA, 14 Jan 1960.

Arbenina, Stella: St. Petersburg, Russ, 27 Sep 1885; d. London, Eng, 26 Apr 1976.

Arbuckle, Andrew: b. Galveston, TX, 5 Sep 1887; d. Los Angeles, CA, 21 Sep 1939.

Arbuckle, Macklyn: b. San Antonio, TX, 9 Jul 1863; d. Waddington, NY, 31 Mar 1931.

Arbuckle, Roscoe (Fatty): b. Smith Center, KS, 24 Mar 1887; d. New York, NY 29 Jun 1933.

Arcaro, Flavia: b. Mejico, TX, 22 Jun 1876; d. New York, NY, 8 Apr 1937.

Archer, Louis A.: b. 1874; d. Los Angeles, CA, ? Aug 1922.

Ardell, Lillian: b. ????; d. New York, NY, 15 Mar 1950.

Arden, Edwin: St. Louis, MO, 13 Feb 1864; d. Forest Hills, NY, 2 Oct 1918.

Arden, Jane: b. 1904; d. Studio City, CA, 21 Mar 1981.

Arendt, Ekkehard: b. Vienna, Austria, 10 Jun 1892; d. 10 May 1954.

Arey, Wayne: b. Rock Falls, IL, 12 Apr 1880; d. New York, NY, 2 Jul 1937.

Arians, Elizabeth: b. 18??; d. 28 Feb 1922.

Arlen, Betty: b. 1905; d. 1966.

Arlen, Richard: b. Charlottesville, VA, 1 Sep 1899; d. Los Angeles, CA, 28 Mar 1976.

Arling, Charles: b. Toronto, Can, 22 Aug c. 1880; d. 19??.

Arliss, Florence M.: b. 1873; d. London, Eng, 11 Mar 1950.

Arliss, George: b. London, Eng, 10 Apr 1868; d. London, Eng, 5 Feb 1946.

Armetta, Henry: b. Palermo, Italy, 4 Jul 1888; d. San Diego, CA, 21 Oct 1945.

Armitage, Pauline: b. 1898; d. New York, NY, 16 Feb 1926.

Armstrong, Billy: b. Bristol, Eng, 14 Jan 1891; d. Sunland, CA, 1 Mar 1924.

Armstrong, Clyde: b. 1879; d. New York, NY, 30 Sep 1937.

Armstrong, Robert: b. Saginaw, MI, 20 Nov 1890; d. Santa Monica, CA, 20 Apr 1973.

Armstrong, Will H.: b. Peoria, IL 18 Dec 1868; d. Los Angeles, CA, 29 Jul 1943.

Arna, Lissa: b. Germany, 1897; d. Berlin, Ger, 22 Jan 1964.

Arnaud, Yvonne: b. Bordeaux, Fr, 20 Dec 1892; d. London, Eng, 20 Sep 1958.

Arno, Sig: b. Hamburg, Ger, 27 Dec 1895; d. Woodland Hills, CA, 17 Aug 1975.

Arnold, Cecile: b. 18??; d. Hong Kong, China, 1931.

Arnold, Edward: b. New York, NY, 18 Feb 1890; d. Encino, CA, 26 Apr 1956.

Arnold, Gertrud: b. Stolp, Poland, 3 Mar 1873; d. 11 Jan 1931.

Arnold, Jessie: b. Lyons, MI, 3 Dec 1884; d. Los Angeles, CA, 5 May 1955.

Arnold, Lois: b. St. Augustine, FL, 1877; d. Philadelphia, PA, 26 Jan 1947.

Arnold, Mabel: b. Texas, 25 Apr 1888; d. Los Angeles, CA, 6 Jan 1964.

Arnold, Marcella: b. 1911; d. Pasadena, CA, 3 Mar 1937.

Arras, Harry L.: b. Buffalo, NY, 31 May 1881; d. Los Angeles, CA, 29 Jan 1942.

Artaud, Antonin: b. Marseille, Fr, 4 Sep 1896; d. Tvry-sur-Seine, Fr, 4 Mar 1948.

Arthur, George K.: b. London, Eng, 27 Jan 1899; d. New York, NY, 30 May 1985.

Arthur, Jean: b, Plattsburg, NY, 17 Oct 1900; d. Carmel, CA, 19 Jun 1991.

Arthur, Johnny: b. Scottdale, PA, 20 May 1883; d. Woodland Hills, CA, 31 Dec 1951.

Arthur, Julia: b. Hamilton, Ont, Can, 3 May 1869; d. Boston, MA, 28 Mar 1950.

Arthur, Louise: b. 1900; d. Los Angeles, CA, 9 Jun 1925.

Arthur, Paul: b. London, Eng, 19 Jul 1859; d. London, Eng, 12 May 1928.

Arundale, Sybil: b. London, Eng, 20 Jun 1882; d. London, Eng, 5 Sep 1965.

Arundell, Teddy: b. Devonshire, Eng, 18??; d. London, Eng, 5 Nov 1922.

Arvidsonp, Linda (Mrs. D. W. Griffith): b. San Francisco, CA, 1884; d. New York, NY, 26 Jul 1949.

Asche, Oscar: b. Geelong, Austral, 26 Jan 1871; d. Marlow, Bucks, Eng, 23 Mar 1936.

Ascher, Anton: b. 1868; d. New York, NY. 30 Sep 1928.

Ash, Gordon: b. England, 1877; d. New York, NY, 20 Apr 1929.

Ash, Jerry (Jerome H. Ash): b. 1893: d. San Francisco, CA, 5 Jan 1953.

Asher, Max: b. Oakland, CA, 5 May 1885; d. Los Angeles, CA, 15 Apr 1957.

Ashley, Arthur H.: b. New York, NY, 6 Oct 1886; d. East Islip, NY, 28 Dec 1970.

Ashley, Beulah: b. Mississippi, 24 Jan 1899; d. Los Angeles, CA, 6 Jul 1965.

Ashton, Dorrit: b. 1873; d. Los Angeles, CA, 25 Jul 1936.

Ashton, Herbert, Jr.: b. San Francisco, CA, 25 Sep 1902; d. San Francisco, CA, 13 Aug 1960,

Ashton, Sylvia: b. Denver, CO, 26 Jan 1880; d. Los Angeles, CA, 18 Nov 1940.

Ashton, Vera: b, Missouri, 28 Feb 1900; d. Los Angeles, CA, 27 Apr 1965.

Ashwell, Lena: b. Wellesley Training Ship, Eng, 25 Sep 1871; d. London, Eng, 13 Mar 1957.

Asquith, Mary: b. 1873; d. Brooklyn, NY, 22 Dec 1942.

Astaire, Adele: b. Omaha, NE, 10 Sep 1898; d. Scottsdale, AZ, 25 Jan 1981.

Astaire, Fred: b. Omaha, NE, 10 May 1899; d. Los Angeles, CA, 22 Jun 1987.

Asther, Niles: b. Hallrup, Den, 17 Jan 1897; d. Stockholm, Sweden, 13 Oct 1981.

Astor, Camille: b. Warsaw, Poland, 1 Sep 1896; d. Los Angeles, CA, 16 Sep 1944.

Astor, Gertrude: b. Lakewood, OH, 9 Nov 1887; d. Los Angeles, CA, 9 Nov 1977.

Astor, Mary: b. Quincy, IL, 3 May 1903; d. Woodland Hills, CA, 25 Sep 1987.

Atherton, Venie: b. 1862; d. New York, NY, 3 Oct 1927.

Atkinson, Evelyn: b. 1900; d. Seattle, WA, 16 Dec 1954.

Atkinson, Frank: b. Blackpool, Eng, 19 Mar 1890; d. Pinner, Eng, 23 Feb 1963.

Atkinson, George A.: b. Liverpool, Eng, 15 Dec 1877; d. Woodland Hills, CA, 1 May 1968.

Atkinson, Josephine: b. ????; d. Los Angeles, CA, 6 Jan 1954.

Atkinson, Maude: b. England, 1885; d. North Hollywood, CA, 7 Mar 1944.

Attie, Joseph M.: b. France, 14 Jun 1892; d. Redondo Beach, CA, 17 Mar 1971.

Atwell, Grace: b. Boston, MA, 13 Jul 1872; d. Los Angeles, CA, 2 Nov 1952.

Atwell, Roy: b. Syracuse, NY, 2 May 1878; d. New York, NY, 6 Feb 1983.

Atwill, Lionel: b. Croydon, Eng, 1 Mar 1885; d. Pacific Palisades, CA, 22 Apr 1946.

Aubrey, James: b. Bolton, Eng, 23 Oct 1887; d. Woodland Hills, CA, 2 Sep 1983.

Auen, Carl: b. Dusseldorf, Ger, 16 Feb 1892; d. Berlin, Ger, ? Jun 1972.

Auer, Florence; b. Albany, NY, 1880; d. New York, NY, 14 May 1962.

Auer, John H.: b. Budapest, Hungary, 3 Aug 1906; d. Riverside, CA, 15 Mar 1975.

Auer, Mischa: b. St. Petersburg, Russ, 17 Nov 1905; d. Rome, Italy, 5 Mar 1967.

Auerbach, Henry L.: b. 18??; d. Oakland, CA, 22 Aug 1916.

Aug, Edna: b. Cincinnati, OH, 1878; d. Willow, NY, 30 Nov 1938.

August, Edwin: b. St. Louis, MO, 10 Nov 1883; d. Los Angeles, CA, 4 Mar 1964.

August Hal: b. 1890; d. Chicago, IL, 21 Sep 1918.

Ault, Marie: b. Wigan, Lancs, Eng, 2 Sep 1870; d. London, Eng, 9 May 1951.

Austen, Leslie: b. London, Eng, 1886; d. 19??.

Austin, Albert: b. Birmingham, Eng, 1885; d. Los Angeles, CA, 17 Aug 1953.

Austin, Charles: b. 1878; d. London, Eng, 14 Jan 1944.

Austin, Frank: b. Mound City, MO, 9 Oct 1877; d. 13 May 1954.

Austin, Jere: b. Minneapolis, MN, 1876; d. Los Angeles, CA, 12 Nov 1927.

Austin, Johanna: b. 1853; d. Los Angeles, CA, 1 Jun 1944.

Austin, William C.: b. Georgetown, Bri Guiana, 12 Jun 1884; d. Orange Co, CA, 15 Jun 1975.

Auzinger, Max (Ben Ali Bey): b. 26 Jul 1839; d. 11 May 1928.

Avery, Charles: b. Chicago, IL, 28 May 1873; d. Los Angeles, CA, 23 Jul 1926.

Avery, Patricia: b. 1903; d. 1973.

Axzelle, Carl: b. Sweden, 11 Apr 1881; d. Malibu, CA, 30 Oct 1958.

Axzelle, Evelyn: b. England, 22 Dec 1890; d. Palm Springs, CA, 11 May 1977.

Aye, Marion: b. Chicago, IL, 5 Apr 1903; d. Los Angeles, CA, 20 Jul 1951.

Ayers, Dudley: b. ????; d. San Francisco, CA, Sep 1930.

Ayerton, Robert: b. 18??; d. 18 May 1924.

Ayling, Robert: b. 18??; d. New York, NY, 28 Aug 1919.

Aylott, Dave: b. London, Eng, 1885; d. England, 31 Oct 1969.

Aynesworth, Allan: b. Sandhurst, Berks, Eng, 14 Apr 1864; d. Camberley, Surrey, Eng, 22 Aug 1959.

Ayres, Agnes: b. Carbondale, IL, 4 Apr 1896; d. Los Angeles, CA, 25 Dec 1940.

Ayres, Sydney: b. New York, 28 Aug 1879; d. Oakland, CA, 9 Sep 1916.

Ayrton, Randle: b. Chester, Cheshire, Eng, 9 Aug 1869; d. Stratford-on-Avon, Eng, 28 May 1940.

B

Babbitt, Orrin: b. 1883; d. Warwick, RI, 5 Jul 1941.

Babcock, Theodore: b. Brooklyn, NY, 14 Feb 1868; d. New York, NY, 7 Sep 1930.

Bach, Olaf: b. 7 Apr 1892; d. 1 Nov 1963.

Bach, Reginald: b. Shepperton, Eng, 3 Sep 1886; d. New York, NY, 6 Jan 1941,

Backus, Frank: b. 18??; d. Buffalo, NY, 14 Jan 1923.

Backus, George: b. Columbus, OH, 1858; d. Merrick, NY, 21 May 1939.

Backus, Lionel C.: b. New York State, 28 Dec 1901; d. Woodland Hills, CA, 10 Jun 1981.

Baclanova, Olga: b. Moscow, Russ, 19 Aug 1899; d. Vevey, Switz, 6 Sep 1974.

Bacon, Frank: b. Marysville, CA, 16 Jan 1864; d. Chicago, IL, 19 Nov 1922.

Bacon, Irving: b. St. Joseph, MO, 6 Sep 1893; d. Los Angeles, CA, 5 Feb 1965.

Bacon, Lloyd: b. San Jose, CA, 16 Jan 1889; d. Burbank, CA, 15 Nov 1955.

Bacon, Walter Scott: b. 13 May 1891; d. Los Angeles, CA, 7 Nov 1973.

Baddeley, Hermione: b. Broseley, Shrops, Eng, 13 Nov 1906; d. Los Angeles, CA, 19 Aug 1986.

Badet, Regina: b. 1876; d. Bordeaux, Fr, ? Nov 1949.

Badgley, Frank C.: b. Ottawa, Can, 1 Jan 1893; d. Ottawa, Can, 9 Sep 1955.

Badgley, Gerald: b. Saginaw, MI, 8 Aug 1885; d. 19??.

Badgley, Helen: b. Saratoga Springs, NY, 1 Dec 1908; d. Phoenix, AZ, 25 Oct 1977.

Baer, Arthur (Bugs): b. Philadelphia, PA, 1886; d. New York, NY, 17 May 1969.

Baggott, King: b. St. Louis, MO, 7 Nov 1879; d. Los Angeles, CA, 11 Jul 1948.

Bailey, Buck (Orlo): b. ????; d. Cleveland, OH, 18 Jun 1923.

Bailey, Edwin D.: b. Oakland, CA, 1873; d. Santa Monica, CA, 22 Jul 1950.

Bailey, Frankie: b. New Orleans, LA, 29 May 1859; d. Los Angeles, CA, 8 Jul 1953.

Bailey, Harry: b. 1880; d. Los Angeles, CA, 9 Aug 1954.

Bailey, Oliver D.: b. 1877; d. Harrison, ME, 12 Jul 1932.

Bailey, Willian Norton: b. Omaha, NE, 26 Sep 1886; d. Los Angeles, CA, 8 Nov 1962.

Baily, George Donald: b. 1863; d. Los Angeles, CA, 11 Dec 1927.

Bainbridge, William H.: b. England, 21 Mar 1853; d. 24 Oct 1931.

Baines, Beulah: b. 1905; d. Banning, CA, 16 Aug 1930.

Baird, Dorothea: b. Teddington, Eng, 20 May 1875; d. Broadstairs, Kent, Eng, 24 Sep 1933.

Baird, Leah: b. Chicago, IL, 20 Jun 1883; d. Los Angeles, CA, 3 Oct 1971.

Baird, Stewart: b. Boston, MA, 1881; d. New York, NY, 28 Oct 1947.

Baker, Mrs. Anna Auer: b. 1860; d. Fort Lee, NJ, 2 Apr 1944.

Baker, Eddie: b. Davis, WV, 17 Nov 1897; d. Los Angeles, CA, 4 Feb 1968.

Baker, Elsie: b. Chicago, IL, 13 Jul 1893; d. Los Angeles, CA, 16 Aug 1971.

Baker, Frank: b. Melbourne, Austral, 11 Oct 1892; d. Woodland Hills, CA, 30 Dec 1980.

Baker, J. Frank (Home Run): b. Trappe, MD, 13 Mar 1886; d. Trappe, MD, 28 Jun 1963.

Baker, Josephine: b. St. Louis, MO, 3 Jun 1903; d. Paris, Fr, 12 Apr 1975.

Baker, Lee: b. Ovid, MI, 12 May 1875; d. Los Angeles, CA, 24 Feb 1948.

Baker, Rex (Snowy): b. Sydney, Austral, 8 Feb 1884; d. 2 Dec 1953.

Baker, William: b. 1888; d. New York, NY, 21 Dec 1916.

Baker, Willis: b. Circleville, OH, 1851; d. Hackensack, NJ, 20 Apr 1932.

Bakewell, William: Los Angeles, CA, 2 May 1908; d. Los Angeles, CA, 15 Apr 1993.

Baldwin, George: b. England, 18??; d. Manila, Philippine Islands, 28 Feb 1923.

Baldwin, Kitty: b. 1853; d. Buffalo, NY, 27 Jul 1934.

Balfour, Augustus: b. Philadelphia, PA, 1866; d. 19??.

Balfour, Betty: b. London, Eng, 27 Mar 1903; d. Surrey, Eng, ? Nov 1978.

Balfour,Charles: b. Rayville, LA, c, 1890; d. May 9, 1912.

Balfour, William: b. 1875; d. New York, NY, 12 Apr 1964.

Ball, Eva Lewis; b. 1881; d. Los Angeles, CA, 6 May 1939.

Ballin, Hugo: b. New York, NY, 1880; d. Santa Monica, CA, 27 Nov 1956.

Ballin, Mabel: b. Philadelphia, PA, 1885; d. Santa Monica, CA, 24 Jul 1958.

Ballmain, Rollo: b. Scotland, 1857; d. Weston-Super-Mare, Somerset, Eng, 5 Dec 1920.

Bamattre, Martha: b. 1892; d. Glendale, CA, 12 Jul 1970.

Bameater, Katherine: b. ????; d. Chicago, IL, 16 Oct 1919.

Bancroft, George: b. Philadelphia, PA, 30 Sep 1882; d. Santa Monica, CA, 2 Oct 1956.

Banker, Bill: b. 1907; d. 25 Sep 1985.

Bankhead, Tallulah: b. Huntsville, AL, 31 Jan 1902; d. New York, NY, 12 Dec 1968.

Banks, Monty: b. Casene, Italy, 18 Jul 1897; d. Arona, Italy, 7 Jan 1950.

Banks, Perry: b. Victoria, Can, 24 Apr 1877; d. Santa Barbara, CA, 10 Oct 1934.

Banky, Vilma: b, Nagydorog, Hungary, 9 Jan 1898; d. Los Angeles, CA, 18 Mar 1991.

Bannerman, Margaret: b. Toronto, Ont, Can, 15 Dec 1896; d. Englewood, NJ, 25 Apr 1976.

Bannister, Harry: b. Holland, MI, 29 Sep 1888; d. New York, NY, 26 Feb 1961.

Banvard, Fifi: b. 1901; d. Sydney, Austral, 24 Jun 1962.

Bara, Lori: b. Cincinnati, OH, 18??; d. Los Angeles, CA, 4 Aug 1965.

Bara, Theda: b. Cincinnati, 22 Jul 1890; d. Los Angeles, CA, 7 Apr 1955.

Barbat, Percy: b. 1883; d. San Antonio, TX, 20 Jan 1965.

Barbee, John: b. 1893; d. Los Angeles, CA, 20 Apr 1981.

Barbier, George W.: b. Philadelphia, PA, 19 Nov 1864; d. Los Angeles, CA, 19 Jul 1945.

Barbour, Edwin Wilbour: b. Philadelphial PA, 18??; d. 14 Sep 1914.

Barclay, Delancey: b. New York, NY, 18??; d, New York, NY, 10 Dec 1917.

Barclay, Don: b. Astoria, OR, 26 Dec 1892; d. Palm Springs, CA, 16 Oct 1975.

Barclay, Eric: b. Sweden, 1897; d. 1936.

Bard, Ben: b. Milwaukee, WI, 26 Jan 1893; d. Los Angeles, CA, 17 May 1974.

Bard, Maria (Migo Bard): b. Switzerland, 7 Jul 1901; d. Germany, 6 Apr 1944.

Baring, Mathilde: b. New Orleans, LA, 1879; d. 19??.

Barker, Adella: b. 1857; d. Amityville, NY, 29 Sep 1930.

Barker, Bradley: b. Hempstead, NY, 1883; d. New York, NY, 29 Sep 1951.

Barker, Corinne: b. 1893; d. New York, NY, 6 Aug 1928.

Barker, Florence: b. Los Angeles, CA, 22 Nov 1891; d. Los Angeles, CA, 15 Feb 1913.

Barker, Reginald: b. Winnipeg, Can, 2 Apr 1886; d. Los Angeles, CA, 23 Feb 1945.

Barleon, Amelia: b. Chicago, IL, 1 Apr 1878; d. Jamaica, NY, 17 Jun 1969.

Barlow, Reginald: b. Cambridge, MA, 17 Jun 1866; d. Los Angeles, CA, 6 Jul 1943.

Barnard, Ivor: b. London, Eng, 13 Jun 1887; d. 30 Jun 1953.

Barnell, Nora Ely: b. 1882; d. Los Angeles, CA, 10 Jul 1933.

Barnes, Frank, b. 1875; d. Bronx, NY, 1 Nov 1940.

Barnes, George: b. 1890; d. Los Angeles, CA, 18 Nov 1949.

Barnes, George E.: b. 1879; d. Honolulu, HI, 3 Mar 1926.

Barnes, J. H. (John Henry): b. Watlington, Oxfs, Eng, 26 Feb 1850; d. London, Eng, 10 Nov 1925.

Barnes, Justus D.: b. Little Falls, NY, 1862; d.Weedsport, NY, 6 Feb 1946.

Barnes, Mac M.: b. ????; d. Los Angeles, CA, 10 Jan 1923.

Barnes, T. Roy: b. Lincolnshire, Eng, 11 Aug 1880; d. Los Angeles, CA, 30 Mar 1937.

Barnes, V. L.: b. Indiana, 1870; d. Los Angeles, CA, 9 Aug 1949.

Barnet, Boris V.: b. Moscow, Russ, 16 Jun 1902; d. 8 Jan 1965.

Barnett, Chester: b. Piedmont, MO, 1885; d. Jefferson City, MO, 22 Sep 1947.

Barr, Clarence: b. Omaha, NE, 1876: 19??.

Barrat, Robert H.: b. New York, NY, 10 Jul 1889; d. Los Angeles, CA, 7 Jan 1970.

Barrett, Charles C.: b. Baltimore, MD, 1871; d. Baltimore, MD, 11 Feb 1929.

Barrett, Minnette: b. Gainesville, GA, 1884; d. Whitestone, NY, 20 Jun 1964.

Barrie, Sir James M.: b. Kirriemuir, Scot, 9 May 1860; d. London, Eng, 19 Jun 1937.

Barrie, Nigel: b. Calcutta, India, 5 Feb 1889; d. England, 8 Oct 1971.

Barringer, Barry: b. Mobile, AL, 25 Jun 1888; d. Los Angeles, CA, 21 May 1938.

Barringer, Ned (Edward): b. 1888; d. Leavenworth, KS, 13 Feb 1976.

Barrington, Herbert: b. England, 1872; d. Tarrytown, NY, 26 Oct 1933.

Barrington, Rutland: b. Penge, Eng, 15 Jan 1853; d. London, Eng, 1 Jun 1922.

Barriscale, Bessie: b. New York, NY, 8 Dec 1984; d. Kentfield, CA, 30 Jun 1965.

Barron, Frederick C.: b. Melbourne, Austral, 1888; d. Central Islip, NY, 9 Oct 1955.

Barrows, Henry A.: b. Saco, ME, 29 Apr 1875; d. Los Angeles, CA, 25 Mar 1945.

Barrows, James O.: b. Copperopolis, CA, 29 Mar 1855; d. Los Angeles, CA, 7 Dec 1925.

Barry, Eddie: b. Philadelphia, PA, Oct 1887, d. 19??.

Barry, Jack: b. Meriden, CT, 26 Apr 1887; d. Shrewsbury, MA, 23 Apr 1961.

Barry, Joan: b. London, Eng, 5 Nov 1901; d. Marbella, Spain, 10 Apr 1989.

Barry, Viola: b. Evanston, IL, 1894; d. Los Angeles, CA, 2 Apr 1964.

Barry, Wesley: b. Los Angeles, CA, 10 Aug 1907; d. Fresno, CA, 11 Apr 1994.

Barrye, Emily: b. 1896; d. Los Angeles, CA, 15 Dec 1957.

Barrymore, Ethel: b. Philadelphia, PA, 15 Aug 1879; d. Beverly Hills, CA, 18 Jun 1959.

Barrymore, John: b. Philadelphia, PA, 15 Feb 1882; d. Los Angeles, CA, 29 May 1942.

Barrymore, Lionel: b. Philadelphia, PA, 28 Apr 1878; d. Van Nuys, CA, 15 Nov 1954.

Barrymore, William: b. Russia, 17 Aug 1899; d. San Diego,CA, 23 Apr 1979.

Bartels, Louis John: b. Bunker Hill, IL, 19 Oct 1895; d. Los Angeles, CA, 4 Mar 1932.

Bartet, Julia: b. Paris, Fr, 1854; d. Paris, Fr, ? Nov 1941.

Barthelmess, Richard: b. New York, NY, 9 May 1895; d. Southampton, NY, 17 Aug 1963.

Bartlett, Elsie: b. ????; d. Daytona Beach, FL, 1944.

Bartlett, Harry W.: b. Pittsburgh, PA, 1862; d. New York, NY, 14 Feb 1933.

Barton, Buzz: b. Los Angeles, CA, 5 Nov 1914; d. 20 Nov 1980.

Barton, Charles T.: b. Sacramento, CA, 25 May 1902; d. Burbank, CA, 5 Dec 1981.

Barton, James: b. Gloucester, NJ, 1 Nov 1890; d. Mineola, NY, 19 Feb 1962.

Barton, Joe: b. 1883; d. Los Angeles, CA, 5 Jul 1937.

Barton, John: b. Germantown, PA, 1 May 1872; d. New York, NY, 23 Dec 1946.

Bary, Leon: b. Paris, Fr, 1880; d. France, 1954.

Baskcomb, A. W.: b. London, Eng, 5 Jul 1880; d. London, Eng, 10 Dec 1939.

Basserman, Albert: b. Mannheim, Ger, 7 Sep 1867; d. Zurich, Switz, 15 May 1952.

Bassett, Russell: b. Milwaukee, WI, 1845; d. New York, NY, 7 May 1918.

Baston, J. Thornton: b. San Francisco, CA, 6 Aug 1892; d. Los Angeles Co, CA, 3 May, 1970.

Batalov, Nikolai: b. Moscow, Russ, 6 Dec 1899; d. 10 Nov 1937.

Batcheff, Pierre: b. 1901; d. Paris, Fr, 13 Apr 1932.

Bateman, Victory: b. New York, NY, 6 Apr 1865; d. Los Angeles, CA, 3 Mar 1926.

Bates, Blanche: b. Portland, OR, 25 Aug 1873; d. San Francisco, CA, 25 Dec 1941.

Bates, Granville: b. Harvard, IL, 7 Jan 1882; d. Los Angeles, CA, 8 Jul 1940.

Bates, Leslie A.: b. Waukegan, IL, ? Jun 1877; d. Los Angeles, CA, 8 Aug 1930.

Bates, Louise Emerald: b. Massachusetts, 28 Dec 1886; d. Los Angeles Co, CA, 11 Jun 1972.

Bates, Tom: b. 1864; d. 11 Apr 1930.

Batley, Dorothy: b. London, Eng, 18 Jan 1902; d. ? Dec 1983.

Batley, Ernest G.; b. England, 1879; d. 1916.

Batley, Ethyle: b. 1879; d. 1917.

Batten, John: b. Rotorua, N. Zealand, 3 Apr 1903; d. Colchester, Eng, 10 Aug 1993.

Battista, Miriam: b. New York, NY, 14 Jul 1914; d. New York, NY, 22 Dec 1980.

Batty, Stephen: b. Budapest, Hungary, 1882; d. Patton, CA, 6 Dec 1938.

Bauer, Arthur: b. Vienna, Austria, 30 Mar 1878; d. 19??.

Bauer, Inez: b. California, 21 Jan 1888; d. Millbrae, CA, 15 May 1975.

Baum, Harry: b. 1915; d. Los Angeles, CA, 31 Jan 1974.

Baur, Harry: b. Montrouge, Fr, 12 Apr 1880; d. Paris, Fr, 8 Apr 1943.

Baxter, Barry: b. England, 5 Aug 1894, New York, NY, 27 May 1922.

Baxter, Thuma Jadee: b. Milton, KY, 15 Jun 1890; d. Los Angeles, CA, 11 Jan 1974.

Baxter, Warner: b. Columbus, OH, 29 Mar 1889; d. Beverly Hills, CA, 7 May 1951.

Bay, Tommy (William): b. Travis County, TX, 22 Feb 1901; d. Burbank, CA, 11 Oct 1933.

Bayer, Charles W.: b. 1893; d. Los Angeles, CA, 28 Nov 1953.

Bayley, Hilda: b. London, Eng, 18??; d. London, Eng, 25 May 1971.

Bayliff, W. Lane: b. London, Eng, 6 Apr 1870; d. Australia, ? Feb 1938.

Bayne, Beverly: b. Minneapolis, MN, 11 Nov 1893; d. Scottsdaple, AZ, 29 Aug 1982.

Baynton, Henry: b. Warwick, Eng, 23 Sep 1892; d. London, Eng, 2 Jan 1951.

Beach, Corra: b. 18 Dec 1880; d. North Hollywood, CA, 5 Oct 1963.

Beal, Frank: b. Cleveland, OH, 11 Sep 1862; d. Los Angeles, CA, 20 Dec 1934.

Beal, Scott: b. Quinnesec, MI, 14 Apr 1890; d. Los Angeles, CA, 10 Jul 1973.

Beale, Frank G. (Plug): b. 18??; d. Los Angeles, CA, 9 Nov 1920.

Beamish, Frank: b. Memphis, TN, 1881; d. New York, NY, 3 Oct 1921.

Beaton, Mary: b. Philadelphia, PA, ????; d. Los Angeles, CA, 25 Jan 1961.

Beatty, George W.: b. 1888; d. South Stroudsburg, NY, 21 Feb 1955.

Beaubien, Julien: b. 1896; d. Long Branch, NJ, 18 Oct 1947.

Beaudet, Louise: b. St. Emilie, Que, Can, 1861; d. New York, NY, 31 Dec 1947.

Beaudine, Harold: b. New York, NY, 29 Nov 1694; d. Los Angeles, CA, 9 May 1949.

Beaudine, William: b. New York, NY, 15 Jan 1892; d. Conoga Park, CA, 18 Mar 1970.

Beaumont, Harry: b. Abilene, KS, 10 Feb 1888; d. Santa Monica, CA, 22 Dec 1966.

Beaumont, Lucy: b. Bristol, Eng, 18 May 1873; d, New York, NY, 24 Apr 1937.

Beaumont, Nellie: b. Ramsgate, Kent, Eng, 1870; d. Concord, NH, 26 Oct 1938.

Beavers, Louise: b. Cincinnati, OH, 8 Mar 1902; d. Los Angeles, CA, 26 Oct 1962.

Beban, George, Sr.: b. San Francisco, CA, 5 Nov 1873; d. Los Angeles, CA, 5 Oct 1928.

Beban, George, Jr.: b. New York, NY, 16 Jun 1914; d. Burbank, CA, 28 Sep 1977.

Bech, Lili: b. Denmark, 29 Dec 1885; d. 1939.

Bechtel, William: b. Berlin, Ger, 12 Jun 1867; d. Los Angeles, CA, 27 Oct 1930.

Bechtel, Mrs. William (Jenny): b. New York, NY, 12 Jun 1861; d. Los Angeles, CA, 21 Oct 1938.

Beck, Ludwig: b. 1887; d. ? Jan 1962.

Becker, Fred G.: b. Chicago, IL, 8 Sep 1882; d. Glendale, CA, 28 Mar 1966.

Bedells, Phyllis: b. Bristol, Gloucs, Eng, 2 Aug 1894; d. London, Eng, 2 May 1985.

Beecher, Ada: b. 1862; d. Los Angeles, CA, 30 Mar 1935.

Beecher, Janet: b. Jefferson City, MO, 21 Oct 1884; d. Washington, CT, 6 Aug 1955.

Beecroft, Victor R.: b. London, Eng, 1882; d. Newport News, VA, 25 Mar 1958.

Beery, Noah: b. Smithville, MO, 17 Jan 1882; d. Los Angeles, CA, 1 Apr 1946.

Beery, Wallace: b. Kansas City, MO, 1 Apr 1885; d. Los Angeles, CA, 15 Apr 1949.

Beery, William C.: b. Clay County, MO, 5 Apr 1879; d. Beverly Hills, CA, 25 Dec 1949.

Begg, Gordon: b. Aberdeen, Scot, 14 Jan 1868; d. ? Feb 1954.

Beggs, Lee: b. Omaha, NE, 1871; d. New York, NY, 18 Nov 1943.

Behmer, Ernst: Konigsberg, Ger, 22 Dec 1875; d. 26 Feb 1938.

Behrle, Fred F.: b. San Diego, CA, 8 Jul 1891; d. San Fernando Valley, CA, 20 May 1941.

Beierle, Alfred: b. Berlin, Ger, 4 Jun 1885; d. 16 Mar 1950.

Belasco, David: b. San Francisco, CA, 25 Jul 1854; d. New York, NY, 14 May 1931.

Belasco, Genevieve: b. London, Eng, 1872; d. New York, NY, 17 Nov 1956.

Belasco, Jay: b. Brooklyn, NY, 11 Jan 1888; d. Santa Monica, CA, ? May 1949.

Belasco,Walter: b. Vancouver, Can, 1864; d. San Francisco, CA, 21 Jun 1939.

Belcher, Alice: b. 1869; d. Los Angeles, CA, 9 May 1939.

Belcher, Charles M.: b. San Francisco, CA, 27 Jul 1872; d. Los Angeles, CA, 10 Dec 1943.

Belcher, Frank H.: b. San Francisco, CA, 1869; d. Brentwood, NY, 27 Feb 1947.

Belfield, Richard W.: b. 23 Jul 1873; d, Los Angeles Co, CA, 2 Jan 1940.

Bell, Digby Valentine: b. Milwaukee, WI, 1849; d. New York, NY, 20 Jun 1917.

Bell, Frederick G.: b. 1879; d. New York, NY, 10 Dec 1930.

Bell, Gaston: b. Boston, MA, 27 Sep 1877; d. Woodstock, NY, 11 Dec 1963.

Bell, Genevieve: b. 1895; d. Los Angeles, CA, 3 Oct 1951.

Bell, Henry B. (Hank): b. Los Angeles, CA, 21 Jan 1892; d. Los Angeles, CA, 4 Feb 1950.

Bell, Marie: b. Begles, Fr, 23 Dec 1900; d. Neuilly, Fr, 15 Aug 1985.

Bell, Monta: b. Washington, DC, 5 Feb 1891; d. Los Angeles, CA, 4 Feb 1958.

Bell, Ralph W.: b. 1883; d. San Francisco, CA, 14 Jul 1936.

Bell, Rex: b. Chicago, IL, 16 Oct 1903; d. Las Vegas, NV, 4 Jul 1962.

Bell, Spencer: b. Lexington, KY, 25 Sep 1887; d. 18 Aug 1935.

Bellamy, George: b. Bristol, Eng, 1866; d. 26 Dec 1944.

Bellamy, Madge: b. Hillsboro, TX, 30 Jun 1899; d. Upland, CA, 24 Jan 1990.

Bellew, Cosmo Kyrle: b. London, Eng, 23 Nov 1885; d. Los Angeles, CA, 25 Jan 1948.

Bellew, Harold Kyrle: b. Prescot, Lancs, Eng, 28 Mar 1855; d. Salt Lake City, UT, 2 Nov 1911.

Bells, Running: b. 1919; d. Glacier Park Reservation, ? Mar 1927.

Belmar, Henry: b. 1849; d. New Castle, PA, 12 Jan 1931.

Belmont, Joseph (Baldy): b. Port Huron, MI, 18 Aug 1875; d. 16 May 1939.

Belmont, Mrs. Morgan: b. 1894; d. New York, NY, 1 Nov 1945.

Belmont, Murray: b. 1889; d. New York, NY, 15 Oct 1922.

Belmont, Ralf: b. Italy, 9 Apr 1882; d. Los Angeles, CA, 21 Sep 1964.

Belmore, Alice: b. London, Eng, 1870; d, New York, NY, 31 Jul 1943.

Belmore, Daisy: b. London, Eng, 30 Jun 1874; d. New York, NY, 12 Dec 1954.

Belmore, Lionel: b. Wimbledon, Eng, 12 May 1868; d. Los Angeles, CA, 30 Jan 1953.

Belmour, Harry: b. San Francisco, CA, 9 Feb 1882; d. 8 Sep 1936.

Beltri, Ricardo: b. 1899; d. Mexico City, Mex, ? May 1962.

Belwin, Alma: b. San Francisco, CA, 1894; d. Boston, MA, 3 May 1924.

Benda, Helena: b. 1903; d. Woodland Hills, CA, 24 Dec 1986.

Benda, Wladyslaw T.: b. Poland, 1875; d. New York, NY, 2 Dec 1948.

Bender, Charles A. (Chief Bender): b. Brainerd, MN, 5 May 1883; d. 22 May 1954.

Bender, Henry: b. Berlin, Ger, 1 Oct 1867; d. 1935.

Bendow, Wilhelm: b. Einbeck, Ger, 29 Sep 1884; d. 29 May 1950.

Benedict, Brooks: b, New York, NY, 6 Feb 18??; d. 1 Jan 1968.

Benedict, Kingsley: b. Buffalo, NY, 14 Nov 1878; d. Woodland Hills, CA, 27 Nov 1951.

Benge, Wilson: b. Greenwich, Eng, 1 Mar 1875; d. Los Angeles, CA, 1 Jul 1955.

Benham, Dorothy: b. Boston, MA, 6 Sep 1910; d. Watertown, WI, 19 Sep 1956.

Benham, Grace: b. Kansas, 25 Jun 1876; d. Pasadena, CA, 19 Nov 1968.

Benham, Harry: b. Valparsiso, IN, 26 Feb 1883; d. Sarasota, FL, 17 Jul 1969.

Benham, Leland: b. Boston, MA, 20 Sep 1905; d. Boynton Beach, FL, 26 Sep 1976.

Benner, Yale Despine: b. New York, 17 Nov 1875; d. San Diego, CA, 29 Sep 1952.

Bennet, Spencer Gordon: b. Brooklyn, NY, 5 Jan 1893; d. Santa Monica, CA, 8 Oct 1987.

Bennet, Mrs. Spencer Gordon: b. 18??; d. Los Angeles Co, CA, 5 Dec,1983.

Bennett, Alma: b. Seattle, WA, 9 Apr 1904; d. Los Angeles, CA, 16 Sep 1958.

Bennett, Barbara: b. Palisades, NJ, 13 Aug 1906; d. Montreal, Can, 8 Aug 1958.

Bennett, Belle: b. Milcoon Rapids, IA, 22 Apr 1891; d. Los Angeles, CA, 4 Nov 1932.

Bennett, Billie: b. Evansville, IN, 23 Oct 1874; d. Los Angeles, CA, 19 May 1951.

Bennett, Catherine: b. Australia, 17 Jan 1901; d. Westwood, CA, 11 Oct 1978.

Bennett, Charles: b. 18??; d. New York, NY, ? Jan 1925.

Bennett, Charles J.: b. Dunedin, New Zealand, 11 Mar 1889; d. Los Angeles, CA, 15 Feb 1943.

Bennett, Chester: b. San Francisco, CA, 18??; d. Hong Kong, 29 Oct 1943.

Bennett, Constance, b. New York, NY, 22 Oct 1905; d. Fort Dix, NJ, 24 Jul 1965.

Bennett, Enid: b. York, Austral, 15 Jul 1893; d. Malibu, CA, 14 May 1969.

Bennett, Frank F.: b. Bakersfield, CA, 15 Sep, 1890; d. Warren Township, NJ, 29 Apr 1957.

Bennett, Hugh S.: b. New York, NY, 1893; d. Malibu, CA, 21 Mar 1950.

Bennett, Joan: b. Palisades, NJ, 27 Feb 1910; d. White Plains, NY, 7 Dec 1990.

Bennett, John Drew: b. Washington, DC, 1884; d. New York, NY, 18 Nov 1944.

Bennett, Joseph: b. Los Angeles, CA, 28 Aug 1894; d. Los Angeles, CA, 3 Dec 1931.

Bennett, Marjorie: b. Perth, Austral, 15 Jan 1895; d. Los Angeles, CA, 14 Jun 1982.

Bennett, Mickey: b. Victoria, Can, 28 Jan 1915; d. Los Angeles, CA, 6 Sep 1950.

Bennett, Richard: b. Deacon's Mills, IN, 21 May 1872; d. Los Angeles, CA, 21 Oct 1944.

Bennett, Wilda: b. Asbury Park, NJ, 19 Dec 1894; d. Winnemucca, NV, 20 Dec 1967.

Benninger, Otto: b. 1893; d. Los Angeles, CA, 3 Mar 1946.

Bennison, Andrew: b. 1887; d. Oxnard, CA, 7 Jan 1942.

Bennison, Louis: b. Oakland, CA, 1883; d. New York, NY, 9 Jun 1929.

Bennoit, Joseph: b. 1875; d. New York, NY, 23 Jun 1925.

Benoit, Victor L.: b. Ottawa, Can, 1877; d. Newburgh, NY, 16 Jan 1943.

Benson, Sir Frank: b. Alresford, Hants. Eng, 4 Nov 1858; d. London, Eng, 31 Dec 1939.

Benson, John William: b. 1862; d. New York, NY, 12 Jul 1926.

Benson, Juliette: b. Massachusetts, 15 Aug 1875; d. Los Angeles, CA, 22 Dec 1962.

Benson, May: b. 18??; d. 29 Sep 1916.

Bent, Buena: b. London, Eng, 1890; d. London, Eng, 17 Dec 1957.

Bent, Marion: b. Bronx, NY, 23 Dec 1879; d. Bronx, NY, 28 Jul 1940.

Bentley, Alice: b. Scanton, PA, 1892; d. Long Island, NY, 3 Sep 1956.

Bentley, Doria: b. ????; d. England, 25 Feb 1944.

Bentley, Grendon: b. Bromyard, Eng, 8 Apr 1877; d. London Eng, 27 Apr 1956.

Benton, Bessie: b. ????; d. Los Angeles, CA, ? Jan 1917.

Benton, Curtis: b. Toledo, OH, 1885; d. Los Angeles, CA, 14 Sep 1938.

Benton, Marie Louise: b. Boston, MA, 1884; d. 19??

Beranger, George Andre: b. Sydney, Austral, 27 Mar 1895; d. Laguna Beach, CA, 8 Mar 1973.

Berangere, Mme.: b. France, 18??; d. Paris, Fr, ? Nov 1928.

Berber, Anita: b. 1899; d. Kreuzberg, Ger, 14 Nov 1928.

Beresford, Harry: b. London, Eng, 4 Nov 1863; d. Los Angeles, CA, 4 Oct 1944.

Berg, Stina: b. Sweden, 1869; d. Sweden, 1930.

Bergen, John: b. ????; d. New York, NY, 25 Aug 1922.

Bergere, Dorothy: b. 1899; d. Harrison, NJ, 12 Jul 1979.

Bergere, Valerie: b. Metz, Fr, 2 Feb 1867; d. Los Angeles, CA, 16 Sep 1938.

Bergman, Henri: b. 1859; d. New York, NY, 9 Jan 1917.

Bergman, Henry: b. San Francisco, CA, 23 Feb 1868; d. Los Angeles, CA, 22 Oct 1946.

Bergner, Elisabeth: b. Drohobycz, Poland, 22 Aug 1900; d. London, Eng, 12 May 1986.

Berkeley, Gertrude: b. Plattsburgh, NY, 1865; d. Los Angeles, CA, 15 Jun 1946.

Berle, Sandra: b. New York, NY, 1877; d. Los Angeles, CA, 31 May 1954.

Berley, Andre: b. France, ????; d. Paris, Fr, 27 Nov 1936.

Berlin, Minnie: b. Germany, 1864; d. New York, NY, 13 Sep 1929.

Berlyn, Ivan: b. England, 1874; d. 11 Dec 1934.

Berman, Bobby Burns: b. London, Eng, 16 Sep 1896; d. San Francisco, CA, 15 Feb 1955.

Bernard, Adolph (Bernard A. Reinold): b. 1860; d. East Islip, NY, 18 Mar 1940.

Bernard, Barney: b. Rochester, NY, 17 Aug 1877; d. New York, NY, 21 Mar 1924.

Bernard, Dorothy: b. Elizabeth, So Africa, 25 Jul 1890; d. Los Angeles, CA, 14 Dec 1955.

Bernard, Harry: b. San Francisco, CA, 13 Jan 1878; d. Los Angeles, CA, 4 Nov 1940.

Bernard, Nan: b. Peabody, KS, ????; d. Princess Bay, NY, 19 Jul 1938.

Bernard, Raymond: b. 1891; d. Paris, Fr, ? Dec 1977.

Bernard, Richard: b. 1865; d. New York, NY, 26 Dec 1925.

Bernard, Sam: b. Birmingham, Eng, 16 Jan 1863; d. 18 May 1927.

Bernardi, Nerio: b. Bologna, Italy, 23 Jul 1899; d. 12 Jan 1971.

Bernhardt, Sarah: b. Paris, Fr, 23 Oct 1844; d. Paris, Fr, 26 May 1923.

Bernoudy, Jane: b. Newcastle, CO, 19 Aug 1893; d. Conoga Park, CA, 28 Oct 1972.

Bernstain, Isadore: b. New York, NY, ? Nov 1877; d. Los Angeles, CA, 18 Oct 1944.

Berrell, George: b. Philadelphia, PA, 16 Dec 1849; d. 20 Apr 1933.

Berry, Aline: b. 1905; d. Los Angeles, CA, 3 Apr 1967.

Berry, James: b. Manchester, Eng, 11 May 1883; d. 1 Aug 1915.

Berry, William Henry: b. London, Eng, 23 Mar 1870; d. Herne Bay, Kent, Eng, 2 May 1951.

Bertini, Francesca: b. Florence, Italy, 11 Apr 1888; d. Rome, Italy, 13 Oct 1985.

Bartone, Alfredo: b. ????; d. ? Mar 1927.

Bertram, Vedah: b. Boston, MA, b. 4 Dec 1891; d. Oakland, CA, 26 Aug 1912.

Bertram, William; b. Walkerton, Ont, Can, 19 Jan 1880; d. Los Angeles, CA, 1 May 1993.

Bertrand, Mary: b, 1881; d. Woodland Hills, CA, 12 May 1955.

Beryl, Eddie: b. 1894; d. Cincinnati, OH, 25 Nov 1922.

Bessent, Marie: b. 1898; d. Los Angeles, CA, 10 Oct 1947.

Besserer, Eugenie: b. Watertown, NY, 25 Dec 1868; d. Los Angeles, CA, 28 May 1934.

Best, Dolly: b. 1899; d. Los Angeles, CA, 6 Oct 1968.

Best, Edna: b. Hove, Sussex, Eng, 3 Mar 1900; d. Geneva, Switz, 18 Sep 1974.

Best, Martin (H. M. Best): b. Chicago, IL, 17 Sep 1880; d. Santa Monica, CA, 2 Nov 1975.

Betts, William F.: b. 1856; d. New York, NY, 5 Apr 1929.

Betz, Matthew: b. St. Louis, MO, 13 Sep 1881; d. Los Angeles, CA, 26 Jan 1938.

Bevan, Billy: b. Orange, Austral, 29 Sep 1887; d, Escondido, CA, 26 Nov 1957.

Bevani, Alexander: b. 1871; d. Los Angeles, CA, 24 Feb 1938.

Bevins, Mabel: b. 18??; d. 23 Dec 1916.

Beyer, Charles W.: b. Newark, NJ, 28 Feb 1893; d. Los Angeles, CA, 28 Nov 1953.

Bianchetti, Suzanne: b. Paris, Fr, 1894; d. Paris, Fr, 17 Oct 1936.

Biancini, Ferrucio: b. Pomponesco, Italy, 18 Aug 1890; d. ? Mar 1955.

Bickel, George L.: b. Saginaw, MI, 17 Feb 1863; d. Los Angeles, CA, 5 Jun 1941.

Biensfeldt, Paul: b. Berlin, Ger, 4 Mar 1869; d. 2 Apr 1933.

Bigelow, Frank: b. 1870; d. 10 Dec 1916.

Bigelow, Fred A.: b. Denver, CO, 1877; d. New York, NY, 8 Dec 1931.

Bilancia, Oreste: b. Catania, Italy, 24 Sep 1881; d. 31 Oct 1945.

Bildt, Paul: b. Berlin, Ger, 19 May 1885; d. Berlin, Ger, 16 Mar 1957.

Billings, Benjamin: b. 1903; d. Los Angeles, CA, 3 May 1923.

Billings, Elmo: b. California, 24 Jun 1912; d. Los Angeles, CA, 6 Feb 1964.

Billings, George A.: b. Preston, MN, 22 Nov 1870; d, Los Angeles, CA, 15 Apr 1934.

Billington, Francelia: b. Dallas, TX, 1 Feb 1895; d. Glendale, CA, 24 Nov 1934.

Binder, Ray Jerome: b. Chicago, IL, 1884; d. 19??.

Bing, Hermam: b. Frankfurt, Ger, 30 Mar 1889; d. Los Angeles, CA, 9 Jan 1947.

Bingham, Cecil: b. 18??; d. London, Eng, 6 May 1925.

Bingham, Stanley J.: b. Cleveland, OH, 28 Apr 1880; d. Riverside Co, CA, 9 Jan 1962.

Binney, Constance: b. New York, NY, 28 Jun 1896; d. Whitestone, NY, ? Nov 1989.

Binney, Faire: b. Pennsylvania, 24 Aug 1900; d. 28 Aug 1957.

Binns, George H.: b. England, 1886; d. Glendale, CA, 27 Oct 1918.

Birkett, Viva: b. Exeter, Devon, Eng, 14 Feb 1887; d. London, Eng, 26 Jun 1934.

Bishop, Alfred: b. Liverpool, Eng, 7 Feb 1848; d. London, Eng, 22 May 1928.

Bishop, Chester: b. New Albany, IN, 7 Feb 1871; d. El Nido, CA, 23 May 1937.

Bishop, Fayette: b. ????; d. 7 Mar 1927.

Bittner, William: b. 1866; d. New York, NY, 5 Jul 1918.

Blache, Herbert: b. London, Eng, 5 Oct 1882; d. Santa Monica, CA, 23 Oct 1953.

Black, Maurice: b. Warsaw, Poland, 14 Jan 1891; d. Los Angeles, CA, 18 Jan 1938.

Black, W. W. b. Irvington, NY, 1871; d. 19??.

Blackhawk, Lawrence: b. ????; d. Los Angeles Go, CA, 10 Aug 1978.

Blackmer, Sidney: b. Salisbury, NC, 13 Jul 1895; d. New York, NY, 5 Oct 1973.

Blackmore, E. Willard: b. 1870; d. St. Louis, MO, 20 Nov 1949.

Blackton, J. Stuart, Sr.: b. Sheffield, Yorks, Eng, 5 Jan 1875; d. Los Angeles, CA, 13 Aug 1941.

Blackton, J. Stuart, Jr.; b. 6 Nov 1897; d. 16 Dec 1968.

Blackton, Paula (Pauline Dean): b. Georgia, 1 Aug 1881; d. Los Angeles, CA, 27 Mar 1930.

Blackton, Violet Virginia: b. 1912; d. 28 Mar 1973.

Blackwell, Carlyle: b. Troy, PA, 20 Jan 1884; d. Miami, FL, 17 Jun 1955.

Blackwell, Jim: b. Richmond, MO, 6 Jun 1876; d. 27 Sep 1932.

Blackwood, Peggy: b. Portland, OR, 15 Jun 1875; d. Los Angeles, CA, 27 Feb 1956.

Blade, Augusta: b. 1871; d. Copenhagen, Denmark, 9 Nov 1953.

Blagoi, George: b. Russia, 1898; d. Los Angeles, CA, 23 Jun 1971.

Blaine, Joan: b. ????; d. New York, NY, 18 Apr 1949.

Blair, Betty: b. 1895; d. Los Angeles Co, CA, 11 Jan 1981.

Blair, Ella S.: b. 1895; d. New York, NY, 11 Dec 1917.

Blair, Sydney: b. San Francisco, CA, 1882; d. 19??.

Blaisdell, Charles (Big Bill): b. 1874; d. Los Angeles, CA, 10 May 1930.

Blaisdell, William: b. 1865; d. Brooklyn, NY, 1 Jan 1931.

Blake, Alva D.: b. Manitou, CO, 31 Mar 1887; d. Los Angeles, CA, 5 Nov 1966.

Blake, Lucy: b. Boston, MA, 1888; d. 19??.

Blake, Marguerite: b. 18??; d. Toronto, Can, 29 Apr 1927.

Blake, Nina: b. 1886; d. New York, NY, 12 Oct 1924.

Blakeley, James: b. Hull, Yorks, Eng, 1873; d. London, Eng, 19 Oct 1915.

Blakemore, Harry D.: b. Gallatin, TN, 1859; d. Bay Shore, NY, 14 Feb 1936.

Blakeslee, Louise: b. 1905; d. New York, NY, 5 Aug 1920.

Blanchar, Pierre: b. Philippeville, Algeria, 30 Jun 1892; d. Paris, Fr, 21 Nov 1963.

Blanchard, Harry: b. 1876; d. Los Angeles, CA, 27 Apr 1944.

Blancke, Kate: b. Cheltenham, Gloucs, Eng, 14 Mar 1860; d; East Islip, NY, 24 Jun 1942.

Bland, R. Henderson: b. England, 18??; d. London, Eng, 20 Aug 1941.

Blandick, Clara: b. Hong Kong, China, 4 Jun 1881; d. Los Angeles, CA, 15 Apr 1962.

Blaney, May: b. England, 6 Jul 1875; d. Wopener, So Africa, 10 Feb 1953.

Blankman, George: b. 1877; d. Los Angeles, CA, 13 Mar 1925.

Bleibtreu, Hedwig: b. Linz, Ger, 23 Dec 1868; d. Vienna, Anstria, 24 Jan 1958.

Bleifer, John: b. Zawiercie, Poland, 26 Jul 1901; d. Los Angeles, CA, 24 Jan 1992.

Bletcher, Arline Roberts: b. 1893; d. Los Angeles, CA, 3 Jul 1992.

Bletcher, Billy: b. Lancaster, PA, 24 Sep 1894; d. Los Angeles, CA, 5 Jan 1979.

Blich, Mrs. Catto (Helen Friedman): b. Germany, 1891; d. Los Angeles, CA, 8 Jun 1926.

Blind, Eric: b. 18??; d. Reading, PA, 31 Dec 1916.

Blinn, Beatrice: b. Wisconsin, 7 Jul 1901; d. Oceanside, CA, 31 Mar 1979.

Blinn, Benjamin F.: b. Allentown, PA, 3 Apr 1872; d. Los Angeles, CA, 28 Apr 1941.

Blinn, Genevieve: b. St. John, New Bruns, Can, 1872; d. Ross, CA, 20 Jul 1956.

Blinn, Holbrook: b. San Francisco, CA, 23 Jan 1872; d. Croton, NY, 24 Jun 1928.

Bliss, Lela: b. Los Angeles, CA, 11 May 1896; d. Woodland Hills, CA, 15 May 1980.

Blood, Adele: b. San Francisco, CA, 23 Apr 1886; d. Harrison, NY, 13 Sep 1936.

Blore, Eric: b. London, Eng, 23 Dec 1887; d. Los Angeles, CA, 1 Mar 1959.

Blossom, Henry Martyn: b. 1867; d. New York, NY, 23 Mar 1919.

Blue, Ben: b. Montreal, Can, 12 Sep 1901; d. Los Angeles, CA, 7 Mar 1975.

Blue, Monte: b. Indianapolis, IN, 11 Jan 1890; d. Milwaukee, WI, 18 Feb 1963.

Blum, Sammy: b. New York, NY, 25 May 1889; d. Los Angeles, CA, 30 May 1945.

Blumenthal-Tamariha, Marie: b. 1859; d. 4 Nov 1938.

Blystone, John G.: b. Rice Lake, WI, 2 Dec 1892; d. Beverly Hills, CA, 6 Aug 1938.

Blythe, Betty: b. Los Angeles, CA, 1 Sep 1893; d. Woodland Hills, CA, 7 Apr 1972.

Blythe, Violet, b. 1890; d. 17 Mar 1983.

Boardman, Claude: b. 1871; d. 10 Dec 1928.

Boardman, Eleanor: b. Philadelphia, PA, 19 Aug 1898; d. Santa Barbara, CA, 12 Dec 1991.

Boardman, True: b. Oakland, CA, 21 Apr 1881; d. Norwalk, CA, 28 Sep 1918.

Boardman, Virginia Eames: b. Ft. Davis, TX, 23 May 1889; d. Los Angeles, CA, 10 Jun 1971.

Bock, Frederick: b. 18??; d. Flushing, NY, 13 Jan 1916.

Boggs, Francis: b. 18??; d. Endendale, CA, 27 Oct 1911.

Bohnen, Michael: b. Koln, Ger, 2 May 1887; d. Berlin, Ger, 26 Apr 1965.

Bois, Curt: b. Berlin, Ger, 5 Apr 1901; d. Berlin, Ger, 25 Dec 1991.

Boland, Eddie: b. San Francisco, CA, 27 Dec 1885; d. Los Angeles, CA, 3 Feb 1935.

Boland, Mary: b. Philadelphia, PA, 28 Jan 1880; d. New York, NY, 23 Jun 1965.

Bolder, Robert: b. London, Eng, 1859; d. Beverly Hills, CA, 10 Dec 1937.

Boles, John: b. Greenville, TX, 27 Oct 1895; d. San Angelos TX, 27 Feb 1969.

Boley, May: b. Washington, DC, 29 May 1881; d. Los Angeles, CA, 7 Jan 1963.

Bombard, Lottie Gertrude: b. 1908; d. Saranac Lake, NY, ? Nov 1913.

Bonanova, Fortunio: b. Palma de Mollorca, Spain, 13 Jan 1895; d. Woodland Hills, CA, 2 Apr 1969.

Bonavita, Jack: b. Philadelphia, PA, 1866; d. Los Angeles, CA, 19 Mar 1917.

Bond, Frank G.: b. Salina, KS, 1886; d. New York, NY, 4 Oct 1929.

Bond, Raymond L.: b. Iowa, 21 Apr 1885; d. San Bernardino Co, CA, 13 Feb 1972.

Bondhill, Gertrude: b. Cincinnati, OH, 1880; d. Chicago, IL, 15 Sep 1960.

Bonillas, Myrta: b. Massachusetts, 3 Nov 1890; d. Los Angeles, CA, 13 Nov 1959.

Bonn, Frank: b. 1873; d. Los Angeles, CA, 4 Mar 1944.

Bonnard, Mario: b. Rome, Italy, 21 Jun 1889; d. Rome, Italy 22 Mar 1965.

Bonner, Joe: b. England, 1882; d. Burbank, CA, 13 Apr 1959.

Bonner, Marjorie: b. Washington, DC, 17 Feb 1905; d. Los Angeles, CA, 28 Sep 1988.

Bonomo, Joe: b. Coney Island, NY, 25 Dec 1902; d. Los Angeles, CA, 28 Mar 1978.

Booker, Harry: b. Kentucky. 1850; d. San Diego, CA, 28 Jun 1924.

Booker, John I.: b. 22 Apr 18 87; d. New Rochelle, NY, 18 Jan 1982.

Boone, Dell: b. Springfield, MO, 28 Feb 1894; d. Burbank, CA, 6 Sep 1960.

Booth, Edwina: b. Provo, UT, 13 Sep 1909; d. Long Beach, CA, 18 May 1991.

Booth, Elmer: b. Los Angeles, CA, 9 Dec 1882; d. Los Angeles, CA, 16 Jun 1915.

Booth, Sydney Barton: b. Boston, MA, 29 Jan 1873; d. Stanford, CT, 5 Feb 1937.

Bordeaux, Joe: b. Colorado, 9 Mar 1886; d. Los Angeles, CA, 10 Sep 1950.

Borden, Eddie: b. Deer Lodge, TN, 1 May 1888; d. Los Angeles, CA, 30 Jun 1955.

Borden, Eugene: b. Paris, Fr, 22 Mar 1897; d. Woodland Hills, CA, 21 Jul 1971.

Borden, Olive: b. Richmond, VA, 20 Jul 1906; d. Los Angeles, CA, 1 Oct 1947.

Borelli, Alda: b. 1882; d. Milan, Italy, 21 May 1961.

Borelli, Lyda: b. Rivarolo Ligure, Italy, 22 Mar 1884; d. Rome, Italy, 1 Jun 1959.

Borello, Edith: b. Italy, 25 Nov 1890; d. Los Angeles, CA, 6 Mar 1974.

Borello, Marco: b. 1899; d. Santa Cruz, CA, 21 Jan 1966.

Borg, Sven-Hugo: b. Winslows, Sweden, 26 Jul 1896; d. Los Angeles, CA, 19 Feb 1981.

Borgato, Agostino: b. Venice, Italy, 30 Jun 1871; d. Los Angeles, CA, 14 Mar 1939.

Borgstrom, Hilda: b. Stockholm, Sweden, 1871; d. Stockholm, Sweden, 2 Jan 1953.

Boring, Edward: b. 18??; d. New York, NY, 18 Jan 1923.

Borland, Barlowe: b. Greenock, Scot, 6 Aug 1877; d. Woodland Hills, CA, 31 Aug 1948.

Boros, Ferike: b. Nagyvard, Hungary, 2 Aug 1880; d. Van Nuys, CA, 16 Jan 1951.

Borup, Doan: b. St. Louis, MO, 27 Jun 1875; d. New York, NY, 2 Oct 1944.

Borzage, Frank: b. Salt Lake City, UT, 23 Apr 1893; d. Los Angeles, CA, 19 Jun 1962.

Bos, Annie: b. Amsterdam, Holland, 10 Dec 1886; d. 3 Aug 1975.

Boshell, Ada: b. 1854; d. Philadelphia, PA, 31 Mar 1924.

Boss, Yale: b. Utica, NY, 18 Oct 1899; d. Augustus GA, 16 Nov 1977.

Bosse, Harriet: b. 1878; d. Oslo, Norway, ? Nov 1961.

Bostwick; Edith: b. Golden, CO, 29 Jan 1882; d. Los Angeles, CA, 3 Dec 1943.

Bosworth, Hobart: b, Marietta, OH, 11 Aug 1867; d. Glendale, CA, 30 Dec 1943.

Boteler, Wade: b. Santa Ana, CA, 3 Oct 1888; d. Los Angeles, CA, 7 May 1943.

Bothwell, John F. (Freckles): b. 1920; d. Long Branch, NJ, 7 Mar 1967.

Bottomley, Roland: b. Liverpool, Eng, 23 Sep 1880; d. New York, NY, 5 Jan 1947.

Boucicault, Dion: b. New York, NY, 23 May 1859; d. Hurley, Bucks, Eng, 25 Jun 1929.

Boucicault, Nina: b. London, Eng, 27 Feb 1867; d. London, Eng, 2 Aug 1950.

Boucicault, Renee: b. 1898; d. New York, NY, 3 Jul 1935.

Boulton, Matthew: b. Lincoln, Eng, 20 Jan 1883; d. Los Angeles, CA, 10 Feb 1962.

Bourber, Aaf: b. Amsterdam, Holland, 17 Oct 1885; d. 23 May 1974.

Bourchier, Arthur: b. Speen, Berks, Eng, 22 Jun 1863; d. Johannesburg, So Africa, 14 September 1927.

Bourke, Fan: b. Brooklyn, NY, 12 Jul 1886; d. Norwalk, CT, 9 Mar 1959.

Bourne, Adeline: b. 1872; d. England, 8 Feb 1965.

Bow, Clara: b. Brooklyn, NY, 29 Jul 1905; d. Los Angeles, CA, 27 Sep 1965.

Bowrs, John: b. Garrett, IN, 25 Dec 1884; d. Malibu Beach, CA, 15 Nov 1936.

Bowers, Lyle: b. Iowa, 22 May 1895; d. Los Angeles, CA, 8 Mar 1943.

Bowes, Clifford W.: b. Pueblo, CO, 14 Nov 1894; d. 6 Jul 1929.

Bowes, Lawrence Alfred: b. Newark, CA, 1 Jan 1885; d. Glendale, CA, 5 Jun 1955.

Bowles, Donald: b. 18??; d. Los Angeles, CA, 3 Oct 1921.

Bowman, Laura: b. 1881; d. Los Angeles, CA, 29 Mar 1957.

Bowman, Lewis Edward: b. 1886; d. 1961.

Bowman, Palmer: b. Brazil, IN, 1884; d. Chicago, IL, 25 Sep 1933.

Bowman, William J: b. Bakersville, NC, 1876; d. San Diego, CA, 1 Jan 1960.

Bowser, Charles: b. 18??; d. 17 Mar 1917.

Boyce, Jack: b. 1885; d. New York, NY, 13 Dec 1923.

Boyd, Ada: b. 1890; d. Barrington, MA, 25 Mar 1978.

Boyd, Betty: b. Kansas City, MO, 11 May 1908; d. Los Angeles, CA, 16 Sep 1971.

Boyd, Storm V.: b. Watertown, NY, 18??; d. Syracuse, NY, 13 Oct 1919.

Boyd, William: b. Cambridge, OH, 5 Jun 1895; d. South Laguna, CA, 12 Sep 1972.

Boyd, William H.: b. New York, NY, 18 Dec 1889; d. Los Angeles, CA, 20 Mar 1935.

Boyer, Charles: b. Figeac Lot, Fr, 28 Aug 1899; d. Phoenix, AZ, 26 Aug 1978.

Boyle, John W.: b. Memphis, TN 1881; d. Los Angeles, CA, 28 Sep 1959.

Boyle, Joseph Clayton: b. Philadelphia, PA, 30 Sep 1888; d. Culver City, CA, 24 Nov 1972.

Boyne, Clifton: b. 1874; d. 16 Dec 1945.

Brabin, Charles J.: b. Liverpool, Eng, 1883; d. Santa Monica, CA, 3 Nov 1957.

Brace, Norman C.: b. 1892; d. New York, NY, 20 Jun 1954.

Bracey, Clara T.: b. 1847; d. Los Angeles, CA, 22 Feb 1941.

Bracey, Sidney: b. Melbourne, Austral, 18 Dec 1877; d. Los Angeles, CA, 5 Aug 1942.

Bracken, Bertram: b. San Antonio, TX, 1879; d. Los Angeles, CA, 1 Nov 1952.

Bradbury, James H. Sr.: b. Old Town, ME, 12 Oct 1857; d. Clifton, NY, 12 Oct 1940.

Bradbury, James H. Jr.: b. New York, NY, 5 Oct 1894; d. Los Angeles, CA, 21 Jun 1936.

Bradbury, Ronald (Robert North Bradbury): b. Walla Walla, WA, 23 Mar 1886; d. Glendale, CA, 24 Nov 1949.

Bradbury, William: b. Portland, OR, 23 Jan 1907; d. Loma Linda, CA, 15 Sep 1971.

Braddell, Maurice: b. England, 1900; d. England, 28 Jul.1990.

Bradley, Amanda: b. 18??; d. New York, NY, 13 Dec 1916.

Bradley, Benjamin R.: b. 1898; d. St. Louis, MO, 29 Sep 1950.

Bradley, Curley (George Courtney): b. Oklahoma, 1911; d. Long Beach, CA, 3 Jun 1985.

Bradley, Estelle: b. Atlanta, GA, 5 Apr 1908; d. Woodland Hills, CA, 28 Jun 1990.

Bradley, Harry C.: b. San Francisco, CA, 15 Apr 1869; d. Los Angeles, CA, 18 Oct 1947.

Bradley, Russell F.: b. Palo Alto, CA, 27 Mar 1894; d. Alameda Co, CA, 17 Dec 1952.

Bradshaw, Eunice: b. 1893; d. 1973.

Bradshaw, Lionel: b. Lima, OH, 10 May 1892; d. Los Angeles, CA, 17 Dec 1918.

Brady, Alice: b. New York, NY, 2 Nov 1892; d. New York, NY, 28 Oct 1939.

Brady, Edwin J.; b. New York, NY, 6 Dec 1889; d. Los Angeles, CA, 31 Mar 1942.

Braham, Harry: b. London, Eng, 1850; d. Staten Island, NY, 21 Sep 1923.

Braham, Horace: b. London, Eng, 29 Jul 1892; d. New York, NY, 7 Sep 1955.

Braham, Lionel: b. England, 1 Apr 1879; d. Los Angeles, CA, 6 Oct 1947.

Brahms, Helene: b. 21 May 1872; d. 22 Jul 1948.

Braidon, Thomas A.: b. England, 1 Mar 1870; d. Los Angeles Co, CA, 22 Jun 1950.

Braithwaite, John: b. 1883; d. Egremont, Cumberland, Eng, ? Oct 1963.

Braithwaite, Dame Lilian: b. Ramsgate, Eng, 1873; d. London, Eng, 17 Sep 1948.

Bramble, A. V.: b. Portsmouth, Eng, 18??; d. 1963.

Bramley, Flora: b. London, Eng, 1909; d. Moline, IL, 23 Jun 1993.

Bramley, Nellie: b. 1889; d. Australia, 10 Jun 1982.

Brand, Mary Spoor: b. 1887; d. 18 Oct 1985.

Brandeis, Madeline: b. San Francisco, CA, 18 Dec 1898; d. Gallup, NM, 27 Jun 1937.

Brandon, Florence: b. 1879; d. London, Eng, 11 Oct 1961.

Brandon, Francis: b. 1886; d. New York, NY, 3 Oct 1924.

Brandon-Thomas, Amy: b. London, Eng, 9 Mar 1890; d. London, Eng, 9 May 1974.

Brandt, Charles C.: b. 1864; d. Philadelphia, PA, 9 Jun 1924.

Brandt, Joseph: b. 18??; d. c. 1916.

Brandt, Louise: b. 1877; d. San Diego, CA, 13 Jul 1959.

Branscombe, Lily: b. New Zealand, 28 Feb 1878; d. San Francisco, CA, 26 Sep 1970.

Brasseur, Pierre: b. Paris, Fr, 22 Dec 1905; d. Brunice, Italy, 14 Aug 1972.

Brausewetter, Hans: b. Malaga, Spain, 27 May 1896; d. 29 Apr 1945.

Brawn, John P.: b. New York, NY, 1869; d. New York, NY, 16 Jun 1943.

Brayfield, George W.: b. ????; d. Denver, CO, 17 Feb 1968.

Brayton, Lily: b. Hindley, Lancs, Eng, 23 Jun 1876; d. Dawlish, Devon, Eng, 30 Apr 1953.

Breamer, Sylvia: b. Sydney, Austral, 9 Jun 1903; d. New York, NY, 7 Jun 1943.

Breen, Harry: b. 18??; d. Riverside Co, CA, 20 Jan 1918.

Breen, Margaret: b. Missouri, 3 Feb 1907; d. Santa Monica, CA, 5 Dec 1960.

Breese, Edmund: b. Brooklyn, NY, 18 Jun 1871; d. New York, NY, 6 Apr 1936.

Brendel, El (Elmer): b. Philadelphia, PA, 25 Mar 1891; d. Los Angeles, CA, 9 Apr 1964.

Brennan, John E.: b. Springfield, MA, 17 Jul 1865; d. Los Angeles, CA, 27 Dec 1940.

Brennan, Robert: b. 1892; d. Los Angeles, CA, 17 Apr 1940.

Brennen, Walter: b. Swampscott, MA, 25 Jul 1894; d. Oxnard, CA, 21 Sep 1974.

Brenon, Herbert: b. Dublin, Ire, 13 Jan 1880; d. Los Angeles, CA, 21 Jun 1958.

Brenon, Juliet: b. 1 Sept 1885; d. Bronx, NY, 18 Nov 1979.

Brenon, Roma: b. Rome, Italy, 1870; d. Brooklyn, NY, 9 Oct 1927.

Brent, Evelyn (Betty Riggs): b. New York, 20 Oct 1899; d. Los Angeles, CA. 4 Jun 1975.

Brent, Romney: b. Saltillo, Mex, 26 Jan 1902; d. Mexico City, Mex, 24 Sep 1976.

Brerton, Tyrone: b. Dublin, Ire, 1894; d. Los Angeles, CA, 25 Apr 1939.

Bressert, Felix: b. Eydtkuhnen, Ger, 2 Mar 1895; d. Los Angeles, CA, 17 Mar 1949.

Bretonne, May: b. 1860; d, Englewood, NJ, 28 Sep 1952.

Bretty, Beatrice: b. 1895; d. Paris, Fr, 4 Sep 1982.

Breyer, Maggie: b. Fort Recovery, OH, 1845; d. Indianapolis, IN, 11 Mar 1931.

Brian, Donald: b. St. Johns, Newfoundland, Can, 17 Feb 1875; d. Great Neck, NY, 22 Dec 1948.

Briant, Roy: b. 1888; d. Los Angeles, CA, 16 Dec 1927.

Brice, Lew: b. New York, NY, 1894; d. Los Angeles, CA, 16 Jun 1966.

Brice, Rosetta (Betty Brice): b. Sunbury, PA, 1892; d. Van Nuys, CA, 15 Feb 1935.

Bricker, Betty: b. 1890; d. Los Angeles, CA, 15 Feb 1954.

Brickert, Carlton: b. Martinsville, IN, 14 May 1890; d. New York, NY, 23 Dec 1943.

Brickley, Charles E.: b. 1891; d. New York, NY, 28 Dec 1949.

Briggs, Hal: b. 1881; d. Rockville Center, NY, 28 Apr 1925.

Briggs, Oscar: b. Wisconsin, 1877; d. Los Angeles, CA, 17 Jan 1928.

Bright, Mildred: b. New York, 30 Apr 1892; d. Woodland Hills, CA, 27 Sep 1967.

Brighton, Albert: b. 1876; d. Grassmere, NY, 11 Jul 1911.

Brinckman, Elsie: b. 1893; d. Los Angeles, CA, 22 Apr 1950.

Brink, Elga: b. 1 Feb 1895; d. ? Dec 1986.

Brinley, Charles E.: b. Yuma, AZ, 15 Nov 1880; d. Los Angeles, CA, 17 Feb 1946.

Brisbane, Arthur: b. 1864; d. New York, NY, 25 Dec 1936.

Briscoe, Lottie: b. St. Louis, MO, 19 Apr 1883; d. New York, NY, 19 Mar 1950.

Brisson, Carl: b. Copenhagen, Den, 24 Dec 1893; d. Copenhagen, Den, 26 Sep 1958.

Britton, Edna: b. 28 Jun 1887; d. Mansfield, MA, 5 Aug 1960.

Britton Hutin: b. Reading, Berks, Eng, 24 Apr 1876; d. England, 3 Sep 1965.

Broad, Kid (William M. Thomas): b. Cornwall, Eng, 3 Mar 1878; d. New York, NY 11 Jun 1947.

Broadley, Edward: b. 1875; d. New York, NY, 24 Nov 1947.

Brock, Tony: b. ????; d. New York, NY, 26 Nov 1924.

Brockwell, Gladys: b. Brooklyn, NY, 26 Sep 1894; d. Los Angeles, CA, 2 Jul 1929.

Broderick, Helen: b. Philadelphia, PA, 11 Aug 1891; d, Beverly Hills, CA, 25 Sep 1959.

Broderick, Lillian: b. New York, NY, 1895; d. Long Island, NY, 28 Mar 1946.

Brodie, Buster: b. Pittsburgh, PA, 11 Oct 1885; d. Los Angeles, CA, 9 Apr 1948.

Brody, Anna G.: b. Poland, 29 Aug 1884; d. New York, NY, 16 Jul 1944.

Brokaw, Charles: b. Columbus, OH, 1898; d. New York, NY, 23 Oct 1975.

Bronson, Betty: b. Trenton, NJ, 17 Nov 1906; d. Pasadena, CA, 19 Oct 1971.

Brook, Clive: b. London, Eng, 1 Jun 1887; d. London, Eng, 17 Nov 1974.

Brooke, Claude: b. Liverpool, Eng, 1853; d. Leonia, NJ, 14 Dec 1933.

Brooke, E. H.: b. 1876; d. 18 Jan 1929.

Brooke, Mrs. E. H.: b. 1835; d. London, Eng, 19 Dec 1915.

Brooke, Myra: b. 1865; d. Amityville, NY, 9 Feb 1944.

Brooke, Tyler: b. New York, NY, 6 Jun 1886; d. Los Angeles, CA, 2 Mar 1943.

Brooke, Van Dyke: b. Detroit, MI, 22 Jun 1859; d. Saratoga Springs, NY, 17 Sep 1921.

Brooker, Tom: b. New York, NY, 25 Jul 1886; d. 29 Jan 1929.

Brooks, Alan: b. Boston, MA, 1888; d. Saranac, NY, 28 Sep 1936.

Brooks, Hank: b. ????; d. Los Angeles, CA, 3 Dec 1925.

Brooks, Louise: b. Cherryvale, KS, 14 Nov 1906; d, Rochester, NY, 8 Aug 1985.

Brophy, Edward B.: b. New York, NY, 27 Feb 1895; d. Los Angeles, CA, 27 May 1960.

Broske, Octavia: b. Pennsylvania, 4 Jun 1886; d. Los Angeles Co, CA, 19 Mar 1967.

Brott, Robert: b. 1881; d. Welfare Island, NY, 15 Aug 1933.

Brough, Mary: b. London, Eng, 16 Apr 1863; d. London, Eng, 30 Sep 1934.

Brower, Otto: b. Grand Rapids, MI, 2 Dec 1895; d. Los Angeles, CA, 25 Jan 1946.

Brower, Robert: b. Point Pleasant, NJ, 14 Jul 1850; d. West Hollywood, CA, 8 Dec 1934.

Brower, Thomas L.: b. Birmingham, AL, 20 Feb 1878; d. 19 Jul 1937.

Brown, Chamberlain: b. 1888; d. New York, NY, 11 Nov 1955.

Brown, Charles D.: b. Council Bluffs, IA, 1 Jul 1887; d. Los Angeles, CA, 25 Nov 1948.

Brown, Everett: b. Texas, 1 Jan 1902; d. 14 Oct 1953.

Brown, Fred G.: b. London, Eng, 1878; d. Toronto, Can, ? Aug 1944.

Brown, Halbert W.: b. 1865; d, New York, NY, 24 Oct 1942.

Brown, Joe E.: b. Holgate, OH, 28 Jul 1892; d. Brentwood, CA, 6 Jul 1973.

Brown, Johnny Mack: b. Dothan, AL, 1 Sep 1904; d. Woodland Hills, CA, 14 Nov 1974.

Brown, Kirke: b. Braddock, PA, 16 Jan 1879; d. Norwood, NJ, 11 Jan 1945.

Brown, Martin: b. Montreal, Can, 22, Jun 1895; d. New York, NY, 13 Feb 1936.

Brown, Maxine: b. Denver, CO, 1897; d. Alameda, CA, 28 Dec 1956.

Brown, Melville W.: b. Portland, OR, 10 Mar 1887; d. Los Angeles, CA, 31 Jan 1938.

Brown, Milton: b. 1875; d. Los Angeles, CA, 31 May 1935.

Brown, Milton: b. 1896; d. Los Angeles, CA, 29 Mar 1948.

Brown, Morgan: b. New York State, 4 Dec 1884; d. Los Angeles Co, CA, 4 Jan 1961.

Brown, Sally Joy: b. 1905; d. 6 May 1986.

Brown, Sedley: b. 29 Feb 1856; d. Los Angeles, CA, 18 Sep 1928.

Brown, Tom: b. New York, NY, 6 Jan 1913; d. Woodland Hills, CA, 3 Jun 1990.

Browne, Bothwell: b. Denmark, 7 Mar 18??; d. Los Angeles, CA, 12 Dec 1947.

Browne, Earle: b. Vallejo, CA, 7 Sep 1872; d. Los Angeles, CA, 29 Nov 1944.

Browne, Lucile: b. Memphis, TN, 18 Mar 1907; d. Lexington, VA, 10 May 1976.

Browne, W. Graham: b. Ireland, 1 Jan 1870; d. Hampstead, Eng, 11 Mar 1937.

Brownell, John C.: b. 1877; d. Starksboro, VT, 27 Aug 1961.

Browning, Tod: b. Louisville, KY, 12 Jul 1882; d. Santa Monica, CA, 6 Oct 1962.

Browning, William E.: b. 1871; d. Laurelton, NY, 21 Dec 1930.

Brownlee, Frank: b. Dallas, TX, 11 Oct 1874; d. Los Angeles Co. CA, 10 Feb 1948.

Bruce, Belle: b. Bridgeport, CT, 18??; d. Winsted, CT, 15 Jun 1960.

Bruce, Beverly: b. Montreal, Can, ????; d. Bryn Mawr, PA, ? Jul 1925.

Bruce, Clifford: b. Toronto, Can, 1885; d. West Camp, NY, 27 Aug 1919.

Bruce, Kate: b. 1858; d. New York, NY, 2 Apr 1946.

Bruce, Tonie Edgar: b. London, Eng, 4 Jun 1892; d. Chertsey, Surrey, Eng, 28 Mar 1966.

Brule, Andre: b. Bordeaux, Fr, 1879; d. Paris, Fr, 14 Feb 1953.

Brundage, Mathilde (Bertha): b. Louisville, KY, 22 Sep 1859; d. Long Beach, CA, 6 May 1939.

Brunel, Adrian: b. Brighton, Eng, 4 Sep 1892; d. Gerrard's Cross, Bucks, Eng, 18 Feb 1958.

Brunel, Irene (Babs): b. 1891; d. 19 Mar 1987.

Brunette, Fritzi: b. Savannah, GA, 27 May 1890; d. Los Angeles, CA, 28 Sep 1943.

Brunius, Pauline: b. Stockholm, Sweden, 10 Feb 1881; d. Stockholm, Sweden, 31 Mar 1954.

Bruns, Edna: b. 1880; d. New York, NY, 23 Jul 1960.

Bruns, Julia: b. St. Louis, MO, 1895; d. New York, NY, 24 Dec 1927.

Brunton, William: b. Canada, 13 Mar 1883; d. Los Angeles Co, CA, 19 Feb 1965.

Bryant, Charles: b. Hartford, Eng, 8 Jan 1879; d. Mt. Kisco, NY, 7 Aug 1948.

Bryant, Jack V.: b. Ayr, Scot, 26 May 1889; d. London, Eng, 2 Mar 1924.

Bryant, Marguerite: b. ????; d. Brooklyn, NY, ? Jan 1951.

Brydone, Alfred: b. Edinburgh, Scot, 9 Dec 1863; d. London, Eng, 26 Nov 1920.

Bryson, Winifred: b, Columbus, OH, 20 Dec 1892; d, Los Angeles, CA, 20 Aug 1987.

Buchanan, Jack: b. Helensburgh, Scot, 2 Apr 1891; d. London, Eng, 20 Oct 1957.

Buck, Ines: b. Oetrichs, SD, 1890; d. Oakland, CA, 6 Sep 1957.

Buck, Nell Roy: b. 1911; d. Van Nuys, CA, 28 Feb 1962.

Buckingham, Thomas: b. Chicago, IL, 1896; d. Los Angeles, CA, 7 Sep 1934.

Buckler, Hugh C.: b. Southampton, Eng, 9 Sep 1881; d. Malibu Lake, CA, 30 Oct 1936.

Buckley, Floyd: b. Chatham, NY, 1874; d. New York, NY, 14 Nov 1956.

Buckley, May: b. San Francisco, CA, 15 Dec 1875; d. c. 1941.

Bucko, Ralph (Buck): b. California, 1891; d. Yakima, WA, 6 Aug 1962.

Buckstone, John C.: b. London, Eng, 1858; d. London, Eng, 24 Sep 1924.

Buckstone, Rowland: b. London, Eng, 29 Mar 1860; d. London, Eng, 13 Sep 1922.

Bucquet, Harold S.: b. England, 1892; d. Los Angeles, CA, 13 Feb 1946.

Buel, Keenan: b. Kentucky, 1873; d. New York, NY, 5 Nov 1948.

Bughart, Charles: b. 1857; d. Los Angeles, CA, 19 Feb 1927.

Buhler, Richard: b. Washington, DC, 1876; d. Washington, DC, 27 Mar 1925.

Bull, Charles Edward: b. Texas, 26 Feb 1881; d. Los Angeles Co, CA, 9 Sep 1971.

Bump, Edmond: b. 1877; d. Los Angeles, CA, 6 Nov 1938.

Bunker, Ralph: b. Boston, MA, 1889; d. New York, NY, 28 Apr 1966.

Bunny, George: b. New York, NY, 17 Jul 1867; d. Los Angeles, CA, 16 Apr 1952.

Bunny, George, Jr.: b. 1893; d. Los Angeles, CA, 8 Dec 1958.

Bunny, John: b. New York, NY, 21 Sep 1863; d. Brooklyn, NY, 26 Apr 1915.

Bunny, John, Jr.: b. 1895; d. Los Angeles, CA, 16 Apr 1971.

Bunton, Laura: b. ????; d. Los Angeles, CA, 6 Jun 1921.

Burani, Michelette: b. Asnieres, Fr, 1882; d. Eastchester, NY, 27 Oct 1957.

Burbank, Goldie (Ruth Harris): b. 1880; d. Toledo, OH, 1 Mar 1954.

Burbeck, Frank: b. Boston, MA, 30 Dec 1856; d. New York, NY, 20 Feb 1930.

Burbridge, Elizabeth (Betty): b. San Diego, CA, 7 Dec 1895; d. Tarzana, CA, 19 Sep 1987.

Burby, Gordon P.: b. New York State, 1882; d. Brightwaters, NY, 17 Oct 1951.

Burchill, William: b. 18??; d. 1 Apr 1930.

Burg, Eugen: b. Berlin, Ger, 6 Jan 1871; d. ? Nov 1944.

Burgess, Earl: b. ????; d. Los Angeles, CA, 5 Feb 1920.

Burghart, Charles: b. ????; d. Los Angeles, CA, 19 Feb 1927.

Burke, Billle: b. Washington, DC; 7 Aug 1885; d. Los Angeles, CA, 14 May 1970.

Burke, J. Frank: b. Hartland, VT, ? Apr 1867; d. Los Angeles, CA, 23 Jan 1918.

Burke, Joseph: b. New York, NY, 1884; d. New York, NY, 17 Dec 1942.

Burke, Thomas F.: b. 18??; d. Los Angeles, CA, 25 Mar 1941.

Burkett, Bartine: b. Robeline, LA, 9 Feb 1898; d. Burbank, CA, 20 May 1994.

Burkhardt, Harry: b. Boston, MA, 27 Sep 1870; d. Los Angeles, CA, 18 Sep 1943.

Burmester, Augusta: b. Hamburg, Ger, 1860; d. Los Angeles, CA, 28 Mar 1934.

Burnett, James (Tex): b. 1904; d. Orange Co, CA, 16 Sep 1984.

Burnham, Nicholas, b. 1860; d. Bernardsville, NJ, 30 Jan 1925.

Burns, Edmund (Edward J. Burns): b. Philadelphia, PA, 27 Sep 1892; d. Los Angeles, CA, 2 Apr 1980.

Burns, Edward W. (Eddie): b. New York, NY, ????; d. 1 Sep 1957.

Burns, Fred: b. Fort Keogh, MT, 24 Apr 1878; d. Los Angeles Co, CA, 18 Jul 1955.

Burns, George J.: b. Utica, NY, 24 Nov 1889; d. Gloversville, NY, 15 Aug 1966.

Burns, James W. (Jim): b. ????; d. San Diego Co, CA, 16 Jul 1975.

Burns, Neal: b, Bristol, PA, 26 Jun 1890; d. Los Angeles, CA, 3 Oct 1969.

Burns, Paul E.: b. Philadelphia, PA, 26 Jan 1881; d. Los Angeles, CA, 17 May 1967.

Burns, Robert Paul (Bobby): b. Philadelphia, PA, 1 Sep 1878; d. Los Angeles Co, CA, 16 Jan 1966.

Burns, William John: b. Baltimore, MD, 19 Oct 1861; d. Sarasota, FL, 14 Apr 1932.

Burr, Edmond: b. ????; d. 16 Jul 1975.

Burr, Eugene: b. Leavenworth, KS, 1884; d. Los Angeles, CA, 7 Jun 1940.

Burress, William: b. New Cornerstone, OH, 19 Aug 1867; d. Los Angeles Co, CA, 30 Oct 1948.

Burris, James (Jim): b. 18??; d. Washington, DC, 2 Jun 1923.

Burrough, Tom: b. Clinton County, IL, 1869; d. Staten Island, NY, 8 Sep 1929.

Burrows, James: b. 1842; d. Lynn, MA, 20 May 1926.

Burt, Ida: b. New Orleans, LA, 1852; d. New York, NY, 26 Oct 1941.

Burt, Laura: b. Isle of Man, UK, 16 Sep 1872; d. Bronx, NY, 16 Oct 1952.

Burt, Nellie: b. ????; d. 3 Nov 1986.

Burt, William P.: b. Peters, MN, 11 Feb 1867; d. Denver, CO, 23 Feb 1955.

Burton, Blanche: b. Baltimore, MD, 1879; d. New York, NY, 24 Jul 1934.

Burton, Charlotte: b. San Francisco, CA, 30 May 1882; d, Los Angeles, CA, 28 Mar 1942.

Burton, Clarence V.: b. Fort Lyons, MO, 10 May 1881; d. Los Angeles, CA, 1 Dec 1933.

Burton, David: b. Odessa, Russ, 22 May 1890; d. New York, NY, 30 Dec 1963.

Burton, Frederick: b. Indianapolis, IN, 20 Oct 1871; d. Woodland Hills, CA, 23 Oct 1957.

Burton, John W.: b. Wisconsin, 7 Jan 1853; d. Los Angeles, CA, 25 Mar 1920.

Burton, Langhorne: b. Somersby, Eng, 25 Dec 1872; d. 6 Dec 1949.

Burton, Ned: b. 1850; d. New York, NY, 11 Dec 1922.

Burton, William H.: b. 11 Apr 1844; d. New York, NY, 15 Mar 1926.

Busch, Mae: b. Melbourne, Austral, 19 Jan 1901; d. Los Angeles, CA, 19 Apr 1946.

Bush, Anita: b. Washington, DC, ????; d. New York, NY, 16 Feb 1974.

Bush, Pauline: b. Lincoln, NE, 22 May 1886; d. La Mesa, CA, 1 Nov 1969.

Bush, Robert Finlay: b. New Haven, CT, 1888; d, Prescott, AZ, 2 Apr 1929.

Bushman, Francis X. Sr.: b. Baltimore, MD, 10 Jan 1883; d. Pacific Palisades, CA, 23 Aug 1966.

Bushman, Francis X., Jr. (Ralph): b. Baltimore, MD, 1 May 1903; d. Los Angeles, CA, 16 Apr 1978.

Buskirk, Bessie: b. Illinois, 21 Mar 1892; d. Los Angeles, CA, 19 Nov 1952.

Buskirk, Hattie: b. Decatur, IL, 7 Aug 1867; d. Los Angeles, CA, 12 Jan 1942.

Buster, Budd: b, Colorado Springs, CO, 14 Jun 1891; d. Los Angeles, CA, 22 Dec 1965.

Butler, Barbara (Babs): b. Ogdensburg, NY, 1902; d. 4 Jan 1975.

Butler, Charles: b. 1856; d. New York, NY, 17 Aug 1920.

Butler, David: b. San Francisco, CA, 17 Dec 1895; d. Los Angeles, CA, 14 Jun 1979.

Butler, Emma Lathrop: b. 24 Mar 1845; d. Englewood, NJ, 8 Mar 1935.

Butler, Frank: b. Oxford, Eng, 28 Dec 1890; d. Los Angeles, CA, 10 Jun 1967.

Butler, Fred J.: b. Idaho, 22 Oct 1867; d. Los Angeles, CA, 22 Feb 1929.

Butler, John A.: b. Canada, 1 May 1884; d. Los Angeles Co, CA, 9 Oct 1967.

Butler, Royal (Roy): b. Atlanta, GA, 4 May 1893; d. Desert Hot Springs, CA, 28 Jul 1973.

Butler, William J. (Daddy): b. Dublin, Ire, 1860; d. Staten Island, NY, 27 Jan 1927.

Butt, Johnny: b. 18??; d. 1930.

Butt,W. Lawson: b. Isle of Jersey, 1883; d. 14 Jan 1956.

Butterfield, Everett: b. Portland, ME, 1885; d. New York, NY, 6 Mar 1925.

Butterfield, Millie: b. ????; d. New York, NY, 19 Apr 1939.

Butterworth, Ernest, Sr.: b, Lancashire, Eng, 16 Dec 1876; d. Rural Pearblossom, CA, 22 Apr 1950.

Butterworth, Ernest, Jr.: b. Lancashire, Eng, 8 May 1905; d. North Hollywood, CA, 2 May 1986.

Butterworth, Frank J.: b. Lancashire, Eng, 12 Dec 1903; d. Burbank, CA, 6 Aug 1975.

Buzzell, Eddie: b. Brooklyn, NY, 13 Nov 1897; d. Los Angeles, CA, 11 Jan 1985.

Buzzi, Pietro: b. Italy, 18??; d. Los Angeles, CA, 16 Feb 1921.

Byers, Nancy: b. 1900; d. 14 Nov 1960.

Byford, Roy: b. London, Eng, 12 Jan 1873; d. London, Eng, 31 Jan 1939.

Byram, Ronald: b. Brisbane, Austral, 18??; d. Calgary, Can, ? Apr 1919.

Byrd, Anthony: b. 1865; d. New York, NY, ? Apr 1925.

Byrens, Myer: b. 1840; d. Los Angeles, CA, 1933.

Byrne, Donn: b. New York, NY, 1889; d. Brandon, Cork, Ire, 18 Jun 1928.

Byrne, Francis M,: b. Newport, RI, 3 Aug 1876; d. New York, NY, 6 Feb 1923.

Byrne, James A.: b. Norwich, CT, 1867; d. Camden, NJ, 19 Mar 1927.

Byrne, John: b. 1862; d. Los Angeles, CA, 14 Feb 1924.

Byrne, John F.: b. 1859; d. Norwich, CT, 19 Sep 1937.

Byron, Marion: b. Dayton, OH, 16 Mar 1911; d. Santa Monica, CA, 5 Jul 1985.

Byron, Paul: b. New York, NY, 1889; d. San Diego, CA, 12 May 1959.

Byron, Royal: b. 20 Feb 1887; d. Trenton, NJ, 4 Mar 1943.

Byron, Walter: b. Leicester, Eng, 11 Jun 1899; d. Signal Hill, CA, 2 Mar 1972.

Bystrom, Walter E.: b. 1894; d. San Diego, CA, 13 Sep 1969.

C

Cabanne, William Christy: b. St. Louis, MO, 16 Apr 1888; d. Philadelphia, PA, 15 Oct 1950.

Cabot, Elliot: b. Boston, MA, 22 Jun 1899; d. New York, NY, 17 Jun 1938.

Cadell, Jean: b. Edinburgh, Scot, 13 Sep 1884; d. London, Eng, 24 Sep 1967.

Cadzaw, William: b. 18??; 28 Oct 1922.

Cahill, Lily: b. Texas, 1885; d. San Antonio, TX, 20 Jul 1955.

Cahill, Marie: b. Brooklyn, NY, 7 Feb 1870; d. New York, NY, 23 Aug 1933.

Cahill, William: b. 1853; d. Brooklyn, NY, 9 Feb 1926.

Cain, Robert: b. Chicago, IL, 4 Jun 1882; d. New York, NY, 27 Apr 1954.

Caine, Derwent Hall: b. Keswick, Eng, 12 Sep 1892; d. Miami, FL, 2 Dec 1971.

Caines, Eleanor: b. Philadelphia, PA, 1880; d. Philadelphia, PA, 2 Jun 1913.

Calapristi, Santo: b. 1897; d. Springfield, PA, 27 Apr 1987.

Caldara, Orme: b. Empire City, OR, 9 Feb 1875; d. Saranac Lake, NY, 21 Oct 1925.

Caldwell, Orville: b. Oakland, CA, 8 Feb 1896; d. Santa Rosa, CA, 24 Sep 1967.

Calhern, Louis: b. Brooklyn, NY, 19 Feb 1895; d. Tokyo, Japan, 12 May 1956.

Calhoun, Alice: b. Cleveland, OH, 21 Nov 1900; d. Los Angeles, CA, 3 Jun 1966.

Calhoun, Patrick: b. Bray, Ire, 1886; d. 19??

Calhoun, Richard A.: b. 1898; d. Los Angeles, CA, 11 Apr 1977.

Calley, Robert S.: b. Oakland, CA, 1889; d. Kansas City, MO, 6 May 1977.

Calliga, George: b. Rumania, 2 Jan 1897; d. Los Angeles Co, CA, 18 Jan 1976.

Calmettes, Andre: b. Paris, Fr, 18 Apr 1861; d. 1942.

Calthrop, Donald: b. London, Eng, 11 Apr 1888; d. London, Eng, 15 Jul 1940.

Calve, Olga, b. Russia, 1899; d. Santa Paula, CA, 12 May 1982.

Calvert, Catherine: b. Baltimore, MD, 20 Apr 1890; d. Uniondale, NY, 18 Jan 1971.

Calvert, Mrs. Charles: b. 1836; d. London, Eng, 20 Sep 1921.

Calvert, E. H. (Elisha Helm): b. Alexandria, VA, 27 Jun 1863; d. Los Angeles, CA, 5 Oct 1941.

Calvert, Louis: b. Manchester, Eng, 25 Nov 1859; d. New York, NY, 9 Jul 1923.

Calvin, Lester: b. Iowa, 1890; d. Orlando, FL, 30 May 1978.

Camelia, Muriel: b. 1913; d. Miami, FL, 15 Nov 1925.

Camerson, Donald C.: b. St. Stephens, Can, 1888; d. West Cornwall, CT, 11 Jul 1955.

Cameron, Gene: b. ????; d. Sentinel, AZ, 16 Nov 1927.

Cameron, Hugh: b. Duluth, MN, 15 May 1879; d. New York, NY, 9 Nov 1941.

Cameron, Rudolph: b. Washington, DC, 24 Oct 1892; d. Los Angeles, CA, 17 Feb 1958.

Cameron, Violet: b. 7 Dec 1839; d. Worthing, Eng, 25 Oct 1919.

Campbell, Allan: b. ????; d. 30 Dec 1917.

Campbell, Colin: b. Falkirk, Scot, 20 Mar 1883; d. Woodland Hills, CA, 25 Mar 1966.

Campbell, Eric: b. Dunoon, Scot, 26 Apr 1879; d. Los Angeles, CA, 20 Dec 1917.

Campbell, Frank G.: b. 1847; d. Los Angeles, CA, 30 Apr 1934.

Campbell, Herbert: b. London, Eng, ? Dec 1844; d. London, Eng, 19 Jul 1904.

Campbell, Margaret: b. St. Louis, MO, 24 Apr 1883; d. Los Angeles, CA, 27 Jun 1939.

Campbell, Webster: b. Kansas City, KS, 25 Jan 1893; d. Liberty, KS, 28 Aug 1972.

Campeau, Frank: b. Detroit, MI, 14 Dec 1864; d. Los Angeles, CA, 5 Nov 1943.

Canfield, William F.: b. 1860; d. New York, NY, 14 Feb 1925.

Cannon, Pomeroy: b. New Albany, IN, 1 Mar 1870; d. Los Angeles, CA, 16 Sep 1928.

Cannon, Raymond: b. Long Hollow, TN, 1 Sep 1893; d. Los Angeles, CA, 7 Jun 1977.

Cansino, Eduardo: b. Madrid, Spain, 1895; d. Pompano Beach, FL, 23 Dec 1968.

Cansino, Eduardo, Jr.: b. New York, NY, 13 Oct 1919; d. Los Angeles, CA, 11 Mar 1974.

Canter, Nellie Bell: b. 1902; d. Pittsburgh, PA, 1 May 1981.

Cantor, Eddie: b. New York, NY, 31 Jan 1892; d. Beverly Hills, CA, 10 Oct 1964.

Cantzen, Conrad: b. New Orleans, LA, 1867; d. New York, NY, 28 Jun 1945.

Canutt, Yakima: b. Colfax, WA, 29 Nov 1895; d. Los Angeles, CA, 24 May 1986.

Capellani, Paul: b, Paris, Fr, 1884; d. 1944.

Capera, Mary: b. ????; d. New York, NY, 21 May 1921.

Capozzi, Alberto A.: b. 8 Jul 1886; d. 27 Jun 1945.

Cappellano, Francesca: b. 1896; d, Los Angeles, CA, 13 Apr 1988.

Caprice, June: b. Arlington, MA, 19 Nov 1899; d. Los Angeles, CA, 9 Nov 1936.

Caress, W. H. (Bill): b. 1883; d. French Lick, IN, 9 Aug 1938.

Carew, James: b. Goshen, IN, 5 Feb 1876; d. London, Eng, 4 Apr 1938.

Carew, Ora: b. Salt Lake City, UT, 13 Apr 1893; d. Los Angeles, CA, 26 Oct 1955.

Carewe, Arthur Edmond: b. Trebizond, Armenia, 30 Dec 1884; d. Santa Monica, CA, 21 Apr 1937.

Carewe, Edwin: b. Gainesville, TX, 5 Mar 1881; d. Los Angeles, CA, Jan 22 1940.

Carewe, Rita (Rita Mason): b. New York, NY, 9 Sep 1909; d. Torrence, CA, 23 Oct 1955.

Carey, Harry: b. New York, NY, 16 Jan 1878; d. Los Angeles, CA, 21 Sep 1947.

Carey, Joyce: b. London, Eng, 30 Mar 1898; d. Los Angeles, CA, 3 May 1993.

Carle, Richard: b. Sommerville, MA, 7 Jul 1871; d. Los Angeles, CA, 28 Jun 1941.

Carleton, Harry G.: b. 1859; d. Boston, MA, 31 Jan 1922.

Carleton, Lloyd B.: b. New York, NY, 1872; d. New York, NY, 8 Aug 1933.

Carleton, Will C.: b. New York, NY, 24 Sep 1872; d. Los Angeles, CA, 21 Sep 1941.

Carleton, William P.: b. London, Eng, 3 Oct 1872; d. Los Angeles, CA, 5 Apr 1947.

Carleton, William T.: b. England, 1859; d. St. John, Bri Col, Can, 28 Sep 1930.

Carlie, Edward: b. 1878; d. Los Angeles, CA, 25 Nov 1938.

Carlisle, Alexandra: b. London, Eng, 15 Jan 1886; d. New York, NY, 21 Apr 1936.

Carlyle, Aileen: b. San Francisco, CA, 5 Mar 1906; d. Los Angeles, CA, 3 May 1984.

Carlyle, Billie: b. Adelaide, Austral, 1901; d. Staines, Eng, 23 Jul 1991.

Carlyle, Francis: b. England, 27 Aug 1868; d. Hartford, CT, 15 Sep 1916.

Carlyle, Richard: b. Guelph, Ont, Can, 21 May 1876; d. San Fernando, CA, 12 Jun 1942.

Carmen, Sybil: b. 1900; d. Paris, Fr, 15 Apr 1929.

Carmi, Maria: b. Florence, Italy, 3 Mar 1880; d. Myrtle Beach, SC, ? Aug 1957.

Carmichael, Myra; b. 1890; d. 22 Oct 1974.

Carminati, Tullio: b. Zara, Dalmatia, Italy, 21 Sep 1894; d. Rome, Italy, 26 Feb 1971.

Carney, George: b. Bristol, Eng, 21 Nov 1887; d. London, Eng, 9 Dec 1947.

Carney, Mary: b. 1904; d. 21 Jul 1984.

Carol, Sue: b. Chicago, IL, 30 Oct 1903; d. Los Angeles, CA, 4 Feb 1982.

Carpenter, Charles: b. 1913; d. Oxnard, CA, 12 Nov 1990.

Carpenter, Frederick L.: b. 1922; d. Oxnard, CA, 31 Mar 1984.

Carpenter, Horace B.: b. Grand Rapids, MI, 31 Jan 1875; d. Los Angeles, CA, 21 May 1945.

Carpenter, Jeanne: b. 1916; d. Oxnard, CA, 5 Jan 1994.

Carpentier, Georges: b. Lens, Fr, 12 Jan 1894; d. Paris, Fr, 27 Oct 1975.

Carr, Alexander: b. Rumni, Russ, 7 Mar 1878; d. Los Angeles, CA, 19 Sep 1946.

Carr, Gladys: b. 1890; d. Los Angeles, CA, 26 Sep 1940.

Carr, John: b. Philadelphia, PA, 19??; d. Los Angeles, CA, 27 Nov 1956.

Carr, Luella: b. Philadelphia, PA, 19??; d. Los Angeles, CA, 16 Jan 1937.

Carr, Mary: b. Philadelphia, PA, 14 Mar 1874; d. Los Angeles, CA, 24 Jun 1973.

Carr, Nat: b. Poltava, Russ, 12 Aug 1886; d. Los Angeles, CA, 6 Jul 1944.

Carr, Percy: b. England, 1875; d. Saranac Lake, NY, 22 Nov 1926.

Carr, Rosemary: b. Philadelphia, PA, 1911; d. Ventura, CA, 24 Sep 1987.

Carr, Sade: b. London, Eng, 1889; d. Carmel, CA, 17 Nov 1940.

Carr, Stephen: b. Philadelphia, PA, 23 Apr 1906; d. North Hollywood, CA, 20 May 1986.

Carr, William G. D.: b. 1867; d. Los Angeles, CA, 13 Feb 1937.

Carre, Bartlett A.: b. Malrose, MA, 10 Jul 1897; d. Los Angeles, CA, 26 Apr 1971.

Carrico, Charles: b. 1888; d. Desert Hot Springs, CA, 18 Jan 1967.

Carrigan, Thomas Jay: b. Lapeer, MI, 13 Apr 1886; d. Lapeer, MI, 2 Oct 1941.

Carrillo, Leo: b. Los Angeles, CA, 6 Aug 1880; d. Santa Monica, CA, 10 8ep 1961.

Carrington, Evelyn C.: b. 22 Sep 1876; d. Los Angeles, CA, 21 Nov 1942.

Carrington, Frank: b. 1902; d. Milburn, NJ, 3 Jul 1975.

Carrington, Murray: b. Upper Norwood, Eng, 13 Mar 1885; d. Clevedon, Somerset, Eng, 2 Dec 1941.

Carroll, Madeline: b. West Bromwich, Staffs, Eng, 26 Feb 1906; d, Marbelle, Spain, 2 Oct 1987.

Carroll, Marcelle: b. Biarritz, Fr, 1897; d. New York, NY, 18 Nov 1936.

Carroll, Nancy: b. New York, NY, 19 Nov 1904; d. New York, NY, 6 Aug 1965.

Carroll, William Arthur: b. New York, NY, 1875; d. Glendale, CA, 26 Dec 1927.

Carson, Madge: b. 18??; d. New York, NY, 16 Sep 1918.

Carter, Calvert: b. Virginia, 23 Oct 1858; d. Long Beach, CA, 26 Aug 1932.

Carter, Harry: b. Louisville, KY, 1879; d. 19??.

Carter, Hubert: b. Great Horton, Yorks, Eng, 1869; d. London, Eng, 26 Mar 1934.

Carter, Leslie: b. 1873; d. 4 Oct 1921.

Carter, Mrs. Leslie: b. Lexington, KY, 10 Jun 1862; d. Santa Monica, CA, 12 Nov 1937.

Carter, Louise: b. Denison, IA, 17 Mar 1875; d. Los Angeles, CA, 10 Nov 1957.

Carter, Monte: b. San Francisco, CA, 1884; d. San Francisco, CA, 14 Nov 1950.

Carter, Nellie Bell: b. 1902; d. 1 May 1981.

Carton, Pauline: b. Geneva, Switz, 7 Apr 1884; d. Paris, Fr, 17 Jun 1974.

Caruso, Enrico: b. Naplest, Italy, 25 Feb 1873; d. Naples, Italy, 2 Aug 1921.

Carver, Kathryn (Kathryn Hill): b. New York, NY, 1906; d. Elmhurst, NY, 18 Jul 1947.

Carver, Louise: b. Davenport, IA, 9 Jun 1868; d. Los Angeles, CA, 19 Jan 1956.

Carvill, Henry J.: b. St. Mary's, Nov Sco, Can, 11 May 1866; d. 11 Mar 1941.

Carville, Virginia: b. 1894; d. Los Angeles, CA, 18 Feb 1982.

Casaleggio, Giovanni: b. 1880; d. Turin, Italy, 11 Nov 1955.

Casanave, Charles: b. Chicago, IL, 1895; d. Rye, NY, 7 May 1958.

Case, Anna: b. Clinton, NJ, 29 Oct 1889; d. New York, NY, 7 Jan 1984.

Casey, Jack: b. Ireland, 15 Aug 1888; d. Los Angeles, CA, 30 Aug 1956.

Casey, Kenneth: b. New York State, 1899; d. Cornwall, NY, 10 Aug 1965.

Casey, Leslie J.: b. Australia, 1891; d. New York, NY, 18 Feb 1942.

Cashier, Isidore: b. Russia, 1887; d. Savannah, GA, 15 Apr 1948.

Cashman, Harry: b. 20 Jun 1870; d. Chicago, IL, 14 Dec 1912.

Cass, Francis: b. ????; d. England, ? May 1927.

Cass, Maurice, b. Vilna, Lithuania, 12 Oct 1884; d. Los Angeles, CA, 8 Jun 1954.

Cassady, James J.: b. Philadelphia, PA, 1869; d. Spokane, WA, 23 Mar 1928.

Cassidy, William E.: b. 1876; d. Cincinnati, OH, 6 Apr 1943.

Cassil, Dorothy: b. 1903; d. Anderson, CA, 19 Apr 1983.

Cassinelli, Dolores: b. Chicago, IL, 4 Jul 1893; d. New Brunswick, NJ, 26 Apr 1984.

Casson, Sir Lewis: b. Birkenhead, Eng, 26 Oct 1875; d. London, Eng, 16 May 1969.

Castle, Irene: b. New Rochelle, NY, 7 Apr 1893; d. Eureka Springs, AR, 25 Jan 1969.

Castle, Vernon: b. Norwich, Eng, 2 May 1887; d. Fort Worth, TX, 15 Feb 1918.

Castleton, Barbara: b. Little Rock, AR, 14 Sep 1895; d. Boca Raton, FL, 23 Dec 1978.

Catlett, Walter: b. San Francisco, CA, 4 Feb 1889; d. Woodland Hills, CA, 14 Nov 1960.

Cavalieri, Lina: b. Rome, Italy, 25 Dec 1874; d. Florence, Italy, 8 Feb 1944.

Cavan, Allan: b. Concord, CA, 25 Mar 1880; d. Los Angeles, CA, 20 Jan 1941.

Cavanagh, Paul: b. Chislehurst, Kent, Eng, 8 Dec 1895; d. Cockeysville, MD, 15 Mar 1964.

Cavanaugh, Hobart: b. Virginia City, NV, 22 Sep 1886; d. Los Angeles, CA, 25 Apr 1950.

Cavanaugh, Lucille: b. 1895; d. Carmel, CA, 13 Jul 1983.

Cavanaugh, William H.: b. New York, NY, 1876; d. 19??.

Cavanna, Elsie: b. Pennsylvania, 30 Jan 1902; d. Los Angeles, CA, 12 May 1963.

Cave, Joseph A.: b. London, Eng, 21 Oct 1823; d. London, Eng, 20 Nov 1912.

Cavender, Glen W.: b. Tucson, AZ, 19 Sep 1883; d. Los Angeles, CA, 9 Feb 1962.

Cavens, Fred: b. Belgium, 30 Aug 1882; d. Woodland Hills, CA, 30 Apr 1962.

Cavin, Jess: b. Indiana, 5 May 1885; d. Los Angeles Co, CA, 20 Jul 1967.

Cawthorne, Joseph: b. New York, NY, 29 Mar 1868; d. Beverly Hills, CA, 21 Jan 1949.

Cazenuve, Paul: b. France, 18??; d. Los Angeles, CA, 22 Jun 1925.

Cecil, Edward: b. San Francisco, CA, 13 Sep 1878; d. Los Angeles, CA, 13 Dec 1940.

Cecil, Mary: b. New York, NY, 1885; d. New York, NY, 21 Dec 1940.

Cecil, Nora: b. Ireland, 23 Oct 1879; d. 19??.

Cederlund, Gosta: b. Stockholm, Sweden, 6 Mar 1888; d. 4 Dec 1980.

Celeste, Olga: b. Sweden, 1887; d. Burbank, CA, 31 Aug 1969.

Celli, Faith: b. London, Eng, 27 Nov 1888; d. Ascot, Eng, 16 Dec 1942.

Cennerazzo, Armando: b. 1886; d. New York, NY, 10 Jan 1962.

Cesar, M: b. 18??; d. ? Sep 1921.

Chadwick, Helene: b. Chadwick, NY, 25 Nov 1897; d. Los Angeles, CA, 5 Sep 1940.

Chagnon, Jack: b. 1880; d. Woonsocket, RI, 21 Jul 1912.

Chaillie, Joseph: b. 1852; d. Amityville, NY, 17 Dec 1924.

Chaliapin, Feodor, Jr.: b. Moscow, Russ, 1905; d. Rome, Italy, 17 Sep 1992.

Challenger, Percy: b. England, 3 Sep 1858; d. Los Angeles, CA, 23 Jul 1932.

Chalmers, Thomas: b. New York, NY, 20 Oct 1884; d. Greenwich, CT, 11 Jun 1966.

Chamberlain, Riley C.: b. Byron, MI, 7 Nov 1854; d. New Rochelle, NY, 22 Jan 1917.

Chamberlin, Belle: b. 1873; d. Los Angeles, CA, 12 Oct 1930.

Chamberlin, J. Raymond: b. 1886; d. Norristown, PA, 2 Dec 1957.

Chambers, Lyster: b. Michigan, 1876; d. New York, NY, 27 Jan 1947.

Chambers, Margaret: b. Kentucky, 16 Oct 1896; d. Los Angeles, CA, 6 Oct 1965.

Chambers, Marie: b. Philadelphia, PA, 1888; d. Paris, Fr, 21 Mar 1933.

Chambers, Ralph W.: b. 1892; d. New York, NY, 16 Mar 1968.

Chance, Frank Leroy: b. Fresno, CA, 19 Sep 1879; d. 14 Sep 1924.

Chandler, Chick: b. Kingston, NY, 18 Jan 1905; d. Laguna Beach, CA, 30 Sep 1988.

Chandler, Clarence: b. 18??; d. Los Angeles, CA, 26 Feb 1915.

Chandler, Edward (Eddie): b. Wilton Junction, IA, 12 Mar 1894; d. Los Angeles Co, CA, 23 Mar 1948.

Chandler, George: b. Waukegan, IL, 30 Jun 1898; d. Los Angeles, CA, 10 Jun 1985.

Chandler, Helen: b. New York, NY, 1 Feb 1906; d. Los Angeles, CA, 30 Apr 1965.

Chandler, Howard: b. ????; d. San Antonio, TX, ? Jan 1933.

Chandler, Lane: b. Culbertson, MT, 4 Jun 1899; d. Los Angeles, CA, 14 Sep 1972.

Chandler, Robert: b. 1860; d. East Islip, NY, 16 Mar 1950.

Chaney, Lon: b. Colorado Springs, CO, 1 Apr 1883; d. Los Angeles, CA, 26 Aug 1930.

Chapin, Alice: b. 1858; d. Keene, NH, 6 Jul 1934.

Chapin, Benjamin C.: b. Bristolville, OH, 1874; d. Liberty, NY, 2 Jun 1918.

Chapin, Harold: b. Brooklyn, NY, 1886; d. France, 26 Sep 1915.

Chaplin, Charles: b. London, Eng, 16 Apr 1889; d. Corsier-Sur-Vevey, Switz, 25 Dec 1977.

Chaplin, Sydney: b. Cape Town, So Africa, 17 Mar 1885; d. Nice, Fr, 15 Apr 1965.

Chapman, Blanche: b. Covington, KY, 1851; d. Rutherford, NJ, 7 Jun 1941.

Chapman, Edythe: b. Rochester, NY, 8 Oct 1863; d. Glendale, CA, 15 Oct 1948.

Charbeneau, Oscar: b. ????; d. Los Angeles, CA, ? Sep 1915.

Charles, John: b. 1835; d. Whitestone, NY, 7 Nov 1921.

Charleson, Mary: b. Dungannon, Ire, 18 May 1890; d. Los Angeles, CA, 3 Dec 1961.

Charsky, Boris: b. Petrograd, Russ, 28 May 1893; d. Inglewood, CA, 1 Jun 1956.

Charters, Spencer: b. Duncannon, PA, 25 Mar 1875; d. Los Angeles, CA, 25 Jan 1943.

Chase, Arline: b. 1900: d. Sierra Madre, CA, 19 Apr 1926.

Chase, Charles (Charles Parrott): b. Baltimore, MD, 20 Oct 1893; d. Los Angeles, CA, 20 Jun 1940.

Chase, Colin: b. Lewiston, ID, 13 Apr 1886; d. Los Angeles, CA, 24 Apr 1937.

Chase, Florence: 1854; d. New York, NY, 12 May 1929.

Chase, George W.: b. Spokane, WA, 1890; d. Woodhaven, NY, 29 Jul 1918.

Chase, Hal (Harold W. Chase): b. Los Catos, CA, 13 Feb 1883; d. Colusas CA, 18 May 1947.

Chase, Pauline: b. Washington, DC. 20 May 1885; d. Tunbridge Wells, Kent, Eng, 3 Mar 1962.

Chatterdon, Arthur B.: b. 1885; d. Absecon, NJ, 9 Oct 1947.

Chatterton, Ruth: b. New York, NY, 24 Dec 1893; d. Norwalk, CT, 24 Nov 1961.

Chatterton, Thomas: b. Geneva, NY, 12 Feb 1881; d. Los Angeles, CA, 17 Aug 1952.

Chautard, Emile: b. Avegon, Fr., 1864; d. Westwood, CA, 24 Apr 1934.

Chauvel, Charles: b. 1897; d. Sydney, Austral, 11 Nov 1959.

Chedister, America: b. Iowa, 21 Oct 1895; d. South Laguna, CA, 1 Nov 1975.

Cheesemam, Martin N.: b. 1859; d. New York, NY, 9 Jun 1924.

Chefe, Jack: b. Kiev, Russ, 1 Apr 1894; d. Los Angeles, CA, 1 Dec 1975.

Cheirel, Jeanne: b. Paris, Fr, 18 Mar 1869; d. Paris, Fr, 2 Nov 1934.

Chene, Dixie: b. Detroit, MI, 31 Jul 1894; d. Los Angeles, CA, 30 Aug 1972.

Chene, Hazel: b. Michigan, 22 Sep 1888; d. Glendale, CA, 28 Apr 1976.

Cheron, Andre: b. France, 24 Aug 1880; d. 26 Jan 1952.

Cherry, Charles: b. Greenwich, Eng, 19 Nov 1872; d. 2 Sep 1931.

Cherry, Malcolm: b. Liverpool, Eng, 17 May 1878; d. London, Eng, 12 Apr 1925.

Cherryman, Rex: b. Grand Rapids, MI, 1896; d. Le Harve, Fr, 10 Aug 1928.

Chesebro, George: b. Minneapolis, MN, 29 Jul 1888; d. Los Angeles, CA, 28 May 1959.

Chesney, Arthur: b. London, Eng, 1882; d. London, Eng, 27 Aug 1949.

Chester, Virginia: b. San Francisco, CA, 27 Aug 1896; d. Oakland, CA, 28 Jul 1927.

Chevalier, Albert: b. London, Eng, 21 Mar 1861; d. London, Eng, 11 Jul 1923.

Chevalier, Maurice: b. Paris, Fr, 12 Sep 1888; d. Paris, Fr, 1 Jan 1972.

Chief Black Hawk (Elmer Attear); b. ????; d. 15 May 1975.

Chief John Big Tree (Issac J. John): b. 1865; d. Onondaga Reservation, NY, ? Jul 1967.

Chief Standing Bear: b. South Dakota, 1865; d. Huntington Park, CA, 20 Feb 1939.

Chief Thunderbird: b. Tongue River, MT, 1867; d. 6 Apr 1946.

Chief White Eagle: b. 1873; d. 1946.

Childers, Naomi: b. Pottstown, PA, 15 Nov 1892; d. Woodland Hills, CA, 8 May 1964.

Chirgwin, George H.: b. London, Eng, 13 Dec 1854; d, London, Eng, 14 Nov 1922.

Chivvis, Frederick W. (Chic): b. White Plains, NY, 2 Dec 1884; d. Reseda, CA, 26 Oct 1963.

Chmara, Gregor: b. Portava, 1893; d. Riverside Co, CA, 3 Feb 1970.

Choux, Jean: b. Geneva, Switz, 1887; d. Paris, Fr, ? Mar 1946.

Chrisander, Nils W.: b. Sweden, 14 Feb 1884; d. 1947.

Christensen, Benjamin: b. Viberg, Denmark, 1879; d. Copenhagen, Denmark, 1959.

Christians, Mady: b. Vienna, Austria, 19 Jan 1900; d. Norwalk, CT, 28 Oct 1951.

Christians, Rudolph: b. Germany, 15 Jan 1869; d. Pasadena, CA, 2 Feb 1921.

Christie, George S.: b. Philadelphia, PA, 27 Feb 1873; d. Toms River, NJ, 20 May 1949.

Christman, Pat: (Ora N.): Meadville, MO, 1882; d. 19??

Christy, Ann: b. Logansport, IN, 31 May 1905; d. Vernon, TX, 14 Nov 1987.

Christy, Ivan W.: b. Denmark, 1887; d. Burbank, CA, 9 May 1949.

Church, Frederick (Montana Bill): b. Quebec, Can, 1889; d. 19??.

Churchill, Berton: b. Toronto, Can, 9 Dec 1876; d. New York, NY, 10 Oct 1940.

Ciannelli, Mrs. Alma: b. 1892; d. Villa San Pietro, Italy, 23 Jul 1968.

Ciannelli, Eduardo: b. Ischia, Italy, 30 Aug 1889; d. Rome, Italy, 8 Oct 1969.

Cichy, Martin: b. New York, NY, 9 Nov 1892; d. Los Angeles Co, CA, 26 Apr 1962.

Cierkes, Vincent: b. 1906; d, Baltimore, MD, 14 Mar 1979.

Cinquevalli, Paul: b. Lissa, Poland, 1859; d. London, Eng, 14 Jul 1918.

Clair, Rene: b. Paris, Fr, 11 Nov 1898; d. Paris, Fr, 15 Mar 1981.

Claire, Gertrude: b. Illinois, 16 Jul 1852; d. Los Angeles, CA, 28 Apr 1928.

Claire, Ina: b. Washington, DC, 15 Oct 1892; d. San Francisco, CA, 21 Feb 1985.

Clare, Madelyn: b. Cleveland, OH, 14 Nov 1894; d. Raleigh, NC, 20 Sep 1975.

Clare, Mary: b. London, Eng, 17 Jul 1894; d. London, Eng, 29 Aug 1970.

Clarence, O. B.: b. London, Eng, 25 Mar 1870; d. Hove, Sussex, Eng, 2 Oct 1955.

Clarens, Elsie: b. 1881; d. New York, NY, 20 Jun 1917.

Clarens, Harry F.: b. 1860; d. New York, NY, 19 Dec 1928.

Clarges, Vernon: b. 1846; d. New York, NY, 11 Aug 1911.

Clark, Andrew J. (Andy): b. New York, NY, ? Mar 1903; d. New Rochelle, NY, 16 Nov 1960.

Clark, Bert: b. London, Eng, 30 Jan 1878; d. New York, NY, 9 May 1922.

Clark, Champ: b. Anderson County, KY, 1850; d. Washington, DC, 1 Mar 1921.

Clark, Charles Dow: b. St. Albans, VT, 1870; d. New York, NY, 26 Mar 1959.

Clark, Davison: b. California, 15 Jan 1881; d. Ventura Co, CA, 4 Nov 1972.

Clark, E. Holman: b. East Hothley, Eng, 22 Apr 1864; d. London, Eng, 7 Sep 1925.

Clark, Edward H.: b. Russia, 6 May 1978; d. Los Angeles, CA, 18 Nov 1954.

Clark, Estelle: b. Warsaw, Poland, 7 May 1898; d. Port Hueneme, CA, 3 Dec 1982.

Clark, Frank: b. Cincinnati, OH, 22 Dec 1857; d. Woodland Hills, CA, 10 Apr 1945.

Clark, Harvey: b. Chelsea, MA, 4 Oct 1885; d. New York, NY, 19 Jul 1938.

Clark, J. A.: b. ????; d. Seattle, WA, 30 May 1921.

Clark, Jack J.: b. 23 Sep 1876; d. Los Angeles, CA, 12 Apr 1947.

Clark, Marguerite: b. Cincinnati, OH, 22 Feb 1883; d. New York, NY, 25 Sep 1940.

Clark, T. C.: b. 1882; d. Los Angeles, CA, 4 Oct 1954.

Clark, Wallis H.: b. Essex, Eng, 2 Mar 1882; d. North Hollywood, CA, 14 Feb 1961.

Clark, Wally: b. 18??; d. Philadelphia, PA, 30 Jan 1920.

Clark, William T.: b. Springfield, OH, 1865; d. Brooklyn, NY, 14 Sep 1925.

Clarke, Betty Ross: b. Pittsburgh, PA, 19 Apr 1896; d. Los Angeles, CA, 31 Jan 1947.

Clarke, Downing: b. Birmingham, Eng, 1859; d. New Haven, CT, 17 Aug 1930.

Clarke, Frank: b. Paso Robles, CA, 29 Dec 1898; d. Los Angeles, CA, 12 Jun 1948.

Clarke, George: b. Bromley, Eng, 11 Apr 1888; d. London, Eng, 21 Dec 1946.

Clarke, Redfield: b. Peru, NY, 18??; d. Detroit, MI, 23 Oct 1928.

Clarke, Westcott B.: b. Jersey City, NJ, 27 Sep 1886; d. Los Angeles Co, CA, 26 Jan 1959.

Clary, Charles: b. Charleston, IL, 24 Mar 1873; d. Los Angeles, CA, 24 Mar 1931.

Clayton, Donald: b. Missouri, 27 Oct 1889; d. 18 Jan 1964.

Clayton, Ethel: b. Champaign, IL, 8 Nov 1883; d. Oxnard, CA, 11 Jun 1966.

Clayton, Frederic: b. 1874; d. New York, NY, 2 Jan 1948.

Clayton, Gilbert: b. Polo, IL, 18 Jan 1859; d. Los Angeles Co, CA, 1 Mar 1950.

Clayton, Hazel: b. 1886; d. Forest Hills, NY, 8 Mar 1963.

Clayton, Lucille: b. ????; d. Birmingham, AL, 26 Jun 1923.

Clayton, Marguerite: b. Ogden, UT, 12 Apr 1891; d. Los Angeles, CA, 20 Dec 1968.

Cleary, Peggy: b. Detroit, MI, 29 Dec 1892; d. Los Angeles, CA, 10 Jan 1972.

Clegg, Valce V.: b. Minnesota, 27 Feb 1888; d. Los Angeles, CA, 29 Jul 1947.

Clements Clay: b. Greentree, KY, 19 May 1888; d. Watertown, NY, 20 Oct 1956.

Clemento, Steve: b. Mexico, 22 Nov 1885; d. Los Angeles, CA, 7 May 1950.

Clements, Dudley: b. New York, NY, 31 Mar 1889; d. New York, NY, 4 Nov 1947.

Clermont, Harvey (Harry): b. 1907; d. Marina del Rey, CA, 28 Jan 1978.

Clerget, Paul: b. France, 1867; d. Paris, Fr, 4 Dec 1935.

Clermont, Rita: b. 4 Mar l894; d. ? Dec 1969.

Cleveland, Anna: b. New Orleans, LA, 1880; d. Manhasset, NY, 7 Jan 1954.

Cliff, Laddie: b. Bristol, Eng, 3 Sep 1891; d. Montana, Switz, 8 Dec 1937.

Cliffe, H. Cooper: b. Oxford, Eng, 19 Jul 1862; d. New York, NY, 1 May 1939.

Clifford, Jack: b. Genoa, Italy, 1680; d. New York, NY, 10 Nov 1956.

Clifford, Kathleen: b. Charlottesville, VA, 16 Feb 1894; d. Los Angeles, CA, 11 Jan 1963.

Clifford, Molly Hamley: b. Exeter, Eng, 1 Aug 1885; d. 7 Jun 1956.

Clifford, William: b. Cincinnati, OH, 27 Jun 1877; d. Los Angeles, CA, 23 Dec 1941.

Clifton, Elmer: b. Chicago, IL, 14 Mar 1890; d. Los Angeles, CA, 15 Oct 1949.

Clifton, Emma: b. Pittsburgh, PA, 1 Nov 1874; d. Los Angeles, CA, 3 Aug 1922.

Clifton, William F.: b. 1855; d. Chicago, IL, 18 Sep 1931.

Cline, Edward F. (Eddie): b. Kenosha, WI, 7 Nov 1892; d. Los Angeles, CA, 22 May 1961.

Clisbee, Edward: b. Santa Rosa, CA, 29 Dec 1878; d. Wenatchee, WA, 24 Jul 1936.

Clive, Henry: b. Melbourne, Austral, 3 Oct 1881; d. Los Angeles, CA, 12 Dec 1960.

Clive, Vincent: b. Upper Norwood, Eng, 18??; d. 11 Apr 1913.

Cloninger, Ralph M.: b. Texas, 20 Apr 1888; d. Los Angeles Co, CA, 17 Jun 1962.

Close, Ivy: b. Stockton-on-Tees, Durham, Eng, 1890; d. Goring, Eng, 4 Dec 1968.

Cloud, Mabel: b. 18??; d. Newkirk, OK, 17 Jun 1921.

Clovelly, Cecil: b. England, 1891; d. New York, NY, 25 Apr 1965.

Cloy, May: b. Minneapolis, MN, 8 May 1892; d. 19??.

Clugston, H. N. (Howard Newkirk Clugston): b. Scotland, 18 Oct 1881; d. Los Angeles, CA, 5 Apr 1944.

Cluzetti, Jules: b. 1861; d. New Orleans, LA, 22 Apr 1927.

Clyde, Andy: b. Blairgowrie, Scot, 25 Mar 1892; d. Los Angeles, CA, 18 May 1967.

Coad, Joyce: b. Wyoming, 14 Apr 1917; d. March Air Force Base, CA, 3 May 1987.

Cobb, Edmund F.: b. Albuquerque, NM, 23 Jun 1892; d. Woodland Hills, CA, 15 Aug 1974.

Cobb, Irvin S.: b. Paducah, KY, 23 Jun 1876; d. New York, NY, 11 Mar 1944.

Cobb, Ty: b. Narrows, GA, 18 Dec 1886; d. Atlanta, GA, 17 Jul 1961.

Coburn, Dorothy: b. Great Falls, MT, 8 Jun 1905; d. Los Angeles, CA, 15 May 1978.

Cochrane, Frank: b. Durham, Eng, 28 Oct 1882; d. London, Eng, 21 May 1962.

Cody, Albert R.: b. Portland, OR, 6 Jun 1885; d. San Francisco, CA, 30 Mar 1966.

Cody, Bill (William J. Cody): b. St. Paul, MN, 5 Jan 1891; d. Santa Monica, CA, 24 Jan 1948.

Cody, Gene: b. Baltimore, MD, 1895; d. Atlanta, GA, 10 Jul 1976.

Cody, Lew: b. Waterville, ME, 22 Feb 1888; d. Los Angeles, CA, 31 May 1934.

Cody, Col. William F. (Buffalo Bill): b. Scott County, IA, 26 Feb 1846; d. Denver, CO, 10 Jan 1917.

Coffee, Lenore: b. San Francisco, CA, 13 Jul 1896; d. Woodland Hills, CA, 2 Jul 1984.

Coffin, C. Hayden: b. Manchester, Eng, 22 Apr 1862; d. London, Eng, 8 Dec 1935.

Cogan, Mrs. Fanny Hay: b. Philadelphia, PA, 1865; d. Los Angeles, CA, 17 May 1929.

Cogan, James P.: b. 18??; d. 21 Sep 1921.

Cogdell, Josephine: b. 1901; d. New York, NY, 2 May 1969.

Coghlan, Charles F.: b. ????; d. Hershey, PA, 18 Mar 1972.

Coghlan, Gertrude Evelyn: b. Hertfordshire, Eng, 1 Feb 1876; d. Bayside, NY, 11 Sep 1952.

Coghlan, Katherine: b. Connecticut, 3 Sep 1889; d. Los Angeles, CA, 20 Sep 1965.

Coghlan, Rose: b. Peterborough, Eng, 18 Mar 1851; d. Harrison NY, 2 Apr 1932.

Cogley, Nick: b. New York, NY, 1869; d. Santa Monica, CA, 20 May 1936.

Cohan, George M.: b. Providence, RI, 3 Jul 1878; d. New York, NY, 5 Nov 1942.

Cohen, Samny: b. Minneapolis, MN, 8 Dec 1902; d. Santa Monica, CA, 30 May 1981.

Cohill, William Wright: b. Pennsylvania, 6 Dec 1882; d. Garberville, CA, 28 Apr 1931.

Coit, Sam: b. Bethlehem, CT, 17 Nov 1872; d. New York, NY, 1 Jan 1933.

Colbourne, Maurice: b. Cuddington, Cheshire, Eng, 24 Sep 1894; d. Perelle, Isle of Guernsey, 22 Sep 1965.

Colburn, Carrie: b. 1858; d. New York, NY, 23 May 1932.

Colby, Herbert: b. 1839; d. Brooklyn, NY, 6 Feb 1912.

Cole, Fred: b. Los Angeles, CA, 21 May 1901; d. Los Angeles, CA, 19 Sep 1964.

Coleman, Charles: b. Sydney, Austral, 22 Dec 1885; d. Woodland Hills, CA, 7 Mar 1951.

Coleman, Don: b. Sheridan, WY, 15 Jan 1893; d. Willits, CA, 16 Dec 1985.

Colenbrander, Col. Johann W.C.B.: b. 18??; d. Africa, 2 Mar 1918.

Collen, Henri: b. 1878; d. Paris, Fr, 25 Jul 1924.

Collett, Lorraine: b. 1893; d. Fresno, CA, 30 Mar 1983.

Collier, Constance: b. Windsor, Eng, 22 Jan 1878; d. New York, NY, 25 Apr 1955.

Collier, William: b. New York, NY, 12 Nov 1866; d. Los Angeles, CA, 13 Jan 1944.

Collier, William, Jr. (Buster): b. New York, NY, 12 Feb 1902; d. San Francisco, CA, 5 Feb 1987.

Collins, Charles E.: b. Anderson County, MO, 23 Jul 1873; d. Los Angeles Co, CA, 15 Apr 1951.

Collins, Eddy: b. 1866; d. Los Angeles, CA, 17 Dec 1916.

Collins, G. Pat: b. Brooklyn, NY, 16 Dec 1895; d. Los Angeles, CA, 5 Aug 1959.

Collins, Jose: b. London, Eng, 23 May 1887; d. London, Eng, 6 Dec 1958.

Collins, May: b. New York, NY, 1906; d. Fairfield, CT, 6 May 1955.

Collins, Monte: b. 1856, d. Los Angeles, CA, 4 Aug 1929.

Collins, Monte, Jr.: b. New York, NY, 3 Dec 1898; d. North Hollywood, CA, 1 Jun 1951.

Collins, Richard: b. 1861; d. 19 Jun 1939.

Collyer, June: b. New York, NY, 19 Aug 1907; d. Los Angeles, CA, 16 Mar 1968.

Colman, Ben: b. 1906; d. Tarzana, CA, 22 Feb 1988.

Colman, Ronald: b. Richmond, Surrey, Eng, 9 Feb 1891; d. Santa Barbara, CA, 19 May 1958.

Colson, Kate: b. 1861; d. Los Angeles, CA, 6 Sep 1944.

Colvig, Vance D.: b. Jacksonville, OR, 11 Sep 1892; d. Woodland Hills, CA, 3 Oct 1967.

Colvin, William G.: b. Sligo, Ire, 20 Jul 1877; d. Los Angeles, CA, 8 Aug 1930.

Coman, Morgan: b. ????; d. ? Mar 1947.

Commerford, Thomas: b. New York, NY, 1855; d. 17 Feb 1920.

Comont, Mathilde: b. Bordeaux, Fr, 9 Sep 1886; d. Los Angeles, CA, 21 Jun 1938.

Compson, Betty: b. Beaver, UT, 18 Mar 1897; d. Glendale, CA, 18 Apr 1974.

Compson, John R. (John R. Cumpson): b. 1868; d. New York, NY, 15 Mar 1913.

Compton, Charles: b. Mount Vernon, NY, 10 Aug 1886; d. 19??.

Compton, Dixie: b. Louisville, KY, 1886; d. 19??

Compton, Fay: b. London, Eng, 18 Sep 1894; d. London, Eng, 12 Dec 1978.

Compton, Juliette: b. Columbus, GA, 3 May 1899; d. Pasadena, CA, 19 Mar 1989.

Compton, Viola: b. London, Eng, 1886; d. Birchington-On-Sea, Eng, 7 Apr 1971.

Comstock, Clarke: b. Yukatan, MN, 7 Jan 1862; d. Los Angeles, CA, 24 May 1934.

Condon, Jackie: b. Los Angeles, CA, 24 Mar 1918; d. Inglewood, CA, 13 Oct 1977.

Cone, Mrs. Nancy Stewart: b. 18??; d. Cincinnati, OH, 23 Nov 1916.

Coniber, Elizabeth Jenkins: b. 1878; d. Caldwell, NJ, 18 Jan 1965.

Conklin, Charles (Heinie): b. San Francisco, CA, 16 Jul 1880; d. Los Angeles, CA, 30 Jul 1959.

Conklin, Chester: b. Oskaloosa, IA, 11 Jan 1886; d. Los Angeles, CA, 11 Oct 1971.

Conklin, Frank: b. Atchison, KS, 15 Apr 1888; d. 6 Jun 1945.

Conklin, Frederick Meade: b. 1874; d. Long Island, NY, 22 Jan 1929.

Conklin, William: b. Brooklyn, NY, 25 Dec 1872; d. Los Angeles, CA, 21 Mar 1935.

Conkwright, Arthur Bliss: b. Sigel, IL, 2 Mar 1882; d. Palm Springs, CA, 3 Feb 1957.

Conlan, Frank: b. Ireland, 1874; d. East Islip, NY, 24 Aug 1955.

Conley, Effie: b. Norwich, CT, 1857; d. 19??.

Conley, George: b. 1887; d. Los Angeles, CA, ? Nov 1929.

Conley, Harry J.: b. 1887; d. Cleveland, OH, 23 Jun 1975.

Conley, Lige: b. Los Angeles, CA, 5 Dec 1899; d. Los Angeles, CA, 11 Dec 1937.

Conley, Onest: b. Evanston, IL, ????; d. Los Angeles Co, CA, 8 Oct 1989.

Conliss, Edward B.: b. 1901; d. Toledo, OH, 3 Aug 1981.

Connelly, Bobby: b. Brooklyn, NY, 4 Apr 1909; d. Lynbrook, NY. 5 Jul 1922.

Connelly, Edward: b. New York, NY, 30 Dec 1855; d. Los Angeles, CA, 20 Nov 1928.

Connelly, Erwin: b. Chicago, IL, ? May 1879; d. Los Angeles, CA, 12 Feb 1931.

Connelly, Jane: b. Port Huron, MI. 2 May 1883; d. Los Angeles, CA, 25 Oct 1925.

Connelly, Marc: b. McKeesport, PA, 13 Dec 1890; d. New York, NY, 21 Dec 1980.

Conness, Robert: b. La Salle County, IL, 24 Dec 1867; d. Portland, ME, 15 Jan 1941.

Connolly, Regina: b. 1892; d. New York, NY, 12 Mar 1926.

Connolly, Walter: b. Cincinnati, OH, 8 Apr 1887; d. Los Angeles, CA, 28 May 1940.

Connor, Edward: b. 18??; d. New York, NY, 14 May 1932.

Connor, Velma: b. 1905; d. Los Angeles, CA, 19 Jul 1987.

Connor, Virginia M.: b. Los Angeles, CA, 28 Jul 1920; d. Rancho Mirage, CA, 27 Feb 1987.

Connors, George (Buck): b. San Sabag TX, 22 Nov 1880; d. 19??.

Conquest, Arthur: b. London, Eng, 1875; d. London, Eng, 6 Dec 1945.

Conrad-Schlenther, Paula: b. Germany, 27 Feb 1860; d. 9 Aug 1938.

Conroy, Larry: b. New York State, 1894; d. New York, NY, 29 Jun 1922.

Constant, Max: b. France, ????; d. Kern Co, CA, 19 May 1943.

Conti, Albert: b. Trieste, Italy, 29 Jar 1887; d. Los Angeles, CA, 18 Jan 1967.

Converse, Thelma Morgan, b. Lucerne, Switz, 1904; d. New York, NY, 25 Jan 1970.

Conville, Robert: b. Maine, 1881; d. Los Angeles Co, CA, 28 Feb 1950.

Conway, Jack: b. Ireland, ????; d. Forest Hills, NY, ? May 1951.

Conway, Jack: b. Graceville, MN, 17 Jul 1887; d. Pacific Palisades, CA, 11 Oct 1952.

Conway, Joseph: b. Philadelphia, PA, c. 1889; d. Philadelphia, PA, 28 Feb 1959.

Conway, Mrs. Lizzie: b. Philadelphia, PA, 1845; d. Milwaukee, WI, 4 May 1916.

Conway, William: b. 1876; d. New York, NY, 13 Oct 1924.

Conyers, Joseph: b. County Mayo, Ire, 1854; d. New York, NY, 25 Jun 1920.

Coogan, Jackie: b. Los Angeles, CA, 26 Oct 1914; d. Santa Monica, CA, 1 Mar 1984.

Coogan, John: b. Syracuse, NY, 1880; d. San Diego, CA, 4 May 1935.

Coogan, Mrs. Lillian: b. 1892; d. Los Angeles, CA, 23 Oct 1977.

Cook, Clyde: b. Port Macquarie, Austral, 16 Dec 1891; d. Carpinteria, CA, 13 Aug 1984.

Cook, Lillian: b. Hot Springs, AR, 1898; d. New York, NY, 14 Mar 1918.

Cook, Warren: b. Boston, MA. 23 May 1878; d. East Islip, NY, 2 May 1939.

Cooke, Albert G. (Al): b. Los Angeles, CA, 1882; d. Santa Monica, CA, 6 Jul 1935.

Cooke, Baldwin C.: b. New York, NY, 10 Mar. 1888; d. Los Angeles, CA, 31 Dec 1953.

Cooke, Ethyle: b. Lynn, MA, 4 Aug 1880; d. Waukesha, WI, 20 Apr 1949.

Cooke, John J.: b. New York State, 1 Oct 1876; d. 2 Oct 1921.

Cooke, Pearl: b. 18??; d. Portland, OR, 15 Dec 1917.

Cooke, Stephen Beach: b, 1898; d. Cooperstown, NY, 16 Sep 1948.

Cooksey, Cartis: b. Indiana, 9 Dec 1891; d. Los Angeles, CA, 19 Apr 1962.

Cookson, S. A.: b. 1869; d. 27 Feb 1947.

Cooley, Frank: b. Natchez, MS, 1870; d. Los Angeles, CA, 6 Jul 1941.

Cooley, Hallam: b. Brooklyn, NY, 8 Feb 1895; d. Tiburon, CA, 20 Mar 1971.

Cooley, James: b. Nelsonvllle, OH, 188O; d. Los Angeles, CA, 5 Nov 1948.

Coombs, Boyce: b. 1890; d. Chicago, IL, 11 Mar 1934.

Coombs, Guy: b. Washington, DC, ? Oct 1882; d. 19??.

Coombs, Jack (Colby Jack): b. LeGrand, IA, 1883; d. Palestine, TX, 15 Apr 1957.

Cooper, Ashley: b. Sydney, Austral, 1882; d. New York, NY, 3 Jan 1952.

Cooper, Claude H.: b. London, Eng, 1881; d. Laurelton, NY, 20 Jul 1932.

Cooper, Dulcie: b. Sydney, Austral, 1904; d. New York, NY, 3 Sep 1981.

Cooper, Earl P.: b. 1886; d. Atwater, CA, 22 Oct 1965.

Cooper, Edna Mae: b. Baltimore, MD, 19 Jul 1900; d. Woodland Hills, CA, 27 Jun 1986.

Cooper, Frank Kemble: b. Worcester, Eng, 22 May 1857; d. New York, NY, 27 Dec 1918.

Cooper, Gary: b. Helena, MT, 7 May 1901; d. Los Angeles, CA, 13 May 1961.

Cooper, George H.: b. Newark, NJ, 18 Dec 1891; d. Tucson, AZ, 9 Dec 1943.

Cooper, Georgia: b. Michigan, 31 Jul 1882; d. Los Angeles, CA, 3 Sep 1968.

Cooper, Gladys: b. London, Eng, 18 Dec 1888; d. Henley-on-Thames, Oxf, Eng, 17 Nov 1971.

Cooper, Harry: b. 1882; d. Los Angeles, CA, 28 Aug 1957.

Cooper, Lillian Kemble: b. London, Eng, 21 Mar 1892; d. Los Angeles, CA, 4 May 1977.

Cooper, Merian C.: b. Jacksonville, FL, 24 Oct 1893; d. Coronado, CA, 21 Apr 1973.

Cooper, Miriam: b. Baltimore, MD, 7 Nov 1894; d. Charlottesville, VA, 12 Apr 1976.

Cooper, Olive: b. 31 Jul 1892; d. Los Angeles, CA, 17 Jun 1987.

Cooper, Tex: b. Texas, 21 Apr 1876; d. Los Angeles, CA, 29 Mar 1951.

Coquelin, Constant-Benoit: b. Boulogne-sur-Mer, Fr, 22 Jan 1841; d. Ont-aux-Dames, Fr, 27 Jar 1909.

Corbett, Ben: b. Hudson, IL, 6 Feb 1892; d. Los Angeles, CA, 19 May 1961.

Corbett, James: b. San Francisco, CA, 1 Sep 1866; d. Bayside, NY, 18 Feb 1933.

Corbin, Virginia Lee: b. Prescott, AZ, 5 Dec 1910; d. Winfield, IL, 4 Jun 1942.

Corda, Maria: b. Deva, Hungary, 4 May 1902; d. 19??.

Cording, Harry: b. England, 26 Apr 1891; d. Sun Valley, CA, 1 Sep 1954.

Corelli, Marie: b. 18??; d. Detroit, MI, 10 May 1954.

Corey, Jim: b. 1883; d. Los Angeles, CA, 10 Jan 1956.

Cornwall, Anne: b. Brooklyn, NY, 17 Jan 1897; d. Van Nuys, CA, 2 Mar 1980.

Corrado, Gino (Eugene Corey): b. Florence, Italy, 9 Feb 1893; d. Woodland Hills, CA, 23 Dec 1982.

Corregan, Donald W.: b. 18??; d. Syracuse, NY, 2 May 1915.

Corrigan, D'Arcy: b. County Cork, Ire, 2 Jan 1870; d. Los Angeles, CA, 25 Dec 1945.

Corrigan, Emmett: b. Amsterdam, Holland, 5 Jun 1871; d. Los Angeles, CA, 29 Oct 1932.

Corrigan, James: b. Ohio, 17 Oct 1867; d. Los Angeles, CA, 28 Feb 1929.

Corrigan, Lloyd: b. San Francisco, CA, 16 Oct 1900; d. Woodland Hills, CA, Nov 1969.

Corsi, Antonio: b. ????; d. Los Angeles, CA, 4 Dec 1924.

Cort, John: b. Woodstock, CT, 1859; d. Stanford, CT, 17 Nov 1929.

Cortez, Armand F.: b. Nimes, Fr, 16 Aug 1880; d. San Francisco, CA, 19 Nov 1948.

Cortez, Ricardo: b. Brooklyn, NY, 19 Sep 1899; d. New York, NY, 28 Apr 1977.

Corthell, Herbert: b. Boston, MA, 20 Jan 1878; d. Los Angeles, CA, 23 Jan 1947.

Cosgrave, Jack: b. Pennsylvania, 29 Sep 1875; d. 27 Jan 1925.

Cosgrave, Luke: b. Ballaghderreen, Ire, 6 Aug 1862; d. Calabasas, CA, 28 Jun 1949.

Cosgrove, Charles: b. Delaware, IA, 17 Nov 1865; d. Los Angeles, CA, 12 Dec 1943.

Cosgrove, Larry Sheldon: b. Baltimore, MD, 1882; d. 19??

Cossar, John Hay: b. London, Eng, 2 Jan 1858; d. Los Angeles, CA, 28 Apr 1935.

Cossart, Ernest: b. Cheltenham, Gloucs, Eng, 24 Sep 1876; d. New York, NY, 21 Jan 1951.

Costa, Sebastiano: b. Italy, 1876; d. New Rochelle, NY, 18 Jul 1935.

Coste, Maurice R.: b. 1875; d. Chatham, Can, 22 Mar 1963.

Costello, Dolores: b. Pittsburgh, PA, 17 Sep 1905; d. Fallbrook, CA, 1 Mar 1979.

Costello, Helene: b. New York, NY, 21 Jun 1903; d. Los Angeles, CA, 26 Jan 1957.

Costello, John L.: b. New York, NY, 1878; d. Los Angeles Co, CA, 29 Jan 1946.

Costello, Mrs. Mae A.: b. Brooklyn, NY, 1882; d. Los Angeles, CA, 2 Aug 1929.

Costello, Maurice: b. Pittsburgh, PA, 22 Feb 1877; d. Los Angeles, CA, 29 Oct 1950.

Costello, William: b. 2 Feb 1898; d. San Jose, CA, 9 Oct 1971.

Cotter, Harry A.: b. Philadelphia, PA, 1880; d. Chicago, IL, 10 Jun 1947.

Cotter, Louise: b. 1884; d. Portland, OR, 11 Jun 1930.

Cotterlly, Mathilde: b. Hamburg, Ger, 7 Feb 1851; d. Tuckerton, NJ, 15 Jun 1933.

Cotton, Lucy: b. Houston, TX, 1891; d. Miami Beach, FL, 12 Dec 1948.

Cotton, Richardson: b. 18??; d. Ephraim, WI, 24 Sep 1916.

Couderc, Pierre M.: b. Paris, Fr, 18 Nov 1896; d. Santa Monica, CA, 6 Oct 1966.

Coulson, Roy: b. Streator, IL, 13 Sep 1890; d. San Bernardino, CA, 10 May 1944.

Coulter, Frazer: b. Smith Falls, Can, 20 Aug 1848; d. East Islip, NY, 26 Jan 1937.

Court, Florence (Lotta Miles): b. 1899; d, Los Angeles, CA, 25 Jul 1937.

Courtenay, William: b. Worcester, MA, 19 Jun 1875; d. Rye, NY, 20 Apr 1933.

Courteney, Fay: b. San Francisco, CA, 7 Oct 1895; d. New York, NY, 18 Jul 1943.

Courtleigh, William: b. Guelph, Ont, Can, 28 Jun 1867; d. Rye, NY, 27 Dec 1930.

Courtleigh, William, Jr.: b. Buffalo, NY, 28 Jun 1892; d. Philadelphia, PA, 13 Mar 1918.

Courtney, Dan: b. 5 Aug 1896; d. Los Angeles, CA, 30 Apr 1982.

Courtney, Oscar W.: b. 1877; d, Chicago, IL, 18 Jun 1962.

Courtot, Marguerite: b. Summit, NJ, 20 Aug 1897; d. Long Beach, CA, 28 May 1986.

Courtwright, William: b. New Milford, IL, 10 Feb 1848; d. Ione, CA, 6 Mar 1933.

Coventry, Florence: b. New Brunswick, Can, 1874; d. New York, NY, 22 Nov 1939.

Covington, Z. Wall: b. Bone Terre, MO, 21 Jan 1876; d. Los Angeles Co, CA, 25 Sep 1941.

Cowan, Lynn: b. Iowa Falls, IA, 8 Jun 1894; d. Pensacola, FL, 29 Aug 1973.

Coward, Noel: b. Teddington, Middlesex, Eng, 16 Dec 1899; d. Blue Harbor, Jamaica, 26 Mar 1973.

Cowie, Laura: b. Aberdeen, Scot, 7 Apr 1892; d. 11 Feb 1969.

Cowl, George: b. Blackpool, Eng, 24 Feb 1878; d. Los Angeles, CA, 4 Apr 1942.

Cowl, Jane: b. Boston, MA, 14 Dec 1885; d. Santa Monica, CA, 22 Jun 1950.

Cowles, Jules: b. Farmington, CT, 7 Oct 1877; d. Los Angeles, CA, 22 May 1943.

Cowper, William C.: b. Manchester, Eng, 1853; d. 13 Jun 1918.

Cox, Robert: b. 1895; d. Phoenix, AZ, 8 Sep 1974.

Cox, Thomas F.: b. 1892; d. La Crescenta, CA, 6 Dec 1914.

Coxen, Edward: b. London, Eng, 8 Aug 1884; d. Los Angeles, CA, 21 Nov 1954.

Coyan, Betty: b. 1901; d. Council Bluffs, IA, 9 Feb 1935.

Coyle, Marion J.: b. 1897; d. North Hollywood, CA, 23 May 1981.

Coyle, Walter V.: b. 1888; d. Freeport, NY, 3 Aug 1948.

Craig, Blanche: b. Culter, ME, 6 Jan 1866; d. Los Angeles, CA, 23 Sep 1940.

Craig, Mrs. Charles G. (Frances): b. Oregon, 10 Oct 1866; d. Los Angeles, CA, 21 Jul 1925.

Craig, Edith: b. Harpenden, Eng, 9 Dec 1869; d. Small Hythe, Kent, Eng, 27 Mar 1947.

Craig, Edith; b. 1908; d. Tenafly, NJ, 2 Mar 1979.

Craig, Edward Gordan: b. Stevenage, Herts, Eng, 16 Jan 1872; d. Vence, Fr, 29 Jul 1966.

Craig, Godfrey: b. Copper Cliff, Ont, Can, 20 Jan 1915; d. Los Angeles, CA, 26 May 1941.

Craig, Nell: b. Princeton, NJ, 13 Jun 1890; d. Woodland Hills, CA, 5 Jan 1965.

Cramer, Richard: b, Bryan, OH, 3 Jul 1890; d. Los Angeles, CA, 9 Aug 1960.

Crampton, Howard: b. New York, NY, 12 Dec 1865; d. 15 Jun 1922.

Crandall, James (Doc): b. Wadena, IN, 8 Oct 1887; d; Bell, CA, 17 Aug 1951.

Crane, Dixie: b. 1888; d. Los Angeles, CA, 18 Nov 1936.

Crane, Ethel Gordon: b. Illinois, 1877; d. San Bernardino, CA, 13 Oct 1930.

Crane, Frank H.: b. San Francisco, CA, 1873; d. Los Angeles, CA, 31 Aug 1948.

Crane, Gardner: b. Boston, MA, 4 Jul 1867; d. Los Angeles, CA, 8 Jun 1939.

Crane, James: b. Rantoul, IL , 9 Aug 1889; d. San Gabriel, CA, 3 Jun 1968.

Crane, Ogden: b. Brooklyn, NY, 1 Sep 1873; d. West Hollywood, CA, 14 May 1940.

Crane, Ward: b. Albany, NY, 18 May 1890; d. Saranac Lake, NY, 21 Jul 1928.

Crane, William H.: b. Leicester, MA, 30 Apr 1845; d. Los Angeles, CA, 7 Mar 1928.

Crane, William H.: b. Brooklyn, NY, 1886; d. Scranton, PA, 22 Jan 1957.

Craske, Leonard: b. England, 1877; d. Boston, MA, 29 Aug 1950.

Craven, Frank: b. Boston, MA, 24 Aug 1875; d. Beverly Hills, CA, 1 Sep 1945.

Craven, Walter: b. 1863; d. Knoxville, TN, 25 Nov 1918.

Crawford, Clifton: b. Edinburgh, Scot, 1875; d. London, Eng, 3 Jan 1920.

Crawford, Capt. Jack: b. County Donegal, Ire, 4 Mar 1847; d. 27 Feb 1917.

Crawford, Joan: b. San Antonio, TX, 23 Mar 1904; d. New York, NY, 10 May 1977.

Crawford, Kathryn: b. Wellsboro, PA, 5 Oct 1908; d. Pasadena, CA, 7 Dec 1980.

Crawford, Sam: b. Wahoo, NE, 18 Apr 1880; d. Los Angeles, CA, 15 Jun 1968.

Crawford, Timothy: b. 1904; d. 13 Jun 1978.

Crawley, Constance: b. London, Eng, 30 Mar 1879; d. Los Angeles, CA, 17 Mar 1919.

Crehan, Joseph: b. Baltimore, MD, 12 Jul 1884; d. North Hollywood, CA, 15 Apr 1966.

Cressall, Maud: b. Demrera, Bri Guiana, 5 Dec 1886; d. Kingsdown, Kent, Eng, ? May 1962.

Cressy, Will M.: b. Bradford, NH, 29 Oct 1864; d. St. Petersburg, FL, 7 May 1930.

Creste, Rene: b. Paris, Fr, 1875; d. 1924.

Crews, Kay C.: b. 1901; d. San Antonio, TX, 29 Nov 1959.

Crews, Laura Hope: b. San Francisco, CA, 12 Dec 1879; d. New York, NY, 13 Nov 1942.

Crimmins, Daniel: b. Liverpool, Eng, 18 May 1863; A. Los Angeles, CA, 12 Jul 1945.

Criner, Lawrence: b. Texas, 19 Jul 1898; d. Los Angeles, CA, 8 Mar 1965.

Crinley, William A.: b. 18??; d. Los Angeles, CA, 1 Jan 1927.

Crisp, Donald: b. Aberfeddy, Scot, 27 Jul 1882; d. Woodland Hills, CA, 25 May 1974.

Criswell, Floyd: b. 17 Jun 1899; d. Los Angeles Co, CA, 28 Dec 1974.

Crittendon, T. D. (Trockwood Dwight Crittendon): b. Oakland, CA, 27 Sep 1878; d. Los Angeles, CA, 17 Feb 1938.

Crocker, Harry: b. San Francisco, CA, 2 Jul 1893; d. Los Angeles, CA, 23 May 1958.

Crocker, May B.: b. 19??; d. New York, NY, 1 Nov 1930.

Crockett, Charles B.: b. Baltimore, MD, 29 Dec 1870; d. Los Angeles, CA, 12 Jun 1934.

Crockett, John: b. ????; d. Los Angeles, CA, 21 Feb 1922.

Croker-King, Charles: b. Rock Holm, Yorks, Eng, 30 Apr 1873; d. 25 Oct 1951.

Crolius, Louise: b. 18??; d. Los Angeles, CA, 1 Jun 1931.

Cronin, Timothy: b. 1860; d. Hawthorne, NY, 6 Jan 1919.

Crosby, Walter Hull: b. ????; d. New York, NY, 14 Apr 1921.

Crosby, Zelda: b. ????; d. New York, NY, 19 Jun 1921.

Crosland, Alan: b. New York, NY, 10 Aug 1894; d. Los Angeles, CA, 16 Jul 1936.

Crosman, Henrietta: b. Wheeling, WV, 2 Sep 1861; d. Pelham Manor, NY, 31 Oct 1944.

Cross, Alfred F.: b. 1891; d. San Diego, CA, 28 Jan 1938.

Cross, Leach: b. New York, NY, 12 Feb 1886; d. New York, NY, 7 Sep 1957.

Cross, Oliver A.: b. New York, NY, 18 Jul 1894; d. Los Angeles Co. CA, 19 Feb 1971.

Cross, Wellington: b. Illinois, 3 Apr 1887; d. New York, NY, 12 Oct 1975.

Croseley, Syd: b. London, Eng, 18 Nov 1885; d. Troon, Scot, ? Nov 1960.

Crosthwaite, Ivy: b. San Diego, CA, 1898; d. Los Angeles, CA, 8 Nov 1962.

Crowell, Josephine: b. Canada, 18??; d. Amityville, NY, 27 Jul 1932.

Crume, Camilla: b. 1874; d. Norwalk, CT, 20 Mar 1952.

Cruster, Aud: b. 1889; d. Moline, IL, 18 May 1938.

Crute, Sally: b. Chattanooga, TN, 1886; d. Miami, FL, 12 Aug 1971.

Cruze, James: b. Five Points, UT, 27 Mar 1884; d. Los Angeles, CA, 3 Aug 1942.

Cruze, Julie Jane: b. New York, NY, 24 Oct 1913; d. San Diego, CA, 27 Jul 1946.

Cruze, Mae: b. Utah, 24 May 1881; d. Los Angeles, CA, 16 Aug 1965.

Cudahy, Michael: b. 1908; d. Los Angeles, CA, 14 Feb 1947.

Cullen, Edward: b. 1895; d. New York, NY, 27 Jul 1964.

Cullington, Margaret: b. New Rochelle, NY, 1886; d. Los Angeles, CA, 18 Jul 1925.

Cullison, Webster: b. Baltimore, MD, 1880; d. Glendale, CA, 7 Jul 1938.

Cumming, Dorothy: b. Burrows, Austral, 12 Apr 1899; d. New York, NY, 10 Dec 1983.

Cummings, Catherine: b. Grantsburg, IL, 1871; d. Los Angeles, CA, 8 Jul 1950.

Cummings, Charles Eugene: b. Indiana, 18??; d. Los Angeles, CA, 4 Oct 1916.

Cummings, Forrest H.: b. San Francisco, CA, 1877; d. Toronto, Can, 15 May 1929.

Cummings, Frances: b. ????; d. New York, NY, 12 Aug 1923.

Cummings, George F.: b. Richmond, VA, 4 Jul 1880; d. Los Angeles Co, CA, 11 Mar 1946.

Cummings, Irving: b. New York, NY, 9 Oct 1888; d. Los Angeles, CA, 18 Apr 1959.

Cummings, Richard H.: b. New Haven, CT, 20 Aug 1858; d. Los Angeles, CA, 25 Dec 1938.

Cummings, Robert: b. Massachusetts, 8 Feb 1865; d. Los Angeles Co, CA, 22 Jul 1949.

Cummings, Ruth (Ruth Sinclair); b. 1894; d. Woodland Hills, CA, 6 Dec 1984.

Cunard, Grace: b. Columbus, OH, 8 Apr 1893; d. Woodland Hills, CA, 19 Jan 1967.

Cunard, Mina: b. Columbus, OH, 16 Dec 1894; d. Woodland Hills CA, 9 Aug 1978.

Cuneo, Lester: b. Chicago, IL, 25 Oct 1888; d. Los Angeles, CA, 1 Nov 1925.

Cunning, Patrick: b. Santa Clara, CA, 23 May 1905; d. Fresno, CA, 13 Mar 1973.

Cunningham, Arthur: b. San Francisco, CA, 1888; d, San Francisco, CA, 29 Nov 1955.

Cunningham, George: b. New York State, 11 Feb 1904; d. Los Angeles, CA, 30 Apr 1962.

Curran, J. P.: b. 18??; d. Sawtelle, CA, 11 Jan 1919.

Curran, Thomas A,: b. Australia, 1879; d. Los Angeles, CA, 24 Jan 1941.

Currie, Clive: b. Birmingham, Eng, 26 Mar 1877; d. London, Eng, 25 May 1935.

Currier, Frank; b. Norwich, CT, 4 Sep 1857; d. Los Angeles, CA, 22 Apr 1928.

Curtis, Allen: b. New York, 1879; d. Santa Anita, CA, 24 Nov 1961.

Curtis, Dick: b. Newport, KY, 11 May 1902; d. Los Angeles, CA, 3 Jan 1952.

Curtis, Jack: b. San Francisco, CA, 28 May 1880; d. Los Angeles, CA, 16 Mar 1956.

Curtis, John W.: b. 1846; d. New York, NY, 21 Jul 1925.

Curtis, Spencer M.: b. 1858; d. Long Beach, CA, 13, Jul 1921.

Cusack, Cyril: b. Durban, So. Africa, 26 Nov 1910; d. London, Eng, 6 Oct 1993.

Custer, Bob: b. Frankfort, KY, 18 Oct 1898; d. Redondo Beach, CA, 27 Dec 1974.

Cuttica, Primo: b. Genoa, Italy, 1876; d. Ilario Legure, Italy ? Oct 1921.

D

Dagnall, Ells: b. 1860; d. England, 26 Dec 1935.

Dagover, Lil: b. Madiven, Java, 30 Sep 1894; d. Germany, 23 Jan 1980,

Dailey, Joseph: b. 1862; d. Englewood, NJ, 23 Sep 1940.

Dalberg, Camille: b. Frankfurt, Ger, 28 Jun 1881; d. 19??.

D'Albrook, Sidney: b. Chicago, IL, 3 May 1886; d. Los Angeles Co, CA, 30 May 1948.

D'Alcy, Jeanne: b. Vaujours, Fr, 20 Mar 1865; d. 1956.

Dale, Dorothy: b. 1883; d. Los Angeles, CA, 13 May 1957.

Dale, Margaret: b. Philadelphia, PA, 6 Mar 1876; d. New York, NY, 23 Mar 1972.

Dale, Marjorie: b. 1897; d. Boston, MA, 21 Apr 1979.

D'Algy, Antoine: b. Spain, 1905; d. 29 Apr 1977.

Dalmores, Aimee: b. 18??; d. 22 Jan 1920.

Dalroy, Harry (Rube): b. 1879; d. Los Angeles, CA, 8 Mar 1954.

Dalsace, Lucien: b. France, 1893; d. Hay-les-Roses, Fr, ? Jul 1980.

Dalton, Charles: b. England, 29 Aug 1864; d. Stamford, CT, 11 Jun 1942.

Dalton, Dorothy: b. Chicago, IL, 22 Sep 1893; d. Scarsdale, NY, 13 Apr 1972.

Dalton, Emmett: b. Bellon, MO, 3 May 1861; d. Los Angeles, CA, 13 Jul 1937.

Dalton, Irene: b. 1901; d. Chicago, IL, 15 Aug 1934.

Daly, Arnold: b. Brooklyn, NY, 4 Oct 1875; d. New York, NY, 13 Jan 1927.

Daly, Hazel: b. 8 Oct c. 1890; d. 19??.

Daly, James L.: b. 1852; d. Philadelphia, PA, 9 Nov 1933.

Daly, Orlando: b. Leamington, Eng, 1873; d. Boston, MA, 17 Jan 1929.

Dalzell, Lydia St. Clair, b. 18??; d. 28 Mar 1974.

d'Ambricourt, Adrienne: b. Paris, Fr, 2 Jun 1878; d. Los Angeles, CA, 6 Dec 1957.

Damia (Marie-Louise Damien): b. 1889; d. Saint Cloud, Fr, 30 Jan 1978.

Damita, Lili: b. Bordeaux, Fr, 10 Jan 1904; d. Palm Beach, FL, 21 Mar 1994.

Damman, Gerhard: b. Cologne, Ger, 30 Mar 1883; d. Bad Ischl, Austria, 21 Feb 1946.

Dampier, Claude: b. Clapham, Eng, 1878; d. London, Eng, 1 Jan 1955.

Damroth, George: b. 1894; d. New York, NY, 10 Feb 1939.

Dan, Zhao: b. 1915; d. Peking, China, 10 Oct 1980.

Dana, Clara L.: b. 1878; d. Los Angeles, CA, 23 Jun 1956.

Dana, Viola: b. Brooklyn, NY, 28 Jun 1897; d. Woodland Hills, CA, 3 Jul 1987.

Dandy, Jess: b. Rochester, NY, 1871; d. Brookline, MA, 15 Apr 1923.

Dane, Karl: b. Copenhagen, Denmark, 12 Oct 1886; d. Los Angeles, CA, 14 Apr 1934.

Danforth, William: b. Syracuse, NY, 13 May 1867; d. Skaneateles, NY, 16 Apr 1941.

Daniels, Bebe: b. Dallas, TX, 14 Jan 1901; d. London, Eng, 16 Mar 1971.

Daniels, Frank: b. Dayton, OH, 1860; d. Palm Beach, FL, 12 Jan 1935.

Daniels, Josephus: b. 1863; d. Raleigh, NC, 15 Jan 1948.

Daniels, Mickey: b. Utah, 11 Oct 1914; d. San Ysidro, CA, 20 Aug 1970.

Daniels, Phyllis: b. 1886; d. London, Eng, 20 Feb 1959.

Daniels, Walter: b. 1875; d. Los Angeles, CA, 30 Mar 1928.

Danis, Ida: b. France, 18??; d. Nice, Fr, 9 Apr 1921.

Dansey, Herbert: b. Rome, Italy, 6 Mar 1870; d. New York, NY, 30 May 1917.

Dansford, Granville: b. 18??; d. Honolulu, HI, 27 Jun 1924.

Darby, John J.: b. Long Beach, CA, 27 Aug 1893; d. Los Angeles Co, CA, 13 Dec 1946.

D'Arcy, Camille: b. 1879; d. Chicago, IL, 26 Sep 1916.

D'Arcy, Hugh A.: b. Paris, Fr, 5 Mar 1843; d. New York, NY, 11 Nov 1925.

D'Arcy, Roy: b. San Francisco, CA, 10 Feb 1894; d. Redlands, CA, 15 Nov 1969.

Dare, Dorris: b. 1899; d. Los Angeles, CA, 16 Aug 1927.

Dare, Eva: b. 18??; d. England, 15 Oct 1931.

Dare, Phyllis: b. London, Eng, 15 Aug 1890; d. Brighton, Eng, 27 Apr 1975.

Dare, Virginia: b. Pennsylvania, 6 Aug 1882; d. Woodland Hills, CA, 8 Jul 1962.

Dare, Zene: b. London, Eng, 4 Feb 1885; d. London, Eng, 11 Mar 1975.

Darien, Frank: b. New Orleans, LA, 18 Mar 1876; d. Los Angeles, CA, 20 Oct 1955.

Dark Cloud (Elizah Tahamont): b. 18??; d. 1918.

Dark Cloud, Beulah: b. 18??; d. Thermolite, CA, 2 Jan 1946.

Darkfeather, Princess Mona: b. Los Angeles, CA, 13 Jan 1881; d. Los Angeles, CA, 3 Sep 1977.

Darley, Brian: b. England, 1858; d. New York, NY, 25 Feb 1924.

Darling, Gladys: b. Chicago, IL, 1898; d. Garden City, CA, 5 Jan 1983.

Darling, Ida: b. New York, NY, 1875; d. Los Angeles, CA, 5 Jun 1936.

Darlings Ruth: b. 18??; d. San Francisco, CA, 11 Sep 1918.

Darmond, Grace: b. Toronto, Can, 20 Nov 1898; d. Los Angeles, CA, 7 Oct 1963.

Darnell, Jean: b. Sherman, TX, 1888; d. Dallas, TX, 19 Jan 1961.

Darnley, Herbert: b. Chatham, Kent, Eng, 1872; d. London, Eng, 7 Feb 1947.

Darnold, Blaine A.: b. 1886; d. Kansas City, MO, 11 Mar 1926.

Darro, Frankie: b. Chicago, IL, 22 Dec 1918; d. Huntington Beach, CA, 26 Dec 1976.

Darrow, Clarence S.: b. Kinsman, OH, 18 Apr 1857; d. Chicago, IL, 13 Mar 1938.

Darrow, John: b. New York, NY, 17 Jul 1907; d. Malibu, CA, 24 Feb 1980.

Darvas, Charles: b. Budapest, Hungary, 2 Mar 1880; d. 14 Apr 1930.

Darwell, Jane: b. Palmyra, MO, 15 Oct 1879; d. Woodland Hills, CA, 13 Aug 1967.

Dashiell, Willard, b. Salisbury, MD, 1867; d. Holyoke, MA, 19 Apr 1943.

Daube, Belle (Harda Daube): b. Northampton, Eng, 1887; d. Los Angeles, CA, 25 May 1959.

Daugherty, Jack (Jack Dougherty): b. Bowling Green, MO, 16 Nov 1895; d. Los Angeles, CA, 16 May 1938.

Daumery, Carrie: b. Amsterdam, Holland, 25 Mar 1863; d. Los Angeles, CA, 1 Jul 1938.

Daven, Andre: b. Paris, Fr, ? Mar 1900; d. Paris, Fr, 17 Nov 1981.

Davenport, A. Bromley (Arthur Bromley Davenport): b. Baginton, Warwick, Eng, 29 Oct 1867; d. London, Eng, 15 Dec 1946.

Davenport, Alice: b. New York, NY, 29 Feb 1864; d. Los Angeles, CA, 24 Jun 1936.

Davenport, Dorothy: b. Boston, MA, 13 Mar 1895; d. Woodland Hills, CA, 12 Oct 1977.

Davenport, Edgar Loomis: b. Roxbury, MA, 7 Feb 1862; d. Boston, MA, 25 Jul 1918.

Davenport, Harry: b. New York, NY, 19 Jan 1866; d. Los Angeles, CA, 9 Aug 1949.

Davenport, Harry J.: b. 7 May 1857; d. Glendale, CA, 20 Feb 1929.

Davenport, Helen (Helene Reynolds): b. 1865; d. New York, NY, 31 May 1928.

Davenport, Kate: b. New York, NY, 7 Jun 1896; d. West Hollywood, CA, 7 Dec 1954.

Davenport, Kenneth: b. Macon, MO, 1879; d. Los Angeles, CA, 10 Nov 1941.

Davenport, Milla: b. Zurich, Switz, 14 Feb 1871; d. Los Angeles, CA, 17 May 1936.

Davenport, William: b. 1867; d. Philadelphia, PA, 11 May 1941.

David, William: b. Vicksburg, MS, 1881; d. East Islip, NY, 10 Apr 1965.

Davidson, Dore: b. New York, NY, 16 Oct 1850; d. New York, NY, 7 Mar 1930.

Davidson, John: b. New York, NY, 25 Dec 1886; d. Los Angeles, CA, 15 Jan 1968.

Davidson, Max: b. Berlin, Ger, 23 May 1875; d. Woodland Hills, CA, 4 Sep 1950.

Davidson, William B.: b. Dobbs Ferry, NY, 16 Jun 1888; d. Santa Monica, CA, 28 Sep 1947.

Davies, David: b. 18??; d. Chicago, IL, ? May 1920.

Davies, Hamilton: b. 18??; d. Los Angeles, CA, 25 May 1922.

Davies, Howard: b. Liverpool, Eng, 18 May 1879; d. Los Angeles, CA, 30 Dec 1947.

Davies, Marion: b. Brooklyn, NY, 3 Jan 1897; d. Los Angeles, CA, 22 Sep 1961.

Davies, Reine: b. Montclair, NJ, 6 Jun 1892; d. Beverly Hills, CA, 2 Apr 1938.

Davies, Rosemary: b. Brooklyn, NY, 15 Jun 1903; d. Bel Air, CA, 20 Sep 1963.

Davis, Ann: b. 1893; d. New York, NY, 3 Sep 1961.

Davis, Conrad: b. 29 Feb 1915; d. Paramount, CA, 22 Dec 1969.

Davis, Edwards: b. Santa Clara, CA, 17 Jun 1867; d. Los Angeles, CA, 17 May 1936.

Davis, Fay: b. Houlton, ME, 15 Dec 1872; d. London, Eng, 26 Feb 1945.

Davis, George: b. Amsterdam, Holland, 7 Nov 1889; d. Los Angeles Co, CA, 19 Apr 1965.

Davis, Glenmore W. (Stuffy): b. 1880; d. Detroit, MI, 20 Aug 1958.

Davis, Hal: b. Ohio, 6 Oct 1909; d. Lancaster, CA, 4 Jan 1960.

Davis, Harry: b. 1874; d. New York, NY, 4 Apr 1929.

Davis, J. Gunnis (James): b. Sunderland, Durham, Eng, 21 Dec 1873; d. Los Angeles, CA, 22 Mar 1937.

Davis, Jackie: b. Los Angeles, CA, 1914; d. Santa Monica, CA, 3 Nov 1992.

Davis, James: b. 18??; d. Chicago, IL, ? Dec 1924.

Davis, Jefferson (Jeff); b. Cincinnati, OH, 1884; d. Cincinnati, OH 5 Apr 1968.

Davis, Mary: b. 1846; d. New York, NY, 24 Jun 1918.

Davis, Mildred: b. Philadelphia, PA, 22 Feb 1901; d. Los Angeles, CA, 18 Aug 1969.

Davis, Morgan: b. Ethel, MO, 2 May 1890; d. Riverside Co, CA, 2 Sep 1941.

Davis, Reed E.: b. 1893; d. 12 Oct 1984.

Davis, Roger: b. 20 Jan 1884; d. Woodland Hills, CA, 3 Mar 1980.

D'Avril, Yola: b. Belgium, 8 Apr 1907; d. Port Hueneme, CA, 2 Mar 1984.

Daw, Marjorie: b. Colorado Springs, CO, 19 Jan 1902; d. Huntington Beach, CA, 18 Mar 1979.

Dawkins, Irma L.: b. Columbia, SC, 25 Mar 1892; d. Raleigh, NC, 13 Oct 1972.

Dawn, Hazel: b. Ogden, UT, 23 Mar 1890; d. New York, NY, 28 Aug 1988.

Dawson, Doris: b. Goldfield, NV, 16 Apr 1909; d. Coral Gables, FL, 20 Apr 1966.

Dawson, Frank: b. England, 4 Jul 1870; d. Los Angeles, CA, 11 Oct 1953.

Dawson, Ivo: d. Rutlandshire, Eng, 13 Dec 1879; d. 7 Mar 1934.

Day, Edith: b. Minneapolis, MN, 10 Apr 1896; d. London, Eng, 1 May 1971.

Day, Frances: b. New York, NY, 16 Dec 1907; d. 1984.

Day, Josette; b. Paris, Fr, 31 Jul 1914; d. Paris, Fr, 29 Jun 1978.

Day, Juliette: b. Boston, MA, 1894; d. Northport, NY, 18 Sep 1957.

Day, Marie L.: b. Troy, NY, 1855; d. Cleveland, OH, 7 Nov 1939.

Day, Shannon (Sylvia Day): b. Austria, 5 Aug 1896; d. New York, NY, 24 Feb 1977.

Dayne, Blanche: b. Troy, NY, 25 Dec 1871; d. Hackensack, NJ, 27 Jun 1944.

Dayton, Frank: b. Boston, MA, 1865; d. New York, NY, 17 Oct 1924.

Daze, Mercedes: b. 1892; d. Los Angeles, CA, 18 Mar 1945.

Dazie, Mlle.: b. 1885; d. Miami Beach, FL, 12 Aug 1952.

Dean, Basil: b. Croydon, Eng, 27 Sep 1888; d. London, Eng, 22 Apr 1978.

Dean, Jack (John W. Dean): b. Bridgeport, CT, 1875; d. New York, NY, 23 Jan 1950.

Dean, Julia: b. St. Paul, MN, 13 May 1878; d. Los Angeles, CA, 18 Oct 1952.

Dean, Louis: b. Wilmington, DE, 1876; d. Honolulu, HI, 8 Apr 1933.

Dean, May: b. ????; d. Jamacia, NY, 28 Aug 1937.

Dean, Nelson: b. 1882; d. Detroit, MI, 19 Dec 1923.

Dean, Priscilla, b. New York, NY, 25 Nov 1896; d. Leonia, NJ, 27 Dec 1987.

Dean, Ralph: b. 21 Mar 1868; d. New York, NY, 15 Sep 1923.

Dean, Rosemary: b. Baltimore, MD, 1898; d. 12 Apr 1990.

Dean, Ruby: b. 1887; d. Cleveland, OH, 23 Feb 1935.

Dean, Wally (W. P. Deal); b. Pennsylvania, 26 Dec 1878; d. 1 Oct 1955.

Deane, Doris: b. La Crosse, WI, 20 Jan 1900; d. Los Angeles, CA, 24 Mar 1974.

Deane, Ralph: b. 1875; d. 4 Feb 1955.

De Angelis: Jefferson: b. San Francisco, CA, 30 Nov 1859; d. Orange, NJ, 20 Mar 1933.

Dearholt, Ashton (Richard Holt): b. Milwaukee, WI, 4 Apr 1894; d. Los Angeles, CA, 27 Apr 1942.

Dearing, Edgar: b. Ceres, CA, 4 May 1893; d. Woodland Hills, CA, 17 Aug 1974.

De Aubry, Diane: b. Sault St. Marie, MI, 1890; d. Santa Monica, CA, 23 May 1969.

Deaves, Ada: b. 1856; d. New York, NY, 18 Sep 1920.

De Balzac, Jeanne: b. France, ????; d. Paris, Fr, ? Apr 1930.

De Barre, Vivian: b. ????; d. Los Angeles, CA, 18 Jul 1985.

De Beck, Billy: b. 1890; d. New York, NY, 11 Nov 1942.

De Becker, Harold: b. London, Eng, 8 Jun 1889; d. Los Angeles, CA, 24 Jul 1947.

De Belleville, Frederick: b. Liege, Belgium, 17 Feb 1857; d. New York, NY, 25 Feb 1923.

De Bosset, Vera: b. St. Petersburg, Russ, 25 Dec 1888; d. New York, NY, 17 Sep 1982.

De Bray, Harold: b. 1874; d. Los Angeles, CA, 31 Oct 1932.

De Briac, Jean F.: b. France, 15 Aug 1891; d. Los Angeles Co, CA, 18 Oct 1970.

De Brugh, Aimee: b. Aberdeen, Scot, 18??; d. 2 Apr 1946.

De Brulier, Nigel: b. Bristol, Eng, 8 Jul 1877; d. Los Angeles, CA, 30 Jan 1948.

Debucourt, Jean: b. Paris, Fr, 19 Jan 1894; d. Paris, Fr, 22 Mar 1958.

De Camp, Frank: b. London, Eng, 1865; d. New York, NY, 18 Dec 1919.

De Carlton, George: b. Boston, MA, 30 Jun 1867; d. Saranac Lake, NY, 15 May 1935.

De Carlton, Grace: b. Boston, MA, 1890: d. Portland, ME, 19??

De Casalis, Jeanne: b. Basutoland, So Africa, 22 May 1892; d. London, Eng, 19 Aug 1966.

Decker, Kathryn Browne: b. Richmond, VA, ????; d. Colombo, Ceylon, 12 Feb 1919.

De Coma, Eddie: b. 1878; d. 30 Jul 1938.

De Conde, Syn M.: b. Brazil, 14 Jun 1894; d. Rio de Janeiro, Brazil, 28 May 1990.

De Cordoba, Pedro: b. New York, NY, 28 Sep 1881; d. Los Angeles, CA, 16 Sep 1950.

De Cordova, Rudolph: b. Kingston, Jamaica, 1860; d. London, Eng, 11 Jan 1941.

De Costa, Morris (Morris Miller): b. 1890; d. Phoenixville, PA, 6 Oct 1957.

De Courcy, Nenette (Nan Boardman): b. New York, NY, 21 Mar 1903; d. Fallbrook, CA, 9 Sep 1984.

Deed, Andre: b. Le Havre, Fr, 24 Feb 1879; d. Paris, Fr, 1938.

Deeley, Ben: b. California, 22 Jan 1878; d. Los Angeles, CA, 23 Sep 1924.

Deer, Diane (Diane Deering): b. 1894; d. New York, NY, 30 May 1979.

Deer, James Young: b. Dakota City, NE, 18??; d. New York, NY, ? Apr 1946.

Deer, John J.: b. 1861; d. St. Regis Reservation, 31 Mar 1940.

De Feraudy, Maurice: b. France, 1859; d. France, 12 May 1932.

De Foe, Annette: b. 1889; d. Los Angeles, CA, 6 Aug 1960.

De Forest, Hal: b. Portugal, 1862; d. New York, NY, 16 Feb 1938.

De Frece, Lauri: b. Liverpool, Eng, 1880; d; Deauville, Fr, 25 Aug 1921.

De Frietas, Cecil: b. 1890; d. Hawthorne, CA, 6 Dec 1925.

De Grasse, Joseph: b. Bathurst, NB, Can, 4 May 1873; d. Los Angeles, CA, 24 May 1940.

De Grasse, Sam: b. Bathurst, NB, Can, 20 Jun 1875; d. Los Angeles, CA, 29 Nov 1953.

DeGrey, Sydney: b. Unn, Eng, 16 Jun 1886; d. Los Angeles Co, CA, 30 Jun 1941.

De Guingand, Pierre: b. Paris, Fr, 6 Jun 1885; d. 10 Jun 1964.

De Haven, Carter: b. Chicago, IL, 5 Oct 1886; d. Woodland Hills, CA, 20 Jul 1977.

De Haven, Evelyn (Evelyn Byrd): b. 1906; d. Los Angeles, CA, 10 Jan 1990.

DeHaven, Flora Parker: b. Perth Amboy, NJ, 1 Sep 1883; d. Los Angeles, CA, 9 Sep 1950.

Dehelly, Jean: b. France, 1896; d. 1964.

De Jonge, Harry: b. 18??; d. Chicago, IL, 13 Mar 1927.

De Kowa, Viktor: b. Hochkirch, Ger, 8 Mar 1904; d. Berlin, Ger, 8 Apr 1973.

De Lacey, John: b. New York, NY, 1872; d. New York, NY, 18 Dec 1924.

De La Cruz, Joseph: b. Mexico, 19 Mar 1892; d. Los Angeles, CA, 14 Dec 1961.

De La Cruz, Juan: b. Copenhagen, Denmark, 4 Jun 1881; d. Orange Co, CA, 12 Nov 1953.

De La Mothe, Leon: b. New Orleans, LA, 1880; d. Woodland Hills, CA, 12 Jun 1943.

De La Motte, Marguerite: b. Duluth, MN, 22 Jun 1902; d. San Francisco, CA, 10 Mar 1950.

Delaney, Charles: b. New York, NY, 9 Aug 1892; d. Los Angeles, CA, 31 Aug 1959.

Delaney, Leo: b. Swanton, VT, 1885; d. New York, NY, 4 Feb 1920.

Delano, Gwen: b. 1882; d. Los Angeles, CA, 20 Nov 1954.

Delargo, Celia: b. 1901; d. San Francisco, CA, 3 Oct 1927.

Delaro, Hattie: b. Brooklyn, NY, 1861; d. New York, NY, 18 Apr 1941.

De Lay, Mel: b. 1900; d. Saugas, CA, 3 May 1947.

Delight, June: b. Rochester, NY, 1898; d. Carmel, GA, 3 Oct 1975.

De Liguoro, Guiseppe: b. Naples, Italy, 10 Jan 1869; d. Rome, Italy, 19 Mar 1944.

De Liguoro, Rina: b. Florence, Italy, 24 Jul 1892; d. Rome, Italy, 7 Apr 1966.

De Lima, Charles: b. 1872; d. Nice, Fr, 8 Aug 1954.

De Limur, Jean: b. Vannes, Brittany, Fr, 1887; d. Paris, Fr, 5 Jun 1976.

De Linsky, Victor: b. Moscow, Russ, 18 Mar 1883; d. Los Angeles, CA, 9 May 1951.

Dell, Rupert L.: b. Oxfordshire, Eng, 1881; d. Los Angeles, CA, 25 Oct 1945.

Del Mar, Claire: b. 1901; d. Carmel, CA, 9 Jan 1959.

Delmar, Kenny: b. Boston, MA, 1911; d. Stamford, CT, 14 Jul 1984.

Delmont, Gene: b. 1895; d. Memphis, TN, 20 Sep 1987.

Delmore, Ralph: b. New York, NY, 18 Dec 1853; d. New York, NY, 21 Nov 1923.

Del Rio, Dolores: b. Durango, Mex, 3 Aug 1905; d. Newport Beach, CA, 11 Apr 1983.

Deltry, William (William Blackwell): b. 18??; d. London, Eng, 8 Oct 1924.

Del Val, Jean (Jean Gauthier): b. Paris, Fr, 17 Nov 1891; d. Pacific Palisades, CA, 13 Mar 1975.

Delysia, Alice: b. Paris, Fr, 3 Mar 1889; d. Brighton, Eng, 9 Feb 1979.

De Main, Gordon (Gordon De Woods): b. Iowa, 28 Sep 1886; d. 5 Mar 1954.

De Mar, Carrie: b. 1 Apr 1876; d. Cold Springs, NY, 23 Feb 1963.

Demarest, William: b. St. Paul, MN, 27 Feb 1892; d. Palm Springs, CA, 27 Dec 1983.

De Max, Edouard: b. Jassy, Romania, 14 Feb 1869; d. Paris, Fr, 28 Oct 1924.

De Me, Shirley: b. 1898; d. Petoskey, MI, 27 Jul 1940.

Demetrio, Anna: b. Rome, Italy, 8 Nov 1892; d. San Mateo Co, CA, 8 Nov 1959.

De Mille, Cecil B.: b. Ashfield, MA, 12 Aug 1881; d. Los Angeles, CA, 21 Jan 1959.

De Mille, Cecilia: b. Orange, NJ, 5 Oct 1908; d. Los Angeles, CA, 23 Jun 1984.

De Mott, John A.: b. 1912; d. San Diego, CA, 19 Mar 1975.

Dempsey, Jack: b. Manassa, CO. 24 Jun 1895; d. New York, NY, 31 May 1983.

Dempsey, Pauline: b. 1868; d. Harlem, NY, ? Sep 1923.

Dempsey, Thomas: b. Philadelphia, PA, 20 Jan 1868; d. Los Angeles, CA, 6 Oct 1947.

Dempster, Carol: b. Deluth, MN, 8 Dec 1901; d. La Jolla, CA, 1 Feb 1991.

Denison, Edwin: b. 1863; d. 26 Jan 1928.

D'Ennery, Guy: b. California, 4 Jun 1884; d. Alameda Co, CA, 17 Oct 1978.

Dennis, Crystal B.: b. Kansas, 15 May 1893; d. Los Angeles Co, CA, 15 Dec 1973.

Dennis, Nadine: b. 1896; d. Studio City, CA, 11 Aug 1979.

Denny, Reginald: b. Richmond, Surrey, Eng, 21 Nov 1891; d. Surrey, Eng, 16 Jun 1967.

Dent, Josephine: b. England, ????; d. 18 Aug 1978.

Dent, Vernon: b. San Jose, CA, 16 Feb 1895; d. Los Angeles, CA, 4 Nov 1963.

Dentler, Marion: b. 24 Feb 1892; d. Kingston, NY, 14 Dec 1988.

Denton, Frank: b. Louth, Lincs, Eng, 1878; d. Flauden, Herts, Eng, 23 Feb 1945.

Denton, George: b. 1865; d. New York, NY, 12 Mar 1918.

De Pew, Joseph: b. Harrison, NJ, 11 Jul 1912; d. Escondido, CA, 30 Oct 1988.

Depp, Harry: b. St. Louis, MO, 22 Feb 1883; d. Los Angeles, CA, 31 Mar 1957.

De Putti, Lya: b. Vecse, Hungary, 10 Jan 1896; d. New York, NY, 27 Nov 1931.

De Ravenne, Arthur: b. Nice, Fr, 13 May 1903; d. Los Angeles, CA, 18 Sep 1962.

De Ravenne, Charles: b. France, 5 Apr 1917; d. Los Angeles, CA, 5 Apr 1977.

De Ravenne, Charline: b. Nice, Fr, 13 May 1882; d. Woodland Hills, CA, 8 May 1962.

De Ravenne, Raymond: b. 1904; d. Los Angeles, CA, 14 Oct 1950.

Derba, Mimi; b. 1894; d. Mexico City, Mex, 14 Jul 1953.

De Remer, Ruby: b. Denver, CO, 9 Jan 1892; d. Beverly Hills, CA, 18 Mar 1984.

De Riso, Camillo: b. Naples, Italy, 1854; d. 2 Apr 1924.

De Roche, Charles: b. Port Vendres, Fr, 7 Jul 1880; d. Paris, Fr, 2 Feb 1952.

De Rosselli, Rex: b. Kentucky, 1876; d. East St. Louis, IL, 21 Jul 1941.

De Rue, Carmen: b. Pueblo, CO. 1908; d. North Hollywood, CA, 28 Sep 1986.

De Rue, Eugene: b. Pueblo, CO, 1885; d. Woodland Hills, CA, 29 Sep 1985.

Derwent, Clarence: b. London, Eng, 23 Mar 1884; d. New York, NY, 6 Aug 1959.

De Segurola, Andreas: b. Madrid, Spain, 1875; d. Barcelona, Spain, 23 Jan 1953.

Desfis, Angelo: b. Greece, 11 Dec 1888; d. Los Angeles, CA, 27 Jul 1950.

Deshon, Florence: b. Tacoma, WA, 1894; d. New York, NY, 4 Feb 1922.

Deshon, Frank: b. 1858; d. South Pasadena, CA, 28 Dec 1918.

De Sica, Vittorio: b. Sora, Italy, 7 Jul 1901; d. Paris, Fr, 13 Nov 1974.

De Silva, Fred: b. Lisbon, Portugal, 7 Feb 1885; d. Norwalk, CA, 16 Feb 1929.

Desjardins, Maxime: b. France, 1861; d. 1 Oct 1936.

Deslys, Gaby: b. Marseilles, Fr, 4 Sep 1881; d. Paris, Fr, 11 Feb 1920.

Desmond, Lucille: b. 1894; d. Los Angeles, CA, 20 Nov 1936.

Desmond, William: b. Dublin, Ire, 23 Jan 1878; d. Los Angeles, CA, 2 Nov 1949.

De Solla, Rachel: b. ????; d. 24 Nov 1920.

Destinn, Emmy: b. Prague, Czech, 26 Feb 1878; d. Budweis, Czech, 28 Jan 1930.

De Tellier, Mariette: b. 1891; d. Cincinnati, OH, 9 Dec 1957.

Deutsch, Ernst: b. Prague, Czech, 16 Sep 1890; d. Berlin, Ger, 22 Mar 1969.

Devant, David: b. London, Eng, 22 Feb 1868; d. London, Eng, 13 Oct 1941

De Vaull, William P.: b. San Francisco, CA, 12 Dec 1870; d. Los Angeles, CA, 4 Jun 1945.

Devere, Arthur: b. Brussels, Belgium, 24 Jun 1883; d. Brussels, Belgium, 23 Sep 1961.

Devere, Francesca: b. 1891; d. Port Townsend, WA, 11 Sep 1952.

Devere, Harry T.: b. New York, 1 Feb 1870; d. 10 Oct 1923.

De Vere, Marjorie: b. 1889; d. New York, NY, 24 Oct 1918.

Devereaux, Jack: b. 22 Mar 1881; d. New York, NY, 19 Jan 1958.

Devereaux, Ora (Grace Gardner): b. 1882; d. Orange, CA, 11 Dec 1951.

De Vernon, Frank: b. 1845; d. New York, NY, 19 Oct 1923.

De Vilbiss, Robert: b. Richmond, CA, 12 Mar 1915; d. Torrance, CA, 4 Mar 1973.

Devine, Andy: b. Flagstaff, AZ, 27 Oct 1905; d. Orange, CA, 18 Feb 1977.

Devine, Jerry: b. Boston, MA, 1908; d. Santa Barbara, CA, 20 May 1994.

Devirys, Rachel: b. 1890; d. Nice, Fr, ? May 1984.

Devoe, Bert: b. 1884; d. Steelton, PA, 17 Jan 1930.

De Vogt, Carl: b. Cologne, Ger, 14 Sep 1885; d. ? Feb 1970.

Devore, Dorothy: b. Fort Worth, TX, 22 Jun 1899; d. Woodland Hills, CA, 10 Sep 1976.

De Vore, James: b. Kansas City, MO, 15 Mar 1890; d. 19??.

De Vries, Henri: b. 1863; d. ? May 1930.

De Weese, Frank: b. 1903; d. Salina, KS, 15 Apr 1928.

Dewey, Elmer (Don Danilo): b. 1884; d. Los Angeles, CA, 28 Oct 1954.

De Winton, Albert: b. 18??; d. Brazil ? May 1934.

De Wolfe, Elsie: b. New York, NY, 20 Dec 1865; d. Versailles, Fr, 12 Jul 1950.

Dexter, Aubrey: b. London, Eng, 29 Mar 1896; d. ? May 1958.

Dexter, Elliott: b. Houston, TX, 29 Mar 1870; d. Amityville, NY, 23 Jun 1941.

Dhelia, France: b. Saint-Lubin-in Vergonnois, Fr, 1898; d. 6 May 1964.

Dial, Patterson: b. Madison, FL, 19 May 1902; d. Los Angeles, CA, 23 Mar 1945.

Dickerson, Jennie: b. Newburgh, NY, 1855; d. Philadelphia, PA, 14 Aug 1943.

Dickey, Paul: b. Chicago, IL, 12 May 1882; d. New York, NY, 8 Jan 1933.

Dickson, Charles (Charles Doblin): b. New York, NY, 1860; d. New York, NY, 11 Dec 1927.

Dickson, John V.: b. Bordentown, NJ, 28 Mar 1875; d. Trenton, NJ, 1 May 1941.

Dickson, Lydia: b. Missouri, 17 Apr 1887; d. Los Angeles, CA, 26 Mar 1928.

Dictor, David: b. 1896; d. Baltimore, MD, ? Aug 1916.

Diegelman, Wilhelm: b. Worbeck, Ger, 28 Sep 1861; d. 1 Mar 1934.

Diehl, Karl Ludwig: b. Halle, Ger, 14 Aug 1896; d. Upper Bavaria, 7 Mar 1958.

Diesel, Gustav: b. Vienna, Austria, 30 Dec 1899; d. Vienna, Austria, 20 Mar 1948.

Dieterle, William: b. Ludwigshafen, Ger, 15 Jul 1893; d. Ottobrunn, Ger, 8 Dec 1972.

Dietl, Frank: b. Lakeville, IN, 15 Nov 1875; d. 24 Jan 1923.

Dietrich, Marlene: b. Berlin, Ger, 27 Dec 1901; d. Paris, Fr, 6 May 1992.

Dieudonne, Albert: b. France, 1892; d. 19 Mar 1976.

Diggins, Eddie: b. San Francisco, CA, 8 Jan 1903; d. Los Angeles, CA, 26 Mar 1927.

Di Golconda, Ligia: b. 1881; d. Mexico City, Mex, ? Jan 1942.

Dill, Max: b. Cleveland, OH, 1877; d. San Frarcisco, CA, 21 Nov 1949.

Dillon, Dick: b. 1896; d. Boston, MA, ? Apr 1961.

Dillon, Edward: b. New York, NY, 1 Jan 1879; d. Los Angeles, CA, 11 Jul 1933.

Dillon, John Francis: b. New York, NY, 26 Nov 1883; d. Los Angeles, CA, 4 Apr 1934.

Dillon, John T.: b. Deal Beach, NJ, 19 Jun 1876; d. Los Angeles, CA, 29 Dec 1937.

Dillon, John Webb: b. London, Eng, 6 Feb 1877; d. Los Angeles, CA, 20 Dec 1949.

Dillon, Tom: b. 1888; d. Burbank, CA, 22 Oct 1965.

Dills, William: b. Burlington, IA, 1878; d. Portland, OR, 25 Mar 1932.

Dime, James: b. Yugoslavia, 19 Dec 1897; d. Woodland Hills, CA, 11 May 1981.

Dion, Hector: b. Boston, MA, 1881; d. 19??.

Dione, Rose: b. Paris, Fr, 1875; d. Los Angeles, CA, 29 Jan 1936.

Di Sangro, Elena: b. Vasto d'Aimone, Italy, 5 Sep 1901; d. 26 Jan 1969.

Ditrichstein, Leo: b. Temesbar, Hungary, 6 Jan 1865; d. Vienna, Austria, 28 Jun 1928.

Ditt, Josephine: b. Chicago, IL, 7 Sep 1868; d. Los Angeles, CA, 18 Oct 1939.

Dittenhoefer, Judge A. J.: b. Charleston, SC, 17 Mar 1835; d. New York, NY, 23 Feb 1919.

Dix, Lillian: b. 1864; d. New York, NY, 10 Oct 1922.

Dix, Mae: b. Lake Ann, MI, 1895; d. Los Angeles, CA, 21 Oct 1958.

Dix, Richard: b. St. Paul, MN, 18 Jul 1893; d. Los Angeles, CA, 20 Sep 1949.

Dixey, Henry E.: b. Boston, MA, 6 Jan 1859; d. Atlantic City, NJ, 25 Feb 1943.

Dixon, Charlotte L.: b. 18??; d. West Palm Beach, FL, ? Oct 1970.

Dixon, Denver (Art Mix): b. Kansas City, MO, 4 Jan 1890; d. Los Angeles, CA, 9 Nov 1972.

Dixon, Henry P.: b. New York, NY, 21 Dec 1869; d. Los Angeles, CA, 3 May 1943.

Doane, Frank: b. England, 18??; d. Port Jefferson, NY, 30 Apr 1943.

Doble, Budd: b. Philadelphia, PA, 10 Oct 1841; d. Los Angeles, CA, 3 Sep 1919.

Doble, Frances: b. Montreal, Can, 1902; d. England, ? Dec 1969.

Doblin, Hugo: b. 1875; d. ? Nov 1960.

Dockstader, Lew: b. Hartford, CT, 7 Aug 1856; d. New York, NY, 26 Oct 1924.

Dodd, Elizabeth: b. 18??; d. Los Angeles, CA, 19 Nov 1928.

Dodd, Ellen: b. 1868; d. New York, NY, 12 Mar 1935.

Dodds, Rev. Neal: b. Fort Madison, IA, 6 Sep 1878; d. Los Angeles, CA, 26 May 1966.

Dolly, Jenny (Jancisi); b. Budapest, Hungary, 25 Oct 1890; d. Los Angeles, CA, 1 Jun 1941.

Dolly, Rosie (Roszika): b. Budapest, Hungary, 25 Oct 1890; d. New York, NY, 1 Feb 1970.

Dolores, Miss (Kathleen Rose): b. 1892; d. Paris, Fr, 7 Nov 1975.

Dominguez, Beatrice: b. San Bernardino, CA, 6 Sep 1897; d. Los Angeles, CA, 27 Feb 1921.

Dominguez, Joe: b. Chihuahua, Mex, 19 Mar 1894; d. Woodland Hills, CA, 11 Apr 1970.

Don, David L.: b. Utica, NY, 1867; d. New York, NY, 27 Oct 1949.

Donaldson, Arthur: b. Norsholm, Sweden, 5 Apr 1869; d. Long Island, NY, 28 Sep 1955.

Donaldson, Lyn: b. New York, NY, 31 Dec 1891; d. Los Angeles, CA, 2 Mar 1966.

Doner, Rose: b. 1905; d. New York, NY, 15 Aug 1926,

Donlevy, Brian: b. Portadown, Ire, 9 Feb 1899; d. Woodland Hills, CA, 5 Apr 1972.

Donlin, Mike: b. Peoria, IL, 30 May 1877; d. Los Angeles, CA, 24 Sep 1933.

Donnelly, Dorothy: b. New York, NY, 28 Jan 1880; d. New York, NY, 3 Jan 1928.

Donnelly, James A.: b. Boston, MA, 1865; d. Los Angeles, CA, 13 Apr 1937.

Donnelly, Leo: b. Philadelphia, PA, 1878; d. Atlantic City, NJ, 20 Aug 1935.

Donnelly, Ruth: b. Trenton, NJ, 17 May 1896; d. New York, NY, 17 Nov 1982.

Donnelly, Thomas: b. Springfield, MA, 1863; d. Springfield, MA, 20 Jul 1923.

Donoghue, Steve: b. 18??; d. London, Eng, 23 Aug 1945.

Donohue, Joseph: b. 1884; d. Flatbush, NY, 24 Oct 1921.

Donovan, Michael Patrick: b. Massachusetts, 29 Nov 1878; d. Los Angeles Co, CA, 11 Nov 1960.

Dooley, Billy: b. Chicago, IL, 8 Feb 1893; d. Los Angeles, CA, 4 Aug 1938.

Dooley, J. Gordon: b. 1899; d. Philadelphia, PA, 24 Jan 1930.

Dooley, Johnny: b. Glasgow, Scot, 1887; d. Yonkers, NY, 7 Jun 1928.

Dooley, Ray: b. Glasgow, Scot, 30 Oct 1896; d. East Hampton, NY, 28 Jan 1984.

Doone, Allen: b. 18??; d. Reno, NV, 4 May 1948.

Dora, Josefine: b. 1868; d. ? May 1944.

Doraldina: b. San Francisco, CA, 1887; d. Los Angeles, CA, 13 Feb 1936.

D'Orcy, Georgia; b. Bordeaux, Fr, 1878; d. 19??.

Dorety, Charles R.: b. San Francisco, CA, 20 May 1898; d. Los Angeles, CA, 2 Apr 1957.

Darian, Charles W.: b. Santa Monica, CA, 1891; d. Albuquerque, NM, 21 Oct 1942.

Doro, Marie: b. Duncannon, PA, 25 May 1882; d. New York, NY, 9 Oct 1956.

Dorsay, Edmund: b. 1897; d. New York, NY, 12 Jun 1959.

D'Orsay, Lawrence: b. Peterborough, Eng, 19 Aug 1853; d. London, Eng, 13 Sep 1931.

Dorsch, Kaethe: b. Neumarkt, Ger, 29 Dec 1889; d. Vienna, Austria, 25 Dec 1957.

Dorziat, Gabrielle: b. Epernay, Fr, 15 Jan 1886; d. Biarritz, Fr, 30 Nov 1979.

Doscher, Doris: b. 24 Jun 1882; d. Farmingdale, NY, 9 Mar 1970.

Dossett, Ghappell; b. London, Eng, 1 Jan 1883; d. Los Angeles Co, CA, 19 Dec 1961.

Doty, Weston: b. Malta, OH, 18 Feb 1913; d. California, 1 Jan 1934.

Doty, Winston: b. Malta, OH, 18 Feb 1913; d. California, 1 Jan 1934.

Doucet, Catherine (Catherine Calhoun): b. Richmond, VA, 20 Jun 1875; d. New York, NY, 24 Jun 1958.

Doucet, H, Paul: b. France, 1886; d. New York, NY, 10 Oct 1928.

Douglas, Byron: b. 1864; d. New York, NY, 21 Apr 1935,

Douglas, Frederick C.: b. Newark, NJ, 1867; d. Los Angeles, CA, 17 Jul 1929.

Douglas, Gilbert: b. Southampton, Eng, 1881; d. Philadelphia, PA, 11 Oct 1959,

Douglas, Gordon: b. New York, NY, 5 Dec 1909; d. Los Angeles, CA, 29 Sep 1993.

Douglas, Kenneth: b. London, Eng, 1873; d. New York, NY, 17 Oct 1923.

Douglas, Royal: b. 1884; d. Cleveland, OH, ? June 1924.

Douglas, Tom: b. Louisville, KY, 4 Sep 1895; d. Guernavaca, Mex, 4 May 1978.

Dove Eyes: b. ????; d. Los Angeles Co, CA, 13 Jul 1969.

Dovey, Alice: b. Plattsmouth, NE, 28 Aug 1885; d. Tarzana, CA, 12 Jan 1969.

Dowlan, William C.: b. St. Paula MN, 21 Sep 1882; d. Los Angeles Co, CA, 6 Nov 1947.

Dowling, Joseph J,: b. Pittsburgh, PA, 4 Sep 1848; d. Los Angeles, CA, 8 Jul 1928.

Downing, Harry: b. 1893; d. Boston, MA, 9 Jan 1972.

Downing, Walter: b. Rochester, NY, 28 Oct 1874; d. Los Angeles, CA, 22 Dec 1937.

Downs, Johnny: b. Brooklyn, NY, 10 Oct 1913; d. Coronado, CA, 6 Jun 1994.

Downs, Rex E.: b. Waterville, OH, 22 Aug 1885; d. Indio, CA, 3 Feb 1975.

Doxat-Pratt, Norman: b. England, 1 Jun 1916; d. 1982.

Doyle, Buddy: b. 1901; d. New York, NY, 9 Nov 1939.

Doyle, Johnny: b. England, 18??; d. Chattanooga, TN; 24 Mar 1919.

Doyle, Larry: b. Caseyville, IL, 31 Jul 1886; d. Saranac Lake, NY, 1 Mar 1974.

Doyle, Regina: b. 1904; d. North Hollywood, CA, 29 Sep 1931.

Drake, Fabia: b. Herne Bay, Eng, 20 Jan 1904; d. London, Eng, 28 Feb 1990.

Drake, Josephine: b. 18??; d. New York, NY, 7 Jan 1929.

Drane, Sam Dade: b. 1869; d. New York, NY, 15 Aug 1916.

Dranem: b. 1869; d. Paris, Fr, 13 Oct 1935.

Draper, Col. T. Waln-Morgan: b. 18??; d. 8 Nov 1915.

Drayton, Alfred: b. Brighton, Eng, 1 Nov 1881; d. London, Eng, 26 Apr 1949.

Dresser, Louise: b. Evansville, IN, 5 Oct 1878; d. Woodland Hills, CA, 24 Apr 1965.

Dressler, Marie: b. Cobourg, Can, 9 Nov 1869; d. Santa Barbara, CA, 28 Jul 1934.

Drew, Ann: b. New York, NY, 13 Jul 1890; d. Miami, FL, 6 Feb 1974.

Drew, Gladys Rankin: b. c. 1874; d. New York, NY, 9 Jan 1914.

Drew, Jerry: b. Bloomfield, IA, 26 Aug 1898; d. Santa Rosa, CA, 14 Nov 1992.

Drew, Lillian: b. Chicago, IL, 1883; d. Chicago, IL, 4 Feb 1924.

Drew, Philip Yale: b. 15 Mar 1880; d. Kensington, Surrey, Eng, 2 Jul 1940.

Drew, Roland: b. Elmhurst, NY, 4 Aug 1900; d. Santa Monica, CA, 17 Mar 1988.

Drew, S. Rankin: b. New York, NY, 1892; d. France, 19 May 1918.

Drew, Sidney: b. New York, NY, 28 Aug 1864; d. New York, NY, 9 Apr 1919.

Drew, Mrs. Sidney (Lucille McVey): b. Sedalia, MO, 18 Apr 1890; d. Los Angeles, CA, 3 Nov 1925.

Drexel, Nancy: b. New York, NY, 6 Apr 1910; d. San Juan Capistrano, CA, 19 Nov 1989.

Driscoll, Frank T. (Tex): b. Indiana, 7 Sep 1889; d. Los Angeles Co, CA, 1 Jun 1970.

Driver, Adabelle: b. England, 6 Dec 1874; d. Monterey Park, CA, 23 Oct 1952.

Dromgold, George: b. Los Angeles, CA, 1894; d. Ft. Lauderdale, FL, 9 Apr 1948.

Drouet, Robert: b. Clinton, IA, 27 Mar 1870; d. New York, NY, 17 Aug 1914.

Druce, Hubert: b. Twickenham, Middlesex, Eng, 20 May 1870; d. New York, NY, 6 Apr 1931.

Drumier, Jack: b. Philadelphia, PA, 1869; d. Clearwater, FL, 21 Apr 1929.

Dryden, Leo: b. London, Eng, 6 Jun 1863; d. London, Eng, 21 Apr 1939.

Dryden, Wheeler: b. London, Eng, 31 Aug 1893; d. Los Angeles, CA, 30 Sep 1957.

Du Brey, Claire: b. Bonners Ferry, ID, 31 Aug 1892; d. Los Angeles, CA, 1 Aug 1993.

Duc, Paul: b. France, 1906; d. ? Sep 1923.

Du Cello, Countess Mary: b. Buffalo, NY, 1864; d. Los Angeles, CA, 20 Nov 1921.

Duchamps, Marcel: b. Blainsville, Normandy, Fr, 28 Jul 1887; d. Neuilly, Fr, 2 Oct 1968.

Ducrow, Tote G.: b. Watsonville, CA, 1858; d. 12 Dec 1927.

Dudley, Bernard: b. Ireland, 1878; d. London, Eng, ? Oct 1964.

Dudley, Charles: b. Fort Grant, AZ, 10 Oct 1883; d. Woodland Hills, CA, 9 Mar 1952.

Dudley, Robert: b. Cincinnati, OH, 13 Sep 1869; d. San Clemente, CA, 12 Nov 1955.

Duff, Sadie: b. 1870; d. New York, NY, 10 Jun 1942.

Duffield, Harry S.: b. 1850; d. Los Angeles, CA, 13 Oct 1921.

Duffy, Jack: b. Pawtucket, RI, 4 Sep 1882; d. Los Angeles, CA, 23 Jul 1939.

Dufkin, Sam: b. 1891; d. Los Angeles, CA, 19 Feb 1952.

Duflos, Hugette: b. Tunisia, 1891; d. Paris, Fr, 12 Apr 1982.

Dufraine, Rosa: b. 1901; d. Duarte, CA, 29 Apr 1935.

Dugan, Tom: b. Dublin, Ire, 1 Jan 1889; d. Redlands, CA, 6 Mar 1955.

Dull, Bunny (Orville 0. Dull), b. Lima, OH, 25 Apr 1890; d. Los Angeles, CA, 29 Dec 1978.

Dullin, Charles: b. Yenne, Fr, 1885; d. Paris, Fr, 11 Dec 1949.

Du Maurier, Sir Gerald: b. London, Eng, 26 Mar 1873; d. London, Eng, 11 Apr 1934.

Dumont, Gordon: b. Milwaukee, WI, 24 Apr 1894; d. Los Angeles Co, CA, 7 Mar 1966.

Dumort, J. M. (J. Monte Dumont): b. Louisiana, 7 Feb 1879; d. Los Angeles Co, CA, 19 Dec 1959.

Dunaew, Nicholas: b. Moscow, Russ, 26 May 1884; d. 19??.

Dunbar, Blanche: b. 1894; d. Los Angeles, CA , 7 Mar 1926.

Dunbar, David: b. West Maitland, Austral, 14 Sep 1886; d. Woodland Hills, CA, 7 Nov 1953.

Dunbar, Dorothy: b. Colorado Springs, C0, 1902; d. Seattle, WA, 23 Oct 1992.

Dunbar, Helen: b. Philadelpha, PA, 10 Oct 1863; d. Los Angeles, CA, 28 Aug 1933.

Dunbar, Jack: b. 1896; d. Edinburgh, Scot, 15 Oct 1961.

Dunbar, Robert: b. Beaver, PA, 1 Jul 1858; d. Los Angeles Co, CA, 16 Jan 1943.

Duncan, Albert E. (Bud): b. Brooklyn, NY, 31 Oct 1883; d. Los Angeles, CA, 26 Nov 1960.

Duncan, Evelyn: b. Los Angeles, CA, 21 Jan 1893; d. Los Angeles, CA, 8 Jun1972.

Duncan, Malcolm: b. Brooklyn, NY, 19 Sep 1881; d. Bay Shore, NY, 2 May 1942.

Duncan, Mary: b. Luttreville, VA, 13 Aug 1895; d. Palm Beach, FL, 9 May 1993.

Duncan, Rosetta: b. Los Angeles, CA, 23 Nov 1896; d. Berwyn, IL, 4 Dec 1959.

Duncan, Taylor E,: b. Kansas City, MO, 4 Jul 1877; d. Los Angeles, CA, 23 Jul 1957.

Duncan, Vivian: b. Los Angeles, CA, 17 Jun 1902; d. Los Angeles, CA, 19 Sep 1986.

Duncan, William: b. Dundee, Scot, 16 Dec 1879; d. Los Angeles, CA, 7 Feb 1961.

Dunham, Maudie: b. Essex, Eng, 1902; d. 3 Oct 1982.

Dunham, Philip Gray: b. London, Eng, 23 Apr 1885; d. Los Angeles, CA, 5 Sep 1972.

Dunkinson, Harry L.: b. New York, NY, 16 Dec 1876; d. 14 Mar 1936.

Dunlap, Louise: b. 1865; d. Los Angeles, CA, 31 Mar 1940.

Dunlap, Scott: b. Chicago, IL, 20 Jun 1892; d. Los Angeles, CA, 30 Mar 1970.

Dunn, Bobby: b. Milwaukee, WI, 28 Aug 1890; d. Los Angeles, CA, 24 Mar 1937.

Dunn, Eddie (Edward F. Dunn): b. Brooklyn, NY, 31 Mar 1896; d. Los Angeles, CA, 5 May 1951.

Dunn, Emma: b. Cheshire, Eng, 26 Feb 1875; d. Los Angeles, CA, 14 Dec 1966.

Dunn, Herbert Stanley: b. 1892; d. Costa Mesa, CA, 14 Apr 1979.

Dunn, J. Malcolm: b. London, Eng, 25 May 1867; d. Beechurst, NY, 10 Oct 1946.

Dunn, John J.: b. New York, NY, 1874; d. Binghamton, NY, ? May 1928.

Dunn, Johnny: b. Binghamton, NY, 1906; d. Bluefield, WV, 2 Apr 1938.

Dunn, Josephine: b. New York, NY, 1 May 1906; d. Thousand, Oaks, CA, 3 Feb 1983.

Dunn, William R.: b. Astoria, NY, 1884; d. 19??.

Dunton, Helen: b. 18??; d. San Francisco, CA, ? Nov 1920.

du Pont, Miss (Marguerite Armstrong): b. Frankfort, KY, 28 Apr 1894; d. Palm Beach, FL, 6 Feb 1973.

Dupree, George: b. Cincinnati, OH, 1874; d. New York, NY, 29 Jul 1951.

Durand, Edouard: b. France, 1871; d. Port Chester, NY, 31 Jul 1926.

Durand, Jean: b. Paris, Fr, 1882; d. Paris, Fr, 1946.

Durant, Thomas: b. 1899; d. Santa Monica, CA, 7 Dec 1984.

Durfee, Minta: b. Los Angeles, CA, 1 Oct 1889; d. Woodland Hills, CA, 9 Sep 1975.

Durham, Lewis: b. New Oxford, PA, 19 Aug 1852; d. 16 Oct 1937.

Durieux, Tilla: b. Vienna, Austria, 18 Aug 1880; d. Berlin, Ger, 21 Feb 1971.

Durkin, James: b. Quebec, Can, 21 May 1879; d. Los Angeles, CA, 12 Mar 1934.

Durning, Bernard J.: b. New York, NY, 1893; d. New York, NY, 29 Aug 1923.

Duryea, George (Tom Keene): b. Smoky Hollow, NY, 30 Dec 1896; d. Woodland Hills, CA, 4 Aug 1963.

Duse, Carlo: b. Udine, Italy, 5 Jan 1899; d. 9 Sep 1956.

Duse, Eleanora: b. Vigerano, Italy, 3 Oct 1859; d. Pittsburgh, PA, 21 Apr 1924.

Dvorak, Ann: b. New York, NY, 2 Aug 1912; d. Honolulu, HI, 10 Dec 1979.

Dwiggins, Jay: b. 18??; d. Los Angeles, CA, 8 Sep 1919.

Dwire, Earl: b. Rockport, MO, 3 Oct 1883; d. Carmichael, CA, 16 Jan 1940.

Dwyer, Ethel: b. Tarrytown, NY, 1898; d. Pittsburgh, PA, 2 Sep 1985.

Dwyer, John T.: b. 1877; d. New York, NY, 7 Dec 1936.

Dwyer, Leslie: b. London, Eng, 28 Aug 1906; d. London, Eng, 26 Dec 1986.

Dwyer, Ruth: b. Brooklyn, NY, 1897; d. Woodland Hills, CA, 2 Mar 1978.

Dyall, Franklin: b. Liverpool, Eng, 3 Feb 1874; d. Worthing, Eng, 8 May 1950.

Dyas, Dave: b. Missouri, 11 Apr 1895; d. 5 Nov 1929.

d'Yd, Jean: b. Paris, Fr, 17 Mar 1880; d. ? May 1964.

Dyer, William: b. Atlanta, GA, 11 Mar 1881; d. Los Angeles, CA, 22 Dec 1933.

E

Eadia, Dennis: b. Glasgow, Scot, 14 Jan 1875; d. London, Eng, 10 Jun 1928.

Eagels, Jeanne: b. Kansas City, MO, 26 Jun 1890; d. New York, NY, 3 Oct 1929.

Eagle, James Crump: b. Norfolk, VA, 10 Sep 1907; d. Los Angeles, CA, 15 Dec. 1959.

Eames, Clare: b. Hartford, CT, 5 Aug 1896; d. London, Eng, 8 Nov 1930.

Earl, Catherine: b. 1886; d. Los Angeles, CA, 14 Aug 1946.

Earlcott, Gladys: b. ????; d. Los Angeles, CA, 18 May 1939.

Earle, Blanche: b. 1883; d. Woodland Hills, CA, 22 Jan 1952.

Earle, Dorothy: b. New Jersey, 4 Stp 1892; d. Los Angeles, CA, 5 Jul 1957.

Earle, Edward: b. Toronto, Ont, Can, 16 Jul 1882; Woodland Hills, CA, 15 Dec 1972.

Earle, Jack: b. Denver, CO, 3 Jul 1906; d. El Paso, TX, 18 Jul 1952.

Earle, Josephine: b. Brooklyn, NY, 23 Feb 1892; d. Brooklyn, NY, ? Aug 1929.

Earles, Harry: b. Germany, 3 Apr 1902; d. Sarasota, FL, 4 May 1985.

Eason, B. Reeves: b. Friars Point, MS, 2 Oct 1886; d. Sherman Oaks, CA, 9 Jun 1956.

Eason, Breezy, Jr.: b. California, 19 Nov 1914; d. Los Angeles, CA, 24 Oct 1921.

East, John M.: b. 1861; d. London, Eng, 18 Aug 1924.

Eaton, Elwyn: b. England, 16 Oct 1864; d. Los Angeles, CA, 30 Apr 1937.

Eaton, Jay K.: b. New Jersey, 17 Mar 1899; d. Los Angeles, CA, 5 Feb 1970.

Eaton, Mabel: b. 18??; a. Chicago, IL, 10 Jan 1916.

Eaton, Mary: b. Norfolk, VA, 29 Jan 1901; d. Los Angeles, CA, 10 Oct 1948.

Eberle, Mrs. Eugene A.: b. Glasgow, Scot, 1841; d. Chatham, NY, ? Jul 1919.

Ebert, Carl: b. 1887; d. Los Angeles, CA, 14 May 1980.

Ebert, Paula: b. Berlin, Ger, 8 Sep 1869; d. 5 Feb 1929.

Eburne, Maude: b. Bronte-on-the-Lake, Can, 10 Nov 1875; d. Los Angeles, CA, 8 Oct 1960.

Eckerline, John Elwood: b. New York, NY, 1884; d. New York, NY, 9 Sep 1926.

Eckersberg, Else: b. 1895; d. Bavaria, ? Nov 1989.

Eckhardt, Oliver J.: b. Missouri, 14 Sep 1873; d, Los Angeles, CA, 15 Sep 1952.

Eddinger, Wallace: b. Albany, NY, 14 Jul 1881; d. Pittsburgh, PA, 8 Jan 1929.

Eddy, Mrs. Augusta F.: b. 1860; d. Staten Island, NY, 21 Sep 1925.

Eddy, Helen Jerome: b. New York, NY, 25 Feb 1897; d. Alhambra, CA, 27 Jan 1990.

Edelstein, "Dad": b. 1845; d. Sydney, Austral, ? Jun 1927.

Edeson, Robert: b. New Orleans, LA, 3 Jun 1868; d. Los Angeles, CA, 24 Mar 1931.

Edgard, Lewis: b. 1878; d. New York, NY, 8 Dec 1917.

Edgren, Robert W.: b. 1874; d. Del Monte, CA, 9 Sep 1939.

Edler, Charles: b. New Jersey, 13 Aug 1864; d. Santa Monica, CA, 29 Mar 1942.

Edlin, Theodore: b. California, 3 Oct 1894; d. Woodland Hills, CA, 7 Jul 1974.

Edmondson, Al: b. Pueblo, CO, 1896; d. 11 May 1954.

Edmondson, Harry B.: b. Baltimore, MD, 1873; d. 19??.

Edmondson, William: b. 1903; d. Los Angeles, CA, 28 May 1979.

Edmunds, Charles: b. New York, 1877; d. 19??.

Edney, Florence: b. London, Eng, 2 Jun 1879; d. New York, NY, 24 Nov 1950.

Edstrom, Katherine: b. 1901; d. Los Angeles, CA, 2 Jun 1973.

Edthofer, Anton: b. Vienna, Austria, 18 Sep 1883; d. 21 Feb 1971.

Edwards, Alan: b. New York, NY, 3 Jun 1892; d. Los Angeles, CA, 8 May 1954.

Edwards, Charles E.: b. 1898; d. Los Angeles, CA, 18 Aug 1978.

Edwards, Edna Park: b. Pittsburgh, PA, 17 Feb 1895; d. Los Angeles, CA, 5 Jun 1967.

Edwards, Edyth Paula: b. Breslau, Ger, 14 May 1899; d. 6 Mar 1956.

Edwards, Eleanor: b. New York, 1882; d. Los Angeles, CA, 22 Oct 1968.

Edwards, Gus: b. Hohensalza, Ger, 18 Aug 1879; d. Los Angeles, CA, 7 Nov 1945.

Edwards, Harry J.: b. London, Can, 1889; d. Los Angeles, CA, 26 May 1952.

Edwards, Henry: b. Weston-Super-Mare, Eng, 18 Sep 1883; d. Chobham, Eng, 2 Nov 1952.

Edwards, John: b. Boston, MA, 1869; d. New York, NY, 16 Oct 1929.

Edwards, Julia: b. 1883; d. Stockton, CA, 16 Apr 1976.

Edwards, Leo: b. Germany, 1886; d. New York, NY, 12 Jul 1978.

Edwards, Mattie: b. 1866; d. Los Angeles, CA, 26 Jun 1944.

Edwards, Nate: b. 1902; d. Los Angeles, CA, 12 Sep 1972.

Edwards, Neely: b. Delphos, OH, 16 Sep 1883; d. Woodland Hills, CA, 10 Jul 1965.

Edwards, Sam: b. San Francisco, CA, 1851; d. Chicago, IL, 2 May 1921.

Edwards, Snitz, b. Budapest, Hungary, 1 Jan 1862; d. Los Angeles, CA, 1 May 1937.

Edwards, Ted: b. Sheffield, Eng, 1884; d. Los Angeles, CA, 29 Sep 1945.

Edwards, Walter: b. Michigan, 8 Jan 1870; d. Honolulu, HI, 12 Apr 1920.

Egan, George: b. 1883; d. Cincinnati, OH, 26 Sep 1943.

Egbert, Albert: b. ????; d. 18 Mar 1942.

Egleston, Ann: b. 1866; d. New York, NY, 18 May 1934.

Ehfe, William C.: b. Payette, ID, 19 Jun 1887; d. Los Angeles, CA, 1 Aug 1940.

Ehrlich, Max b. Berlin, Ger, ????; d. Auschwitz, Ger, 1943.

Eibenschutz, Lia: b. 19 Mar 1899; d. ? Mar 1985.

Eilers, Sally: b. New York, NY, 11 Dec 1908; d. Woodland Hills, CA, 5 Jan 1978.

Ekert, Alexander: b. 1875; d. ? Nov 1920.

Ekman, Gosta: b. Stockholm, Sweden, 28 Dec 1890; d. Stockholm, Sweden, 12 Jan 1938.

Ekman, John: b. Stockholm, Sweden, 1880; d. 1949.

Elder, Ruth: b. Anniston, AL, 8 Sep 1905; d. San Francisco, CA, 9 Oct 1977.

Eldridge, Anna Mae: b. 1894; d. Van Nuys, CA, 17 Apr 1950.

Eldridge, Charles E.: b. Saratoga Springs, NY, 1854; d. New York, NY, 29 Oct 1922.

Eldridge, Florence: b. Brooklyn, NY, 5 Sep 1901; d. Santa Barbara, CA, 1 Aug 1988.

Eline, Mrs. Grace: b. 1874; d. New York, NY, 24 Jul 1935.

Eline, Marie: b. Milwaukee, WI, 27 Feb 1905; d. Longview, WA, 3 Jan 1981.

Elizondo, Joaquin: b. 1896; d. Los Angeles, CA, 15 Jan 1952.

Elkas, Edward: b. New York, NY, 8 Feb 1862; d. 19??.

Ellery, Arthur: b. 1870; d. Elizabeth, NJ, 27 Aug 1945.

Ellingford, William: b. 1863; d. Los Angeles, CA, 20 May 1936.

Elliott, Frank: b. Cheshire, Eng, 11 Feb 1880; d. ? Jul 1970.

Elliott, Gertrude: b. Rockland, ME, 14 Dec 1874; d. Kent, Eng, 24 Dec 1950.

Elliott, Gordon (Wild Bill Elliott): b. Pattonsburg, MO, 16 Oct 1903; d. Las Vegas, NV, 26 Nov 1965.

Elliott, John H.: b. Pella, IA, 5 Jul 1876; d. Los Angeles, CA, 12 Dec 1956.

Elliott, Lillian: b. Canada, 24 Apr 1874; d. Los Angeles, CA, 15 Jan 1959.

Elliott, Madge: b. London, Eng, 12 May 1898; d. New York, NY, 8 Aug 1955.

Elliott, Maxine: b. Rockland, ME, 5 Feb 1871; d. Cannes, Fr, 5 Mar 1940.

Elliott, Milton: b. Gadsden, AL, 1896; d. Los Angeles, CA, 2 Aug 1920.

Elliott, Robert: b. Ohio, 9 Oct 1879; d. Los Angeles, CA, 15 Nov 1951.

Elliott, William: b. Boston, MA, 4 Dec 1885; d. New York, NY, 5 Feb 1932.

Ellis, Diane: b. Los Angeles, CA, 20 Dec 1909; d. Madras, India, 15 Dec 1930.

Ellis, Edward: b. Coldwater, MI, 12 Nov 1870; d. Beverly Hills, CA, 26 Jul 1952.

Ellis, Frank B.: b. Oklahoma, 26 Feb 1897; d. Los Angeles, CA, 23 Feb 1969.

Ellis, George: b. 1891; d. Bloomington, IL, ? Mar 1929.

Ellis, Houston: b. 1893; d. Delana, CA, 13 Feb 1928.

Ellis, Lillian: b. 1911; d. Copenhagen, Denmark, 21 Feb 1951.

Ellis, Robert: b. Brooklyn, NY, 27 Jun 1892; d. Los Angeles, CA, 29 Dec 1974.

Elliston, Grace: b. Memphis, TN, 1878; d. Lenox, MA, 14 Dec 1950.

Elliston, Mark: b. 1889; d. Chicago, IL, 27 Feb 1925.

Ellsler, Effie: b. Cleveland, OH, 17 Sep 1855; d. Los Angeles, CA, 8 Oct 1942.

Elmer, Billy (William E. Johns): b. Council Bluffs, IA, 25 Apr 1869; d. Los Angeles, CA, 24 Feb 1945.

Elmer, Clarence Jay: b. San Francisco, CA, 1886; d. 19??.

Elmore, Pearl: b. Kansas City, MO, 1879; d. 19??.

Elsie, Lily: b. Worsley, Lancs, Eng, 8 Apr 1886; d. Pelehouse Common, Sussex, Eng, 16 Dec 1962.

Elsom, Isobel: b. Chesterton, Eng, 16 Mar 1893; d. Woodland Hills, CA, 12 Jan 1981.

Eltinge, Julian: b. Newtonville, MA, 14 May 1882; d. New York, NY, 7 Mar 1941.

Elton, Edmund J.: b. England, 5 Feb 1871; d. Los Angeles, CA, 4 Jan 1952.

Elvey, Maurice: b. Darlington, Durham, Eng, 11 Nov 1887; d. Brighton, Eng, 28 Aug 1967.

Elvidge, June: b. St. Paul, MN, 30 Jun 1893; d. Eatontown, NJ, 1 May 1965.

Elvin, Joe: b. London, Eng, 29 Nov 1862; d. London, Eng, 3 Mar 1935.

Elwell, George H.: b. 1896; d. Los Angeles, CA, 13 Nov 1916.

Ely, Eleazer: b. 1839; d. Cooperstown, NY, 9 Feb 1929.

Ely, Harry: b. 1883; d. Los Angeles, CA, 15 Jul 1951.

Ely, S. Gilbert: b. 1858; d. Osgood, IN, ? Apr 1920.

Elzer, Karl Conrad: b. Karlsruhe, Ger, 2 Aug 1881; d. Rottach- Egern, Bavaria, 30 Aug 1938.

Emden, Margaret: b. ????; d. England, 13 Feb 1946.

Emerick, Bessie: b. Rochester, IN, 1875; d. Boston, MA, 13 Dec 1939.

Emerson, John: b. Sandusky, OH, 28 May 1871; d. Pasadena, CA, 7 Mar 1956.

Emerson, Ralph (Walter): b. Kalispell, MT, 9 Aug 1899; d. West Lafayette, IN, 22 Feb 1984.

Emery, Gilbert: b. Naples, NY, 11 Jun 1875; d. Los Angeles, CA, 28 Oct 1945.

Emery, Gilbert W.: b. 1882; d. Los Angeles, CA, 31 Dec 1934.

Emery, Pollie: b. Bolton, Eng, 10 May 1875; d. London, Eng, 31 Oct 1958.

Emery, Winifred: b. Manchester, Eng, 1 Aug 1862; d. Bexhill, Sussex, Eng, 15 Jul 1924.

Emmet, Katherine: b. San Francisco, CA 1882; d. New York, NY, 6 Jun 1960.

Emmons, Louise: b. 1862; d. Los Angeles, CA, 6 Mar 1935.

Emney, Fred, Sr.: b. London, Eng, 5 Mar 1865; d. New Malden, Surrey, Eng, 7 Jan 1917.

Empey, Guy: b. Ogden, UT, 11 Dec 1883; d. Wadsworth, KS, 22 Feb 1963.

Empress, Marie: b. 18??; d. At sea c. 1919.

Encinas, Lalo: b. Arizona, 27 Jun 1886; d. Los Angeles, CA, 5 May 1959.

Endresse, Clara: b. 20 Mar 1898; d. Los Angeles, CA, 2 Dec 1979.

Engel, Alexander: b. 4 Jun 1902; d. Saarbrucken, Ger, ? Aug 1968.

Engel, Joseph W.: b. 1883; d. New York, NY, 18 Apr 1943.

England, Daisy: b. 1862; d. 7 Mar 1943.

Engle, Billy: b. Austria, 28 May 1889; d. Woodland Hills, CA, 28 Nov 1966.

Englisch, Lucie: b. Baden, Austria, 8 Feb 1897; d. Erlangen, Ger, ? Oct 1965.

English, Harry: b. 1861; d. Englewood, NJ, 3 Apr 1939.

English, Robert: b. Cheltenham, Eng, 2 Dec 1878; d. 19??.

Ennis, Harry: b. 1880; d. Brooklyn, NY, 12 Oct 1924.

Ens, William (Eagle Eye): b. Fort Thomas, AZ, 1877; d. Los Angeles, CA, 17 Jan 1927.

Enstedt, Howard: b. Illinois, 7 May 1906; d. 13 Dec 1928.

Entwistle, Harold: b. London, Eng, 5 Sep 1865; d. Los Angeles, CA, 1 Apr 1944.

Entwistle, Robert: b. London, Eng, 1872; d. Brooklyn, NY, 19 Dec 1922.

Epping, Florence Luella: b. 1888; d. 1986.

Erastoff, Edith: b. Helsinki, Finland, 1887; d. 1945.

Eric, Fred: b. Peru, IN, 1874; d. New York, NY, 16 Apr 1935.

Erickson, Bob: b. Minneapolis, MN, 10 Oct 1898; d. Los Angeles, CA, 21 Jan 1941.

Erickson, Knute: b. Norrkoping, Sweden, 27 May 1870; d. Los Angeles, CA, 31 Dec 1945.

Errol, Leon: b. Sydney, Austral, 3 Jul 1881; d. Los Angeles, CA, 12 Oct 1951.

Erskine, Wallace: b. England, 8 Aug 1862; d. Massapequa, NY, 6 Jan 1943.

Erwin, June: b. 1918; d. Carmichael, CA, 27 Dec 1965.

Erwin, Madge H.: b. ????; d. Alameda Co, CA, 30 Jun 1967.

Erwin, Stuart: b. Squaw Valley, CA, 14 Feb 1903; d. Beverly Hills, CA, 21 Dec 1967.

Escoffier, Paul: b. ????; d. Paris, Fr, 30 Jul 1941.

Esdale, Charles: b. 1873; d. New York, NY, 10 Jul 1937.

Esmelton, Frederick: b. Melbourne, Austral, 22 Jun 1872; d. Los Angeles, CA, 23 Oct 1933.

Esmond, Annie: b. Surrey, Eng, 27 Sep 1873; d. 4 Jan 1945.

Esmond, H. V. (Harry Vernon): b. London, Eng, 30 Nov 1869; d. Paris, Fr, 17 Apr 1922.

Esmonde, Merceita: b. Philadelphia, PA, 1869; d. Brooklyn, NY, 22 Nov 1929.

Espinosa, Edouard: b. London, Eng, 2 Feb 1872; d. Worthing, Sussex, Eng, 23 Mar 1950.

Esser, Peter: b. Germany, 1896; d. Dusseldorf, Ger, 23 Jun 1970.

Estabrook, Howard: b. Detroit, MI, 11 Jul 1884; d. Woodland Hills, CA, 16 Jul 1978.

Ethier, Alphonse: b. Virginia City, NV, 10 Dec 1874; d. Los Angeles, CA, 5 Jan 1943.

Ettlinger, Karl: b. Frankfurt, Ger, 22 Jan 1882; d. 8 May 1946.

Europe, James R.: b. Mobile, AL, 1878; d. Boston, MA, 9 May 1919.

Evans, Cecilia: b. Oxford, KS, 7 May 1902; d. San Rafaels, CA, 11 Nov 1960.

Evans, Charles E.: b. Rochester, NY, 6 Sep 1856; d. Santa Monica, CA, 16 Apr 1945.

Evans, Dame Edith: b. London, Eng, 8 Feb 1888; d. Cranbrook, Kent, Eng, 14 Oct 1976.

Evans, Edith: b. 1894; d. Morristown, NJ, 12 Oct 1962.

Evans, Esther: b. 1883; d. Santa Monica, CA, 7 Nov 1943.

Evans, Fred (Pimple): b. England, 1889; d. 1951.

Evans, Fred: b. 1840; d. Bristol, Eng, 31 Oct 1909.

Evans, Helen St. Clair: b. 1905; d. Los Angclcs, CA, 6 Jun 1927.

Evans, Herbert D.: b. London, Eng, 16 Apr 1882; d. San Gabriel, CA, 10 Feb 1952.

Evans, Jack: b. North Carolina, 5 Mar 1893; d. Los Angeles, CA, 7 Mar 1950.

Evans, Joe: b. 1891; d. 1967.

Evans, Madge: b. New York, NY, 1 Jul 1909; d, Oakland, NJ, 26 Apr 1981.

Evans, Will: b. London, Eng, 29 May 1873; d. London, Eng, 11 Apr 1931.

Evans, William A.: b. 1876; d. Los Angeles, CA, ? Sep 1937.

Evelyn, Fay: b. 1895; d. Washington, DC, 22 Jun 1947.

Evelyn, Mildred: b. 26 Sep 1898; d. England, 1989.

Evelynne, May: b. 1856; d. Los Angeles, CA, 3 Apr 1943.

Evennett, Wallace: b. London, Eng, 17 Dec 1887; d. ? Oct 1973.

Everest, Barbara: b. London, Eng, 19 Jun 1890; d. London, Eng, 9 Feb 1968.

Evers, Ernest P.: b. Villa Ridge, IL, 12 Sep 1874; d. Los Angeles, CA, 22 Jul 1945.

Everton, Paul: b. New York, NY, 19 Sep 1868; d. Los Angeles, CA, 26 Feb 1948.

Evesson, Isabelle: b. 18??; d. Stamford, CT, 9 Aug 1914.

Eysoldt, Gertrude: b. Pirna, Ger, 11 Nov 1870; d. Ohlstadt, Ger, 6 Jan 1955.

Eyton, Bessie: b. Santa Barbara, CA, 5 Jul 1890; d. 19??.

F

Faassen, William b. 1897; d. 15 Apr 1978.

Faber, Leslie: b. Newcastle-on-Tyne, Eng, 30 Aug 1879; d. London, Eng, 5 Aug 1929.

Fahreny, Milton: b. Dayton, OH, 24 Jun 1872; d. Culver City, CA, 26 Mar 1941.

Fair, Elinor: b. Richmond, VA, 21 Dec 1903; d. Seattle, WA, 26 Apr 1957.

Fair, Joyce (Clare Boothe Luce): b. New York, NY, 10 Apr 1903; d. Washington, DC, Oct 1987.

Fair, Virginia: b. Comstock, TX, 23 Aug 1899; d. Los Angeles, CA, 5 Sep 1948.

Fairbanks, Douglas, Sr.: b. Denver, CO, 23 May 1883; d. Santa Monica, CA, 12 Dec 1939.

Fairbanks, Flobelle: b. 1908; d. New York, NY, 5 Jan 1969.

Fairbanks, Fred T.: b. 1871; d. Coney Island, NY, 15 May 1927.

Fairbanks, Madeleine: b. New York, NY, 15 Nov 1900; d, New York, NY, 26 Jan 1989.

Fairbanks, Marion: b. New York, NY, 15 Nov 1900; d. New York, NY, 20 Sep 1973.

Fairbanks, William: b. St. Louis, MO, 24 May 1889; d. Los Angeles, CA, 1 Apr 1945.

Fairbrother, Sydney: b. London, Eng, 31 Jul 1872; d. London, Eng, 10 Jan 1941.

Fairchild, Ray: b. 1872; d. Ohio, 20 Apr 1918.

Faire, Virginia Brown: b. Brooklyn, NY, 26 Jun 1904; d. Laguna Beach, CA, 30 Jun 1980.

Fairfax, Lance: b. New Zealand, ? Apr 1899; d. ? Jan 1974.

Fairfax, Lettice: 26 Mar 1876; d. 25 Dec 1948.

Falconett, Renee: b. Sermano, Corsica, 1892; d. Buenos Aires, Argentina, 12 Dec 1946.

Falkenstein, Julius: b. 1877; d. 9 Dec 1933.

Fanning, Frank B.: b. Los Angeles, CA, 25 Dec 1879; d. Los Angeles, CA, 1 Mar 1934.

Farebrother, Violet: b. Grimsby, Lincs, Eng, 22 Aug 1888; d. Eastbourne, Sussex, Eng, 27 Sep 1969.

Ferjeon, Herbert: b. San Francisco, CA, 27 Oct 1879; d. London, Eng, 3 May 1945.

Farley, Dot: b. Chicago, IL, 6 Feb 1881; d. Woodland Hills, CA, 21 May 1971.

Farley, James Lee: b. Waldron, AR, 8 Jan 1882; d. Pacoima, CA, 12 Oct 1947.

Farnum, Dustin: b. Hampton Beach, NH, 27 May 1874; d. New York, NY, 3 Jul 1929.

Farnum, Franklyn: b. Boston, MA, 5 Jun 1878; d. Los Angeles, CA, 4 Jul 1961.

Farnum, William: b. Boston, MA, 4 Jul 1876; d. Los Angeles, CA, 5 Jun 1953.

Farrar, Geraldine: b. Melrose, MA, 28 Feb 1882; d. Ridgefield, CT, 11 Mar 1967.

Farrar, Margaret: b. Kansas City, MO, 8 Apr 1901; d, Los Angeles, CA, 9 Aug 1925.

Farrell, Charles: b. Onset Bay, MA, 9 Aug 1902; d. Palm Springs, CA, 6 May 1990.

Farrell, Charles: b. Dublin, Ire, 6 Aug 1900; d. London, Eng, 27 Aug 1988.

Farrell, Glenda: b. Enid, OK, 30 Jun 1904; d. New York, NY, 1 May 1971.

Farren, Fred: b. London, Eng, 1874; d. London, Eng, 7 May 1956.

Farren, George F.: b. Boston, MA, 14 Sep 1858; d. New York, NY, 21 Apr 1935.

Farren, William: b. 2 Aug 1853; d. London, Eng, 7 Sep 1937.

Farrington, Adele: b. Brooklyn, NY, 1867; d. Los Angeles, CA, 19 Dec 1936.

Farrington, Frank: b. England, 8 Jul 1873; d. Los Angeles, CA, 27 May 1924.

Fatima, "La Belle": b. Syria, 1880; d. Venice, CA, 14 Mar 1921.

Faulkner, John: b. 18??; d. 1940.

Faulkner, Ralph C., Sr.: b. San Antonio, TX, 1890; d. Washington, DC, 21 Aug 1948.

Faulkner, Ralph: b. Aberdeen, WA, 1891; d. Burbank, CA, 28 Jan 1987.

Faussett, Jimmy, Jr.: b. 1878; d. Los Angeles, CA, 13 Nov 1940.

Faust, Martin J.: b. Poughkeepsie, NY, 16 Jan 1886; d. Los Angeles, CA, 19 Jul 1943.

Faversham, William: b. London, Eng, 12 Feb 1868; d. Bay Shore, NY, 7 Apr 1940.

Favor, Edward M.: b. 1856; d. Brooklyn, NY, 10 Jan 1936.

Fawcett, Charles S.: b. 1855; d. London, Eng, 23 Nov 1922.

Fawcett, George: b. Fairfax County, VA, 25 Aug 1860; d. Nantucket, MA, 6 Jun 1939.

Fay, Elfie: b. 11 Jan 1881; d. Los Angeles, CA, 18 Sep 1927.

Fay, Essie: b. 1883; d. St. Petersburg, FL, 7 Apr 1949.

Fay, Hugh: b. New York State, 18??; d. Los Angeles, CA, 4 Dec 1926.

Fay, Jack: b. 1903; d. Los Angeles, CA, 15 Nov 1928.

Fay, Olive: b. 1925; d. Los Angeles, CA, 23 Nov 1977.

Fay, W. G. (Billy): b. Dublin, Ire, 12 Nov 1872; d. London, Eng, 27 Oct 1947.

Faye, Julia: b. Richmond, VA, 24 Sep 1893; d. Santa Monica, CA, 6 Apr 1966.

Faylauer, Adolph: b. Ohio, 16 Nov 1882; d. Los Angeles, CA, 11 Jan 1961.

Fazenda, Louise: b. Lafayette, IN, 17 Jun 1889; d. Los Angeles, CA, 17 Apr 1962.

Fealy, Margaret: b. Memphis, TN, 18 Jul 1865; d. Woodland Hills, CA, 11 Feb 1955.

Fealy, Maude: b. Memphis, TN, 4 Mar 1883; d. Woodland Hills, CA, 9 Nov 1971.

Fearnley, Jane: b. c. 1885; d. 19??.

Featherly, William: b. 1870; d. Los Angeles, CA, 11 May 1925.

Featherston, Vane: London, Eng, 16 Dec 1864; d. Maidenhead, Berks, Eng, 6 Nov 1948.

Feld, Fritz: b. Berlin, Ger, 15 Oct 1900; d. Santa Monica, CA, 18 Nov 1993.

Feldman, Gladys: b. 28 Sep 1891; d. New York, NY, 12 Feb 1974.

Felix, George: b. 1866; d. New York, NY, 12 May 1949.

Fellowes, Rockcliffe: b. Ottawa, Can, 17 Mar 1883; d. Los Angeles, CA, 28 Jan 1950.

Fellows, Robert: b. Los Angeles, CA, 23 Aug 1903; d. Los Angeles, CA, 11 May 1969.

Felt, Edward: b. 1857; d. New York, NY, 7 Jul 1928.

Felton, Verna: b. Salines, CA, 20 Jul 1890; d. North Hollywood, CA, 14 Dec 1966.

Fenimore, Ford: b. 18??; d. El Paso, TX, 20 Apr 1941.

Fenner, Walter: b. Akron, OH, 1882; d. Los Angeles, CA, 7 Nov 1947.

Fenton, Leslie: b. Liverpool, Eng, 12 Mar 1902, d. Montecito, CA, 25 Mar 1978.

Fenton, Mabel: b. Van Buren Co, MI, 29 Mar 1868; d. Los Angeles, CA, 19 Apr 1931.

Fenton, Mark: b. Crestline, OH, 11 Nov 1866; d. Los Angeles, CA, 29 Jul 1925.

Fenwick, Harry: b. Cincinnati, OH, 1 Aug 1880; d. 24 Dec 1932.

Fenwick, Irene: b. Chicago, IL, 5 Sep 1887; d. Beverly Hills, CA, 24 Dec 1936.

Feodoroff, Leo: b. Odessa, Russ, 1867; d. Long Beach, NY, 23 Nov 1949.

Ferguson, Al: b. Rosslarre, Ire, 19 Apr 1888; d. Burbank, CA, 4 Dec 1971.

Ferguson, Barney: b. 1853; d. Bernardsville, NJ, 28 Aug 1924.

Ferguson, Casson: b. Alexandria, LA, 29 May 1891; d. Los Angeles, CA, 12 Feb 1929.

Ferguson, Elsie: b. New York, NY, 19 Aug 1883; d. New London, CT, 15 Nov 1961.

Ferguson George S.: b. 1884; d. Los Angeles, CA, 24 Apr 1944.

Ferguson Helen: b. Decatur, IL, 23 Jul 1901; d. Clearwater, Fl, 14 Mar 1977.

Ferguson, Hilda: b. Baltimore, MD, 1903; d. New York, NY, 3 Sep 1933.

Ferguson Lile: b. ????; d. Yuma, AZ, 21 Nov 1921.

Ferguson, Mattie: b. Indianapolis, IN, 1862; d. New York, NY, 31 Mar 1929.

Ferguson, William J.: b. Baltimore, MD, 8 Jun 1845; d. Baltimore, MD, 3 May 1930.

Fern, Frtizie: b. Akron, OH, 19 Sep 1901; d. Los Angeles, CA, 20 Sep 1932.

Fernandes, Nascimento: b. Faro, Portugal, 6 Nov 1886; d. Lisbon, Portugal, 15 Aug 1955.

Fernandez, Bijou: b. New York, NY, 1877; d. New York, NY, 7 Nov 1961.

Fernandez, George M.: b. 1864; d. 1923.

Fernandez, Roy: b. 1888; d. Los Angeles, CA, 22 Jun 1927.

Ferrari, Martin: b. Russia, 1879; d. 18 May 1927.

Fetchit, Stepin: b. Key West, FL, 30 May 1902; d. Woodland Hills, CA, 19 Nov 1985.

Fetherston, Eddie: b. New York, NY, 9 Sep 1896; d. Yucca Valley, CA, 12 Jun 1965.

Feyder, Jacques: b. Ixelles, Belgium, 21 Jul 1886; d. Rives de Prangins, Switz, 24 May 1948.

Ffolliott, Gladys, b. Ireland, 1879; d. London, Eng, 1 Feb 1928.

Field, Alexander: b. London, Eng, 6 Jun 1892; d. London, Eng, ? Aug 1971.

Fields Ben: b. England, 1878; d. Los Angeles, CA, 21 Oct 1939.

Field, George: b. San Francisco, CA, 18 Mar 1877; d. California, 9 Mar 1925.

Field, Gladys: b. San Francisco, CA, 18??; d. Mt. Vernon, NY, 2 Sep 1920.

Field, Madalynne: b. Michigan, 1 Apr 1907; d. Palm Springs, CA, 1 Oct 1974.

Fielding, Edward: b. Brooklyn, NY, 19 Mar 1875; d. Los Angeles, CA, 10 Jan 1945.

Fielding, Margaret: b. Jersey City, NJ, 22 Jun 1895; d. Los Angeles, CA, 25 Nov 1974.

Fielding, Minnie: b. 1871; d. 22 Jul 1936.

Fielding, Romaine: b. Kentucky, 26 May 1879; d. Los Angeles, CA, 15 Dec 1927.

Fields, Herbert: b, New York, NY, 26 Jul 1897; d. New York, NY, 24 Mar 1958.

Fields, Lew: b. New York, NY, 1 Jan 1867; d. Beverly Hills, CA, 20 Jul 1941.

Fields, W. C.: b. Philadelphia, PA, 29 Jan 1880; d. Pasadena, CA, 25 Dec 1946.

Fierce, Louis: b. 1852; d. Bernardsville, NJ, 11 Mar 1926.

Figman, Max: b. Vienna, Austria, 1868; d. Bayside, NY, 13 Feb 1952.

Figman, Oscar: b. 1882; d. Neponsit, NY, 18 Jul 1930.

Fijewski, Tadzio: b. Poland, 14 Aug 1911; d. 1977.

Fillmore, Clyde: b. McCannelsville, OH, 25 Sep 1875; d. Santa Monica, CA, 19 Dec 1946.

Fillmore, Nellie: b. 1864; d. Winthrop, MA, 20 Jun 1942.

Filson, Al W.: b. Blufton, IN, 27 Jan 1857; d. 14 Nov 1925.

Finch, Flora: b. Sussex, Eng, 17 Jun 1869; d. Los Angeles, CA, 4 Jan 1940.

Finch, Veronica Cavendish: b. 1900; d. New York, NY, 16 Jul 1924.

Findlay, John: b. England, 1858; d. New York, NY, 10 Apr 1918.

Findlay, Ruth: b. New York, 1904; d. New York, NY, 13 Jul 1949.

Findlay, Thomas B.: b. Guelph, Ont, Can, 28 Dec 1873; d. Aylmer, Que, Can, 29 May 1941.

Fine, Budd: b. Connecticut, 9 Feb 1894; d. West Los Angeles, CA, 9 Feb 1966.

Finlay, Robert: b. New Haven, CT, 1888; d. Prescott, AZ, 2 Apr 1929.

Finlayson, James H.: b. Falkirk, Scot, 27 Aug 1887; d. Los Angeles, CA, 9 Oct 1953.

Finley, Ned: b. 10 Jul 18??; d. New York, NY, 27 Sep 1920.

Finn, Adelaide: b. 4 Jan 1894; d. Addingham, PA, 20 Jan 1978.

Fiorenza, Alfredo: b. Italy, 1868; d. Los Angeles, CA, 24 Feb 1931.

Fischer, David G.: b. 1891; d. Hartford, CT, 21 Apr 1939.

Fischer, Margarita: b. Missouri Valley, IA, 12 Feb 1886; d. Encinitas, CA; 11 Mar 1975.

Fischer, Robert C.: b. Danzig, Ger, 28 May 1881; d. San Diego, CA, 11 Mar 1973.

Fischer-Koeppe, Hugo: b. 13 Feb 1890; d. 31 Dec 1937.

Fisher, Alfred C.: b. Bristol, Eng, 14 Jan 1849; d. Glendale, CA, 26 Aug 1933.

Fisher, Charles: b. 18??; d. 1 Jul 1916.

Fisher, George: b. Republic, MI, 10 Aug 1891; d. Sawtelle, CA, 13 Aug 1960 .

Fisher, Harry, Jr.: b. Boston, MA, 13 Sep 1885; d. Los Angeles, CA, 21 May 1917.

Fisher, Harry E.: b. Bristol, Eng, 1868; d. New York, NY, 28 May 1923.

Fisher, Lawrence (Larry): b. New York, NY, 19 Apr 1891; d. 6 Dec 1937.

Fisher, Maggie (Maggie Halloway): b. Manchester, Eng, 10 Jun 1854; d. Glendale, CA, 3 Nov 1938.

Fisher, Millicent: b. Ashville, NC, 4 Feb 1896; d. Ventura, CA, 1 Jan 1979.

Fisher, Sallie: b. Wyoming, 10 Aug 1880; d. Palms, CA, 8 Jun 1950.

Fisher, William: b. 1868; d. Los Angeles, CA, 4 Jul 1933.

Fiske, Minnie Maddern: b. New Orleans, LA, 19 Dec 1865; d. Hollis, NY, 15 Feb 1932.

Fitz-Allen, Adelaide: b. 1856; d. New York, NY, 26 Feb 1935.

Fitzgerald, Cissy: b. England, 1873; d. Ovingdean, Sussex, Eng, 5 May 1941.

Fitzgerald, Edward P.: b. 1883; d. Buffalo, NY, 1 May 1942.

Fitzgerald, Florence Dimock: b. 1889; d. Hartford, CT, 31 Jan 1962.

Fitzgerald, James M.: b. Mississippi 19 Apr 1896; d. Los Angeles, CA, 21 Jan 1919.

Fitzhamon, Lewin: b. Aldingham, Eng, 5 Jun 1869; d. London, Eng, 10 Oct 1961.

Fitzharris, Edward: b. England, 1890; d. Woodland Hills, CA, 12 Oct 1974.

Fitzhugh, Venita: b. 1895; d. Philadelphia, PA, 1 Jan 1920.

Fitzmaurice, George: b. Paris, Fr, 13 Feb 1895; d. Los Angeles, CA, 13 Jun 1940.

Fitzroy, Emily: b. London, Eng, 24 May 1860; d. Gardena, CA, 3 Mar 1954.

Fitzroy, Louis: b. Sault Saint Marie, MI, 24 Nov 1870; d. Los Angeles, CA, 26 Jan 1947.

Fix, Paul: b. Dobbs Ferry, NY, 13 Mar 1901; d. Santa Monica, CA, 14 Oct 1983.

Flagg, James Montgomery: b. Pelham Manor, NY, 18 Jun 1877; d. New York, NY, 27 May 1960.

Flanagan, Edward J.: b. St. Louis, MO, 1880; d. Los Angeles, CA, 18 Aug 1925.

Flanagan, Hugh: b. 18??; d. New York, NY, 26 Dec 1925.

Flanagan, Rebecca C,: b. Philadelphia, PA, 10 Feb 1878; d. Los Angeles, CA, 30 Jan 1938.

Flateau, George: b. France, 1882; d. Paris, Fr, 13 Feb 1953.

Flatow, John L.: b. 18??; d. Washington, DC, 3 Oct 1922.

Flaum, Mayer: b. 1900; d. Los Angeles, CA, 26 Apr 1990.

Fleck, Frederick: b. New York, NY, 4 Jun 1692; d. Los Angeles, CA, 9 Nov 1961.

Fleming, Alice: b. Brooklyn, NY, 9 Aug 1882; d, New York, NY, 6 Dec 1952.

Fleming, Carroll: b. Lexington, KY, 1865; d. Bronx, NY, ? May 1930.

Fleming, Caryl Stacy: b. Cedar Rapids, IA, 1894; d. Beverly Hills, CA, 2 Sep 1940.

Fleming, Claude: b. Camden, NSW, Austral, 22 Feb 1884; d. Sydney, Austral, 23 Mar 1952.

Fleming, Ian: b. Melbourne; Austral, 10 Sep 1888; d. London, Eng, 1 Jan 1969.

Fleming, Robert: b. Ontario, Can, 19 Feb 1878; d. 4 Oct 1933.

Fletcher, Art: b. Collinsville, IL, 5 Jan 1885; d. Los Angeles, CA, 6 Feb 1950.

Fletcher, Bramwell, b. Bradford, York, Eng, 20 Feb 1904; d. Westmoreland, NH, 22 Jun 1988.

Fletcher, Cecil B.: b. Northampton, Eng, 18??; d. Romford, Essex, Eng, ? Nov 1918.

Fletcher, Ora: b. ????; d. ? Feb 1920.

Flint, Hazel: b. 1893; d. Los Angeles, CA, 18 Aug 1959.

Flint, Helen: b. Chicago, IL, 14 Jun 1898; d. Washington, DC, 9 Sep 1967.

Florath, Albert: b. Bielefeld, Ger. 14 Dec 1888; d. Gailsdorf- Nordwuertemberg, Ger, 10 Mar 1957.

Floresco, Michel: b. Italy, ????; d. Venice, Italy, ? Oct 1925.

Florey, Robert: b. Paris, Fr, 14 Sep 1900; d. Santa Monica, CA, 16 May 1979.

Flowers, Bess: b. Sherman, TX, 23 Mar 1898; d. Woodland Hills, CA, 26 Jul 1984.

Flowerton, Consuelo: b. 1900; d. New York, NY, 21 Dec 1965.

Flugrath, Edna: b. Brooklyn, NY, 29 Dec 1893; d. San Diego, CA, 6 Apr 1966.

Fluker, Mack A.: b. Los Angeles, CA, 22 Apr 1903; d. Los Angeles, CA, 28 Apr 1929.

Flynn, Hazel E.: b. Chicago, IL, 31 Mar 1899; d. Santa Monica, CA, 15 May 1964.

Flynn, Maurice B. (Lefty): b. Greerwich, CT, 26 May 1892; d. Camden, SC, 4 Mar 1959.

Fogel, Vladimir: b. 18??; d. 8 Jun 1929.

Fogg, Orian: b. 1849; d. New York, NY, 24 May 1923.

Follansbee, Oliver: b. Illinois, 18 Sep 1890; d. Los Angeles, CA, 4 Apr 1969.

Fonda, Gloria: b. St. Paul, MN, 1896; d. Alamos, Sonora, Mex, 20 Jan 1978.

Fones, Gilbert, A.: b. Arkansas, 13 Sep 1887; d. Los Angeles, CA, 5 Oct. 1965.

Fonss, Olaf: b. Denmark, 1882; d. Copenhagen, Denmark, 4. Nov 1949.

Fontanne, Lynne: b. Woodford, Essex, Eng, 6 Dec 1887; d. Genesee Depot, WI, 30 Jul 1983.

Foote, Courtenay: b. Harrogate, Eng, 18??; d. Italy, 4 Mar 1925.

Forbes, Harris L.: b. Annapolis, MD, 5 Feb 1877; d. Glendale, CA, 26 Oct 1956.

Forbes, Mary: b. London, Eng, 1 Jan 1883; d. Beaumont, CA, 22 Jul 1974.

Forbes, Mary E.: b. Rochester, NY, 8 Nov 1879; d. Los Angeles, CA, 20 Aug 1964.

Forbes, Norman: b. Scotland, 24 Sep 1858; d. London, Eng, 28 Sep 1932.

Forbes, Ralph: b. London, Eng, 30 Sep 1905; d. New York, NY, 31 Mar 1951.

Forbes-Robertson, Eric: b. 1865; d. London, Eng, 9 Mar 1935.

Forbes-Robertson, Sir Johnston: b. London, Eng, 16 Jan 1853; d. Dover, Eng, 6 Nov 1937.

Force, Floyd Charles: b. South Line, MI, 22 Mar 1876; d. Los Angeles, CA, 9 Jun 1947.

Ford, Fenton: b. 1878; d. Los Angeles, CA, 1 May 1938.

Ford, Francis: b. Portland, ME, 15 Aug 1881; d. Los Angeles, CA, 5 Sep 1953.

Ford, Harrison: b. Kansas City, MO, 16 Mar 1884; d. Woodland Hills, CA, 2 Dec 1957.

Ford, John: b. Cape Elizabeth, ME, 1 Feb 1894; d. Palm Desert, CA, 31 Aug 1973.

Ford, Lettie: b. 1847; d. New York, NY, 26 Sep 1936.

Ford, Marty: b. 1900; d. Los Angeles, CA, 12 Nov 1954.

Ford, Philip: b. Portland, ME, 16 Oct 1900; d. Woodland Hills, CA, 12 Jan 1976.

Forde, Arthur: b. Plymouth, Eng, 29 Jul 1871; d. Culver City, CA, 30 Dec 1952.

Forde, Eugene: b. Providence, RI, 8 Nov 1896; d. Port Hueneme, CA, 27 Feb 1986.

Forde, Eugenie: b. New York, NY, 22 Jun 1879; d. Van Nuys, CA, 5 Sep 1940.

Forde, Hal: b. Ireland, 1877; d. Philadelphia, PA, 4 Dec 1955.

Forde, Stanley H.: b. Buffalo, NY, 9 Feb 1878; d. New York, NY, 28 Jan 1929.

Forde, Victoria: b. New York, NY, 21 Apr 1896; d. Los Angeles, CA, 24 Jul 1964.

Forde, Walter: b. Bradford, Yorks, Eng, 21 Apr 1896; d. Santa Monica, CA, 7 Jan 1984.

Fordred, Dorice: b. Port Elizabeth, So Africa, 25 Nov 1902; d. London, Eng, 4 Aug 1980.

Forest, Frank: b. St. Paul, MN, 17 Oct 1896; d. Santa Monica, CA, 23 Dec 1976.

Forest, Jean: b. Paris, Fr, 27 Sep 1912; d. 27 Mar 1980.

Forest, Karl: b. Vienna, Austria, 12 Nov 1874; d. 3 Jun 1944.

Forman, Tom: b. Mitchell County, TX. 22 Feb 1893; d. Venice, CA, 7 Nov 1926.

Forman, Tom B.: b. Minnesota, 29 Oct 1891; d. Los Angeles, CA, 16 Nov 1951.

Formby, George: b. Wigan, Lancs, Eng, 26 May 1904; d. Preston, Lancs, Eng, 6 Mar 1961.

Formes, Karl, Jr.: b. London, Eng, 3 Jul 184l; d. Los Angeles, CA, 18 Nov 1939.

Forrest, Allan: b. Brooklyn, NY, 1 Sep 1889; d. Detroit, MI, 25 Jul 1941.

Forrest, Arthur: b. Bayreuth, Ger, 1859; d. New York, NY, 14 May 1933.

Forrest, Belford: b. 1878; d. Los Angeles, CA, 1 May 1938.

Forrest, Mabel: b. Illinois, 5 Nov 1894; d. Woodland Hills, CA, 5 Jul 1967.

Forrester, Frederick: b. 1872; d. New York, NY, 14 Oct 1952.

Forsberg, Edwin: b. Cleveland, OH, 1872; d. New York, NY, 11 May 1947.

Forst, Willi: b. Vienna, Austria, 1903; d. Vienna, Austria, 12 Aug 1980.

Forster, Hedda: b. Frankfort-on-the-Main, Ger, 27 Jun 1895; d. Berlin, Ger, 2 Jan 1933.

Forster, Oscar,: b. New York, NY, 17 Feb 1885; d. 19??.

Foster, Rudolf: b. Groebming, Ger, 30 Oct 1884; d. Vienna, Austria, 25 Oct 1968.

Forsythe Robert: b, Belfast, Ire, 1876; d. New York, NY, 9 Feb 1922.

Forsythe, Victor Clyde: b. 1886; d. Pasadena, CA, 24 May 1962.

Fortescue, Viola: b. Columbus, GA, 1875; d. New York, NY, 16 Sep 1953.

Fortier, Herbert: b. Toronto, Can; 1867; d. Philadelphia, PA, 16 Feb 1949.

Fortune, Edmund: b. Geneva, NY, 27 Mar 1851; d. 21 Sep 1939.

Fortune, Wallace: b. 1884; d. New York, NY, 12 Jan 1926.

Foshay, Harold: b. Brooklyn, NY, 1884; d. Charleston, SC, 23 Feb 1953.

Foss, Darrell Burton: b, Oconomowoc, WI, 28 Mar 1892; d. Los Angeles, CA, 15 Sep 1962.

Foss, Kenelm: b. England, 13 Dec 1885; d. London, Eng, 28 Nov 1963.

Foster, Fern: b. Somerville, MA, 2 Oct 1885; d. Somerville, MA, 10 Jun 1949.

Foster, Flora (Billy Foster); b. Boston, MA, 1898; d. Chicago, IL, 16 Sep 1914.

Foster, Helen: b. Independence, KS, 23 May 1906; d. Los Angeles, CA, 25 Dec 1982.

Foster, J. Morris: b. Foxbert, PA, 9 Sep 1881; d. Burbank, CA, 24 Apr 1966.

Foster, May: b. Illinois, 27 Mar 1873; d. Los Angeles, CA, 6 Jan 1951.

Fouce, Frank: b. Hawaii, 26 Oct 1899; d. Los Angeles, CA, 11 Jan 1962.

Fougers, Pierre: b. France, ????; d. Paris, Fr, 28 Nov 1922.

Fougez, Anna: b. 1895; d. Santa Marinella, Italy, ? Sep 1966.

Fowler, Brenda: b. Jamestown, ND, 16 Feb 1883; d. Los Angeles, CA, 27 Oct 1942.

Fowler, John C.: b. New York, NY. 25 Jul 1869; d. Los Angeles, CA, 27 Jun 1952.

Fowler, Robert G.: b. California, 10 Aug 1883; d. San Jose, CA, 15 Jun 1966.

Fox, Harry: b. New York State, 25 May 1882; d. Los Angeles, CA, 20 Jul 1959.

Fox, John, Jr.: b. 18??; d. Big Stone Gap, VA, 6 Jul 1919.

Fox, Josephine: b. 1869; d. Englewood, NJ, 2 Aug 1953.

Fox, Virginia: b. Charleston, WV, 19 Apr 1902; d. Santa Monica, CA, 14 Oct 1982.

Foxe, Earle: b. Oxford, OH, 25 Dec 1891; d. Los Angeles, CA, 10 Dec 1973.

Foy, Bryan: b. Chicago, IL, 8 Dec 1896; d. Los Angeles, CA, 20 Apr 1977.

Foy, Charles: b. Illinois, 12 Jan 1898; d. Los Angeles, CA, 22 Aug 1984.

Foy, Eddie: b. New York, NY, 9 Mar 1854; d. Kansas City, MO, 16 Feb 1928.

Foy, Eddie, Jr.: b. New Rochelle, NY, 4 Feb 1905; d. Woodland Hills, CA, 15 Jul 1983.

Foy, Harry: b. 1868; d. New York, NY, 4 Mar 1931.

Foy, Madeline: b. 21 Sep 1903; d. Los Angeles, CA, 5 Jul 1988.

Foy, Mary: b. 19??; d. Los Angeles, CA, 13 Dec 1987.

Foy, Patrick C.: b. 18??; d. New York, NY, 4 Sep 1920.

Foy, Richard: b. 1905; d. Dallas, TX, 4 Apr 1947.

Frahrney, Milton J.: b. 1871; d. Culver City, CA, 26 Mar 1941.

Fralick, Allen (Freddie): b. Detroit, MI, 4 Jun 1888; d. Los Angeles, CA, 13 May 1958.

Frame, Park B.: b. Seattle, WA, 1888; d. San Bernardino, CA, 2 Jun 1943.

France, C. V. (Charles): b. Bradford, Eng, 30 Jun 1868; d. Gerrards Cross, Eng, 13 Apr 1949.

France, Claude: b. Austria, 1893; d. Paris, Fr, 2 Jan 1928.

Francen, Victor: b. Tirlemont, Belgium, 5 Aug 1888; d. Aix-en- Provence, Fr, 17 Nov 1977.

Frances, Rose: b. Milwaukee, WI, 1881; d. Los Angeles, CA, 27 Jan 1962.

Francis, Alec B.: b. London, Eng, 2 Dec 1867; d. Los Angeles, CA, 6 Jul 1934.

Francis, Eve: b. Brussels, Belgium, 1896; d. Neuilly, Fr, 6 Dec 1980.

Francis, Noel: b. Temple, TX, 31 Aug 1906; d. California, 30 Oct 1959.

Francis, Olin: b. Mooresville, MS, 13 Sep 1892; d. Los Angeles, CA, 30 Jun 1952.

Francisco, Betty: b. Little Rock, AR, 26 Sep 1900; d. Corona, CA, 25 Nov 1950.

Franck, John L.: b. Louisville, KY, 31 Jul 1852; d. Los Angeles, CA, 22 Oct 1920.

Franey, William: b. Chicago, IL, 23 Jun 1889; d. Los Angeles, CA, 6 Dec 1940.

Frank, Alexander: b. England, 1866; d. Long Island, NY, 14 Dec 1939.

Frank, Christian J.: b. New York, 13 Mar 1890; d. Los Angeles, CA, 10 Dec 1967.

Frank, Harry: b. Berlin, Ger, 15 Oct ????; d. 1948.

Frank, J. Herbert: b. New York, NY, 12 May 1885; d. Los Angeles, CA, 9 Mar 1926.

Frank, William: b. 1880; d. Los Angeles, CA, 23 Dec 1925.

Franke, Constant: b. Brussels, Belgium, 5 May 1893; d. Los Angeles, CA, 31 Oct 1943.

Frankel, Franchon: b. St. Louis, MO, 28 Apr 1874; d. Los Angeles, CA, 12 Aug 1937.

Franklin, Alberta: b. 1897; d. Mountain View, CA, 14 Mar 1976.

Franklin, Irene: b. St. Louis, MO, 13 Jun 1876; d. Englewood, NJ, 16 Jun 1941.

Franklin, Martha: b. Germany, 13 Nov 1868; d. Los Angeles, CA, 19 Apr 1929,

Franklin, Rupert: b. 1862; d. Los Angeles, CA, 14 Jan 1939.

Franklin, Sidney: b. 1870; d. Los Angeles, CA, 18 Mar 1931.

Franklyn, Beth: b. 1873; d. Baltimore, MD, 5 Mar 1956.

Franklyn, Irwin: b. New York, NY, 8 Jan 1904; d. Los Angeles, CA, 7 Sep 1966.

Frankman, Charles U.: b. New York, NY, 23 Sep 1883; d. 19??.

Franz, Joseph J.: b. Utica, NY, 12 Oct 1883; d. Los Angeles Co. CA, 9 Sep 1970.

Fraser, Alec: b. Fife, Scot, 16 Feb 1884; d. London, Eng, 20 Jun 1956.

Fraser, Harry L.: b. San Francisco, CA, 31 Mar 1889; d. Pomona Valley, CA, 8 Apr 1974.

Frawley, William: b. Burlington, IA, 26 Feb 1887; d. Los Angeles, CA, 3 Mar 1966.

Frazer, Nitra: b. 1888; d. Englewood, NJ, 2 May 1979.

Frazer, Robert W.: b. Farmington, MA, 29 Jun 1889; d. Los Angeles, CA, 17 Aug 1944.

Frazin, Gladys: b. 1901; d. New York, NY, 9 Mar 1939.

Frederici, Blanche: b. Brooklyn, NY, 21 Jan 1878; d. Visalia, CA, 23 Dec 1933.

Frederick, Freddie Burke: b. San Francisco, CA, 13 Jan 1921; d. Glendale, CA, 31 Jan 1986.

Frederick, Pauline: b. Boston, MA, 12 Aug 1885; d. Los Angeles, CA, 19 Sep 1938.

Fredericks, William: b. 1861; d. Astoria, NY, 2 Mar 1931.

Freear, Louie: b. 26 Nov 1871; d. London, Eng, 23 Mar 1939.

Freeman, Maurice: b. 1872; d. Bay Shore, NY, 26 Mar 1953.

Freeman, William B.: b. 1870; d. Brockton, MA, 7 Jun 1932.

Fregoli, Leopoldo: b. Rome, Italy, 2 Jul 1867; d. 26 Nov 1936.

Freil, Rayamond A. (Dick): b. 1894; d. Yonkers, NY, 24 May 1939.

Fremont, Al W.: b. Cohoes, NY, 23 Feb 1860; d. Los Angeles, CA, 16 Jan 1930.

French, Charles K.: b. Columbus, OH, 17 Jan 1860; d. Los Angeles, CA, 2 Aug 1952.

French, George B: b. Storm Lake, IA, 14 Apr 1883; d. Los Angeles, CA, 9 Jun 1961.

French, Helen K.: b. Ohio, 13 Feb 1863; d. Los Angeles, CA, 12 Mar 1917.

French, Herbert C. (Bert): b. 1891; d. New London, CT, 27 Jan 1924.

Fresnay, Pierre: b. Paris, Fr, 4 Apr 1897; d. Paris, Fr, 9 Jan 1975.

Frey, Callie: b. 1875; d. Los Angeles, CA, 29 Apr 1948.

Fric, Martin: b. Prague, Czech, 2 Mar 1902; d. 1968.

Friebus, Theodore: b. Washington, DC, 1879; d. New York, NY, 26 Dec 1917.

Friedberger, Louis: b. Germany, 18??; d. Los Angeles, CA, 16 Feb 1924.

Friedgen, Raymond: b. New York, NY, 1893; d. Los Angeles, CA, 1 Mar 1966.

Friedman Henry: b. 1897; d. Bryn Mawr, PA, 18 Aug 1983.

Fries, Otto H.: b. St. Louis, MO, 28 Oct 1887; d. 15 Sep 1938.

Friganza, Trixie: b. Grenola, KS, 29 Nov 1870; d. Flintridge, CA, 27 Feb 1955.

Frink, Lola B.: b. 1900; d. Chicago, IL, 15 Nov 1952.

Frisby, Mildred: b. 18??; d. 1939.

Frith, Thomas Preston: b. 1883; d. Los Angeles, CA, 7 Jan 1945.

Fritsch, Willy: b. Kattowitz, Ger, 27 Jan 1901; d. Hamburg, Ger, 12 Jul 1973.

Frohlich, Gustav: b. Hanover, Ger, 21 Mar 1902; d. Lugano, Switz, 22 Dec 1987.

Frye, Dwight: b. Salina, KS, 22 Feb 1899; d, Los Angeles, CA, 7 Nov 1943.

Fuchs, Oskar: b. Germany, 9 Jan 1866; d. 19 Oct 1927.

Fuller, Irene: b. 1898; d. Los Angeles, CA, 20 Mar 1945.

Fuller, Jesse: b. Jonesboro, GA, 12 Mar 1896; d. Oakland, CA, 29 Jan 1976.

Fuller, Lew H.: b. 1887; d. Chicago, IL, 13 Nov 1939.

Fuller, Mary: b. Washington, DC, 5 Oct 1888; d. Washington, DC, 9 Dec 1973.

Fulton, Maude: b. Eldorado, KS, 14 May 1881; d. San Fernando, CA, 9 Nov 1950.

Fung, Willie: b. Canton, China, 3 Mar 1896; d. Los Angeles, CA, 16 Apr 1945.

Furey, Barney: b. Boise, ID, 7 Sep 1886, d. Los Angeles, CA, 18 Jan 1938.

Furey, James A.: b. Ogdensburg, NY, 10 May 1865; d. New York, NY, 7 Jul 1930.

Furniss, Harry: b. Wexford, Ire, 1854; d. Hastings, Eng, 15 Jan 1925.

Fursman, Georgia May: b. 1860; d. 10 Feb 1926.

G

Gaal, Franciska: b. Budapest, Hungary, 1 Feb 1901; d. New York, NY, 13 Aug 1972.

Gable, Clark: b. Cadiz, OH, 1 Feb 1901; d. Los Angeles, CA, 16 Nov 1960.

Gabriel, Carl: b, 18??; d. Munich, Ger, ? Feb 1931.

Gabriel, Jean (Jean G. Citarella): b. 1898; d. Newark, NJ, 9 Oct 1977.

Gabrio, Gabriel: b. Reims, Fr, 1888; d. 2 Nov 1946.

Gaden, Alexander: b. Montreal, Can, 20 Feb 1880; d. 19??.

Gaidarov, Vladimir: b. 25 Jul 1893; d. 17 Dec 1976.

Gail, Jane: b. Salem, NY, 16 Aug 1890; d. 19??.

Gaillard, Robert: b. Adrian, MI, 14 Nov 1868; d. Glendale, CA, 24 Sep 1941.

Galbraith, Joseph: b. 18??; d. Los Angeles, CA, 4 Mar 1918.

Gale, Alice: b. Philadelphia, PA, 5 Dec 1858; d. New York, NY, 27 Mar 1941.

Gale, Lillian: b. 8 Jun 1885; d. Englewood, NJ, 2 Apr 1972.
Gale, Marguerite: b. 1885; d. Amsterdam, NY, 20 Aug 1948.
Galeen, Henrik: b. Holland, 1882; d. Rochester, NY, 30 Jul 1949.
Gallagher, Frank: b. 1901; d. Burbank, CA, 16 Feb 1929.
Gallagher, Ray: b. San Francisco, CA, 17 Apr 1885; d. Camarillo, CA, 6 Mar 1953.
Gallagher, Richard (Skeets): b. Terre Haute, IN, 28 Jul 1886; d. Santa Monica, CA, 22 May 1955.
Gallaher, Donald: b. Illinois, 25 Jun 1895; d. Los Angeles, CA, 14 Aug 1961.
Gallatin, Alberta: b. Campbell County, WV, 1861; d. New York, NY, 25 Aug 1948.
Gallery, Tom: b. Chicago, IL, 27 Nov 1898; d. Encino, CA, 25 Aug 1993.
Galli, Georges: b. Paris, Fr, 1902; d. Marseilles, Fr, 3 Jul 1982.
Galli-Curci, Amelita: b. Milan, Italy, 18 Nov 1882; d. La Jolla, CA, 26 Nov 1963.
Galvani, Ciro: b. Castel San Pietro, Italy, 10 Apr 1867; d. Castel San Pietro, Italy, 28 Jan 1956.
Galvani, Dino: b. Milan, Italy, 27 Oct 1890; d. London, Eng, 14 Sep 1960.
Gambarelli, Maria: b. Spezia, Italy, 1900; d. Huntington, NY, 4 Feb 1990.
Gamble, Fred (Fred Gambold): b. Indianapolis, IN, 26 Oct 1868; d. Los Angeles, CA, 17 Feb 1939.
Gamble, Warburton: b. England, 1883; d. 27 Aug 1945.
Gamboa, Elias: b. Mexico, 20 Jul 1895; d. Los Angeles, CA, 9 Dec 1959.
Gance, Able: b. Paris, Fr, 25 Oct 1889; d. Paris, Fr, 10 Nov 1981.
Gane, Nolan: b. Houma, LA, 18??; d. 12 Feb 1915.
Gant, Harry: b. Des Moines, IA, 11 Feb 1881; d. Sunland, CA, 26 Jul 1967.
Gantvoort, Carl: b. Bowling Green, KY, 1883; d. Los Angeles, CA, 28 Sep 1935.
Ganzhorn, John W.: b. Ft. Thomas, AR, 21 Mar 1881; d, Los Angeles, CA, 19 Sep 1956.
Garavaglia, Ferruccio: b. San Zenone, Poland, 1 May 1868; d. 29 Apr 1912.
Garbo, Greta: b. Stockholm, Sweden, 18 Sep 1905; d. New York, NY, 15 Apr 1990.
Garbutt, Frank A: b. 1869; d. Los Angeles, CA, 19 Nov 1947.
Garcia, Allan (Al Ernest Garcia): b. San Francisco, CA, 11 Mar 1887; d. Los Angeles, CA, 4 Sep 1938.
Garcia, May: b. 1868; d. New York, NY, 17 Aug 1950.
Garcia, Sara: b. Mexico, 1895; d. Mexico City, Mex, 21 Nov 1980.
Gardel, Carlos: b. Toulouse, Fr, 11 Dec 1890; d. Medellin, Columbia, 24 Jun 1935.
Gardelle, Yvonne (aka Yvonne Chappelle): b. Chicago, IL, 7 Oct 1897; d. Oceanside, CA, 21 Jul 1979.
Garden, Mary: b. Aberdeen, Scot, 20 Feb 1874; d. Aberdeen, Scot, 3 Jan 1967.
Gardin, Vladimir; b. Russia, 18 Jan 1877; d. Moscow, Russ, 28 May 1965.

Gardiner, Don: b. 1902; d. Los Angeles, CA, 5 Jun 1926.

Gardiner, Reginald: b. Wimbledon, Surrey, Eng, 27 Feb 1903; d. Westwood, CA, 7 Jul 1980.

Gardner, Amelia: b. Pittsburgh, PA, 4 Sep 1866; d. Baltimore, MD, 11 Jan 1947.

Gardner, Cyril: b. Paris, Fr, 30 May 1898; d. Los Angeles, CA, 30 Dec 1942.

Gardner, George: b. 1868; d. East Islip, NY, 12 May 1929.

Gardner, Helen: b. 2 Sep 1884; d. Orlando, FL, 20 Nov 1968.

Gardner, Jack: b. 1873; d. Encino, CA, 30 Sep 1950.

Gardner, Jack: b. 1876; d. Glendale, CA, 29 Dec 1929.

Gardner, Peter: b. 1898; d. Studio City, CA, 13 Nov 1953.

Gardner, Shayle: b. Auckland, New Zealand, 22 Aug 1890; d. 17 May 1945.

Garland, Franklyn: b. 1864; d. Los Angeles, CA, 5 May 1945.

Garnett, Tay: b. Los Angeles, CA, 13 Jun 1894; d. Sawtelle, CA, 3 Oct 1977.

Garon, Pauline: b. Montreal, Can, 9 Sep 1901; d. San Bernardino, CA, 27 Aug 1965.

Garrick, Richard T.: b. Ireland, 27 Dec 1878; d. Los Angeles, CA, 21 Aug 1962.

Garrison, Lindley Miller: b. Camden, NJ, 28 Nov 1864; d. Sea Bright, NJ, 18 Oct 1932.

Garrity, Harry: b. New Jersey, 15 Nov 1872; d. Los Angeles, CA, 13 Dec 1928.

Garry, Claude: b. 1877; d. Paris, Fr, ? Aug 1918.

Garry, Joseph: b. 14 Aug 1877; d. Marietta, OH, 7 Jun 1954.

Gartner, Adolph: b. 1879; d. Los Angeles, CA, 9 Jan 1958.

Garvie, Edward: b. Meriden, CT, 30 Oct 1864; d. New York, NY, 17 Feb 1939.

Garvin, Anita: b. New York, NY, 11 Feb 1906; d. Woodland Hills, CA, 7 Jul 1994.

Garwood, William: b. Springfield, MO, 28 Apr 1884; d. Los Angeles, CA, 28 Dec 1950.

Gaskell, Charles L.: b. New Bern, NC, 29 Jan 1870; d. Los Angeles, CA, 9 Dec 1943.

Gaston, George: b. 1844; d. Englewood, NJ, 14 Jan 1937.

Gaston, Mae: b. Boston, MA, c, 1890; d. 19??.

Gastrock, Philip: b. Louisiana, 26 Oct 1876; d. Woodland Hills, CA, 10 Apr 1956.

Gauntier, Gene: b. Kansas City, MO, c. 1880; d. Cuernavaca, Mex, 18 Dec 1966.

Gauthier, Suzanne: b. 1926; d. Los Angeles, CA, 26 Jan 1988.

Gavin, John F.: b. 18??; d. Bronte, Austral, ? Feb 1938.

Gaxton, William: b. San Francisco, CA, 2 Dec 1893; d. New York, NY, 2 Feb 1963.

Gay, Charles: b. France, 1887, d. Newport Beach, CA, 23 Feb 1950.

Gay, Maisie: b. London, Eng, 7 Jan 1883; d. London, Eng, 13 Sep 1945.

Gay, Walter: b. 18???; d. 8 Jan 1936.

Gaye, Howard: b. Hitchin, Hertfordshire, Eng, 18??; d. London, Eng, 26 Dec 1955.

Gayer, Echlin Philip: b. 1878; d. New York, NY, 14 Feb 1926,

Gaynor, Janet: b. Philadelphia, PA, 6 Oct 1906; d. Palm Springs, CA, 14 Sep 1984.

Gaynor, Ruth: b. 1902; d. Seattle, WA, 28 May 1919.

Gaynor, Mayor William J.: b. Oneida, NY, 1851; d. Aboard Ship, 10 Sep 1913.

Gear, Luella: b. New York, NY, 5 Sep 1897; d. New York, NY, 3 Apr 1980.

Geary, Maine (Bud): b. Salt Lake City, UT, 15 Feb 1898; d. Los Angeles, CA, 22 Feb 1946.

Gebhardt, Frank: b. 18??; d. 23 May 1951.

Gebhardt, George M.: b. Basle, Switz, 1879; d. Edensdale, NY, 2 May 1919.

Gebhart, Albert: b. 1887; d. East Orange, NJ, 4 Jan 1950.

Gebuehr, Otto: b. Kettwig, Ger, 19 May 1877; d. Wiesbaden, Ger, 13 Mar 1954.

Gee, George: b. Yorkshire, Eng, 1895; d. Coventry, Warwick, Eng, 17 Oct 1959.

Gee, George D.: b. 18??; d. Brooklyn, NY, ? Dec 1917.

Gehring, Viktor: b. 10 Jan 1889; d. 24 Apr 1978.

Gehrung, Gene: b. 1882; d. Jacksonville, FL, 19 Oct 1938.

Geldert, Clarence: b. St. John, New Bruns, Can, 9 Jun 1867; d. Los Angeles, CA, 13 May 1935.

Gamelli, Enrico: b. Milan, Italy, 1841; d. 7 May 1926.

Gemier, Firmin: b. Aubervilliers, Fr, 13 Feb 1865; d. Paris, Fr, 26 Nov 1933.

Gemore, Charles: b. Philippines, 15 Aug 1903; d. Los Angeles, CA, 19 Aug 1961.

Genaro, Frankie: b. 1901; d. Staten Island, NY, 12 Dec 1966.

Gendron, Pierre (Leon Gendron): b. Toledo, OH, 4 Mar 1896; d. Los Angeles, CA, 27 Nov 1956.

George, A. E.: b. Lincoln, Eng, 22 Jul 1869; d. London, Eng, 10 Nov 1920.

George, Franklyn: b. Oil City, PA, 1881; d. Aberdeen, WA, 16 Feb 1951.

George, George M.: b. St. Louis, MO, 1889; d. Los Angeles Co, CA, 28 Nov 1960.

George, Gladys: b. Patten, ME, 13 Sep 1904; d. Los Angeles, CA, 8 Dec 1954.

George, Heinrich: b. Stettin, Ger, 9 Oct 1883; d. Russian Internment Camp, 27 Sep 1946.

George, Johh: b. Syria, 21 Jan 1898; d. Los Angeles, CA, 25 Aug 1968.

George, Maude: b. Riverside, CA, 15 Aug 1888; d. Sepulveda, CA, 10 Oct 1963.

George, Voya: b. 1895; d. New York, NY, 8 May 1951.

Geraghty, Carmelita: b. Rushville, IN, 21 Mar 1901; d. New York, NY, 7 Jul 1966.

Gerald, Jim: b. France, 1889; d. 1958.

Gerald, Pete: b. Piacenza, Italy, 1864 d. 19??.

Gerard, Carl: b. Copenhagen; Denmark, 28 Sep 1885; d. Los Angeles, CA, 6 Jan 1966.

Gerard, Joseph Smith: b. 1871; d. Woodland Hills, CA, 20 Aug 1949.

Gerard, Teddie: b. Buenos Aires, Argentina, 2 May 1892; d. London, Eng, 31 Aug 1942.

Gerasch, Alfred: b. Berlin, Ger, 17 Aug 1877; d. ? Aug 1955.

Gerber, Neva: b. Chicago, IL, c. 1892; d. 19??.

Gerdes, Emily: b. Jefferson, KS, 29 Dec 1890; d. Los Angeles, CA, 17 Sep 1974.

Germonprez, Valerie: b. 14 Apr 1897; d. Sherman Oaks, CA, 22 Oct 1988.

Gerold, Hermen: b. Austria, 1862; d. New York, NY, 19 Nov 1920.

Gerrard, Charles: b. Carlow, Ire, 25 Dec 1887; d. 19??.

Gerrard, Douglas: b. Dublin, Ire, 12 Aug 1891; d. Los Angeles, CA, 5 Jun 1950.

Gerrard, Gene: b. London, Eng, 31 Aug 1892; d. Sidmouth, Devon, Eng, 1 Jun 1971.

Gerron, Kurt: b. Berlin, Ger, 11 May 1897; d. Auschwitz, Ger, 28 Oct 1944.

Gerson, Paul: b. England, 1871; d. Los Angeles, CA, 5 Jun 1957.

Gert, Valeska: b. Berlin, Ger, 11 Jan 1896; d. 18 Mar 1978.

Gerwing, George: b. Colorado, 25 Nov 1902; d. Riverside, CA, 9 Jan 1979.

Getchell, Sumner: b. Oakland, CA, 20 Oct 1906; d. Sebastopol, CA, 21 Sep 1990.

Ghione, Emilio: b. Turin, Italy, 1879; d. Turin, Italy, 7 Jan 1930.

Giacomino (Giuseppe Cirenia): b. 1884; d. Milan, Italy, ? Aug 1956.

Gibbons, Rose: b. 1886; d. Oakland, CA, 13 Aug 1964.

Gibbs, Joseph F.: b. England, 18??; d. New York, NY, 14 Apr 1921.

Gibbs, Robert Paton: b. Scranton, PA, 1860; d. Clifton, NY, 22 Feb 1941.

Gibler, Mrs. Margaret May: b. Pittsburgh, PA, 1895; d. Paterson, NJ, 21 Feb 1994.

Giblyn, Charles: b. Watertown, NY, 6 Sep 1871; d. Los Angeles, CA, 14 Mar 1934.

Gibney, Louise: b. 1896; d. Santa Maria, CA, 22 Sep 1986.

Gibson, Charles Dana: b. Roxbury, MA, 14 Sep 1867; d. New York, NY, 23 Dec 1944.

Gibson, Dorothy: b. Hoboken, NJ, 18??; d. Paris, Fr, 20 Feb 1946.

Gibson, Helen: b. Cleveland, OH, 27 Aug 1894; d. Roseburg, OR, 10 Oct 1977.

Gibson, Hoot (Edward): b. Tekamah, NE, 6 Aug 1892; d. Woodland Hills, CA, 23 Aug 1962.

Gibson, James Edwin: b. Jefferson, IN, 24 Oct 1865; d. Redondo Beach, CA, 13 Oct 1938,

Gibson, Kenneth: b. Sandusky, OH, 17 Jan 1898; d. Los Angeles Co, CA, 26 Nov 1972.

Gibson, Margaret (Patricia Palmer): b. Colorado Springs, CO. 14 Sep 1895; Los Angeles, CA, 21 Oct 1964.

Gifford, Ada: b. Rahway, NJ, 22 May c. 1885; d. 19??.

Gigli, Beniamino, b. Recanati, Italy, 20 Mar 1890; d. Rome, Italy, 30 Nov 1957.

Gignoret, Gabriel: b. France, 1879; d. Paris, Fr, 16 Mar 1937.

Gilbert, Billy: b. Louisville, KY, 12 Jan 1894; d. Los Angeles, CA, 23 Sep 1971.

Gilbert, Billy: b. California, 15 Sep 1891; d. Los Angeles, CA, 29 Apr 1961.

Gilbert, Joe: b. 1902; d. Los Angeles, CA, 26 May 1959.

Gilbert, John: b. Logan, UT, 10 Jul 1899; d. Los Angeles, CA, 9 Jan 1936.

Gilbert, Mae Edwards: b. 1871; d. Los Angeles, CA, 18 Aug 1947.

Gilbert, Maude: b. 24 May 1883; d. Laguna Beach, CA, 7 Jul 1953.

Gilbert, Mercedes: b. Jacksonville, FL, 1894; d. New York, NY, 1 Mar 1952.

Gilbert, Walter: b. Brooklyn, NY, 1887; d. Brooklyn; NY, 12 Jan 1947.

Giles, Anna: b. Illinois, 23 Nov 1873; d. Los Angeles, CA, 2 Feb 1973.

Gilfeather, Daniel: b. Boston, MA, 1854; d. Long Beach, CA, 2 May 1919.

Gill, Basil: b. Birkenhead, Eng, 10 Mar 1877; d. Hove, Eng, 23 Apr 1955.

Gill, Robert Stowe: b. 18??; d. France, ? Sep 1918.

Gillespie, Albert T. (Bert): b. Hancock, MI, 1888; d. ? May 1922.

Gillespie, Edward C.: b. 1874; d. New York, NY, 23 Jul 1918.

Gillespie, William: b. Aberdeen, Scot, 24 Jan 1894; d. 19??.

Gillette, Elma: b. 3 Jul 1874; d. Los Angeles, CA, 9 Jul 1941.

Gillette, William: b. Hartford, CT, 24 Jul 1853; d. Hartford, CT, 29 Apr 1937.

Gillingwater, Claude: b. Louisiana, MO, 2 Aug 1870; d. Beverly Hills, CA, 1 Nov 1939.

Gillis, William S,: b. Texas, 17 Nov 1867; d. Los Angeles, CA, 24 Apr 1946.

Gillman, Rita: b. Roanoke, VA, 1898; d. Conoga Park, CA, 14 Nov 1986.

Gillmore, Frank: b. New York, NY, 14 May 1867; d. New York, NY, 29 Mar 1943.

Gills, Norbert M.: b. 18??; d. San Francisco, CA, 21 Feb 1920.

Gilman, Ada: b. 6 Oct 1854; d. Holmesburg, PA, 18 Dec 1921.

Gilman, Fred: b. 1903; d. Capistrano Beach, CA, 30 Mar 1988.

Gilmore, Barney: b. 1869; d. Los Angeles, CA, 19 Apr 1949.

Gilmore, Douglas: b. Boston, MA, 25 Jun 1903; d. New York, NY, 26 Jul 1950.

Gilmore, Faye: b. 1900; d. 12 Aug 1984.

Gilmore, Helen: b. Washington, DC, 4 Jan 1862; d. Los Angeles, CA, 16 Nov 1936.

Gilmour, John H.: b. Ottawa, Can, 1857; d. New York, NY, 24 Nov 1922.

Gilpin, Charles S.: b. Richmond, VA, 1879; d. Eldredge Park, NJ, 6 May 1930.

Gingold, Baroness Helene: b. 18??; d. 10 Dec 1926.

Ginn, Hayward J.: b. Virginia City, NV, 8 Sep 1878; d. Los Angeles, CA, 14 Feb 1926.

Ginn, Wells Watson: b. Bellefontaine, OH, 1891; d. Cincinnati, OH, 15 Apr 1959.

Girard, Joseph W.: b. Williamsport, PA, 2 Apr 1871; d. Woodland Hills, CA, 21 Aug 1949.

Girardot, Etienne: b. London, Eng, 22 Feb 1856; d. Los Angeles, CA, 10 Nov 1939.

Gish, Dorothy: b. Massillon, OH, 11 Mar 1898; d. Rapallo, Italy, 4 Jun 1968.

Gish, Lillian: b. Springfield, OH, 14 Oct 1893; d. New York, NY, 27 Feb 1993.

Gish, Mrs. Mary: b. Urbana, IL, 1860; d. New York, NY, 16 Sep 1948.

Glaser, Lulu: b. Allegheny, PA, 2 Jun 1874; d. Norwalk, CT, 5 Sep 1958.

Glass, Gaston: b. Paris, Fr, 31 Dec 1895; d. Santa Monica, CA, 11 Nov 1965.

Glassner, Erika: b. Germany, 28 Feb 1896; d. 1951.

Glaum, Louise: b. Baltimore, MD, 4 Sep 1900; d. Los Angeles, CA, 25 Nov 1970.

Glazer, Eve F.: b. Pennsylvania, 4 Jun 1903; d. Los Angeles, CA, 29 Jun 1960.

Gleason, Adda: b. Chicago, IL, 19 Dec 1888; d. Woodland Hills, CA, 6 Feb 1971.

Gleason, Fred: b. 1854; d. New York, NY, 9 Jun 1933.

Gleason, James: b. New York, NY, 23 May 1882; d. Los Angeles, CA, 12 Apr 1959.

Gleason, Mina: b. 1858; d. Beverly Hills, CA, 27 Jun 1931.

Gleckler, Robert: b. Pierre, SD, 11 Jan 1887; d. Los Angeles, CA, 25 Feb 1939.

Glendinning, Ernest: b. Ulverston, Eng, 19 Feb 1884; d. South Coventry, CT, 17 May 1936.

Glendon, J. Frank: b. Choteau, MT, 25 Oct 1866; d. Los Angeles, CA, 17 Mar 1937.

Glenn, Forrest: b. Marissa, IL, 1900; d. Saranac Lake, NY, 24 Aug 1954.

Glennon, Herbert (Bert): b. Araconda, MT, 19 Nov 1893; d. Los Angeles, CA, 29 Jun 1967.

Glickman, Ellis P.: b. Kiev, Russ, 1869; d. Chicago, IL, 3 Oct 1931.

Gliddon, John: b. 24 Aug 1897; d. Worthing, Eng, 18 Jul 1990.

Glover, Emlye: b. ????; d. Los Angeles, CA, ? Sep 1923.

Glover, Gertrude: b. Chicago, IL, 21 Sep 1895; d. Boulder, CO, 1 Mar 1977.

Glowner, M. Lee: b. California, 21 Oct 1866; d. California, 9 Jul 1923.

Glyn, Elinor: b. Isle of Jersey, 17 Oct 1864; d. London, Eng, 23 Sep 1943.

Glynne, Mary: b. Penarth, Wales, 25 Jan 1895; d. London, Eng, 19 Sep 1954.

Goddard, Alf: b. London, Eng, 28 Nov 1897; d. 25 Feb 1981.

Godowsky, Dagmar: b. Petrograd, Russ, 24 Nov 1896; d. New York, NY, 13 Feb 1975.

Goetz, Curt: b. Mainz, Ger, 17 Nov 1888; d. 12 Sep 1960.

Goetz, E.Ray: b. Buffalo, NY, 12 Jun 1886; d. Greenwich, CT, 12 Jun 1954.

Goetz, Paul P. (Pop): b. 1865; d. Los Angeles, CA, 26 Sep 1929.

Goetzke, Bernhard: b. Danzig, Ger, 1883; d. Berlin, Ger, 7 Oct 1964.

Gofton, E. Story: b. England, 1847; d. 1 May 1939.

Goines, Betty: b. 1904; d. ? Jan 1929.

Going, Frederica: b. New York, NY, 13 Aug 1895; d. New York, NY, 11 Apr 1959.

Goldberg, Rube L.: b. San Francisco, CA, 4 Jul 1883; d. New York, NY, 7 Dec 1970.

Golden, Olive Fuller (Olive Carey): b. New York, NY, 31 Jan 1896; d. Carpinteria, CA, 13 Mar 1988.

Golden, Ruth Fuller: b. New York, NY, 19 May 1901; d. Los Angeles, CA, 15 Aug 1931.

Goldin, Sidney M.: b. 1880; d. New York, NY, 19 Sep 1937.

Goldstein, Abe: b. 1895; d. Los Angeles, CA, 9 Feb 1990.

Goldsworthy, John H.: b. England, 28 Apr 1884; d. Los Angeles, CA, 10 Jul 1958.

Gollan, Campbell (David Gollan); b. Cults, Scot, 1866; d. New York, NY, 13 Dec 1916.

Gombell, Minna: b. Baltimore, MD, 28 May 1893; d. Santa Monica, CA, 14 Apr 1973.

Gondi, Harry: b. 1900; d. Hamburg, Ger, ? Oct 1968.

Gonzalez, Myrtle: b. Los Angeles, CA, 28 Sep 1891; d. Los Angeles, CA, 22 Oct 1918.

Good, Frank B.: b. Columbus, OH, 3 Oct 1884; d. Los Angeles, CA, 1 Jun 1939.

Goodall, Grace: b. San Francisco, CA, 12 Jun 1889; d. Los Angeles Co, CA, 27 Sep 1940.

Goode, Lizzie: b. 18??; d. New York, NY, 27 Jan 1921.

Goodfriend, Pliny: b. Drayton, ND, 5 Sep 1891; d. Santa Monica, CA, 20 Jan 1981.

Goodrich, Charles W.: b. 1861; d. Norwalk, CT, 20 Mar 1931.

Goodrich, Edna: b. Logansport, IN, 22 Dec 1883; d. New York, NY, 26 May 1971.

Goodrich, Katherine: b. Austin, TX, 1880; d. 19??.

Goodwin, George: b. 1864; d. England, 12 Jul 1926.

Goodwin, Harold: b. Peoria, IL, 1 Dec 1902; d. Woodland Hills, CA, 12 Jul 1987.

Goodwin, Nat C.: b. Boston, MA, 25 Jul 1857; d, New York, NY, 31 Jan 1919.

Goodwins, Leslie: b. London, Eng, 17 Sep 1899; d. Los Angeles, CA, 8 Jan 1969.

Gorcey, Bernard: b. Switzerland, 1888; d. Los Angeles, CA, 11 Sep 1955.

Gordon, A. George: b. 1882; d. Chicago, IL, 27 Dec 1953.

Gordon, Alice: b. St. Andrews, Scot, 1879; d. 19??.

Gordon, C. Henry: b. New York, NY, 17 Jun 1884; d. Los Angeles, CA, 3 Dec 1940.

Gordon, Edward: b. 1886; d. Los Angeles, CA, 10 Nov 1938.

Gordon, Gloria: b. 1881; d. Los Angeles, CA, 21 Nov 1962.

Gordon, Hal: b. London, Eng, 18 Apr 1894; d. 1946.

Gordon, Harris: b. Glenside, PA, 4 Jul 1884; d. Burbank, CA, 31 Mar 1947.

Gordon, Harry G.: b. Buffalo, NY, 1884; d. 20 Nov 1948.

Gordon, Huntley: b. Montreal, Can, 8 Oct 1887; d. Los Angeles, CA, 8 Dec 1956.

Gordon, James: b. Pittsburgh, PA, 23 Apr 1871; d. Los Angeles, CA, 12 May 1941.

Gordon, Julia Swayne: b. Columbus, OH, 29 Oct 1878; d. Los Angeles, CA, 28 May 1933.

Gordon, Kitty: b. Folkestone, Kent, Eng, 22 Apr 1878; d. Brentwood, NY, 26 May 1974.

Gordon, Leon: b. Brighton, Eng, 12 Jan 1894; d. 4 Jan 1960.

Gordon, Marian: b. 1897; d. Los Angeles, CA, 8 Jan 1927.

Gordon, Mary: b. Glasgow, Scot, 16 May 1882; d. Pasadena, CA, 23 Aug 1963.

Gordon, Maude Turner: b. Franklin, IN; 10 Nov 1868; d. Los Angeles, CA, 12 Jan 1940.

Gordon, Paul: b. Brooklyn, NY, 1883; d. Florence, Italy, 3 May 1929.

Gordon, Peter: b. Naples, Italy, 1887; d. Los Angeles, CA, 25 May 1943.

Gordon, Phyllis: b. Suffolk, VA, c. 1889; d. 194?.

Gordon, Richard H: b. Philadelphia, PA, 1893; d. Los Angeles, CA, 20 Sep 1956.

Gordon, Robert: b. Kansas, 3 Mar 1895; d. Victorville, CA, 26 Oct 1971.

Gordon, Roy: b. Ohio, 18 Oct 1884; d. Sherman Oaks, CA, 23 Jul 1972.

Gordon, Ruth: b. Wollaston, MA, 30 Oct 1896; d. Edgartown, MA, 28 Aug 1985.

Gordon, Vera: b. Edkerternoslav, Russ, 11 Jun 1886; d. Beverly Hills, CA, 8 May 1948.

Gordoni, Arthur: b. New York State, 17 Mar 1893; d. Los Angeles, CA, 10 Aug 1966.

Gore, Rosa: b. Now York, NY, 15 Sep 1866; d. Los Angeles, CA, 4 Feb 1941.

Gorman, Baby Eerly: b. 1906; d. Dover, NJ, 20 May 1982.

Gorman, Charles: b. 1865; d. New York, NY, 25 Jan 1928.

Gorman, Eddie: b. Jersey City, NJ, 1872; d. New York, NY, 28 Jun 1919.

Gorman, James J.: b. 1860; d. Boston, MA, 14 Aug 1921.

Gosford, Alice Peckham: b. Rhode Island, 1886; d. New York, NY, 23 Jan 1919.

Gosnell, Evelyn: b. 1895; d. New York, NY, 11 Nov 1946.

Gott, Barbara: b. Stirling, Scot, ????; d. 18 Nov 1944.

Gottout, John: b. 18??; d. 1934.

Gottschalk, Ferdinand: b. London, Eng, 28 Feb 1858; d. London, Eng, 10 Nov 1944.

Goudal, Jetta: b. Amsterdam, Holland, 12 Jul 1891; d. Los Angeles, CA, 14 Jan 1985.

Gough, John: b. Boston, MA, 22 Sep 1894; d. Los Angeles, CA, 29 Jun 1968.

Gould, Billy: b. New York, NY, 1869; d. New York, NY, 1 Feb 1950.

Gould, Myrtle: b. 1880; d. Los Angeles, CA, 25 Feb 1941.

Goulding, Alf: b. Melbourne, Austral, 26 Jan 1896; d. Los Angeles, CA, 25 Apr 1972.

Goulding, Edmund: b. London, Eng, 20 Mar 1891; d. Los Angeles, CA, 24 Dec 1959.

Gove, Otis M.: b. 1852; d. Los Angeles, CA, 23 Jan 1931.

Gowland, Gibson: b. Carlisle, Eng, 4 Jan 1877; d. London, Eng, 9 Sep 1951.

Grace, Dick: b. Minnesota, 10 Jan 1898; d. Los Angeles Co, CA, 25 Jun 1965.

Grady, James H.: b. 1869; d. Lynn, MA, 17 Feb 1941.

Graetz, Paul: b. Berlin, Ger, 4 Aug 1889; d. Los Angeles, CA, 16 Feb 1937.

Graham, Ben R.: b. 1851; d. New Brighton, NY, 25 Mar 1924.

Graham, Charlie: b. Carthage, MS, 16 Feb 1895; d. Los Angeles, CA, 9 Oct 1943.

Graham, Frederick: b. 1866; d. Sharon, CT, 26 Sep 1947.

Graham, Harry: b. London, Eng, 1874; d. London, Eng, 30 Oct 1936.

Graham, Robert: b. Baltimore, MD, 17 Dec 1858; d. New York, NY, 17 Jul 1916.

Graham, Violet: b. England, 9 Nov 1890; d. 1967.

Grahame, Bert: b. 1892; d. England, 23 Mar 1971.

Gran, Albert: b. Bergen, Norway, 4 Aug 1862; d. Los Angeles, CA, 16 Dec 1932.

Granach, Alexander: b. Werbowitz, Poland, 18 Apr 1890; d. New York, NY, 14 Mar 1945.

Granby, Joseph: b. Boston, MA, 24 Mar 1885; d. Los Angeles, CA, 22 Sep 1965.

Grandais, Suzanne: b. Paris, Fr, 14 Jul 1893; d. France, 18 Aug 1920.

Grandee, George: b. Bridgeport, CT, 22 May 1903; d. Long Beach, CA, 1 Aug 1985.

Grandin, Elmer: b. 1861; d. Patchogue, NY, 19 May 1933.

Grandin, Ethel: b. New York, NY, 3 Mar 1894; d. Woodland Hills, CA, 27 Sep 1988.

Grandon, Francis J. (Frank Grandin): b. Chicago, IL, 1879; d. Los Angeles, CA, 11 Jul 1929.

Grange, Red (Harold E. Grange): b. Forksville, PA, 13 June 1903; d. Lake Wales, FL, 28 Jan 1991.

Granger, Elsa G.: b. Australia, 1904; d. New York, NY, 8 Feb 1955.

Granger, Maude: b. 1851; d. New York, NY, 17 Aug 1928.

Granstedt, Greta: b. Malmo, Sweden, 13 Jul 1907; d. Los Angeles, CA, 7 Oct 1987.

Grant, Corinne: b. New Orleans, LA, 1888; d. 19??.

Grant, Henry Clay: b. New York State, 1885; d. New York, NY, 30 Nov 1953.

Grant, Lawrence: b, Bournemouth, Eng, 30 Oct 1869; d. Santa Barbara, CA, 19 Feb 1952.

Grant, Sydney: b. Boston, MA, 20 Feb 1873; d. Los Angeles, CA, 12 Jul 1953.

Grant, Valentine: b. Indiana, 14 Feb 1881; d. Orange Co, CA, 12 Mar 1949.

Granville, Audrey: b. 1911; d. Encino, CA, 20 Oct 1972.

Granville, Charlotte: b. London, Eng, 9 May 1860; d. Los Angeles, CA, 8 Jul 1942.

Granville, Louise: b. Sydney, Austral, 29 Sep 1895; d. Woodland Hills, CA, 22 Dec 1968.

Granville, Taylor: b. 1877; d. Los Angeles, CA, 14 Apr 1923.

Grassby, Bertram: b. Lincolnshire, Eng, 23 Dec 1880; d. Scottsdale, AZ, 7 Dec 1953.

Grassby, Mrs. Bertram (Gertrude): b. 1877; d. Los Angeles, CA, 6 Apr 1962.

Grasso, Giovanni: b. Sicily, 1875; d. 13 Oct 1930.

Gratton, Lawrence: b. Concord, NH, 1870; d. New York, NY, 9 Dec 1941.

Grauer, Ben: b. New York, NY, 2 Jun 1908; d. New York, NY, 31 May 1977.

Grauman, Sid: b. Indianapolis, IN, 17 Mar 1879; d. Los Angeles, CA, 4 Mar 1950.

Graves, George: b. London, Eng, 1 Jan 1876; d. London, Eng, 2 Apr 1949.

Graves, Kathryn: b. Minnesota, 1 Dec 1899; d. San Diego, CA, 26 Feb 1977.

Graves, Ralph: b. Cleveland, OH, 23 Jan 1900; d. Santa Barbara, CA, 18 Feb 1977.

Graves, Robert, Jr.: b. New York, NY, 22 Oct 1888; d. 19 Aug 1954.

Gravet, Fernard: b. Brussels, Belgium, 25 Dec 1904; d. Paris, Fr, 2 Nov 1970.

Gravina, Cesare: b. Naples, Italy, 23 Jan 1858; d. Italy, c. 1954.

Gray, Betty: b. Passaic, NJ, 1895; d. New York, NY, ? Jun 1919.

Gray, Dorothy: b. Los Angeles, CA, 23 Oct 1922; d. Los Angeles, CA, 9 May 1976.

Gray, George G.: b. 1894; d. Asheville, NC, 8 Sep 1967.

Gray, Gilda: b. Krakow, Poland, 24 Oct 1899; d. Los Angeles, CA, 22 Dec 1959.

Gray, Gloria (Lillian Halpren): b. 1900; d. Walla Walla, WA, 4 Apr 1918.

Gray, Lawrence: b. San Francisco, CA, 28 Jul 1898; d. Mexico City, Mex, 2 Feb 1970.

Gray, Phyllis: b. 1887; d. Los Angeles, CA, 21 Jan 1922.

Graybill, Joseph: b. Milwaukee, WI, 1877; d. New York, NY, 3 Aug 1913.

Greeley, Evelyn: b. Austria, 3 Nov 1888; d. Palm Beach, FL, 25 Mar 1975.

Green, Alfred E.: b. Perris, CA, 11 Jul 1889; d. Los Angeles, CA, 4 Sep 1960.

Green, Burton: b. 1874; d. Mount Vernon, NY, 17 Nov 1922.

Green, Dorothy: b. Petrograd, Russ, 1892; d. New York, NY, 16 Nov 1963.

Green, Duke: b. 18??; d. Woodland Hills, CA, 22 Nov 1984.

Green, Emily: b. Philadelphia, PA, 1888; d. Willow Grove, PA, 26 Mar 1980.

Green, Fred E.: b. 1890; d. San Mateo, CA, 5 Aug 1940.

Green, Judd: b. 1866; d. 1932.

Green, Kenneth: b. 1908; d. Los Angeles, CA, 24 Feb 1969.

Green, Margaret: b. New York, 1890; d. New York, NY, 30 Jan 1967.

Green, William B.: b. 1852; d. Utica, NY, 10 Apr 1926.

Greene, Clay M.: b. San Francisco, CA, 1850; d. San Francisco, CA, 5 Sep 1933.

Greene, Helen: b. New York, NY, 1896; d. Oakland, CA, 10 Oct 1947.

Greene, Kempton: b. Shreveport, LA, 28 Jun 1890; d. 19??.

Greene, Walter D.: b. Baltimore, MD, 1872; d. Great Neck, NY, 20 Feb 1941.

Greenleaf, Mace: b. Maine, 18??; d. Philadelphia, PA, 23 Mar 1912.

Greenwood, Charlotte: b. Philadelphia, PA, 25 Jun 1890; d. Beverly Hills, CA, 18 Jan 1978.

Greenwood, Hubert F.: b. England, 1 Apr 1884; d. Los Angeles Co, CA, 7 Apr 1950.

Greenwood, Winifred: b. Geneseo, NY, 1 Jan 1885; d. Woodland Hills, CA, 23 Nov 1961.

Greer, Julian: b. London, Eng, 1870; d. New York, NY, 15 Apr 1928.

Greet, Ben: b. London, Eng, 24 Sep 1857; d. London, Eng, 17 May 1936.

Greet, Clare: b. England, 14 Jun 1871; d. London, Eng, 14 Feb 1939.

Gregg, Arnold (Arnold Gray): b. Toledo, OH, 20 Apr 1899; d. Alpine, CA, 3 May 1936.

Gregori, Ferdinand: b. Germany, 13 Apr 1870; d. 12 Dec 1928.

Gregor, Nora: b. Gorizia, Italy, ????; d. Santiago, Chile, 20 Jan 1949.

Gregory, Dora: b. Dulwich, Eng, 2 Sep 1872; d. London, Eng, 5 Mar 1954.

Gregory, Edna: b. Winnipeg, Can, 25 Jan 1905; d. Los Angeles, CA, 3 Jul 1965.

Gregory, Ena (Marion Douglas): b. Sydney, Austral, 18 Apr 1906; d. Laguna Beach, CA, 13 Jun 1993.

Gregory, Gilbert: b. 18??; d. 9 Dec 1919.

Gregory, William H.: b. 18??; d. Los Angeles, GA, 24 Dec 1926.

Gresham, Edith: b. 1897; d. Riverdale, NY, 31 Dec 1976.

Gretler, Heinrich: b. Zurich, Switz, 1 Oct 1897; d. Zurich, Switz, 30 Sep 1977.

Grey, Gloria: b. Portland, OR, 23 Oct 1909; d. Los Angeles, CA, 22 Nov 1947.

Grey, Jane: b. Middlebury, VT, 22 May 1883; d. New York, NY, 9 Nov 1944.

Grey, Katherine: b. San Francisco, CA, 27 Dec 1873; d. Orleans, MA, 21 Mar 1950.

Grey, Leonard: b. England, 18??; d. New York, NY, 3 Aug 1918.

Grey, Lillian: b. 18??; d. Los Angeles, CA, 22 Apr 1985.

Grey, Olga: b. Budapest, Hungary, 1897; d. Los Angeles, CA, 25 Apr 1973.

Grey, Ray: b. 1899; d. Glendale, CA, 18 Apr 1925.

Grey, Robert Henry: b. Oakland, CA, 17 Jul 1891; d. Los Angeles, CA, 26 Apr 1934.

Gribbon, Eddie: b. New York, NY, 3 Jan 1890; d. Los Angeles, CA, 28 Sep 1965.

Gribbon, Harry: b. New York, NY, 9 Jun 1885; d. Los Angeles, CA, 28 Jul 1961.

Griffen, Nannie: b. 18??; d. New York, NY, 17 Jul 1925.

Griffies, Ethel: b. Sheffield, Eng, 26 Apr 1878; d. London, Eng, 9 Sep 1975.

Griffin, Carleton E.: b. New York, NY, 23 May 1893; d. Los Angeles, CA, 24 Jul 1940.

Griffin, Frank L.: b. 1889; d. Los Angeles, CA, 17 Mar 1953.

Griffin, Gerald: b. Pittsburgh, PA, 1854; d. Venice, CA, 16 Mar 1919.

Griffin, Phyllis: b. 18??; d. London, Eng, 20 Feb 1959.

Griffith, Corinne: b. Texarkana, TX, 21 Nov 1894; d. Santa Monica, CA, 13 Jul 1979.

Griffith, D. W.: (David Wark Griffith): b. La Grange, KY, 22 Jan 1875; d. Los Angeles, CA, 23 Jul 1948.

Griffith, Edward H.: b. Illnois, 23 Aug 1888; d. South Lagana, CA, 3 Mar 1975.

Griffith, Gordon: b. Chicago, IL, 4 Jul 1907; d, Los Angeles, CA, 12 Oct 1958.

Griffith, Harry: b. Indiana, 19 Jul 1866; d. Pasadena, CA, 4 May 1926.

Griffith, Katherine: b. San Francisco, CA, 30 Sep 1876; d. Los Angeles, CA, 17 Oct 1921.

Griffith, Raymond: b. Boston, MA, 23 Jan 1887; d. Los Angeles, CA, 25 Nov 1957.

Griffith, Robert E.: b. Methuen, MA, 1907; d. Port Chester, NY, 7 Jun 1961.

Grimes, Thomas: b. Marysville, KS, 4 Nov 1887; d. Tujunga, CA, 19 Aug 1934.

Grimwood, Herbert: b. Walthamstow, Eng, 7 Mar 1875; d. England, 1 Dec 1929.

Gripp, Harry: b. Tyrone, PA, 20 Nov 1885; d. 19??.

Grisel, Louis R.: b. Newcastle, DE, 26 Nov 1849; d. Fort Lee, NJ, 19 Nov 1928.

Griswold, Grace: b. Astabula, OH, 1872; d. New York, NY, 13 Jun 1927.

Griswold, James: b. New Britain, CT, 30 Apr 1882; d. Glendale, CA, 4 Oct 1935.

Griswold, Nathaniel: b. 18??; d. Albany, NY, ? Nov 1918.

Grock (Charles A. Wettach): b. Reconvilier, Switz, 10 Jan 1880; d. Imperia, Italy, 14 Jul 1959.

Gronau, Ernst Alfred: b. Memel, Ger, 21 Aug 1887; d. 11 Aug 1938.

Gross, William J.: b. 1837; d. Brooklyn, NY, 11 Apr 1924.

Grossmith, Ena: b. London, Eng, 14 Aug 1896; d. London, Eng, 20 Mar 1944.

Grossmith, George: b. London, Eng, 11 May 1874; d. London, Eng, 6 Jun 1935.

Grossmith, Lawrence: b. London, Eng, 29 Mar 1877; d. Los Angeles, CA, 21 Feb 1944.

Grossmith, Weedon: b. London, Eng, 9 Jun 1852; d. London, Eng, 14 Jun 1919.

Grosso, Paul (Kansas): b. 1897; d. Fort Bragg, CA, 5 Jul 1979.

Grover, Leonard, Sr.: b. Springwater, NY, 9 Dec 1835; d. New York, NY, 7 Mar 1926.

Grover, Leonard, Jr.: b. Baltimore, MD, 1859; d. Brooklyn, NY, 24 Mar 1947.

Groves, Fred: b. London, Eng, 8 Aug 1880; d. London, Eng, 4 Jun 1955.

Grundgens, Gustaf: b. Dusseldorf, Ger, 22 Dec 1899; d. Manila, Philippines, 7 Oct 1963.

Gruning, Ilka: b. Vienna, Austria, 4 Sep 1876; d. 14 Nov 1964.

Gsell, Henry: b. 1889; d. 19??.

Guard, A. Sully: b. 18??; d. Jacksonville, FL, 21 Mar 1916.

Guard, Kit: b. Hals, Denmark, 5 May 1894; d. Los Angeles, CA, 18 Jul 1961.

Gudgeon, Bernard C.: b. Oklahoma, 1889; d. Bergen, NJ, 22 Oct 1948.

Guensta, F. F.: b. Pittsburgh, PA, 16 Feb 1862; d. Glendale, CA, 28 Mar 1936.

Guest, Frederick: b. 18??; d. New York, NY, 20 Jan 1922.

Guilbert, Yvette: b. Paris, Fr, 20 Jan 1865; d. Aix-en-Provence, Fr, 3 Feb 1944.

Guinan, Texas: b. Waco, TX, 12 Jan 1884; d. Vancouver, Can, 5 Nov 1933.

Guise, Thomas S.: b. Detroit, MI, 18??; d. 1930.

Guitry, Sacha: b. St. Petersburg, Russ, 21 Feb 1885; d. Paris, Fr, 24 Jul 1957.

Guitty, Madeline: b. 1871; d. Paris, Fr, 12 Apr 1936.

Gullan, Campbell: b. Glasgow, Scot, 18??; d. New York, NY, 1 Dec 1939.

Gunn, Charles: b. Wisconsin, 31 Jul 1883; d. Los Angeles, CA, 6 Dec 1918.

Gunn, Earl: b. Michigan, 8 May 1901; d. San Francisco, CA, 14 Apr 1963.

Gurney, Edmund: b. Ireland, 1851; d. New York, NY, 14 Jan 1925.

Gustafason, Alva: b. Stockholm, Sweden, 1904; d. Stockholm, Sweden, 1926.

Guthrie, Charles W.: b. 1871; d. Washington, DC, 30 Jun 1939.

Gwenn, Edmund: b. Glamorgan, Wales, 26 Sep 1875; d. Woodland Hills, CA, 6 Sep 1959.

Gwynne, Harold William: b. 18??; d. Kew Gardens, NY, ? Aug 1927.

Gwyther, Geoffrey: b. 1890; d. 27 Jul 1944.

Gys, Leda: b. Rome, Italy, 10 Mar 1892; d. 2 Oct 1957.

H

Haack, Kathe: b. Berlin, Ger, 11 Aug 1893; d. Berlin, Ger, 5 May 1986.

Haas, Hugo: b. Brno, Czech, 19 Feb 1901; d. Vienna, Austria, 1 Dec 1968.

Hackathorne, George: b. Pendleton, OR, 13 Feb 1896; d. Los Angeles, CA, 25 Jun 1940.

Hackenschmidt, George: b. Estonia, 1877; d. London, Eng, 19 Feb 1968.

Hackett, Florence: b. Buffalo, NY, 1882, d. New York, NY, 21 Aug 1954.

Hackett, James K.: b. Wolf Island, Ont, Can, 6 Sep 1869; d. Paris, Fr, 8 Nov 1926.

Hackett, Jeanette: b. 1898; d. New York, NY, 16 Aug 1979.

Hackett, Lillian: b. Chicago, IL, 11 Oct 1896; d. Los Angeles, CA, 28 Feb 1973.

Hackett, Raymond: b. New York, NY, 15 Jul 1902; d. Los Angeles, CA, 7 Jul 1958.

Haddock, William F.: b. Portsmouth, NH, 27 Nov 1877; d. New York, NY, 30 Jun 1969.

Haddon, Peter: b. Rawtenstall, Eng, 31 Mar 1898; d. London, Eng, 7 Sep 1962.

Hadley, Bert: b. Walla Walla, WA, 12 Apr 1882; d. 19??.

Hadley, Hap (Alvan C. Hadley): b. Findlay, IL, 16 Mar 1895, d. New York, NY, 4 Aug 1976.

Haefeli, Charles: b. New York State, 16 Jul 1887; d. Los Angeles, CA, 12 Feb 1955.

Hagen, Charles F.: b. 1872; d. Los Angeles, CA, 13 Jun 1958.

Hagen, Walter: b. Rochester, NY, 21 Dec 1892; d. Traverse City, MI, 5 Oct 1969.

Hagenbruch, Charlotte: b. Austria, 1895; d. Lichtenstein, 19 May 1968.

Hagney, Frank: b. Sydney, Austral, 20 Mar 1884; d. Los Angeles, CA, 25 Jun 1973.

Hahn, Phillip: b. Amsterdam, Holland, 1884; d. NY, 4 Aug 1976.

Haine, Horace J.: b. 1868; d. New York, NY, 26 Sep 1940.

Haines, Louis: b. 1877; d. New York, NY, 25 Jul 1929.

Haines, Rhea: b. Indiana, 2 Oct 1894; d. Los Angeles, CA, 12 Mar 1964.

Haines, Robert Terrell: b. Muncie, IN, 3 Feb 1870; d. New York, NY, 6 May 1943.

Haines, WIlliam: b. Staunton, VA, 1 Jan 1900; d. Los Angeles, LA, 16 Dec 1973.

Hale, Alan: b. Washington, DC, 10 Feb 1892; d. Los Angeles, CA, 22 Jan 19, 1950.

Hale, Bobbie: b. London, Eng, 27 May 1886; d. 27 Sep 1977.

Hale, Creighton: b. Cork, Ire, 24 May 1882; d. South Pasadena, CA, 9 Aug 1965.

Hale, Georgia: b. St. Joseph, MO, 25 Jun 1896; d. Los Angeles, CA, 7 Jun 1985.

Hale, Walter: b. Chicago, IL, 4 Aug 1869; d. New York, NY, 4 Dec 1917.

Hales, Ethelbert: b. New Zealand, 1882, d. Riverdale, NY, 26 Jan 1933.

Haley, Jack: b. Boston, MA, 10 Aug 1899; d. Los Angeles, CA, 6 Jun 1979.

Hall, Alexander: b. Boston, MA, 11 Jan 1895; d. San Francisco, CA, 30 Jul 1968.

Hall, Ben: b. Brooklyn, NY, 18 Mar 1899; d. North Hollywood, CA, 20 May 1985.

Hall, Charlie: b. Birmingham, Eng, 19 Aug 1899; d. North Hollywood, CA, 7 Dec 1959.

Hall, Donald: b. Nuree, East India, 14 Aug 1868, d. Woodland Hills, CA, 18 Jul 1948.

Hall, Dorothy: b. Bradford, PA, 1906; d. New York, NY, 3 Feb 1953.

Hall, Edna: b. 1886; d. Culver City, CA, 17 Jul 1945.

Hall, Ella: b. New Jersey, 17 Mar 1896; d. Canoga Park, CA, 3 Sep 1981.

Hall, Ethel: b. ???? d. Merecd, CA, 28 Jun 1927.

Hall, Gabrielle: b. Missouri, 18 Apr 1898; d. El Cajon, CA, 1 Jan 1967.

Hall, George Edwardes: b. Brooklyn, NY, 1872; d. Los Angeles, CA, 1 Jul 1922.

Hall, George Edwardes, Jr.: b. Brooklyn, NY, 1901; d. ? Dec 1991.

Hall, George, M.: b. Sweden, 1890; d. Saranac Lake, NY, 24 Apr 1930.

Hall, Howard: b. Michigan, 30 May 1867; d. Long Beach, CA 25 Jul 1921.

Hall, J. Albert: b. Calcutta, India, 1884; d. Cumberland, MD, 18 Apr 1920.

Hall, James: b. Dallas, TX, 22 Oct 1900; d. Jersey City, NJ, 7 Jun 1940.

Hall, Jane: b. Winona, MN, 15 Feb 1880; d. St. Paul, MN, 13 Oct 1975.

Hall, John: b. 1878; d. Los Angeles, CA, 25 Apr 1936.

Hall, Laura Nelson: b. Philadelphia, PA, 11 Jul 1876; d. 19??.

Hall, Lillian: b. Brooklyn, NY, 15 Mar 1896; d. Los Angeles, CA, 18 Mar 1959.

Hall, Louis Leon: b. Oneida, NY, 1879; d. Houghton, ME, 17 Apr 1930.

Hall, Maud: b. New Orleans, LA, 1881; d. Liberty, NY, 1 May 1938.

Hall, May: b. 11 Sep 1877; d. 21 Dec 1962.

Hall, Nelson: b. 1881; d. Philedelphia, PA, 28 Jul 1944.

Hall, Thurston: b. Boston, MA, 10 May 1882; d. Beverly Hills, CA, 20 Feb 1958.

Hall, Willard Lee: b. Altoona, PA, 1863; d. San Francisco, CA, 30 Oct 1936.

Hall, Winter: b. Christchurch, New Zealand, 21 Jun 1872; Los Angeles, CA, 10 Feb 1947.

Hall-Davis, Lillian: b. Hampstead, London, Eng, 1897; d. London, Eng, 25 Oct 1933.

Hallam, Henry: b. London, Eng, 1867; d. 9 Nov 1921.

Hallard, C. M. (Charles M. Hallard): b. Edinburgh, Scot, 26 Oct 1865; d. Farnham, Surrey, Eng, 21 Mar 1942.

Hallatt, Henry: b. Whitehaven, Eng, 1 Feb 1888; d. Cambridge, Eng, 24 Jul 1952.

Haller, Ernest: b. Los Angeles, CA, 31 May 1896; d. Marina del Rey, CA, 21 Oct 1970.

Hallett, Albert: b. 1870; d. Los Angeles, CA, 3 Apr 1935.

Halliburton, Jeanne: b. 1895; d. Falls Church, VA, 23 Jan 1986.

Halliday, John: b. Brooklyn, NY, 11 Sep 1880; d. Honolulu, HI, 17 Oct 1947.

Halliday, Lena: b. London, Eng, ????; d. 19 Dec 1937.

Halligan, William: b. Illinois, 29 Mar 1883; d. Woodland Hills, CA, 28 Jan 1957.

Hallor, Edith: b. Washington, DC, 26 May 1896; d. Newport Beach, CA, 21 May 1971.

Hallor, Ethel: b. 1882, d. 1967.

Hallor, Ray: b. Washington, DC, 11 Jan 1900, d. Palm Springs, CA, 16 Apr 1944.

Halls, Ethel May: b. 1882; d. Woodland Hills, CA, 16 Sep 1967.

Halm, Harry: b. Germany, 1898; d. ? Nov 1980.

Halstan, Margaret E.: b. London, Eng:, 25 Dec 1879; d. Hornchurch, Essex, Eng, 8 Jan 1967.

Halton, Charles: b. Washington, DC, 16 Mar 1876; d. Los Angeles, CA, 16 Apr 1959.

Ham, Harry: b. Napanee, Ont, Can, 1891; d. Beverly Hills, CA, 27 Jul 1943.

Hamer, Fred: b. Lancashire, Eng, 1873; d. Los Angeles, CA, 30 Dec 1953.

Hamill, Lucille: b. Carthage, NY, 1902; d. New York, NY, 17 Jun 1939.

Hamilton, Gordon: b. Coytesville, NJ, 1884; d. Fort Lee, NJ, 16 Jan 1939.

Hamilton, Hale: b. Fort Madison, IA, 28 Feb 1880; d. Los Angeles, CA, 19 May 1942.

Hamilton, Jack (Shorty): b. Chicago, IL, 9 Nov 1879; d. Los Angeles, CA, 7 Mar 1925.

Hamilton, John: b. Philadelphia, PA, 16 Jan 1887; A. Los Angeles, CA, 15 Oct 1958.

Hamilton, John F.: b. New York, NY, 7 Nov 1893; d. Paramus, NJ, 11 Jul 1967.

Hamilton, Laurel Lee: b. ???? d. Los Angeles, CA, 15 Dec 1955.

Hamilton, Lloyd V.: b. Oakland, CA, 19 Aug 1891; d. Los Angeles, CA, 18 Jan 1935.

Hamilton, Mahlon: b. Baltimore, MD, 15 Jun 1880; d. Woodland Hills, CA, 20 Jun 1960.

Hamilton, Neil: b. Lynn, MA, 9 Sep 1897; d. Escondido, CA, 24 Sep 1984.

Hamlin, William Hugh: b. 1885; d. Los Angeles, CA, 27 Sep 1951.

Hammer, Ina: b. ????; d. Brattleboro, VT, 9 Aug 1953.

Hammerstein, Elaine: b. Philadelphia, PA, 16 Jun 1897; d. Tia Juana, Mex, 13 Aug 1948.

Hammerstein, Stella: b. New York. NY, 2 Jan 1880; d. Englewood, NJ, 7 Jun 1975.

Hammond, C. Norman (Charles): b. San Jose, CA, 1878; d. New York, NY, 5 Jun 1941.

Hammond, Virginia: b. Staunton, Va, 20 Aug 1893; d. Washington, DC, 6 Apr 1972.

Hampden, Walter: b. Brooklyn, NY, 30 Jun 1879; d. Los Angeles, CA, 11 Jun 1955.

Hamper, Genevieve: b. Greenville, MI, 1889; d. New York, NY, 13 Feb 1971.

Hampton, Crystal: b. ????; d. New York, NY, 17 Jun 1922.

Hampton, Faith: b. 1909; d. Los Angeles, CA, 31 Mar 1949.

Hampton, Grayce: b. Devonshire, Eng, 28 Mar 1876; d. Los Angeles, CA, 20 Dec 1963.

Hampton, Hope: b. Houston, TX, 19 Feb 1897; d. New York, NY, 23 Jan 1982.

Hampton, Louise: b. Stockport, Eng, 1880; d. London, Eng, 10 Feb 1954.

Hamrick, Burwell: b. 1906; d. Los Angeles, CA, 21 Sep 1970.

Handforth, Ruth: b. Springfield, MA, 11 Jul 1882; d. Los Angeles Co, CA, 10 Sep 1965.

Handworth, Harry: b. 18??; d. Brooklyn, NY, 22 Mar 1916.

Handworth, Octavia: b. New York, NY, 24 Dec 1887; d. Hemet, CA, 3 Oct 1978.

Handyside, Clarence: b. Montreal, Can, 1854; d. Philadelphia, PA, 20 Dec 1931.

Hanford, Charles B.: b. Sutter Creek, CA, 5 May 1859; d. Washington, DC, 16 Oct 1926.

Hanft, Jules: b. Jersey City, NJ, 16 Sep 1859; d. 6 Aug 1936.

Hanlon, Alma: b. New Jersey, 30 Apr 1890; d. Monterey, CA, 26 Oct 1977.

Hanlon, Edward: b. Manchester, Eng, 1854; d. St. Petersburg, FL, 15 Mar 1931.

Hanna, Franklyn: b. Missouri, 1875; d. 19 Jan 1931.

Hannah, James: b. 1906; d. Fresno, CA, 11 Sep 1978.

Hanneford, Edwin (Poodles): b. Barnley, Eng, 1892; d. Kattskill Bay, NY, 9 Dec 1967.

Hanneman, Frederick G.: b. 1914; d. Santa Barbara, CA, 3 Oct 1980.

Hanray, Lawrence: b. London, Eng, 16 May 1874; d. 28 Nov 1947.

Hansel, Howell: b. Indiana, 1860; d. New York, NY, 5 Nov 1917.

Hansen, Einar: b. Stockholm, Sweden, 15 Jun 1899; d. Santa Monica, CA, 3 Jun 1927.

Hansen, Juanita: b. Des Moines, IA, 3 Mar 1895; d. Los Angeles, CA, 26 Sep 1961.

Hansen, Max: b. Mannheim, Ger, 22 Dec 1887; d. 13 Nov 1961.

Hanson, Frank (Spook): b. Brooklyn, NY, 1874; d. New York, NY, 16 Jun 1924.

Hanson, Gladys: b. Atlanta, GA, 5 Sep 1883; d. Atlanta, GA, 23 Feb 1973.

Hanson, Lars: b. Goteborg, Sweden, 1887; d. Stockholm, Sweden, 8 Apr 1965.

Harbacher, Karl: b. Austria, 2 Nov 1879; d. 8 Mar 1943.

Harbaugh, Carl: b. Washington, DC, 10 Nov 1886; d. Woodland Hills, CA, 26 Feb 1960.

Harbaugh, William: b. 1899; d. Yuma., AZ, 19 Oct 1924.

Harben, Hubert: b. London, Eng, 12 Jul 1878; d. London, Eng, 24 Aug 1941.

Harcourt, Gerald: b. 1886; d. Sydney, Austral, 1 Jun 1924.

Harcourt, Peggy: b. ????; d. Hewlett, NY, 31 Jul 1916.

Harcourt, William: b. Gallatin, TN, 1866; d. New York, NY, 27 Nov 1923.

Harden, Viola: b. 1897; d. Miami Beach, FL, ? Aug 1988.

Hardin, Neil Cameron: b. Louisiana, MO, 20 Sep 1880; d. Louisiana, MO, 22 Nov 1969.

Harding, Alma: b. ????; d. Woodstock, NY, 17 Oct 1961.

Harding, J. Rudge: b. Elvethan, Eng, 1862; d. 24 Apr 1932.

Harding, Lyn: b. Newport, Wales, 12 Oct 1867; d. Southend, Sussex, Eng, 26 Dec 1952.

Hards, Ira M.: b. Geneva, IL, 1873; d. West Norwalk, CT, 2 May 1938.

Hardwicke, Sir Cedric: b. Stourbridge, Eng, 19 Feb 1893; d. New York, NY, 6 Aug 1964.

Hardy, Loo: b. Berlin, Ger, 1898; d. London, Eng, 1934.

Hardy, Oliver: b. Atlanta, GA, 18 Jan 1892; d. North Hollywood, CA, 7 Aug 1957.

Hardy, Sam: b. New Haven, CT, 21 Mar 1883; d. Los Angeles, CA, 16 Oct 1935.

Hare, F. Lumsden: b. Cashel, Ire, 27 Apr 1875; d. Los Angeles, CA, 28 Aug 1964.

Hare, Sir John: b. Giggleswick, Eng, 16 May 1844; d. London, Eng, 28 Dec 1921.

Harker, Gordon: b. London, Eng, 7 Aug 1885; d. London, Eng, 2 Mar 1967.

Harkins, Dixie: b. 1906; d. Jacksonville, FL, 1 Sep 1963.

Harlam, Macey: b. New York, NY, 18??; d. Saranac Lake, NY, 17 Jun 1923.

Harlan, Kenneth: b. Boston, MA, 26 Jul 1895; d. Sacramento, CA, 6 Mar 1967.

Harlan, Otis: b. Zanesville, OH, 29 Dec 1865; d. Martinsville, IN, 20 Jan 1940.

Harlan, Richard: b. Lima, Peru, 19 Apr 1900; d. San Clemente, CA, 20 Oct 1968.

Harlan, Viet: b. Berlin, Ger, 22 Sep 1899; d. Capri, Italy, 13 Apr 1964.

Harley, Edwin: b. Philadelphia, PA, 1848; d. Milwaukee, WI, 29 Oct 1933.

Harlow, Jean: b. Kansas City, KS, 3 Mar 1911; d. Los Angeles, CA, 7 Jun 1937.

Harmon, Pat: b. Lewiston, IL, 3 Feb 1886; d. Riverside, CA, 26 Nov 1958.

Harolde, Ralf: b. Pittsburgh, PA, 17 May 1899; d. Santa Monica, CA, 1 Nov 1974.

Harr, Silver: b. Idaho, 21 Sep 1892; d. Los Angeles Co, CA, 19 Sep 1968.

Harrigan, William: b. New York, NY, 27 Mar 1894; d. New York, NY, 1 Feb 1966.

Harriman, Moses H.: b. 1861; d. East Islip, NY, 16 Sep 1928.

Harrington, George: b. 18??; d. England, 14, Jun 1922.

Harrington, John, b. Riverside Co, CA, 23 Jul 1882; d. San Francisco Co, CA, 9 Sep 1945.

Harris, Averell: b. ????; d. New York, NY, 25 Sep 1966.

Harris, Bernard: b. 1892; d. Encino, CA, 12 Jul 1981.

Harris, Carolina (Caroline E. Barthelmess): b. 1867; d. New York, NY, 23 Apr 1937.

Harris, Charles K.: b. Poughkeepsie, NY, 1 May 1865; d. New York, NY, 22 Dec 1930.

Harris, Elmer: b. Chicago, IL, 11 Jan 1878; d. Washington, DC, 6 Sep 1966.

Harris, Georgie: b. Liverpool, Eng, 19 Jun 1898; d. England, 14 Mar 1986.

Harris, Joseph: b. Maine, 11 Jan 1870; d. Los Angeles, CA, 11 Jun 1953.

Harris, Katherine: b. 1893; d. New York, NY, 2 May 1927.

Harris, Leonore: b. New York, NY, 1879; d. New York, NY, 27 Sep 1953.

Harris, Marcia: b. Providence, RI, 14 Feb 1880; d. 19??.

Harris, Mildred: b. Cheyenne, WY, 29 Nov 1902; d. Los Angeles, CA, 20 Jul 1944.

Harris, Mitchell; b. New York, NY, 1883; d. New York, NY, 16 Nov 1948.

Harris, Sadie: b. 1892; d. New York, NY, 15 May 1933.

Harris, Mrs. Sam H. (Alice-Nolan): b. 1888; d. New York, NY, 24 Nov 1930.

Harris, Wadsworth: b. Boston, MA, 9 Oct 1864; d. Los Angeles, CA, 1 Nov 1942.

Harris, Winifred: b. England, 1879; d. Evanston, IL; 18 Apr 1972.

Harrison, Jimmy: b. Texas, 26 May 1908; d. Woodland Hills, CA, 9 Nov 1977.

Harrison, Mark: b. 1864; d. 1 Jun 1952.

Harrison, Mona K.: b. Edinburgh, Scot, 18??; d. 2 Jan 1957.

Harrison, Saul E.: b. Brenham, TX, 1888; d. New York, NY, 13 Oct 1944.

Harrison, Stanley: b. Glasgow, Scot, 1877; d. New York, NY, 16 Feb 1950.

Harron, Charles: b. ????; d. Los Angeles, CA, 24 Dec 1915.

Harron, John: b. New York, NY, 31 Mar 1903; d. Seattle, WA, 24 Nov 1939.

Harron, Robert: b. New York, NY, 24 Apr 1893; d. New York, NY, 5 Sep 1920.

Harron, Tessie: b. New York, NY, 16 Feb 1896; d. Los Angeles, CA, 9 Nov 1918.

Hart, Albert: b. Liverpool, Eng, 6 Dec 1875; d. Los Angeles, CA, 10 Jan 1940.

Hart, Florence: b. ????; d. Germantown, PA, 30 Mar 1960.

Hart, Fred: b. ????; d. Chicago, IL, 9 Nov 1927.

Hart, James T.: b. 1868; d. Los Angeles, CA, 12 Aug 1926.

Hart, Joseph: b. Boston, MA, 8 Jun 1864; d. New York, NY, 3 Oct 1921.

Hart, Lewis O.: b. 1847, d. Staten Island, NY, 9 Jan 1920.

Hart, Lucia (Sunshine): b. Indianapolis, IN, 6 Jul 1886; d. Los Angeles, CA, 3 Jan 1930.

Hart, Neal: b. Richmond, NY, 7 Apr 1879; d. Los Angeles, CA, 2 Apr 1949.

Hart, William S.: b. Newburgh, NY, 6 Dec 1864; d. Los Angeles, CA, 23 Jun 1946.

Hart, William Valentine (Pop): b. 1867; d. New York, NY, 14 Oct 1925.

Harte, Betty: b. Lebanon, PA, 1882; d. Los Angeles, CA, 3 Jan 1965.

Hartford, David: b. Rockland, MI, 11 Jan 1873; d. Los Angeles, CA, 29 Oct 1932.

Hartford, Harry: b. 1851; d. Bernardsville, NJ, 20 Sep 1925.

Hartigan, Patrick C.: b. New York, NY, 21 Dec 1881; d. Los Angeles, CA, 8 May 1951.

Hartigan, William: b. 1866; d. Johannesburg, So Africa, 3 Jul 1920.

Hartley, Charles: b. 1852; d. Fort Lee, NJ, 13 Oct 1930.

Hartley, Helen: b. 1892; d. Denison, TX, 30 Oct 1954.

Hartman, Ferris, b. 1861; d. San Francisco, LA, 1 Sep 1931.

Hartman, Gretchen (Greta Arbin, Sonia Markova): b. Chicago, IL, 28 Aug 1897; d. Los Angeles, CA, 27 Jan 1979.

Hartman, Jonathan W. (Pop): b. Louisville, KY, 1872; d. Tampa, FL, 19 Oct 1965.

Hartman, Ruth: b. Illinois, 3 Apr 1893; d. Los Angeles, CA, 9 Jul 1956.

Hartmann, Paul: b. Furth, Ger, 8 Jan 1889; d. 30 Jun 1977.

Hartmann, Sadakichi: b. 1866; d. St. Petersburg, FL, 21 Nov 1944.

Hartsell, Harold: b. 1874; d. Beechurst, NY, 1 Oct 1930.

Harty, Veola: b. 1896; d. New York, NY, 13 Jul 1936.

Harvey, Clarence: b. 1865; d. New York, NY, 3 May 1945.

Harvey, Donald (James H. Brundage): b. 1863; d. Los Angeles, CA, 1 Feb 1931.

Harvey, Fletcher: b. 1865; d. Bay Shore, NY, 8 Sep 1931.

Harvey, Forrester: b. County Cork, Ire, 27 Jun 1884; d. Laguna Beach, CA, 14 Dec 1945.

Harvey, Georgia: b. Nova Scotia, Canada, 1875; d. New York, NY, 17 May 1960.

Harvey, Herman (Hank): b. 1849; d. Los Angeles, CA, 4 Dec 1929.

Harvey, John M. (Jack): b. Cleveland, OH, 1881; d. Los Angeles, CA, 10 Nov 1954.

Harvey, Lee F.: b. 1895; d. Philadelphia, PA, 19 Apr 1950.

Harvey, Lew P.: b. Wisconsin, 6 Oct 1887; d. Los Angeles Co, CA, 19 Dec 1953.

Harvey, Lillian: b. Edmonton, Eng, 19 Jan 1906; d. Antibes, Fr, 27 Jul 1968.

Harvey, Paul: b. Sandwich, IL, 10 Sep 1882; d. Los Angeles, CA, 15 Dec 1955.

Harvey, Rupert: b. Ironbridge, Eng, 1 Jan 1887; d. London, Eng, 7 Jul 1954.

Harwood, John: b. London, Eng, 29 Feb 1876; d. London, Eng, 26 Dec 1944.

Hasegawa, Kazuo: b. Japan, 29 Feb 1908; d. Japan, ? Apr 1984.

Haskel, Leonhard: b. Seelow, Ger, 7 Apr 1872; d. 30 Dec 1923.

Haskin, Harry R.: b. 1870; d. 7 Feb 1953.

Haskin, Charles Wilson: b. 1868; d. New York, NY, 10 Jun 1927.

Hassell, George: b. Birmingham, Eng, 4 May 1881; d. Chatsworth, CA, 17 Feb 1937.

Hastings, Adelaide: b. 18??; d. Toledo, OH, 22 May 1921.

Hastings, Carey: b. New Orleans, LA, 18??; d. New York, NY, c. 1929.

Haswell, Miss Percy: Austin, TX, 30 Apr 1871; d. Nantucket, MA, 13 Jun 1945.

Hatch, Harry E.: b. 1882; d. New York, NY, 22 Oct 1926.

Hatch, William Riley: b. Cleveland, OH, 2 Sep :1862; d. Bay Shore, NY, 6 Sep 1925.

Hathaway, Henry: b. Sacramento, CA, 13 Mar 1898; d. Los Angeles, CA, 11 Feb 1985.

Hathaway, Jean (Jane Hathaway): b. Hungary, 15 Jun 1876; d. Los Angeles, CA, 23 Aug 1938.

Hathaway, Joan: b. ????; d. Los Angeles, CA, 6 Feb 1981.

Hathaway, Lillian: b. Liverpool, Eng, 1876; d. Englewood Cliffs, NJ, 12 Jan 1954.

Hathaway, Rhody: b. San Francisco, CA, 5 Oct 1868; d. Los Angeles, CA,18 Feb 1944.

Hatswell, Donald R. O.: b. England, 3 Jul 1898; d. Encino, CA, 29 Jun 1976.

Hatton, Clare: b. 1869; d. Denver, CO, 26 Jun 1943.

Hatton, Dick (Edward Hatton): Kentucky, 1886; d. Los Angeles, CA, 9 Jul 1931.

Hatton, Frances: b. Nebraska, 19 Oct 1886; d. Palmdale, CA, 16 Oct 1971.

Hatton, Raymond: b. Red Oak, IA, 7 Jul 1887; d. Palmdale, CA, 21 Oct 1971.

Hauber, William C.: b. Brownsville, MN, 1891; d. Los Angeles, CA, 17 Jul 1929.

Haught, Albert: b. Dallas, TX, 30 Apr 1899; d. Los Angeles, CA, 29 Oct 1936.

Haupt, Ulrich: b. Prussia, 8 Aug 1887; d. Santa Maria, CA, 5 Aug 1931.

Havel, Joe: b. 1869; d. Los Angeles, CA, 24 Jan 1932.

Havens, Beckwith: b. 1890; d. New York, NY, 7 May 1969.

Haver, Phyllis: b. Douglas, KS, 6 Jan 1899; d. Falls Village, CT, 19 Nov 1960.

Havez, Jean C.: b. Baltimore, MD, 1870; d. Beverly Hills, CA, 11 Feb 1925.

Haviland, Auguste: b. 18??; d. New York, NY, 25 Oct 1925.

Haviland, Rena: b. 1878; d. Woodland Hills, CA, 20 Feb 1954.

Hawkins, Puny: b. ????; b. Wichita, KS, 30 Mar 1947.

Hawks, Charles Monroe: b. 1874; d. Los Angeles, CA, 15 Dec 1951.

Hawley, Allen Burton: b. Albany, NY, 1895; d. Troy, NY, 12 Sep 1975.

Hawley, H. Dudley: Styal, Cheshire, Eng, 1879; d. New York, NY, 29 Mar 1941.

Hawley, Ormi: b, Holyoke, MA, 1889; d. Rome, NY, 3 Jun 1942.

Hawley, Wanda (Wanda Petit): b. Scranton, PA, 30 Jul 1895; d. Los Angeles, CA, 18 Mar 1963.

Hawthorne, David: b. Kettering, Eng, 1888; d. 18 Jun 1942.

Hawtrey, Sir Charles: b. Slough, Eng, 21 Sep 1858; d. London, Eng, 30 Jul 1923.

Hay, Mary: b. Fort Bliss, TX, 22 Aug 1901; d. Inverness, CA, 4 Jun 1957.

Hayakawa, Sessue: b. Nanaura, Japan, 10 Jun 1890, d. Tokyo, Japan, 23 Nov 1973.

Hayden, J. Charles: b. Frederick, MD, 1876; d. Baltimore, MD, ? Oct 1943.

Haydock, John: b. New York, NY, 1845; d. New York, NY, 19 Jan 1918.

Haye, Helen: b. Assam, India, 28 Aug 1874; d. London, Eng, 1 Sep 1957.

Hayes, Carrie: b. 1879; d. Philadelphia, PA, 22 Dec 1954.

Hayes, E. J. (Edmond J. Hayes): b. 1866; d. Los Angeles, CA, 12 Jun 1921.

Hayes, Frank: b. San Francisco, LA, 17 May 1871; d. Los Angeles, CA, 28 Dec 1923.

Hayes, George (Gabby): b. Wellesville, NY, 7 May 1885; d. Burbank, CA, 9 Feb 1969.

Hayes, Helen: b. Washington, DC, 10 Oct 1900; Nyack, NY, 17 Mar 1993.

Hayes, Helen, M.: b. Chattanooga, TN, ????; d. ? Jul 1974.

Hayes, Sidney: b. 1865; d. Beverly Hills, CA, 2 May 1940.

Hayes, William: b. 1887; d. Los Angeles, CA, 13 Jul 1937.

Hayman, Adam Charles: b. New York, NY, 1880; d. Niagara Falls, NY, 11 Jul 1945.

Haynes, Manning: b. Lyminster, Eng, 18??; d.1957.

Haynes, Marie: b. South Sutton, NH, 10 May 1865; d. Amityville, NY, 3 Apr 1934.

Haynes, Minna Gale (Minna Gale): b. New Jersey, 26 Sep 1869; d. Riverside, CT, 4 Mar 1944.

Hazelton, Joseph: b. 1853; d. Los Angeles, CA, 8 Oct 1936.

Hearn, Edward: b. Dayton, WA, 6 Sep 1888; d. Los Angeles, CA, 15 Apr 1963.

Hearn, Fred G.: b. Louisville, KY, 20 Dec 1871; d. Pasadena, CA, 20 Jan 1923.

Heath, Frank: b. 1892; d. Los Angeles, CA, 31 Oct 1952.

Heatherley, Clifford; b. Preston, Lancs, Eng, 8 Oct 1888; d. London, Eng, 15 Sep 1937.

Heazlet, Eva (Eva McKenzie): b. Cecil, OH, 5 Nov 1889; d. Los Angeles, CA, 15 Sep 1967.

Hebert, Mrs. Helen: b. Brooklyn, NY, 6 Apr 1873; d. Los Angeles, CA, 27 Oct 1946.

Hebert, Henry J. (H. J. Herbert): b. Providence, RI, 12 Nov 1879; d. Los Angeles, CA, 18 Jan 1956.

Hechy, Alice: b. Anklam, Ger, 21 Jul 1898; d. 1973.

Heck, Stanton: b. Wilmington, DE, 8 Jan 1877; d. Los Angeles, CA, 16 Dec 1929.

Hedlund, Guy: b. Connecticut, 21 Aug 1884; d. Culver City, CA, 29 Dec 1964.

Hedman, Martha: b. Ostersund, Sweden, 12 Aug 1888; d. 19??.

Hedqvist, Ivan: b. Stockholm, Sweden, 8 Jun 1880; d. 23 Aug 1935.

Heggie, Oliver P.: b. Angaston, Austral, 16 Sep 1879; d. Los Angeles, CA, 7 Feb 1936.

Heidemann, Paul: b. Koln, Ger, 26 Oct 1884; d. Berlin, Ger, 20 Jun 1968.

Heisey, Mart E:. b. 1865; d. Chicago, IL, 21 Apr 1925.

Heisler, Elfriede: b. 31 Mar 1885; d. 21 Feb 1919.

Held, Anna: b. Paris, Fr, 18 Mar 1873; d. New York, NY, 12 Aug 1918.

Heller, William (Owen Dale): b. 1851; d. San Francisco, CA, 21 Feb 1919.

Hellum, Barney: b. Seavyanv, Norway, 1 Jan 1895; d. 22 Dec 1935.

Helmore, Arthur: b. 1858; d. 14 Jun 1941.

Helms, Ruth b. 1897; d. Los Angeles, CA, 27 Oct 1960.

Helston, Wally (Walter Ellis): b. England, 1873; d. Wildwood, NJ, 1 Sep 1933.

Helton, Percy: b. New York, NY, 31 Jan 1894; d. Los Angeles, CA, 11 Sep 1971.

Heming, Violet: b. Leeds, Eng, 27 Jan 1895; d. New York, NY, 4 Jul 1981.

Hemingway, Marie: b. Yorkshire, Eng, 1893; d. 11 Jan 1939.

Hemming, Alfred: b. London, Eng, 1851; d. New York, 17 Dec 1942.

Hemphill, Frank: b. Mobile, AL, 6 Oct 1870; d. Oakland, CA, 12 Dec 1966.

Henabery, Joseph: b. Omaha, NE, 15 Jan 1887; d. Woodland Hills, CA, 18 Feb 1976.

Henckles, Paul: b. Hurth, Ger, 9 Sep 1885; d. Kettwich, Ger, 27 May 1967.

Hendee, Harold F.: b. 4 Dec 1879; d. New York, NY, 24 Jun 1966.

Henderson, Del: b. St. Thomas, Ont, Can, 5 Jul 1877; d. Los Angeles, CA, 2 Dec 1956.

Henderson, George A.: b. New York, NY, 1851; d. San Francisco, CA, 28 Nov 1923.

Henderson, Grace: b. Ann Arbor, MI, 1860; d. New York, NY, 30 Oct 1944.

Henderson, Jack: b. Syracuse, NY, 1878; d. New York, NY, 1 Jan 1957.

Henderson, Lucius J.: b. Aldo, IL, 1860; d. New York, NY, 18 Feb 1947.

Henderson, Ted, b. California, 6 Jul 1888; d. Santa Paula, CA, 19 Jul 1962.

Henderson, V. Talbot: b. Phelps Mills, NY, 9 Feb 1879; d. Los Angeles, CA, 24 May 1946.

Hendricks, Ben, Sr.: b. Buffalo, NY, 1868; d. Los Angeles, CA, 30 Apr 1930.

Hendricks, Ben, Jr.: b. New York, NY, 2 Nov 1893; d. Los Angeles, CA, 15 Aug 1938.

Hendricks, Dudley C.: b. La Grange, KY, 3 Aug 1870; d. Pasadena, CA, 3 Feb 1942.

Hendricks, John B.: b. 1873; d. Elizabeth, NJ, 26 Feb 1949.

Hendricks, Louis: b. Buffalo, NY, 1861; d. New York, NY, 18 Dec 1923.

Hendrie, Anita: b. 1868; d. Brooklyn, NY, 15 Apr 1940.

Hendrie, Ernest: b. England, 10 Jun 1859; d. Windsor, Eng, 11 Mar 1929.

Hendrix, Noah (Shorty): b. Missouri, 20 Dec 1889; d. Los Angeles Co, CA, 4 Mar 1973.

Henley, Hobart: b. Louisville, KY, 23 Nov 1886; d. Beverly Hills, CA, 22 May 1964.

Henley, Rosina: b. 18 Nov 1890; d. New York, NY, ? Jul 1978.

Hennecke, Clarence R.: b. Omaha, NE, 16 Sep 1894; d. Santa Monica, CA, 28 Aug 1969.

Hennessey, David: b. 1852; d. Chicago, IL, 24 Mar 1926.

Hennessey, John: b. Boston, MA, 1853; d. New York, NY, 15 May 1920.

Henning, Uno: b. Sweden, 1895; d. 16 May 1970.

Henri, Louie (Lady Lytton): b. 1863; d. Surbiton, Eng, 2 May 1947.

Henrikson, Anders: b. Stockholm, Sweden, 1896; d. Sweden, 1965.

Henry, Charlotte: b. Brooklyn, NY, 3 Mar 1913; d. San Diego, CA, 11 Apr 1980.

Henry, Gale: b. Bear Valley, CA, 15 Apr 1893; d. Palmdale, CA, 17 June 1972.

Henry, John: b. 1880; d. Winthrop, MA, 12 Aug 1958.

Henry, S. Creagh: b. Isle of Guernsey, 1 Jul 1863; d. 26 Feb 1946.

Henry, William (Bill): b. Los Angeles, CA, 10 Nov 1918; d. Los Angeles, CA, 10 Aug 1982.

Henson, Leslie: b. London, Eng, 3 Aug 1891; d. Harrow Weald, Eng, 2 Dec 1957.

Hepworth, Cecil M.: b. London, Eng, 1874; d. Greenford, Middlesex, Eng, 9 Feb 1953.

Herbert, Henry: b. London, Eng, 1879; d. Flushing, NY, 20 Feb 1947.

Herbert, Holmes: b. Mansfield, Eng, 30 Jul 1878; d. Los Angeles CA, 26 Dec 1956.

Herbert, Hugh: b. Binghamton, NY, 10 Aug 1885; d. Los Angeles, CA, 12 Mar 1952.

Herbert, Joseph: b. Liverpool, Eng, 1867; d. New York, NY, 18 Feb 1923.

Herbert, Sidney: b. England, 18??; d. London, Eng, 24 Dec 1927.

Herford, William B.: b. Yorkshire, Eng, 5 May 1853; d. 27 Dec 1934.

Heriat, Philippe: b. Paris, Fr, 15 Sep 1898; d. Paris, Fr, 10 Oct 1971.

Heritage, Clarence: b. 1854; d. New York, NY, 27 Oct 1940.

Herlein, Lillian: b. 11 Mar 1895; d. New York, NY, 13 Apr 1971.

Herlinger, Karl: b. Vienna, Austria, 1880; d. Los Angeles, CA, 8 Feb 1949.

Herman, Al: b. Scotland, 25 Feb 1887; d. Los Angeles, CA, 2 Jul 1967.

Herman, Jay: b. 18??; d. Bridgeport, CT, 20 Feb 1928.

Herman, Milton: b. 1896; d. New York, NY, 21 Jan 1951.

Hernandez, Albert: b. Mexico, 1899; d. Los Angeles, CA, 2 Jan 1948.

Hernandez, Anna (Anna Dodge): b. River Falls, WI, 19 Oct 1867; d. Los Angeles, CA, 4 May 1945.

Hernandez, George F.: b. Placerville, CA, 6 Jun 1863; d. Los Angeles, CA, 31 Dec 1922.

Herrick, Jack: b. Hungary, 4 Feb 1891; d. Los Angeles Co, CA, 18 Jun 1952.

Herring, Aggie: b. San Francisco, CA, 4 Feb 1876; d. Santa Monica, CA, 28 Oct 1939.

Herring, Jess: b. Missouri, 29 Oct 1895; d. Los Angeles Co, CA, 5 Mar 1953.

Herrmann, Julius E.: b. Germany, 13 Jun 1883; d. 1977.

Herschfield, Harry: b. 1885; d. New York, NY, 15 Dec 1974.

Hersholt, Allan: b. Copenhagen, Denmark, 1914; d. Los Angeles, CA, 19 Feb 1990.

Hersholt, Jean: b. Copenhagen, Denmark, 12 Jul 1886; d. Los Angeles, CA, 2 Jun 1956.

Herz, Ralph: b. Paris, Fr, 25 Mar 1878; d. Atlantic City, NJ, 12 Jul 1921.

Herzfeld, Guido: b. Berlin, Ger, 1865; d. 16 Nov 1923.

Herzinger, Charles W.: b. San Francisco, CA, 10 Aug 1864; d. Los Angeles, CA, 18 Feb 1953.

Herzog, Charles L. (Buck): b. Baltimore, MD, 9 Jul 1885; d. Baltimore, MD, 5 Feb 1970.

Herzog, Frederic: b. 1868; d. Glendale, CA, 2 Mar 1928.

Heslewood, Tom: b. Hessle, York, Eng, 8 Apr 1868; d. 28 Apr 1959.

Heslop, Charles: b. Thames Ditton, Eng, 8 Jun 1883; d. London, Eng, 13 Apr 1966.

Hesse, Baron William: b. Moscow, Russ, 22 Jul 1885; d. Los Angeles, CA, 3 Apr 1936.

Hessling, Catherine: b. Morionvillers, Alsace, Fr, 1899; d. 1979.

Hester, James: b. 1867; d. Brooklyn, NY, 16 Feb 1924.

Hesterberg, Trude: b. Berlin, Ger, 2 May 1892; d. Munich, Ger, 31 Aug 1967.

Hevener, Gerald: b. Philadelphia, PA, 30 Apr 1873; d. 19??.

Hewlett, Ben: b. Oakland, CA, 27 Feb 1892; d. Santa Monica, CA, 16 Aug 1948.

Hewston, Alfred H.: b. San Francisco, CA, 12 Sep 1882; d. Los Angeles, CA, 6 Sep 1947.

Heyes, Herbert: b. Vader, WA, 3 Aug 1889; d. Los Angeles, CA, 31 May 1958.

Hiatt, Ruth: b. Cripple Creek, CO, 6 Jan 1906; d. Montrose, CA, 21 Apr 1994.

Hibbard, Edna: b. California, 1895; d. New York, NY, 26 Dec 1942.

Hickman, Alfred: b. England, 25 Feb 1872; d. Los Angeles, CA, 9 Apr 1931.

Hickman, Charles H.: b. 1876; d. 19 Sep 1938.

Hickman, Howard: b. Columbia, MO, 9 Feb 1880; d. Los Angeles LA, 30 Dec 1949.

Hickok, Lida: b. 1863; d. Los Angeles, CA, 23 Aug 1928.

Hickok, Rodney: b. 1892; d. Los Angeles, CA, 9 Mar 1942.

Hicks, Eleanor: b. 1886; d. Aurora, IL, 11 Jul 1936.

Hicks, Russell: b. Baltimore, MD, 4 Jun 1895; d. Los Angeles, CA, 1 Jun 1957.

Hicks, Sir Seymour: b. St. Hélier, Isle of Jersey, 30 Jan 1871; d. Fleet, Hants, Eng, 6 Apr 1949.

Hiers, Walter: b. Cordele, GA, 18 Jul 1893; d. Los Angeles, CA, 27 Feb 1933.

Higby, Wilbur: b. Merdian, MS, 21 Aug, 1867; d. Los Angeles, CA, 1 Dec 1934.

Higgins, David H.: b. Chicago, IL, 21 Jun 1858; d. Brooklyn, NY, 29 Jun 1936.

Hignett, H. R.: b. Ringway, Cheshire, Eng, 29 Jan 1870; d. 17 Dec 1959.

Hildebrand, Hilde: b. Hanover, Ger, 10 Sep 1897; d. 28 Apr 1976.

Hildebrand, Lo: b. 1894; d. Los Angeles, CA, 11 Sep 1936.

Hildebrand, Rodney: b. Illinois, 22 Mar 1892; d. Los Angeles, CA, 22 Feb 1962.

Hilforde, Mary: b. Carbondale, PA, 1853; d. Amityville, NY, 12 Dec 1927.

Hill, Al: b. New York, NY, 14 Jul 1892; d. Los Angeles Co, CA, 14 Jul 1954.

Hill, Arthur: b. 1875; d. Los Angeles, CA, 9 Apr 1932.

Hill, Arthur R.: b. 1890; d. Los Angeles, CA, 17 Apr 1941.

Hill, Ben: b. 1894; d. Dallas, TX, 30 Nov 1969.

Hill, Doris: b. Roswell, NM, 21 Mar 1905; d. Kingman, AZ, 3 Mar 1976.

Hill, Dudley: b. Baltimore, MD, 1880; d. Wilkesboro, NC, 7 Jan 1960.

Hill, Josephine: b. San Francisco, CA, 3 Oct 1899; d. Palm Springs, CA, 17 Dec 1989.

Hill, Kenneth: b. Boston, MA, ????; d. St. Mortiz, Switz, 15 Jan 1929.

Hill, Maud: b. St. Louis, MO, 1885; d. 19??.

Hill, Robert F.: b. Fort Rohen, Can, 14 Apr 1886; d. Los Angeles, CA, 18 Mar 1966.

Hill, Thelma: b. Emporia, KS, 12 Dec 1906; d. Culver City, CA, 11 May 1938.

Hill, Wesley: b. Baltimore, MD, 1875; d. New York, NY, 10 Dec 1930.

Hilliard, Ernest: b. New York, NY, 31 Jan 1890; d. Santa Monica, CA, 3 Sep 1947.

Hilliard, Harry S.: b. Cincinnati, OH, 24 Oct 1886; d. St. Petersburg, FL, 21 Apr 1966.

Hilliard, Mrs. Mack (Hazel Clayton): b. 1886; d. Forest Hills, NY, 8 Mar 1963.

Hillis, Houston: b. ????; d. Bakersfield, CA, 12 Feb 1928.

Hilton, Frank: b. 1871; d. New York, NY, 16 Feb 1932.

Hilton, Haran: b. 1900; d. Los Angeles, LA, ? Aug 1930.

Hinckley, William L.: b. 1894; d. New York, NY, 4 May 1918.

Hinds, Nina: b. 1904; d. Reno, NV, 24 May 1961.

Hines, Charles J.: b. Pittsburgh, PA, 1891; d. Los Angeles, CA, 16 Jul 1936.

Hines, Johnny: b. Golden, CO, 25 Jul 1895; d. Los Angeles, CA, 24 Oct 1970.

Hines, Samuel E.: b. 1881; d. Los Angeles, CA, 16 Nov 1939.

Hippe, Lew: b. 1880; d. Los Angeles, CA, 19 Jul 1952.

Hitchcock, Alfred: b. London, Eng, 13 Aug 1899; d. Los Angeles, CA, 29 Apr 1980.

Hitchcock, Raymond: b. Auburn, NY, 22 Oct 1865; d. Beverly Hills, CA, 24 Nov 1929.

Hitchcock, Walter: b. Walden, MA, 1872; d. New York, NY, 23 Jun 1917.

Hively, Georgenia: b. 1891; d. North Hollywood, CA, 21 May 1977.

Hoagland, Harland: b. 1895; d. Los Angeles, CA, 9 Jan 1971.

Hoban, Stella: b. 1890; d. Muskegon, MI, 24 Jan 1962.

Hobbs, Jack: b. London, Eng, 28 Sep 1893; d. Brighton, Eng, 4 Jun 1968.

Hoch, Emil H.: b. Pforzheim, Ger, 21 Oct 1866; d. Los Angeles, CA, 13 Oct 1944

Hockey, Harry G.: b. London, Eng, 1864; d. New York, NY, 3 Feb 1936.

Hodd, Joseph B.: b. 1896; d. Philadelphia, PA, 26 Jun 1965.

Hodges, William C.: b. Newbury Township, OH, 6 Feb 1876; d. Claridon Township, OH, 27 Jul 1961.

Hodgins, Leslie: b. 1885; d. St. Louis, MO, ? Sep 1927.

Hoeflich, Lucie: b. Hannover, Ger, 20 Feb 1883; d. Berlin, Ger, 9 Oct 1956.

Hoerbiger, Paul: b. Budapest, Hungary, 29 Apr 1893; d. Vienna, Austria, 18 Mar 1981.

Hoey, Dennis: b. London, England, 30 Mar 1893; d. Palm Beach, FL, 25 Jul 1960.

Hoey, Herbert: b. Atlanta, GA, 24 Sep 1894; d. Miami Shores, FL, 7 Dec 1970.

Hoey, Iris: b. London, Eng, 17 Jul 1885; d. London, Eng, 13 May 1979.

Hoffman, Eberhard: b. Germany, 1883; d. Denville, NJ, 16 Jun 1957.

Hoffman, Gertrude: b. Montreal, Can, 1898; d. Washington, DC, 3 Jun 1955.

Hoffman, Gladys: b. ???? d. San Francisco, CA, 5 Feb 1962.

Hoffman, Otto: b. New York, NY, 2 May 1879; d. Woodland Hills, CA, 23 Jun 1944.

Hoffmann, Ernst, b. Berlin, Ger, 7 Dec 1880; d. 27 Apr 1945.

Hogan, Earl (Hap): b. ????; d. Los Angeles, CA, 14 Oct 1944.

Hogan, James P: b. 1891; d. North Hollywood, CA, 4 Nov 1943.

Hohl, Arthur: b. Pittsburgh, PA, 21 May 1889; d. Santa Monica, CA, 10 Mar 1964.

Holbrook, John Knight: b. Ripley, TN, 18??; d. Los Angeles, CA, 17 Nov 1934.

Holden, Harry M.: b. Franklin, OH, 1868; d. Woodland Hills, CA, 4 Feb 1944.

Holden, William: b. Rochester, NY, 22 May 1872; d. Los Angeles, CA, 2 Mar 1932.

Holding, Thomas: b. Blackheath, Kent, Eng, 25 Jan 1880; d. New York, NY, 4 May 1929.

Holland, Cecil: b. Gravesend, Eng, 29 Mar 1887; d. Los Angeles, CA, 29 Jun 1973.

Holland, Clifford: b. ????; d. Los Angeles, CA, 26 Sep 1990.

Holland, Edna: b. New York, NY, 20 Sep 1895; d. Los Angeles, CA, 4 May 1982.

Holland, Joseph: b. 1859; d. New York, NY, 25 Sep 1926.

Holland, Mildred: b. Chicago, IL, 9 Apr 1869; d. New York, NY, 27 Jan 1944.

Holland, Ralph: b. 1888; d. Los Angeles, CA, 7 Dec 1939.

Holles, Anthony: b. London, Eng, 31 Jan 1901; d. 4 Mar 1950.

Hollingshead, Gordon: b. Garfield, NJ, 8 Jan 1891; d. Balboa, CA, 8 Jul 1952.

Hollingsworth, Alfred: b. New York State, ? Apr 1869; d. Glendale, CA, 19 Jun 1926.

Hollingsworth, Harry: b. Los Angeles, CA, 3 Sep 1868; d. Inglewood, CA, 4 Nov 1947.

Hollis, Hylda: b. Philadelphia, PA, 10 Jul 1891; d. Woodland Hills, CA, 9 Dec 1961.

Hollis, T. Beresford (Jack): b. London, Eng, 1859; d. Amityville, NY, 15 Dec 1940.

Hollister, Alice: b. Worcester, MA, 28 Sep 1886; d. Costa Mesa, CA, 24 Feb 1973.

Hollister, Doris: b. New York State, 2 Dec 1906; d. Tustin, CA, 26 Jul 1990.

Hollister, George K., Jr.: b. 6 Jun 1908; d. Vista, CA, 22 Jan 1976.

Holloway, Carol: b. Williamstown, MA, 30 Apr 1892; d. 19??.

Holloway, Stanley: b. London, Eng, 1 Oct 1890; d. Littlehampton, Eng, 30 Jan 1982.

Holloway, Sterling: b. Cedartown, GA. 4 Jan 1905; d. Los Angeles, CA, 22 Nov 1992.

Holly, Mary: b. 1887; d. Palm Springs, CA, 17 May 1976.

Holm, Dary: b. Germany, 16 Apr 1897; d. ? Aug 1960.

Holm, Magda: b. Sweden, 1899; d. 10 Oct 1982.

Holman, Harry: b. Lebanon, MO, 15 Mar 1862; d. Los Angeles, CA, 3 May 1947.

Holman, Richard: b. 1900; d. San Francisco, CA, 12 Aug 1955.

Holmes, Burton: b. Chicago, IL, 8 Jan 1870; d. Los Angeles, CA, 22 Jul 1958.

Holmes, Gilbert (Pee Wee): b. Miles City, MT, 15 Jun 1895; d. Los Angeles, CA, 17 Aug 1936.

Holmes, Helen: b. Chicago, IL, 19 Jun 1893; d. Los Angeles, CA, 8 Jul 1950.

Holmes, Milton: b. Syracuse, NY, 30 Jul 1907; d. Los Angeles, CA, 19 Sep 1987.

Holmes, Phillips: b. Grand Rapids, MI, 22 Jul 1907; d. Armstrong, Ont, Can, 12 Aug 1942.

Holmes, Rapley: b. Canada, 1868; d. Strathroy, Ont, Can, 11 Jan 1928.

Holmes, Stuart: b. Chicago, IL, 10 Mar 1884; d. Los Angeles, CA, 29 Dec 1971.

Holmes, Taylor: b. Newark, NJ, 16 May 1878; d. Los Angeles, CA, 30 Sep 1959.

Holmes-Gore, Arthur: b. England, 1871; d. Dardanelles, 12 Aug 1915.

Holmes-Gore, Dorothy: b. London, Eng, 26 May 1896; d. London, Eng, 14 Oct 1977.

Holmquist, Sigrid: b. Baros, Sweden, 1899; d. Sydney, Austral, 9 Jul 1970.

Holt, Edwin: b. Maine, 12 Apr 18??; d. 5 Jul 1920.

Holt, Helen: b. 1890; d. Vancouver, Can, 17 Jan 1927.

Holt, Jack: b. New York, NY, 31 May 1888; d. Sawtelle, CA, 18 Jan 1951.

Holt, Skip: b. 1921; d. 2 Feb 1986.

Holt, Tim: b. Los Angeles, CA, 5 Feb 1918; d. Shawnee, OK, 15 Feb 1973.

Holtz, Tenen: b. Russia, 27 Feb 1887; d. 1 Jul 1971.

Holubar, Allen J.: b. San Francisco, CA, 3 Aug 1890; d. Los Angeles, CA, 20 Nov 1923.

Homan, Gertrude: b. 1880; d. Glen Grove, NY, 29 May 1951.

Homans, Robert: b. Malden, MA, 8 Nov 1877; d. Los Angeles, CA, 27 Jul 1947.

Homolka, Oscar: b. Vienna, Austria, 12 Aug 1898; d. Sussex, Eng, 27 Jan 1978.

Honda, Frank K.: b. 1884; d. New York, NY, 3 Feb 1924.

Honn, Eldon: b. 1890; d. San Diego, CA, 11 Aug 1927.

Hood, Joseph B.: b. 1896; d. Philadelphia, PA, 26 Jun 1965.

Hood, Wally: b. Whittier, CA, 9 Feb 1895; d. Los Angeles, CA, 2 May 1965.

Hoops, Arthur: b. Middletown, CT, 1870; d. Long Island, NY, 16 Sep 1916.

Hope, Evelyn: b. London, Eng, 18??; d. 23 Dec 1966.

Hope, Gloria: b. Pittsburgh, PA, 9 Nov 1899; d. Pasadena, CA, 29 Oct 1976.

Hope, Maidie: b. London, Eng, 15 Feb 1881; d. London, Eng, 18 Apr 1937.

Hopkins, Ben: b. Buffalo, NY, 9 May 1870; d. Los Angeles, CA, 8 Feb 1941.

Hopkins, Clyde E.: b. Garrett, KS, 25 Jun 1893; d. Los Angeles, CA, 19 Nov 1958.

Hopper, De Wolf: b. New York, NY, 30 Mar 1858; d, Kansas City, MO, 23 Sep 1935.

Hopper, Edna Wallace: b. San Francisco, CA, 17 Jan 1874; d. New York, NY, 14 Dec 1959.

Hopper, Hedda: b. Hollidaysburg, PA, 2 Jun 1890; d. Los Angeles, CA, 1 Feb 1966.

Hopper, William: b. New York, NY, 26 Jan 1915; d. Palm Springs, CA, 6 Mar 1970.

Hopton, Russell: b. New York, NY, 18 Feb 1900; d. North Hollywood, CA, 7 Apr 1945.

Horan, Charles T.: b. New York, NY, 1882; d. Los Angeles, CA, 11 Jan 1928.

Horne, Edna (Frankie Ashley): b. 1886; d. Culver City, CA, 17 Jul 1945.

Horne, Harold (Hal): b. Boston, MA, 12 Aug 1896; d. New York, NY, 8 Jun 1955

Horne, James W.: b. San Francisco, CA, 14 Dec 1881; d. Los Angeles, CA, 29 Jun 1942.

Horne, William T.: b. Batavia, IL, 4 Jun 1869; d. Los Angeles Co, CA, 15 Dec 1942.

Horner, Louise: b. 6 Jun 1877; d. Los Angeles, CA, 6 Feb 1962.

Hornick, Harry: b. Charleston, SC, ????; d. 7 Feb 1975.

Horning, Benjamin: b. 1853; d. Los Angeles, CA, 18 Jan 1936.

Horsley, David: b. 1874; d. Los Angeles, CA, 23 Feb 1933.

Horton, Clara: b. Brooklyn, NY, 29 Jul 1904; d. Whittier, CA, 4 Dec 1976.

Horton, Edward Everett: b. Brooklyn, NY 18 Mar 1887; d. Encino, CA, 29 Sep 1970.

Horwitz, Joseph: b. 1858; d. Mt. Clemens, MI, 26 Oct 1922.

Hosford, Maud: b. 1864; d. Corinth, VT, 14 Oct 1935.

Hoskins, Allen G. (Farina): b. Boston, MA, 9 Aug 1920; d. Oakland, CA, 26 Jul 1980.

Hotaling, Arthur D.: b. Albany, NY, 3 Feb 1873; d. near San Pedro, CA, 13 Jul 1938.

Hotaling, Frank: b. 1900; d. Woodland Hills, CA, 13 Apr 1977.

Hotely, Mae: b. Maryland, 7 Oct 1872; d. Coronado, CA, 6 Apr 1954.

Houdini, Harry: b. Budapest, Hungary, 24 Mar 1874; d. Detroit, MI, 31 Oct 1926.

House, Chandler: b. Colorado, 26 Jan 1904; d. Westminster, CA, 17 Mar 1982.

House, Jack: b. Texas, 18 Feb 1887; d. Los Angeles, CA, 20 Nov 1963.

House, Newton: b. Holly, CO, 1 Nov 1911; d. Colton, CA, 23 Jul 1987.

Housman, Arthur: b. New York, NY, 10 Oct 1889; d. Los Angeles, CA, 8 Apr 1942.

Houston, Renee: b. Johnston, Scot, 24 Jul 1902; d. London, Eng, 9 Feb 1980.

Howard, Arthur B.: b. 1857; Ware, MA, ? May 1928.

Howard, Bert: b. Salmon Falls, NH, 7 Aug 1878; d. Los Angeles, CA, 27 Oct 1958.

Howard, Charles Ray: b. San Diego, CA, 1882; d. New York, NY, 28 Jun 1947.

Howard, Constance: b. Omaha, NE, 4 Oct 1906; d. San Diego, CA, 5 Dec 1985.

Howard, David: b. Philadelphia, PA, 6 Oct 1896; d. Los Angeles, CA, 21 Dec 1941.

Howard, Ernest: b. Falls Village, CT, 1875; d. Brooklyn, NY, 8 Nov 1940.

Howard, Frances: b. Omaha, NE, 4 Jun 1903; d. Beverly Hills, CA, 2 Jul 1976.

Howard, George W.: b. Philadelphia, PA, 1873; d. New York, NY, 25 Aug 1928.

Howard, Gertrude: b. Hot Springs, AR, 2 Oct 1893; d. Los Angeles, CA, 30 Sep 1934.

Howard, Harold: b. Rutland, NY, 22 Aug 1870; d. Woodland Hills, CA, 9 Dec 1944.

Howard, Helen: b. Colorado Springs, CO, 2 May 1899; d. Los Angeles, CA, 13 Mar 1927.

Howard, Leslie: b. London, Eng, 3 Apr 1893; d. Bay of Biscay, 1 Jun 1943.

Howard, May: b. 1870; d. Los Angeles, CA, 1 Feb 1935.

Howard, Norah: b. London, Eng, 12 Dec 1901; d. 2 May 1968.

Howard, Peter (Pete the Hermit): b. Knocklong, Ire, 26 Jun 1878; d. Los Angeles, CA, 14 Mar 1969.

Howard, Vincente: b. Los Angeles, CA, 19 Jul 1869; d. Los Angeles Co, CA, 2 Nov 1946.

Howard, Walter: b. Leamington Spa, Eng, 7 Mar 1866; d. London, Eng, 6 Oct 1922.

Howard, Warda: b. San Francisco, CA, 1881; d. New York, NY, 17 Mar 1943.

Howard, William: b. Germany, 1883; d. Los Angeles, CA, 23 Jan 1944.

Howe, Betty: b. New York, NY, 23 May 1895; d. New York, NY, 21 Jun 1969.

Howe, Walter: b. London, Eng, 12 Apr 1879; d. Toronto, Can, 31 Jul 1957.

Howell, Alice: b. New York, NY, 5 May 1888; d. Los Angeles, CA, 12 Apr 1961.

Howes, Bobby: b. London, Eng, 4 Aug 1895; d. London, Eng, 27 Apr 1972.

Howes, Reed: b. Washington, DC, 5 Jul 1900; d. Woodland Hills, CA, 6 Aug 1964.

Howland, Jobyna: b. Indianapolis, IN, 31 Mar 1880; d. Los Angeles, CA, 7 Jun 1936.

Howlin, Olin: b. Denver, CO. 10 Feb 1886; d. Los Angeles, CA, 19 Sep 1959.

Howson, Albert: b. Brooklyn, NY, 3 Feb 1881; d. Jamaica, NY, 2 Aug 1960.

Hoxie, Al: b. Lewis County, ID, 7 Oct 1901; d. Redlands, CA, 6 Apr 1982.

Hoxie, Jack: b. Kingfisher, OK, 11 Jan 1885; d. Elkhart, KS, 27 Mar 1965.

Hoyt, Arthur: b. Georgetown, CO, 19 Mar 1874; d. Woodland Hills, CA, 4 Jan 1953.

Hoyt, Helen: b. 1904; d. Orange Co. CA, 9 Apr 1979.

Hoyt, Julia: b. New York, NY, 1897; d. New York, NY, 31 Oct 1955.

Huber, Charles C.: b. Illinois, 11 Jul 1885; d. Altadena, CA, 19 May 1960.

Hubert, Harold: b. 1858; d. New York, NY, 31 Mar 1916.

Hudson, Eric: b. Nottingham, Eng, 23 Nov 1862; d. New York, NY, 4 Oct 1918.

Huff, Forrest: b. 22 Aug 1876; d. New York, NY, 21 Aug 1947.

Huff, Justina: b. Columbus, GA, 8 Sep 1893; d. Philadelphia, PA, 29 Jun 1977.

Huff, Louise: b. Columbus, GA, 4 Nov 1895; d. New York, NY, 22 Aug 1973.

Hughes, Gareth: b. Llanelli, Wales, 23 Aug 1894; d. Woodland Hills, CA, 1 Oct 1965.

Hughes, Lloyd: b. Bisbee, AZ, 21 Oct 1897; d. San Gabriel, CA, 6 Jun 1958.

Hughes, Roy: b. Kinmundy, IL, 11 Jan 1894; d. 12 Jan 1928.

Hughes, Rupert: b. Lancaster, MO, 31 Jan 1872; d. Los Angeles, CA, 9 Sep 1956.

Hughes, Rush: b. Ohio, 15 Jan 1910; d. Studio City, CA, 16 Apr 1958.

Hughes, Thomas A.: b. 1887; d. Los Angeles, CA, 25 Nov 1953.

Hughes, Yvonne: b. 1900; d. New York, NY, 26 Dec 1950.

Hughston, Regan: b. Chicago, IL, 3 Sep 1875; d. Siasconset, MA, 2 Oct 1951.

Hulbert, Jack: b. Ely, Cambridge, Eng, 24 Apr 1892; d. London, Eng, 25 Mar 1978.

Hulburd, H. L. (Bud): b. 19??; d. Burbank, CA, 10 Feb 1973.

Hulette, Gladys: b. Arcade, NY, 21 Jul 1896; d. Montebello, CA, 8 Aug 1991.

Huley, Pete: b. 1892; d. Vancouver, Can, 6 Feb 1973.

Hull, Arthur Stuart: b. Pennsylvania, 8 May 1878; d. Los Angeles, CA, 28 Feb 1951.

Hull, Henry: b. Louisville, KY, 3 Oct 1890; d. Cornwall, Eng, 8 Mar 1977.

Hull, Shelly: b. Louisville, KY, 1885; d. New York, NY, 14 Jan 1919.

Humberstone, H. Bruce: b. Buffalo, NY, 18 Nov 1903; d. Woodland Hills, CA, 11 Oct 1984.

Humbert, George: b. Florence, Italy, 29 Jul 1880; d. Los Angeles, CA, 8 May 1963.

Hume, Benita: b. London, Eng, 14 Oct 1906; d. Egertan, Eng, 1 Nov 1967.

Hume, Ilean: b. Toronto, Can, 26 Feb 1896; d. Studio City, CA, 20 Nov 1978.

Hummel, Mary R.: b. 1889; d. Los Angeles, CA, 16 Feb 1946.

Humphrey, Bessie: b. Boston, MA, 18??; d. Los Angeles, CA; 8 Mar 1933.

Humphrey, Orral: b. Louisville, KY, 3 Apr 1880; d. Los Angeles, CA, 12 Aug 1929.

Humphrey, William J.: b. Chicopee Falls, MA, 2 Jan 1874; d. Los Angeles, CA, 4 Oct 1942.

Humphreys, Cecil: b. Cheltenham, Gloucs, Eng, 21 Jul 1883; d. New York, NY, 6 Nov 1947.

Hungerford, Mona: b. England, 1900; d. New York, NY, 17 Jul 1942.

Hunt, Gov. George W. P.: b. 1 Nov 1856; d. Phoenix, AZ, 24 Dec 1934.

Hunt, Jay: b. Philadelphia, PA, 4 Aug 1855; d. Los Angeles, CA, 18 Nov 1932.

Hunt, Madge: b. New York, NY, 27 Nov 1875; d. Los Angeles, CA, 2 Aug 1935.

Hunt, Martita: b. Buenos Aires, Argent, 30 Jan 1900; d. London, Eng, 13 June 1969.

Hunt, Rea M.: b. New Mexico, 5 Nov 1892; d. Los Angeles, CA, 21 Jun 1961.

Hunter, Edna: b. Toledo, OH, 1876; d. New York, NY, 5 Feb 1920.

Hunter, Glenn: b. Highland Hills, NY, 26 Sep 1894; d. New York, NY, 30 Dec 1945.

Hunter, Harrison: b. 18??; d. Boston, MA, 2 Jan 1923.

Hunter, Ian: b. Cape Town, So Africa, 13 Jun 1900; d. London, Eng, 23 Sep 1975.

Hunter, Kenneth: b. South Africa, 19 Feb 1882; d. Los Angeles, CA, 21 Dec 1961.

Hunter, Richard: b. California, 21 Apr 1875; d. Santa Monica, CA, 22 Dec 1962.

Huntington, Wright: b. 1866; d. New York, NY, 21 Sep 1916.

Huntley, Fred W.: b. London, Eng, 29 Aug 1864; d. Los Angeles, CA, 1 Nov 1931.

Huntley, Hugh: b. London, Eng, 14 Dec 1889; d. Laguna Beach, CA, 9 Feb 1977.

Huntress, Mary: b. Richmond, VA, ????; d. Manila, Philippines, 11 Dec 1933.

Hurley, Julia: b. Greenwich Village, NY, 1847; d. New York, NY, 4 Jun 1927.

Hurlock, Madeline: b. Federalsburg, MD, 12 Dec 1899; d. New York, NY, 4 Apr 1989.

Hurst, Brandon: b. London, Eng, 30 Nov 1866; d. Los Angeles, CA, 15 Jul 1947.

Hurst, Paul: b. Traver, CA, 15 Oct 1888; d. Los Angeles, CA, 27 Feb 1953.

Hurt, Mary: b. 1889; d. Los Angeles, CA, 6 Oct 1976.

Hutchins, Bobby (Wheezer): b. Tacoma, WA, 29 Mar 1925; d. Merced, CA, 17 May 1945.

Hutchins, George C.: b. 1869; d. 10 Oct 1952.

Hutchins, Richard: b. 1876; d. New York, NY, 5 Sep 1950.

Hutchison, Charles A.: b. Pittsburgh, PA, 3 Dec 1879; d. Los Angeles, CA, 30 May 1949.

Hutchison, William: b. Edinburgh, Scot, 16 May 1869; d. Los Angeles, CA, 7 Sep 1918.

Huth, Harold: b. Huddersfield, York, Eng, 20 Jan 1892; d. London, Eng, 26 Oct 1967.

Hutton, Leona: b. 1892; d. Toledo, OH, 1 Apr 1949.

Hyams, John: b. Syracuse, NY, 6 Jul 1869; d. Los Angeles, CA, 9 Dec 1940.

Hyams, Leila: b. New York, NY, 1 May 1905; d. Bel-Air, CA, 4 Dec 1977.

Hyatt, Clayton: b. ????; d. Windsor, Can, ? Jan 1932.

Hylan, Donald: b. 1899; d. New York, NY, 20 Jun 1968.

Hyman, Louis: b. 1875; d. 3 Aug 1929.

Hymer, John B.: b. 1876; d. Los Angeles, CA, 16 Jun 1953.

Hynes, John E.: b. 1853; d. Los Angeles, CA, 12 Apr 1931.

Hytten, Olaf: b. Glasgow, Scot, 3 Mar 1888; d. Los Angeles, CA, 11 Mar 1955.

I

Ikonnikoff, Alexander: b. Kiev, Russ, 1884; d. Los Angeles, CA, 17 Nov 1936.

Illian, Isolde: b. Milwaukee, WI, 28 May 1898; d. Beverly Hills, CA, 5 Nov 1963.

Illington, Margaret: b. Bloomington, IL, 23 Jul 1881; d. Miami Beach, FL, 11 Mar 1934.

Illington, Marie: b. London, Eng, 1856; d. London, Eng, 3 Feb 1927.

Imboden, David C.: b. Kansas City, MO, 6 Mar 1887; d. Kansas City, MO, 18 Mar 1974.

Imboden, Hazel Bourne: b. Washburn, IL, ????; d. Kansas City, MO, 8 Oct 1956.

Impekoven, Sabine: b. 1889; d. 5 May 1970.

Imperio, Pastora: b. Seville, Spain, 1889; d. Madrid, Spain, 14 Sep 1979.

Inagaki, Hiroshi: b. Japan, 1905; d. Tokyo, Japan, 21 May 1980.

Ince, John E.: b. New York, NY, 29 Aug 1878; d. Los Angeles, CA, 10 Apr 1947.

Ince, Ralph W.: b. Boston, MA, 16 Jan 1882; d. London, Eng, 11 Apr 1937.

Ince, Thomas H.: b. Newport, RI, 16 Nov 1882; d. Beverly Hills, CA, 19 Nov 1924.

Inescourt, Elaine: b. London, Eng, 1877; d. Brighton, Eng, 7 Jul 1964.

Ingalls, Bernice: b. 1895; d. Jacksonville, FL, 25 Feb 1987.

Ingersoll, William: b. Lafayette, IN, 9 Oct 1860; d. Los Angeles, CA, 7 May 1936.

Ingleton, George: b. 1861; d. Dark Canyon, CA, 19 May 1926.

Inglis, W. A. (Gus): b. 1882; d. Burbank, CA, 4 Aug 1952.

Ingraham, Harris: b. London, Eng, 1881; d. 19??.

Ingraham, Lloyd: b. Rochelle, IL, 30 Nov 1874; d. Calabasas, CA 4 Apr 1956.

Ingram, Carl: b. Atchison, KS, 1878; d. 19??.

Ingram, Rex: b. (Rex Hitchcock): b. Dublin, Ire, 15 Jan 1893; d. Los Angeles, CA, 21 Jul 1950.

Ingram, Rex: b. Cairo, IL, 20 Oct 1895; d. Los Angeles, CA, 19 Sep 1969.

Ingram, William D.: b. 1857; d. New York, NY, 2 Feb 1926.

Intropidi, Ethel: b. New York, NY, 1896; d. New York, NY, 18 Dec 1946.

Irvine, Robin: b. London, Eng, 21 Dec 1901; d. London, Eng, 28 Apr 1933.

Irving, Ethel (Birdie): b. England, 5 Sep 1869; d. Bexhill-on-Sea, Eng, 3 May 1963.

Irving H. B.: b. London, Eng, 5 Aug 1870; d. London, Eng, 17 Oct 1919.

Irving, Margaret: b. Pittsburgh, PA, 18 Jan 1898; d. Stanton, CA, 5 Mar 1988.

Irving, Mary Jane: b. Columbia, SC, 20 Oct 1913; d. Bel Air, CA, 17 Jul 1983.

Irving, Paul: b. Boston, MA, 24 Aug 1877; d. Los Angeles, CA, 8 May 1959.

Irving, William J.: b. Hamburg, Ger, 17 May 1893; d. Los Angeles, CA, 25 Dec 1943.

Irwin, Boyd: b. Brighton, Eng, 12 Mar 1880; d. Woodland Hills, CA, 22 Jan 1957.

Irwin, Charles W.: b. Ireland, 31 Jan 1887; d. Woodland Hills, CA, 12 Jan 1969.

Irwin, May: b. Whitby, Can, 27 Jun, 1862; d. New York, NY, 22 Oct 1938.

Irwin, Wallace: b. Oneida, NY, 15 Mar 1875; d. Southern Pines, NC, 14 Feb 1959.

Irwin, Will: b. Oneida, NY, 14 Sep 1873; d. New York, NY, 24 Feb 1948.

Isbert, Jose: b. Madrid, Spain, 3 Mar 1886; d. Madrid, Spain, 28 Nov 1966.

Ishii, Kan: b. 1901; d. Tokyo, Japan, 29 Apr 1972.

Ito, Michio: b. Tokyo, Japan, 13 Apr 1892; d. Tokyo, Japan, 6 Nov 1961.

Ivan, Rosalind: b. London, Eng, 27 Nov 1880; d. New York, NY, 6 Apr 1959.

Ivans, Elaine: b. New York, NY, 1900; d. New York, NY, 5 Apr 1975.

Ives, Charlotte: b. 27 Nov 1891; d. ? Sep 1976.

Ivins, Perry: b. Trenton, NJ, 19 Nov 1894; d. Los Angeles, CA, 22 Aug 1963.

J

Jaccard, Jacques: b. New York, 11 Sep 1886; d. Los Angeles Co, CA, 24 Jul 1960.

Jack, T. C.: b. 1882; d. Los Angeles, CA, 4 Oct 1954.

Jackie, William: b. 1890; d. San Francisco, CA, 19 Sep 1954.

Jackson, Ethel (Ethel Kent): b. New York, NY, 31 Jul 1883; d. Los Angeles, CA, 27 Jul 1952.

Jackson, Joe: b. Vienna, Austria, 1875; d. New York, NY, 14 May 1942.

Jackson, Orin C.: b. Terre Haute, IN, 1874; d. 19??.

Jackson, Selmer: b. Lake Mills, IA, 7 May 1888; d. Burbank, CA, 30 Mar 1971.

Jackson, Thomas E.: b. New York, NY, 4 Jul 1886; d. Tarzana, CA, 7 Sep 1967.

Jacob, Naomi: b. Ripon, Eng, 1 Jul 1884; d. Sirmione, Italy, 27 Aug 1964.

Jacobini, Maria: b. Rome, Italy, 17 Feb 1890; d. 20 Nov 1944.

Jagger, Dean: b. Lima, OH, 7 Nov 1903; d. Santa Monica, CA, 5 Feb 1991.

Jahnke, Marion Diggs: b. 1890; d. 6 May 1986.

Jahr, Adolf: b. 1894; d. Stockholm, Sweden, 19 Apr 1964.

James, Alf P.: b. Australia, 12 Oct 1865; d. Los Angeles, CA, 9 Oct 1946.

James, Eddie: b. 1880; New York, NY, 22 Dec 1944.

James, Gardner: b. New York, NY, 16 Mar 1903; West Los Angeles, CA, 23 Jun 1953.

James, Gladden: b. Zanesville, OH, 1892; d. Los Angeles, CA, 28 Aug 1948.

James, Horace D.: b. Baltimore, MD, 17 Jan 1853; d. Orange, NJ, 16 Oct 1925.

James, Jesse, Jr.: b. 1876; d. Los Angeles Co, CA, 26 Mar 1951.

James, Walter: b. Chattanooga, TN, 3 Jun 1882; d. Gardenia, CA, 27 Jun 1946.

Jamison, Bud (William): b. Vallejo, CA, 15 Feb 1894; d. Los Angeles, CA, 30 Sep 1944.

Janis, Elsie: b. Columbus, OH, 16 Mar 1889; d. Los Angeles, CA, 26 Feb 1956.

Janney, Leon: b. Ogden, UT, 1 Apr 1917; d. Guadalajara, Mex, 28 Oct 1980.

Jannings, Emil: b. Rorschach, Switz, 26 Jul 1886; d. Zinkenbach, Austria, 2 Jan 1950.

Jansen, Marie: b. Boston, MA, 1849; d. Milford, MA, 20 Mar 1914.

Janson, Victor: b. Riga, Russ, 25 Sep 1884; d. Berlin, Ger, ? Jul 1960.

Janssen, Walter: b. Krefeld, Ger, 7 Feb 1887; d. 1 Jan 1976.

Jaray, Hans: b. Vienna, Austria, 24 Jun 1906; d. Vienna, Austria, 6 Jan 1990.

Jarrett, Arthur L.: b. Marysville, CA, 5 Feb 1884; d. New York, NY, 12 Jun 1960.

Jarrett, Dan: b. 4 Apr 1894; d. Los Angeles, CA, 13 Mar 1938.

Jarrett, Daniel: b. Wales, 1854; d. Brooklyn, NY, 23 Sep 1917.

Jarrott, John: b. 1883; d. New York, NY, 14 Jun 1938.

Jarvis, Jean: b. Denver, CO, 23 May 1903; d. Los Angeles, CA, 16 Mar 1933.

Jarvis, Sydney: b. Toronto, Can, 11 Jan 1878; d. Los Angeles, CA, 6 Jan 1939.

Jay, Dorothy: b. 1908; d. Los Angeles, CA, 28 Jul 1936.

Jay, Ernest: b. London, Eng, 18 Sep 1893; d. London, Eng, 8 Feb 1957.

Jeans, Isabel: b. London, Eng, 16 Sep 1891; d. London, Eng, 4 Sep 1985.

Jeans, Ursula: b. Simla, India, 5 May 1906; d. London, Eng, 21 Apr 1973.

Jeayes, Allan: b. London, Eng, 19 Jan 1885; d. London, Eng, 20 Sep 1963.

Jeffers, John S.: b. 1874; d. Long Beach, NY, 3 Jan 1939.

Jeffers, William L.: b. 1898; d. Los Angeles, CA, 18 Apr 1959.

Jefferson, Daisy: b. 1889; d. Los Angeles, CA, 3 Jun 1967.

Jefferson, Joseph: b. Philadelphia, PA, 20 Feb 1829; d. Palm Beach, FL, 23 Apr 1905.

Jefferson, Thomas: b. New York, NY, 10 Sep 1856; d. Los Angeles, CA, 2 Apr 1932.

Jefferson, William Winter: b. London, Eng, 1875; d. Honolulu, HI, 10 Feb 1946.

Jeffrey, Hugh S.: b. Belfast, Ire, 1873; d. Los Angeles, CA, 18 Jan 1927.

Jeffries, James J.: b. Carroll, OH, 15 Apr 1875; d. Burbank, CA, 3 Mar 1953.

Jelley, Herbert E.: b. Pittsburgh, PA, 1886; d. 19??.

Jenkins, Elizabeth b. 1879; d. 18 Jan 1965.

Jenks, Lela B.: b. 1870; d. Los Angeles, CA, 15 Apr 1939.

Jenks, Si (Howard H. Jenkins): b. Norristown, PA, 23 Sep 1876; d. Woodland Hills, CA, 6 Jan 1970.

Jennings, Al: b. Virginia, 25 Nov 1863; d. Tarzana, CA, 26 Dec 1961.

Jennings, DeWitt: b. Cameron, MO, 21 Jun 1872; d. Los Angeles, CA, 28 Feb 1937.

Jennings, S. E.: b. Chicago, IL, 8 Apr 188O; d. 3 Feb 1932.

Jensen, Eulalie: b. St. Louis, MO, 24 Dec 1884; d. Los Angeles, CA, 7 Oct 1952.

Jepp, Mary: b. West Point, MS, 1 Oct 1898; d. Monterey, CA, 28 Apr 1980.

Jepson, Kate: b. Clinton, NY, 1869; d. Philadelphia, PA, 27 Sep 1923.

Jerome, Elmer: b. Illinois, 30 Jan 1872; d. Los Angeles Co, CA, 10 Aug 1947.

Jerrold, Mary: b. London, Eng, 4 Dec 1877; d. London, Eng, 3 Mar 1955.

Jeske, George: b. 1891; d. Los Angeles, CA, 28 Oct 1951.

Jessel, George: b. New York, NY, 3 Apr 1898; d. Los Angeles, CA, 23 May 1981.

Jett, Sheldon: b. 1901; d. New York, NY, 1 Feb 1960.

Jewett, Ethel: b. Portland, OR. c. 1889; d. 19??.

Jiminez, Soledad: b. Saintander, Spain, 28 Feb 1874; d. Woodland Hills, CA, 17 Oct 1966.

Jobson, Edward: b. Philadelphia, PA, 29 Feb 1861; d. San Jose, CA, 7 Feb 1925.

Joby, Hans: b. Kronstadt, Hungary, 3 Aug 1884; d. Los Angeles, CA, 1 May 1943

John, Georg: b. ????; d. 1934.

Johns, Bertram: b. Plymouth, Eng, 1874; d. Los Angeles, CA, 9 May 1934.

Johnson, Arthur V.: b. Cincinnati, OH, 1 Jun 1876; d. Philadelphla, PA, 17 Jan 1916.

Johnson, Benjamin: b. 1866: d. New York, NY, 23 Jun 1928.

Johnson, Burges: b. 1873: d. Schenectady, NY, 13 Feb 1963.

Johnson, Edith: b. Rochester, NY, 10 Aug 1894; d. Los Angeles, CA, 5 Sep 1969.

Johnson, Emory: b. San Francisco, CA, 1894; d. San Mateo, CA, 18 Apr 1960.

Johnson, Jack: b. Galveston, TX, 31 Mar 1878; d. Raleigh, NC, 10 Jun 1946.

Johnson, John Lester: b. South Carolina, 13 Aug 1893; d. Los Angeles, CA, 27 Mar 1968.

Johnson, Kenneth: b. 1912; d. Los Angeles, CA, 1 Nov 1974.

Johnson, Martin: b. Rockford, IL, 9 Oct 1884; d. Newhall, CA, 13 Jan 1937.

Johnson, Noble: b. Marshall, MO, 18 Apr 1881; d. Yucaipa, CA, 9 Jan 1978.

Johnson, Orrin: b. Louisville, KY, 1 Dec 1865; d. Neenah, WI, 24 Nov 1943.

Johnson, Osa: b. Chanute, KS, 14 Mar 1894; d, New York, NY, 7 Jan 1953.

Johnson, Pauline: b. England, 1900; d. England, 1947.

Johnson, Richard: b. Denver, CO, 1891; d. 19??.

Johnson, Tefft: b. Washington, 23 Sep 1887; d. ? Oct 1956.

Johnson, Victor L.: b. New York, NY, 1907; d. Honolulu, HI, 16 May 1988.

Johnston, J. W.: b. Kilkee , Ire, 2 Oct 1876; d. Los Angeles, CA, 29 Jul 1946.

Johnston, Julanne: b. Indianapolis, IN, 1 May 1900; d. Grosse Pointe, MI, 26 Dec 1988.

Johnston, Lorimer: b. Maysville, KY, 2 Nov 1858; d. Los Angeles, CA, 20 Feb 1941.

Johnston, Mac: b. Doniphan, MO, 1906; d. Mt. Vernon, MO, 22 Mar 1977.

Johnston W. Ray: b. Bristow, IA, 2 Jan 1892; d. Los Angeles, CA, 14 Oct 1966.

Johnstone, Justine: b. Englewood, NJ, 31 Jan 1895; d. Santa Monica, CA, 3 Sep 1982.

Johnstone, Lamar: b . Fairfax, VA, 1886; d. Palm Springs CA, 21 May 1919.

Jolivet, Rita: b. Paris, Fr. c. 1890; d. Barcelona, Spain, 26 Jul 1962.

Jolson, Al: b. Srednik, Lithuania, 26 May 1886; d. San Francisco, CA, 23 Oct 1950.

Jonassen, Frank: b. Utah, 1881; d. 19??,

Jones: Beulah Hall: b. Goliad, TX, 28 Jun 1900; d. Los Angeles, CA, 8 Oct 1952.

Jones, Buck (Charles): b. Vincennes, IN, 4 Dec 1889; d. Boston, MA, 30 Nov 1942.

Jones, Elizabeth (Tiny): b. Wales, 25 Nov 1875; d. Los Angeles, CA, 21 Mar 1952.

Jones, Freda M.: b. 1897; d. Los Angeles, CA, 24 Oct 1976.

Jones, Hazel: b. England, 17 Oct 1896; d. New York, NY, 13 Nov 1974.

Jones, J. Parks: b. Cincinnati, OH, 22 Aug 1890; d. Los Angeles, CA, 11 Jan 1950.

Jones, Jessie: b. Garden City, KS, 1892; d. 19??.

Jones, Johnny (Edward Peil, Jr.): b. Wisconsin, 18 Nov 1907; d. San Andreas, CA, 7 Nov 1962.

Jones, Mark: b. California, 9 Dec 1889; d. Los Angeles, CA, 14 Apr 1965.

Jones, Morgan: b. Denver, CO, 1879; d. New York, NY, 21 Sep 1951.

Jones, Paul Meredith: b. Bristol, TN, 1897; d. North Hollywood, CA, 30 Dec 1966.

Jones, Paul R. (John Byrd): b. 1910; d. New Milford, CT, 24 Feb 1987.

Jones, R. D.: b. ????; d. Marsfield, OR, 12 Jun 1925.

Jones, Sam: b. Birkenhead, Eng, 1863; d. Bournemouth, Eng, 25 Aug 1952.

Jones, Wallace: b. London, Eng, 1883; d. Los Angeles, CA, 7 Oct 1936.

Jordan, Egon: b. 19 Mar 1902; d. 27 Dec 1978.

Jordan, Sid: b. Muskogee, OK, 12 Aug 1889; d. 30 Sep 1970.

Jordon, Harry J.: b. 1902; d. Los Angeles, CA, 7 Jun 1945.

Jordon, Jules: b. Birmingham, Eng, 1871; d. Toledo, OH, 22 Jul 1925.

Jorge, Paul: b. France, 1849; d. France, 31 Dec 1928.

Jorgensen, Emilius A.: b. Denmark, 15 Mar 1888; d. 5 Dec 1963.

Jose, Edward: b. Antiwerp, Belgium, ????; d. Nice, Fr, 18 Dec 1930.

Jose, Richard J.: b. Lanner, Cornwall, Eng, 5 Jun 1870; d. San Francisco, CA, 20 Oct 1941.

Joslin, Margaret: b. Cleveland, OH, 6 Aug 1883; d. Glendale, CA, 14 Oct 1956.

Jossenberger, Phil (Phil Rich): b. 1896; d, Woodland Hills, CA, 22 Feb 1956.

Jossey, William J.: b. Macon, GA, 1867; d. Macon, GA, 25 Jun 1937.

Joube, Romuald: b. 1876; d. 1949.

Jouvet, Louis: b. Crozon, Fr, 24 Dec 1887; d. Paris, Fr, 16 Aug 1951.

Joy, Ernest C.: b. Iowa; 20 Jan 1878; d. Los Angeles, CA, 12 Feb 1924.

Joy, Leatrice: b. New Orleans, LA, 7 Nov 1893; d. Riverdale, NY, 13 May 1965.

Joyce, Alice: b. Kansas City, MO, 1 Oct 1890; d. Los Angeles, CA, 9 Oct 1955.

Joyce, Anna: b. 1912; d. Hialeah, FL, 23 Nov 1986.

Joyce, Natalie: b. Norfolk, VA, 1902; d. San Diego, CA, 9 Nov 1992.

Joyce, Peggy Hopkins: b. Norfolk, VA, 1893; d. New York, NY, 12 Jun 1957.

Joyner, Francis: b. New Orleans, LA, 1887; d. 19??.

Joyzelle, Rosamonde: b. England, 10 Jun 1883; d. Richmond, CA, 12 Jul 1964.

Judd, John: b. 1893; d. Los Angeles Co, CA, 7 Oct 1950.

Judels, Charles: b. Amsterdam, Holland, 17 Aug 1882; d. San Francisco, CA, 14 Feb 1969.

Judson, Sheldon: b. 1896; d. Los Angeles, CA, 5 Feb 1923.

Julian, Rupert: b. Auckland, New Zealand, 26 Jan 1879; d. Los Angeles, CA, 27 Dec 1943.

June (June Tripp): b. Blackpool, Eng, 11 Jun 1901; d. New York, NY, 14 Jan 1985.

June, Mildred: b. St. Louis, MO, 1906; d. Los Angeles, CA, 19 Jun 1940.

Junior, John: b. Minneapolis, MN, 17 Dec 1890; d. 19??.

Junkerman, Hans: b. Stuttgart, Ger, 24 Feb 1872; d. Berlin, Ger, 12 Jun 1943.

K

Kachalov, Vassili I.: b. Vilnius, Lithuania, 11 Feb 1875; d. Moscow, Russ, 30 Sep 1948.

Kademova, Litka: b. Bulgaria, 1908; d. Marina, CA, 15 Oct 1979.

Kaelred, Katherine: b. England, 9 May 1882; d. 19??.

Kahanamoku, Duke: b. Honolulu, HI, 24 Aug 1890; d. Honolulu, HI, 22 Jan 1968.

Kahn, Otto: b. Mannheim, Ger, 21 Feb 1867; d. New York, NY, 29 Mar 1934.

Kahn, Richard C.: b. 1896; d. Los Angeles, CA, 28 Jan 1960.

Kaiser-Heyl, Willi: b. Frankfort, Ger, 4 Aug 1876; d. 2 Dec 1953.

Kaiser-Tietz, Erich: b. 1878; d. 22 Nov 1928.

Kalich, Bertha: b. Lemberg, Poland, 17 May 1874; d. New York, NY, 18 Apr 1939.

Kalich, Jacob: b. Rymanov, Poland, 18 Nov 1891; d. Lake Mahopac, NY, 16 Mar 1975.

Kaliz; Armand: b. Paris, Fr, 23 Oct 1887; d. Los Angeles, CA, 1 Feb 1941.

Kalkhurst, Eric: b. 1902; d. Washington, DC, 13 Oct 1957.

Kaminska, Ida: b. Odessa, Russ, 4 Sep 1899; d. New York, NY, 21 May 1980.

Kampers, Fritz: b. Garmisch-Partenkirchen, Ger, 14 Jul 1891; d. Garmisch-Partenkirchen, Ger, 1 Sep 1950.

Kane, Diana: b. Birmingham, AL, 10 Jan 1901; d. Beverly Hills, CA, 20 Apr 1977.

Kane, Eddie: b. St. Louis, MO, 12 Aug 1889; d. Los Angeles, CA, 30 Apr 1969.

Kane, Gail: b. Philadelphia, PA, 10 Jul 1887; d. Augusta, ME, 17 Feb 1966.

Kane, Lida: b. 1885; d. New York, NY, 7 Oct 1955.

Kapoor, Prithvi Raj: b. India, 1906; d. Bombay, India, 29 May 1972.

Kappeler, Alfred: b. Zurich, Switz, 1877; d. New York, NY, 29 Oct 1945.

Karels, Harvey: b. Illinois, 4 Mar 1905; d. Los Angeles, CA, 17 Nov 1975.

Karl, Roger: b. France, 1882; d. Paris, Fr, 4 May 1984.

Karloff, Boris: b. Dulwich, Eng, 23 Nov 1887; d. Midhurst, Sussex, Eng, 2 Feb 1969.

Karno, Fred: b. Exeter, Eng, 26 May 1866; d. Parkstone, Eng, 17 Sep 1941.

Karns, Roscoe: b. San Bernardino, CA, 7 Sep 1891; d. Los Angeles, CA, 6 Feb 1970.

Karr Darwin: b. Almond, NY, 25 Jul 1875; d. Los Angeles, CA, 31 Dec 1945.

Kastner, Bruno: b. Soest, Prussia, 3 Jan 1890; d. Kreuznach, Ger, 10 Jun 1932.

Kasznar, Kurt: b. Vienna, Austria, 12 Aug 1913; d. Santa Monica, CA, 6 Aug 1979.

Kaufman, Joseph: b. Russia, 1882; d. New York, NY, 1 Feb 1918.

Kay, Honey Beatrice: b. New York, NY, 11 Apr 1907; d. Los Angeles, CA, 8 Nov 1986.

Kay, Marjorie: b. ????; d. Hartford, CT, 25 Jun 1949.

Kaye, Albert P.: b. Ringwood, Eng, 1878; d. Washingtonville, NY, 7 Sep 1946.

Kayser, Charles Willy: b. Metz, Ger, 28 Jan 1881; d. 10 Jul 1942.

Kayssler, Friedrich: b. Neurode/Grafschaft, Glatz, Ger, 7 Apr 1874; d. Kleinmachnow, Ger, 24 Apr 1945.

Keane, Doris: St. Joseph, MI, 12 Dec 1881; d. New York, NY, 25 Nov 1945.

Keane, Edward: b. New York, NY, 28 May 1884; d. Los Angeles Co, CA, 12 Oct 1959.

Keane, Raymond: b. Denver, CO, 6 Sep 1906; d. Los Angeles, CA, 24 Aug 1973.

Kearney, John L.: b. New York, NY, 1871; d. New York, NY, 3 Aug 1945.

Keatan, A. Harry: b. Russia, 26 May 1896; d. Los Angeles, CA, 18 Jun 1966.

Keaton, Buster: b. Piqua, KS, 4 Oct 1895; d. Woodland Hills, CA, 1 Feb 1966.

Keaton, Joseph: b. Terre Haute, IN, 1867; d. Los Angeles, CA, 13 Jan 1946.

Keaton, Louise: b. 1901; d. Van Vuys, CA, 18 Feb 1981.

Keaton, Myra: b. Modale, IA, 1877; d. Los Angeles, CA, 21 Jul 1955.

Keckley, Jane: b. Charleston, SC, 10 Sep 1876; d. South Pasadena, CA, 14 Aug 1963.

Keefe, Cornelius (Jack Hill): b. Boston, MA, 13 Jul 1900; d. Los Angeles, CA, 11 Dec 1972.

Keefe, Zena: b. San Francisco, CA, 26 Jun 1896; d. Danvers, MA, 16 Nov 1977.

Keen, Malcolm: b. Bristol, Eng, 8 Aug 1887; d. London, Eng, 30 Jan 1970.

Keenan, Frank: b. Dubuque, IA, 8 Apr 1858; d. New York, NY, 24 Feb 1929.

Keenan, Harry G.: b. Richmond, IN, 15 Jun 1867; d. Santa Ana, CA, 18 Apr 1944.

Keene, Mattie: b. 1862; d. New York, NY, 1 Sep 1944.

Keener, Hazel: b. Fairbury, IL 22 Oct 1904; d. Pacific Grove, CA, 7 Aug 1979.

Keh Lu: b. ????; d. ? May 1922.

Keightley, Cyril: b. Wellington, N. Zealand, 10 Nov 1875; d. New York, NY, 14 Aug 1929.

Keinz, Barbara Leona: b. 1888; d. Oklahoma City, OK, 4 Nov 1939.

Keith, Donald: b. Boston, MA, 6 Sep 1903; d. Los Angeles, CA, 1 Aug 1969.

Keith, Eugene: b. 1879; d. New York, NY, 6 Feb 1955.

Keith, Ian: b. Boston, MA, 27 Feb 1899; d. New York, NY, 26 Mar 1960.

Keith, Isabelle: b. New York, NY, 1898; d. Mill Valley, CA, 20 Jul 1979.

Keith, Robert: b. Fowler, IN, 10 Feb 1898; d. Los Angeles, CA, 23 Dec 1966.

Kelcy, Herbert: b. London, Eng, 10 Oct 1956; d. Bayport, NY, 10 Jul 1917.

Keleher, Daniel F.: b. 1869; d. New Rochelle, NY, ? Jun 1917.

Kellard, Ralph: b. New York, NY, 16 Jun 1882; d. New York, NY, 5 Feb 1955.

Keller, Alfred S.: b. Pennsylvania, 1911; d. Palisades, CA, 6 Sep 1989.

Keller, Brooklyn: b. Lakeland, FL, 20 Mar 1890; d. 19??.

Keller, Gertrude: b. Denver, CO, 1881; d. Los Angeles, CA, 12 Jul 1951.

Keller, Helen: b. Tyscynbuam, AL, 27 Jun 1881; d. Westport, CT, 1 Jun 1968.

Keller, Nell Clark: b. 1876; d. Tacoma, WA, 2 Sep 1965.

Kellerd, John E.: b. London, Eng, 14 May 1863; d. Yonkers, NY, 6 Jun 1929.

Kellerman, Annette: b. Sydney, Austral, 6 Jul 1887; d. Southport, Austral, 5 Nov 1975.

Kellino, Roy: b. London, Eng, 22 Apr 1912; d. Los Angeles, CA, 18 Nov 1956.

Kellino, Will P.: b. London, Eng, 1873; d. 1958.

Kellogg, Cornelia: b. 1877; d. Los Angeles, CA, 21 Feb 1934.

Kelly, Dorothy: b. Philadelphia, PA, 12 Feb 1894; d. Minneapolis, MN, 31 May 1966.

Kelly, Fanny: b. 1876; d. Los Angeles, CA, 27 Jun 1925.

Kelly, Gregory: b. New York, NY, 16 Mar 1891; d. New York, NY, 9 Jul 1927.

Kelly, Harry: b. New York, 1873; d. New York, NY, 19 Mar 1936.

Kelly, James T.: b. Castlebar, Ire, 10 Jul 1854: d. 12 Nov 1933.

Kelly, John: b. Boston, MA, 29 Jun 1901; d. Los Angeles Co, CA, 9 Dec 1947.

Kelly, John T.: b. Boston, MA,, 26 Aug 1852; d. New York, NY, 16 Jan 1922.

Kelly, Kitty: b. New York, NY, 27 Apr 1902; d. Los Angeles, CA, 29 Jun 1968.

Kelly, Margot: b. 1893; d. New York, NY, 10 Mar 1976.

Kelly, Nan: b. 1895; d. Camarillo, CA, 26 Oct 1978.

Kelly, Patrick J.: b. Philadelphia, PA, 18 Jul 1891; d. 19 Mar 1938.

Kelly, Paul: b. Brooklyn, NY, 9 Aug 1899; d. Los Angeles, CA, 6 Nov 1956.

Kelly, Renee: b. London, Eng, 4 Jun 1888; d. London, Eng, 28 Aug 1965.

Kelly, Robert H.: b. Chicago, IL, 1875; d. Lewistown, ME, 19 Jun 1949.

Kelly, Scotch (James Steele): b. 1889; d. Isle of Man, 19 Feb 1967.

Kelly, William J.: b. Newburyport, MA, 16 Jun 1875; d. New York, NY, 17 May 1949.

Kelsey, Fred A.: b. Sandusky, OH, 20 Aug 1884; d. Woodland Hills, CA, 2 Sep 1961.

Kelso, Mayme: b. Columbus, OH, 28 Feb 1867; d. South Pasadena, CA, 5 Jun 1946.

Kemp, Everett: b. Shelbyville, IL, 1874; d. Kansas City, MO, 1 Oct 1958.

Kemp, Mae (Mary Lange): b. 1877; d. New York, NY, 6 Feb 1926.

Kendall, Harry: b. Australia, 1872; d. Brooklyn, NY, 27 Jul 1936.

Kendall, Henry: b. London, Eng, 28 May 1897; d. France, 9 Jun 1962.

Kennard,Victor: b. Hackensack, NJ, 1887; d. Bridgeport, CT, 14 Aug 1953.

Kennedy, Charles Rann: b. Derby, Eng, 11 Feb 1871; d. Westwood, CA, 16 Feb 1950.

Kennedy, Edgar: b. Monterey, CA, 26 Apr 1890; d. Los Angeles, CA, 9 Nov 1948.

Kennedy, John F.: b. ????; d. Los Angeles, CA, 6 Nov 1960.

Kennedy, Leo A.: b. Wilmington, DE, 1883; d. New York, NY, 11 Dec 1939.

Kennedy, Madge: b. Chicago, IL, 19 Apr 1891; d. Woodland Hills, CA, 9 Jun 1987.

Kennedy, Merna: b. Kankakee, IL, 7 Sep 1908; A. Los Angeles, CA, 20 Dec 1944.

Kennedy, Tom: b. New York, NY, 15 Jul 1885; d. Woodland Hills, CA, 6 Oct 1965.

Kenneth, Harry D.: b. 1854; d. Newark, NJ, 18 Jan 1929.

Kenney, Jack: b. Illinois, 16 Nov 1886; d. Los Angeles, CA, 26 May 1964.

Kenny, Colin: b. Dublin, Ire, b. 4 Dec 1888; d. Los Angeles Co. CA, 2 Dec 1968.

Kent, Arnold: b. Florence, Italy, 21 Jan 1899; d. Los Angeles, CA, 28 Sep 1928.

Kent, Charles: b. London, Eng, 18 Jun 1852; d. Brooklyn, NY, 21 May 1923.

Kent, Crawford: b. London, Eng, 12 Oct 1881; d. Los Angeles, CA, 14 May 1953.

Kent, Kate: b. 1864; d. Van Nuys, CA, 11 Dec 1934.

Kent, Larry: b. Liverpool, Eng, 15 Sep 1900; d. Los Angeles, CA, 7 Nov 1967.

Kent Raymond: b. 1886; d. New York, NY, 1 Nov 1948.

Kent, S. Miller: b. 1882; d. Amityville, NY, 12 Nov 1948.

Kent, Stapleton: b. England, 15 May 1883; d. Los Angeles Co. CA, 3 Apr 1962.

Kent, William: b. St. Paul, MN, 1886; d. New York, NY, 4 Oct 1945.

Kenton, Erle C.: b. Norboro, MO, 1 Aug 1896; d. Glendale, CA, 28 Jan 1980.

Kentuck, Joe: b. ????; d. Lapwai, ID, 7 Feb 1923.

Kenyon, Doris: b. Syracuse, NY, 5 Sep 1897; d. Beverly Hills, CA, 1 Sep 1979.

Kenyon, Robert: b. 1889; d. Chicago, IL, 19 Dec 1928.

Keogh, Thomas J.: b. 18??; d. Colon, MI, 3 Jun 1925.

Keough, Edwin: b. 18??; d. New York, NY, 17 Aug 1920.

Keppens, Emile: b. France, ????; d. France, ? Oct 1926.

Ker, Paul: b. 1875; d. New York, NY, 31 Mar 1929.

Kerby, Frederick: b. Hamilton, Can, 1877; d. Saginaw, MI; 4 Apr 1927.

Kerby, Marion: b. 1877; d. Los Angeles, CA, 16 Dec 1956.

Kern, Cecil: b. Portland, OR, 1892; d. New York, NY, 4 Jun 1928.

Kern, Hal C.: b. Anaconda, MT, 14 Jul 1894; d. Los Angeles, CA, 24 Feb 1985.

Kerr, Frederick: b. London, Eng, 11 Oct 1858; d. London, Eng, 2 May 1933.

Kerr, Robert: b. Burlington, CT, 1895; d. Porterville, CA, 5 Sep 1960.

Kerrick, Tom: b. 1895; d. Los Angeles, CA, 27 Apr 1927.

Kerrigan, J. Warren: b. Louisville, KY, 25 Jul 1879; d. Los Angeles, CA, 9 Jun 1947.

Kerrigan, Joseph M.: b. Dublin, Ire, 16 Dec 1884; d. Los Angeles, CA, 29 Apr 1964.

Kerrigan, Kathleen: b. New Albany, IN, 11 Apr 1868; d. San Fernando, CA, 27 Jan 1957.

Kerrigan, William W.: b. Louisville, KY, 25 Jul 1879; d. Los Angeles, CA, 20 Feb 1953.

Kerry, Norman: b. Rochester, NY, 16 Jun 1889; d. Los Angeles, CA, 12 Jan 1956.

Kershaw, Eleanor: b. Missouri, 19 Nov 1884; d. Palos Verdes, CA, 13 Sep 1971.

Kershaw, Willette: b. Clifton Heights, MO, 17 Jun 1882; d. Honolulu, HI, 4 May 1960.

Kerwood, Dick: b. Virginia, 8 Oct 1892; d. Pico Canyon, CA, 15 Oct 1924.

Kessel, Adam: b. 1866; d. Keesville, NY, 21 Sep 1946.

Key, Kathleen: b. Buffalo, NY, 1 Apr 1907; d. Woodland Hills, CA, 22 Dec 1954.

Keys, Nelson: b. London, Eng, 7 Aug 1886; d. London, Eng, 26 Apr 1939.

Kidd, Jim: b. Texas, 1846; d. Los Angeles, CA, 9 Dec 1916.

Kidd, Kathleen: b. England, 1899; d. Toronto, Can, 23 Feb 1961.

Kilgour, Joseph: b. Ayr, Can, 11 Jul 1863; d. East Islip, NY, 20 Apr 1933.

Kilpack, Bennett: b. England, 6 Feb 1883; d. Santa Monica, CA, 17 Aug 1962.

Kimball, Edward M.: b. Keokuk, IA, 26 Jun 1859; d. Los Angeles, CA, 4 Jan 1938.

Kimball, Louis: b. Marshalltown, IA, 19 May 1889; d. Orlando, Fl, 29 Jan 1936.

Kimball, Pauline Garrett: b. Chicago, IL, 15 Mar 1860; d. Los Angeles, CA, 11 Dec 1919.

Kimura, Massa Kich: b. Japan, 1890; d. New York, NY, 3 Nov 1918.

King, Ada: b. London, England, 1862; d. 8 Jun 1940.

King, Allyn: b. 1901; d. New York, NY, 30 Mar 1930.

King, Anita: b: Chicago, IL, 1889; d. Los Angeles, CA, 10 Jun 1963.

King, Boyd: b. 1906; d. Los Angeles, CA, 19 Feb 1940.

King, Burton L.: b. Cincinnati, OH, 25 Aug 1877; d. Los Angeles, CA, 4 May 1944.

King, Carlton: b. St. Louis, MO. 15 Dec 1881; d. Glendale, CA, 6 Jul 1932.

King, Charles L.: b. Dallas, TX, 21 Feb 1895; d. Los Angeles, CA, 7 May 1957.

King, Claude: b. Northampton, Eng, 15 Jan 1876; d. Los Angeles, CA, 18 Sep 1941.

King, Emmett C.: b. Griffin, GA, 31 May 1865; d. Los Angeles, CA, 21 Apr 1953.

King, Henry: b. Christianburg, VA, 24 Jan 1886; d. Toluca Lake, CA, 29 Jan 1982.

King, Joseph (Joe): b. Austin, TX, 9 Feb 1883; d. Woodland Hills, CA, 11 Apr 1951.

King, Leslie: b. Baltimore, MD, 1876; d. Amityville, NY, 10 Oct 1947.

King, Louis: b. Christianburg, VA, 28 Jun 1898; d. Los Angeles, CA, 7 Sep 1962.

King, Lucille: b. 1886; d. ? Aug 1977.

King, Mollie: b. New York, NY, 16 Apr 1898; d. Ft. Lauderdale, FL, 28 Dec 1981.

King, Nellie: b. 1895; d. West Palm Beach, FL, 1 Jul 1935.

King, Will: b. Brooklyn, NY, 1886; d. Oakland, CA, 22 Jan 1958.

Kingdon, Dorothy (Dorothy Van Raven): b. Auburn, NY, 1894; d. Los Angeles, CA, 31 Mar 1939.

Kingdon, Frank: b. Providence, RI, 1865; d. Englewood, NJ, 9 Apr 1937.

Kingsley, Florida: b. Jacksonville, FL, 1879; d. Bay Shore, NY, 19 Mar 1937.

Kingston, Natalie: b. Vallejo, CA, 19 May 1905; d. West Hills, CA, 2 Feb 1991.

Kingston, Winifred: b. London, Eng, 11 Nov 1894; d. La Jolla, CA, 3 Feb 1967.

Kinsella, Kathleen: b. Liverpool, Eng, 1878; d.: Washington, 25 Mar 1961.

Kinsey, Arlene: b. 1891; d. 30 Jan 1984.

Kipling, Richard: b. New York, 21 Aug 1879; d. Los Angeles Co, CA, 11 Mar 1965.

Kirby, David: b. St. Louis, MO, 16 Jul 1883; d. Los Angeles, CA, 4 Apr 1954.

Kirby, Ollie (Ollie Kirkby): b. Philadelphia, PA, 26 Sep 1886; d. Glendale, CA, 7 Oct 1964.

Kirby, William W.: b. Germany, 4 Apr 1876; d. Los Angeles, CA, 17 Apr 1914.

Kirk, Bertha W.: b. 1883; d. Los Angeles, CA, 9 Sep 1928.

Kirk, Jack: b. 1895; d. Ketchican, AK, 3 Sep 1948.

Kirkham, Kathleen: b. Menominee, MI, 15 Apr 1895; d. Santa Barbara, CA, 7 Nov 1961.

Kirkland, David: b. San Francisco, CA, 26 Nov 1878; d. Los Angeles, CA, 27 Oct 1964.

Kirkland, Hardee: b. Savannah, GA, 23 May 1868; d. California, 18 Feb 1929.

Kirkwood, James: b. Grand Rapids, MI, 22 Feb 1875; d. Woodland Hills, CA, 24 Aug 1963.

Kirkwood, Ray: b. Dotter, PA, 16 Jun 1893; d. Levittown, NY, ? Feb 1973.

Kirtley, Virginia: b. Bowling Green, MO, 11 Nov 1883; d. Sherman Oaks, CA, 19 Aug 1956.

Kitchen, Fred: b. 15 Jun 1872; d. Hampton Hill, Eng, 1 Apr 1951.

Klein, Julius: b. Hungary, 1886; d. Los Angeles, CA, 16 Jul 1966.

Klein, Robert: b. Paris, Fr, 16 May 1880; d. Los Angeles Co, CA, 21 Dec 1960.

Kleine-Rogge, Rudolf: b. Cologne, Ger, 24 Nov 1888; d. Craz, Austria, 30 Apr 1955.

Kley, Fred: b. Baltimore, MD, 14 Aug 1885; d. Los Angeles, CA, 14 Mar 1944.

Kline, Ben: b. Birmingham, AL, 11 Jul 1894; d. Los Angeles, CA, 7 Jan 1974.

Kling, Saxon: b. 1892; d. Marion, OH, 29 Jul 1940.

Klinger, Warner: b. Stuttgart, Ger, 23 Oct 1903; d. 23 Jun 1972.

Klitzsch, Edgar: b. 11 Jul 1887; d. 15 Feb 1955.

Klopfer, Eugen: b. Thalheim, Ger, 10 Mar 1886; d. Wiesbaden, Ger, 3 Mar 1950.

Kluppell, Kitty: b. Holland, 1897; d. 13 Oct 1982.

Knabb, Harry G.: b. 1891; d. Cincinnati, OH, 17 Dec 1955.

Knabenshue, Roy: b. 1876; d. Los Angeles, CA, 6 Mar 1960.

Knight, Henry K. (Hank): b. 1847; d. Los Angeles, CA, 21 Apr 1930.

Knight, James: b. Canterbury, Kent, Eng, 4 May 1891; d. c. 1984.

Knight, Lillian: b. 1881; d. Pomona, CA, 16 May 1946.

Knight, Percival: b. Scotland, 1875; d. Montreux, Switz, 27 Nov 1923.

Knighton, Percy: b. Cismont, VA, 14 May 1898; d. Little Rock, AR, 1 Jun 1971.

Knoles, Harley: b. Rotherham, Eng, 1880; d. London, Eng, 6 Jan 1936.

Knott, Adelbert (Ethelbert): b. 1859; d. Los Angeles, CA, 3 May 1933.

Knott, Clara: b. Indiana, 19 Jan 1871; d. Los Angeles, CA, 11 Nov 1926.

Knott, Lydia: b. Tyner, IN, 1 Oct 1866; d. Woodland Hills, CA, 30 Mar 1955.

Knowland, Alice: b. Fort Fairfield, ME, 6 Oct 1879; d. Los Angeles, CA, 27 May 1930.

Knowles, J. Harry: b. England, 18??; d. Orange, FL, ? Sep 1923.

Knowles, R. G. (Richard George Knowles): b. Hamilton, Can, 7 Oct 1858; d. London, Eng, 1 Jan 1919.

Knox, Hugh B. (Hugo B. Koch): b. 1881; d. Seattle, WA, 9 Sep 1926.

Knox, Teddy: b. Gateshead, Eng, 12 Jul 1894; d. England, 1 Dec 1974.

Kobs, Alfred: b. 1881; d. Los Angeles, CA, 20 Oct 1929.

Koerner, Hermine: b. 1882; d. Vienna, Austria, 14 Dec 1960.

Kohler, Fred: b. Kansas City, MO, 21 Apr 1888; d. Los Angeles, CA, 28 Oct 1938.

Kohlmar, Lee: b. Furth, Ger, 27 Feb 1873; d. Los Angeles, CA, 14 May 1946.

Kolb, Clarence: b. Cleveland, OH, 31 Jul 1874; d. Los Angeles, CA, 25 Nov 1964.

Kolb, Therese: b. Altkirch, Fr, 19 Jan 1856; d. Levallois-Perret, Fr, 19 Aug 1935.

Kolker, Henry: b. Quincy, IL, 13 Nov 1870; d. Los Angeles, CA, 15 Jul 1947.

Koller, Hermine: b. Germany, ????; d. Geneva, Switz, ? Mar 1920.

Komai, Tetsu: b. Kumamoto, Japan, 23 Apr 1894; d. Gardena, CA, 10 Oct 1970.

Konstam, Phyllis: b. London, Eng, 14 Apr 1907; d. Somerset County, Eng, 20 Aug 1976.

Kopp, Erwin: b. Berlin, Ger, 3 Jul 1877; d. 24 Apr 1928.

Korayim, Mohamed: b. Egypt, 1898; d. Cairo, Egypt, 27 May 1972.

Korff, Arnold: b. Vienna, Austria, 2 Aug 1870; d. New York, NY, 2 Jun 1944.

Kornman, Mary: b. Idaho Falls, ID, 27 Dec 1915; d. Glendale, CA, 1 Jun 1973.

Kornman, Verna: b. 1897; d. Santa Bathara, CA, 20 May 1986.

Kortman, Robert: b. Philadelphia, PA, 24 Dec 1887; d. Long Beach, CA, 13 Mar 1967.

Kortner, Fritz: b. Vienna, Austria, 12 May 1892; d. Munich, Ger, 22 Jul 1970.

Kosloff, Theodore: b. Moscow, Russ, 22 Jan 1882; d. Los Angeles, CA, 22 Nov 1956.

Kotsonaros, George: b. Nauplie, Greece, ????; d. Eutaw, AL, 13 Jul 1933.

Koupal, T. Morse: b. New York, NY, 24 Mar 1890; d. Toledo, OH, 29 Mar 1970.

Koval-Samborsky, Ivan: b. Russia, 16 Sep 1893; d. 1962.

Krahly, Hanns: b. Germany, 1885; d. Los Angeles, CA, 11 Nov 1950.

Kramer, Ida: b. 1878; d. Brooklyn, NY, 14 Oct 1930.

Kramer, Leopold: b. Prague, Czech, 29 Sep 1869; d. 29 Oct 1942.

Kramer, Wright: b. Somerville, MA, 19 May 1875; d. Los Angeles, CA, 14 Nov 1941.

Kranz, Alfred: b. Brooklyn, NY, 1869; d. Providence, RI, 2 Dec 1937.

Kraus, Charles: b. Budapest, Hungary, 1866; d. New York, NY, 12 Jul 1931.

Krause, Charles: b. France, 18??; d. ? Oct 1926.

Krauss, Werner: b. Gestungshausen, Ger, 23 Jun 1884; d. Vienna, Austria, 20 Oct 1959.

Kraussneck, Arthur: b. Ostpreussen, Ger, 9 Apr 1856; d. 21 Apr 1941.

Krimer, Harry: b. 10 Mar 1896; d. 4 Jan 1991.

Kroell, Adrienne: b. 1892; d. Evanston, IL, 2 Oct 1949.

Kronert, Max: b. 18??; d. 22 Jul 1925.

Kruger, Harold (Stubby): b. Honolulu, HI, 23 Sep 1897; d. Los Angeles, CA, 7 Oct 1965.

Kruger, Otto: b. Toledo, OH, 6 Sep 1885; d. Woodland Hills, CA, 6 Sep 1974.

Kruger, Paul: b. Eau Claire, WI, 24 Jul 1895; d. 6 Nov 1960.

Kuehne, Edna: b. 1897; d. Los Angeles, CA, 31 Jul 1922.

Kuhn, Evelyn: b. 1893; d. 29 Jun 1976.

Kuhne, Friedrich, b. 1869; d. ? Oct 1958.

Kunkel, George: b. 1867; d. Los Angeles, CA, 8 Nov 1937.

Kupfer, Margarethe: b. Freystadt, Ger, 10 Apr 1881; d. 11 May 1953.

Kusell, Maurice L.: b. 1902; d. Los Angeles, CA, 2 Feb 1992.

Kutschera, Viktor: b. Austria, 2 May 1863; d. 20 Jan 1933.

Kuwa, George K.: b. Japan, 7 Apr 1885; d. 13 Oct 1931.

Kyle, Austin C.: b. 1893; d. France, 10 Nov 1916.

Kyle, Howard: b. Shullsburg, WI, 22 Apr 1861; d. New York, NY, 1 Dec 1950.

L

La Badie, Florence: b. New York, NY, 27 Apr 1888; d. Ossining, NY, 13 Oct 1917.

La Badie, Hubert: b. 1866; d. Brighton, MI, 15 Sep 1942.

La Bey, Louis: b. Lafontaine, Can, 1870; d. 19??.

La Bissenier, Erin: b. Minnesota, 5 Aug 1901; d. Los Angeles Co, CA, 22 Sep 1976.

La Brake, Harrison: b. 1888; d. Malone, NY, 2 Dec 1933.

Lackaye, Helen: b. Washington, DC, 10 Jan 1883; d. Jersey City, NJ, 19 Oct 1940.

Lackaye, James M.: b. Washington, DC, 5 Dec 1867; d. New York, NY, 8 Jun 1919.

Lackaye, Ruth: b. Oregon City, OR, 1869; d. 19??.

Lackaye, Wilton: b. London County, VA, 30 Sep 1862; d. New York, NY, 21 Aug 1932.

Lackteen Frank: b. Lebanon, 29 Aug 1894; d. Los Angeles, CA, 8 Jul 1968.

Ladd, Schuyler: b. 1877; d. Alhambra, CA, 14 Apr 1961.

La Deaux, Evelyn: b. 1905; d. Philadelphia, PA, ? Mar 1944.

Laemmle, Carl, Sr.: b. Laupheim, Ger, 17 Jan 1867; d. Beverly Hills, CA, 24 Sep 1939.

La Fayette, Ruby: b. Augusta, KY, 22 Jul 1844; d. Los Angeles, CA, 3 Apr 1935.

Lagrange, Louise: b. Oran, Algeria, 18 Aug 1898; d. Paris, Fr. ? Mar 1979.

Laidlaw, Ethan: b. Butte, MT, 25 Nov 1899; d. Los Angeles, CA, 25 May 1963.

Laidlaw, Roy: b. Comber, Can, 25 Mar 1883; d. Los Angeles, CA, 2 Feb 1936.

Laidley, Alice: b. 1903; d. Paris, Fr, 25 Jun 1926.

Laing, Alfred B.: b. 1890; d. Los Angeles, CA, 3 Aug 1976.

Lair, Grace: b. 18??; d. Cleveland, OH, 5 Jan 1955.

Laite, Charles: b. Warwick, Eng, 15 Jun 1883; d. Cleveland, OH, 17 Feb 1937.

La Jana: b. Berlin, Ger, 24 Feb 1905; d. Berlin, Ger, 13 Mar 1940.

Lake, Alice: b. Brooklyn, NY, 12 Sep 1895; d. Los Angeles, CA, 15 Nov 1967.

Lake, Arthur: b. Corbin, KY, 17 Apr 1905; d. Indian Wells, CA, 9 Jan 1987.

Lake, Florence: b. Charleston, SC, 27 Nov 1904; d. Woodland Hills, CA, 11 Apr 1980.

Lalor, Frank: b. Washington, DC, 20 Aug 1869; d. New York, NY, 15 Oct 1932.

Lamac, Karl: b. 1898; d. Hamburg, Ger, 2 Aug 1952.

La Marr, Barbara: b. North Yakima, WA, 28 Jul 1896; d. Altadena, CA, 30 Jan 1926.

La Marr, Richard: b. Italy, 6 Nov 1895; d. 24 Apr 1975.

Lambart, Capt. Harry: b. Dublin, Ire, 9 Jul 1876; d. London, Eng, 11 Jun 1949.

Lambert, Albert: b. France, 18??; d. Paris, Fr, ? Aug 1918.

Lambert, Charlotte: b. 1857; d. Central Islip, NY, 8 Sep 1935.

Lambert, Clara: b. 18??; d. 1921.

Lambert, Ernest: b. Ireland, 1874; d. New York, NY, 27 Jan 1945.

Lambert, Glen: b. Richmond, VA, 28 Jan 1896; d. Jacksonville Beach, FL, 9 Dec1973.

Lambert, Toby (Skinny): b. Edmonton, Can, 17 Sep 1916; d. 14 Jun 1972.

La Meri: b. Louisville, KY, 1898; d. San Antonio, TX, 7 Jan 1988.

Lamont, Charles: b. San Francisco, CA, 5 May 1895; d. Woodland Hills, CA, 11 Sep 1993.

Lamont, Harry: b. New York, NY, 17 Jun 1882; d. Venice, CA, 8 May 1957.

Lamont, Jack: b. 1893; d. Cleveland, OH, 28 Feb 1956.

Lampin, Georges: b. St. Petersburg, Russ, 1901; d. Pau, Fr, 11 May 1979.

Lampton, Dee: b. Fort Worth, TX, 1898; d. New York, NY, 2 Sep 1919.

Lancaster, John: b. Richmond, VA, 1857; d. Washington, DC, 11 Oct 1935.

Lance, Chief Buffalo Child Long: b. 18??; d. Los Angeles, CA, 20 Mar 1932.

Lanchester, Elsa: b. London, Eng, 28 Oct 1902; d. Woodland Hills, CA, 26 Dec 1986.

Landa, Max: b. Vienna, Austria, 1880; d. 9 Nov 1933.

Landau, David: b. Philadelphia, PA, 9 Mar 1879; d. Los Angeles, CA, 20 Sep 1935.

Landi, Elissa: b. Venice, Italy, 6 Dec 1904; d. Kingston, NY, 21 Oct 1948.

Landis, Cullen: b. Nashville, TN, 9 Jul 1895; d. Bloomfield Hills, MI, 26 Aug 1975.

Landis, Margaret: b. Nashville, TN, 31 Aug 1890; d. Oakland, CA, 8 Apr 1981.

Landreth, Gertrude Griffith: b. New York, 26 Feb 1897; d. Palo Alto, CA, 25 Nov 1969.

Lane, Adele: b. New Jersey, 17 Jul 1877; d. Los Angeles, CA, 24 Oct 1957.

Lane, Allan (Rocky): b. Mishawaka, IN, 22 Sep 1909; d. Woodland Hills, CA, 27 Oct 1973.

Lane, Charles: b. Madison, IL, 25 Jan 1869; d. Van Nuys, CA, 17 Oct 1945.

Lane, Dorothy: b. 1905; d. New York, NY, 7 Oct 1923.

Lane, Harry J.: b. 1876; d. New York, NY, 27 Oct 1943.

Lane, Lupino: b. London, Eng, 16 Jun 1892; d. London, Eng, 10 Nov 1959.

Lane, Nora: b. Chester, IL, 12 Sep 1905; d. Glendale, CA 16 Oct 1948.

Lang, Fritz: b. Vienna, Austria, 5 Dec 1890; d. Los Angeles, CA, 2 Aug 1976.

Lang, Howard: b. New Orleans, LA, 12 May 1874; d. Los Angeles, CA, 26 Jan 1941.

Lang, Louise: b. 1907; d. Los Angeles, CA, 2 Feb. 1977.

Lang, Matheson: b. Montreal, Can, 15 May 1879; d. Bridgetown, Barbados, 11 Apr 1948.

Lang, Peter: b. 29 May 1859; d. New York, NY, 20 Aug 1932.

Lang, Walter: b. Memphis, TN, 10 Aug 1896; d. Palm Springs, CA, 7 Feb 1972.

Langdon, Harry: b. Council Bluffs, IA, 15 Jun 1884; d. Los Angeles, CA, 22 Dec 1944.

Langdon, Lillian: b. New Jersey, 1861; d. Santa Monica, CA, 8 Feb 1943.

Langer, Gilda: b. 1896; d. 23 Jan 1920.

Langford, Martha: b. 18??; d. Syracuse, NY, 21 Apr 1935.

Langhanke, Otto L.: b. 1871; d. Los Angeles, CA, 3 Feb 1943.

Langley, Herbert: b. 1888; d. London, Eng, ? Sep 1967.

Langtry, Lillie: b. Isle of Jersey, 13 Oct 1851; d. Monaco, 12 Feb 1929.

Lani, Maria: b. Warsaw, Poland, 1906; d. Paris, Fr, 11 Mar 1954.

Lanning, Edward: b. Iowa, 21 Sep 1870; d. Los Angeles, CA, 19 Sep 1918.

Lanning, Frank L.: b. Marion, IA, 14 Aug 1872; d. Los Angeles, CA, 17 Jun 1945.

Lanning, George: b. Marion, IA, 20 Feb 1877; d. Los Angeles Co, CA, 5 Jun 1941.

Lanphier, Fay: b. 1906; d. Oakland, CA, 21 Jun 1959.

La Pearl, Harry: b. Danville, IL, 1885; d. Los Angeles, CA, 13 Jan 1946.

La Plante, Beatrice: b. Paris, Fr, 1900; d. 19??.

La Plante, Violet (Violet Avon): b. Missouri, 17 Jan 1908; d. La Jolla, CA, 1 Jun 1984.

Lardner, Ring: b. Miles City, MI, 6 Mar 1885; d. Easthampton, NY, 25 Sep 1933.

La Reno, Dick: b. New York, NY, 31 Oct 1863; d. Los Angeles, CA, 26 Jul 1945.

Larimore, Earle: b. Portland, OR, 2 Aug 1899; d. New York, NY, 22 Oct 1947.

Larkin, Dolly: b. New York, NY, 19 Apr 1891; d. 19??.

Larkin, George: b. New York, NY, 11 Nov 1887; d. New York, NY, 27 Mar 1946.

Larkin, John: b. 1874; d. Los Angeles, CA, 19 Mar 1936.

La Roche, Edward: b. 1879; d. New York, NY, 26 Dec 1935.

La Rocque, Rod: b. Chicago, IL, 29 Nov 1896; d. Beverly Hills, CA, 15 Oct 1969.

Larrimore, Francine: b. Verdun, Fr, 22 Aug 1897; d. New York, NY, 7 Mar 1975.

Larsen, Viggo: b. Copenhagen, Dermark, 14 Aug 1880; d. Germany, 6 Jan 1957.

La Rue, Grace: b. Kansas City, MO, 1882; d. Burligame, CA, 12 Mar 1956.

La Rue, Jean: b. 1901; d. San Antonio, TX, ? Jun 1956.

Lasker, Dr. Emmanual: b. Berlin, Ger, 24 Dec 1868; d. New York, NY, 11 Jan 1941.

Lasker, Myles: b. 1893; d. New York, NY, 7 Dec 1940.

Latham, Joseph W., Sr.: b. 1890; d. Valley Cottage, NY, 10 Oct 1970.

Latimer, Alice: b. 18??; d. Wynnewood, PA, 15 May 1930.

Latimer, Henry: b. 1876; d. London, Eng, 25 Jan 1963.

La Torre, Charles: b. New York, NY, 15 Apr 1894; d. Los Angeles, CA, 2 Feb 1990.

Lauder, Sir Harry: b. Portobello, Scot, 14 Aug 1870; d. Strathaven, Scot, 26 Feb 1950.

Laughlin, Anna: b. Sacramento, CA, 11 Oct 1885; d. New York, NY, 6 Mar 1937.

Laughton, Charles: b. Scarborough, Eng, 1 Jul 1899; d. Los Angeles, CA, 15 Dec 1962.

Laurel, Mae: b. Australia, 24 May 1886; d. Sayville, NY, 1969.

Laurel, Stan: b. Ulverston, Eng, 16 Jun 1890; d. Santa Monica, CA, 23 Feb 1965.

Laurell, Kay: b. New Castle, PA, 1890; d. London, Eng, 31 Jan 1927.

Laurie, Edward: b. 18??; d. London, Eng, 9 Jan 1919.

La Varnie, Laura: b. Jefferson City, MO, 2 Mar 1853; d. Los Angeles, CA, 18 Sep 1939.

La Vere, June: b. 1903; d. Woodland Hills, CA, 7 Feb 1991.

Laverne, Dorothy: b. 1910; d. Los Angeles, CA, 29 Dec 1940.

La Verne, Lucille: b. Memphis, TN, 7 Nov 1869; d. Culver City, CA, 4 Mar 1945.

Lavigne, Maurice: b. 1887; d. New York, NY, 24 Jun 1952.

Law, Burton: b. Ouray, CO, 22 Oct 1877; d. Los Angeles Co, CA, 2 Nov 1963.

Law, Donald: b. Tampa, FL, 1920; d. Meadville, PA, 5 Feb 1959.

Law Rodman: b. Massachusetts, 1885; d. Greenville, SC, 14 Oct 1919.

Law, Walter: b. Farmersville, OH, 26 Mar 1876; d. Los Angeles, CA, 8 Aug 1940.

Lawford, Betty: b. London, Eng, 1910; d. New York, NY, 20 Nov 1960.

Lawford, Ernest: b. England, 20 Apr 1870; d. New York, NY, 26 Dec 1940.

Lawrence, Eddy: b. San Francisco, CA, 1881; d. San Diego, CA, 5 Dec 1931.

Lawrence, Florence: b. Hamilton, Ont, Can, 1 Jan 1890; d. Beverly Hills, CA, 28 Dec 1938.

Lawrence, Gerald: b. London, Eng, 23 Mar 1873; d. London, Eng, 16 May 1957.

Lawrence, Lillian: b. Alexander, WV, 17 Feb 1868; d. Beverly Hills, CA, 7 May 1926.

Lawrence, Raymond: b. London, Eng, 8 Dec 1888; d. Los Angeles Co, CA, 28 May 1976.

Lawrence, William E. (Babe): b. Brooklyn, NY, 22 Aug 1896; d. Los Angeles, CA, 28 Nov 1947.

Lawson, Eleanor; b. Illinois, 23 Dec. 1875; d. Pasadena, CA, 22 Mar 1966.

Lawson, John: b. Hollingworth, Eng, 9 Jan 1865; d. London, Eng, 25 Nov 1920.

Lawson, Louise: b. ????; d. New York, NY, 8 Feb 1924.

Lawson, Stan: b. 1909; d. Los Angeles, CA, 17 Jul 1977.

Lawton, Thais: b. Louisville, KY, 18 Jun 1878; d. New York, NY, 18 Dec 1956.

Lay, Irving T.: b. 18??; d. Seneca Falls, NY, ? Mar 1932.

Laymon, Gene: b. Michigan City, IN, 25 Jul 1889; d. Los Angeles, CA, 6 Jun 1946.

Lazzeri, Tony: b. San Francisco, CA, 6 Dec 1903; d. San Francisco, CA, 6 Aug 1946.

Leach, John: b. 1853; d. Chicago, IL, ? Mar 1918.

Leahy, Eugene: b. Limerick, Ire, 14 Mar 1883; d. London, Eng, ? Mar 1967.

Leahy, Margaret: b. London, Eng, 17 Aug 1902; d. Los Angeles, CA, 17 Feb 1967.

Learn, Alice: b. 18??; d. New York, NY, 23 Nov 1984.

Learn, Bessie: b. San Diego, CA, 30 Aug 1888; d. Burbank, CA, 5 Feb 1987.

Leary, Gilda: b. London, Eng, 1896; d. New York, NY, 17 Apr 1927.

Leary, Nolan: b. Rock Island, IL, 26 Apr 1889; d. Los Angeles, CA, 12 Dec 1987.

Lease, Rex: b. Central City, WV, 11 Feb 1899; d. Los Angeles, CA, 3 Jan 1966.

Le Bargy, Charles: b. La Chapelle, Fr, 1858; d. Nice, Fr, 5 Feb 1936.

Lebedeff, Ivan: b. Uspoliai, Lithuania, 18 Jun 1894; d. Los Angeles, CA, 31 Mar 1953.

Lebius, Aenderly: b. Tilsit, Ger, 6 Dec 1867; d. Berlin, Ger, 5 Mar 1921.

Leblanc, Georgette: b. Rouen, Fr. 1876; d. Cannes, Fr. 26 Oct 1941.

Le Brandt, Gertrude: b. 1863; d. Los Angeles, CA, 28 Aug 1955.

Le Brun, Mignon b. New York, NY, 4 Jan 1888; d. Los Angeles, CA, 20 Sep 1941.

Lederer, Gretchen: b. Cologne, Ger, 23 May 1891; d. Anaheim, CA, 20 Dec 1955.

Lederer, Otto: b. Prague, Czech, 17 Apr 1886; d. Woodland Hills, CA, 3 Sep 1965.

Lederer, Pepi: b. Chicago, IL, 18 Mar 1910; d. Los Angeles, CA, 11 Jun 1935.

Lederman, D. Ross: b. Lancaster, PA, 12 Dec 1894; d. Los Angeles, CA, 24 Aug 1972.

Ledoux, Fernand: b. Tirlemont, Belgium, 24 Jan 1897; d. Paris, Fr, 21 Sep 1993.

Lee, Annabelle: b. ????; d. Santa Monica, CA, 8 Sep 1989.

Lee, Auriol: b. London, Eng, 13 Sep 1880; d. Hutchinson, KS, 2 Jul 1941.

Lee, Bessie: b. 1906; d. Pittsburgh, PA, 28 Jun 1972.

Lee, Carolyn: b. New York, NY, 1858; d. New York, NY, 11 Jan 1920.

Lee, Charles T.: b. 1882; d. Los Angeles, CA, 14 Mar 1927.

Lee, Duke R.: b. Prince Henry Co, VA, 13 May 1881; d. Los Angeles, CA, 1 Apr 1959.

Lee, Elizabeth Borders: b. 1892; d. San Antonio, TX, 1985.

Lee, Etta: b. 1906; d. Eureka, CA, 27 Oct 1956.

Lee, Florence: b. Vermont, 12 Mar 1888; d. Los Angeles, CA, 1 Sep 1962.

Lee, Frankie: b. Gunnison, CO, 1 Jun 1912; d. 19??.

Lee, Gwen: b. Hasting, NE, 12 Nov 1904; d. Reno, NV, 20 Aug 1961.

Lee, Harry: b. Richmond, VA, 1 Jun 1872; d. Los Angeles, CA, 8 Dec 1932.

Lee, Jane: b. 1912; d. New York, NY, 17 Mar 1957.

Lee, Jennie: b. California, 1850; d. Los Angeles, CA, 4 Aug 1925.

Lee, Lila: b. Union Hill, NJ, 25 Jul 1905; d. Saranac Lake, NY, 13 Nov 1973.

Lee, Moe: b. 1884; d. Chicago, IL, 5 Jan 1966.

Lee, Norma: b. Newport, KY, 1899; d. New York, NY, 12 Dec 1980.

Lee, Raymond: b. Los Angeles, CA, 1910; d. Canoga, CA, 26 Jun 1974.

Lee, Richard Lawrence: b. New York, NY, 1 Jun 1872; d. New York, NY, 24 Jul 1931.

Lee, Rowland V.: b. Findlay, OH, 6 Sep 1891; d. Palm Desert, CA, 21 Dec 1975.

Lefaur, Andre: b. France, 25 Jul 1879; d. Paris, Fr, 4 Dec 1952.

Lefebvre, Rene: b. Nice, Fr, 8 Mar 1898; d. ? May 1991.

Leffingwell, George B.: b. Meadeville, PA, 18 May 1885; d. Downing, CA, 27 Apr 1934.

Leffler, Hermann: b. Quedlinburg, Ger, 3 Oct 1864; d. 21 Nov 1929.

Legal, Ernst: b. Schlieben, Ger, 2 May 1881; d. Berlin, Ger, 29 Jun 1955.

Le Guere, George: b. Memphis, TN, 17 Jul 1887; d. New York, NY, 21 Nov 1947.

Lehr, Anna: b. New York, NY, c. 1885; d. 19??.

Lehrman, Henry (Pathe): b. Vienna, Austria, 30 Mar 1886; d. Los Angeles, CA, 7 Nov 1946.

Leiber, Fritz: b. Chicago, IL, 31 Jan 1882; d. Pacific Palisades, CA, 14 Oct 1949.

Leicester, Ernest: b. 11 Jun 1866; d. London, Eng, 5 Oct 1939.

Leigh, Frank: b. London, Eng, 18 Apr 1876; d. Los Angeles, CA, 9 May 1948.

Leigh, Lisle: b. Salt Lake City, UT, 1879; d. New York, NY, 18 May 1927.

Leigh, Philip: b. England, 1880; d. New York, NY, 19 Jun 1935.

Leighton, Daniel: b. 1880; d. Los Angeles, CA, 20 Jan 1917.

Leighton, Harry: b. New York, NY, 14 Jun 1866; d. Bay Shore, NY, 30 May 1926.

Leighton, Lillianne: b. Auroaville, WI, 17 May 1874; d. Woodland Hills, CA, 19 Mar 1956.

Lely, Durward: b. Arbroath County, Scot, 2 Sep 1852; d. Glasgow, Scot, 29 Feb 1944.

Lem, Betty: b. ????; d. Los Angeles, CA, 10 Dec 1986.

Le Maire, George: b. Fort Worth, TX, 1884; d. New York, NY, 20 Jan 1930.

Le Maire, William: b. Fort Worth, TX, 21 Dec 1892; d. Los Angeles, CA, 11 Nov 1933.

La Mans, Marcel: b. Antwerp, Belgium, 1897; d. Lyons, NJ, 9 Jan 1946.

Le Moyne, Charles: b. Illinois, 27 Jun 1880; d. Los Angeles, CA, 13 Sep 1956.

Lennard, Arthur: b. Plumstead, Eng, 8 Mar 1867; d. Shoreham-by-Sea, Eng, 14 Jan 1954.

Lennox, Vera: b. Thornton Heath, Eng, 25 Nov 1904; d. England, 7 Dec 1984.

Leno, Dan: b. London, Eng, 20 Dec 1860; d. London, Eng, 31 Oct 1904.

Leno, Dan, Jr.: b. 1892; d. London, Eng, 2 Jan 1962.

Lenox, Fred: b. 1864; d. New York, NY, 28 Nov 1930.

Lentz, Irene (Irene): b. Montana, 8 Dec 1907; d. Los Angeles, CA, 15 Nov 1962.

Lenz, Andrew Francis: b. 1876; d. New York, NY, 27 Apr 1946.

Leon, Pedro: b. Tucson, AZ, 29 Jun 1878; d. 14 Jul 1931.

Leonard, Benny: b. New York, NY, 1896; d. New York, NY, 18 Apr 1947.

Leonard, Gus: b. Marseilles, Fr, 1856; d. Los Angeles, CA, 27 Mar 1939.

Leonard, Harry: b. c. 1857; d. Los Angeles, CA, 1 Sep 1917.

Leonard, Jack: b. England, 18??; d. Los Angeles, CA, ? Oct 1921.

Leonard, James: b. 1868; d. Glendale, CA, 4 Jul 1930.

Leonard, Marion: b. Ohio, 9 Jan 1881; d. Woodland Hills, CA, 9 Jan 1956.

Leonard, Minnie: b. 1873; d. Los Angeles, CA, 2 Jan 1940.

Leonard, Robert: b. Poland, 22 Feb 1849; d. Brooklyn, NY, 5 Jan 1948.

Leonard, Robert: Z.: b. Chicago, IL, 7 Oct 1889; d. Los Angeles, CA, 27 Aug 1968.

Leone, Henry: b. Constantinople, Italy, 30 Mar 1858; d. Mt. Vernon, NY, 9 Jun 1922.

Leong, James B.: b. Shanghai, China, 2 Nov 1889; d. Los Angeles Co, CA, 16 Dec 1967.

Leonidov, Leonid: b. Odessa, Russ, 3 Jun 1873; d. Moscow, Russ, 6 Aug 1941.

Le Roy, Mervyn: b. San Francisco, CA, 15 Oct 1900; d. Beverly Hills, CA, 13 Sep 1987.

Le Saint, Edward J.: b. Cincinnati, OH, 13 Dec 1870; d. Los Angeles, CA, 10 Sep 1940.

Leslie, Eleanor: b. London, Eng, 1874; d. Glendale, CA, 14 Jun 1929.

Leslie, Gladys: b. New York, NY, 5 Mar 1899; d. Boynton Beach, FL, 2 Oct 1976.

Leslie, Lilie: b. Scotland, 1892; d. Los Angeles, CA, 8 Sep 1940.

Leslie, Marguerite: b. Ostersund, Sweden, 3 Apr 1884; d. 1958.

Lessey, George A.: b. Amherst, MA, 8 Jun 1879; d. Westbrook, CT, 3 Jun 1947.

L'Estelle, Eleanor Scott: b. 1880; d. Los Angeles, CA, 25 Apr 1962.

Lester, Kate: b. Norfolk, Eng, 1857; d. Los Angeles, CA, 12 Oct 1924.

Lester, Louise: b. Milwaukee, WI, 8 Aug 1867; d. Los Angeles, CA, 17 Nov 1952.

L'Estrange, Dick: b. Asheville, NC, 27 Dec 1889; d. Burbank, CA, 19 Nov 1963.

L'Estrange, Julian: b. England, 6 Aug 1878; d. New York, NY, 22 Oct 1918.

Le Strange, Norman: b. ????; d. London, Eng, 5 Jun 1936.

Lett, Robert: b. 18??; d. West Orange, NJ, ? Mar 1916.

Letta, Vin Sini: b. 18??; d. Chicago, IL, 4 May 1921.

Lettinger, Rudolf: b. 26 Oct 1865; d. 21 Mar 1937.

Leubas, Louis: b. 1870; d. Digne, Fr, 29 Aug 1932.

Leudesdorff-Tormin, Philine: b. 1894; d. 30 Apr 1924.

Levall, G. E.: b. 18??; d. Coalinga, CA, ? Feb 1922,

Le Valle, Cleo: b. ????; d. Del Mar, CA, ? Aug 1925.

Levance, Cal: b. Canada, 18??; d. Toronto, Can, 6 Sep 1951.

Le Veque, Eddie: b. Juarez, Mex, 1896; d. Los Angeles, CA, 28 Jan 1989.

Levering, James: b. Bristol, Eng, 1861; d. 19??.

Levesque, Marcel: b. Paris, Fr, 6 Dec 1877; d. ? Feb 1962.

Le Viness, Carl: b. New York, NY, 6 Jul 1885; d. Los Angeles, CA, 15 Oct 1964.

Lewis, Ada: b. New York, NY, 1875; d. Hollis, NY, 24 Sep 1925.

Lewis, Charles H.: b. 1850; d. 3 Nov 1928.

Lewis, Edgar: b. Holden, MO, 22 Jun 1872; d. Los Angeles, CA, 21 May 1938.

Lewis, Eric: b. Northampton, Eng, 23 Oct 1855; d. Margate, Eng, 1 Apr 1935.

Lewis, Eva: b. St. Louis, MO, 1881; d. Los Angeles, CA, 6 May 1939.

Lewis, Fred: b. Kingston-on Thames, Eng, 23 Dec 1860; d. England, 25 Dec 1927.

Lewis, Frederick G.: b. Oswego, NY, 14 Feb 1873; d. Amityville, NY, 19 Mar 1946.

Lewis, Gordon: b. Harrison, AR, 1890; d. Tucson, AZ, 17 Mar 1933.

Lewis, Harry: b. 1886; d. Los Angeles, CA, 18 Nov 1950.

Lewis, Ida: b. New York State, 1855; d. Los Angeles, CA, 21 Apr 1935.

Lewis, James H. (Daddy): b. 1850; d. Pawtucket, RI, 3 Nov 1928.

Lewis, Mrs. Jeffreys: b. London, Eng, 1857; d. New York, NY, 28 Apr 1926.

Lewis, Martin: b. London, Eng, 8 Sep 1888; d. Farnborough, Kent, Eng, ? Apr 1970.

Lewis, Mary: b. Hot Springs, AR, 7 Jan 1900; d. New York, NY, 31 Dec 1941.

Lewis, Mitchell: b. Syracuse, NY, 26 Jun 1880; d. Los Angeles, CA, 24 Aug 1956.

Lewis, Ralph: b. Inglewood, IL, 28 Oct 1872; d. Los Angeles, CA, 4 Dec 1937.

Lewis, Richard: b. 1869; d. Los Angeles, CA, 30 Apr 1935.

Lewis, Sam: b. 1878; d. Los Angeles, CA, 28 Apr 1963.

Lewis, Tom: b. St. John, New Bruns, Can, 17 May 1867; d. New York, NY, 19 Oct 1927.

Lewis, Vera: b. New York, NY, 10 Jun 1873; d. Woodland Hills, CA, 8 Feb 1956.

Lewis, Walter P.: b. Albany, NY, 10 Jun 1866; d. 30 Jan 1932.

Leyton, George: b. New Orleans, LA, 24 Apr 1864; d. London, Eng, 5 Jun 1948.

Leyva, Frank: b. 26 Oct 1897; d. 25 Feb 1981.

Libbey, J. Aldrich: b. 1872; d. San Francisco, CA, 29 Apr 1925.

Libeau, Gustave: b. Brussels, Belgium, 8 Nov 1877; d. 1957.

Licho, Edgar Adolph: b. Russia, 1876; d. Los Angeles, CA, 11 Oct 1944.

Liddy, James: b. 1895; d. New York, NY, 18 Feb 1936.

Lieb, Herman: b. Chicago, IL, 9 Mar 1873; d. Tucson, AZ, 9 Mar 1966.

Lieberman, Jacob: b. 1879; d. Philadelphia, PA, 16 Feb 1956.

Liedtke, Harry: b. Konigsberg, Ger, 12 Oct 1882; d. Bad Saarow-Pieskow, Ger, 28 Apr 1945.

Liggett, Louis: b. Hungary, 30 May 1864; d. Los Angeles, CA, 27 Nov 1928.

Ligon, Grover: b. Kerney, MO, 1 Feb 1885; d. Los Angeles, CA, 3 Mar 1965.

Lillard, Charlotte: b. New Orleans, LA, 1893; d. Los Angeles, CA, 4 Mar 1946.

Lillford, Harry: b. ????; d. New York, NY, 9 Jan 1931.

Lillie, Beatrice: b. Toronto, Can, 29 May 1894; d. London, Eng, 20 Jan 1989.

Lillie, Maj. Gordon W. (Pawnee Bill): b. Bloomington, IL, 14 Feb 1860; d. Pawnee, OK, 3 Feb 1942.

Lincoln, Caryl: b. Oakland, CA, 16 Nov 1908; d. Woodland Hills, CA, 20 Feb 1983.

Lincoln, E. K. (Edward Klink Lincoln): b. Johnstown, PA, 8 Aug 1884; d. Los Angeles, CA, 9 Jan 1958.

Lincoln, Elmo: b. Rochester, IN, 6 Feb 1889; d. Los Angeles, CA, 27 Jun 1952.

Lindau, Rolf: b. Thale, Ger, 21 Aug 1904; d. Santa Monica, CA, 27 Jul 1969.

Linden, Einar: b. Sweden, 26 Jun 1886; d. Los Angeles, CA, 19 Oct 1954.

Linder, Max: b. St. Loubes, Fr, 16 Dec 1883; d. Paris, Fr, 31 Oct 1925.

Lindley, Bert: b. Chicago, IL, 3 Dec 1873; d. Los Angeles Co, CA, 12 Sep 1953.

Lindroth, Helen: b. 3 Dec 1874; d. Boston, MA, 5 Oct 1956.

Lindsay, James: b. Devonshire, Eng, 26 Feb 1869; d. Melbourne, Austral, 9 Jun 1928.

Lindsay, Marquerita: b. 1883; d. Los Angeles, CA, 26 Dec 1955.

Ling, Ritchie: b. London, Eng, 1867; d. New York, NY, 5 Mar 1937.

Lingham, Thomas G.: b. Indianapolis, IN, 7 Apr 1870; d. Woodland Hills, CA, 19 Feb 1950.

Link, Adolf: b. Budapest, Hungary, 15 Sep 1881; d. New York, NY, 23 Sep 1933.

Lingham, Thomas G.: b. Indianapolis, IN, 7 Apr 1870; d. Woodland Hills, CA, 19 Feb 1950.

Link, Adolf: b. Budapest, Hungary, 15 Sep 1881; d. New York, NY, 23 Sep 1933.

Link, William: b. 1867; d. Los Angeles, CA, 17 Apr 1937.

Linow, Ivan: b. Latvia, 1888; d. 19??.

Lion, Leon M.: b. London, Eng, 12 Mar 1879; d. Brighton, Eng, 28 Mar 1947.

Lipscomb, W. P. b. Merton, Surrey, Eng, 1887; d. London, Eng, 24 Jul 1958.

Lipton, Sir Thomas: b. Glasgow, Scot, 10 May 1850; d. London, Eng, 2 Oct 1931.

Lissenko, Nathalie: b. Russia, c. 1886; d. 1969.

Lister, Francis: b. London, Eng, 2 Apr 1899; d. London, Eng, 28 Oct 1951.

Liston, Hudson: b. Belfast, Ire, 1841; d. Amityville, NY, 15 Sep 1929.

Liston, Millicent: b. 1859; d. New York, NY, 20 Feb 1920.

Litson, Mason N.: b. New York, NY, 1878; d. Los Angeles, CA, 19 Dec 1949.

Little, Ann: b. Sisson, CA, 7 Feb 1891; d. Los Angeles, CA, 21 May 1984.

Little, Chief Edward: b. 1868; d. Detroit, MI, 10 Jan 1928.

Littlefield, Emma: b. New York, NY, 12 Jan 1883; d. Farmingdale, NY, 23 Jun 1934.

Littlefield, Lucien: b. San Antonio, TX, 16 Aug 1895; d. Los Angeles, CA, 4 Jun 1960.

Livesey, Roger: b. Barry, Wales, 25 Jun 1906; d. Watford, Herts, Eng, 4 Feb 1976.

Livesey, Sam, b. Flintshire, Wales, 14 Oct 1873; d. London, Eng, 7 Nov 1936.

Livingston, Margaret: b. Salt Lake City, UT, 25 Nov 1895; d. Warrington, PA, 13 Dec 1984.

Livingston, Robert: b. Quincy, IL, 9 Dec 1904; d. Tarzana, CA, 7 Mar 1988.

Livingstone, Frank H.: b. San Francisco, CA, 1870; d. Oakland, CA. 26 Nov 1932.

Llewellyn, Fewlass: b. Hull, Yorks, Eng, 5 Mar 1866; d. London, Eng, 16 Jun 1941.

Lloyd, Albert S.: b. 1884; d. Los Angeles, CA, 10 Jul 1964.

Lloyd, Alice: b. London, Eng, 20 Oct 1873; d. London, Eng, 16 Nov 1949.

Lloyd, Charles M.: b. Virginia, 1870; d. Los Angeles, CA, 4 Dec 1948.

Lloyd, Doris: b. Liverpool, Eng, 3 Jul 1896; d. Santa Barbara, CA, 21 May 1968.

Lloyd, Ethel: b. Brooklyn, NY, 18??; d. Brooklyn, NY, 12 Jan 1923.

Lloyd, Frank: b. Glasgow, Scot, 2 Feb 1887; d. Los Angeles, CA, 10 Aug 1960.

Lloyd, Frederick W.: b. London, Eng, 15 Jan 1880; d. Hove, Sussex, Eng, 24 Nov 1949.

Lloyd, Gaylord E.:b. Burchard, NE, 1888; d. Beverly Hills, CA, 1 Sep 1943.

Lloyd, Harold: b. Burchard, NE, 20 Apr 1893; d. Los Angeles, CA, 8 Mar 1971.

Lloyd, James Darsie: b. 1864; d. Los Angeles, CA, 17 Dec 1947.

Lloyd, Marie: b. London, Eng, 12 Feb 1870; d. London, Eng, 7 Oct 1922.

Lloyd, Rollo: b. Akron, OH, 22 Mar 1883; d. Los Angeles, CA, 24 Jul 1938.

Loback, Marvin: b. Tacoma, WA, 21 Nov 1896; d. Los Angeles, CA, 18 Aug 1938.

Locke, William J.: b. Barbados, BWI, 20 Mar 1863; d. Paris, Fr, 15 May 1930.

Locklear, Lt. Omer: b. Fort Worth, TX, 28 Oct 1891; d. Los Angeles, CA, 2 Aug 1920.

Lockwood, Harold: b. Brooklyn, NY, 12 Apr 1887; d. New York, NY, 19 Oct 1918.

Loder, John: b. London, Eng, 1 Mar 1898; d. Selborne, Eng, 26 Dec 1988.

Lodge, Ben: b. 18??; d. Long Island, NY, 10 Jan 1927.

Lodi, Theodore: b. Russia, 1876; d. 6 Mar 1947.

Loff, Jeanette: b. Cronno, ID, 9 Oct 1906; d. Los Angeles, CA, 4 Aug 1942.

Loftus, Cecilia: b. Glasgow, Scot, 22 Oct 1876; d. New York, NY, 12 Jul 1943.

Loftus, WIlliam C.: b. 1862; d. Los Angeles, CA, 11 Mar 1931.

Logan, Jacqueline: b. Corsicana, TX, 30 Nov 1902; d. Melbourne, FL, 4 Apr 1983.

Logan, Stanley: b. London, Eng, 12 Jun 1885; d. New York, NY, 30 Jan 1953.

Lohman, Zalla: b. Yugoslavia, 1906; d. Los Angeles, CA, 17 Jul 1967.

Lombard, Carole: b. Fort Wayne, IN, 6 Oct 1908; d. Las Vegas, NV, 16 Jan 1942.

Lombardi, Dillo: b. Parma, Italy, 10 Jan 1858; d. Civita Castellan, Italy, 15 Jul 1935.

London, Babe (Jean): b. Des Moines, IA, 1901; d. Woodland Hills, CA, 29 Nov 1980.

London, Tom (Leonard T. Clapham): b. Louisville, KY, 24 Aug 1889; d. Los Angeles, CA, 5 Dec 1963.

Lonergan, Lester: b. Ireland, 28 Apr 1869; d. Lynn, MA, 13 Aug 1931.

Long, Frederic: b. 1857; d. Los Angeles, CA, 18 Oct 1941.

Long, Luray (Luray Roble): b. Wisconsin, 3 Dec 1890; d. Los Angeles, CA, 2 Jan 1919.

Long, Nicholas, Sr.: b. 1851; d. New York, NY, 16 Apr 1926.

Long, Nicholas, Jr.: b. Greenlawn, NY, 1906; d. New York, NY, 31 Aug 1949.

Long, Sally: b. Kansas City, MO, 5 Dec 1901; d. Newport Beach, CA, 12 Aug 1987.

Long, Walter H.: b. Milford, NH, 5 Mar 1879; d. Los Angeles, CA, 4 Jul 1952.

Longden, John: b. West Indies, 11 Nov 1900; d. 26 May 1971.

Longfellow, Malvina: b. Virginia, 30 Mar c. 1890; d. 19??.

Longford, Raymond: b. 1868; d. 2 Apr 1959.

Longman, Edward G.: b. Brooklyn, NY, 1881; d. Miami, FL, 14 Apr 1969.

Longworth, Edward O.: b. 1893; d. Los Angeles, CA, 27 Nov 1927.

Lonsdale, Harry: b. Worcester, Eng, 6 Dec 18??; d. 12 Jul 1923.

Loomes, Harry E.: b. 18??; d. Philadelphia, PA, 17 Mar 1946.

Loos, Anita: b. Sissons, CA, 26 Apr 1889; d. New York, NY, 18 Aug 1981.

Loos, Theodore: b. Zwingenberg, Ger, 18 May 1883; d. Stuttgart, Ger, 27 Jun 1954.

Lopez, Carlos: b. Durango, Mex, 4 Nov 1887; d. Tapachula, Mex, 13 Feb 1942.

Loraine, Robert: b. Liscard, Cheshire, Eng, 14 Jan 1876; d. London, Eng, 23 Dec 1935.

Lorch, Theodore A.: b. Springfield, IL, 29 Sep 1880; d. Camarillo, CA, 11 Nov 1947.

Lord, Del: b. Grimsley, Can, 7 Oct 1894; d. Calabasas, CA, 23 Mar 1970.

Lord, Phillips H.: b. Hartford, VT, 13 Jul 1902; d. Ellsworth, MO, 19 Oct 1975.

Lorenz, John A.: b. Buffalo, NY, 1887; d. Paramus, NJ, 30 Apr 1972.

Lorimer, Enid: b. 1888; d. Sydney, Austral, 15 Jul 1982.

Lorraine, Emily: b. England, 1878; d. New York, NY, 6 Jul 1944.

Lorraine, Harry: b. Brighton, Eng, 1866; d. 19??.

Lorraine, Jean: b. 1907; d. Alameda Co, CA, 24 Jan 1958.

Lorraine, Leota: b. Kansas City, MO, 14 Mar 1899; d. Los Angeles, CA, 9 Jul 1974.

Lorraine, Lillian: b. San Francisco, CA, 1 Jan 1892; d. New York, NY, 17 Apr 1955.

Lorraine, Louise: b. San Francisco, CA, 1 Oct 1902; d. Sacramento, CA, 2 Feb 1981.

Lorraine, Marie: b. Sydney, Austral, ????; d. London, Eng, 5 Mar 1982.

Lorraine, Tui (Tui Bow): b. New Zealand, 19 Oct 1906; d. Alderly, Austral, 25 Mar 1993.

Lorre, Peter: b. Rosenberg, Hungary, 26 Jun 1904; d. Los Angeles, CA, 23 Mar 1964.

Lorys, Denise: b. ????; d. Paris, Fr, 19 Nov 1930.

Losee, Frank: b. Brooklyn, NY, 12 Jun 1856; d. Yonkers, NY, 14 Nov 1937.

Lotto, Claire: b. ? Mar 1898; d. ? Aug 1952.

Louis, Maude: b. Oregon, 19 Feb 1884; d. Glendale, CA, 14 Mar 1976.

Louis, Willard: b. San Francisco, CA, 19 Apr 1882; d. Glendale, CA, 22 Jul 1926.

Louise, Anita: b. New York, NY, 9 Jan 1915; d. Los Angeles, CA, 25 Apr 1970.

Love, Bessie: b. Midland, TX, 10 Sep 1898; d. London, Eng, 26 Apr 1986.

Love, Mabel: b. England, 16 Oct 1874; d. Weybridge, Surrey, Eng, 15 May 1953.

Love, Montague: b. Portsmouth, Eng, 1877; d. Beverly Hills, CA, 17 May 1943.

Lovely, Louise: b. Sydney, Austral, 1896; d. Hobart, Austral, 18 Mar 1980.

Lovett, Shaw: b. New York, NY, 22 Mar 1896; d. Escondido, CA, 27 Dec 1971.

Low, Warren: b. Pittsburgh, PA, 12 Aug 1905; d. Woodland Hills, CA, 27 Jul 1989.

Lowe, Edmund: b. San Jose, CA, 3 Mar 1890; d. Woodland Hills, CA, 20 Apr 1971.

Lowe, James B.: b. Georgia, 12 Oct 1879; d. Los Angeles, CA, 19 May 1963.

Lowell, Helen: b. New York, NY, 2 Jun 1866; d. Los Angeles, CA, 28 Jun 1937.

Lowell, Joan: b. Berkeley, CA, 23 Nov 1902; d. Brasilia, Brazil, 7 Nov 1967.

Lowell, John (John Lowell Russell): b. Pleasant Valley, IA, 22 Apr 1875; d. Los Angeles, CA, 19 Sep 1937.

Lowery, William A.: b. St. Louis, MO, 22 Jul 1885; d. Los Angeles Co, CA, 15 Nov 1941.

Loy, Myrna: b. Helena, MT, 2 Aug 1905; d. New York, NY, 14 Dec 1993.

Lubetty, Madeline: b. ????; d. Miami, FL, ? Sep 1968.

Lubitsch, Ernst: b. Berlin, Ger, 28 Jan 1892; d. Bel-Air, CA, 30 Nov 1947.

Luby, Edna: b. New York, NY, 12 Oct 1891; d. New York, NY, 1 Oct 1928.

Lucas, Samuel: b. Washington, OH, 1840; d. New York, NY, 10 Jan 1916.

Lucas, Wilfred: b. Canada, 30 Jan 1871; d. Los Angeles, CA, 13 Dec 1940.

Lucenay, Harry: b. Marseilles, Fr, 8 May 1887; d. Los Angeles, CA, 28 May 1944.

Luckett, Edith: b. 16 Jul 1896; d. Phoenix, AZ. 26 Oct 1987.

Lucy, Arnold: b. Tottenham, Middlesex, Eng, 1865; d. 15 Dec 1945.

Luddy, Barbara: b. Great Falls, MT, 25 May 1908; d. Los Angeles, CA, 1 Apr 1979.

Luden, Jack: b. Reading, PA, 8 Feb 1902; d. San Quentin, CA, 15 Feb 1951.

Ludwig, Edward: b. Russia, 1899; d. Santa Monica, CA, 20 Aug 1982,

Luff, William: b. London, Eng, 31 May 1872; d. England, 15 Mar 1960.

Lufkin, Sam: b. Utah, 8 May 1891; d. Los Angeles, CA, 19 Feb 1952.

Lugg, William: b. Portsmouth, Eng, 4 Jun 1852; d. 1940.

Lugosi, Bela: b. Lugos, Hungary, 20 Oct 1882; d. Los Angeles, CA, 16 Aug 1956.

Lukas, Paul: b. Budapest, Hungary, 26 May 1894; d. Tangier, Morocco, 15 Aug 1971.

Lumiere, Auguste: b. Besancon, Fr, 19 Oct 1862; d. Lyon, Fr, 10 Apr 1954.

Lund, O. A. C.: b. Stockholm, Sweden, c. 1890; d. 1963.

Lund, Richard: b. Goteborg, Sweden, 1885; d. Sweden, 17 Sep 1960.

Lundequist, Gerda: b. Stockholm, Sweden, 14 Feb 1871; d. ? Oct 1959.

Lunt, Alfred: b. Milwaukee, WI, 19 Aug 1892; d. Chicago, IL, 3 Aug 1977.

Lupino, Barry: b. London, Eng, 7 Jan 1882; d. Brighton, Eng, 25 Sep 1962.

Lupino, Mark: b. 1869; d. London, Eng, 4 Apr 1930.

Lupino, Wallace: b. Edinburgh, Scot, 23 Jan 1898; d. Ashford, Middlesex, Eng, 11 Oct 1961.

Luther, Anna: b. Newark, NJ, 7 Jul 1897; d. Los Angeles, CA, 16 Dec 1960.

Lyel, Viola: b. Hull, Yorks, Eng, 9 Dec 1900; d. 14 Aug 1972.

Lyell, Lottie: b. Australia, 1890; d. Sydney, Austral, 21 Dec 1925.

Lygo, Mary (Irene Fuller): b. ????; d. Los Angeles, CA, 1 Jun 1927.

Lyle, Clinton: b. California, 27 Aug 1883; d. Los Angeles Co, CA, 26 Jun 1950.

Lyle, Lynston: b. 1856; d. London, Eng, 19 Feb 1920.

Lynch, Helen: b. Billings, MT, 6 Apr 1900; d. Miami, FL, 2 Mar 1965.

Lynch, Jim: b. 18??; d. Chicago, IL, 20 Apr 1916.

Lyndon, Alice: b. 1874; d. Los Angeles, CA, 9 Jul 1949.

Lynn, Emmett: b. Muscatine, IA, 14 Feb 1897; d. Los Angeles, CA, 20 Oct 1958.

Lynn, Sharon: b. Weatherford, TX, 9 Apr 1910; d. Los Angeles, CA, 26 May 1963.

Lyon, Ben: b. Atlanta, Ga, 6 Feb 1901; d. At Sea, 22 Mar 1979.

Lyon, Esther: b. 30 Oct 1869; d. New York, NY, 15 Jul 1958.

Lyons, Cliff (Tex): b. South Dakota, 4 Jul 1901; d. Los Angeles, CA, 6 Jan 1974.

Lyons, Eddie: b. Beardstown, IL, 25 Nov 1886; d. Pasadena, CA, 30 Aug 1926.

Lyons, Fred: b. 18??; d. 16 Mar 1921.

Lyons, Harry M.: b. Illinois, 12 Nov 1879; d. Los Angeles, CA, 13 Mar 1919.

Lytell, Bert: b. New York, NY, 24 Feb 1885; d. New York, NY, 28 Sep 1954.

Lytell, Wilfred: b. New York, NY, 1892; d. Salem, NY, 10 Sep 1954.

Lytton, Doris: b. Manchester, Eng, 23 Jan 1893; d. London, Eng, 3 Dec 1953.

Lytton, L. Rogers: b. New Orleans, LA, 1867; d. 9 Aug 1924.

Lyvenden, Lord (Percy Vernon): b. Kettering, Eng, 29 Dec 1857; d. London, Eng, 25 Dec 1926.

M

Mac, Nila: b. Arkansas City, KS, 29 Oct 1891; d. New York, NY, 20 Jan 1953.

MacAdams, Rhea: b. 1884; d. Placerville, CA, 20 Jul 1982.

McAlister, Mary: b. Los Angeles, CA, 27 May 1909; d. Del Mar, CA, 1 May 1991.

McAllister, Paul: b. Brooklyn, NY, 30 Jun 1875; d. Santa Monica, CA, 8 Jul 1955.

McAlpine, Jane: b. 1896; d. Long Branch, NJ, 19 Oct 1947.

McAtee, Clyde: b. 1881; d. Calabasas, CA, 20 Feb 1947.

McAvoy, May: b. New York, NY, 8 Sep 1901; d. Sherman Oaks, CA, 26 Apr 1984.

MacBride, Donald: b. New York, NY, 23 Jun 1893; d. Los Angeles, CA, 21 Jun 1957.

McBride, Edith: b. 18??; d. New York, NY, 10 Dec 1926.

MacBride, Olivia: b. Hemet, CA, 1896; d. Anaheim, CA, 27 Aug 1976.
McCabe, George F.: b. Chicago, IL, 1865; d. Bellview, NY, 17 Dec 1917.
McCabe, Harry: b. Chicago, IL, 1879; d. Los Angeles, CA, 11 Feb 1925.
McCabe, John: b. 1879; d. Buffalo, NY, 19 Jun 1929.
McCabe, May: b. Indianapolis, IN, 1873; d. New York, NY, 22 Jun 1949.
McCall, Lizzie: b. Buffalo, NY, 4 Jul 1857; d. New York, NY, 18 Apr 1942.
McCall, William: b. Delaven, IL, 19 May 1870; d. Los Angeles, CA, 10 Jan 1938.
McCallum, John: b. England, 1 Mar 1863; d. Los Angeles, CA, 19 Feb 1923.
McCann, Charles Andrew: b. 18??; d. Paris, Fr. ? Sep 1927.
McCarthy, Earl: b. Fort Wayne, IN, 1906; d. Los Angeles, CA, 28 May 1933.
McCarthy, John P.: b. San Francisco, CA, 17 Mar 1865; d. Pasadena, CA, 4 Sep 1962.
McCarthy, Lillah: b. Cheltenham, Gloucs, Eng, 22 Sep 1875; d. London, Eng, 15 Apr 1960.
McCarthy, Myles: b, Toronto, Can, 27 Apr 1874; d. Los Angeles, CA, 27 Sep 1928.
McCauley, Edna: b. Detroit, MI, 18??; d. Rome, Italy, 28 Jan 1919.
McCauley, Jack: b. New York State, 1901; d. Menlo Park, CA, 13 Jun 1980.
McCay, Neil: b. 1869; d. Englewood, NJ, 10 Apr 1933.
McCay, Winsor: b. Spring Lake, MI, 1872; d. Sheepshead Bay, NY, 26 Jul 1934.
McClellan, Robert Francis: b. 1888; d. 20 Mar 1973.
McClelland, Donald: b. New York, NY, 29 Sep 1903; d. New York, NY, 15 Nov 1955.
McCloskey, Elizabeth: b. 1872; d. Los Angeles, CA, 8 Jan 1942.
McClure, Frank: b. 1895; d. Los Angeles, CA, 23 Jan 1960.
McClure, Irene: b. ????; d. Bakersfield, CA, 4 Sep 1928.
McCollum, H. H.: b. Wilkes-Barre, PA, 1887; d. New York, NY, 19 Dec 1938.
McComas, Carroll: b. Alburquerque, NM, 27 Jun 1886; d. New York, NY, 9 Nov 1962.
McComas, Kandall (Breezy Brisbane): b. Holton, KS, 29 Oct 1916; d. Lake Isabella, CA, 15 Oct 1981.
McComas, Ralph C.: b. California, 8 Sep 1889; d. San Francisco, CA, 13 Jul 1924.
McConnell, Gladys: b. Oklahoma City, OK, 22 Oct 1905; d. Fullerton, CA, 4 Mar 1979.
McConnell, Mollie: b. Indiana, 24 Sep 1865; d. Los Angeles, CA, 9 Dec 1920.
McCord, Mrs. Lewis: b. Philadelphia, PA, 18??; d. Harrisburg, PA, 24 Dec 1917.
McCord, Vera: b. 1877; d. New York, NY, 3 Mar 1949.
McCormack, Billie: b. 1876; d. Santa Monica, CA, 31 Jan 1935.
McCormack, Frank: b. Washington, DC, 1876; d. Connecticut, 22 May 1941.

McCormick, Alyce (Joy Auburn): b. Chicago, IL, 13 Jan 1901; d. Los Angeles, CA, 6 Jan 1932.

McCormick, Merrill: b. Denver, CO. 5 Feb 1892; d. San Gabriel, CA, 19 Aug 1953.

McCoy, Gertrude, b. Sugar Valley, GA. 30 Jun 1890; d. Atlanta, GA, 17 Jul 1967.

McCoy, Harry: b. Philadelphia, PA, 10 Dec 1889; d. Los Angeles, CA, 1 Sep 1937.

McCoy, Horace: b. 1897; d. Beverly Hills, CA, 16 Dec 1955.

McCoy, Tim: b. Saginaw, MI, 10 Apr 1891; d. Nogeles, AZ, 29 Jan 1978.

McCrea, Joel: b. Los Angeles, CA, 5 Nov 1905; d. Woodland Hills, CA, 20 Oct 1990.

McCreery, Joey: b. ????; d. Orange Co, CA, 1 May 1989.

McCullough, Philo: b. San Bernardino, CA, 16 Jun 1893; d. Burbank, CA, 5 Jun 1981.

McCullough, Ralph: b. Laramie, WY, 2 Sep 1895; d. Los Angeles, CA, 25 Dec 1943.

McCullum, Bartlett: b. 18??; d. Philadelphia, PA, 25 Mar 1916.

McCutcheon, George Barr: b. Tippecanoe County, IN, 26 Jul 1866; d. New York, NY, 23 Oct 1928.

McCutcheon, Wallace: b. New York, NY, 23 Dec 1894; d. Los Angeles, CA, 27 Jan 1928.

McDaniel, George: b. Atlanta, GA, 1885; d. San Fernando, CA, 20 Aug 1944.

McDermott, John W.: b. Green River, WY, 9 Sep 1892; d. Los Angeles, CA, 22 Jul 1946.

McDermott, Joseph: b. 1890; d. Los Angeles, CA, 6 Mar 1923.

MacDermott, Marc: b. Australia, 24 Jul, 1881; d, Glendale, CA, 5 Jan 1929.

Macdona, Charles T.: b. Dublin, Ire, 1860; d. Brighton, Eng, 15 Nov 1946.

McDonald, Charles: b. 1876; d. Tucson, AZ, 7 Aug 1953.

McDonald, Charles B.: b. Springfield, MA, 26 May 1886; d. Hollywood, FL, 29 Dec 1964.

MacDonald, Donald; b. Denison, TX, 13 Mar 1898; d. New York, NY, 9 Dec 1959.

McDonald, Francis: b. Erlanger, KY, 22 Aug 1889; d. Los Angeles, CA, 18 Sep 1968.

MacDonald, J. Farrell: b. Waterbury, CT, 14 Apr 1875; d. Los Angeles, CA, 2 Aug 1952.

McDonald, Jack: b. San Francisco, CA, 17 Sep 1880; d. 19??.

MacDonald, Katherine: b. Pittsburgh, PA, 14 Dec 1891; d. Santa Barbara, CA, 4 Jun 1956.

MacDonald, Wallace: b. Mulgrave, Nova Scotia, Can, 5 May 1891; d. Santa Barbara, CA, 30 Oct 1978.

McDowell, Claire: b. New York, NY, 2 Nov 1878; d. Woodland Hills, CA, 23 Oct 1966.

MacDowell, Melbourne: b. South River, NJ, 22 Nov 1857; d. Decator, CA, 18 Feb 1941.

McDowell, Nelson: b. Greenfield, MO, 14 Aug 1870; d. Los Angeles, CA, 3 Nov 1947.

McDuff, James: b. 1863; d. Bay Shore, NY, 31 Mar 1937.

McDunnough, Walter S.: b. Montreal, Can; 15 Dec 1863; d. Los Angeles, CA, 1 Jul 1942.

Mace, Fred: b. Philadelphia, PA, 22 Aug 1878; d. New York, NY, 21 Feb 1917.

Mace, Wynn: b. South Pasadena, CA, 3 Aug 1890; d. Los Angeles Co, CA, 15 Jan 1955.

McEvoy, Dorothea: b. 1896; d. La Jolla, CA, 6 Feb 1976.

McFadden, Bernarr: b. Mill Springs, MO, 16 Aug 1868; d. Jersey City, NJ, 12 Oct 1955.

MacFadden, Gertrude: b. 1900; d. Los Angeles, CA, 3 Jun 1967.

McFadden, Ivor: b. San Francisco, CA, 6 Aug 1887; d. Los Angeles, CA, 14 Aug 1942.

McFarland, Carroll A.: b. 1885; d. Portland, OR, 1 Mar 1935.

MacFayden, Harry: b. Milwaukee, WI, 1875; d. New York, NY, 13 Nov 1940.

McGarry, Garry: b. Franklin, PA, 17 Oct 1889; d. New York, NY, 15 Nov 1927.

McGaugh, Wilbur: b. California, 12 Mar 1895; d. Los Angeles, CA, 31 Jan 1965.

McGee, James L.: b. Brownsville, NE, 7 Jun 1873; d. Los Angeles, CA, 15 Feb 1936.

MacGill, Moyna: b. Belfast, Ire, 10 Dec 1895; d. Santa Monica, CA, 25 Nov 1975.

McGlynn, Frank: b. San Francisco, CA, 26 Oct 1866; d. Newburgh, NY, 18 May 1951.

McGlynn, Frank, Jr.: b. Marin County, CA, 9 Jul 1904; d. 29 Mar 1939.

McGowan, John P.: b. Terowie, Austral, 24 Feb 1880; d. Los Angeles, CA, 26 Mar 1952.

McGowan, Jack W.: b. Muskegon, MI, 1892; d. New York, NY, 28 May 1977.

McGrail, Walter: b. Brooklyn, NY, 19 Oct 1888; d. San Francisco, CA, 19 Mar 1970.

McGrath, Larry: b. New York State, 28 Aug 1888; d. Los Angeles, CA, 6 Jul 1960.

McGrath, Thomas: b. 1867; d. Fort Wayne, IN, 22 Apr 1937.

McGraw, John J.: b. Truxton, NY, 7 Apr 1873; d. New York, NY, 24 Feb 1934.

MacGregor, Harmon: b. New York, NY, 1889; d. Marblehead, MA, 4 Dec 1948.

McGregor, Malcolm: b. Newark, NJ, 13 Oct 1892; d. Los Angeles, CA, 29 Apr 1945.

MacGregor, Norval: b. River Falls, WI, 3 Apr 1862; d. 21 Nov 1933.

McGuire, Benjamin: b. 1875; d. New York, NY, 10 Apr 1925.

McGuire, Kathryn: b. Peoria, IL, 6 Dec 1903; d. Los Angeles, CA, 10 Oct 1978.

McGuire, Tom: b. Milford, CT, 1 Sep 1869; d. Los Angeles, CA, 6 May 1954.

McHugh, Catherine: b. Montana, 1870; d. Los Angeles, CA, 25 Mar 1954,

McHugh, Charles P.: b. Philadelphia, PA, 20 Jul 1870; d. Los Angeles, CA, 21 Oct 1931.

McHugh, Frank: b. Homestead, PA, 23 May 1899; d. Greenwich, CT, 11 Sep 1981.

McHugh, Grace: b. 1888; d. Canon City, CO, 1 Jul 1914.

McHugh, Jack: b. Montana, 1913; d. Las Vegas, NV, 13 Jan 1983.

McHugh, Matt: b. Connellsville, PA, 22 Jan 1894; d. North Ridge, CA, 22 Feb 1971.

McIllwain, William A.: b. 1862; d. Los Angeles, CA, 27 May 1933.

McInnis, John (Stuffy): b. Gloucester, MA, 19 Sep 1890; d. Ipswich, MA, 16 Feb 1960.

McIntosh, Burr: b. Wellsville, OH, 21 Aug 1862; d. Los Angeles, CA, 28 Apr 1942.

McIntyre, Frank: b. Ann Arbor, MI, 25 Feb 1879; d. Ann Arbor, MI, 8 Jun 1949.

McIntyre, Molly: b. Glasgow, Scot, ????; d. New York, NY, 29 Jan 1952.

McIvor, Mary: b. Barnesville, OH, 31 Aug 1904; d. Los Angeles, CA, 28 Feb 1941.

Mack, Andrew: b. Boston, MA, 25 Jul 1863; d. Bayside, NY, 21 May 1931.

Mack, Betty: b. Illinois, 30 Nov 1901; d. Placerville, CA, 5 Nov 1980.

Mack, Billy: b. ????; d. New York, NY, 27 Jan 1961.

Mack, Charles: b. 1878; d. Los Angeles, CA, 29 Nov 1956.

Mack, Charles E.: b. White Cloud, KS, 22 Nov 1887; d. Mesa, AZ, 11 Jan 1934.

Mack, Charles Emmett: b. Scranton, PA, 25 Nov 1900; d. Riverside, CA, 17 Mar 1927.

Mack, Dick: b. 1854; d. San Francisco, CA, 4 Feb 1920.

Mack, George E.: b. Boston, MA, 1866; d. Cheyenne, WY, 20 May 1948.

Mack, Hayward: b. Albany, NY, 1879; d. Los Angeles, CA, 24 Dec 1921.

Mack, Helen: b. Rock Island, IL, 13 Nov 1913; d. Beverly Hills, CA, 13 Aug 1986.

Mack, Hughie: b. Brooklyn, NY, 1884; d. Santa Monica, CA, 13 Oct 1927.

Mack, James T.: b. Chicago, IL, 1871; d. Los Angeles, CA, 12 Aug 1948.

Mack, Joseph P.: b. Boleneva, Italy, 4 May 1878; d. Los Angeles, CA, 8 Apr 1946.

Mack, Max: b. Halberstadt, Ger, 21 Oct 1884; d. London, Eng, ? Mar 1973.

Mack, Rose: b. 1866; d. New York, NY, 9 Oct 1927.

Mack, Wilbur: b. Binghamton, NY, 29 Jul 1873; d. Los Angeles, CA, 13 Mar 1964.

Mack, Willard: b. Morrisburgh, Ont, Can, 18 Sep 1873; d. Brentwood Heights, CA, 18 Nov 1934.

Mack, William B.: b. Bay City, MI, 8 Apr 1872; d. Islip, NY, 13 Sep 1955.

Mackaill, Dorothy: b. Hull, Eng, 4 Mar 1903; d. Honolulu, HI, 12 Aug 1990.

Mackay, Charles D.: b. Philadelphia, PA, 15 Oct 1867; d. Fort Lee, NJ, 19 Nov 1935.

Mackay, Edward J.: b. 1874; d. Elizabeth, NJ, 26 Dec 1948.

Mackaye, Dorothy: b. 1898; d. Los Angeles, CA, 5 Jan 1940.

McKee, Lafayette: b. Morrison, IL, 23 Jan 1872; d. Temple City, CA, 10 Aug 1959.

McKee, Raymond: b. Indiana, 7 Dec 1892; d. Long Beach, CA, 3 Oct 1984.

McKee, Scott A.: b. Glasgow, Scot, 9 May 1881; d. Los Angeles Co, CA, 17 Apr 1945.

McKeen, Lawrence, Jr. (Snookums): b. 1 Sep 1924; d. Los Angeles, CA, 2 Apr 1933.

MacKenna, Kenneth: b. Canterbury, NH, 19 Aug 1899; d. Los Angeles, CA, 15 Jan 1962.

McKentry, Elizabeth: b. 1899; d. New York, NY, 3 Sep 1920.

MacKenzie, Donald: b. Edinburgh, Scot, 17 Apr 1879; d. Jersey City, NJ, 21 Jul 1972.

McKenzie, Ella: b. 19??; d. Los Angeles, CA, 23 Apr 1987.

McKenzie, Ida Mae: b. 1912; d. Los Angeles, CA, 29 Jun 1986.

MacKenzie, Murdock: b. 18??; d. 28 Oct 1923.

McKenzie, Robert B.: b. Ballymania, Ire, 22 Sep 1880; d. Manunuck, RI, 8 Jul 1949.

McKey, William: b. Louisiana, 1862; d. New York, NY, 3 Jan 1918.

McKim, Robert: b. San Jacinto, CA, 26 Aug 1886; d. Los Angeles, CA, 4 Jun 1927.

Mackin, William: b. 1883; d. Los Angeles, CA, 9 Sep 1928.

McKinnel, Norman: b. Maxwellton, New Bruns, Can, 10 Feb 1870; d. London, Eng, 29 Mar 1932.

McKinnon, Al, b. San Francisco, CA, 18??; d. San Francisco, CA, 11 Jan 1927.

Mackley, Arthur J.: b. Portsmouth, Eng, 3 Jul 1865; d. Los Angeles, CA, 21 Dec 1926.

McKnight, Anna: b. 1908; d. Los Angeles, CA, 25 Mar 1930.

McLaglen, Clifford: b. Capetown, So Africa, 1892; d. Huddersfield, Yorks, Eng, ? Sep 1978.

MeLaglen, Cyril: b. England, 9 Sep 1899; d. Ferris, CA, 11 Jul 1987.

McLeglen, Kenneth: b. England, 1901; d. 20 Jan 1979.

McLaglen, Victor: b. Tunbridge Wells, Kent, Eng, 10 Dec 1886; d. Newport Beach, CA, 7 Nov 1959.

MacLane, Barton: b. Columbia, SC, 25 Dec 1902; d. Santa Monica, CA, 1 Jan 1969.

MacLane, Mary: b. Winnipeg, Can, 2 May 1881; d. Chicago, IL, 6 Aug 1929.

MacLaren, Ian: b. Lynmouth, Devon, Eng, 1 May 1875; d. Woodland Hills, CA, 10 Apr 1952.

MacLaren, Mary: b. Pittsburgh, PA, 19 Jan 1896; d. West Hollywood, CA, 9 Nov 1985.

McLarnie, Thomas: b. North Adams, MA, 1871; d. Brighton, MA, 1 Dec 1931.

McLaughlin, Gibb: b. Sunderland, Eng, 19 Jul 1884; d. 1960.

McLaughlin, Harry (Tex): b. 18??; d. Syracuse, NY, 21 Sep 1920.

MacLean, Douglas: b. Philadelphia, PA, 10 Jan 1890; d. Beverly Hills, CA, 9 Jul 1967.

McLean, Larry: b. Cambridge, MA, 18 Jul 1881; d. Boston, MA, 14 Mar 1921.

MacLean, R. D.: b. New Orleans, LA, 7 Mar 1859; d. Los Angeles, CA, 27 Jun 1948.

McLennan, Rodney: b. Melbourne, Austral, 28 Dec 1901; d. 27 Nov 1973.

McLeod, Elsie: b. c. 1890; d. 19??.

McLeod, Tex (Alexander): b. Gonzales, TX, 11 Nov 1889; d. Brighton, Eng, 12 Feb 1973.

McManus, George: b. St. Louis, MO. 23 Jan 1884; d. Santa Monica, CA, 22 Oct 1954.

MacMillan, Violet: b. Grand Rapids, MI, 4 Mar 1887; d. Grand Rapids, MI, 28 Dec 1953.

McMurphy, Charles: b. North Vernon, IN, 31 Jul 1892; d. Los Angeles Co, CA, 24 Oct 1969.

McNamara, Ted: b. Australia, 1868; d. Ventura, CA, 3 Feb 1928,

McNamee, Donald: b. 1897; d. Los Angeles, CA, 17 Jul 1940.

McNamee, Graham: b. Washington, DC, 10 Jul 1888; d. New York, NY, 9 May 1942.

McNaughton, Charles: b. Walthamstow, Essex, Eng, 24 Apr 1878; d. Los Angeles Co, CA, 4 Dec 1955.

McNaughton, Harry: b. Englahd 1896; d. Amityville, NY, 26 Feb 1967.

MacNaughton, Tom: b. England, 1 Jul 1867; d. St. Albans, Eng, 28 Nov 1923.

McNeil, Frank A.: b. Missouri, 18 Nov 1867; d. Los Angeles, CA, 27 Feb 1918,

McNeil, Norman: b. Charleston, SC, 27 Oct 1891; d. 17 Dec 1938.

McNish, Frank E.: b. Camden, NJ, 14 Dec 1853; d. Chicago, IL, 27 Dec 1924.

McNulty, Harold: b. 1903; d. Los Angeles, CA, 6 Jun 1978.

Macollum, Barry: b. Ireland, 6 Apr 1889; d. West Los Angeles, CA, 22 Feb 1971.

MacPherson, Harry Fransworth: b. 1882; d. Sawtelle, CA, 5 Aug 1951,

MacPherson, Jeanie: b. Boston, MA, 18 May 1887; d. Los Angeles, CA, 26 Aug 1946.

MacQuarrie, Albert: b. San Francisco, CA, 8 Jan 1882; d. Los Angeles, CA, 17 Feb 1950.

MacQuarrie, Frank M: b. San Francisco, CA, 27 Jan 1875; d. Los Angeles, CA, 25 Dec 1950.

MacQuarrie, Murdoch: b. San Francisco, CA, 25 Aug 1878; d. Los Angeles, CA, 20 Aug 1942.

McQuoid, Buddie (Edwin): b. 1910; d. Los Angeles, CA, 15 Jul 1950.

McQuoid, Rose Lee: b. Arizona, 26 Oct 1886; d. Los Angeles, CA, 4 May 1962.

McRae, Bruce: b. India, 15 Jan 1867; d. New York, NY, 7 May 1927.

McRae, Duncan; b. London, Eng, 1881; d. London, Eng, 4 Feb 1931.

MacRae, Gordon: b. East Orange, NJ, 12 Mar 1921; d. Lincoln, NE, 24 Jan 1986.

McVeigh, John: b. 1875; d. 2 Jul 1914.

McWade, Edward: b. Washington, DC, 14 Jan 1865; d. Los Angeles, CA, 17 May 1943.

McWade, Margaret: b. Illinois, 3 Sep 1872; d. Los Angeles, CA, 1 Apr 1956.

McWade, Robert, Sr.: b. Long Sault Rapids, Can, 25 Jan 1835; d. New York, NY, 5 Mar 1913.

McWade, Robert, Jr.: b. Buffalo, NY, 17 Jun 1872; d. Culver City, CA, 19 Jan 1938.

Macy, Carlton: b. 1861; d. Bay Shore, NY, 17 Oct 1946.

Macy, Maud Hall: b. 1881; d. Liberty, NY, 1 May 1938.

Madden, Golda: b. Nebraska, 17 Jul 1886; d. Los Angeles, CA, 26 Oct 1960.

Madison, Cleo: b. Bloomington, IL, 1883; d. Burbank, CA, 11 Mar 1964.

Madison, Harry: b. 1877; d. Los Angeles, CA, 8 Jul 1936.

Madsen, Harald: b. Silkeborg, Denmark, 20 Nov 1890; d. 13 Jul 1949.

Magee, Harriett: b. 1878; d. Los Angeles, CA, 19 Apr 1954.

Maggi, Luigi: b. Turin, Italy, 21 Dec 1867; d. Turin, Italy, 22 Aug 1946.

Magri, Count Primo: b. 1849; d. Middlesboro, MA, 31 Oct 1920.

Magrill, George: b. Brooklyn, NY, 5 Jan 1900; d. Los Angeles, CA, 30 May 1952.

Maguire, Edward: b. 1867; d. New York, NY. 10 Apr 1925.

Maguire, Thomas: b. Milford, CT, 7 Sep 1869; d. North Hollywood, CA, 21 Jun 1934.

Mahoney, Wilkie: b. San Miguel, CA, 1897; d. Los Gatos, CA, 30 Jul 1976.

Mahoney, Will: b. Helena, MT, 5 Feb 1894; d. Melbourne, Austral, 9 Feb 1967.

Maigne, Charles: b. Richmond, VA, 11 Nov 1881; d. San Francisco, CA, 28 Nov 1929.

Mailes, Charles H.: b. Halifax, Nova Scotia, Can, 25 May 1870; d. Los Angeles, CA, 17 Feb 1937.

Maines, Dan: b. 1868; d. Los Angeles, CA, 2 Jan 1934.

Maiori, Antonio: b. 1869; d. Brooklyn, NY, 30 Jul 1938.

Maison, Edna: b. San Francisco, CA, 17 Aug 1892; d. Los Angeles, CA, 11 Jan 1946.

Maitland, Gertrude: b. Boston, MA, 1880; d. New York, NY, 28 Dec 1938.

Maitland, Lauderdale: b. London, Eng, 1877; d. London, Eng, 28 Feb 1929.

Maja, Zelma: b. Sweden, 11 Feb 1883; d. Palo Alto, CA, 28 May 1972.

Majeroni, George: b. Melbourne, Austral, 11 Jan 1877; d. Saranac Lake, NY, 5 Aug 1924.

Majeroni, Mario: b. Italy, 1870; d. New York, NY, 18 Nov 1931.

Makarenko, Daniel: b. 1879; d. Philadelphia, PA, 6 Mar 1957.

Malan, William: b. New York, NY, 2 Nov 1867; d. Los Angeles, CA, 13 Feb 1941.

Malatesta, Fred: b. Naples, Italy, 18 Apr 1889; d. Burbank, CA, 8 Apr 1952.

Maley, Denman: b. Holyoke, MA, 1876; d. Collingsworth, NJ, 22 May 1927.

Maljan, Abdul (Terrible Turk): b. 1882; d. Los Angeles, CA, 7 Sep 1944.

Malleson, Miles: b. Croydon, Eng, 25 May 1888; d. London, Eng, 15 Mar 1969.

Mallon, Catherine: b. 9 Mar 1906; d. Los Angeles, CA, 13 Feb 1929.

Malloy, John J.: b. Dover, DE, 1898; d. Los Angeles, CA, 9 Feb 1968.

Malone, Florence: b. ????; d. Lyons, NY, 4 Mar 1956.

Malone, Molly (Edith Greaves): b. 1889; d. Los Angeles, CA, 14 Feb 1952.

Maloney, Leo D.: b. San Jose, CA, 1888; d. New York, NY, 2 Nov 1929.

Mandel, Frances Wakefield: b. 1891; d. Batavia, NY; 26 Mar 1943.

Mander, Miles: b. Wolverhampton, Eng, 14 May 1888; d. Los Angeles, CA, 8 Feb 1946.

Mandeville, William C.: b. Louisville, KY, 1867; d. New York, NY, 19 Apr 1917.

Mandy, Jerry: b. Utica, NY, 5 Jun 1892; d. Los Angeles, CA, 1 May 1945.

Manes, Gina: b. Paris, Fr, 7 Apr 1893; d. Toulouse, Fr, 6 Sep 1989.

Manley, Charles (Daddy): b. Ireland, 25 Sep 1830; d. Los Angeles, CA, 26 Feb 1916.

Mann, Bertha: b. Atlanta, GA, 21 Oct 1893; d. Los Angeles, CA, 20 Dec 1967.

Mann, Cato: b. 1887; d. Belleaire Bluffs, FL, 14 Dec 1977.

Mann, Hank (David W. Lieberman): b. New York, NY, 28 May 1887; d. South Pasadena, CA, 25 Nov 1971.

Mann, Louis: b. New York, NY, 20 Apr 1865; d. New York; NY, 15 Feb 1931.

Mann, Margaret: b. Aberdeen, Scot, b Apr 1868; d. Los Angeles, CA, 4 Feb 1941.

Mann, Ned H.: b. Redkey, IN, 1893; d. La Jolla, CA, 1 Jul 1967.

Mann, Stanley: b. England, 30 Aug 1883; d. Los Angeles, CA, 10 Aug 1953.

Mannering, Lewin: b. Poland, 19 Jan 1876; d. London, Eng, 7 Jun 1932.

Manners, Lady Diana: b. London, Eng, 29 Aug 1892; d. London, Eng, 16 Jun 1986.

Mannes, Florence Vensen: b. 1896; d. Los Angeles, CA, 30 Oct 1964.

Mannheim, Lucie: b. Berlin, Ger, 30 Apr 1895; d. Braunlage, Ger, 28 Jul 1976.

Manning, Aileen: b. Boulder, CO, 20 Jan 1886; d. Los Angeles, CA, 25 Mar 1946.

Manning, Ambrose: b. 1861; d. Brixham, Eng, 22 Mar 1940.

Manning, Jack: b. 1880; d. Yonkers, NY, 18 Jun 1938.

Manning, Joseph: b. 18??; d. Los Angeles, CA, 31 Jul 1946.

Manning, Marjorie: b. 1898; d. Los Angeles, CA, 3 Jun 1922.

Manon, Marcia (Camille Ankewich): b. Paris, Fr, 28 Oct 18??; d. Victorville, CA, 12 Apr 1973.

Mansfield, Alice: b. 1858; d. 17 Feb 1938.

Mansfield, Duncan: b. 1897; d. Los Angeles, CA, 15 Sep 1971.

Mansfield, Lucille (Pauline Daly); b. 1890; d. Santa Monica, CA, 14 Aug 1981.

Mansfield, Martha: b. Mansfield, OH, 14 Jul 1899; d. San Antonio, TX, 30 Nov 1923.

Mantell, Robert Bruce: b. Irvine, Scot, 7 Feb 1854; d. Atlantic Highlands, NJ, 27 Jun 1928.

Mantell, Robert Bruce, Jr.: b. Atlantic Highlands, NJ, 1909; d. Los Angeles, CA, 24 Oct 1933.

Manzini, Italia Almirante: b. Taranto, Italy, 1890; d. ? Oct 1941.

Marba, Joseph: b. Peabody, MA, 19 Oct 1879; d. 7 Sep 1938.

Marble, John S.: b. Buffalo, NY, 18 May 1844; d. New York, NY, 23 Jun 1919.

Marburgh, Bertram: b. New York, 17 May 1875; d. Woodland Hills, CA, 22 Aug 1956.

Marceline (Marceline Orbes): b. Zaragoza, Spain 15 May 1873; d. New York, NY, 5 Nov 1927.

March, Frederic: b. Racine, WI, 31 Aug 1897; d. Los Angeles, CA, 14 Apr 1975.

Marchal, Arlette: b. Paris, Fr, 29 Jan 1902; d. Paris, Fr, 9 Feb 1984.

Marche, Gazelle: b. Utica, NY, 1892; d. New York, NY, 26 Feb 1935.

Marcotti, Margaret: b. Los Angeles, CA, 1913; d. San Diego, CA, 8 Apr 1985.

Marcus, James: b. New York, NY, 21 Jan 1867; d. Los Angeles, CA, 15 Oct 1937.

Maretskaya, Vera Petrovana: b. Moscow, Russ, 1906; d. Moscow, Russ, ? Aug 1978.

Margolis, Charles (Doc): b. 1874; d. Glendale, CA, 22 Sep 1926.

Mari, Febo: b. Messina, Italy, 18 Jan 1884; d. 6 Jun 1939.

Marievsky, Josef: b. Russia, 1 Jan 1888; d. 27 Apr 1971.

Marinoff, Fania: b. Odessa, Russ, 20 Mar 1890; d. Englewood, NJ, 17 Nov 1971.

Marion, Edna: b. Chicago, IL, 12 Dec 1906; d. Los Angeles, CA, 2 Dec 1957.

Marion, Frances: b. San Francisco, CA, 18 Nov 1888; d. Los Angeles, CA, 12 May 1973.

Marion, George F., Sr.: b. San Francisco, CA, 16 Jul 1860; d. Carmel, CA, 30 Nov 1945.

Marion, Oskar: b. 2 Apr 1896; d. ? Mar 1986.

Marion, William: b. California, 12 Jan 1878; d. Los Angeles Co, CA, 3 Jan 1957.

Maris, Mona: b. Buenos Aires, Arg, 7 Nov 1903; d. Buenos Aires, Arg, 23 Mar 1991.

Mark, Michael: b. Russia, 15 Mar 1886; d. Woodland Hills, CA, 3 Feb 1975.

Marke, Sid: b. 1896; d. Pittsburgh, PA, 30 May 1985.

Markey, Enid: b. Dillon, CO, 22 Feb 1896; d. Bay Shore, NY, 15 Nov 1981.

Marks, Lou: b. 1895; d. Little Neck, NY, 11 Dec 1987.

Marks, Willis: b. Rochester, MN, 20 Aug 1865; d. Los Angeles, CA, 6 Dec 1952.

Marlborough, Leah: b. 1869; d. 21 Dec 1953.

Marlo, George M.: b. New York, NY, 1884; d. New York, NY, 5 Feb 1970.

Marlowe, James C.: b. 1865; d. New York, NY, 4 Sep 1926.

Marlowe, June: b. St. Cloud, MN, 6 Nov 1903; d. Burbank, CA, 10 Mar 1984.

Marmont, Percy: b. London, Eng, 25 Nov 1883; d. London, Eng, 3 Mar 1977.

Marnac, Jeanne: b. 1896; d. 1976.

Marquard, Rube: b. Cleveland, OH, 1889; d. Baltimore, MD, 2 Jun 1980.

Marr, Hans: b. Breslau, Poland, 22 Jul 1878; d. 30 Mar 1949.

Marr, William: b. San Francisco, CA, 1893; d. New York, NY, 15 May 1960.

Marriott, Charles: b. London, Eng, 1859; d. Los Angeles, CA, 7 Dec 1917.

Marriott, Moore: b. West Drayton, Eng, 14 Sep 1885; d. London, Eng, 11 Dec 1949.

Mars, Severin: b. 1878; d. 17 Jul 1921.

Marsh, Della: b. 18??; d. Ithaca, NY, 6 May 1973.

Marsh, Mae: b. Madrid, NM, 9 Nov 1895; d. Hermosa Beach, CA, 13 Feb 1968.

Marsh, Marguerite (Marguerite Loveridge): b. Lawrence, KS, 1892; d. New York, NY, 8 Dec 1925.

Marsh, Mitzie (Mother): b. 18??; d. Los Angeles, CA, 22 Feb 1928.

Marshall, Boyd: b. Fort Clinton, OH, 1885; d. New York, NY, 9 Nov 1950.

Marshall, George E.: b. Chicago, IL, 29 Dec 1891; d. Los Angeles, CA, 17 Feb 1975.

Marshall, Herbert: b. London, Eng, 23 May 1890; d. Beverly Hills, CA, 22 Jan 1966.

Marshall, Tully: b. Nevada City, CA, 13 Apr 1864; d. Encino, CA, 10 Mar 1943.

Marstini, Rosita: b. Nancy, Fr, 19 Sep 1887; d. Los Angeles, CA, 24 Apr 1948.

Martell, Alphonse: b. Strasbourg, Fr, 27 Mar 1890; d. San Diego Co, CA, 18 Mar 1976.

Martin, Chris-Pin: b. Tucson, AZ, 19 Nov 1893; d. Los Angeles, CA, 27 Jun 1953.

Martin, Frank Wells: b. 1880; d. Los Angeles, CA, 9 Aug 1941.

Martin, Glenn L.: b. Marksburg, IA, 17 Jan 1886; d. Baltimore, MD, 4 Dec 1955.

Martin, Jacques: b. 1853; d. New York, NY, 15 Aug 1917.

Martin, Mrs. Jacques: b. 1863; d. New York, NY, 11 Jul 1936.

Martin, John E.: b. Philadelphia, PA, 1855; d. New York, NY, 22 Nov 1933.

Martin, Silver Moon (Michael); b. 1891; d. Comanche, OK, 20 Jan 1969.

Martin, Townsend: b. New York, NY, 1896; d. New York, NY, 22 Nov 1951.

Martin, Vivian: b. Sparata, MI, 22 Jul 1893; d. New York, NY, 16 May 1987.

Martindel, Edward: b. Hamilton, OH, 28 Jul 1873; d. Woodland Hills, CA, 4 May 1955.

Martin-Harvey, Sir John: b. Wivenhoe, Essex, Eng, 22 Jun 1867; d. London, Eng, 14 May 1944.

Martin-Harvey, Muriel: b. London, Eng, 4 Oct 1891; d. Northwood, Middlesex, Eng, 15 Dec 1988.

Martinoff, M. T.: b. 18??; d. Koslov, Russ, 1928.

Marx, Harpo: b. New York, NY, 23 Nov 1888; d. Los Angeles, CA, 28 Sep 1964.

Marx, Max: b. 18??; d. Universal City, CA, 1925.

Masi, Philip W.: b. Norfolk, VA, 1888; d. New York, NY, 12 Dec 1922.

Mason, Ann: b. Virginia, 1898; d. New York, NY, 6 Feb 1948.

Mason, Buddy: b. Pennsylvania, 30 Oct 1902; d. Woodland Hills, CA, 15 Apr 1975.

Mason, Dan: b. Syracuse, NY, 9 Feb 1857; d. Baersville, NY, 6 Jul 1929.

Mason, Eliza: b. England, ????; d. New York, NY, 21 Jan 1925.

Mason, Evelyn M.: b. 1892; d. Los Angeles, CA, 29 Oct 1926.

Mason, Gregory: b. 1889; d. Greenwich, CT, 29 Nov 1968.

Mason, Haddon: b. London, Eng, 21 Feb 1898; d. London, Eng, 30 Apr 1966.
Mason, James: b. Paris, Fr, 3 Feb 1889; d. Los Angeles, CA, 7 Nov 1959.
Mason, John B.: b. Orange, NJ, 28 Oct 1858; d. Stamford, CT, 12 Jan 1919.
Mason, Leroy: b. Baltimore, MD, 2 Jul 1903; d. Los Angeles, CA, 13 Oct 1947.
Mason, Louis: b. Danville, KY, 1 Jun 1888; d. Los Angeles, CA, 12 Nov 1959.
Mason, Margery Land: b. ????; d. Tucson, AZ, 21 Nov 1968.
Mason, Mary: b. Pasadena, CA, 1911; d. New York, NY, 13 Oct 1980.
Mason, Reginald: b. San Francisco, CA, 27 Jun 1875; d. Hermosa Beach, CA, 10 Jul 1962.
Mason, Shirley: b. Brooklyn, NY, 6 Jun 1901; d. Los Angeles, CA, 27 Jul 1979.
Mason, Sidney L.: b. Paterson, NJ, 1886; d. New York, NY, 1 Mar 1923.
Mason, William (Smiling Billy): b. 1888; d. Orange, NJ, 24 Jan 1941.
Masson, Tom: b. Essex, CT, 21 Jul 1866; d. Glen Ridge, NJ, 18 Jun 1934.
Mathe, Edouard: b. 1886; d. 1934.
Mather, Sydney: b. 1876; d. New York, NY, 18 Apr 1925.
Mathes, Allen: b. 1885; d. New York, NY, 13 Aug 1934.
Mathewson, Christy: b. Factoryville, PA, 12 Aug 1880; d. Saranac Lake, NY, 7 Oct 1925.
Mathot, Leon: b. France, 5 Mar 1896; d. Paris, Fr, 6 Mar 1968.
Matieson, Otto: b. Copenhagen, Denmark, 27 Mar 1893; d. Stafford, AZ, 19 Feb 1932.
Matray, Frnst: b. Budapest, Hungary, 27 May 1891; d. Los Angeles, CA, 12 Nov 1978.
Matson, Thomas: b. 1888; d. Woodland Hills, CA, 1 Feb 1978.
Matthews, A. E. (Matty): b. Bridlington, York, Eng, 22 Nov 1869; d. Bushy Heath, Eng, 25 Jul 1960.
Matthews, Dorcas: b. England, 5 Nov 1890; d. Berkley, CA, 24 Jan 1969.
Matthews, Dorothy: b. New York, NY, 13 Feb 1912; d. Los Angeles, CA, 18 May 1977.
Matthews, Jessie: b. London, Eng, 11 Mar 1907; d. London, Eng, 19 Aug 1981.
Matthews, Junius Conyers: b. Illinois, 12 Jun 1890; d. Los Angeles Co, CA, 18 Jan 1978.
Matthison, Edith Wynne: b. Birmingham, Eng, 23 Nov 1875; d. Los Angeles, CA, 23 Sep 1955.
Mattox, Martha: b. Natchez, MS, 1879; d. Sidney, NY, 2 May 1933.
Mattraw, Scotty: b. Evans Mills, NY, 19 Oct 1880; d. Los Angeles, CA, 9 Nov 1946.
Maturin, Eric: b. India, 30 May 1883; d. London, Eng, 17 Oct 1957.

Maude, Arthur: b. Pontefract, York, Eng, 1881; d. 19??.

Maude, Beatrice: b. California, 22 Jul 1892; d. Los Angeles, CA, 14 Oct 1984.

Maude, Charles R.: b. 1882; d. 14 Nov 1943.

Maude, Cyril: b. London, Eng, 24 Apr 1862; d. Torquay, Devon, Eng, 20 Feb 1951.

Maupain, Ernest (Ernest Maupi): b. Toulon, Fr, 1881; d. France, 10 Jan 1949.

Maurice (Maurice O.L. Mouvet); b. 17 Mar 1887; d. Lausanne, Switz, 18 May 1927.

Maurice, Mary: b. Morristown, OH, 15 Nov 1844; d. Port Carbon, PA, 30 Apr 1918.

Maurice, Newman: b. 18??; d. London, Eng, 11 Sep 1920.

Maurus, Gerda: b. Croatia, 25 Aug 1909; d. Duesseldorf, Ger, 25 Aug 1968.

Mawson, Edward R.: b. 1862; d. New York, NY, 20 May 1917.

Maxam, Louella: b. St. Augustine, FL, 10 Jun 1896; d. Burbank, CA, 3 Sep 1970,

Maxim, Hudson: b. Orneville, ME, 3 Feb 1853; d. Hopatocong, NJ, 6 May 1927.

Maximov, Vladimir: b. 27 Jul 1880; d. 22 Mar 1937.

Maxwell, Jane: b. 1851; d. Wilmington, CA, ? Aug 1924.

Maxwell, Vera: b. New York, NY, 1892; d. New York, NY, 1 May 1950.

Maxwell-Willshire, Gerard: b. 1893; d. London, Eng, 3 Apr 1947.

May, Alyce: b. Los Angeles, CA, c. 1915; d. Rose Rito Beach, Mex, 31 Dec 1980.

May, Ann: b. Cincinnati, OH, 25 Nov 1899; d. Los Angeles, CA, 26 Jul 1985.

May, Doris (Doris Lee,): b. Seattle, WA, 15 Oct 1902; d. Camarillo, CA, 12 May 1984.

May, Edna: b. Syracuse, NY, 2 Sep 1875; d. Lausanne, Switz, 2 Jan 1948.

May, Eva: b. 1901; d. Baden, Austria, 11 Sep 1924.

May, Harold R.: b. 1903; d. Los Angeles, CA, 16 Sep. 1973.

May, Mia: b. Vienna, Austria, 2 Jun 1884; d. Los Angeles, CA, 28 Nov 1980.

Mayakovsky, Vladimir: b. Bagdadi, Georgia, 19 Jul 1893; d. Moscow, Russ, 14 Apr 1930.

Mayall, Herschel, b. Warren County, KY, 12 Jul 1863; d. Detroit, MI, 10 Jun 1941.

Maydoch, John: b. 1894; d. New York, NY, ? Jan 1918.

Maye, Jimsy: b. Spokane, WA, 1893; d. Jackson, OR, 10 Apr 1968.

Maye, Leola: b. 1891; d. Glendale, CA, 17 Apr 1928.

Mayhew, Kate: b. Indianapolis, IN, 2 Sep 1853; d. New York, NY, 16 Jun 1944.

Maynard, Harry: b. 1898; d. Saratoga, CA, 23 Jul 1976.

Maynard, Ken: b. Vevey, IN, 21 Jul 1895; d. Woodland Hills, CA, 23 Mar 1973.

Maynard, Kermit: b. Vevey, IN, 20 Sep 1897; d. North Hollywood, CA, 16 Jan 1971.

Mayne, Clarice: b. London, Eng, 6 Feb 1886; d. London, Eng, 16 Jan 1966.

Mayne, Eric: b. Dublin, Ire, 28 Apr 1865; d. Los Angeles, 9 Feb 1947.

Mayne, Ernie: b. 1874; d. Brighton, Eng, 15 May 1937.

Mayo, Albert: b. 1887; d. Los Angeles, CA, 20 May 1933.

Mayo, Archie: b. New York, NY, 1891; d. Guadalajara, Mex, 4 Dec 1968.

Mayo, Edna: b. Philadelphia, PA, 23 Mar 1895; d. San Francisco, CA, 5 May 1970.

Mayo, Frank: b. New York, NY, 28 Jun 1889; d. Laguna Beach, CA, 9 Jul 1963.

Mayo, Harry: b. Helena, MT, 11 Mar 1898; d. Woodland Hills, CA, 6 Jan 1964.

Mayo, Margaret: b. Brownsville, IL, 19 Nov 1882; d. Ossining, NY, 25 Feb 1951.

Mayo, Rose: b. 1877; d. Atlantic City, NJ, 25 Jul 1936.

Mdivani, David (David Manor): b. Batumi, Georgia, 4 Feb 1904; d. Los Angeles, CA, 5 Aug 1984.

Meade, Charles A.: b. Rutland, VT, 1876; d. New York, NY, 14 Sep 1949.

Meakin, Charles: b. Utah, 2 Oct 1879; d. Los Angeles, CA, 17 Jan 1961.

Meakin, Ruth Eldredge: b. 1879; d. Los Angeles, CA, 3 Nov 1939.

Mears, Benjamin S.: b. 1872; d. Cliffside Park, NJ, 27 Jan 1952.

Measor, Adele: b. Ireland, 2 Sep 1860; d. 9 Jun 1933.

Medcraft, Russell G.: b. 1897; d. New York, NY, 28 Sep 1962.

Meech, Edward: b. 1892; d. Findlay, OH, 2 Mar 1952,

Meech, George T.: b. Chicago, IL, 1866; d. Jamaica, NY, 29 Mar 1941.

Meehan, Lew: b. Minnesota, 7 Sep 1890; d. Los Angeles Co, CA, 10 Aug 1951.

Meehan, William E.: b. New York State, 1885; d. Kingsbridge, NY, 23 Mar 1920.

Meek, Donald: b. Glasgow, Scot, 14 Jul 1878; d. Los Angeles, CA, 18 Nov 1946.

Meek, Kate: b. New York, NY, 1838; d. New York, NY, 4 Sep 1925.

Meeker, George: b. Brooklyn, NY, 5 Mar 1904; d. Carpinteria, CA, 19 Aug 1984.

Mahaffey, Blanche: b. Cincinnati, OH, 28 Jul 1908; d. Los Angeles, CA, 31 Mar 1968.

Mehnert, Lothar: b. Berlin, Ger, 21 Feb 1875; d. 30 Nov 1926.

Meighan, Thomas: b. Pittsburgh, PA, 9 Apr 1879; d. Great Neck, NY, 8 Jul 1936.

Meister, Otto L.: b. 1869; d. Milwaukee, WI, 10 Jul 1944.

Melesh, Alex: b. Kiev, Russ, 28 Oct 1890; d. Los Angeles, CA, 4 Mar 1949.

Melford, Austin: b. Alverstoke, Eng, 21 Aug 1884; d. London, Eng, 19 Aug 1971.

Melford, George H.: b. Rochester, NY, 19 Feb 1877; d. Los Angeles, CA, 25 Apr 1961.

Melford, Louise Leroy: b. 1880; d. North Hollywood, CA, 15 Nov 1942.

Melford, Mark: b. 18??; d. London, Eng, 4 Jan 1914.

Melies, Georges: b. Paris, Fr. 8 Dec 1861; d. Paris, Fr, 21 Jan 1938.

Meller, Raquel: b. Madrid, Spain, 1888; d. Barcelona, Spain, 26 Jul 1962.

Mellish, Fuller, Sr.: b. London, Eng, 3 Jan 1865; d. New York, NY, 7 Dec 1936.

Mellish, Fuller, Jr.: b. 1895; d. Forest Hills, NY, 8 Feb 1930.

Melrose, Rhoda: b. 1892; d. Los Angeles, CA, 25 Feb 1985.

Melville, Emilie: b. Philadelphia, PA, 1852; d. San Francisco, CA, 20 May 1932.

Melville, Rose: b. Terre Haute, IN, 30 Jan 1873; d. Lake George, NY, 8 Oct 1946.

Menahan, Jean: b. ????; d. Washington, DC, 18 May 1963.

Mendes, Lothar: b. Berlin, Ger, 19 May 1894; d. London, Eng, 25 Feb 1974.

Menjou, Adolphe: b. Pittsburgh, PA, 18 Feb 1890; d. Los Angeles, CA, 29 Oct 1963.

Menjou, Henri: b. Pittsburgh, PA, 2 Jun 1891; d. West Los Angeles, CA, 27 Jan 1956.

Mercanton, Jean: b. France, 17 May 1902; d. 5 Nov 1947.

Mercer, Beryl: b. Seville, Spain, 13 Aug 1882; d. Santa Monica, CA, 28 Jul 1939.

Meredith, Anne: b. ????; d. London, Eng, 8 Jan 1961.

Meredith, Charles H.: b. Knoxville, PA, 27 Aug 1894; d. Los Angeles, CA, 28 Nov 1964.

Meredith, Jane: b. 1885; d. New York, NY, 15 Feb 1945.

Meredith, Joan: b. ? Feb 1905; d. Los Angeles, CA, 13 Oct 1980.

Meredyth, Bess: b. Buffalo, NY, 12 Feb 1889; d. Woodland Hills, CA, 13 Jul 1969.

Merivale, Philip: b. Rehutia, India, 2 Nov 1886; d. Los Angeles, CA, 12 Mar 1946.

Merkel, Una: b. Covington, KY, 10 Dec 1903; d. Los Angeles, CA, 2 Jan 1986.

Merkert, Delbert (Bert): b. 1875; d. North East, PA, 28 Jun 1953.

Merkle, Fred: b. Watertown, WI, 10 Dec 1888; d. Daytona Beach, FL, 2 Mar 1956.

Merkyl, Wilmuth (John Merkyl); b. Iowa, 2 Jun 1885; d. Los Angeles, CA, 1 May 1954.

Merlo, Anthony: b. Italy, 1 Oct 1886; d. Woodland Hills, CA, 25 Apr 1976.

Merriam, Charlotte: b. Sheridan, IL, 5 Apr 1906; d. Los Angeles, CA, 10 Jul 1972.

Merriam, Harold A.: b. 1876; d. Elmsford, NY, 21 Dec 1937.

Merrick, Tom: b. Hanford, CA, 1894; d. Los Angeles, CA, 26 Apr 1927.

Merrill, Frank: b. Newark, NJ, 21 Mar 1893; d. Los Angeles, CA, 12 Feb 1966.

Merrill, Walter: b. Bangor, PA, 22 Apr 1906; d. Los Angeles, CA, 10 Jan 1985,

Merson, Billy: b. Nottingham, Eng, 29 Mar 1881; d. London, Eng, 25 Jun 1947.

Merton, Collette: b. New Orleans, LA, 7 Mar 1907; d. Los Angeles, CA, 24 Jul 1968.

Messinger, Buddy: b. San Francisco, CA, 26 Oct 1907; d. Los Angeles, CA, 25 Oct 1965.

Messinger, Josephine: b. 1885; d. Los Angeles, CA, 3 Mar 1968.

Messinger, Marie: b. Coeur D'Alene, ID, 1906; d. Woodland Hills, CA, 4 Apr 1987.

Messlein, John: b. 1899; d. Weehawken, NJ, 25 Aug 1920.

Metcalfs Earle: b. Newport, KY, 11 Mar 1890; d. Burbank, CA, 26 Jan 1928.

Metz, Albert: b. 1886; d. North Hollywood, CA, 20 Aug 1940.

Metzetti, Otto: b. 1891; d. Los Angeles, CA, 31 Jan 1949.

Metsetti, Victor: b. 1895; d. Los Angeles, CA, 21 Aug 1949.

Meusel, Bob: b. San Jose, CA, 19 Jul 1896; d. Downey, CA, 28 Nov 1977.

Meusel, Emil (Irish): b. Oakland, CA, 9 Jun 1893; d. Long Beach, CA, 1 Mar 1963.

Meyer, Johannes: b. Brieg, Silesia, 18??; d. Marburg-Lahn, Ger, 25 Jan 1976.

Meyer, Otto: b. Germany, 1851; d. Jamaica, NY, 8 Nov 1921.

Meyer, Torben: b. Copenhagen, Denmark, 1 Dec 1884; d. Woodland Hills, CA, 22 May 1975.

Michel, Gaston: b. France, 1856; d. Lisbon, Port, ? Nov 1921.

Michelena, Beatriz: b. New York, NY, 22 Feb 1890; d. San Francisco, CA, 10 Oct 1942.

Michelena, Vera: b. New York, NY, 16 Jun 1884; d. Bayside, NY, 26 Aug 1961.

Middlemass, Robert M.: b. New Britain, CT, 3 Sep 1885; d. Los Angeles, CA, 11 Sep 1949.

Middleton, Charles: b. Elizabethtown, KY, 3 Oct 1879; d. Los Angeles, CA, 22 Apr 1949.

Midgley, Fannie: b. Cincinnati, OH, 26 Nov 1879; d. Los Angeles, CA, 4 Jan 1932.

Midgley, Florence: b. 1890; d. Los Angeles, CA, 16 Nov 1949.

Mikhoels, Salomon M.: b. Dvinsk, Russ, 1890; d. Moscow, Russ, 1948.

Milar, Adolph: b. Germany, 19 Apr 1886; d. Santa Clara Co. CA, 25 May 1950.

Milash, Robert E.: b. New York, NY, 18 Apr 1885; d. Woodland Hills, CA, 14 Nov 1954.

Milcrest, H. M. (Howard): b. 1892; d. Huachuca Mountains, AZ, 23 Nov 1920.

Miles, David: b. Milford, CT, 1871; d. New York, NY, 28 Oct 1915.

Miles, Gen. Nelson A.: b. Westminster, MA, 8 Aug 1839; d. Washington, DC, 15 May 1925.

Milestone, Lewis: b. Odessa, Russ, 30 Sep 1895; d. Los Angeles, CA, 25 Sep 1980.

Milford, Arthur: b. Lamar, CO. 1902; d. Santa Monica, CA, 23 Dec 1991.

Milford, Bliss: b. c. 1890; d. 19??.

Miljan, John: b. Lead City, SD, 8 Nov 1892; d. Los Angeles, CA, 24 Jan 1960.

Millar, Adelqui: b. Concepcion, Chile, 5 Aug 1891; d. Santiago, Chile, 7 Aug 1956.

Millard, Evelyn: b. London, Eng, 18 Sep 1869; d. London, Eng, 9 Nov 1941.

Millarde, Harry E.: b. Cincinnati, OH, 12 Nov 1885; d. New York, NY, 2 Nov 1931.

Millen, Frank H.: b. 1861; d. Albuquerque, NM, 26 Dec 1931.

Miller, Ashley: b. Cincinnati, OH, 11 Aug 1867; d. New York, NY, 19 Nov 1949.

Miller, Carl: b. Wichita County, TX, 9 Aug 1893; d. Honolulu, HI, ? Feb 1979.

Miller, Diana: b. Seattle, WA, 18 Mar 1902; d. Monrovia, CA, 18 Dec 1927.

Miller, E. G. (Edward): b. Eastbourne, Eng, 22 Dec 1881; d. Los Angeles Co, CA, 1 Dec 1948.

Miller, Gertie: b. 1878; d. Chiddingford, Eng, 25 Apr 1952.

Miller, Harold A.: b. California, 31 May 1894; d. Los Angeles Co, CA, 18 Jul 1972.

Miller, Henry, Jr.: b. 22 May 1889; d. Mexico City, Mex, ? Apr 1927.

Miller, Hugh J.: b. Berwick-on-Tweed, Eng, 22 May 1889; d. Los Angeles, CA, 11 May 1956.

Miller, Jack: b. 1888; d. San Diego, CA, 25 Sep 1928.

Miller, Jane: b. 18??; d. New York, NY, 20 Sep 1936.

Miller, Juanita: b. 1880; d. Oakland, CA, 9 Apr 1970,

Miller, Ruby: b. London, Eng, 14 Jul 1889; d. Chichester, Eng, 2 Apr 1976.

Miller, Ruth: b. 1903; d. Santa Monica, CA, 13 Jun 1981.

Miller, Seton T.: b. Chehalis, WA, 3 May 1902; d. Woodland Hills, CA, 29 Mar 1974.

Miller, W. Chrystie: b. New York, NY, 10 Aug 1843; d. Staten Island, NY, 23 Sep 1922.

Miller, Walter: b. Dayton, OH, 9 Mar 1892; d. Los Angeles, CA, 30 Mar 1940.

Miller, William (Ranger Bill): b. Kutztown, PA, 5 Mar 1887; d. Los Angeles, CA, 12 Nov 1939.

Millett, Arthur Nelson: b. Pittsfield, ME, 21 Apr 1874; d. Los Angeles Co, CA, 24 Feb 1952.

Millman, Bird: b. 1895; d. Canon City, CO, 5 Aug 1940.

Millner, Marietta: b. Vienna, Austria, 1906; d. Badenweiler, Ger, 26 Jun 1929.

Mills, Alyce: b. Pittsburgh, PA, 16 Feb 1899; d. Ft. Lauderdale, FL, 27 Apr 1990.

Mills, Bob: b. Detroit, MI, 1898; d. Colorado, 16 Oct 1934.

Mills, Frank: b. Kendall, MI, 1870; d. Michigan, 11 Jun 1921.

Mills, Frank C.: b. Washington, 26 Jan 1891; d. Los Angeles, CA, 18 Aug 1973.

Mills, Joseph S.: b. 1875; d. Los Angeles, CA, 19 Oct 1935.

Mills, Thomas R.: b. England, 28 Jun 1878; d. Woodland Hills, CA, 29 Nov 1953.

Millsfield, Charles (Monsieur Pompon): b. Netherlands, 6 Nov 1876; d. Los Angeles Co, CA, 18 Sep 1962.

Milne, Minnie: b. Syria, 1872; d. New York, NY, 9 Apr 1932.

Miltern, John: b. New Britain, CT, 13 Jul 1870; d. Los Angeles, CA, 15 Jan 1937.

Milton, Billy: b. London, Eng, 8 Dec 1905; d. Northwood, Eng, 22 Nov 1989.

Milton, Maud: b. Gravesend, Eng, 24 Mar 1859; d. Ryde, Isle of Wright, Eng, 19 Nov 1945.

Milward, Dawson: b. London, Eng, 13 Jul 1870; d. London, Eng, 15 May 1926.

Miner, Daniel: b. 1880; d. Los Angeles, CA, 24 Jun 1938.

Minetti, Maria: b. 18??; d. London, Eng, 9 Dec 1971.

Minter, Mary Miles: b. Shreveport, LA, 1 Apr 1902; d. Santa Monica, CA, 5 Aug 1984.

Minter, William F.: b. 1892; d. Los Angeles, CA, 13 Jul 1937.

Mintz, Jack: b. 1895; d. Woodland Hills, CA, 19 Jan 1983.

Minzey, Frank: b. Massachusetts, 1879; d. Lake George, NY, 12 Nov 1949.

Mistinguett: b. Enghien-les-Bains, Val-d'Oise, Fr, 5 Aug 1875; d. Paris, Fr, 5 Jan 1956.

Mitchell, Abbie: b. 1883; d. New York, NY, 16 Mar 1960.

Mitchell, Belle: b. Michigan, 24 Sep 1889; d. Woodland Hills, CA, 12 Feb 1979.

Mitchell, Bruce: b. Freeport, IL, 16 Nov 1880; d. Los Angeles, CA, 26 Sep 1952.

Mitchell, Charles J.: b. New York, NY, 17 May 1879; d. Los Angeles, CA, 13 Dec 1929.

Mitchell, Dodson: b. Memphis, TN, 23 Jan 1868; d. New York, NY, 2 Jun 1939.

Mitchell, Grant: b. Columbus, OH, 17 Jun 1874; d. Los Angeles, CA, 1 May 1957.

Mitchell, Howard M.: b. Pittsburgh, PA, 11 Dec 1887; d. Los Angeles, CA, 4 Oct 1958.

Mitchell, Leslie: b. Brandon, Manitoba, Can, 1885; d. Vancouver, Can, 25 Oct 1965.

Mitchell, Rhea: b. Portland, OR, 10 Dec 1893; d. Los Angeles, CA, 16 Sep 1957.

Mix, Art (George Kesterson): b. Illinois, 18 Jun 1896; d. Riverside Co, CA, 7 Dec 1972.

Mix, Ruth: b. Dewey, OK, 13 Jul 1912; d. Corpus Christi, TX, 21 Sep 1977.

Mix, Tom: b. DuBois, PA, 6 Jan 1880; d. Florence, AZ. 12 Oct 1940.

Modjeska, Felix B.: b. Omaha, NE, 6 Aug 1887; d. Newport Beach, CA, 29 Mar 1940.

Modot, Gaston: b. Paris, Fr, 30 Dec 1887; d. 19 Feb 1970.

Moehring, Carl F. (Kansas): b. Ohio, 9 Jul 1897; d. Los Angeles Co, CA, 3 Oct 1968.

Mohan, Earl John: b. Pueblo, CO, 1889; d. Los Angeles, CA, 15 Oct 1928.

Mojica, Jose: b. San Gabriel, Mex, 14 Sep 1899; d. Lima, Peru, 20 Sep 1974.

Moldaner, Karin: b. Stockholm, Sweden, 20 May 1889; d. Vardinge/Stockholm, Sweden, 1978.

Molina, Joe: b. Arizona, 23 May 1899; d. Woodland Hills, CA, 16 Dec 1977.

Molyneaux, Eileen: b. Pietermaritzburg, Natal, So Africa, 26 Aug 1893; d. Bryn Mawr, PA, 13 Apr 1962.

Monahan, Joseph A., Sr.: b. 1882; d. Teaneck, NJ, 9 Nov 1931.

Monberg, George: b. Illinois, 9 Aug 1890; d. 7 Mar 1925.

Moncrieff, Murray: b. 18??; d. 21 May 1949.

Moncries, Edward: b. Brooklyn, NY, 1859; d. Los Angeles, CA, 22 Mar 1938.

Mong, William V.: b. Chambersburg, PA, 25 Jun 1875; d. Los Angeles, CA, 11 Dec 1940.

Monica, Maria: b. 1899; d. Las Vegas, NV, 29 Oct 1991.

Monkman, Phyllis: b. London, Eng, 8 Jan 1892; d. London, Eng, 2 Dec 1976.

Monroe, Frank: b. Jersey City, NJ, 1864; d. Bay Shore, NY, 19 Jun 1937.

Montague, Frederic: b. London, Eng, 1864; d. Los Angeles, CA, 2 Jul 1919.

Montague, Monte: b. Somerset, KY, 23 Apr 1891; d. Burbank, CA, 6 Apr 1959.

Montague, Rita: b. Illinois, 16 May 1883; d. Los Angeles, CA, 5 May 1962.

Montana, Lewis (Bull): b. Vogliera, Italy, 16 May 1887; d. Los Angeles, CA, 24 Jan 1950.

Montano, A.: b. Barbados, West Indies, 18??; d. Long Island, NY, 6 Sep 1914.

Monterey, Carlotta: b. San Francisco, CA, 28 Dec 1888; d. Westwood, NJ, 18 Nov 1970.

Montgomery, Betty: b. ????; d. 1 Jan 1922.

Montgomery, David C.: b. St. Joseph, MO, 21 Apr 1870; d. Chicago, IL, 20 Apr 1917.

Montgomery, Earl T.: b. Santa Cruz Co, CA, 24 May 1894; d. Los Angeles Co, CA, 28 Oct 1966.

Montgomery, Frank E.: b. Petrolia, PA, 14 Jun 1877; d. Los Angeles, CA, 18 Jul 1944.

Montgomery, Jack T.: b. Nebraska, 14 Nov 1891; d. Los Angeles, CA, 21 Jan 1962.

Montgomery, Mabel: b. Brooklyn, NY, 18??; d. Honolulu, HI, 20 Jul 1942.

Montgomery, Marian (Marian Baxter); b. 1896; d. Woodland Hills, CA, 7 Feb 1977.

Monti, Carlotta: b. 20 Jan 1907; d. Woodland Hills, CA 8 Dec 1993.

Montt, Christina: b. Chile, 1897; d. Los Angeles, CA, 22 Apr 1969.

Moody, Mrs. William Vaughn: b. 18??; d. Chicago, IL, 22 Feb 1932.

Mooers, De Sacia: b. Michigan, 19 Nov 1888; d. Los Angeles, CA, 11 Jan 1960.

Moon, Donna (Donna Drew): b. 18??; d. Helena, MT, 24 Oct 1918.

Moon, Morse: b. 18??; d. Helena, MT, 17 Oct 1918.

Moore, Cleve: b. Port Huron, MI, 10 Jun 1904; d. Miami, FL, 25 Jan 1954.

Moore, Colleen: b. Port Huron, MI, 19 Aug 1900; d. Templeton, CA, 25 Jan 1988.

Moore, Eva: b. Brighton, Eng, 9 Feb 1870; d. Maidenhead, Eng, 27 Apr 1955.

Moore, Florence: b. Philadelphia, PA, 13 Nov 1886; d. Darby, PA, 23 Mar 1935.

Moore, Frank F.: b. Philadelphia, PA, 1880; d. Los Angeles, CA, 28 May 1924.

Moore, Gladys C.: b. 1864; d. Jackson Heights, NY, 5 Sep 1937.

Moore, Hilda: b. England, 1886; d. New York, NY, 18 May 1929.

Moore, Ida: b. Ohio, 1 Mar 1882; d. Los Angeles Co, CA, 26 Sep 1964.

Moore, Joe: b. County Meath, Ire, 1896; d. Santa Monica, CA, 22 Aug 1926.

Moore, Lucia: b. Louisiana, 1867; d. New York, NY, ? Apr 1932.

Moore, Mary: b. London, Eng, 3 Jul 1861; d. London, Eng, 6 Apr 1931.

Moore, Mary: b. 18??; d. France, ? Jan 1919.

Moore, Matt: b. County Meath, Ire, 8 Jan 1888; d. Los Angeles, CA, 20 Jan 1960.

Moore, Owen: b. County Meath, Ire, 12 Dec 1886; d. Beverly Hills, CA, 9 Jun 1939.

Moore, Percy: b. Montreal, Can, 1878; d. New York, NY, 8 Apr 1945.

Moore, Rex: b. 26 Feb 1900; d. Los Angeles Co, CA, 21 Apr 1975.

Moore, Scott: b. 1889; d. Miami Beach, FL, 18 Dec 1967.

Moore, Tom: b. County Meath, Ire, 1 May 1883; d. Santa Monica, CA, 12 Feb 1955.

Moore, Unity: b. Galway, Ire, 27 Jul 1894; d. London, Eng, ? Feb 1981.

Moore, Victor: b. Hammonton, NJ, 24 Feb 1876; d. East Islip, NY, 23 Jul 1962.

Moore, Vin: b. Mayville, NY, 1878; d. Los Angeles, CA, 5 Dec 1949.

Moorehouse, Bert: b. Illinois, 20 Nov 1894; d. Los Angeles, CA, 26 Jan 1954.

Moran, Frank: b. Ohio, 18 Mar 1887; d. Los Angeles, CA, 14 Dec 1967.

Moran, George: b. Elwood, KS, 3 Oct 1881; d. Oakland, CA, 1 Aug 1949.

Moran, Lee: b. Chicago, IL, 23 Jun 1888; d. Woodland Hills, CA, 24 Apr 1961.

Moran, Leo D.: b. 1889; d. Tucson, AZ, 8 Mar 1927.

Moran, Lois: b. Pittsburgh, PA, 1 Mar 1909; d. Sedona, AZ, 13 Jul 1990.

Moran, Percy: b. Ireland, 18??; d. 1958.

Moran, Polly: b. Chicago, IL, 28 Jun 1883; d. Los Angeles, CA, 25 Jan 1952.

Morand, M. R.: b. 1861; d. 5 Mar 1922.

Morante, Milburn M.: b. San Francisco, CA, 6 Apr 1887; d. Pacoima, CA, 28 Jan 1964.

Mordant, Edwin: b. Baltimore, MD, 22 Dec 1868; d. Los Angeles, CA, 16 Feb 1942.

Morel, Dene: b. England, 17 Jan 1901; d. ? Oct 1928.

Morena, Erna: b. Aschaffenburg, Bavaria, 24 Apr 1892; d. Munich, Ger, 21 Jul 1962.

Moreno, Antonio: b. Madrid, Spain, 26 Sep 1887; d. Beverly Hills, CA, 15 Feb 1967.

Moreno, Marguerite: b. Paris, Fr, 1871; d. Touzac, Lot, Fr, 14 Jul 1948.

Moreno, T. B. (Skyball): b. 1890; d. Los Angeles, CA, 25 Oct 1938.

Morey, Harry T.: b. Charlotte, MI, 1873; d. Brooklyn, NY, 24 Jan 1936.

Morey, Henry A.: b. 1848; d. Astoria, NY, 8 Jan 1929.

Morgan, Boyd F. (Red): b. Waurika, OK, 1915; d. Tarzana, CA, 8 Jan 1988.

Morgan, Byron: b. Carthage, MO, 24 Oct 1889; d. Los Angeles, CA, 22 May 1963.

Morgan, Fitzroy: b. England, 18??; d. 25 Oct 1912.

Morgan, Frank: b. New York, NY, 1 Jun 1890; d. Los Angeles, CA, 18 Sep 1949.

Morgan, Gene: b. Racine, WI, 12 Mar 1893; d. Santa Monica, CA, 15 Aug 1940.

Morgan, Harry R. (Cy): b. Pomeroy, OH, 10 Nov 1878; d. Wheeling, WV, 28 Jun 1962.

Morgan, Jackie: b. Aberdean, SD, 7 Jul 1916; d. Brea, CA, 25 Jul 1981.

Morgan, Margaret: b. Ontario, Can, 1895; d. Glendale, CA, 29 Aug 1926.

Morgan, Paul: b. Vienna, Austria, 1 Oct 1886; d. ? Jan 1939.

Morgan, Ralph: b. New York, NY, 6 Jul 1883; d. New York, NY, 11 Jun 1956.

Morgan, Ruth: b. Columbus, OR, ????; d. Venice, CA, 28 Jun 1917.

Moriarty, Marcus: b. 18??; d. New York, NY, 21 Jun 1916.

Morison, Lindsay: b. Newcastle-on-Tyne, Eng, 18??; d. New Rochelle, NY, 22 Feb 1917.

Morlay, Gaby: b. Angers, Fr, 8 Jun 1893; d. Nice, Fr, 4 Jul 1964.

Morley, Jay: b. Port Orange, FL, 14 Jul 1890; d. Santa Monica, CA, 9 Nov 1976.

Morne, Maryland: b. England, 1900; d. Los Angeles, CA, 18 Jul 1935.

Morosco, Walter: b. San Francisco, CA. 1899; d. Coronado, CA, 30 Dec 1948.

Morrell, George: b. California, 10 Apr 1871; d. Los Angeles, CA, 28 Apr 1955.

Morrell, Louis: b. 1873; d. Elgin, IL, 11 Jul 1945.

Morris, Adrian M. b. Mt. Vernon, NY, 12 Jan 1907; d. Los Angeles, CA, 30 Nov 1941.

Morris, Chester: b. New York, NY, 16 Feb 1901; d. New Hope, PA, 11 Sep 1970.

Morris, Diana: b. California, 21 Jul 1906; d. Los Angeles, CA, 19 Feb 1961.

Morris, Gordon: b. 1899; d. Los Angeles, CA, 7 Apr 1940.

Morris, Jack J. (Jack Maurice,): b. 1904; d. Sherman Oaks, CA, 21 Apr 1990.

Morris, Johnny: b. New York, NY, 15 Jun 1887; d. Los Angeles, CA, 7 Oct 1969.

Morris, Lee: b. Missouri, 23 Jun 1863; d. 6 Feb 1933.

Morris, Margaret: b. Minneapolis, MN, 7 Nov 1898; d. Los Angeles, CA, 7 Jun 1968.

Morris, Reginald: b. New Jersey, 25 Jun 1886; d. Los Angeles, CA, 16 Feb 1928.

Morris, Richard: b. Boston, MA, 1861; d. Los Angeles, CA, 11 Oct 1924.

Morris, William: b. Boston, MA, 1 Jan 1861; d. Los Angeles, CA, 11 Jan 1936.

Morrison, Adrienne: b. New York, NY, 1 Mar 1883; d. New York, NY, 20 Nov 1940.

Morrison, Anna Marie: b. 1884; d. Los Angeles, CA, 5 Jul 1972.

Morrison, Anne: b. 18??; d. Los Angeles, CA, 7 Apr 1967.

Morrison, Arthur: b. St. Louis, MO, 1 May 1877; d. Los Angeles, CA, 20 Feb 1950.

Morrison, C. P. (Chick): b. Mt. Morrison, CO, 3 Apr 1878; d. Los Angeles, CA, 20 Jun 1924.

Morrison, Ernie (Sunshine Sammy): b. New Orleans, LA, 20 Dec 1912; d. Lynwood, CA, 24 Jul 1989.

Morrison, Florence: b. 1871; d. New York, NY, 8 May 1928.

Morrison, Howard Priestly: b. Baltimore, MD, 1872; d. Kew Gardens, NY, 26 Jan 1938.

Morrison, James: b. Matoon, IL, 15 Nov 1888; d. New York, NY, 15 Nov 1974.

Morrison, Louis: b. Portland, ME, 8 Feb 1866; d. Los Angeles, CA, 22 Apr 1946.

Morrison, Meta: b. 1892; d. Chicago, IL, 28 Nov 1982.

Morrison, Pete (George): b. Denver, CO, 8 Aug 1890; d. Los Angeles, CA, 5 Feb 1973.

Morrissey, Betty: b. Brooklyn, NY, 1908; d. New York, NY, 20 Apr 1944.

Morrissey, Will: b. New York, NY, 19 Jun 1887; d. Santa Barbara, CA, 16 Dec 1957.

Morrow, Jane (Gladys Rankin): b. 1874; d. New York, NY, 9 Jan 1914.

Morse, Karl: b. 1888; d. Los Angeles, CA, 22 Jan 1936.

Morse, Salmi: b. 18??; d. c. 1913.

Mortimer, Dorothy: b. 1898; d. New York, NY, 15 Feb 1950.

Mortimer, Edmund: b. New York State, 1880; d. Los Angeles, CA, 21 May 1944.

Mortimer, Henry: b. Toronto, Can, 14 Aug 1882; d. Whitby, Can, 20 Aug 1952.

Morton, Charles: b. Illinois, 28 Jan 1908; d. North Hollywood, CA, 26 Oct 1966.

Morton, Drew: b. 1855; d. New York, NY, 4 Sep 1916.

Morway, Jacques: b. Hungary, 1843; d. 6 May 1914.

Mosjoukine, Ivan: b. Penza, Russ, 1889; d. Paris, Fr, 18 Jan 1939.

Moskivin, Ivan M.: b. Moscow, Russ, 18 Jun 1874; d. Moscow, Russ, 16 Feb 1946.

Moskowitz, Jennie: b. Romania, 1868; d. New York, NY, 26 Jul 1953.

Mosley, Frederick C.: b. 1854; d. Staten Island, NY, 9 Mar 1927.

Mosquini, Marie: b. Los Angeles, CA, 3 Dec 1902; d. Los Angeles, CA, 21 Feb 1983.

Moulton, Edwin (Buck): b. New York, 8 Apr 1891; d. Los Angeles, CA, 7 May 1959.

Mounet-Sully, Jean: b. Bergerac, Fr, 27 Feb 1841; d. Paris, Fr, 1 Mar 1916.

Mouvet, Maurice: b. Switzerland, 1886; d. Lausanne, Switz, 17 Mar 1989.

Mower, Jack: b. California, 5 Sep 1890; d. Los Angeles, CA, 6 Jan 1965.

Moyea, John W.: b. 18??; d. ? Aug 1912.

Moylan, Catherine: b. Dallas, TX, 1904; d. Fort Worth, TX, 9 Sep 1969.

Moyles, Dan: b. 1873; d. New York, NY, 25 Sep 1933.

Mozart, George: b. Great Yarmouth, Eng, 15 Feb 1864; d. London, Eng, 10 Dec 1947.

Mudd, E. Virginia: b. 1893; d. San Antonio, TX, 21 May 1979.

Mudie, Leonard: b. England, 11 Apr 1883; d. Los Angeles, CA, 14 Apr 1965.

Muir, Helen: b. 1864; d. Los Angeles, CA, 2 Dec 1934.

Mulcaster, George H.: b. London, Eng, 27 Jun 1891; d. England, 19 Jan 1964.

Muldoon, William: b. 25 May 1845; d. Purchase, NY, 3 Jun 1933.

Mulgrew, Thomas G.: b. 1889; d. Providence, RI, 3 Dec 1954.

Mulhall, Jack: b. Wappinger Falls, NY, 7 Oct 1887; d. Woodland Hills, CA, 1 Jun 1979.

Mulhauser, James: b. Brooklyn, NY, 31 Oct 1889; d. Beverly Hills, CA, 15 Jun 1939.

Mullally, Jode: b. New Orleans, LA, 19 Nov 1886; d. Philadelphia, PA, 23 Dec 1918.

Munier, Ferdinand: b. San Diego, CA, 3 Dec 1889; d. Los Angeles, CA, 27 May 1945.

Munro, Douglas: b. London, Eng, 18??; d. Birmingham, Eng, 27 Jan 1924.

Munson, Byron: b. Chicago, IL, 29 Jun 1900; d. Burbank, CA, 28 Jul 1989.

Munson, Ona: b. Portland, OR, 16 Jun 1906; d. New York, NY, 11 Feb 1955.

Muratore, Lucien: b. Marseilles, Fr, 29 Aug 1878; d. Paris, Fr, 16 Jul 1954.

Murdock, Ann: b. Port Washington, NY, 10 Nov 1890; d. Lucerne, Switz, 22 Apr 1939.

Murnane, Allan L.: b. Philadelphia, PA, 1882; d. New Rochelle, NY, 2 Apr 1950.

Murnau, F. W.: Bielefled, Ger, 28 Dec 1888; d. Santa Barbara, CA 11 Mar 1931.

Murphy, Ada: b. England, 6 Jan 1887; d. Encino, CA, 25 Aug 1961.

Murphy, Charles B.: b. Independence, MO, 12 Dec 1881; d. Bakersfield, CA, 11 Jun 1942.

Murphy, Eddie: b. Nincock, NY, 2 Oct 1891; d. Dunmore, PA, 21 Feb 1969.

Murphy, Edna: b. New York, NY, 17 Nov 1899; d. Santa Monica, CA, 3 Aug 1974.

Murphy, Jimmy: b. San Francisco, CA, 1894; d. Syracuse, NY, 15 Sep 1924.

Murphy, John Daly: b. Chicago, IL, 5 Feb 1873; d. New York, NY, 20 Nov 1934.

Murphy, John T.: b. Helena, MT, 24 Aug 1879; d. Los Angeles Co, CA, 7 Jul 1955.

Murphy, Joseph J.: b. California, 16 May 1877; d. San Jose, CA, 31 Jul 1961.

Murphy, Maurice: b. Seattle, WA, 3 Oct 1913; d. Los Angeles, CA, 23 Nov 1978.

Murray, Bobby: b. St. Albans, VT, 4 Jul 1898; d. Nashua, NH, 4 Jan 1979.

Murray, Charlie: b. Laurel, IN, 22 Jun 1872; d. Los Angeles, CA, 29 Jul 1941.

Murray, David Mitchell: b. 1853; d. Long Island, NY, 20 Oct 1923.

Murray, Edgar: b. 1892; d. Los Angeles, CA, 16 Oct 1959,

Murray, Elizabeth: b. 25 Apr 1871; d. Philadelphia, PA, 27 Mar 1946.

Murray, James: b. New York, NY, 9 Feb 1901; d. New York, NY, 10 Jul 1936.

Murray, James Sylvester: b. England, 1862; d. Bronx, NY, 17 Oct 1939.

Murray, John (Red): b. Arnot, PA, 4 Mar 1884; d. Sayre, PA, 4 Dec 1958.

Murray, John T.: b. Australia, 28 Aug 1886; d. Woodland Hills, CA, 12 Feb 1957.

Murray, Mae: b. Portsmouth, VA, 10 May 1889; d. Los Angeles, CA, 23 Mar 1965.

Murray, Marion: b. 1885; d. New York, NY, 11 Nov 1951.

Murray, Tom: b. Stonefoot, IL, 8 Sep 1874; d. North Hollywood, CA, 27 Aug 1935.

Murth, Florence: b. Boswell, PA, 20 Jan 1897; d. Durarte, CA, 29 Mar 1934.

Musidora (Jeanne Roques): b. Paris, Fr, 1889; d. Paris, Fr. ? Dec 1957.

Muslili, Boots: b. 1916; d. Norfolk, MA, 23 Sep 1967.

Mussette, Charles: b. London, Eng, 1876; d. Bernardsville, NJ, 6 Dec 1939.

Mussey, Francine: b. ????; d. Paris, Fr, 26 Mar 1933.

Mussolini, Benito: b. Dovia di Predappio, Italy, 29 Jul 1883; d. Como Province, Italy, 28 Apr 1945.

Musson, Bennet: b. Cario, IL, 1866; d. Amityville, NY, 17 Feb 1946.

Myers, Carmel: b. San Francisco, CA, 4 Apr 1901; d. Los Angeles, CA, 9 Nov 1980.

Myers, Harry C.: b. New Haven, CT, 5 Sep 1882; d. Los Angeles, CA, 25 Dec 1938.

Myles, Norbert: b. Wheeling, WV, 29 Aug 1887; d. Los Angeles, CA, 15 Mar 1966.

N

Nagel, Beth: b. Chicago, IL, 9 Apr 1877; d. Beverly Hills, CA, 29 Oct 1936.

Nagel, Conrad: b. Keokuk, IA, 16 Mar 1897; d. New York, NY, 24 Feb 1970.

Nairn, Ralph: b. Scotland, 1873; d. London, Eng, ? Dec 1934.

Naldi, Nita: b. New York, NY, 1 Apr 1897; d. New York, NY, 17 Feb 1961.

Nally, William: b. ????; d. New York, NY, ? Mar 1929.

Namara, Marguerite: b. Cleveland, OH, 19 Nov 1888; d. Spain, 3 Nov 1974.

Nanook: b. Alaska, ????; d. ? Nov 1925.

Nansen, Betty: b. Copenhagen, Den, 19 Mar 1873; d. Copenhagen, Den, 15 Mar 1943.

Napier, Diane: b. Bath, Eng, 1906; d. London, Eng, 12 Mar 1982.

Napierkowska, Stacia: b. Paris, Fr, 16 Dec 1886; d. Paris, Fr, 11 May 1945.

Nardelli, George: b. France, 21 Oct 1895; d. Los Angeles Co, CA, 16 Sep 1973.

Nares, Anna: b. 1870; d. Flushing, NY, 19 Dec 1915.

Nares, Owen: b. Maiden Erleigh, Eng, 11 Aug 1888; d. Brecon, Wales, 30 Jul 1943.

Nash, Florence: b. Troy, NY, 2 Oct 1888; d. Los Angeles, CA, 2 Apr 1950.

Nash, George Frederick: b. Philadelphia, PA, 1873; d. Amityville, NY, 30 Dec 1944.

Nash, June: b. 1911; d. Hampton Bays, NY, 8 Oct 1979.

Nash, Mary: b. Troy, NY, 15 Aug 1885; d. Brentwood, CA, 3 Dec 1976.

Natheaux, Louis: b. Pine Bluff, AR, 10 Dec 1894; d. Los Angeles, CA, 23 Aug 1942.

Nazimova, Alla: b. Yalta, Crimea, 4 Jun 1878; d. Los Angeles, CA, 13 Jul 1945.

Neal, Lloyd: b. Michigan, 20 Oct 1861; d. Los Angeles Co, CA, 19 Aug 1952.

Neason, Hazel: b. Pittsburgh, PA. 16 Aug c. 1890; d. New York, NY, 24 Jan 1920.

Nedell, Bernard: b. New York, NY, 14 Oct 1893; d. Los Angeles, CA. 23 Nov 1972.

Negri, Pola: b. Lipno, Poland, 31 Dec 1897; d. San Antonio, TX, 1 Aug 1987.

Neilan, Marshall: b. San Bernardino, CA, 11 Apr 1891; d. Woodland Hills, CA, 26 Oct 1958.

Neill, James: b. Savannah, GA, 29 Sep 1860; d. Los Angeles, CA, 15 Mar 1931.

Neill, Richard R.: b. Philadelphia, PA, 12 Nov 1875; d. Woodland Hills, CA, 8 Apr 1970.

Neill, Roy William: b. Queenstone Harbor, Ire, 1887; d. London, Eng, 14 Dec 1946.

Neilson, Lois: b. Tulare, CA, 1898; d. 9 Jul 1990.

Neilson-Terry, Dennis: b. London, Eng, 21 Oct 1895; d. Bulawayo, So Rhodesia, 14 Jul 1932.

Neilson-Terry, Julia: b. London, Eng, 12 Jun 1868; d. London, Eng, 27 May 1957.

Neilson-Terry, Phyllis: b. London, Eng, 15 Oct 1892; d. London, Eng, 25 Sep 1977.

Nelson, Evelyn: b. Chloride, AZ, 13 Nov 1899; d. Los Angeles, CA, 16 Jun 1923.

Nelson, Frank: b. 1872; d. California, 27 Nov 1932.

Nelson, Harold: b. Boston, MA, 26 Aug 1864; d. Los Angeles, CA, 26 Jan 1937.

Nelson, Hilda: b. 1881; d. New York, NY, ? Jan 1919.

Nelson, Jack: b. Memphis, TN, 1892; d. 19??.

Nelson, Lottie: b. California, 13 Mar 1875; d. Los Angeles, CA, 8 May 1966.

Nelson, Sam: b. Whittier, CA, 31 May 1896; d. Los Angeles, CA, 1 May 1963.

Nelson-Ramsey, John: b. ????; d. London, Eng, 5 Apr 1929.

Nero, Curtis: b. Muskogee, OK, 3 Apr 1906; d. Los Angeles Co, CA, 28 Jan 1942.

Nesbit, Evelyn: b. Tarentum, PA, 25 Dec 1884; d. Santa Monica, CA, 17 Jan 1967.

Nesbitt, Cathleen: b. Liskeard, Cheshire, Eng, 24 Nov 1888; d. London, Eng, 2 Aug 1982.

Nesbitt, Miriam: b. Chicago, IL, 14 Sep 1873; d. Los Angeles, CA, 11 Aug 1954.

Nesbitt, Thomas: b. England, 1890; d. Johannesburg, So Africa, 31 Mar 1927.

Nesmith, Ottola: b. Washington, DC, 12 Dec 1889; d. Los Angeles, CA, 7 Feb 1972.

Ness, Ole M.: b. 1888; d. North Hollywood, CA, 19 Jul 1953.

Nestell, Bill: b. California, 3 Mar 1893; d. Bishop, CA, 18 Oct 1966.

Neu, Oscar F.: b. Buffalo, NY, 22 Jun 1886; d. Crestwood, NY, 26 Aug 1957.

Neumann, Lotte: b. Germany, 5 Aug 1899; d. Bavaria, Ger 26 Feb 1977.

Neville, George: b. Boston, MA, 17 Oct 1865; d. New York, NY, 18 Aug 1932.

Neville, Harry: b. Launceston, Tasmania, 24 Mar 1867; d. Rockville Center, NY, 25 Jan 1945.

Nevius, B. A.: b. ????; d. Leon, IA, ? Aug 1928.

Newall, Guy: b. Wright, Eng, 25 May 1885; d. London, Eng, 25 Feb 1937.

Newberg, Frank A.: b. Pennsylvania, 9 Oct 1886; d. Woodland Hills, CA, 4 Nov 1969.

Newcomb, Mary: b. North Adams, MA, 24 Aug 1893; d. Dorchester, Eng, 26 Dec 1966.

Newcombe, Caroline: b. Shreveport, LA, 1872; d. New York, NY, 17 Dec 1941.

Newman, Horace: b. 1863; d. New York, NY, 13 Nov 1947.

Newman, John Koch: b. 1864; d. New York, NY, 2 Mar 1927.

Newman, Lur Barden: b. ????; d. 1 Dec 1918.

Newman, Nell: b. 1881; d. Los Angeles, CA, ? Aug 1931.

Newmeyer, Fred C.: b. Central City, CO, 9 Aug 1888; d. Woodland Hills, CA, 24 Apr 1967.

Newton, Charles Lindner: b. Rochester, NY, 1874; d. 1926.

Newton, Irving (Fig): b. 1898; d. Sherman Oaks, CA, 13 Jun 1980.

Niblo, Fred: b. York, NE, 6 Jan 1874; d. New Orleans, LA, 11 Nov 1948.

Nichols, Anne: b. Dales Mill, GA, 26 Nov 1891; d. Englewood Cliffs, NJ, 15 Sep 1966.

Nichols, George: b. Rockford, IL, 1864; d. Los Angeles, CA, 20 Sep 1927.

Nichols, George Jr.: b. San Francisco, CA, 5 May 1897; d. Los Angeles, CA, 13 Nov 1939.

Nichols, Guy: b. ????; d. Hempstead, NY, 23 Jan 1928.

Nichols, Marguerite: b. Los Angeles, CA, 1900; d. Los Angeles, CA, 17 Mar 1941.

Nicholson, John: b. Charleston, IL, 1873; d. New York, NY, 24 Jun 1934.

Nicholson, Lillian: b. 1881; d. Los Angeles Co, CA, 31 Mar 1949.

Nicholson, Paul: b. Orange, NJ, 1877; d. Santa Monica, CA, 2 Feb 1935.

Nickols, Walter: b. 1853; d. New York, NY, 25 Dec 1927.

Nicol, Joseph E.: b. 1856; d. Bernardsville, NJ, 31 May 1926.

Nielsen, Asta: b. Copenhagen, Den, ? Oct 1881; d. Copenhagen, Den, 24 May 1972.

Nigh, William: b. Berlin, WI, 12 Oct 1881; d. Burbank, CA, 27 Nov 1955.

Night, Harry (Hank): b. 1847; d. Los Angeles, CA, 24 Apr 1930.

Nile, Grace Dunbar: b. ????; d. Lakewood, CO, 14 Nov 1958.

Nillson, Carlotta: b. Stockholm, Sweden, 1878; d. New York, NY, 31 Dec 1951.

Nilsson, Anna Q.: b. Ystad, Sweden, 30 Mar 1888; d. Hemet, CA, 11 Feb 1974.

Nissen, Greta: b. Oslo, Norway, 30 Dec 1906; d. Montecito, CA, 15 May 1988.

Nitter, Erna: b. Berlin, Ger, 28 Aug 1888; d. Hamburg, Ger, 17 Jun 1986.

Nixon, Marion: b. Superior, WI, 20 Oct 1904; d. Los Angeles, CA, 13 Feb 1983.

Noa, Julian: b. 1879; d. New York, NY, 26 Nov 1958.

Nobles, Dolly: b. Cincinnati, OH, 1863; d. New York, NY, 6 Oct, 1930.

Nobles, Milton: b. Almont, MI, 28 Sep 1847; d. Brooklyn, NY, 14 Jun 1924.

Nobles, Milton, Jr.: b. Brooklyn, NY, 1893; d. Chester, PA, 22 Feb 1925.

Noel, Billy: b. Canada, 1885; d. New Rochelle, NY, 13 Aug 1969.

Nolan, Mary: b. Louisville, KY, 18 Dec 1905; d. Los Angeles, CA, 31 Oct 1948.

Noll, Karel: b. Czechoslovakia, 1880; d. Prague, Czech, ? Mar 1928.

Nomis, Leo: b. Iowa, ????; d. Los Angeles, CA, 5 Feb 1932.

Noon, Paisley: b. Los Angeles, CA, 1897; d. Los Angeles, CA, 27 Mar 1932.

Norcross, Frank M.: b. Boston, MA, 10 Jul 1857; d. Glendale, CA 12 Sep 1926.

Nordstrom, Clarence: b. Chicago, IL, 13 Mar 1893; d. East Orange, NJ. 13 Dec 1968.

Norman, Amber: b. Utah, 6 Jun 1901; d. 21 Oct 1972.

Norman, Gertrude: b. London, Eng, 19 May 1848; d. Los Angeles, CA, 20 Jul 1943.

Norman, Josephine: b. Vienna, Austria, 12 Nov 1904; d. Roslyn, NY, 24 Jan 1951.

Normand, Claire: b. Paris, Fr, 1891; d. 19??.

Normand, Mabel: b. Staten Island, NY, 9 Nov 1892; d. Monrovia, CA, 23 Feb 1930.

Norrie, Claude: b. Scotland, 1872; d. Chicago, IL, 10 May 1916.

Norris, Anna: b. Sweden, 1860; d. ? Jul 1957.

Norris, William: b. New York, NY, 15 Jun 1870; d. West Bronxville, NY, 20 Mar 1929.

North, Joseph B.: b. England, 27 Dec 1873; d. Woodland Hills, CA, 8 Jan 1945.

North, Robert (Bobby): b. New York, NY, 2 Feb 1884; d. Los Angeles, CA, 13 Aug 1976.

North, Wilfred: b. London, Eng, 16 Jan 1863; d. Los Angeles, CA, 3 Jun 1935.

Northpole, John: b. Yugoslavia, 23 Dec 1892; d. Los Angeles Co, CA, 26 Feb 1964.

Northrup, Harry S.: b. Paris, Fr, 31 Jul 1875; d. Los Angeles, CA, 2 Jul 1936.

Norton, Barry: b. Buenos Aires, Argentina, 16 Jun 1909; d. Los Angeles, CA, 25 Aug 1956.

Norton, Cecil A.: b. 1895; d. Los Angeles, CA, 30 Nov 1955.

Norton, Edgar: b. England, 11 Aug 1868; d. Woodland Hills, CA, 6 Feb 1953.

Norton, Elda: b. Canada, 21 Apr 1891; d. Los Angeles, CA, 15 Apr 1947.

Norton, Fletcher: b. San Francisco, CA, 4 Aug 1877; d. Los Angeles, CA, 3 Oct 1941.

Norton, Frederick: b. ????; d. 15 Dec 1946.

Norwood, Eille: b. York, Eng, 11 Oct 1861; d. London, Eng, 24 Dec 1948.

Norworth, Ned: b. 1889; d. New York, NY, 12 Feb 1940.

Nosher, Edith: b. 1894; d. 13 Jul, 1929.

Nosseck, Max: b. Nakel, Poland, 19 Sep 1902; d. Bad Wiesse, Ger, 29 Sep 1972.

Nova, Hedda: b. Odessa, Russ, c. 1890; d. 19??.

Novak, Eva: b. St. Louis, MO, 14 Feb 1898; d. Woodland Hills, CA, 17 Apr 1988.

Novak, Jane: b. St. Louis, MO, 12 Jan 1896; d. Woodland Hills, CA, 1 Feb 1990.

Novarro, Ramon: b. Durango, Mex, 6 Feb 1899; d. Los Angeles, CA, 31 Oct 1968.

Novelli, Amleto: b. Bologna, Italy, 18 Oct 1885; d. Italy, 16 Apr 1924.

Novelli, Ermete: b. Lucca, Italy, 5 May 1851; d. Rome, Italy, 30 Jan 1919.

Novello, Ivor: b. Cardiff, Wales, 15 Jan 1893; d. London, Eng, 6 Mar 1951.

Novello, Roselle: b. 1896; d. Los Angeles, CA, 16 Jan 1992.

Nowell, Nedgewood: b. Portsmouth, NH, 1878; d. Philadelphia, PA, 17 Jan 1957.

Noyes, Joseph (Skeets): b. New Orleans, LA, 19 Sep 1868; d. Los Angeles, CA, 18 Apr 1936.

Nuemann, Charles: b. 1883; d. Glendale, CA, 16 Jul 1927.

Nugent, Elliott: b. Dover, OH, 20 Sep 1897; d. New York, NY, 9 Aug 1980.

Nugent, Moya: b. 1901; d. London, Eng, 26 Jan 1954.

Nunn, Wayne: b. 1881; d. New York, NY, 17 Dec 1947.

Nye, Carroll: b. Canton, OH, 4 Oct 1901; d. Encino, CA, 17 Mar 1974.

Nye, G. Raymond: b. Tamaqua, PA, 1889; d. 19??.

Nye, Ned: b. 1871; d. Los Angeles, CA, 10 Dec 1924.

Nye, Tom F.: b. 1847; d. 13 Jan 1925.

Nystrom, Ulrica: b. France, ????; d. France, ? Nov 1923.

O

Oaker, John: b. Ottawa, Can, 1893; d. 19??.

Oakie, Jack: b. Sedalia, MO, 12 Nov 1903; d. Los Angeles, CA, 23 Jan 1978.

Oakland, Vivien: b. Oakland, CA, 20 May 1895; d. Los Angeles, CA, 1 Aug 1958.

Oakley, Annie: b. Patterson Township, OH, 13 Aug 1860; d. Greenville, OH, 4 Nov 1926.

Oakley, Florence: b. 1891; d. Los Angeles, CA, 25 Sep 1956.

Oakley, Laura: b. Oakland, CA, 10 Jul 1879; d. Altadena, CA, 30 Jan 1957.

Oakman, Wheeler: b. Washington, DC, 21 Feb 1890; d. Van Nuys, CA, 19 Mar 1949.

O'Beck, Ferdinand J.: b. Philadelphia, PA, 1881; d. Los Angeles, CA, 31 Jan 1929.

Obenaus, Richards A. (Richard Bernard): b. 1875; d. Kingston, NY, 17 Dec 1941.

Ober, Mrs. Adelaide D.: b. 1841; d. Hastings-on-Hudson, NY, 8 Feb 1922.

Ober, George: b. Baltimore, MD, 1849; d. Hastings-on-Hudson, NY, 17 Nov 1912.

Ober, Kirt: b, 1875; d. Huntington Beach, CA, 31 May 1939.

Ober, Robert: b. Bunker Hill, IL, 3 Sep 1881; d. New York, NY, 7 Dec 1950.

Oberle, Mrs. Florence: b. Tarrytown, NY, 1870; d. Los Angeles, CA, 10 Jul 1943.

O'Brien, Barry: b. London, Eng, 23 Dec 1893; d. London, Eng, 25 Dec 1961.

O'Brien, Daniel J.: b. 1874; d. San Francisco, CA, 12 Oct 1933.

O'Brien, Eugene: b. Boulder, CO, 14 Nov 1860; d. Los Angeles, CA, 29 Apr 1966.

O'Brien, George: b. San Francisco, CA, 19 Apr 1900; d. Broken Arrow, OK, 4 Sep 1985.

O'Brien, Pat: b. Milwaukee, WI, 11 Nov 1899; d. Santa Monica, CA, 15 Oct 1983.

O'Brien, Lt. Pat: b. California, ????; d. Los Angeles, CA, 18 Dec 1920.

O'Brien, Terence: b. Dublin, Ire, 25 Oct 1887; d. Welwyn, Herts, Eng, 13 Oct 1970.

O'Brien, Tom: b. San Diego, CA, 25 Jul 1890; d. Los Angeles, CA, 8 Jun 1947.

O'Byrne, Patsy: b. Kansas, 28 Jul 1884; d. Woodland Hills, CA, 18 Apr 1968.

O'Connor, Charles F.: b. 1897; d. New York, NY, 7 Nov 1979.

O'Connor, Edward: b. Dublin, Ire, 20 Feb 1862; d. New York, NY, 14 May 1932.

O'Connor, Frank: b. New York, 11 Apr 1882; d. Los Angeles, CA, 22 Nov 1959.

O'Connor, Harry M.: b. Chicago, IL, 27 Apr 1873; d. Woodland Hills, CA, 10 Jul 1971.

O'Connor, John: b. 1874; d. Santa Monica, CA, 10 Sep 1941.

O'Connor, Kathleen: b. Dayton, OH, 7 Jul 1894; d. Los Angeles, CA, 24 Jun 1957.

O'Connor, Kathryn Kennedy: b. Cortland, NY, 1894; d. Albuquerque, NM, 16 Nov 1965.

O'Connor, Louis J.: b. Providence, RI, 28 Jun 1879; d. Los Angeles, CA, 7 Aug 1959.

O'Connor, Loyola: b. St. Paul, MN, c. 1880; d. 19??.

O'Connor, Robert Emmett: b. Milwaukee, WI, 18 Mar 1885; d. Los Angeles, CA, 4 Sep 1962.

O'Dare, Peggy (Peggy O'Day): b. New York, NY, 19 Jun 1900; d. Santa Monica, CA, 25 Nov 1964.

O'Davoren, Vesey, b. 1889; d. Los Angeles, CA, 30 May 1989.

O'Day, Dawn (Anne Shirley): b. New York, NY, 17 Apr 1918; d. Los Angeles, CA, 4 Jul 1993.

O'Day, William: b. 1862; d. Bernardsville, NJ, 14 May 1926.

O'Dell, Edna: b. 1896; d. Woodland Hills, CA, 11 Jun 1987.

O'Dell, Georgia: b. 1893; d. Los Angeles Co, CA, 6 Sep 1950.

O'Dell, Maude: b. Beaufort, SC, 10 Nov 1871; d. New York, NY, 27 Feb 1937.

O'Dell, "Shorty" (Solomon Schwartz): b. ????; d. New York, NY, 11 Nov 1924.

Odemar, Fritz: b. Hanover, Ger, 31 Jan 1890; d. Munich, Ger, 3 Jun 1955.

O'Donnell, Spec (Walter): b. Fresno, CA, 9 Apr 1911; d. Woodland Hills, CA, 14 Oct 1986.

O'Donovan, Fred: b, Dublin, Ire, 14 Oct 1889; d. London, Eng, 19 Jul 1952.

Oettel, Walter (Wally): b. 17 Aug 1891; d. Woodland Hills, CA, 21 Jul 1980.

Offerman, George: b. Hoboken, NJ, 29 Apr 1879; d. Los Angeles, CA, 5 Mar 1938.

Offerman, George, Jr.: b. Chicago, IL, 14 Mar 1917; d. New York, NY, 14 Jan 1963.

O'Flynn, Paddy: b. Pittsburgh, PA, 19 Jan 1896; d. Los Angeles, CA, 11 Dec 1961.

Ogden, Vivia: b. 21 Mar 18??; d. 22 Dec 1952.

Ogle, Charles: b. Steubenville, OH, 5 Jun 1865; d. Long Beach, CA, 11 Oct 1940.

O'Grady, Tom: b. 1901; d. Los Angeles Co, CA, 31 Aug 1942.

O'Hara, George: b. Idaho, 22 Feb 1899; d. Los Angeles, CA, 16 Oct 1966.

O'Hara, John: b. 1859; d. St. Kilda, Austral, 15 Jul 1929.

O'Hara, Shirley: b. New York, NY, 23 May 1910; d. Los Angeles, CA, 5 May 1979.

Okazaki, Bob: b. 1902; d. Los Angeles, CA, 28 May 1985.

O'Keefe, Arthur J.: b. 1874; d. Los Angeles, CA, 29 Mar 1959.

O'Keefe, Loraine: b. Kansas, 23 Nov 1894; d. Los Angeles, CA, 12 Sep 1924.

Oland, Warner: b. Umea, Sweden, 3 Oct 1880; d. Stockholm, Sweden, 6 Aug 1938.

Olcott, Sidney: b. Toronto, Can, 20 Sep 1872; d. Los Angeles, CA, 16 Dec 1949.

Oldfield, Barney: b. York Township, OH, 29 Jan 1878; d. Beverly Hills, CA, 4 Oct 1946.

Oldring, Rube: b. New York, NY, 30 May 1884; d. Bridgeton, NJ, 9 Sep 1961.

Olive, Edyth: b. Newton Abbott, Eng, 1872; d. London, Eng, 7 Nov 1956.

Oliver, Edna May: b. Malden, MA, 9 Nov 1883; d. Los Angeles, CA, 9 Nov 1942.

Oliver, Guy: b. Chicago, IL, 25 Sep 1878; d. Los Angeles, CA, 1 Sep 1932.

Oliver, Ted: b. Kentucky, 2 Feb 1892; d. Los Angeles, CA, 30 Jun 1957.

Oliver, Virgil Jr.: b. 1916; d. Baton Rouge, LA, 3 Jun 1968.

Olivette, Marie: b. 1893; d. New York, NY, 15 Mar 1959.

Olmstead, Gertrude: b. Chicago, IL, 13 Nov 1904; d. Beverly Hills, CA, 18 Jan 1975.

O'Loughlin, John Carr: b. Dublin, Ire, 1886; d. 19??.

Olsen, Lauritz: b. Copenhagen, Denmark, 10 Aug 1872; d. 9 May 1955.

O'Madigan, Isabel: b. St. Louis, MO, 16 Oct 1871; d. Los Angeles, CA, 23 Jan 1951.

O'Malley, Charles E.: b. 1897; d. Los Angeles, CA, 29 Jul 1958.

O'Malley, Pat: b. Forest City, PA, 3 Sep 1890; d. Van Nuys, CA, 21 May 1966.

O'Malley, Rex: b. London, Eng, 2 Jan 1901; d. New York, NY, 1 May 1976.

O'Malley, Thomas E.: b. 1856; d. Brooklyn, NY, 5 May 1926.

Ondra, Anny: b. Tarnow, Poland, 15 May 1903; d, Hamburg, Ger, 28 Feb 1987.

O'Neil, Frank: b. ????; d. New York, NY, 8 Dec 1917.

O'Neil, Nance: b. Oakland, CA, 8 Oct 1874; d. Englewood, NJ, 7 Feb 1965.

O'Neil, Peggy: b. Buffalo, NY, 1897; d. London, Eng, 7 Jan 1960.

O'Neil, Sally: b. Bayonne, NJ, 23 Oct 1908; d. Galesburg, IL, 18 Jun 1968 .

O'Neill, Edward: b. Bombay, India, 1867; d. 19?? .

O'Neill, Jack: b. Philadelphia, PA, 1883; d. Los Angeles, CA, 20 Aug 1957.

O'Neill, James: b. Kilkenny, Ire, 15 Nov 1847; d. New London, CT, 10 Aug 1920.

O'Neill, James (Tip): b. Philadelphia, PA, 1863; d. Los Angeles, CA, 8 Oct 1938.

O'Neill, Johnny P.: b. 1862; d. Sydney, Austral, 14 Sep 1930.

Ong, Dana DeMoss: b. Richmond, OH, 3 Jul 1874; d. Los Angeles, CA, 31 Dec 1948.

Ongley, Amy: b. Roanoke, VA, 1886; d. New York, NY, 4 Dec 1926.

Onno, Ferdinand: b. Czarnowitz, Russ, 19 Oct 1881; d. 1970.

Opp, Julie: b. New York, NY, 28 Jan 1871; d. New York, NY, 8 Apr 1921.

O'Ramey, Georgia: b. Mansfield, OH, 31 Dec 1886; d. New Haven, CT, 2 Apr 1928.

Ordysnki, Richard: b. Poland, 1878; d. 13 Aug 1953.

O'Reilly, Tex (Edward O'Reilly): b. Texas, 1880; d. Sunmount, NY, 8 Dec 1946.

Orla, Resel: b. 1889; d. 23 Jul 1931.

Orlamond, Madge B,: b. St. Charles, MN, 15 Jan 1861; d. Los Angeles, CA, 22 Jun 1947.

Orlamond, William, b. Copenhagen, Den, 1 Aug 1867; d. Los Angeles, CA, 23 Apr 1957.

Orlando, Guido: b. Italy, 1907; d. Los Angeles, CA, 22 May 1988.

Ormonde, Eugene: b. Boston, MA, 18??; d. Saratoga Springs, NY, 16 Jul 1922.

O'Rourke, Eugene: b. New York, NY, 28 Jul 1863; d. Washington, DC, 30 Oct 1917.

O'Rourke, Thomas: b. 1872; d. Queens, NY, 16 Oct 1958.

Orska, Maria: b. Nikolajeff, Russ, 16 Mar 1893; d. Vienna, Austria, 16 May 1930.

Ortego, Art: b. California, 9 Feb 1890; d. Burbank, CA, 24 Jul 1960.

Orth, Louise: b. Denver, CO. 1891; d. 19??.

Ortin, Miguel: b. Spain, 1891; d. 10 May 1978.

Osborne, Bud: b. Knox County, TX, 20 Jul 1884; d. Los Angeles, CA, 2 Feb 1964.

Osborne, George: b. 1848; d. San Francisco, CA, 11 Aug 1916.

Osborne, Jefferson: b. Saginaw, MI, 1872; d. Hondo, CA, 11 Jun 1932.

Osborne, Rowland: b. Fulton, NY, 1875; d. New York, NY, 19 Apr 1920.

Osborne, Vivienne: b. Des Moines, IA, 10 Dec 1896; d. Malibu, CA, 10 Jun 1961.

Osterman, Kathryn: b. Toledo, OH, 5 May 1883; d. New York, NY, 25 Aug 1956.

Ostriche, Muriel: b. New York, NY, 24 Mar 1896; d. St. Petersburg, FL, 3 May 1989.

O'Sullivan, Tony: b. 18??; d. New York, NY, 4 Jul 1920.

Oswalda, Ossi: b. Prague, Czech, 2 Feb 1899; d. Berlin, Ger, 1 Jan 1948.

Otis, Elita Proctor: b. Cleveland, OH, 1851; d. Pelham, NY, 10 Aug 1927.

Ott, Frederick P.: b. 1860; d. West Orange, NJ, 24 Oct 1936.

Otte, Henri Rolph: b. 1879; d. San Francisco, CA, 17 Dec 1930.

Ottiano, Rafaela: b. Venice, Italy, 4 Mar 1888; d. Boston, MA, 15 Aug 1942.

Otto, Arthur: b. 18??; d. Tacoma, WA. ? Jan 1918.

Otto, Henry: b. St. Louis, MO, 8 Aug 1877; d. Los Angeles, CA, 3 Aug 1952.

Otto, Paul: b. ????; d. 25 Nov 1943.

Otton, William G.: b. England, 1852; d. New York, NY, 7 Mar 1930.

Oupenskaya, Maria: b. Tula, Russ, 29 Jul 1876; d. Los Angeles, CA, 3 Dec 1949.

Overton, Evart Emerson: b. Osborne, OH, 5 Aug 1889; d. Riverdale, NY, 27 Jan 1949.

Ovey, George: b. Trenton, MO, 13 Dec 1870; d. Los Angeles, CA, 13 Sep 1951.

Owen, Catherine Dale: b. Louisville, KY, 28 Jul 1903; d. New York, NY, 7 Sep 1965.

Owen, Cecil: b. London, Eng, 2 Jun 1873; d. Rockville Center, NY, 25 Jul 1928.

Owen, Reginald: b. Wheathampstead, Herts, Eng, 5 Aug 1887; d. Boise, ID, 5 Nov 1972.

Owen, Seena (Signe Auen): b. Spokane, WA, 14 Nov 1894; d. Los Angeles, CA, 15 Aug 1966.

Owen, Tudor: b. Wales, 20 Jan 1898; d. Los Angeles Co, CA, 13 Mar 1979.

Owens, William: b. New York, 1863; d. Chicago, IL, 20 Aug 1926.

Owsley, Monroe: b. Atlanta, GA, 11 Aug 1900; d. San Francisco, CA, 7 Jun 1937.

P

Pabst, Georg W.: b. Raudnitz, Bohemia, 27 Aug 1885; d. Vienna, Austria, 29 May 1967.

Packard, Clayton L,: b. Washington, 6 Mar 1887; d. San Diego, CA, 7 5ep 1931.

Padden, Sarah: b. England, 16 Oct 1881; d. Los Angeles, CA, 4 Dec 1967.

Paddock, Charles: b. Gainesville, TX, 8 Nov 1900; d. Sitka, AK 22 Jul 1943.

Padilla, Ema: b. Mexico City, Mex, 1900; d. Mexico City, Mex, 2 Jul 1966.

Padjan, Jack (Jack Duane): b. Montana, 14 Dec 1887; d. Riverside Co, CA, 1 Feb 1960.

Padula, Vincent: b. Argentina, 1900; d. Glendale, CA, 16 Jan 1967.

Pagano, Bartholomeo (Maciste): b. San Ilario, Italy, 27 Sep 1878; d. Genoa, Italy, 24 Jun 1947.

Pagay, Sofie: b. Berlin, Ger, 22 Apr 1857; d. 23 Jan 1937.

Pagden, Leonard: b. 1862; d. 24 Mar 1928.

Page, Bob: b. 1886; d. 23 Jul 1943.

Page, James E.: b. England, 1870; d. London, Eng, 26 Mar 1930.

Page, Norman: b. Nottingham, Eng, 1876; d. London, Eng, 4 Jul 1935.

Paget, Alfred: b. 18??; d. c. 1925.

Paget, Doriel: b. 1897; d. England, ? Aug 1991.

Paige, Jean: b. Paris, IL, 3 Jul 1895; d. Los Angeles, CA, 15 Dec 1990.

Paige, Mabel: b. New York, NY, 19 Dec 1880; d. Van Nuys, CA, 8 Feb 1954.

Palasthy, Alexander: b. Hungary, 1877; d. Los Angeles, CA, 16 Mar 1948.

Palermi, Mimmo: b. Italy, 1917; d. 1925.

Palfi, Lotte (Lotte Andor): b. Bochum, Ger, 28 Jul 1903; d. New York, NY, 8 Jul 1991.

Pallay, Fran: b. Atlanta, GA, 1904; d. Brentwood, CA, 6 Nov 1981.

Pallenberg, Max: b. Vienna, Austria, 18 Dec 1877; d. Karlevy Vary, Czech, 20 Jun 1934.

Pallette, Eugene: b. Winfield, KS, 8 Jul 1889; d. Los Angeles, CA, 3 Sep 1954.

Palmer, Corliss: b. Edison, GA, 25 Jul 1909; d. Camarillo, CA, 27 Aug 1952.

Palmer, Inda: b. 18??; d. Ridgewood, NJ, 16 Apr 1923.

Palmer, Jack F.: b. Toronto, Can, 27 Apr 1866; d. Los Angeles, CA, 27 Sep 1928.

Palmer, Lorle: b. 1878; d. New York, NY, 21 Jul 1952.

Palmer, Lorna: b. 1907; d. Los Angeles, CA, 14 Jun 1928.

Palombi, Augusto: b. ????; d. Rome, Italy, 5 Feb 1924.

Pangborn, Franklin: b. Newark, NJ, 23 Jan 1889; d. Santa Monica, CA, 20 Jul 1958.

Pann, Peter: b. Hamburg, Ger, 1872; d. New York, NY, 29 Dec 1948.

Pannaci, Charles: b. 1904; d. Long Branch, NJ, 15 Feb 1927.

Panzer, Paul: b. Wurzburg, Bavaria, 3 Nov 1872; d. Los Angeles, CA, 16 Aug 1958.

Pape, Lionel: b. England, 17 Apr 1877; d. Woodland Hills, CA, 21 Oct 1944.

Papke, Billy: b. Spring Valley, IL, 17 Sep 1886; d. Newport Beach, CA, 26 Nov 1936.

Pardee, C. W. (Doc): b. 1885; d. Glendale, AZ, 17 Jul 1975.

Park, Custer B.: b. Missouri, 4 Nov 1899; d. Los Angeles, CA, 25 Sep 1955.

Park, Josephine: b. 18??; d. Glen Falls, NY, 12 Jan 1931.

Parke, William Sr.: b. Bethlehem, PA, 1873; d. New York, NY, 28 Jul 1941.

Parker, Adele,: b. Plainsfield, NJ, 1885; d. Cleveland, OH, 20 Jan 1966.

Parker, Albert: b. New York State, 1887; d. London, Eng, 10 Aug 1974.

Parker, Barnett: b. Batley, Eng, 11 Sep 1886; d. Los Angeles, CA, 5 Aug 1941.

Parker, Cecil: b. Hastings, Eng, 3 Sep 1897; d. Brighton, Eng, 20 Apr 1971.

Parker, Lucy: b. 1863; d. New York, NY, 21 Mar 1947.

Parker, Marion: b. 18??; d. Venice, CA, ? Nov 1920.

Parker, Vivien: b. 1896; d. Bronx, NY, 2 Feb 1974.

Parkes, Edward: b. New York, NY, 1893; d. Los Angeles, CA, 24 Jul 1985.

Parkhurst, Frances: b. 18??; d. Caldwell, NJ, 31 Dec 1969.

Parkington, Beulah: b. ????; d. Los Angeles, CA, 7 Nov 1958.

Parlo, Dita: b. Stettin, Ger, 4 Sep 1906; d. Paris, Fr, 13 Dec 1971.

Parmalee, Philip: b. 18??; d. c. 1913.

Parr, Charles T.: b. 1843; d. New York, NY, 3 Nov 1923.

Parr, Walter: b. 18??; d. 1913.

Parrish, Helen: b. Columbus, GA, 12 Mar 1922; d. Los Angeles, CA, 22 Feb 1959.

Parrish, Laura Reese: b. 1887; d. Los Angeles, CA, 15 Aug 1977.

Parrish, Mary Catherine: b. 1873; d. Los Angeles Co, CA, 13 Sep 1951.

Parrott, James: b. Baltimore, MD, 2 Aug 1892; d. Los Angeles, CA, 10 May 1939.

Parry, Harvey: b. California, 23 Apr 1900; d. Sherman Oaks, CA, 18 Sep 1985.

Parsons, Carola: b. ????; d. New York, NY, 18 Dec 1958.

Parsons, Baby (Harriet Parsons): b. Burlington, IA, 23 Aug 1906; d. Santa Monica, CA, 2 Jan 1983.

Parsons, "Smiling Billy": b. Middletown, NY, 14 Aug 1878; d. Los Angeles, CA, 28 Sep 1919.

Pasha, Kalla: b. New York, NY, 1879; d. Talmadge, CA, 10 Jun 1933.

Patch, Wally: b. London, Eng, 26 Sep 1888; d. London, Eng, 27 Oct 1970.

Pates, Gwendolyn: b. Texas, 1893; d. 19??.

Paton, Charles, b. London, Eng, 31 Jul 1874; d. 10 Apr 1970.

Paton, Stuart: b. Glasgow, Scot, 23 Jul 1883; d. Woodland Hills, CA, 16 Dec 1944.

Patrick, Ethel: b. 1887; d. Beverly Hills, CA, 18 Sep 1944.

Patrick, Jerome: b. New Zealand, 1883; d. New York, NY, 26 Sep 1923.

Patterson, Elizabeth: b. Savannah, TN, 22 Nov 1874; d. Los Angeles, CA, 31 Jan 1966.

Patterson, Joy W.: b. 1906; d. Santa Ana, CA, 23 Mar 1959.

Patterson, Starke: b. 1899; d. Jonesboro, AR, ? May 1951.

Patton, William (Bill): b. Amarillo, TX, 2 Jun 1894; d. Los Angeles Co, CA, 12 Dec 1951.

Paul, Albert: b. Berlin, Ger, 2 Feb 1856; d. Dresden, Ger, 5 Aug 1928.

Paul, Fred: b. Lausanne, Switz, 1880; d. 19??.

Paul, Logan: b. Ayr, Scot, 1849; d. Brooklyn, NY, 15 Jan 1932.

Paul, Val: b. Denver, CO, 10 Apr 1886; d. Los Angeles, CA, 23 Mar 1962.

Paulder, Maria: b. Tetschon-Bodenbach, Ger, 20 Jun 1903; d. Munich, Ger, 17 Aug 1990.

Paulig, Albert: b. Germany, 1872; d. Germany, 19 Mar 1933.

Pauline, J. Robert: b. 1874; d. Rochester, NY, 11 Nov 1942.

Paulsen, Harold: b. Elmshorn, Ger, 26 Aug 1895; d. Hamburg, Ger, 4 Aug 1954.

Paulsen, Lina: b. Germany, ????; d. 17 Nov 1932.

Paumier, Alfred (Alfred Hodgson): b. Liverpool, Eng, 14 Nov 1870; d. 25 Jan 1951.

Pauncefort, Claire: b. England, ????; d. Worthing, Eng, 23 Nov 1924.

Pauncefort, George: b. San Francisco, CA, 24 Nov 1869; d. Los Angeles, CA, 25 Mar 1942.

Pavanelli, Livio: b. Copparo, Italy, 7 Sep 1881; d. 29 Apr 1958.

Pavlova, Anna: b. St. Petersburg, Russ, 31 Jan 1881; d. The Hague, Holland, 23 Jan 1931.

Pawle, Lennox: b. London, Eng, 27 Apr 1872; d. Los Angeles, CA, 22 Feb 1936.

Paxton, George: b. England, 1862; d. Fort Lee, NJ, 19 Feb 1914.

Paxton, Sidney: b. London, Eng, 25 Jun 1860; d. Montauk, NY, 13 Oct 1930.

Payne, Douglas: b. England, 1875; d. England, 3 Aug 1965.

Payne, Edmund: b. London, Eng, 1865; d. London, Eng, 1 Jul 1914.

Payne, Edna: b. New York, NY, 5 Dec 1891; d. Los Angeles, CA, 31 Jan 1953.

Payne, Louis: b. Elmira, NY, 13 Jan 1873; d. Woodland Hills, CA, 14 Aug 1953.

Paynter, Corona: b. Canada, 1898; d. Los Angeles, CA, 29 Jul 1986.

Payson, Blanche: b. Santa Barbara, CA, 20 Sep 1881; d. Los Angeles, CA, 4 Jul 1964.

Payton, Claude: b. Centerville, IA, 30 Mar 1882; d. Los Angeles, CA, 1 Mar 1955.

Payton, Corse: b. Centerville, IA, 18 Dec 1867; d. Brooklyn, NY, 23 Feb 1934.

Payton, Gloria: b. New York, NY, 2 Aug 1897; d. Louisiana, MO, 1 Aug 1989.

Payton, Lucy: b. Kansas, 12 Oct 1877; d. Louisiana, MO, 15 Jan 1969.

Peacock, Kim: b. Watford, Herts, Eng, 24 Mar 1901; d. Emsworth, Hants, Eng, 26 Dec 1966.

Peacock, Lillian: b. Scottsdale, Pa, 23 Oct 1889; d. Los Angeles, CA, 18 Aug 1918.

Pearce, George C.: b. New York, NY, 26 Jun 1865; d. Los Angeles, CA, 12 Aug 1940.

Pearce, Peggy: b. Long Beach, CA, 4 Jun 1894; d. Burbank, CA, 26 Feb 1975.

Pearson, Molly: b. Edinburgh, Scot, 1876; d. Newton, CT, 26 Jan 1959.

Pearson, Virginia: b. Louisville, KY, 7 Mar 1888; d. Los Angeles, CA, 6 Jun 1958.

Peckham, Frances Miles: b. 1893; d. New York, NY, 7 Jun 1959.

Peer, Heinrich: b. Vienna, Austria, 25 Nov 1867; d. 13 May 1927.

Peer, Helen: b. New York, NY, 1898; d. New Rochelle, NY, 6 May 1942.

Peers, Joan: b. Chicago, IL, 19 Aug 1909; d. San Francisco, CA, 11 Jul 1975.

Pegg, Vester: b. Appleton City, MO, 23 Jan 1889; d. Los Angeles, CA, 19 Feb 1951.

Peil, Edward J.: b. Racine, WI, 18 Jan 1883; d. Los Angeles, CA, 29 Dec 1958.

Peile, Kinsey: b. Allahabad, India, 20 Dec 1862; d. 13 Apr 1934.

Pemberton, Henry W.: b. Richmond, VA, 1875; d. Orlando, FL, 26 Jul 1952.

Pemberton, Patricia: b. ????; d. 9 Mar 1929.

Penbroke, Harry: b. 1887; d. Los Angeles, CA, 14 Sep 1960.

Pendleton, Gaylord: b. New York State, 16 Sep 1908; d. Pasadena, CA, 3 Oct 1984.

Pendleton, Nat: b. Davenport, IA, 9 Aug 1895; d. La Jolla, CA, 11 Oct 1967.

Penman, Lea: b. Red Cloud, NE, 1895; d. Los Angeles, CA, 12 Oct 1962.

Pennell, Richard O.: b. Jersey City, NJ, 21 Feb 1866; d. Los Angeles, CA, 22 Mar 1934.

Pennick, Jack: b. Portland, OR, 7 Dec 1895; d. Manhattan Beach, CA, 16 Aug 1964.

Pennington, Ann: b. Camden, NJ, 23 Dec 1892; d. New York, NY, 4 Nov 1971.

Pennington, Edith Mae: b. ????; d. Shreveport, LA, 16 May 1964.

Penwarden, Duncan: b. Nova Scotia, Can, 9 Feb 1880; d, Jackson Heights, NY, 13 Feb 1930.

Pepper, Helsey James: b. 1874; d. Los Angeles, CA, 9 Sep 1928.

Percival, Walter C.: b. Chicago, IL, 1887; d. Los Angeles, CA, 28 Jan 1934.

Percy, Eileen: b. Belfast, Ire, 21 Aug 1900; d. Beverly Hills, CA, 29 Jul 1973.

Percy, Fred: b. London, Eng, 1852; d. Brixton, Eng, 15 Jul 1926.

Perdue, Derelys: b. Illinois, 22 Mar 1902; d. Los Angeles, CA, 30 Sep 1989.

Periolat, George E.: b. Chicago, IL, 1873; d. Los Angeles, CA, 20 Feb 1940.

Periot, Arthur: b. 1899; d. Monterey, CA, 24 Feb 1929.

Perkins, Dr. James M.: b. Farmington, MO, 1863; d. Denver, CO, 28 Oct 1926.

Perkins, Jean (Daredevil): b. 1899; d. Riverside, CA, 24 Dec 1922.

Perkins, Osgood: b. West Newton, MA, 16 May 1892; d. Washington, DC, 21 Sep 1937.

Perkins, Walter E.: b. Biddeford, ME, 1870; d. Brooklyn, NY, 3 Jun 1925.

Perley, Anna: b. 1849; d. Los Angeles, CA, 20 Jan 1937.

Perley, Charles G.: b. Riverside, CA, 1885; d. Santa Ana, CA, 10 Feb 1933.

Perret, Leonce: b. Niort, Fr, 13 May 1880; d, Paris, Fr, 14 Aug 1935.

Perrin, Jack: b. Three Rivers, MI, 25 Jul 1896; d. Los Angeles, CA, 17 Dec 1967.

Perrins, Leslie: b. Moseley, Eng, 1902; d. Esher, Eng, 13 Dec 1962.

Perry, Anna Day: b. 1853; d. Peak Island, ME, 28 Oct 1928.

Perry, Antoinette: b. Denver, CO, 27 June 1888; d. New York, NY, 28 Jun 1946.

Perry, Charles Emmett: b. New York, 26 Dec 1901; d. Los Angeles, CA, 26 Feb 1967.

Perry, Ida: b. Berlin, Ger, 16 Feb 1877; d. ? Sep 1966.

Perry, Jack: b. ????; d. 7 Oct 1971.

Perry, Jessie: b. Aurora, IN, 1 Sep 1876; d. Los Angeles Co, CA, 6 Jul 1944.

Perry, Kathryn: b. New York, NY, 1897; d. Woodland Hills, CA, 14 Oct 1983.

Perry, Pauline: b. 1882; d. San Diego, CA, 7 Sep 1985.

Perry, Robert E.: b. New York, NY, 26 Dec 1878; d. Los Angeles, CA, 8 Jan 1962.

Perry, Walter L., b. San Francisco, CA, 14 Sep 1868; d. Los Angeles Co, CA, 22 Jan 1954.

Persse, Thomas: b. Lembrick, Ire, 4 Sep 1862; d. Venice, CA, 17 Apr 1920.

Pertwee, Roland: b. Brighton, Eng, 15 May 1885; d. London, Eng, 26 Apr 1963.

Peters, Frederick: b. Waltham, MA, 30 Jun 1884; d. Los Angeles, CA, 23 Apr 1963.

Peters, House: b. Bristol, Gloucs, Eng, 12 Mar 1880; d. Woodland Hills, CA, 7 Dec 1967.

Peters, Capt. John: b. Germany, ????; d. Santa Rosa, CA, 21 Oct 1940.

Peters, John S.: b. Ohio, 31 Dec 1894; d. San Fernando, CA, 7 Nov 1963.

Peters, Page: b. 1889; d. Hermosa Beach, CA, 22 Jun 1916.

Petersen, Ernst: b. 1860; d. 26 Mar 1930.

Petley, Frank B.: b. Old Charlton, Eng, 28 Mar 1872; d. 12 Jan 1945.

Petra, Hortense: b. ????; d. Los Angeles, CA, 8 Jul 1982.

Petroff, Paul: b. Denmark, 1908; d. Antwerp, Bel, 27 Apr 1981.

Petrova, Olga: b. Tur Brook, Eng, 10 May 1884; d. Clearwater, FL, 30 Nov 1977.

Petrovitch, Ivan: b. Novi Sad, Yugoslavia, 1 Jan 1896; d. Munich, Ger, 12 Oct 1962.

Peukert, Leo: b. 1886; d. ? Jan 1944.

Peukert-Impekoven, Sabine: b. Germany, 1890; d. Frankfurt, Ger, 5 May 1970.

Peyton, Lawrence (Larry): b. Hartford, KY, 18??; d. France, ? Oct 1918.

Phelps, Buster (Silas V. Phelps): b. Los Angeles, CA, 5 Nov 1926; d. Los Angeles, CA, 10 Jan 1983.

Phelps, Frarcher: b. 1898; d. 2 Nov 1972.

Phelps, Lee: b. Pennsylvania, 15 May 1893; d. Culver City, CA, 19 Mar 1953.

Philbin, Mary: b. Chicago, IL, 16 Jul 1903; d. Huntington Beach, CA, 7 May 1993.

Philbrick, William H.: b. 18??; d. Chelsea, MA, 20 Oct 1955.

Philipp, Adolph: b. Hamburg, Ger, 29 Jan 1864; d. New York, NY, 30 Jul 1936.

Philley, Virginia: b. 1890; d. Ft. Wayne, IN, 10 Feb 1980.

Phillips, Albert: b. Edwardsville, IN, 1875; d. New York, NY, 24 Feb 1940.

Phillips, Alex, Sr.: b. Canada, 1900; d. Mexico City, Mex, 14 June 1977.

Phillips, Auguatua: b. Rensselaer, IN, 1 Aug 1874; d. 19??.

Phillips, Charles: b. 1904; d. Los Angeles, CA, 25 May 1958.

Phillips, Clement K.: b. ????; d. Hayward, CA, 4 Oct 1928.

Phillips, Dorothy: b. Baltimore, MD, 30 Oct 1889; d. Woodland Hills, CA, 1 Mar 1980.

Phillips, Edna: b. Canada, 26 Feb 1878; d. Los Angeles, CA, 26 Feb 1952.

Phillips, Edward (Eddie): b. Philadelphia, PA, 14 Aug 1899; d. North Hollywood, CA, 22 Feb 1965.

Phillips, Edwin R.: Providence, RI, 18??; d. Coney Island, NY, 29 Aug 1915.

Phillips, Festus (Dad): b. 1872; d. Los Angeles, CA, 5 Sep 1955.

Phillips, Helene (Mrs. Helene Evans): b, Massachusetts, 21 May 1875; d. Santa Monica, CA, 24 Jul 1955.

Phillips, Kate: b. Essex, Eng, 28 Jul 1856; d. London, Eng, 9 Sep 1931.

Phillips, Kember (Tubby): b. Bloemfontein, So Africa, 1884; d. London, Eng, 26 Apr 1930.

Phillips, Minna: b. Sydney, Austral, 1 Jun 1885; d. New Orleans, LA, 17 Jan 1963.

Phillips, Norma: b. Baltimore, MD, 1893; d. New York, NY, 11 Nov 1931.

Phillips, Norman: b. 1892; d. Culver City, CA, 11 Feb 1931.

Phipps, Sally: b. San Francisco, CA, 24 May 1909; d. New York, NY, 17 Mar 1978.

Picha, Hermann: b. Charlottenburg, Ger, 1865; d. 7 Jan 1936.

Pick, Lupu: b. Jassy, Romania, 2 Jan 1886; d. Berlin, Ger, 7 Mar 1931.

Picker, Sylvia: b. 1916; d. Los Angeles, CA, 25 Sep 1981.

Pickett, Bill: b. ????; d. Oklahoma, 1932.

Pickett, Ingram B.: b. 1898; d. Santa Fe, NM, 14 Feb 1963.

Pickford, Charlotte: b. 1873; d. Los Angeles, CA, 22 Mar 1928.

Pickford, Jack: b. Toronto, Can, 18 Aug 1896; d. Paris, Fr, 3 Jan 1933.

Pickford, Lottie: b. Toronto, Can, 9 Jun 1895; d. Beverly Hills, CA, 9 Dec 1936.

Pickford, Mary: b. Toronto, Can, 8 Apr 1893; d. Santa Monica, CA, 29 May 1979.

Pidgeon, Walter: b. East St. John, New Bruns, Can, 23 Sep 1897; d. Santa Monica, 25 Sep 1984.

Piel, Harry: b. Dusseldorf, Ger, 12 Jul 1892; d. Munich, Ger, 27 Mar 1963.

Pierade, Jean Pierre; b. Charleroi, Belgium, ????; d. Paris, Fr, 28 Aug 1937.

Pierce, Evelyn: b. Del RIo, TX, 5 Feb 1908; d. Oyster Bay, NY, 9 Aug 1960.

Pierce, Frances: b. 18??; d. Los Angeles, CA, 25 Nov 1913.

Piercc, Jack P.: b. 1889; d. Los Angeles, CA, 19 Jul 1968.

Pierce, James: b. Freedom, IN, 8 Aug 1900; d. Apple Valley, CA, 12 Nov 1983.

Pieri, Vittori: b. Italy, 18??; d. Turin, Italy, ? May 1926.

Pierre, Anatole: b. 18??; d. New Orleans, LA, ? Feb 1926.

Pierson, Leo: b. Abilene, KS, 25 Dec 1888; d. Los Angeles, CA, 2 Oct 1943.

Piggott, Tempe: b. England, 2 Feb 1884; d. Woodland Hills, CA, 6 Oct 1962.

Pike, Harry J.: b. New York, NY, 1873; d. New York, NY, 18 Dec 1919.

Pike, William: b. Salt Lake City, UT, c. 1888; d. 19??.

Pila, Maximo: b. Santanda, Spain, 30 Jan 1885; d. Los Angeles, CA, 2 Aug 1939.

Pilcer, Harry: b. New York, NY, 29 Apr 1885; d. Cannes, Fr, 14 Jan 1961.

Pilkington, Paul: b. 1877; d. 26 Jan 1918.

Pinchot, Rosamond: b. New York, NY, 26 Oct 1904; d. Old Brookville, NY, 24 Jan 1938.

Pine, Ed: b. 1904; d. Woodland Hills, CA, 9 May 1950.

Pinero, Arthur Wing: b. London, Eng, 24 May 1855; d. London, Eng, 23 Nov 1934.

Pingree, Earl M.: b. Illinois, 4 Mar 1887; d. Los Angeles Co, CA, 12 Jul 1958.

Pinson, Lucile: b. Ramsey, IL, 1 Jun 1900; d. Van Nuys, CA, 12 Jan 1977.

Pitti, Ben: b. 1893; d. Culver City, CA, 26 Jul 1955.

Pitts, ZaSu: b. Parsons, KS, 3 Jan 1898; d. Los Angeles, CA, 7 Jun 1963.

Pittschau, Werner: b. Germany, 1903; d. Spandau, Ger ? Oct 1928.

Pixley, Gus: b. 1864; d. Saranac Lake, NY, 2 Jun 1923.

Plank, Eddie: b. Gettysburg, PA, 31 Aug 1875; d. Gettysburg, PA, 24 Feb 1926.

Platen, Karl: b. 6 Mar 1877; d. ? Jul 1952.

Playfair, Sir Nigel: b. London, Eng, 1 Jul 1874; d. London, Eng, 19 Aug 1934.

Playter, Wellington: b. Rawcliff, Eng, 9 Dec 1879; d. Oakland, CA, 15 Jul 1937.

Plimmer, Walter, Jr.: b. 1901; d. Lexington, Ky, 18 Sep 1968.

Plumb, Hay: b. England, 1883; d. 1960.

Plummer, Lincoln: b. Maryland, 28 Sep 1875; d. Los Angeles, CA, 14 Feb 1928.

Plunkett, Walter: b. Oakland, CA, 5 Jun 1902; d. Santa Monica, CA, 8 Mar 1982.

Podesta, Maria Esther: b. Argentina, 1896; d. Buenos Aires, Arg, 18 Sep 1983.

Poff, Lon: b. Bedford, IN, 8 Feb 1870; d. Los Angeles Co, CA, 8 Aug 1952.

Pohl, Max: b. 10 Dec 1885; d. 7 Apr 1935.

Pointer, Anton: b. Salzburg, Ger, 8 Dec 1890; d. 8 Sep 1949.

Pola, Isa: b. Pologne, Italy, 1909; d. Milan, Italy, 15 Dec 1984.

Polanski, Goury: b. Russia, 1893; d. Los Angeles, CA, 17 Oct 1976.

Polidor (Ferdinando Guillaume): b. France, 19 May 1887; d. 3 Dec 1977.

Polini, Emile: b. 18??; d. England, 31 Jul 1927.

Polla, Pauline M.: b. 1868; d. Albany, NY, 9 Apr 1940.

Pollar, Gene: b. New York, NY, 1892; d. Ft. Lauderdale, FL, 20 Oct 1971.

Pollard, Daphne: b. Melbourne, Austral, 19 Oct 1894; d. Los Angeles, CA, 22 Feb 1978.

Pollard, Harry: b. Republic City, KS, 23 Jan 1879; d. Pasadena, CA, 6 Jul 1934.

Pollard, Snub (Harry): b. Melbourne, Austral, 9 Nov 1889; d. Burbank, CA, 19 Jan 1962.

Polo, Eddie: b. Italy, 1 Feb 1875; d. Los Angeles, CA, 14 Jun 1961.

Polo, Sam: b. California, 7 Nov 1872; d. Woodland Hills, CA, 3 Oct 1966.

Ponder, Jack: b. Shreveport, LA, 20 Nov 1903; d. Los Angeles Co, CA, 5 Aug 1970.

Ponto, Erich: b. Lubeck, Ger, 14 Dec 1884; d. Stuttgart, Ger, 4 Feb 1957.

Pope, Unola B.: b. 1884; d. Fremont, OH, 1 Feb 1938.

Porcasi, Paul: b. Palermo, Italy, 1 Jan 1879; d. Los Angeles, CA, 8 Aug 1946.

Porten, Henny: b. Magdeburg, Ger, 7 Apr 1888; d. Berlin, Ger, 15 Oct 1960.

Porter, Caleb: b. London, Eng, 1 Sep 1867; d. London, Engt 13 Mar 1940.

Porter, Edward D.: b. Columbus, TN, 26 May 1881; d. Los Angeles, CA, 29 Jul 1939.

Porter, Paul, Sr.: b. 1886; d. New York, NY, 17 Oct 1957.

Post, Charles A. (Buddy): b. Salt Lake City, UT, 3 Nov 1897; d. Los Angeles Co, CA, 20 Dec 1952.

Post, Guy Bates: b. Seattle, WA, 22 Sep 1875; d. Los Angeles, CA, 16 Jan 1968.

Post, Wilmarth H.: b. ????; d. Rutherford, NJ, 25 Aug 1930.

Postance, William C. F.: b. 1875; d. Hoboken, NJ, 14 Apr 1953.

Potel, Victor: b. Lafayette, IN, 12 Oct 1889; d. Los Angeles, CA, 8 Mar 1947.

Potter, Billy: b. 1874; d. New York, NY, 2 Apr 1961.

Potts, Hank: b. 26 May 1896; d. Los Angeles, CA, 1 Apr 1980.

Potts, Walter L.: b. 1873; d. Indianapolis, IN, 25 Feb 1943.

Pounds, Charles Courtice: b. London, Eng, 30 May 1862; d. Kingston, Eng, 21 Dec 1927.

Pouyet, Eugene: b. France, 23 Aug 1883; d. Alameda Co, CA, 22 May 1950.

Powell, David: b. Glasgow, Scot, 17 Dec 1894; d. New York, NY, 16 Apr 1925.

Powell, Dick: b. 18??; d. Hales Corner, WI, 26 Sep 1948.

Powell, Russell: b. Indianapolis, IN, 16 Sep 1875; d. Los Angeles, CA, 28 Nov 1950.

Powell, Soldene: b. 1860; d. New York, NY, 12 Apr 1915.

Powell, W. Templer: b. 18??; d. 29 Jun 1949.

Powell, William: b. Pittsburgh, PA, 29 Jul 1892; d. Palm Springs, CA, 5 Mar 1984.

Power, Jule: b. Portland, OR, 18??; d. Los Angeles, CA, 14 Feb 1932.

Power, Paul: b. Chicago, IL, 7 Dec 1902; d. North Hollywood, CA, 5 Apr 1968.

Power, Tyrone, Sr.: b. London, Eng, 2 May 1869; d. Los Angeles, CA, 30 Dec 1931.

Power, Mrs. Tyrone (Patia Reaume): b. ????; d. Canterbury, NH, 29 Sep 1959.

Powers, Francis: b. Marner, VA, 4 Jun 1865; d. Santa Monica, CA, 10 May 1940.

Powers, John H.: b. 1885; d. New York, NY, 17 Jan 1941.

Powers, Lucille: b. San Antonio, TX, 18 Nov 1911; d. El Monte, CA, 11 Sep 1981.

Powers, May: b. ????; d. Louisville, KY, 24 Jul 1961.

Powers, Tom: b. Owensboro, KY, 7 Jul 1890; d. Manhattan Beach, CA, 9 Nov 1955.

Powley, Bryan: b. Reading, Eng, 16 Sep 1871; d. London, Eng, ? Dec 1962.

Poynter, Beulah: b. St. Joseph, MO, 6 Jun 1886; d. 19??.

Pradot, Marcelle: b. 1902; d. Paris, Fr, 24 Jun 1982.

Pratt, Gilbert W.: b. Providence, RI. 1891; d. Los Angeles, CA, 10 Dec 1954.

Pratt, Jack: b. St. John, New Bruns, Can, 12 Jan 1878; d. Los Angeles, CA, 24 Dec 1938.

Pratt, Lynn: b. Sylvan Center, MI, 18 Jan 1863; d. New York, NY, 9 Jan 1930.

Pratt, Purnell B.: b. Bethel, IL, 20 Oct 1885; d. Los Angeles, CA, 25 Jul 1941.

Pray, Anna M.: b. 1891; d. New York, NY, 30 Jun 1971.

Prazsky, Beda: b. 15 Jun 1914; d. 6 Aug 1975.

Preer, Evelyn: b, Chicago, IL, 26 Jul 1896; d. Los Angeles, CA, 17 Nov 1932.

Prejean, Albert: b. Paris, Fr. 27 Oct 1893; d. Paris, Fr. 1 Nov 1979.

Preobrazhenskaya, Olga: b. Russia, 1885; d. 1966.

Prestelle, Mae: b. Iowa, 4 Jul 1878; d. Los Angeles, CA, 29 Apr 1952.

Pretty, Arline: b. Washington, DC, 5 Sep 1885; d. Los Angeles, CA, 14 Apr 1978.

Prevert, Pierre: b. Paris, Fr, 26 May 1906; d. Paris, Fr, 6 Apr 1988.

Prevost, Marie: b. Sarnia, Ont, Can, 6 Nov 1898; d. Los Angeles, CA, 20 Jan 1937.

Price, Kate: b. County Cork, Ire, 13 Feb 1872; d. Los Angeles, CA, 4 Jan 1943.

Price, Mark: b. Ireland, 18??; d. New York, NY, 31 Mar 1917.

Price, Nancy: b. Kimber, Worcs, Eng, 3 Feb 1880; d. Worthing, Eng, 31 Mar 1970.

Price, Stanley L.: b. Kansas, 31 Dec 1892; d. Los Angeles, CA, 13 Jul 1955.

Price, Ted: b. 1882; d. Newhall, CA, 13 Mar 1928.

Primrose, Daisy: b. 1889; d. Los Angeles, CA, 19 Nov 1927.

Prince, Adelaide: b. London, Eng, 14 Dec 1866; d. Shawnee-on- Delaware, PA, 4 Apr 1941.

Prince, Arthur: b. London, Eng, 17 Nov 1881; d. London, Eng, 14 Apr 1948.

Prince, Charles (Rigadin): b. Maisons-Lafite, Fr, 1872; d. Paris, Fr, 18 Jul 1933.

Prince, John T.: b. Boston, MA, 11 Sep 1871; d. Los Angeles, CA, 23 Dec 1937.

Pringle, Aileen: b. San Francisco, CA, 27 Jul 1895; d. New York, NY, 16 Dec 1989.

Pringle, John: b. 1862; d. Los Angeles, CA, 12 Aug 1929.

Prior, Herbert: b. Oxford, Eng, 2 Jul 1867; d. Los Angeles, CA, 3 Oct 1954.

Prouty, Jed: b. Boston, MA, 6 Apr 1879; d. New York, NY, 10 May 1956.

Prussing, Margaret: b. Highland, IL, 29 Mar 1890; d. Los Angeles Co, CA, 13 Jan 1944.

Pryce, Col. C. Rhys: b. 18??; d. ? Feb 1915.

Psilander, Valdemar: b. Copenhagen, Den, 9 May 1884; d. 16 Mar 1917.

Pudovkin, Vsevolod: b. Penza, Russ, 28 Feb 1893; d. Russia, 30 Jun 1953.

Puffy, Charles H.: b. Budapest, Hungary, 3 Nov 1884; d. 1942.

Puglia, Frank: b. Sicily, 9 Mar 1892; d. South Pasadena, CA, 25 Oct 1975.

Purviance, Edna: b. Lovelock, NV, 21 Oct 1894; d. Woodland Hills, CA, 13 Jan 1958.

Q

Quaranta, Lydia: b. Turin, Italy, 1891; d. Italy, 5 Mar 1928.

Quartaro, Nena: b. New York, NY, 17 Mar 1908; d. Woodland Hills, CA, 23 Nov 1985.

Quartermaine, Charles: b. Richmond, Eng, 30 Dec 1877; d. ? Aug 1958.

Quartermaine, Leon: b. Richmond, Eng, 24 Sep 1876; d. London, Eng, 25 Jun 1967.

Quattrociocchi, Nicky: b. Palermo, Sicily, ????; d. Palermo, Sicily ? Apr 1968.

Querio, Isa: b. 1893; d. 1976.

Quillan, Eddie: b. Philadelphia, PA, 31 Mar 1907; d. Burbank, CA, 19 Jul 1990.

Quillan, John: b. Philadelphia, PA, 25 Jun 1906; d. Los Angeles, CA, 27 Aug 1985.

Quillan, Joseph F.: b. Glasgow, Scot, 27 Jul 1884; d. Los Angeles, CA, 16 Nov 1952.

Quillan, Joseph: b. 1916; d. Los Angeles, CA, 6 Apr 1961.

Quillan, Mrs. Sarah: b. 1879; d. Los Angeles, CA, 3 Aug 1969.

Quimby, Casius C.: b. 1873; d. Bridgeport, CT, 12 Feb 1944.

Quimby, Margaret: b. Minnesota, 1905; d. Minneapolis, MN, 26 Aug 1965.

Quinlan, Gertrude: b. Boston, MA, 25 Feb 1875; d. New York, NY, 29 Nov 1963.

Quinn, Jack: b. ????; d. New York, NY, 10 Dec 1929.

Quinn, James: b. 1884; d. New York, NY, 30 Nov 1919.

Quinn, James T.: b. New Orleans, LA, 17 Jul 1885; d. 21 Aug 1940.

Quinn, Joe: b. 1899; d. Los Angeles, CA, 20 May 1974.

Quinn, John P.: b. St. Louis, MO, 1851; d. Philadelphia, PA, 18 Apr 1916.

Quirk, Billy (William A. Quirk): b. Jersey City, NJ, 29 Mar 1873; d. Los Angeles, CA, 20 Apr 1926.

R

Rabagliat, Alberto: b. Milan, Italy, 26 Jun 1906; d. Rome, Italy, 7 Mar 1974.

Rachlitz, Violet: b. ????; d. New York, NY, 12 Jan 1916.

Radcliffe, Violet: b, 1908; d. c. 1926.

Rader, William E.: b. St. Louis, MO, 12 Aug 1890; d. Los Angeles, CA, 7 Feb 1947.

Rae, Claire: b. 1889; d. Canton, OH, 7 Jul 1938.

Rafferty, Patrick C.: b. 18??; d. Utica, NY, ? Apr 1935.

Raglan, James: b. Redhill, Surrey, Eng, 6 Jan 1901; d. London, Eng, 15 Nov 1961.

Rahm, Knute Olof: b. Sweden, 20 Mar 1876; d. Los Angeles, CA, 23 Jul 1957.

Rahn, Bruno: b. 1898; d. Berlin, Ger, 15 Sep 1927.

Raimu, Jules: b. Toulon, Fr, 17 Dec 1883; d. Paris, Fr, 20 Sep 1946.

Raine, Adelaide: b. 4 Jan 1894; d. Drexel Hills, PA, 20 Jan 1978.

Rainer, Robert Richard: b. 1889; d. West Los Angeles, CA, 25 Aug 1960.

Rains, Claude: b. London, Eng, 10 Nov 1889; d. Laconia, NH, 30 May 1967.

Rains, Fred: b. London, Eng, 1875; d. London, Eng, 3 Dec 1945.

Rajas, Louis: b. ????; d. Redondo Beach, CA, ? Mar 1921.

Raker, Lorin: b. Joplin, MO, 8 May 1891; d. Woodland, Hills, CA, 25 Dec 1959.

Rale, M. W. (Michael W. Pale): b. 25 Mar 1877; d. Englewood, NJ, 8 Jul 1940.

Raleigh, Mrs. Cecil (Saba Raleigh): b. England, 1866; d. London, Eng, 22 Aug 1923.

Ralli, Paul: b. Greece, 2 Mar 1903; d. Los Angeles, CA, 4 Sep 1953.

Ralph, Hanna: b. 25 Sep 1885; d. Berlin, Ger, 25 Mar 1978.

Ralph, Jessie: b. Gloucester, MA, 5 Nov 1865; d. Gloucester, MA, 30 May 1944.

Ralston, Bradford: b. 1906; d. ? Mar 1991.

Ralston, Esther: b. Bar Harbor, ME, 17 Sep 1902; d. Ventura, CA, 14 Jan 1994.

Ralston, Howard: b. Bar Harbor, ME, 25 Jul 1904; d. Los Angeles, CA, 1 Jun 1992.

Ralston, Jobyna: b. South Pittsburgh, TN, 21 Nov 1900; d. Woodland Hills, CA, 22 Jan 1967.

Rambeau, Marjorie: b. San Francisco, CA, 15 Jul 1889; d. Palm Springs, CA, 7 Jul 1970.

Rambova, Natacha: b. Salt Lake City, UT, 19 Jan 1897; d. Pasadena, CA, 5 Jun 1966.

Rameau, Emil: b. Berlin, Ger, 13 Aug 1888; d. 9 Sep 1957.

Ramirez, Pepita: b. 1902; d. Los Angeles, CA, 27 Dec 1927.

Ramsey, John Nelson: b. 1863; d. London, Eng, 5 Apr 1929.

Ranaldi, Frank: b. 1905; d. Los Angeles, CA, 2 May 1933.

Rand, Ayn: b. Russia, 1905; d. New York, NY, 6 Mar 1982.

Rand, John F.: b. New Haven, CT, 1878; d. Los Angeles, CA, 25 Jan 1940.

Rand, Sally: b. Hickory County, MO, 2 Jan 1904; d. Glendora, CA, 31 Aug 1979.

Randall, Bernard: b. Odessa, Russ, 4 Jul 1884; d. New York, NY, 17 Dec 1954.

Randall, Harry: b. 1860; d. London, Eng, 18 May 1932.

Randall, Jack (Addison Randall): b. San Fernando, CA, 12 May 1906; d. Conoga Park, CA, 16 Jul 1945.

Randall, Rae: b. 1909; d. Los Angeles, CA, 7 May 1934.

Randall, William: b. Rochester, NY, 1877; d. Elizabeth, NY, 22 Apr 1939.

Randolph, Anders: b. Viborg, Den, 18 Dec 1870; d. Los Angeles, CA, 2 Jul 1930.

Randolph, Dorothy: b. ????; d. Atlanta, GA. 10 Mar 1918.

Randolph, Louise: b. Fort Leavenworth, KS, 12 Mar 1870; d. Port Chester, NY, 2 Nov 1953.

Ranier, Richard: b. California, 6 Nov 1889; d. Los Angeles, CA, 25 Aug 1960.

Rankin, Arthur: b. New York, NY, 30 Aug 1900; d. Los Angeles, CA, 23 Mar 1947.

Rankin, Caroline (Spike): b. Pittsburg, PA, 22 Aug 1880; d. Los Angeles Co, CA, 2 Feb 1953.

Rankin, Doris: b. 1880; d. Washington, DC, 1946.

Ranous, William V.: b. New York State, 12 Mar 1857; d. Santa Monica, CA, 1 Apr 1915.

Ransom, Edith: b. 1905; d. Seattle, WA, 26 Jan 1933.

Ranson, Nellie Crawford: b. 1876; d. 16 Nov 1964.

Rappe, Virginia: b. Chicago, IL, 1896; d. San Francisco, CA, 9 Sep 1921.

Rapport, Helena: b. 1884; d. New York, NY, 5 Dec 1954.

Raquello, Edward: b. Warsaw, Poland, 14 May 1900; d. 24 Aug 1976.

Rasmussen, Maurine: b. Illinois, 16 May 1883; d. Los Angeles, CA, 5 May 1962.

Rasp, Fritz: b. Bayreuth, Ger, 13 May 1891; d. Graefelfing, Ger, 30 Nov 1976.

Ratcliffe, E. J. (E. J. Radcliffe): b. London, Eng, 10 Mar 1863; d. Los Angeles, CA, 28 Sep 1948.

Rathbone, Basil: b. Johannesburg, So Africa, 13 Jun 1892; d. New York, NY, 21 Jul 1967.

Rathbone, Guy B.: b. Liverpool, Eng, 28 May 1884; d. 21 Apr 1916.

Ratner, Anna: b. 1892; d. Chicago, IL, 2 Jul 1967.

Rattenberry, Harry L.: b. Sacramento, CA, 14 Nov 1857; d. Los Angeles, CA, 9 Dec 1925.

Rau, William: b. 1893; d. Los Angeles, CA, 28 Sep 1925.

Raucourt, Jules: b. Brussels, Belgium, 8 May 1890; d. Los Angeles, CA, 30 Jan 1967.

Rauscher, William: b. 18??; d. Mount Vernon, NY, c. 1962.

Ravenscroft, Ralph: b. 1871; d. Rochester, IN, 18 May 1934.

Rawlinson, Herbert: b. Brighton, Eng, 15 Nov 1885; d. Los Angeles, CA, 12 Jul 1953.

Rawlston, Zelma: b. Germany, 1868; d. New York, NY, 30 Oct 1915.

Ray, Albert: b. New Rochelle, NY, 28 Aug 1897; d. Los Angeles, CA, 8 Feb 1944.

Ray, Allene: b. San Antonio, TX, 2 Jan 1901; d. Temple City, CA; 5 May 1979.

Ray, Charles: b. Jacksonville, IL, 15 Mar 1891; d. Los Angeles, CA, 23 Nov 1943.

Ray, Emma: b. 1871; d. Los Angeles, CA, 3 Jan 1935.

Ray, Estelle Goulding: b. 1888; d. Los Angeles, CA, 1 Aug 1970.

Ray, Helen: b. Fort Stockton, TX, 1879; d. Wolfeboro, NH, 2 Oct 1965.

Ray, Jack: b. 1917; d. Montclair, CA, 31 Oct 1975.

Ray, Johnny: b. Wales, 1859; d. Los Angeles, CA, 4 Sep 1927.

Ray, Marjorie: b. 1890; d. San Diego, CA, 22 Jul 1924.

Ray, Naomi: b. 1893; d. New York, NY, 13 Mar 1966.

Rayford, Alma: b. Muskopee, OK, 24 Mar 1903; d. El Paso, TX, 14 Feb 1987.

Raymond, Charles: b. London, Eng, 1858; d. 1930.

Raymond, Cyril: b. Bognor Regis, Eng, 1897; d. London, Eng, 21 Mar 1973.

Raymond, Frances (Frankie Raymond): b. Selma, MA, 24 May 1869; d. Los Angeles, CA, 18 Jun 1961.

Raymond, Helen: b. Philadelphia, PA, 1885; d. New York, NY, 26 Nov 1965.

Raymond, Jack: b. 1892; d. Los Angeles, CA, 7 Jul 1942.

Raymond, Jack: b. Minneapolis, MN, 14 Dec 1901; d. Santa Monica, CA, 5 Dec 1951.

Raymond, Jack: b. Wimborne, Dorsetshire, Eng, 1886; d. London, Eng, 20 Mar 1953.

Raymond, Pete: b. Minneapolis, MN, 1871; d. New York, NY, 30 Mar 1927.

Rayner, Minnie: b. London, Eng, 2 May 1869; d. London, Eng, 13 Dec 1941.

Razetto, Stella: b. San Diego, CA, 17 Dec 1881; d. Malibu Beach, CA, 21 Sep 1948.

Read, Didde: b. Australia, 1899; d. Los Angeles, CA, 6 Feb 1932.

Read, Opie: b. Nashville, TN, 22 Dec 1852; d. Chicago, IL, 2 Nov 1939.

Reader, Ralph: b. Crewkerne, Somerset, Eng, 25 May 1903; d. London, Eng, 13 May 1982.

Readick, Frank M.: b. 1861; d. New York, NY. 26 Aug 1924.

Ready, Mike: b. Troy, NY, 21 Aug 1858; d. Los Angeles, CA, 26 Mar 1936.

Reals, Grace: b. 18??; d. New York, NY, 31 Aug 1925.

Reardon, Edmund H. (Ned): b. 18??; d. New York, NY, 4 Feb 1916.

Reaume, Helen: b. Kentucky, 18??; d. Cincinnati, OH, 1 Nov 1924.

Redding, Eugene: b. Montreal, Can, 20 May 1870; d. Montreal, Can, ? Apr 1937.

Redding, Harry: b. 1882; d. New York, NY, 9 Mar 1949.

Reddway, Eddie: b. 1870; d. Reading, PA, 9 Apr 1919.

Redgrave, Roy: b. 1872; d. Sydney, Austral, 25 May 1922.

Redman, Frank E.: b. New York State, 1879; d. Englewood, NJ, 24 Jul 1940.

Redmond, Elmer E.: b. Pennsylvania, 5 May 1887; d. Los Angeles Co, CA, 18 Jul 1955.

Red Wing, Princess: b. Winnebago, NV, 13 Feb 1884; d. New York, NY, 12 Mar 1974.

Redwing, Rodd: b. New York State, 24 Aug 1904; d. Los Angeles, CA, 30 May 1971.

Reed, Bob: b. 1869; d. London, Eng, 27 Sep 1927.

Reed, Dave: b. 1872; d. New York, NY, 11 Apr 1946.

Reed, Donald: b. Mexico City, Mex, 23 Jul 1901; d. Westwood, CA, 28 Feb 1973.

Reed, Florence: b. Philadelphia, PA, 10 Jan 1883; d. East Islip, NY, 21 Nov 1967.

Reed, George E.: b. 1890; d. Camden, NJ, 11 Jun 1952.

Reed, George H.: b. Macon, GA, 27 Nov 1866; d. Woodland Hills, CA, 6 Nov 1952.

Reed, Julian: b. 1864; d. Englewood, NJ, 28 May 1934.

Reed, Vivian: b. Chicago, IL, 1893; d. Woodland Hills, CA, 19 Jul 1989.

Reeves, Billy: b. London, Eng, 1864; d. N. Ixworth, Suffolk, Eng, 29 Dec 1943.

Reeves, Kynaston: b. London, Eng, 29 May 1893; d. London, Eng, 10 Dec 1971.

Reeves, Myrtle: b. Atlanta, GA, 1897; d. Garden Grove, CA, 18 Jan 1983.

Reeves, Robert Jasper: b. Marlin, TX, 28 Jan 1892; d. Los Angeles, CA, 13 Apr 1960.

Reeves-Smith, H.: b. Scarborough, Eng, 1863; d. Elwell, Surrey, Eng, 29 Jan 1938.

Regan, Edgar J.: b. 1880; d. San Francisco, CA, 21 Jun 1938.

Regas, George: b. Sparta, Greece, 9 Nov 1890; d. Los Angeles, CA, 13 Dec 1940.

Regas, Pedro: b. Sparta, Greece, 18 Apr 1897; d. Los Angeles, CA, 10 Aug 1974.

Regno, Ugo Del: b. 1897; d. 14 Jun 1981.

Rehan, Mary: b. 1887; d. Rochester, MN, 28 Aug 1963.

Rehfeld, Curt: b. Dresden, Ger, 11 Feb 1881; d. 24 Mar 1934.

Rehkopf, Paul: b. Germany, 1872; d. ? June 1949.

Reicher, Frank: b. Munich, Ger, 2 Dec 1875; d. Playa del Reys, CA, 19 Jan 1965.

Reicher, Hedwiga; b. Oldenburg, Ger, 12 Jun 1884; d. Los Angeles, CA, 2 Sep 1971.

Reichert, Kittens: b. Yonkers, NY, 3 Mar 1910; d. Louisville, KY, 11 Jan 1990.

Reid, Hal (James Halleck Reid): b. Cedarville, OH, 14 Apr 1862; d. New York, NY, 22 May 1920.

Reid, Mrs. Hal (Bertha Westbrook): b. 18??; d, Newark, NJ, 28 Jul 1939.

Reid, Leslie: b. Canada, 18??; d. 1917.

Reid, Mary: b. Gibraltar, 29 Aug 1895; d. New York, NY, 18 Jul 1979.

Reid, Wallace: b. St. Louis, MO, 15 Apr 1891; d. Los Angeles, CA, 18 Jan 1923.

Reid, Wallace, Jr.: b. Los Angeles, CA, 1917; d. Santa Monica, CA, 26 Feb 1990.

Reimers, Georg: b. 1870; d. Vienna, Austria, 15 Apr 1936.

Reinach, Edward: b. 18??; d. Beverly Hills, CA, 2 Aug 1936.

Reinhardt, John: b. Austria, 1901; d. Berlin, Ger, 6 Aug 1953.

Reinwald, Hanni: b. Degerloch, Ger, 24 Aug 1903; d. 1978.

Reisner, Charles F. (Chuck): b. Minneapolis, MN, 14 Mar 1887; d. La Jolla, CA, 24 Sep 1962.

Reithe, Aloise D.: b. Los Angeles, CA, 1890; d. Los Angeles, CA, 5 Sep 1943.

Rejane, Gabrielle: b. Paris, Fr, 6 Jun 1857; d. Paris, Fr, 14 Jun 1920.

Relph, George: b. Cullercoats, Eng, 27 Jan 1888; d. London, Eng, 24 Apr 1960.

Remus, Romola: b. ????; d. Chicago, IL, 17 Feb 1987.

Remy, Dick, Sr.: b. 1873; d. Los Angeles, CA, 1 Jun 1947.

Renaldo, Duncan: b. Spain, 23 Apr 1904; d. Santa Barbara, CA, 3 Sep 1980.

Renavent, Georges: b. Paris, Fr, 23 Apr 1893; d. Guadalajara, Mex, 2 Jan 1969.

Renfro, James Lige (Rennie): b. Denison, TX, 30 Sep 1892; d. Redding, CA, 2 Mar 1962.

Renick, Ruth: b. Galveston, TX, 1893; d. Los Angeles, CA, 7 May 1984.

Rennie, James: b. Toronto, Can, 18 Apr 1890; d. New York, NY, 31 Jul 1965.

Renoir, Pierre: b. Paris, Fr, 21 Mar 1885; d. Paris, Fr, 11 Mar 1952.

Requa, Charles: b. New York State, 20 Mar 1892; d. Los Angeles Co, CA, 11 Dec 1967.

Reuter-Eichberg, Adele: b. Germany, 18??; d. 4 Oct 1928.

Revel, Mollie: b. 1848; d. 31 Dec 1932.

Revelle, Hamilton: b. Gibraltar, 31 May 1872; d. Nice, Fr, 11 Apr 1958.

Revier, Dorothy: b. San Francisco, CA, 18 Apr 1904; d. Los Angeles, CA, 19 Nov 1993.

Reville, Alma: b. London, Eng, 23 Sep 1897; d. Bel Air, CA, 6 Jul 1982.

Rex, Will: b. 1692; d. 12 May 1916.

Rey, Harry: b. 1178; d. ? Jul 1910.

Reynolds, E. Vivian: b. London, Eng, 24 Jun 1866; d. 13 May 1952.

Reynolds, Edna: b. New York, NY, 10 Feb 1888; d. 19??.

Reynolds, Genevieve: b. New York, NY, ????; d. Chicago, IL, 25 Jan 1922.

Reynolds, Harrington: b. 1852; d. Christchurch, New Zealand, 15 Oct 1919.

Reynolds, Lynn F.: b. Harlem, IA, 7 May 1891; d. Los Angeles, CA, 25 Feb 1927.

Reynolds, Noah: b. 18??; d. Philadelphia, PA, 19 Sep 1948.

Reynolds, Robert R.: b. Asheville, NC, 18 Jun 1884; d. Asheville, NC, 13 Feb 1963.

Reynolds, Tom: b. London, Eng, 9 Aug 1866; d. 25 Jul 1942.

Reynolds, Vera: b. Richmond, VA, 25 Nov 1899; d. Woodland Hills, CA, 22 Apr 1962.

Reynolds, Wilson: b. Louisville, KY. 1870; d. Ossining, NY, 10 Apr 1938.

Rhein-Schradling, Otto Franz: b. 18??; d. Milwaukee, WI, 30 Apr 1952.

Rhodes, Billie: b. San Francisco, CA, 15 Aug 1894; d. Los Angeles, CA, 12 Mar 1988.

Rhodes, Little Billy: b. Illinois, 1 Feb 1894; d. Los Angeles, CA, 24 Jul 1967.

Rhodes, Percy W.: b. 1871; d. ? Nov 1956.

Rhudin, Fridolf: b. Munkfors, Sweden, 1895; d. 6 Mar 1935.

Rial, Louise: 1850; d. New York, NY, 9 Aug 1940.

Rice, Emmit B.: b. 1884; d. Los Angeles, CA, 23 Mar 1939.

Rice, Fanny: b. Lowell, MA, 4 Feb 1859; d. New York, NY, 10 Jul 1936.

Rice, Frank: b. Muskegan, MI, 13 May 1892; d. Los Angeles, CA, 9 Jan 1936.

Rice, Grantland: b. 1881; d. New York, NY, 13 Jul 1954.

Rice, Herbert: b. 1888; d. Chicago, IL, ? Jul 1938.

Rice, Ivy: b. 1898; d. Los Angeles, CA, 8 Nov 1962.

Rice, John C.: b. Sullivan County, NY, 7 Apr 1858; d. Philadelphia, PA, 5 Jun 1915.

Rice, Roy: b. New York, NY, 4 Apr 1887; d. Visalia, CA, 29 Dec 1966.

Rich, Helen: b. Pittsburgh, PA, 1897; d. New York, NY, 28 Aug 1963.

Rich, Irene: b. Buffalo, NY, 13 Oct 1891; d. Santa Barbara, CA, 22 Apr 1988.

Rich, John: b. 18??; d. New York, NY, 27 Aug 1912.

Rich, Lillian: b. Herne Hill, London, Eng, 1 Jan 1900; d. Woodland Hills, CA, 5 Jan 1954.

Rich, Vivian: b. Philadelphia, PA, 26 May 1893; d. Los Angeles, CA, 17 Nov 1957.

Richard, Frida: b. Vienna, Austria, 1 Nov 1873; d. Salzburg, Austria, 12 Sep 1946.

Richards, Charles: b. Indianpolis, IN, 16 Dec 1899; d. Los Angeles, CA, 29 Jul 1948.

Richards, Cicely: b. London, Eng, 1850; d. London, Eng, 8 Apr 1933.

Richardson, Frank: b. 18??; d. Murrieta Springs, CA, 29 Jan 1913.

Richardson, Frank: b. Philadelphia, PA, 6 Sep 1898; d. Philadelphia, PA, 30 Jan 1962.

Richardson, Jack: b. New York, NY, 18 Nov 1883; d. c. 17 Nov 1957.

Richepin, Jean: b. Medeah, Algeria, 4 Feb 1849; d. Paris, Fr, 12 Dec 1926.

Richman, Al: b. New Orleans, LA, 21 May 1885; d. Los Angeles, CA, 20 Apr 1936.

Richman, Charles: b. Chicago, IL, 12 Jan 1870; d. Bronx, NY, 1 Dec 1940.

Richmond, Warner: b. Racine, WI, 11 Jan 1886; d. Los Angeles, CA, 19 Jun 1948.

Richter, Hans: b. Berlin, Ger, 1868; d. Lacarno, Switz, 1 Feb 1976.

Richter, Paul: b. Vienna, Austria, 1 Apr 1895; d. Vienna, Austria, 30 Dec 1961.

Rickard, George L. (Tex): b. Sherman, TX, 2 Jan 1870; d. Miami Beach, FL, 5 Jun 1929.

Ricketts, Thomas: b. London, Eng, 15 Jan 1853; d. Los Angeles, CA, 19 Jan 1939.

Ricks, Archie: b. California, 29 Feb 1896; d. Los Angeles Co, CA, 10 Jan 1962.

Ricksen, Lucille: b. Chicago, IL, 22 Aug 1909; d. Los Angeles, CA, 13 Mar 1925.

Ricksen, Marshall: b. Illinois, 19 Dec 1907; d. Oakland, CA, 16 Jan 1975.

Rickson, Joe: b. Clearcreek, MT, 6 Sep 1880; d. Los Angeles Co, CA, 8 Jan 1958.

Riddell, George: b. England, 1864; d. New York, NY, 19 Mar 1944.

Ridgely, Cleo: b. New York, NY, 12 May 1894; d. Glendale, CA, 18 Aug 1962.

Ridges, Stanley: b. Southampton, Eng, 1892; d. Westbrook, CT, 22 Apr 1951.

Ridgeway, Fritzi: b. Missoula, MT, 8 Apr 1898; d. Lancaster, CA, 29 Mar 1961.

Riechers, Helene: b. Germany, 1869; d. Berlin, Ger, 24 Jul 1957.

Rieck, Arnold: b. 22 Jun 1876; d. Leipzig, Ger, 7 Nov 1924.

Rieck, Johnnie H.: b. Denmark, 20 Nov 1880; d. Greenville, SC, 26 Oct 1956.

Riegal, Charles Henry: b. 1857; d. Briarcliff, NY, 21 Oct 1935.

Riemann, Johannes: b. Berlin, Ger, 31 May 1887; d. Constance, Ger, 30 Sep 1959.

Ries, William J.: b. 1895; d. Los Angeles, CA, 16 Nov 1955.

Riga, Nadine: b. 1909; d. Los Angeles, CA, 11 Dec 1968.

Rigby, Arthur: b. London, Eng, 27 Sep 1900; d. Worthing, Eng, 25 Apr 1971.

Rigby, Edward: b. Ashford, Kent, Eng, 5 Feb 1879; d. London, Eng, 5 Apr 1951.

Riley, George: b. Rochester, NY. 3 Dec 1897; d. Los Angeles, CA, 30 May 1972.

Riley, Jack (Slim): b. 1895; d. Newhall, CA, 9 Jul 1933.

Riley, James Whitcomb: b. Greerfield, IN, 7 Oct 1853; d. Indianapolis, IN, 22 Jul 1916.

Rilla, Walter: b. Neukirchen, Ger, 1894; d. 21 Nov 1980.

Ring, Blanche: b. Boston, MA, 24 Apr 1877; d. Santa Monica, CA, 13 Jan 1961.

Ring, Cyril: b. Massachusetts, 5 Dec 1892; d. Los Angeles, CA, 17 Jul 1967.

Rin-Tin-Tin: b. 1916; d. Los Angeles, CA, 8 Aug 1932.

Ripley, Raymond: b. 1891; d. Los Angeles, CA, 7 Oct 1938.

Risdon, Elizabeth: b. Wandsworth, Eng, 26 Apr 1887; d. Santa Monica, CA, 20 Dec 1958.

Rishell, Myrtle: b. Portland, OR, 12 Sep 1877; d. Los Angeles, CA, 12 Sep 1942.

Rising, William S.: b. 1851; d. New York, NY, 5 Oct 1930.

Ristelhueber, Joseph H.: b. 1847; d. Los Angeles, CA, 28 Feb 1943.

Ritchie, Charles: b. 18??; d. Chattanooga, TN, 25 May 1931.

Ritchie, Edith: b. 18??; d. Philadelphia, PA, 24 Mar 1916.

Ritchie, Franklin: b. Ritchie, PA, 26 Jun 1865; d. Santa Barbara, CA, 25 Jan 1918.

Ritchie, Perry V.: b. Kansas, 28 Nov 1887; d. Los Angeles, CA, 27 Jul 1918.

Ritchie, William (Billie): b. Glasgow, Scot, 14 Sep 1878; d. Los Angeles, CA, 6 Jul 1921.

Ritter, Esther: b. Illinois, 30 Mar 1902; d. Los Angeles, CA, 30 Dec 1925.

Ritter, George: b. 18??; d. ? Dec 1919.

Ritterband, Gerhard: b. 1904; d. Berlin, Ger, ? Oct 1959.

Rittner, Rudolf: b. Weissbach, Ger, 30 Jun 1869; d. 4 Feb 1943.

Ritz, Al: b. Newark, NJ, 27 Aug 1901; d. New Orleans, LA, 22 Dec 1965.

Rivero, Julian: b. Galveston, TX, 25 Jul 1890; d. Los Angeles, CA, 24 Feb 1976.

Rivers, Fernand: b. 1882; d. Nice, Fr, ? Aug 1960.

Riviere, Fred (Curly): b. England, 1875; d. Los Angeles, CA, 6 Nov 1935.

Roach, Bert: b. Washington, DC, 21 Aug 1891; d. Los Angeles, CA, 16 Feb 1971.

Roach, Hal: b. Elmira, NY, 19 Jan 1892; d. Bel-Air, CA, 2 Nov 1992.

Roanne, Andre: b. Paris, Fr, 22 Sep 1896; d. ? Sep 1959.

Roarks C. F. (Counsellor): b. Indiana, 26 Apr 1860; d. 15 Nov 1929.

Robards, Jason: b. Hillsdale, MI, 31 Dec 1892; d. Sherman Oaks, CA, 4 Apr 1963.

Robards, Willis L.: b. Texas, 1 Jan 1873; d. Los Angeles, CA, 3 Nov 1921.

Robbins, Marcus B.: b. 3 Jan 1868; d. Los Angeles, CA, 5 Apr 1931.

Robbins, Roy (Skeeter Bill): b. Glen Rock, WY, 16 Jul 1887; d. Los Angeles, CA, 28 Nov 1933.

Robbins, Walter: b. Chicago, IL, 18 Oct 1888; d. Los Angeles Co, CA, 13 Jul 1965.

Roberts, Anna: b. 18??; d. Quebec, Can, ? Nov 1915.

Roberts, Arthur: b. London, Eng, 21 Sep 1852; d. London, Eng, 27 Feb 1933.

Roberts, Charles B. (Jack): b. ????; d. Los Angeles, CA, 14 Sep 1927.

Roberts, Desmond: b. London, Eng, 5 Feb 1894; d. 11 Jan 1968.

Roberts, Edith: b. New York, NY, 17 Sep 1899; d. Los Angeles, CA, 20 Aug 1935.

Roberts, Evelyn: b. Reading, Eng, 28 Aug 1886; d. 30 Nov 1962.

Roberts, Florence: b. New York, NY, 14 Feb 1871; d. Los Angeles, CA, 17 Jul 1927.

Roberts, Florence: b. Frederick, MD, 16 Mar 1861; d. Los Angeles, CA, 6 Jun 1940.

Roberts, George: b. England, 1845; d. London, Eng, 25 Apr 1930.

Roberts, Hans: b. 1874; d. Jamaica, NY, 2 May 1954.

Roberts, Joseph: b. 1870; d. Los Angeles, CA, 28 Oct 1923.

Roberts, Ralph Arthur: b. Meerane, Ger, 2 Oct 1886; d. Berlin, Ger, 12 Mar 1940.

Roberts, Stephen: b. Summerville, MA, 23 Nov 1895; d. Los Angeles, CA, 17 Jul 1936.

Roberts, Theodore: b. San Francisco, CA, 8 Oct 1861; d. Los Angeles, CA, 14 Dec 1928.

Roberts, Thomas Benton: b. ????; d. Los Angeles, CA, 11 May 1987.

Roberts, Walter C.: b. 18??; d. South Haven, MI, 21 Mar 1926.

Robertshaw, Jerrold: b. Allerton, York, Eng, 28 Mar 1866; d. London, Eng, 14 Feb 1941.

Robertson, James Francis: b. 1869; d. Nyack, NY, 18 May 1942.

Robertson, James (Scotty): b. 1859; d. Los Angeles, CA, 13 Nov 1936.

Robertson, Jean: b. Australia, 1894; d. Sydney, Austral, ? Aug 1967.

Robertson, John S.: b. London, Ont, Can, 14 Jun 1878; d. Escondido, GA, 5 Nov 1964.

Robertson, Lolita: b. California, c. 1890; d. 19??.

Robertson, Orie O.: b. Illinois, 9 Jan 1881; d. Los Angeles, CA, 14 Apr 1964.

Robertson, Willard: b. Runnels, TX, 1 Jan 1886; d. Los Angeles Co, CA, 5 Apr 1948.

Robeson, Paul: b. Princeton, NJ, 9 Apr 1898; d. Philadelphia, PA, 23 Jan 1976.

Robey, Sir George: b. London, Eng, 20 Sep 1869; d. Saltdean, Sussex, Eng, 29 Nov 1954.

Robinne, Gabrielle: b. 1890; d. ? Dec 1980.

Robinson, Edward G.: b. Bucharest, Romania, 12 Dec 1893; d. Los Angeles, CA, 26 Jan 1973.

Robinson, Forrest: b. New York State, 2 Aug 1858; d. Los Angeles, CA, 6 Jan 1924.

Robinson, Frances: b. Fort Wadsworth, NY, 26 Apr 1916; d. Los Angeles, CA, 16 Aug 1971.

Robinson, Gertrude: b. New York, NY, 1891; d. Woodland Hills, CA, 19 Mar 1962.

Robinson, Harry T.: b. Des Moines, IA, 1 Jun 1872; d. Los Angeles, CA, 8 Sep 1946.

Robinson, J. A.: b. 1891; d. Phoenix, AZ, 15 May 1936.

Robinson, Legal W.: b. 1877; d. New York, NY, ? Jan 1919.

Robinson, Ruth: b. Kansas, 18 Aug 1887; d. Los Angeles Co, CA, 17 Mar 1966.

Robinson, Spike: b. 1884; d. Maywood, CA, 13 Jul 1942.

Robinson, Walter Charles: b. England, 1872; d. 1942.

Robson, Andrew: b. Hamilton, Ont, Can; 1868; d. Los Angeles, CA, 26 Apr 1921.

Robson, May: b. Melbourne, Austral, 19 Apr 1858; d. Los Angeles, CA, 20 Oct 1942.

Robson, Philip: b. Edinburgh, Scot, 18??; d. New York, NY, 6 May 1919.

Robson, Robert: b. Neenah, WI, 1870; d. New York, NY, 3 Jun 1947.

Robson, Mrs. Stuart (May Waldron): b. 1868; d. Louisville, LA, 22 Dec 1924.

Robson, Stuart, Jr.: b. ????; d. New York, NY, 21 Aug 1946.

Robyns, William: b. St. Louis, MO, 1855; d. Los Angeles, CA, 22 Jan 1936.

Roccardi, Albert: b. Rome, Italy, 9 May 1864; d. 14 May 1934.

Roche, John C.: b. Penn Yan, NY, 6 May 1893, Los Angeles, CA, 10 Nov 1952.

Rock, Charles: b. Vellore, East Indies, 30 May 1866; d. London, Eng, 12 Jul 1919.

Rock, Joseph (Joe): b. New York, NY, 25 Dec 1892; d. Sherman Oaks, CA, 5 Dec 1984.

Rock, William (Billy): b. Bowling Green, KY, 1875; d. Philadelphia, PA, 27 Jun 1922.

Rock, William T.: b. 1853; d. Oyster Bay, NY, 27 Jul 1916.

Rockwell, Florence: b. St. Louis, MO, 9 Jul 1887; d. Stamford, CT, 24 Mar 1964.

Roden, Edelaine: b. 1901; d. Los Angeles, CA, 26 Mar 1989.

Roderick, Leslie: b. 1907; d. Los Angeles, CA, 16 Aug 1927.

Rodgers, Eugene: b. 1867; d. Los Angeles, CA, 9 Mar 1919.

Rodgers, Walter L.: b. Ohio, 31 Aug 1886; d. Los Angeles, CA, 24 Apr 1951.

Rodman, Victor: b. Arkansas, 6 Aug 1892; d. Los Angeles, CA, 29 Jun 1965.

Rodney, Earl: b. Toronto, Can, 4 Jun 1888; d. Los Angeles, CA, 16 Dec 1932.

Rodolfi, Eleuterio: b. Italy, 1876; d. 1935.

Roe, Bassett: b. Folkestone, Kent, Eng, 10 Sep 1860; d. 2 Nov 1934.

Roels, Marcel: b. Antwerp, Belgium, 12 Jan 1894; d. Brussels, Belgium, 27 Dec 1973.

Rogers, Bessie: b. 1884; d. Venice Beach, CA, 5 Mar 1930.

Rogers, Carl D.: b. 1898; d. Houston, TX, 2 Mar 1965.

Rogers, Charles A.: b. England, 15 Jan 1887; d. Los Angeles, CA, 20 Dec 1956.

Rogers, Joseph: b. Lebanon, Syria, 10 Apr 1871; d. Los Angeles, CA, 27 Dec 1942.

Rogers, Lora: b. 1874; d. Providence, RI, 23 Dec 1948.

Rogers, Louise Mackintosh: b. 1865; d. Beverly Hills, CA, 1 Nov 1933.

Rogers, Lucretia Harris: b. 18??; d. Los Angeles, CA, ? Aug 1923.

Rogers, Mildred: b. Nebraska, 14 Apr 1899; d. Los Angeles, CA, 14 Apr 1973.

Rogers, Rena: b. Illinois, 7 Jun 1900; d. Los Angeles, CA, 19 Feb 1966.

Rogers, Robert M.: b. 1862; d. New York, NY, 15 Dec 1916.

Rogers, Rod: b. ????; d. Tamarac, FL, 23 Feb 1983.

Rogers, Will: b. Clarmore, OK, 4 Nov 1879; d. South Barrow, AK, 15 Aug 1935.

Rogers, Will, Jr.: b. New York, NY, 20 Oct 1912; d. Tubac, AZ, 9 Jul 1993.

Roland, Frederick: b. Toronto, Can, 12 Nov 1885; d. Los Angeles, CA, 2 Jun 1936.

Roland, Gilbert: b. Juarez, Mex, 11 Dec 1905; d. Beverly Hills, CA, 15 May 1994.

Roland, Ruth: b. San Francisco, CA, 26 Aug 1892; d. Los Angeles, CA, 22 Sep 1937.

Rollan, Henri: b. Paris, Fr, 23 Mar 1888; d. 23 Jun 1967.

Rolland, Edna: b. Neenah, WI, 182?; d. Colorado Springs, CO, 26 Nov 1915.

Rollens, Jacques (Jack Rollens): b. Chicago, IL, 13 Oct 1902; d. Los Angeles, CA, 19 Mar 1955.

Rollow, Preston J.: b. Fredericksburg, VA, 1871; d. New York, NY, 20 May 1947.

Romain, George E.: b. Bordeaux, Fr, 1878; d. Philadelphia, PA, 7 May 1929.

Roman, Frank: b. Granada, Spain, 25 Sep 1908; d. Santa Monica, CA, 23 Mar 1987.

Romanov, Natasha Galitzine: b. 1906; d. Menlo Park, CA, 28 Mar 1989.

Rome, Bert: b. 1887; d. Chelan, WA, 25 Aug 1946.

Rome, Betty: b. ????; d. Los Angeles Co, CA, 12 Feb 1973,

Rome, Stewart: b. Newbury, Berks, Eng, 30 Jun 1886; d. Newbury, Berks, Eng, 26 Feb 1965.

Romer, Leila: b. 1878; d. Los Angeles, CA, 10 Feb 1944.

Romero, Ramon: b. Jacksonville, FL, 1908; d. Los Angeles, CA, 4 Jul 1981.

Rooke, Irene: b. Bridgeport, Dorset, Eng, 1878; d. Chesham, Bucks, Eng, 14 Jun 1958.

Rooney, Pat (Fred): b. 1891; d. Los Angeles, CA, 15 Jun 1933.

Rooney, Pat, II: b. New York, NY, 4 Jul 1880; d. New York, NY, 9 Sep 1962.

Rooney, Pat, III: b. 1 Apr 1909; d. South Sutton, MA, 5 Nov 1979.

Roosevelt, Buddy: b. Meeker, CO, 25 Jun 1898; d. Meeker, CO, 6 Oct 1973.

Roosevelt, Theodore: b. New York, NY, 27 Oct 1858; d. Oyster Bay, NY, 6 Jan 1919.

Roper, Jack: b. Mississippi, 25 Mar 1904; d. Woodland Hills, CA, 28 Nov 1966.

Roquemore, Henry: b. Marshall, TX, 13 Mar 1888; d. Beverly Hills, CA, 30 Jun 1943.

Rork, Ann: b. Darien, CT, 12 Jun 1908; d, Nashville, TN, 23 Jan 1988.

Rorke, Ina: b. Portugal, 1868; d. Morristown, NJ, 23 Apr 1944.

Rorke, Kate: b. London, Eng, 22 Feb 1866; d. Little Hadham, Herts, Eng, 31 Jul 1945.

Rorke, Mary: b. London, Eng, 14 Feb 1858; d. London, Eng, 12 Oct 1938.

Rosanova, Rosa (Rosa Rose): b. Odessa, Russ, 23 Jun 1869; d. Santa Monica, CA, 29 May 1944.

Rosar, Annie: b. Vienna, Austria, 17 May 1888; d. Vienna, Austria, 1 Aug 1963.

Rosay, Francoise: b. Paris, Fr, 19 Apr 1891; d, Paris, Fr, 28 Mar 1974.

Roscoe, Albert: b. Nashville, TN, 23 Aug 1888; d. Los Angeles, CA, 8 Mar 1933.

Rose, Berthold: b. Germany, 30 Mar 1870; d. 8 Mar 1925.

Rose, Blanche: b. Detroit, MI, 1878; d. Los Angeles, CA, 5 Jan 1953.

Rose, Robert: b. 1868; d. Los Angeles, CA, 1 Jun 1936.

Rose, Ruth: b. 16 Jan 1896; d. Santa Monica, CA, 8 Jun 1978.

Roseleigh, Jack: b. Tennessee, 1887; d. 5 Jan 1940.

Roselle, William: b. New York, NY, 1878; d. Bronx, NY, 1 Jun 1945.

Rosen, Jimmy: b. Russia, 1885; d. New York, NY, 1 Jun 1940.

Rosenberg, Sarah: b. Poland, 1 Jul 1874; d. Los Angeles, CA, 16 Jun 1964.

Rosenblatt, Cantor Josef: b. New York, NY, 9 May 1882; d. Jerusalem, Israel, 19 Jun 1933.

Rosener, George M.: b. Brooklyn, NY, 23 May 1879; d. Los Angeles Co, CA, 29 Mar 1945.

Rosing, Bodil: b. Copenhagen, Den, 27 Dec 1877; d. Los Angeles, CA, 31 Dec 1941.

Rosley, Adrian: b. Rumania, 28 Oct 1888; d. Los Angeles, CA, 5 Mar 1937.

Rosmer, Milton: b. Southport, Lancs, Eng, 4 Nov 1881; d. Chesham, Bucks, Eng 7 Dec 1971.

Rose, Arthur: b. 1880; d. Los Angeles Co, CA, 17 Feb 1955.

Ross, Blanche: b. 1890; d. Paris, Fr, 29 May 1969.

Ross, Bob: b. Vancouver, Can, 1925; d. Vancouver, Can, 17 Apr 1982.

Ross, Charles J.: b. Montreal, Can, 18 Feb 1859; d. North Asbury Park, NJ, 15 Jun 1918.

Ross, Churchill: b. Lafayette, IN, 29 Jan 1901; d. Los Angeles, CA, 23 May 1962.

Ross, Marion (Marion Roland): b. 1898; d, Seattle, WA, 23 Jul 1966.

Ross, Thomas W.: b. Boston, MA, 22 Jan 1875; d. Torrington, CT, 14 Nov 1959.

Rossitto, Angelo: b. 1908; d. Los Angeles, CA, 21 Sep 1991.

Rosson, Arthur H.: b. London, Eng, 24 Aug 1887; d. Los Angeles, CA, 17 Jun 1960.

Resson, Harold (Hal): b. New York, NY, 1895; d. Palm Beach, FL, 6 Sep 1988.

Rosson, Helene: b. Newport, RI, 14 Jun 1897; d. Palm Beach, FL, 5 May 1985.

Rosson, Queenie (Ethel): b. 24 Feb 1889; d. West Palm Beach, FL, 19 Dec 1978.

Rosson, Richard: b. New York, NY, 4 Apr 1893; d. Los Angeles, CA, 31 May 1953.

Roth, Ann: b. 1913; d. ? Jan 1979.

Roth, Lillian: b. Boston, MA, 13 Dec 1910; d. New York, NY, 12 May 1980.

Roth, Sandy: b. 1889; d. Beverly Hills, CA, 4 Nov 1943.

Rothauser, Edouard: b. Budapest, Hungary, ? Jan 1876; d. 24 Jan 1956.

Rothe, Anita: b. Alexandria, VA, 1867; d. Bronx, NY, 9 Jan 1944.

Rothier, Leon: b. Rheims, Fr, 1875; d. New York, NY, 6 Dec 1951.

Roubert, Matty: b. New York State, 22 Jan 1907; d. Honolulu, HI, 17 May 1973.

Roughwood, Owen: b. London, Eng, 9 Jun 1876; d. 30 May 1947.

Roux, Antonio: b. Mexico, 7 May 1901; d. Woodland Hills, CA, 9 Nov 1976.

Rouversi, Ermanno: b. Milan, Italy, 5 Oct 1903; d. 28 Dec 1968.

Rowan, Ernest: b. 1886; d. Hampton, VA, 30 Sep 1960.

Rowlands, Art: b. Oakland, CA, 26 Aug 1897; d. Los Angeles, CA, 25 May 1944.

Royce, Brigham: b. Memphis, TN, 1864; d. Baltimore, MD, 7 Mar 1933.

Royce, Julian: b. Bristol, Eng, 26 Mar 1870; d. London, Eng, 10 May 1946.

Royce, Riza: b. Lancaster, PA, 18 Jul 1903; d. Los Angeles, CA, 20 Oct 1980.

Royce, Ruth: b. Versailles, MO, 6 Feb 1893; d. Los Angeles, CA, 7 May 1971.

Royce, Teddy: b. 1840; d. London, Eng, 24 Jan 1926.

Royer, Harry: b. Missouri, 6 Oct 1890; d. Los Angeles, CA, 1 Aug 1951.

Royston, Roy: b. London, Eng, 5 Apr 1899; d. ? Oct 1976.

Ruben, J. Walter: b. New York, NY, 14 Aug 1899; d. Los Angeles, CA, 4 Sep 1942.

Ruben, Jose: b. Paris, Fr, 1889; d. New York, NY, 28 Apr 1969.

Rubens, Alma: b. San Francisco, CA, 19 Feb 1897; d. Los Angeles, CA, 21 Jan 1931.

Rubinstein, Ida: b. St. Petersburg, Russ, 1883; d. Paris, Fr, 20 Sep 1960.

Ruby, Mary: b. Brooklyn, NY, 1894; d. New York, NY, 13 Dec 1987.

Rudami, Rosa: b. New York State, 1899; d, Albany, NY, 2 Feb 1966.

Rudhyar, Dane: b, Paris, Fr, 1895; d. San Francisco, CA, 14 Sep 1985.

Rudolph, Oscar: b. Cleveland, OH, 1911; d. Encino, CA, 1 Feb 1991.

Ruge, Billy: b. New York, 1885; d. 19??.

Ruggles, Charles: b. Los Angeles, CA, 8 Feb 1886; d. Santa Monica, CA, 23 Dec 1970.

Ruggles, Wesley: b. Los Angeles, CA, 11 Jun 1889; d. Santa Monica, CA, 8 Jan 1972.

Runnel, Albert F.: b. St. Paul, MN, 1891; d. Clearwater, FL, 4 Jan 1974.

Runyon, Damon: b. Manhattan, KS, 4 Oct 1864; d. New York, NY, 10 Dec 1946.

Rushton, Roland: b. Australia, 18??; d. New York, NY, 5 Nov 1925.

Ruskin, Jacob: b. 1886; d. New Rochelle, NY, 6 Nov 1962.

Ruskin, Shimen: b. Vilna, Poland, 25 Feb 1907; d. Los Angeles, CA, 23 Apr 1976.

Russell, Albert: b. New York, NY, 2 Aug 1890; d. Los Angeles, CA, 4 Mar 1929.

Russell, Byron: b. Clonmel, Ire, 1884; d. New York, NY, 4 Sep 1963.

Russell, Dan: b. Birmingham, Eng, 1875; d. Dallas, TX, 19 Mar 1925.

Russell, Edd X.: b. New York, 27 May 1878; d. Los Angeles, CA, 17 Nov 1966.

Russell, Evangeline: b. New York, NY, 18 Aug 1902; d. Los Angeles Co, CA, 22 Feb 1966.

Russell, Frank: b. 1857; d. New York, NY, 12 Aug 1925.

Russell, Hattie: b. 1850; d. Long Branch, NJ, 12 Aug 1918.

Russell, James Gordon: b. Piedmont, AL, 11 Jan 1883; d. Los Angeles, CA, 21 Apr 1935.

Russell, Jean: b. ????; d. New York, NY, 8 Jul 1922.

Russell, Lillian: b. Clinton, IA, 4 Dec 1861; d. Pittsburgh, PA, 6 Jun 1922.

Russell, William: b. New York, NY, 12 Apr 1886; d. Los Angeles, CA, 18 Feb 1929.

Rutan, Charles Hart: b. Brooklyn, NY, 6 Jul 1892; d. Los Angeles Co, CA, 17 Jul 1968.

Ruth, Babe (George Herman): b. Baltimore, MD, 6 Feb 1895; d. New York, NY, 16 Aug 1948.

Ruth, Marshall: b. Marshalltown, IA, 24 Dec 1898; d. Los Angeles, CA, 17 Jan 1953.

Rutherford, Jack: b. England, 12 Apr 1893; d. Patagonia, AZ, 21 Aug 1982.

Ryan, Annie: b. 1863; d. Los Angeles, CA, 14 Feb 1943.

Ryan, Chet: b. Spearfish, SD, 17 May 1889; d; Los Angeles Co, CA, 20 Jan 1943.

Ryan, Joe: b. Crook County, WY, 23 May 1887; d. Riverside Co, CA, 23 Dec 1944.

Ryan, Mary: b. Brooklyn, NY, 11 Nov 1885; d. Cranford, NJ. 2 Oct 1948.

Ryan, Robert J,: b. Pipestone, MN, 16 Apr 1896; d. Los Angeles Co, CA, 27 Nov 1958.

Ryckmam, Chester: b. 1897; d. Fort Rosecrans, CA, 6 Nov 1918.

Ryley, J. H. (James H. Ryley): b. 1841; d. 28 Jul 1922.

Ryley, Phil: b. ????; d. Los Angeles, CA, ? Oct 1937.

Ryno, William H.: b. New York, NY, 8 Oct 1864; d. 3 Dec 1939.

S

Sabato, Alfredo: b. Italy, 23 Mar 1894; d. Los Angeles Co, CA, 10 Feb 1956.

Sabin, Catherine J.: b. 1889; d. New York, NY, 19 May 1943.

Sack, Nathaniel: b. Libau, Russ, 15 Jul 1880; d. New York, NY, 2 Jul 1966.

Sackville, Gordon: b. Peterborough, Ont, Can, 1880; d. Los Angeles, CA, 6 Aug 1926.

Sadler, Josie: b. New York, c. 1871; d. c. 1933.

Sage, Byron: b. 1914; d. Los Angeles, CA, 14 Jan 1974.

Sage, Stuart: b. Sioux Falls, SD, 1893; d. New York, NY, 4 Mar 1926.

Sainpolis, John (John St. Polis): b. New Orleans, LA, 24 Nov 1873; d. Los Angeles, CA, 8 Oct 1946.

St. Audrie, Stella: b. 1876; d. 11 May 1925.

St. Clair, Jacques: b. ????; d. ? Apr 1929.

St. Clair, Malcolm: b. Los Angeles, CA, 17 May 1897; d. Pasadena, CA, 1 Jun 1952.

St. Claire, Adah: b. New York, NY, 1854; d. Amityville, NY, 16 Aug 1928.

St. Denis, Ruth: b. Newark, NJ, 20 Jan 1878; d. Los Angeles, CA, 21 Jul 1968.

St. George, Jenny: b. 18??; d. Freehold, NJ, 15 Apr 1938.

St. James, William H.: b. 1876; d. New York, NY, 23 Jul 1931.

St. John, Al (Fuzzy): b. Santa Ana, CA, 10 Sep 1892; d. Lyons, GA, 21 Jan 1963.

St. Leo, Leonard: b. England, 1 May 1894; d. Los Angeles Co, CA, 9 Feb 1977.

St. Pierre, Clara: b. 1866; d. Santa Monica, CA, 30 Jan 1942.

Saintsbury, H. A.: b. London, Eng, 18 Dec 1869; d. London, Eng, 19 Jun 1939.

Sais, Marin: b. San Rafael, CA, 2 Aug 1890; d. Woodland Hills, CA, 31 Dec 1971.

Sakall, S. Z. (Cuddles): b. Budapest, Hungary, 2 Feb 1883; d. Los Angeles, CA, 12 Feb 1955.

Saker, Annie: b. 13 Mar 1882; d. Essex, Eng, 8 Oct 1932.

Sale, Charles (Chic): b. Huron, SD, 25 Aug 1885; d. Los Angeles, CA, 7 Nov 1936.

Sale, Frances: b. 1892; d. Los Angeles, CA, 6 Aug 1969.

Sale, Virginia: b. Urbana, IL, 1899; d. Woodland Hills, CA, 23 Aug 1992.

Salfner, Heinz: b. Munich, Ger, 31 Dec 1877; d. 13 Oct 1945.

Salisbury, Monroe: b. Angola, NY, 6 May 1876; d. San Bernardino, CA, 7 Aug 1935.

Salmonova, Lyda: b. Prague, Czech, 1889; d. Prague, Czech, 1968.

Salter, Harold (Hal): b. Atlanta, GA, 8 Apr 1886; d. Los Angeles, CA, 9 May 1928.

Salter, Harry: b. 18??; d. c. 1920.

Salter, Lou: b. Quimper, Fr, 1902; d. 21 Oct 1948.

Salter, Thelma: b. 1909; d. Los Angeles, CA, 17 Nov 1953.

Salvini, Alessandro: b. Italy, 6 Aug 1890; d. 24 Jul 1955.

Sampson, Teddy: b. New York, NY, 8 Aug 1898; d. Woodland Hills, CA, 24 Nov 1970.

Samson, Ivan: b. Brighton, Eng, 28 Aug 1894; d. London, Eng, 1 May 1963.

Samuel, Andy: b. Los Angeles, CA, 10 Apr 1909; d. Colton, CA, 5 Mar 1992.

Sandberg, Robert Albert: b. Chicago, IL, 6 Oct 1887; d. 19??.

Sande, Earle H.: b. Croton, SD, 13 Nov 1898; d. 19 Aug 1968.

Sanderson, Julia: b. Springfield, MA, 20 Aug 1887; d. Springfield, MA, 27 Jan 1975.

Sandow, Eugene: b. Kenigsburg, Ger, 10 Apr 1867; d. London, Eng, 14 Oct 1925.

Sandrock, Adele: b. Rotterdam, Holland, 19 Aug 1863; d. Berlin, Ger, 30 Aug 1937.

Sanford, Albert: b. New York, NY, 1893; d. New York, NY, 10 Feb 1953.

Sanford, Stanley J. (Tiny): b. Osage, IA, 26 Feb 1894; d. Los Angeles Co, CA, 29 Oct 1961.

Sanger, Bert: b. 1894; d. Blackpool, Eng, ? Aug 1968.

Sansberry, Hope (Virginia Staunton): b. 1896; d. Laguna Hills, CA, 14 Dec 1990.

Santley, Frederic: b. Salt Lake City, UT, 20 Nov 1887; d. Los Angeles, CA, 14 May 1953.

Santley, Joseph: b. Salt Lake City, UT, 10 Jan 1889; d. Los Angeles, CA, 8 Aug 1971.

Santley, Laurene: b. 1868; d. Los Angeles, CA, 22 Sep 1933.

Santoro, Jack: b. New York, NY, 18 Apr 1898; d. Los Angeles, CA, 23 Oct 1980.

Santschi, Thomas: b. Missouri, 24 Oct 1880; d. Los Angeles, CA, 9 Apr 1931.

Sargeantson, Kate: b. Wales, 18??; d. New York, NY, 16 Feb 1918.

Sargent, Alfred Maxwell: b. 1861; d. Kalamazoo, MI, ? Jan 1949.

Sargent, Lewis: b. Los Angeles, CA, 19 Aug 1903; d. Los Angeles, CA, 19 Nov 1970.

Sarno, Hector V.: b. Naples, Italy, 24 Apr 1880; d. Pasadena, CA, 16 Dec 1953.

Sarony, Gilbert: b. 18??; d. Pittsburgh, PA, 15 Dec 1910.

Sass, Edward: b. 1858; d. New Malden, Surrey, Eng, 15 Nov 1916.

Satie, Erik: b. Honfleur, Fr, 17 May 1866; d. France, 1 Jul 1925.

Sauerman, Carl J.: b. Stockholm, Sweden, 1868; d. Brooklyn, NY, 9 Apr 1924.

Saum, Clifford: b. Columbus, OH, 18 Dec 1882; d. Glendale, CA, 5 Mar 1943.

Saunders, Alice: b. Holyoke, MA, 4 Sep 1872; d. Los Angeles Co. CA, 25 Jul 1953.

Saunders, Florence: b. Valparaiso, Chile, 1890; d. London, Eng, 24 Jan 1926.

Saunders, Jackie: b. Philadelphia, PA, 6 Oct 1892; d. Palm Springs, CA, 14 Jul 1954.

Saunders, Lucille: b. 18??; d. San Francisco, CA, 8 Jan 1919.

Saunders, Nellie Park: b. Saginaw, MI, 1869; d. Greenwood, SC, 3 Mar 1942.

Saville, Gus: b. Peekskill, NY, 1857; d. Los Angeles, CA, 25 Mar 1934.

Saville, Ruth: b. Allessandro, CA, 1893; d. Los Angeles, CA, 31 Mar 1985.

Savo, Jimmy: b. New York, NY, 1895; d. Terni, Umbria, Italy, 6 Sep 1960.

Sawamura, Kunitaro: b. 1905; d. Tokyo, Japan, 26 Nov 1974.

Sawyer, Laura: b. 1885; d. Matawan, NJ, 7 Sep 1970.

Saxe, Templer: b. Redhill, Surrey, Eng, 22 Aug 1865; d. Cincinnati, OH, 17 Apr 1935.

Saxon, Hugh: b. New Orleans, LA, 14 Jan 1869; d. Beverly Hills, CA, 14 May 1945.

Saylor, Syd: b. Chicago, IL, 24 May 1895; d. Los Angeles, CA, 21 Dec 1962.

Sayres, Margaret: b. 1868; d. Asheville, NC, 17 Apr 1937.

Scaduto, Joseph: b. New York, NY, 28 May 1898; d. Los Angeles, CA, 19 Oct 1943.

Scanlon, Edward: b. New York, NY, 1883; d. Weehawken, NJ, 31 Aug 1949.

Scannell, John J.: b. 1887; d. Jackson Heights, NY, 18 Feb 1926.

Scardon, Paul: b. Melbourne, Austral, 6 May 1874; d. Fontana, CA, 17 Jan 1954.

Schable, Robert: b. Hamilton, Ont, Can, 31 Aug 1873; d. Los Angeles, CA, 3 Jul 1947.

Schacht, Gustav: b. 1876; d. New York, NY, 8 Oct 1943.

Schade, Fritz: b. Germany, 188O; d. Los Angeles, CA, 17 Jun 1926.

Schaefer, Albert: b. Galveston, TX, 1 May 1916; d. Los Angeles, CA, 26 Oct 1942.

Schaefer, Anne: b. St, Louis, MO, 10 Jul 1870; d. Los Angeles, CA, 3 May 1957.

Schaefer, Charles N.: b. 12 Feb 1863; d. Los Angeles, CA, 5 Feb 1939.

Schaeffer, Otis: b. 1907; d. Norwalk, CT, 8 Jun 1962.

Schang, Wally: b. South Wales, NY, 22 Aug 1889; d. St. Louis, MO, 6 Mar 1985.

Scharpegge, Ernie: b. ????; d. Milwaukee, WI, 11 Mar 1940.

Schauffuss, Hans Joachim: b. Germany, 28 Dec 1918; d. 27 Oct 1941.

Scheff, Fritzi: b. Vienna, Austria, 30 Aug 1879; d. New York, NY, 8 Apr 1954.

Schenck, Earl O.: b. Columbus, OH, 13 May 1889; d. 19??.

Schenstrom, Carl: b. Copenhagen, Den, 13 Nov 1881; d. 10 Apr 1942.

Schildkraut, Joseph: b. Vienna, Austria, 22 Mar 1895; d. New York, NY, 21 Jan 1964.

Schildkraut, Rudolph: b. Constantinople, Turkey, 27 Apr 1862; d. Los Angeles, CA, 15 Jul 1930.

Schipa, Carlo: b. Italy, 1900; d. Los Angeles, CA, 25 Aug 1988.

Schlettow, Hans Adelbert: b. Frankfurt, Ger, 11 Jun 1888; d. Berlin, Ger, 30 Apr 1945.

Schmitt, Joseph: b. 1871; d. Los Angeles, CA, 25 Mar 1935.

Schnall, Ida: b. 18??; d. Los Angeles, CA, 14 Feb 1973.

Schneider, James: b. New York State, 15 Dec 1881; d. Los Angeles, CA, 14 Feb 1967.

Schnell, Georg Heinrich: b. Germany, 11 Apr 1878; d. 31 Mar 1951.

Scholz, Robert: b. 1886; d. 10 Oct 1927.

Schramm, Karla: b. Los Angeles, CA, 1 Feb 1891; d. Los Angeles, CA, 17 Jan 1980.

Schreck, Max: b. Berlin, Ger, 6 Sep 1879; d. Munich, Ger, 19 Feb 1936.

Schroder, Arthur: b. 20 Nov 1892; d. 4 Feb 1986.

Schultz, Harry: b. Germany, 11 Mar 1883; d. Los Angeles, CA, 4 Jul 1935.

Schultz, Joseph: b, 1866; d. Chicago, IL, 1 Oct 1916.

Schumaker, Ida C.: b. ????; d. Los Angeles Co, CA, 25 Aug 1969.

Schumann-Heink, Ferdinand: b. Hamburg, Ger, 9 Aug 1893; d. Los Angeles, CA, 15 Sep 1958.

Schumann-Heink, Henry: b. Hamburg, Ger, 24 Jun 1886; d. Los Angeles, CA, 28 Mar 1951.

Schumm, Harry: b. Chicago, IL, 27 Sep 1877; d. Los Angeles, CA, 4 Apr 1953.

Schuszel, Reinhold: b. Hamburg, Ger, 7 Nov 1886; d. Munich, Ger, 11 Sep 1954.

Schuster, Harold: b. Cherokee, IA, 1 Aug 1902; d. Westlake Village, CA, 19 Jul 1986.

Schwaiger, Franz: b. Germany, 1880; d. 2 Dec 1926.

Schwartz, Maurice: b. Sedikor, Russ, 18 Jun 1890; d. Tel Aviv, Israel, 10 May 1960.

Schwed, Blanche: b. 1906; d. New York, NY, 4 Jul 1983.

Scott, Blanche: b. Rochester, NY, 1885; d. Rochester, NY, 12 Jan 1970.

Scott, Carrie: b. 1870; d. New York, NY, 18 Dec 1928.

Scott, Cyril: b. Banbridge, County Down, Ire, 9 Feb 1866; d. Flushing, NY, 16 Aug 1945.

Scott, Fred: b. Los Angeles, CA, 14 Feb 1902; d. Palm Springs, CA, 16 Dec 1991.

Scott, Frederick T.: b. 18??; d. Staten Island, NY, 22 Feb 1942.

Scott, Gertrude: b. Sevenoaks, Kent, Eng, 18??; d. England, 23 Dec 1951.

Scott, Gregory: b. Sandy, Eng, 15 Dec 1879; d. 19??.

Scott, Lois: b. ????; d. Los Angeles, CA, ? Sep 1924.

Scott, Mabel Julienne: b. Minneapolis, MN, 2 Nov 1892; d. Los Angeles, CA, 1 Oct 1976.

Scott, Markle: b. 1873; d. Los Angeles, CA, 4 Jul 1958.

Scott, Peggy: b. 1901; d. London, Eng, 26 Aug 1926.

Scott, Walter F.: b. Baltimore, MD, 1879; d. New York, NY, 5 Mar 1940.

Scott, Walter K.: b. 18??; d. Washington, DC, 9 Apr 1958.

Scott-Gatty, Alexander: b. Ecclesfield, Yorks, Eng, 3 Oct 1876; d. London, Eng, 6 Nov 1937.

Seabury, Forrest: b. 1876; d. Los Angeles Co. CA, 15 Feb 1944.

Seabury, Ynez: b. Oregon, 26 Jun 1907; d. Sherman Oaks, CA, 11 Apr 1973.

Seagram, Wilfred: b. England, 1884; d. New York, NY, 28 May 1938.

Sealy, Lewis A.: b. Dublin, Ire, 1851; d. New York, NY, 19 Mar 1931.

Seaman, Marjorie: b. Pennsylvania, 21 Jun 1900; d. Los Angeles, CA, 9 Mar 1923.

Searle, Kamuela C.: b. Hawaii, 29 Aug 1890; d. Los Angeles, CA, 14 Feb 1924.

Searles, Cora B.: b. 1859; d. Los Angeles, CA, 4 Mar 1935.

Sears, Allan D.: b. San Antonio, TX, 9 Mar 1887; d. Los Angeles, CA, 18 Aug 1942.

Sears, Zelda: b. Brockway, MI, 21 Jan 1873; d. Los Angeles, CA, 19 Feb 1935.

Seastrom, Dorothy: b. Texas, ????; d. Dallas, TX, ? Feb 1930.

Seastrom, Victor: b. Varmland, Sweden, 20 Sep 1879; d. Stockholm, Sweden, 3 Jan 1960.

Seaton, Scott: b. Sacramento, CA, 11 Mar 1871; d. Los Angeles, CA, 3 Jun 1968.

Sebastian, Dorothy: b. Birmingham, AL, 26 Apr 1905; d. Los Angeles, CA, 8 Apr 1957.

Sedan, Rolfe: b. New York, NY, 20 Jan 1896; d. Pacific Palisades, CA, 16 Sep 1982.

Seddon, Margaret: b. Washington, DC, 18 Nov 1872; d. Philadelphia, PA, 17 Apr 1968.

Sedgwick, Edward: b. Galveston, TX, 7 Nov 1889; d. Los Angeles, CA, 7 May 1953.

Sedgwick, Eileen: b. Galveston, TX, 17 Oct 1898; d. Marina del Rey, CA, 15 Mar 1991.

Sedgwick, Josie: b. Galveston, TX, 13 Mar 1896; d. Santa Monica, CA, 30 Apr 1973.

See, Edward: b. New York, NY, 1855; d. New York, NY, 17 Feb 1923.

Seed, David: b. New York, NY, 8 Jul 1888; d. Brooklyn, NY, 3 Nov 1960.

Seeley, Jemes L.: b. Rushville, IL, 1867; d. New York, NY, 15 Feb 1943.

Seelos, Annette: b. California, 1891; d. New York, NY, 23 Oct 1918.

Seely, Sybil: b. 2 Jan 1900; d. Culver City, CA, 26 Jun 1984.

Seger, Lucia Backus: b. 1873; d. New York, NY, 17 Jan 1962.

Seiter, Robert: b. 1909; d. St. Petersburg, FL, 12 Jan 1986.

Seiter, William A.: b. New York, NY, 10 Jun 1892; d. Beverly Hills, CA, 26 Jul 1964.

Seitz, George B.: b. Boston, MA, 3 Jan 1888; d. Los Angeles, CA, 8 Jul 1944.

Selbie, Evelyn: b. Louisville, KY, 6 Jul 1871; d. Woodland Hills, CA, 6 Dec 1950.

Selby, Norman (Kid McCoy): b. Rushvllle, IN, 13 Oct 1873; d. Detroit, MI, 18 Apr 1940.

Sellon, Charles: b. Boston, MA, 24 Aug 1870; d. Los Anpeles, CA, 26 Jun 1937.

Selwyn, Edgar: b. Cincinnati, OH, 20 Oct 1875; d. Los Angeles, CA, 13 Feb 1944.

Selwynne, Clarissa: b. London, Eng, 26 Feb 1886; d. Los Angeles, CA, 13 Jun 1948.

Semels, Harry: b. New York, NY, 20 Nov 1887; d. Los Angeles, CA, 2 Mar 1946.

Semmler, Gustav Adolf: b. 14 Mar 1885; d. Berlin, Ger, 24 Feb 1968.

Semon, Larry: b. West Point, NY, 16 Jul 1889; d. Victorville, CA, 8 Oct 1928.

Sennett, Mack: b. Danville, Que, Can, 17 Jan 1880; d. Woodland Hills, CA, 5 Nov 1960.

Seragnoli, Oreste: b. Italy, 10 Jul 1883; d. 13 Apr 1965.

Serda, Julia: b. Vienna, Austria, 1875; d. Dresden, Ger, 3 Nov 1965.

Sergis, Simone: b. ????; d. Los Angeles Co, CA, 12 Jul 1971.

Serrano, Vincent: b. New York, NY, 17 Feb 1866; d. New York, NY, 11 Jan 1935.

Servaes, Dagney: b. Berlin, Ger, 10 Mar 1897; d. ? Jul 1961.

Servanti, Luigi: b. Italy, 1885; d. 1976.

Sesti, Claire: b. New York, NY, 23 May 1913; d. Boynton Beach, FL, 29 Jan 1990.

Sever, Alfred: b. 1891; d. New York, NY, 26 Mar 1953.

Severin-Mars, M.: b. Bordeaux, Fr, 1873; d. France, 17 Jul 1921.

Sewall, Allan D.: b. Massachusetts, 23 Jul 1882; d. Los Angeles, CA, 20 Jan 1954.

Sewall, Lucile: b. 1888; d. Los Angeles, CA, 15 Dec 1976.

Seybolt, Eleanor: b. 1885; d. New York, NY, 17 Sep 1947.

Seyler, Athene: b. London, Eng, 31 May 1889; d. London, Eng, 12 Sep 1990.

Seymour, Clarine: b. Brooklyn, NY, 9 Dec 1898; d. New York, NY, 25 Apr 1920.

Seymour, Harry: b. New York, NY, 22 Jun 1891; d. Los Angeles, CA, 11 Nov 1967.

Shackleford, Floyd: b. Iowa, 7 Sep 1905; d. 17 Dec 1972.

Shafer, Mollie: b. California, 1872; d. Los Angeles, CA, 19 Nov 1940.

Shaffner, Mrs. Lillian: b. 1862; d. Los Angeles, CA, 10 Jan 1930.

Shaiffer, Howard C. (Tiny): b. 1917; d. Burbank, CA, 24 Jan 1967.

Shain, John Howard: b. 1903; d. Bryn Mawr, PA, 6 Dec 1979.

Shannon, Alexander K.: b. Harve, Fr, 1862; d. New York, NY, 7 Mar 1932.

Shannon, Cora: b. Illinois, 30 Jan 1869; d. Woodland Hills, CA, 27 Aug 1957.

Shannon, Mrs. Dale: b. 18??; d. New York, NY, 1 Jun 1923.

Shannon, Effie: b. Cambridge, MA, 13 May 1867; d. Bay Shore, NY, 24 Jul 1954.

Shannon, Ethel: b. Denver, CO, 22 May 1898; d. Los Angeles, CA, 10 Jul 1951.

Shannon, Frank Connolly, b. Ireland, 27 Jul 1874; d. Los Angeles, CA, 1 Feb 1959.

Shannon, Jack: b. Ohio, 31 Aug 1892; d. North Hollywood, CA, 27 Dec 1968.

Shanor, Peggy: b. West Virginia, 1896; d. New York, NY, 30 May 1935.

Sharkey, Tom (Sailor): b. Dundalk, Ire, 26 Nov 1873; d. San Francisco, CA, 17 Apr 1953.

Sharp, Henry: b. Riga, Latvia, 19 Feb 1887; d. Brooklyn, NY, 10 Jan 1964.

Sharp, Ramona: b. Longwood, MO, 9 May 1901; d. Glendale, CA, 26 Apr 1941.

Sharpe, David: b. St. Louis, MO, 1909; d. Altadena, CA, 30 Mar 1980.

Shattuck, Truly: b. San Miguel, CA, 27 Jul 1876; d. Woodland Hills, CA, 6 Dec 1954.

Shaw, Brinsley: b. 18??; d. 19??.

Shaw, Buddy: b. 1906; d. Los Angeles, CA, 29 Aug 1976.

Shaw, C. Montague: b. Adelaide, Austral, 23 Mar 1882; d. Woodland Hills, CA, 6 Feb 1968.

Shaw, George Bernard: b. Dublin, Ire, 26 Jul 1855; d. Ayot St. Lawrence, Eng, 2 Nov 1950.

Shaw, Harold: b. England, 3 Nov 1877; d. Los Angeles, CA, 30 Jan 1926.

Shaw, Lewis: b. London, Eng, 6 May 1910; d. 13 Jul 1987.

Shaw, Oscar: b. Philadelphia, PA, 11 Oct 1887; d. Little Neck, NY, 6 Mar 1967.

Shawn, Ted: b. Kansas City, MO, 21 Oct 1891; d. Orlando, FL , 9 Jan 1972.

Shdanoff, Elsa Schreiber: b. Vienna, Austria, 1900; d. Los Angeles, CA, 8 Jan 1982.

Shea, Bird: b. ????; d. Los Angeles, CA, 23 Nov 1924.

Shea, Louis: b. 1870; d. New York, NY, 13 Jul 1925.

Shea, Thomas E.: b. East Cambridge, MA, 1861; d. East Cambridge, MA, 23 Apr 1940.

Shea, William J.: b. Dumfries, Scot, 1861; d. Brooklyn, NY, 5 Nov 1918.

Shean, Al: b. Dornum, Ger, 12 May 1868; d. New York, NY, 12 Aug 1949.

Shearer, Athole: b. Montreal, Can, 20 Nov 1900; d. Los Angeles, CA, 17 Mar 1985.

Shearer, Edith F.: b. Canada, 1873; d. Garden Grove, CA, 2 Jul 1958.

Shearer, Norma: b. Montreal, Can, 10 Aug 1900; d. Woodland Hills, CA, 12 Jun 1983.

Sheehan, John J.: b. Oakland, CA, 22 Oct 1885; d. Los Angeles, CA, 15 Feb 1952.

Sheer, William A.: b. Birmingham, Eng, 18??; d. New York, NY, 10 Jul 1933.

Sheerer, Will E.: b. 18??; d. Yonkers, NY, 24 Dec 1915.

Sheffield, Reginald: b. London, Eng, 18 Feb 1901; d. Pacific Palisades, CA, 8 Dec 1957.

Shelby, Charlotte: b. Shreveport, LA, 19 Dec 1877; d. Santa Monica, CA, 13 Mar 1957.

Shelby, Margaret: b. San Antonio, TX, 16 Jun 1900; d. Los Angeles, CA, 21 Dec 1939.

Sheldon, Jerome: b. Ohio, 13 Aug 1890; d. Los Angeles, CA, 15 Apr 1962.

Sheldon, Kathryn: b. Cincinnati, OH, 22 Sep 1879; d. Los Angeles Co, CA, 25 Dec 1975.

Sheldon, Marion: b. Cambridge, MA, 3 May 1885; d. Los Angeles, CA, 28 Feb 1944.

Sheldon, Suzanne: b. Rutland, VT, 24 Jan 1875; d. London, Eng, 21 Mar 1924.

Shelton, James: b. Paducah, KY, 1913; d. Miami, FL, 2 Sep 1975.

Shelton, Marie: b. Atlanta, GA, ????; d. Los Angeles, CA, 13 Mar 1949.

Shepard, Iva: b. Cincinnati, OH, 23 Apr 1886; d. Arcadia, CA, 26 Jan 1973.

Shepley, Ruth: b. Providence, RI, 29 May 1892; d. New York, NY, 16 Oct 1951.

Sheppard, Bert: b. 1882; d. Cassopolis, MT, 18 Aug 1929.

Sherart, Georgia: b. 1862; d. Los Angeles, CA, 24 Jan 1929.

Sheridan, Frank: b. Boston, MA, 11 Jun 1869; d. Los Angeles, CA, 24 Nov 1943.

Sherman, Evelyn: b. Iowa, 11 Dec 1882; d. Los Angeles Co, CA, 19 Apr 1974.

Sherman, Lowell: b. San Francisco, CA, 11 Oct 1888; d. Los Angeles, CA, 28 Dec 1934.

Sherman, Mary: b. Russia, 1887; d. Santa Monica, CA, 13 Aug 1980.

Sherrill, Jack: b. Atlanta, GA, 14 Apr 1898; d. Honolulu, HI, 26 Nov 1973.

Sherry, J. Barney: b. Philadelphia, PA, 4 Mar 1874; d. Philadelphia, PA, 22 Feb 1944.

Sherwood, Arthur W.: b. Los Angeles, CA, ????; d. Joplin, MO, 14 Mar 1986.

Sherwood, Clarence L.: b. Shiloh, LA, 5 Jan 1884; d. Los Angeles Co, CA, 15 Jan 1941.

Sherwood, Lydia: b. London, Eng, 5 May 1906; d. London, Eng, 20 Apr 1989.

Sherwood, William (Billy): b. New Orleans, LA, 1896; d. Washington, DC, 24 May 1918.

Sherwood, Yorke: b. England, 14 Dec 1873; d. Los Angeles, CA, 27 Sep 1958.

Shields, Ernest W.: b. Chicago, IL, 5 Aug 1884; d. Los Angeles, CA, 13 Dec 1944.

Shields, Sandy: b. 1873; d, New York, NY, 3 Aug 1923.

Shields, Sydney: b. New Orleans, LA, 1888; d. New York, NY, 19 Sep 1960.

Shine, John L.: b. Manchester, Eng, 28 Mar 1854; d. New York, NY, 16 Oct 1930.

Shine, Wilfred: b. Manchester, Eng, 12 Jul 1863; d. Kingston, Surrey, Eng, 14 Mar 1939.

Shipmen, Nell: b. Victoria, Bri Col, Can, 25 Oct 1892; d. Cabazon, CA, 23 Jan 1970.

Shirley, Arthur: b, Hobart, Tasmania, 31 Aug 1886; d. 19??.

Shirley, Bobbie: b. ????; d. 13 Feb 1970.

Shirley, Jessie: b. 1866; d. Spokane, WA, 30 May 1918.

Shirley, Tom: b. 1900; d. New York, NY, 24 Jan 1962.

Short, Antrim: b. Cincinnati, OH, 11 Jul 1900; d. Woodland Hills, CA, 24 Nov 1972.

Short, Florence: b. Springfield, MA, 1893; d. Los Angeles, CA, 10 Jul 1946.

Short, Gertrude: b. Cincinnati, OH, 6 Apr 1900; d. Los Angeles, CA, 31 Jul 1968.

Short, Harry: b. 1876; d. New York, NY, 17 Aug 1943.

Short, Hassard: b. Eddington, Lincs, Eng, 15 Oct 1877; d. Nice, Fr, 9 Oct 1956.

Short, Lewis W.: b. Dayton, OH, 14 Feb 1875; d. Los Angeles, CA, 26 Apr 1958.

Shotwell, Marie: b. New York, NY, 1886; d. Long Island, NY, 18 Sep 1934.

Shultz, Harry: b. 1883; d. Los Angeles, CA, 4 Jul 1935.

Shumway, Leonard C.: b. Salt Lake City, UT, 4 Mar 1884; d. Los Angeles, CA, 4 Jan 1959.

Shumway, Walter: b. Cleveland, OH, 26 Aug 1884; d. Woodland Hills, CA, 13 Jan 1965.

Sibley, Lucy: b. 18??; d. 30 Dec 1945.

Sidman, Sam: b. 1871; d. Pinewald, NJ, 3 Jan 1948.

Sidney, George: b. Nagynichal, Hungary, 15 Mar 1877; d. Los Angeles, CA, 29 Apr 1945.

Sidney, Scott: b. Philadelphia, PA, 1872; d. Elstres, Eng, 20 Jul 1928.

Siebel, Peter: b. 1884; d. Long Beach, CA, 4 Mar 1949.

Siegel, Bernard: b. Lemberg, Poland, 19 Apr 1868; d. Los Angeles, CA, 9 Jul 1940.

Siegmann, George: b. New York, NY, 8 Feb 1882; d. Los Angeles, CA, 22 Jun 1928.

Signoret, Gabriel: b. Marseilles, Fr, 15 Nov 1878; d. Paris, Fr, 16 Mar 1937.

Signoret, Jean: b. Cavaillon, Fr, 1885; d. Paris, Fr, 10 Oct 1923.

Silbert, Jacob: b. 1870; d. New York, NY, 19 Apr 1937.

Silbert, Liza: b. Rumania, 1880; d. Miami, FL, 29 Nov 1965.

Sills, Milton: b. Chicago, IL, 12 Jan 1882; d. Los Angeles, CA, 15 Sep 1930.

Silvaney, Elsa: b. 10 Feb 1898; d. Toowoomba, Austral, 22 Aug 1983.

Silver, Christine: b. London, Eng, 17 Dec 1884; d. London, Eng, 23 Nov 1960.

Silver, Pauline: b. South Dakota, 13 Feb 1888; d. West Hollywood, CA, 2 Jan 1969.

Silverwood, Don: b. ????; d. Reno, NV, 10 Jan 1928.

Sima, Oskar: b. 31 Jul 1900; d. ? Jun 1969.

Simmons, Earl: b. 1889; d. New York, NY, 10 Jan 1934.

Simon, Michel: b. Geneva, Switz, 9 Apr 1895; d. Paris, Fr, 30 May 1975.

Simon, Sol S.: b. Sacramento, CA, 15 Dec 1864; d. Los Angeles, CA, 24 Apr 1940.

Simon-Girard, Aime: b. Paris, Fr, 1889; d. ? Jun 1950.

Simpson, Fanny: b. 18??; d. Woodstock, NY, 17 Oct 1961.

Simpson, Grant M.: b. Sioux Falls, SD, 1885; d. Asheville, NC, 5 Jan 1932.

Simpson, Ivan: b. Glasgow, Scot, 4 Feb 1875; d. New York, NY, 12 Oct 1951.

Simpson, John: b. 18??; d. New York, NY, 17 Jun 1918.

Simpson, Russell: b. San Francisco, CA, 17 Jun 1880; d. Los Angeles, CA, 12 Dec 1959.

Sinclair, Daisy: b. New York, NY, 1878; d. New York, NY, 14 Jan 1929.

Sinclair, Richard C.: b. 18??; d. Brooklyn, NY, 16 Sep 1926.

Sinclair, Upton: b. Baltimore, MD, 20 Sep 1878; d. Bound Brook, NJ, 25 Nov 1968.

Singer, Marian: b. England, 1851; d. Long Island, NY, 21 Nov 1924.

Singh, Bhogwan: b. India, 22 Sep 1883; d. Woodland Hills, CA, 6 Mar 1962.

Singleton, Joseph E.: b. Melbourne, Austral, 1881; d. 19??.

Sini'letta, Vic (Victor A. Smith): b. ????; d. Chicago, IL, 4 May 1921.

Sipperly, Ralph W.: b. 1890; d. Bangor, ME, 9 Jan 1928.

Sipple, Crete: b. Missouri, 18 Nov 1882; d. Los Angeles, CA, 20 Feb 1972.

Sisson, Vera: b. Colorado, 31 Jul 1891; d. Salinas, CA, 6 Aug 1954.

Sitgreaves, Marion: b. ????; d. East Islip, NY, 2 Feb 1961.

Skinner, Cornelia Otis: b. Chicago, IL, 30 May 1901; d. New York, NY, 9 Jul 1979.

Skinner, Harold Otis: b. 1889; d. San Diego, CA, 14 Sep 1922.

Skinner, Otis: b. Cambridge, MA, 28 Jun 1858; d. New York, NY, 4 Jan 1942.

Skipworth, Alison: b. London, Eng, 25 Jul 1863; d. New York, NY, 5 Jul 1952.

Slater, Bob: b. 1869; d. New York, NY, 20 Jun 1930.

Slavin, John C.: b, New York, NY, 1869; d. New York, NY, 27 Aug 1940.

Sleeman, Phil: b. England, 28 Feb 1891; d. Los Angeles Co, CA, 19 Sep 1953.

Sleeper, Martha: b. Lake Bluff, IL, 24 Jan 1904; d. Beaufort, SC, 25 Mar 1983.

Slezak, Walter: b. Vienna, Austria, 3 Mar 1902; d. Flower Hill, NY, 22 Apr 1983.

Sloan, Tod: b. Bunker Hill, TN, 10 Aug 1874; d. Los Angeles, CA, 21 Dec 1933.

Sloan, William Hope: b. 1864; d. Amityville, NY, 12 Jan 1933.

Sloane, Olive: b. 16 Dec 1896; d. London, Eng, 28 Jun 1963.

Sloman, Edward: b. London, Eng, 19 Jul 1885; d. Woodland Hills, CA, 29 Sep 1972.

Slott, Nate David: b. Chicago, IL, 22 Apr 1902; d. Los Angeles, CA, 26 Sep 1963.

Small, Edna: b. 1898; d. Cincinnati, OH, 14 Jul 1917.

Small, Edward: b. Brooklyn, NY, 1 Feb 1891; d. Los Angeles, CA, 25 Jan 1977.

Smalley, Phillips: b. Brooklyn, NY, 7 Aug 1865; d. Los Angeles, CA, 2 May 1939.

Smart, H. F. (Ray Archer): b. England, 18??; d. Los Angeles, CA, 22 Jul 1923.

Smiley, Charles: b. 1855; d. Los Angeles, CA, 22 Jun 1925.

Smiley, Joseph W.: b. Boston, MA, 18 Jun 1881; d. New York, NY, 2 Dec 1945.

Smirrova, Dina: b. Russia, 24 Feb 1889; d. 16 Jan 1947.

Smith, Albert E.: b. England, 1878; d. Los Angeles, CA, 1 Aug 1958.

Smith, Albert J.: b. Chicago, IL, 15 Feb 1894; d. Los Angeles, CA, 11 Apr 1939.

Smith, Arlene: b. Arena, WI, 1892; d. Los Angeles, CA, 12 Jan 1984.

Smith, Arthur T.: b. 1878; d. Norwalk, CT, 14 Apr 1958.

Smith, C. Aubrey: b. London, Eng, 21 Jul 1863; d. Beverly Hills, CA, 20 Dec 1948.

Smith, Charles H.: b. Washington, IL, 3 Oct 1865; d. Los Angeles, CA, 11 Jul 1942.

Smith, Clifford: b. Richmond, IN, 1886; d. Los Angeles, CA, 17 Sep 1937.

Smith, Cyril: b. Peterhead, Scot, 4 Apr 1892; d. London, Eng, 5 Mar 1963.

Smith, Dick: b. 18??; d. Los Angeles, CA, 7 Feb 1937.

Smith, Dwight: b. Vevey, IN, 1857; d. Monsey, NY, 30 May 1949.

Smith, Gerald Oliver: b. London, Eng, 26 Jun 1892; d. Woodland Hills, CA, 28 May 1974.

Smith, Edward (Gunboat): b. Philadelphia, Pa, 12 Dec 1887; d. Leesburg, FL, 6 Aug 1974.

Smith, Howard I: b. Attleboro, MA, 12 Aug 1894; d. Los Angeles, CA, 10 Jan 1968.

Smith, J. Sebastian: b. Southwell, Notts, Eng, 3 Oct 1869; d. 15 Jan 1948.

Smith, Jack: b. 1896; d. Los Angeles, CA, 14 Jan 1944.

Smith, Jess: b. Pittsburgh, PA, 9 Mar 1897; d. Los Angeles, CA, 11 Apr 1965.

Smith, Leonard R,: b. 1889; d. San Antonio, TX, 9 Jul 1958.

Smith, Margaret M.: b. England, 9 Jul 1881; d. Los Angeles, CA, 9 Dec 1960.

Smlth, Mark: b. New York, NY, 16 Apr 1887; d. New York, NY, 9 May 1944.

Smith, Oscar: b. Topeka, KS, 28 Oct 1885; d. Los Angeles Co, CA, 18 Mar 1956.

Smith, Paul Gerard: b. Omaha, NE, 14 Sep 1894; d. San Diego, CA, 4 Apr 1968.

Smith, Pete: b. New York, NY, 4 Sep 1892; d. Santa Monica, CA, 12 Jan 1979.

Smith, Pleasant (Jimmy Dee Smith): b. 1886; d. Las Vegas, NV, 12 Mar 1969.

Smith, Sidney C.: b. Faribault, MN, 28 Feb 1893; d. Los Angeles, CA, 4 Jul 1928.

Smithson, Laura: b. Stockton-on-Tees, Eng, 14 Feb 1885; d. London, Eng, 20 Dec 1963.

Smitterick, Grover: b. ????; d. New York, NY, ? Sep 1914.

Smoller, Dorothy: b. Memphis, TN, 1901; d. New York, NY, 9 Dec 1926.

Smythe, Florence: b. California, 19 Apr 1878; d. Los Angeles, CA, 29 Aug 1925.

Snegoff, Leonid: b. Russia, 15 May 1883; d. Los Angeles, CA, 22 Feb 1974.

Snelling, Minnette: b. 1878; d. Los Angeles, CA, 19 Dec 1945.

Snodgrass, Smythe: b. 1887; d. Bayonne, NJ, 3 Oct 1921.

Snow, Marguerite: b. Salt Lake City, UT, 9 Sep 1889; d. Woodland Hills, CA, 17 Feb 1958.

Snow, Mortimer: b. Brigham City, UT, 19 Nov 1868; d. East Islip, NY, 20 Jun 1935.

Snowden, Carolynne: b. Oakland, CA, 1900; d. Los Angeles, CA, 6 Sep 1985.

Snyder, Matt: b. 22 Mar 1835; d. San Francisco, CA, 17 Jan 1917.

Sodders, Carl: b. 18??; d. Dayton, OH, 18 Dec 1958.

Sojin (Sojin Kamiyama): b. Sendai, Japan, 30 Jan 1891; d. Tokyo, Japan, 28 Jul 1954.

Sokoll, Mike: b. Poland, 1891; d. 24 Aug 1991.

Sokoloff, Vladimir: b. Moscow, Russ, 24 Dec 1889; d. Los Angeles, CA, 15 Feb 1962.

Solovitch, Don: b. ????; d. Manti, UT, 6 Jan 1928.

Somerest, Pat: b. London, Eng, 28 Feb 1897; d. Apple Valley, CA, 20 Apr 1974.

Sondermann, Emil: b. Germany, 1861; d. 29 Aug 1927.

Sorter, Irma: b. Colorado, 3 Nov 1904; d. Santa Clara Co, CA, 3 Sep 1968.

Sosso, Pietro: b. Italy, 20 Nov 1869; d. San Francisco, CA, 25 Apr 1961.

Sothern, E. H.: b. New Orleans, LA, 6 Dec 1859; d. New York, NY, 28 Oct 1933.

Sothern, Harry: b. London, Eng, 26 Apr 1883; d. Fort Lee, NJ, 22 Feb 1957.

Sothern, Hugh (Roy Sutherland): b. Anderson County, KS, 20 Jul 1881; d. Los Angeles, CA, 13 Apr 1947.

Sothern, Jean: b. Philadelphia, PA, 1895; d. Chicago, IL, 8 Jan 1924.

Sothern, Sam: b. London, Eng, 1865; d. Los Angeles, CA, 21 Mar 1920.

Sotomayer, Jose: b. 1904; d. Mexico City, Mex, 24 Jan 1967.

Soule, Mrs. Leona Cardona: b. 1864; d. New York, NY, 15 Feb 1928.

Souper, Kay: b. ????; d. 2 Jan 1947.

Soussanin, Nicholas: b. Yalta, Russ, 1889; d. New York, NY, 27 Apr 1975.

Southard, Harry D.: b. Buffalo, NY, 1886; d. New York, NY, 27 Apr 1939.

Southwick, Albert P.: b. 1876; d. New York, NY, 19 Jan 1929.

Southwick, Dale: b. 1913; d. Long Beach, CA, 29 Apr 1968.

Sovern, Clarence: b. 1900; d. Burbank, CA, 13 Mar 1929.

Sowards, George: b. Missouri, ????; d. Los Angeles Co, CA, 20 Dec 1975.

Sowards, Len: b. Missouri, 17 Oct 1892; d. Sawtelle, CA, 20 Aug 1962.

Sparks, Ned: b. Guelph, Ont, Can, 19 Nov 1883; d. Victorville, CA, 3 Apr 1957.

Spaulding, George: b. Colorado, 6 Jul 1881; d. Los Angeles, CA, 23 Aug 1959.

Spaulding, Nellie Parker: b. Machias, ME, 4 Aug 1870; d. Glendale, CA, 18 Jun 1945.

Speaker, Tris: b. Hubbard, TX, 4 Apr 1888; d. Whitney, TX, 8 Dec 1958.

Spear, Harry: b. Los Angeles, CA, 25 Dec 1912; d. Los Angeles, CA, 11 Feb 1969.

Spear, Rita: b. 19??; d. Los Angeles, CA, 9 Nov 1968.

Speelmans, Hernann: b. Urdingen, Ger, 14 Aug 1904; d. 9 Feb 1960.

Spellman, Leora: b. 1891; d. Los Angeles, CA, 4 Sep 1945.

Spence, Ralph: b. Key West, FL, 4 Nov 1889; d. Woodland Hills, CA, 21 Dec 1949.

Spencer, Fred: b. Pueblo, CO, 1901; d. Los Angeles, CA, 13 Oct 1952.

Spencer, George Soule: b. Wisconsin, 25 Sep 1874; d. Los Angeles Co, CA, 7 Aug 1949.

Spencer, James: b. 1893; d. Los Angeles Co, CA, 28 Jun 1943.

Spencer, Robert: b. 1900; d. New York, NY, 4 Sep 1939.

Spencer, Walter: b. Murray, UT, 17 Sep 1882; d. Long Beach, CA, 8 Sep 1927.

Spere, Charles: b. Lincoln, NE, 17 Jul 1897; d. Los Angeles, CA, 20 Apr 1945.

Spingler, Harry: b. Buffalo, NY, 3 Aug 1889; d. Woodland Hills, CA, 22 Apr 1953.

Spofford, Charles (Baby): b. Los Angeles, CA, 10 Dec 1915; d. Los Angeles, CA, 29 Sep 1935.

Spong, Hilda: b. London, Eng, 14 May 1875; d. Ridgefield, CT, 16 May 1955.

Spooner, Cecil: b. New York State, 29 Jan 1875; d. Sherman Oaks, CA, 13 May 1953.

Spooner, Edna May: b. Centerville, IA, 10 May 1873; d. Sherman Oaks, CA, 14 Jul 1953.

Spooner, Franklin E.: b. Centerville, IA, 16 Apr 1860; d. Monterey Park, CA, 14 Jan 1943.

Spottswood, James: b. Washington, DC, 1882; d. New York, NY, 11 Oct 1940.

Sprotte, Bert: b. Chemnitz, Ger, 9 Dec 1870; d. Los Angeles Co, CA, 30 Dec 1949.

Squire, Ronald: b. Tiverton, Devon, Eng, 25 Mar 1886; d. London, Eng, 16 Nov 1958.

Squires, Jack: b. New York, NY, 1894; d. New York, NY, 21 Jun 1938.

Stallard, Ernest: b. 1864; d. Chicago, IL, 18 Oct 1929.

Stamper, F. Pope: b. Richmond, Surrey, Eng, 20 Nov 1880; d. 12 Nov 1950.

Stamp-Taylor, Enid: b. Monkseaton, Eng, 12 Jun 1904; d. London, Eng, 13 Jan 1946.

Standing, Gordon H.: b. London, Eng, 24 Nov 1887; d. Los Angeles, CA, 21 May 1927.

Standing, Sir Guy: b. London, Eng, 1 Sep 1873; d. Los Angeles, CA, 24 Feb 1937.

Standing, Guy, Jr.: b. New York, NY, 12 Apr 1904; d. Reseda, CA, 14 Nov 1954.

Standing, Herbert, Sr.: b. London, Eng, 13 Nov 1846; d. Los Angeles, CA, 5 Dec 1923.

Standing, Herbert, Jr.: b. London, Eng, 1884; d. New York, NY, 23 Sep 1955.

Standing, Jack: b. London, Eng, 10 Feb 1886; d. Los Angeles, CA, 26 Oct 1917.

Standing, Joan: b. England, 21 Jun 1903; d. Houston, TX, 3 Feb 1979.

Standing, Percy D.: b. England, c. 1882; d. 19??.

Standing, Wyndham: b. London, Eng, 24 Aug 1881; d. Los Angeles, CA, 1 Feb 1963.

Standish, Joseph W.: b. 1865; d. Cleveland, OH, 27 Oct 1943.

Stanford, Arthur: b. Philadelphia, PA, 24 Aug 1878; d. New Bedford, MA, 21 Jul 1917.

Stanford, Henry: b. Ramleh, Egypt, 22 Jan 1872; d. Staten Island, NY, 18 Feb 1921.

Stanley, Edwin: b. Chicago, IL, 22 Nov 1880; d. Los Angeles, CA, 25 Dec 1944.

Stanley, Forrest: b. New York, NY, 21 Aug 1889; d. Los Angeles, CA, 27 Aug 1969.

Stanley, George C.: b. San Francisco, CA, 29 Jan 1875; d. 19??.

Stanley, Henry: b. New York, NY, 25 Jan 1864; d. 19??.

Stanley, Minnie: b. 1874; d. New York, NY, 1 Apr 1948.

Stanmore, Frank: b. London, Eng, 10 Mar 1877; d. Gravesend, Eng, 15 Aug 1943.
Stanton, Fred R.: b. 1881; d. Los Angeles, CA, 27 May 1925.
Stanton, Larry T.: b. Ohio, 22 Oct 1893; d. Los Angeles, CA, 9 May 1955.
Stanton, Paul: b. Illinois, 21 Dec 1884; d. Los Angeles Co, CA, 9 Oct 1955.
Stanton, Will: b. London, Eng, 18 Sep 1885; d. Los Angeles, CA, 18 Dec 1969.
Stanwood, Rita: b. Salem, MA, 15 Jan 1888; d. Los Angeles, CA, 15 Nov 1961.
Stanwyck, Barbara: b. Brooklyn, NY, 16 Jul 1907; d. Los Angeles, CA, 20 Jan 1990.
Stark, Dick: b. Grand Rapids, MI, 1911; d. Sotogrande, Spain, 12 Dec 1986.
Stark, Kurt: b. 18??; d. 1916.
Stark, Leighton: b. 18??; d. Mawasquam, NJ, 20 Jul 1924.
Stark, Mabel: b. 1889; d. Thousand Oaks, CA, 20 Apr 1968.
Starke, Pauline: b. Joplin, MO, 10 Jan 1900; d. Santa Monica, CA, 3 Feb 1977.
Starkey, Bert: b. Manchester, Eng, 10 Jan 1880; d. Los Angeles, CA, 10 Jun 1939.
Starr, Frederick: b. San Francisco, CA, 1878; d. Los Angeles, CA, 20 Aug 1921.
Starr, Harry: b. 1877; d. Harrison, OK, 23 Feb 1921.
Starrett, Charles: b. Athol, MA, 28 Mar 1903; d. Borrego Springs, CA, 22 Mar 1986.
Steadman, Vera: b. Monterey, CA, 21 Jun 1900; d. Long Beach, CA, 14 Dec 1966.
Stecker, A. S. (Algernon Stecker): b. 1892; d. Los Angeles, CA, 23 Jun 1924.
Stedman, Lincoln: b. Denver, Co. 18 May 1906; d. Los Angeles, CA, 22 Mar 1948.
Stedman, Marshall: b. Bethel, ME, 1874; d. Laguna Beach, CA, 16 Dec 1943.
Stedman, Myrtle: b. Chicago, IL, 3 Mar 1885; d. Los Angeles, CA, 8 Jan 1938.
Steele, Agnes: b. 1882; d. Los Angeles Co, CA, 3 Mar 1949.
Steele, Bob: b. Portland, OR, 23 Jan 1907; d. Burbank, CA, 21 Dec 1988.
Steele, Clifford: b. 1878; d. Los Angeles, CA, 5 Mar 1940.
Steele, Minnie: b. Australia, 1881; d. Los Angeles, CA, 5 Jan 1949.
Steele, Vernon: b. Santiago, Chile, 18 Sep 1882; d. Los Angeles, CA, 23 Jul 1955.
Steele, Willian (William Gettinger): b. San Antonio, TX, 28 Mar 1889; d. Los Angeles, CA, 13 Feb 1966.
Steelman, Henry Paul (Hank): b. 1902; d. Atascadero, CA, 30 Jan 1939.
Steelman, Hosea E.: b. Cincinnati, OH, 31 Mar 1876; d. Los Angeles Co, CA, 4 Jul 1953.
Steers, Larry: b. Indiana, 14 Feb 1888; d. Los Angeles, CA, 15 Feb 1951.
Steger, Julius: b. Vienna, Austria, 4 Mar 1870; d. Vienna, Austria, 25 Feb 1959.
Steidl, Robert: b. Germany, 1861; d. 24 Apr 1927.
Stein, Geoffrey: b. Washington, DC, 1869; d. Amityville, NY, 28 May 1930.
Steiner, Elio: b. 9 Mar 1905; d. Rome, Italy, 6 Dec 1965.

Steiner, Sigfrit: b. Bale, Ger, 31 Oct 1906; d. Munich, Ger, 21 Mar 1988.

Steinrueck, Albert: b. Wettenburg-Walkdeck, Ger, 20 May 1872; d. Berlin, Ger, 2 Feb 1929.

Stembridge, J. S.: b. Milledgeville, GA, 9 Feb 1869; d. Los Angeles Co, CA, 31 Oct 1942.

Sten, Anna: b. Kiev, Russ, 3 Dec 1908; d. New York, NY, 12 Nov 1993.

Stepanek, Karel: b. Brno, Czech, 29 Oct 1899; d. 5 Jan 1981.

Stephenson, Henry: b. Granada, Bri W. Indies, 16 Apr 1871; d. San Francisco, CA, 24 Apr 1956.

Steppling, John C.: b. Essen, Ger, 8 Aug 1870; d. Los Angeles, CA, 6 Apr 1932.

Sterler, Fritz: b. 12 Apr 1886; d. 24 Apr 1920.

Sterling, Edythe: b. Kansas City, KS, 29 Oct 1892; d. Los Angeles, CA, 5 Jun 1962.

Sterling, Ford: b. La Crosse, WI, 3 Nov 1880; d, Los Angeles, CA, 13 Oct 1939.

Sterling, Jane: b. New York, NY, 1866; d. Middlebury, VT, 30 Dec 1956.

Sterling, Merta: b. 1882; d. Los Angeles, CA, 14 Mar 1944.

Starling, Richard: b. New York, NY, 30 Aug 1880; d. Douglaston, NY, 15 Apr 1959.

Stern, Louis: b. New York, NY, 10 Jan 1860; d. Los Angeles, CA, 15 Feb 1941.

Sternroyd, Vincent: b. Highgate, London, Eng, 8 Oct 1857; d. London, Eng, 3 Nov 1948.

Stevens, Charles: b. Solomonsville, AZ, 26 May 1893; d. Los Angeles, CA, 22 Aug 1964.

Stevens, Edwin: b. California, 16 Aug 1860; d. Los Angeles, CA, 1 Jan 1923.

Stevens, Emily: b. New York, NY, 27 Feb 1882; d. New York, NY, 2 Jan 1928.

Stevens, Evelyn: b. Brooklyn, NY, 1891; d. New York, NY, Aug 28, 1938.

Stevens, George: b. Oakland, CA, 18 Dec 1904; d. Lancaster, CA, 8 Mar 1975.

Stevens, George S.: b. London, Eng, 1860; d. Brooklyn, NY, 20 Aug 1940.

Stevens, Jessie: b. ????; d. Palmyra, NY, ? Jun 1922.

Stevens, Landers: b. San Francisco, CA, 17 Feb 1877; d. Los Angeles, CA, 19 Dec 1940.

Stevens, Lynn: b. 1898; d, Worcester, MA, 28 Mar 1950.

Stevens, Morton L.: b. Marlboro, MA, 1890; d. Marlboro, MA, 5 Aug 1959.

Stevenson, Charles A.: b. Dublin, Ire, 6 Nov 1851; d. Los Angeles, CA, 2 Jul 1929.

Stevenson, Charles E.: b. Sacramento, CA, 13 Oct 1887; d. Palo Alto, CA, 4 Jul 1943.

Stevenson, Douglas: b. Versailles, KY, 1885; d. Versailles, KY, 31 Dec 1934.

Stevenson, John: b. 1884; d. New York, NY, 10 Aug 1922.

Steward, Maynon: b. 1880; d. 25 Dec 1932.

Stewart, Anita: b. Brooklyn, NY, 17 Feb 1895; d. Beverly Hills, CA, 4 May 1961.

Stewart, Danny: b. 1907; d. Honolulu, HI, 15 Apr 1962.

Stewart, Etta: b. ????; d. 23 Apr 1929.

Stewart, George: b. Brooklyn, NY, 27 Jun 1888; d. Los Angeles, CA, 24 Dec 1945.

Stewart, Grant: b. England, 18 Apr 1866; d. Woodstock, NY, 18 Aug 1929.

Stewart, Hamilton: b. 18??; d. Oxford, Eng, 15 May 1924.

Stewart, Julia: b. Edinburgh, Scot, c. 1880; d. Philadelphia, PA, c. 1940.

Stewart, Katherine: b. Sandwich, Eng, 1868; d. New York, NY, 24 Jan 1949.

Stewart, Lucille Lee: b. Brooklyn, NY, 25 Dec 1889; d. Hemet, CA, 8 Jan 1982.

Stewart, Melville: b. London, Eng, 17 Feb 1869; d. Sea Gate, NY, 5 Aug 1915.

Stewart, Nellie: b. 1859; d. Sydney, Austral, 20 Jun 1931.

Stewart, Richard: b. 18??; d. c. 1938.

Stewart, Roy: b. San Diego, CA, 17 Oct 1884; d. Westwood, CA, 26 Apr 1933.

Stiller, Mauritz: b. Helsinki, Finland, 17 Jul 1883; d. Stockholm, Sweden, 8 Nov 1928.

Stine, Charles J.: b. 1869; d. Bay Shore, NY, 5 Jan 1934.

Stinson, Mortimer E.: b. New York State, 25 Dec 1871; d. 20 Jul 1927.

Stites, Frank: b. Indiana, 28 Feb 1882; d. Universal City, CA, 15 Mar 1915.

Stockdale, Carl: b. Worthington, MN, 19 Feb 1874; d. Woodland Hills, CA, 15 Mar 1953.

Stockfield, Betty: b. Sydney, Austral, 15 Jan 1905; d. London, Eng, 26 Jan 1966.

Stockwell, Winifred: b. 1894; d. New Hope, MN, 8 Feb 1981.

Stoddard, Belle: b. Remington, OH, 13 Sep 1869; d. Los Angeles, CA, 13 Dec 1950.

Stoeckel, Joe: b. Munich, Ger, 27 Sep 1894; d. Munich, Ger, 14 Jun 1959.

Stoffer, Josephine: b. Baltimore, MD, 18??; d. New York, NY, 25 Oct 1922.

Stokes, Olive M.: b. Oklahoma, 10 Apr 1887; d. Los Angeles Co, CA, 1 Nov 1972.

Stone, Arthur Taylor: b. St. Louis, MO, 28 Nov 1883; d. Los Angeles, CA, 4 Sep 1940.

Stone, Dorothy: b. Brooklyn, NY, 3 Jun 1905; d. Montecito, CA, 24 Sep 1974.

Stone, Florence: b. 1880; d. Los Angeles, CA, 25 Aug 1950.

Stone, Fred: b. Longmont, CO, 19 Aug 1873; d. Los Angeles, CA, 6 Mar 1959.

Stone, Gene (Eugene): b. 1892; d. 21 Feb 1947.

Stone, George E.: b. Lodz, Poland, 18 May 1903; d. Woodland Hills, CA, 26 May 1967.

Stone, Jack: b. London, Eng, 26 Nov 1906; d. 8 Apr 1962.

Stone, Lewis: b. Worcester, MA, 15 Nov 1879; d. Los Angeles, CA, 13 Sep 1953.

Stone, Mrs. Robert E.: b. 18??; d. 5 Nov 1916.

Stonehouse, Ruth: b. Denver, CO, 28 Sep 1892; d. Los Angeles, CA, 12 May 1941.

Storey, Edith: b. New York, NY, 18 Mar 1892; d. Northport, NY, 9 Oct 1967.

Storey, Fred: b. London, Eng, 20 Jun 1861; d. London, Eng, 4 Dec 1917.

Storey, Helen: b. 1903; d. Chicago, IL, 26 Apr 1935.

Storm, Jerome: b. Denver, CO, 11 Nov 1890; d. Hot Springs, CA, 10 Jul 1958.

Stormont, Leo: b. 18??; d. 28 Jan 1923.

Stowe, Leslie: b. Homer, LA, 1866; d. Englewood, NJ, 16 Jul 1949.

Stowell, William H,: b. Boston, MA, 13 Mar 1885; d. Elizabethville, So Africa, 24 Nov 1919.

Straner, John: b. 1846; d. St. Louis, MO, ? Jul 1912.

Strassborg, Morris: b. 1897; d. South Laguna, CA, 8 Feb 1974.

Stratton, Eugene: b. Buffalo, NY, 8 May 1861; d. London, Eng, 15 Sep 1918.

Stratton, Gene: b. 1915; d. Los Angeles, CA, 16 Aug 1966.

Straus, Clement: b. New York State, 27 Sep 1886; d. Los Angeles, CA, 8 Aug 1915.

Strauss, William H.: b. New York, NY, 13 Jun 1885; d. Los Angeles, CA, 5 Aug 1943.

Strayer, Frank: b. Altoona, PA, 7 Sep 1891; d. Los Angeles, CA, 3 Feb 1964.

Street, Julian: b. Chicago, IL, 1880; d. Lakeville, CT, 19 Feb 1947.

Strickland, Helen: b. Boston, MA, 1863; d. New York, NY, 11 Jan 1938.

Strickland, Hugh: b. 1885; d. Los Angeles, CA, 2 May 1941.

Strickland, Mabel: b. 1897; d. 3 Jan 1976.

Striker, Joseph: b. New York, NY, 1899; d. Livingston, NJ, 24 Feb 1974.

Strong, Eugene: b. Wisconsin, 9 Aug 1893; d. Los Angeles, CA, 25 Jun 1962.

Strong, Fred: b. 18??; d. 1938.

Strong, Jay: b. Cleveland, OH, 1897; d. New York, NY, 1 Dec 1953.

Strong, Forter: b. St. Joseph, MO, 1879; d. New York, NY, 11 Jun 1923.

Strongheart, Nipo: b. Yakima Reservation, WA, 15 May 1891; d. Los Angeles, CA, 30 Dec 1966.

Stryker, Gustave: b. Chicago, IL, 1866; d. New York, NY, 3 Jun 1943.

Stuart, Donald: b. London, Eng, 2 Dec 1898; d. Los Angeles, CA, 22 Feb 1944.

Stuart, Iris: b. 2 Feb 1903; d. New York, NY, 21 Dec 1936.

Stuart, Jean: b. California, 13 Jul 1906; d. Los Angeles, CA, 23 Nov 1926.

Stuart, John: b. Edinburgh, Scot, 18 Jul 1898; d. London, Eng, 17 Oct 1979.

Stuart, Leslie: b. ????; d. Los Angeles Co., CA, 3 Apr 1977.

Stuart, Nick: b. Romania, 10 Apr 1903; d. Biloxi, MS, 7 Apr 1973.

Stuart, Ralph R.: b. 1890; d. New York, NY, 4 Nov 1952.

Stuart, Simeon: b. 15 May 1864; d. 1939.

Studiford, Grace: b. 1877; d. Long Beach, NY, 21 Oct 1947.

Stuewe, Hans: b. Germany, 14 May 1901; d. Berlin, Ger, 13 May 1976.

Sturgis, Eddie: b. Washington, DC, 22 Oct 1881; d. Los Angeles, CA, 13 Dec 1947.

Sturz, Louis: b. 1885; d. Florida, 13 Feb 1958.

Styan, Arthur: b. 18??; d. Melbourne, Austral, ? Jan 1926.

Subject, Evelyn: b. Chicago, IL, ????; d. Temple City, CA, 22 Apr 1975.

Sulky, Leo: b. Cincinnati, OH, 6 Dec 1874; d. Los Angeles Co, CA, 3 Jun 1957.

Sullivan, Anne: b. Feeding Hills, MA, 11 Apr 1866; d. Queens, NY, 20 Oct 1936.

Sullivan, Charles: b. Louisiana, 24 Apr 1899; d. Los Angeles Co, CA, 25 Jun 1972.

Sullivan, Daniel J.: b. 1874; d. New York, NY, 23 Feb 1937.

Sullivan, Frederick: b. London, Eng, 18 Jul 1872; d. Los Angeles, CA, 24 Jul 1937.

Sullivan, James E.: b. 1864; d. 1 Jun 1931.

Sullivan, John Maurice: b. Washington DC. 24 Sep 1875; d. Los Angeles, CA, 8 Mar 1949.

Sullivan, William A. (Billy): b. Worcester, MA, 1891; d. Great Neck, NY, 23 May 1946.

Sulzner, William: b. New Jersey, 18 Mar 1883; d. New York, NY, 6 Nov 1941.

Summers, Edna Lee: b. 12 Dec 1895; d. San Diego Co, CA, 1 Nov 1989.

Summers, Leonora: b. 1898; d. Woodland Hills, CA, 29 Jun 1976.

Summerville, Amelia: b. Kildare, Ire, 15 Oct 1862; d. New York, NY, 21 Jan 1934.

Summerville, Slim (George J.): b. Alburquerque, NM, 10 Jun 1892; d. Laguna Beach, CA, 5 Jan 1946.

Sumner, Frederick: b. 1874; d. New York, NY, 11 Jan 1942.

Sumner, Verlyn: b. Lakefield, MN, 7 Jun 1897; d. Bremerton, WA, 10 Feb 1935.

Sunshine, Baby (Pauline Flood): b. California, 1 Dec 1915; d. Los Angeles, CA, 19 Oct 1917.

Sunshine, Marion: b. Kentucky, 1894; d. New York, NY, 25 Jan 1963.

Supple, Cuyler C.: b. Germantown, PA, 13 Feb 1894; d. Los Angeles, CA, 3 May 1944.

Suratt, Valeska: b. Terre Haute, IN, 28 Jun 1882; d. Washington, DC, 2 Jul 1962.

Sutch, Herbert: b. London, Eng, 29 Jun 1884; d. 22 Jan 1939.

Sutherland, A. Edward (Eddie): b. London, Eng, 5 Jan 1897; d. Palm Springs, CA, 31 Dec 1973.

Sutherland, Anne: b. Washington, DC, 1 Mar 1867; d. Brentwood, NY, 22 Jun 1942.

Sutherland, Dick: b. Benton, KY, 23 Dec 1881; d. Los Angeles, CA, 3 Feb 1934.

Sutherland, John: b. Scotland, 1845; d. Brooklyn, NY, 31 Aug 1921.

Sutherland, Victor: b. Paducah, KY, 24 Feb 1889; d. Los Angeles, CA, 29 Aug 1968.

Sutton, Brad: b. 1863; d. Richmond, NY, 19 Aug 1932.

Sutton, Charles: b. 1856; d. Englewood, NJ, 22 Jul 1935.

Sutton, Susie: b. ????; d. New York, NY, 2 Feb 1956.

Sutton, William: b. 1877; d. West Los Angeles, CA, 10 Sep 1955.

Swain, Mack: b. Salt Lake City, UT, 16 Feb 1876; d. Tacoma, WA, 25 Aug 1935.

Swallow, Ernest: b. South Dakota, 24 Dec 1886; d. Los Angeles Co, CA, 13 Dec 1967.

Swan, Paul: b. Ashland, IL, 5 Jun 1883; d. Bedford Hills, NY, 1 Feb 1972.

Swanson, Gloria: b. Chicago, IL, 27 Mar 1897; d. New York, NY, 4 Apr 1983.

Swanstrom, Karin: b. Norrkoping, Sweden, 13 Jun 1873; d. 5 Jul 1942.

Swartz, Sara: b. 1899; d. Woodland Hills, CA, 30 Mar 1949.

Sweatnam, Willis P.: b. Zanesville, OH, 1854; d. New York, NY, 25 Nov 1930.

Sweeney, Jack: b. 1889; d. Los Angeles, CA, 12 Apr 1950.

Sweet, Blanche: b. Chicago, IL, 8 Jun 1896; d. New York, NY, 6 Sep 1986.

Sweet, Harry: b. Colorado, 1901; d. Big Bear, CA, 18 Jun 1933.

Swenson, Alfred G.: b. Salt Lake City, UT, 1883; d. Staten Island, NY, 28 Mar 1941.

Swete, Lyall (Edward L. Swete): b. Warrington, Eng, 25 Jul 1865; d. London, Eng, 19 Feb 1930.

Swickard, Charles F.: b. Germany, 21 Mar 1868; d. Fresno, CA, 12 May 1929.

Swickard, Joseph: b. Coblenz, Ger, 26 Jun 1866; d. Los Angeles, CA, 1 Mar 1940.

Swinley, Ion: b. Barnes, Surrey, Eng, 27 Oct 1891; d. London, Eng, 16 Sep 1937.

Sydmeth, Louise: b. London, Eng, 1868; d. New York, NY, 26 Nov 1938.

Sydney, Aurele: b. 18??; d. Madrid, Spain, ? May 1920.

Sydney, Basil: b. London, Eng, 23 Apr 1894; d. London, Eng, 10 Jan 1968.

Sylva, Marguerite: b. Brussels, Belgium, 10 Jul 1875; d. Glendale, CA, 21 Feb 1957.

Sylvani, Gladys: b. England, 1885; d. Alexandria, VA, 20 Apr 1953.

Sylvano, Wanda: b. Paris, Fr, ????; d. Paris, Fr, 8 Apr 1926.

Sylvester, Frank L.: b. 1868; d. Los Angeles, CA, 17 Dec 1931.

Sym, Igo: b. Innsbruck, Austria, 3 Jul 1896; d. 7 Mar 1941.

T

Taber, Richard: b. Long Branch, NJ, 31 Oct 1885; d. New York, NY, 16 Nov 1957.

Tabler, P. Dempsey: b. Tennessee, 23 Nov 1876; d. San Francisco, CA, 7 Jun 1956.

Tabor, Rose: b. 18??; d. Chicago, IL, 19 Sep 1925.

Taggart, Ben L.: b. New York, NY, 5 Apr 1889; d. Santa Monica, CA, 17 May 1947.

Takada, Minoru: b. ????; d. Tokyo, Japan, 28 Dec 1977.

Talazac, Odette: b. ????; d. France, 1948.

Talbot, Mae: b. Indiana, 1869; d. Glendale, CA, 4 Aug 1942.

Talbot, Joseph B. (Slim): b. Hamilton, IL, 1895; d. Boulevard, CA, 25 Jan 1973.

Taliaferro, Edith: b. Richmond, VA, 21 Dec 1893; d. Newton, CT, 2 Mar 1958.

Taliaferro, Mabel: b. New York, NY, 21 May 1887; d. Honolulu, HI, 24 Jan 1979.

Talma, Zolya: b. ????; d. Los Angeles Co, CA, 26 Nov 1983.

Talmadge, Constance: b. Brooklyn, NY, 19 Apr 1900; d. Los Angeles, CA, 23 Nov 1973.

Talmadge, Margaret (Peg): b. 18??; d. Los Angeles, CA, 28 Sep 1933.

Talmadge, Natalie: b. Brooklyn, NY, 29 Apr 1899; d. Santa Monica, CA, 19 Jun 1969.

Talmadge, Norma: b. Jersey City, NJ, 26 May 1897; d. Las Vegas, NV, 24 Dec 1957.

Talmadge, Richard: b. Munich, Ger, 3 Dec 1896; d. Carmel Valley, CA, 25 Jan 1981.

Tamara (Tamara Swann): b. Russia, 1910; d. Lisbon, Port, 22 Feb 1943.

Tanaka, Kinuyo: b. Tokyo, Japan, 29 Nov 1910; d. 21 Mar 1977.

Tanaka, Shoji: b. 1886; d. New York, NY, 19 Oct 1918.

Tanguay, Eva: b. Marbleton, Que, Can, 1 Aug 1878; d. Los Angeles, CA, 11 Jan 1947.

Tannahill, Myrtle: b. 18 May 1886; d. Yorktown Heights, NY, 25 Jul 1977.

Tannaura, Philip: b. New York, NY, 28 Mar 1897; d. Beverly Hills, CA, 7 Dec 1973.

Tanner, James J.: b. 1873; d. Los Angeles, CA, 3 Apr 1934.

Tanner, Marion: b. Buffalo, NY, 1891; d. New York, NY, 30 Oct 1985.

Tansey, Mrs. Emma: b. Louisville, KY, 12 Sep 1870; d. Los Angeles, CA, 23 Mar 1942.

Tansey, Johnny: b. New York State, 8 Oct 1901; d. North Hollywood, CA, 28 Apr 1971.

Tansey, Robert Emmett: b. Brooklyn, NY, 28 Jun 1897; d. Los Angeles, CA, 17 Jun 1951.

Tansey, Sheridan James: b. New York, NY, 29 Jul 1906; d. Sacramento, CA, 12 Apr 1961.

Tantlinger, Verne: b. 1863; d. Los Angeles, CA, 27 Feb 1939.

Tapley, Rose: b. Petersburg, VA, 30 Jun 1881; d. Woodland Hills, CA, 23 Feb 1956.

Taptuka, Clarence S.: b. 1898; d. Albuquerque, NM, 8 Nov 1967.

Tarbutt, Frazer: b. Toronto, Can, 1896; d; France, 16 Jun 1918.

Tarron, Elsie: b. 30 Sep 1903; d. Los Angeles, CA, 24 Oct 1990.

Tashman, Lilyan: b. Brooklyn, NY, 23 Oct 1899; d. New York, NY, 21 Mar 1934.

Tata, Paul M.: b. 1883; d. Memphis, TN, 30 Mar 1962.

Tate, Cullen B.: b. Paducah, KY, 10 Mar 1896; d. Los Angeles, CA, 12 Oct 1947.

Tate, Harry: b. Scotland, 4 Jul 1872; d. London, Eng, 14 Feb 1940.

Taurog, Norman: b. Chicago, IL, 23 Feb 1899; d. Rancho Mirage, CA, 7 Apr 1981.

Tavares, Arthur: b. California, 10 Jan 1884; d. Los Angeles Co, CA, 27 May 1954.

Tavernier, Albert: b. 1859; d. Boston, MA, 3 Nov 1929.

Taylor, Alma: b. London, Eng, 3 Jan 1895; d. London, Eng, ? Jan 1974.

Taylor, Avonne: b. Springfield, OH, 12 Feb 1899; d. Cleveland, OH, 20 Mar 1992.

Taylor, Beth: b. 1889; d. Los Angeles, CA, 1 Mar 1951.

Taylor, E. Forrest: b. Bloomington, IL, 29 Dec 1883; d, Garden Grove, CA, 19 Feb 1965.

Taylor, Estelle: b. Wilmington, DE, 20 May 1894; d. Los Angeles, CA, 15 Apr 1958.

Taylor, Josephine: b. 1891; d. Calumet City, IL, 26 Nov 1964.

Taylor, Julia: b. 20 Sep 1878; d. Los Angeles, CA, 4 Dec 1976.

Taylor, Lark (John Lark Taylor): b. Nashville, TN, 1881; d. Nashville, TN, 26 Mar 1946.

Taylor, Laurette: b. New York, NY, 1 Apr 1884; d. New York, NY, 7 Dec 1946.

Taylor, Ruth Lee: b. Grand Rapids, MI, 15 Jan 1907; d. Palm Springs, CA, 12 Apr 1964.

Taylor, Stanley: b. Campbell, MN, 3 Mar 1900; d. Inglewood, CA, 27 Nov 1980.

Taylor, William Desmond: b. Carlow, Ire, 26 Apr 1867; d. Los Angeles, CA, 1 Feb 1922.

Taylor, William H. (Billy): b. Brownsville, TX, 9 Jul 1829; d. Los Angeles, CA, 26 Dec 1930.

Taylor, Wilton: b. 1869; d. 24 Jan 1925.

Tead, Phillips: b. Somerville, MA, 29 Sep 1893; d. Los Angeles Co, CA, 9 Jun 1974.

Teare, Ethel: b. Phoenix, AZ, 11 Jan 1894; d. San Mateo, CA, 4 Mar 1959.

Tearle, Conway: b. New York, NY, 17 May 1878; d. Los Angeles, CA, 1 Oct 1938.

Tearle, Godfrey: b. New York, NY, 12 Oct 1884; d. London, Eng, 8 Jun 1953.

Tedmarsh, William J.: b. London, Eng, 3 Feb 1876; d. 10 May 1937.

Tedro, Henrietta: b. 1885; d. Los Angeles, CA, 25 Jul 1948.

Teje, Tora: b. Stockholm, Sweden, 7 Jan 1893; d. 30 Apr 1973.

Tell, Alma: b. New York, NY, 27 Mar 1898; d. San Francisco, CA, 29 Dec 1937.

Tell, Olive: b. New York, NY, 1894; d. New York, NY, 6 Jun 1951.

Tellegen, Lou: b. Oedenrode, Holland, 26 Nov 1883; d. Los Angeles, CA, 29 Oct 1934.

Tellegen, Mike: b. Russia, 20 Apr 1885; d. Los Angeles Co, CA, 16 Aug 1970.

Tello, Alfonso Sanchez: b. 8 Mar 1905; d. La Jolla, CA, 18 Apr 1979.

Temary, Elza: b. 1904; d. Tucson, AZ, 15 Feb 1968.

Tempest, Marie: b. London, Eng, 15 Jul 1862; d. London, Eng, 15 Oct 1942.

Tempest, Tom: b. 1876; d. Skowhegan, ME, 14 Dec 1955.

Temple, Richard: b. England, 1873; d. New York, NY, 14 Oct 1954.

Templeton, Olive: b. 1883; d. New York, NY, 29 May 1979.

Tenbrook, Harry: b. Norway, 9 Oct 1887; d. Woodland Hills, CA, 14 Sep 1960.

Ten Eyck, Lillian: b. New Jersey, 22 Apr 1886; d. Los Angeles Co, CA, 6 Dec 1966.

Tengroth, Birgit: b. Stockholm, Sweden, 13 Jul 1915; d. 21 Sep 1983.

Tennant, Barbara: b. London, Eng, 19 May 1892; d. 19??.

Tennant, Dorothy: b. San Francisco, CA, 10 Jul 1865; d. West Palm Beach, FL, 3 Jul 1942.

Tennyson, Gladys: b. Texas, 2 Nov 1894; d. Yuba City, CA, 27 Apr 1983.

Terhune, Albert Payson: b. Newark, NJ, 21 Dec 1872; d. Pompton Lakes, NJ, 18 Feb 1942.

Terriss, Ellaline: b. Stanley, Falkland Islands, 13 Apr 1871; d. London, Eng, 16 Jun 1971.

Terriss, Tom: b. London, Eng, 28 Sep 1874; d. New York, NY, 8 Feb 1964.

Terry, Alice (Alice Taafe): b. Vincennes, IN, 24 Jul 1899; d. Burbank, CA, 22 Dec 1987.

Terry, Don: b. Natick, MA, 8 Aug 1902; d. Oceanside, CA, 6 Oct 1988.

Terry, Dame Ellen: b. Coventry, Eng, 27 Feb 1848; d. Small Hythe, Kent, Eng, 21 Jul 1928.

Terry, Ethel Grey: b. Oakland, CA, 2 Oct 1891; d. Los Angeles, CA, 6 Jan 1931.

Terry, Fred: b. London, Eng, 9 Nov 1863; d. London, Eng, 17 Apr 1933.

Terry, Tex: b. Terre Haute, IN, 22 Aug 1902; d. 18 May 1985.

Tetzlaff, Teddy: b. 1883; d. Santa Ana, CA, 1929.

Te Wan, Madame Sul (Nellie Conley): b. 1873; d. Los Angeles, CA, 1 Feb 1959.

Thalasso, Arthur: b. Ohio, 26 Nov 1883; d. Los Angeles Co, CA, 13 Feb 1954.

Thanhouser, Gertrude: b. Beauvoir, MS, 23 Apr 1880; d. Glen Cove, NY, 29 May 1951.

Tharp, Norman: b. England, 18??; d. London, Eng, 2 Apr 1921.

Thatcher, Evelyn (Eva): b. Omaha, NE, 14 Mar 1862; d. Los Angeles, CA, 28 Sep 1942.

Thatcher, Heather: b. London, Eng, c. 1894; d. London, Eng, 15 Jan 1987.

Theby, Rosemary: b. St. Louis, MO, 8 Apr 1885; d. 19??.

Thesiger, Ernest: b. London, Eng, 15 Jan 1879; d. London, Eng, 14 Jan 1961.

Thiele, Wilhelm: b. Vienna, Austria, 10 May 1890; d. Woodland Hills, CA, 7 Sep 1975.

Thimig, Hermann: b. Vienna, Austria, 3 Oct 1890; d. Vienna, Austria, 7 Jul 1982.

Thom, Norman: b. Greenup, KY, 19 Oct 1877; d. 24 May 1931.

Thomas, Calvin L.: b. Kansas City, KS, 1885; d. Caldwell, NJ, 26 Sep 1964.

Thomas, Edward: b. Red Bank, NJ, 20 Dec 1884; d. Los Angeles, CA, 29 Dec 1943.

Thomas, Frank M.: b. St. Joseph, MO, 13 Jul 1889; d. Tujunga, CA, 25 Nov 1989.

Thomas, Gretchen: b. 1897; d. Los Angeles, CA, 1 Nov 1964.

Thomas, Gus (Gustave): b. Toronto, Can, 1865; d; Everett, WA, 3 May 1926.

Thomas, Jameson: b. London, Eng, 27 Mar 1888; d. Sierra Madre, CA, 10 Jan 1939.

Thomas, John Charles: b. Meyersdale, PA, 6 Sep 1889; d. Apple Valley, CA, 13 Dec 1960.

Thomas, Olive: b. Charleori, PA, 20 Oct 1894; d. Paris, Fr, 10 Sep 1920.

Thomas, Virginia: b. ????; d. Los Angeles, CA, 12 Jan 1955.

Thomas, Walter: b. England, 1867; d. New York, NY, 21 Mar 1917.

Thomashefsky, Boris: b. Kiev, Russ, 12 May 1868; d. New York, NY, 9 Jul 1939.

Thompson, Al (Albert): b. Pennsylvania, 21 Sep 1884; d. Los Angeles Co, CA, 1 Mar 1960.

Thompson, Blackie (Clarence Bergen): b. 1877; d. Los Angeles, CA, 17 May 1936.

Thompson, David H.: b. New York, NY, 4 May 1886; d. Los Angeles, CA, 20 May 1957.

Thompson, Duane: b. Red Oaks IA, 1908; d. Los Angeles, CA, 15 Aug 1970.

Thompson, Frederick A.: b. Montreal, Can, 7 Aug 1869; d. Los Angeles, CA, 23 Jan 1925.

Thompson, Hal: b. 1894; d. 3 Mar 1966.

Thompson, Hugh E.: b. St. Louis, MO, 1887; d. 19??.

Thompson, John: b. 18??; d. ? May 1917.

Thompson, Keene: b. 1886; d. Los Angeles, CA, 11 Jul 1937.

Thompson, Lotus: b. Sydney, Austral, 22 Aug 1906; d. Burbank, CA, 19 May 1963.

Thompson, Margaret: b. Trinidad, CO, 26 Oct 1889; d. Los Angeles, CA, 26 Dec 1969.

Thompson, May: b. Birmingham, Eng, 1890; d. Devon, PA, 18 Nov 1978.

Thompson, Molly: b. 1879; d. Culver City, CA, 14 Feb 1928.

Thompson, Nick J.: b. Houston, TX, 11 Feb 1889; d. Los Angeles, CA, 22 Apr 1980.

Thompson, Raymond: b. 1898; d. Cordova, AK, 29 Jun 1927.

Thompson, Therese: b. Anna, IL, 1876; d. Los Angeles, CA, 16 Sep 1936.

Thompson, Walker: b. Lexington, KY, 1888; d. Chicago, IL, 19 Sep 1922.

Thompson, William H.: b. Glasgow, Scot, 24 Apr 1852; d. New York, NY, 4 Feb 1923.

Thomson, Archibald: b. Elmira, NY, 1901; d. New York, NY, 22 Sep 1981.

Thomson, Fred C.: b. Pasadena, CA, 26 Feb 1890; d. Los Angeles, CA, 25 Dec 1928.

Thomson, Kenneth: b. Pittsburgh, PA, 7 Jan 1899; d. Los Angeles, CA, 26 Jan 1967.

Thomson, Polly: b. Glasgow, Scot, 1884; d. Bridgeport, CT, 20 Mar 1960.

Thorn, John: b. 1880; d. Mercer, PA, 28 Aug 1935.

Thornby, Robert T.: b. New York, NY, 27 Mar 1888; d. Los Angeles Co, CA, 6 Mar 1953.

Thorndike, Russell: b. Rochester, Kent, Eng, 6 Feb 1885; d. London, Eng, 7 Nov 1972.

Thorndike, Sybil: b. Gainsborough, Eng, 24 Oct 1882; d. London, Eng, 9 Jun 1976.

Thorndike, Lucyle: b. Seattle, WA, 1885; d. Los Angeles, CA, 17 Dec 1935.

Thorne, Frank A.: b. Philadelphia, PA, 12 Oct 1881; d. North Hollywood, CA, 28 May 1953.

Thorne, Richard: b. 1905; d. Los Angeles, CA, 31 Jan 1957.

Thorne, Robert: b. 18 Aug 1880; d. New York, NY, 3 Jul 1965.

Thorne, William L,: b. Fresno, CA, 14 Oct 1878; d. Fresno, CA, 10 Mar 1948.

Thornton, Edith: b. New York, NY, 9 Jan 1896; d. Glendale, CA, 13 Feb 1984.

Thornton, Richard: b. 1873; d. New York, NY, 9 May 1936.

Thorp, Ruth: b. Hartford, CT, 1890; d. 1971.

Thorpe, Richard: b. Hutchinson, KS, 24 Feb 1896; d. Palm Springs, CA, 1 May 1991.

Thumb, Mrs. General Tom (Lavina Warren, Adele Cox):,b. Middlesboro, MA, 1841; Middlesboro, MA, 25 Nov 1919.

Thumb, Tom (Darius Adner Alder): b. 1842; d. Los Angeles, CA, 24 Sep 1926.

Thurman, Mary: b. Richfield, UT, 27 Apr 1894; d. New York, NY, 22 Dec 1925.

Thurston, Charles E.: b. Oconto, WI, 10 Aug 1868; d. Los Angeles, CA, 4 Mar 1940.

Thurston, Howard: b. Columbus, OH, 20 Jul 1869; d. Miami Beach, FL, 13 Apr 1936.

Tidblad, Inga: b. Stockholm, Sweden, 29 May 1901; d. Stockholm, Sweden, 12 Sep 1975.

Tidmarsh, Ferdinand: b. Philadelphia, PA, 1883; d. Philadelphia, PA, ? Nov 1922.

Tiedtke, Jakob: b. Berlin, Ger, 23 Jun 1875; d. Berlin, Ger, 30 Jan 1960.

Tietjen, Charles L.: b. New York, NY, 18??; d. New York, NY, 25 Dec 1938.

Tighe, Harry: b. New Haven, CT, 27 Jun 1885; d. Old Lyme, CT, 10 Feb 1935.

Tilbury, Zeffie: b. London, Eng, 20 Nov 1863; d. Los Angeles, CA, 22 Jul 1950.

Tilden, William T.: b. Germantown, PA, 10 Feb 1893; d. Los Angeles, CA, 4 Jun 1953.

Tilghman, William M.: b. Fort Dodge, IA, 4 Jul 1854; d. Oklahoma, 1 Nov 1924.

Tilley, Vesta: b. Worcester, Eng, 13 May 1864; d. London, Eng, 16 Sep 1952.

Tilton, Edwin Booth: b. Chicago, IL, 15 Sep 1859; d. Los Angeles, CA, 16 Jan 1926.

Tincher, Fay: b. Topeka, KS, 17 Apr 1884; d. Brooklyn, NY, 11 Oct 1983.

Tinney, Frank: b. Philadelphia, PA, 29 Mar 1878; d. Northport, NY, 28 Nov 1940.

Tisdale, Franklin M.: b. 1871; d. Los Angeles, CA, 14 Feb 1947.

Tissot, Alice: b. France, 1890; d. Paris, Fr, 5 May 1971.

Titheradge, Dion: b. Melbourne, Austral, 30 Mar 1886; d. London, Eng, 16 Nov 1934.

Titheradge, Madge: b. Melbourne, Austral, 2 Jul 1887; d. Fetcham, Surrey, Eng, 13 Nov 1961.

Titmuss, Phyllis: b. London, Eng, 14 Jan 1900; d. 6 Jan 1946.

Titterington, Morris M.: b. ????; d. Snyder, PA, ? Jul 1928.

Titus, Fred: b. 18??; d. Los Angeles, CA, ? Feb 1918.

Titus, Lydia Yeamena: b. Australia, 1866; d. Los Angeles, CA, 29 Dec 1929.

Tobin, Frank: b. 18??; d. Omaha, NE, 20 Jul 1913.

Todd, Harry: b. Allegheny, PA, 13 Dec 1863; d. Glendale, CA, 15 Feb 1935.

Todd, Thelma: b. Lawrence, MA, 29 Jul 1905; d. Los Angeles, CA, 16 Dec 1935.

Toler, Hooper: b. Witchita, KS, 1891; d. Los Angeles, CA, 2 Jun 1922.

Toler, Sidney: b. Warrensburg, VA, 28 Apr 1888; d. Los Angeles, CA, 12 Feb 1947.

Tollaire, August: b. Paris, Fr, 7 Mar 1866; d. Los Angeles Co, CA, 15 Jan 1959.

Tolly, Frank: b. 18??; d. New York, NY, 26 Nov 1924.

Tolnaes, Gunnar: b. Cristiania, Norway, 7 Feb 1879; d. 9 Nov 1940.

Tolstol, Countess (Sophie Behra): b. 1846; d. Trasnay Polyana, Russ, 4 Nov 1919.

Tomamoto, Thomas: b. Japan, 1879; d. New York, NY, 29 Sep 1924.

Tomick, Frank: b. 1895; d. Los Angeles Co, CA, 29 Oct 1966.

Tonaka, Shoji: b. 18??; d. New York, NY, 19 Oct 1918.

Tonge, H. Assheton: b. 1872; d. New York, NY, 2 Apr 1927.

Tonge, Philip: b. London, Eng, 26 Apr 1897; d. Los Angeles, CA, 28 Jan 1959.

Tooker, William H.: b. New York, NY, 2 Sep 1869; d. Los Angeles, CA, 10 Oct 1936.

Tordesilla, Jesus: b. Spain, 1893; d. Madrid, Spain, 24 Mar 1973.

Tornek, Anna: b. 1896; d. Woodland Hills, CA, 12 Aug 1985.

Tornek, Jack: b. Russia, 2 Jan 1888; d. Los Angeles Co, CA, 18 Feb 1974.

Torpe, Marie: b. 1904; d. Woodland Hills, CA, 28 Jul 1967.

Torpey, Lester: b. 1899; d. Weehawken, NJ, 25 Aug 1920.

Torrence, David: b. Edinburgh, Scot, 17 Jan 1864; d. Woodland Hills, CA, 26 Dec 1951.

Torrence, Ernest: b. Edinburgh, Scot, 26 Jun 1878; d. New York, NY, 15 May 1933.

Torres, Raquel: b. Senora, Mex, 11 Nov 1908; d. Los Angeles, CA, 10 Aug 1987.

Toto (Armando Novello): b. Geneva, Switz, 1888; d. New York, NY, 15 Dec 1938.

Toto, Billie: b. 1904; d. New York, NY, 24 Dec 1928.

Totten, Edyth: b. 1885; d. New York, NY, 12 Nov 1953.

Totten, Joseph Byron: b. Brooklyn, NY, 1870; d. New York, NY, 29 Apr 1946.

Toulout, Jean: b. Paris, Fr, 28 Sep 1887; d. 18 Oct 1962.

Tourneur, Jacques: b. Paris, Fr, 12 Nov 1904; d. Bergerec, Fr, 19 Dec 1977.

Tourneur, Maurice: b. Paris, Fr, 2 Feb 1873; d. Paris, Fr, 4 Aug 1961.

Tower, Halsey: b. Buffalo, NY, 5 Oct 1889; d. Los Angeles, CA, 24 Nov 1939.

Towne, Charles Hanson: b. 1877; d. New York, NY, 28 Feb 1949.

Townley, Jack: b. Kansas City, MO, 3 Mar 1897; d. Los Angeles Co, CA, 15 Oct 1960.

Townsend, Anna: b. Utica, NY, 5 Jan 1845; d. Los Angeles, CA, 11 Sep 1923.

Townsend, Genevieve: b. 1899; d. Switzerland, 1 May 1927.

Tracey, Thomas F.: b. County Cork, Ire, 1880; d. New York, NY, 27 Aug 1961.

Tracy, Helen: b. Jacksonville, FL, 7 May 1850; d. Staten Island, NY, 5 Sep 1924.

Trader, George Henry: b. Sunderland, Durham, Eng, 1865; d. East Islip, NY, 12 Mar 1951.

Trafton, Herbert: b. 20 Jun 1893; d. San Diego, CA, 1 Sep 1979.

Trainor, Leonard: b. Talaquah, OK, 24 Feb 1879; d. Santa Monica, CA, 28 Jul 1940.

Trask, Wayland: b. New York State, 16 Jul 1887; d. Los Angeles, CA, 18 Nov 1918.

Trautman, Ludwig: b. 1886; d. Berlin, Ger, 24 Jan 1957.

Travers, Richard C.: b. Hudson Bay Trading Post, Can, 15 Apr 1885; d. San Pedro, CA, 20 Apr 1935.

Traverse, Madlaine: b. Cleveland, OH, 1 Aug 1875; d. Cleveland, OH, 7 Jan 1964.

Travis, Charles W.: b. 1861; d. Brooklyn, NY, 14 Aug 1917.

Travis, Don: b. Winfield, KS, 17 Nov 1898; d. Newport Beach, CA, 28 Jul 1970.

Tree, Chief John Big: b. 1865; d. Syracuse, NY, 6 Jul 1967.

Tree, Helen Maude (Lady Tree): b. London, Eng, 5 Oct 1858; d. London, Eng, 7 Aug 1937.

Tree, Sir Herbert Beerbohm: b. London, Eng, 17 Dec 1853; d. London, Eng, 2 Jul 1917.

Trenkor, Luis: b. Ortiseip Italy, 4 Oct 1893; d. Bolzano, Italy, 12 Apr 1990.

Trenor, Frank A.: b. Watervliet, NY, 1876; d. Watervliet, NY, 4 Dec 1941.

Trent, Jack B.: b. Texas, 24 Aug 1896; d. Los Angeles Co, CA, 1 Aug 1961.

Trento, Guido: b. Italy, 21 Jun 1892; d. San Francisco, CA, 31 Jul 1957.

Trenton, Pell: b. New York, NY, c. 1890; d. 19??.

Treptow, Otto: b. Germany, 18??; d. 3 Mar 1924.

Tresham, Jennie: b. 1881; d. Portland, OR, 18 Dec 1913.

Treskoff, Olga: b. Glenlyon, PA, 1902; d. New York, NY, 23 Apr 1938.

Trevelyan, Hilda: b. England, 4 Feb 1880; d. London, Eng, 10 Nov 1959.

Trevelyn, Una: b. Memphis, TN, 1896; d. Los Angeles, CA, 14 May 1948.

Trevor, Ann: b. London, Eng, 1899; d. England, ? Jul 1970.

Trevor, Hugh: b. Yonkers, NY, 28 Oct 1903; d. Los Angeles, CA, 10 Nov 1933.

Trevor, Norman: b. Calcutta, India, 23 Jun 1877; d. Norwalk, CA, 30 Oct 1929.

Triller, Armand: b. Bucharest, Romania, 20 Mar 1883; d. 12 Dec 1939.

Trimble, George S.: b. Brooklyn, NY. 10 Oct 1874; d. Philadelphia, PA, 23 Feb 1925.

Trimble, Larry: b. Robbinston, ME, 15 Feb 1885; d. Woodland Hills, CA, 8 Feb 1954.

Trimmingham, Ernest: b. 1879; d. 6 Feb 1942.

Trotsky, Leon: b. Yanovka, Ukraine, 8 Nov 1879; d. Mexico City, Mex, 20 Aug 1940.

Troubetzkoy, Youcca: b. Los Angeles, CA, 12 Dec 1905; d. Palm Beach, FL, 22 Apr 1992.

Troutman, Ivy: b. Long Branch, NJ, 23 Sep 1883; d. Tinton Falls, NJ, 12 Jan 1979.

Trouve, Roger Karl: b. 1881; d. 4 May 1984.

Trow, William: b. Illinois, 19 Oct 1890; d. Los Angeles, CA, 2 Sep 1973.

Trowbridge, Charles: b. Vera Cruz, Mex, 10 Jan 1882; d. Los Angeles, CA, 30 Oct 1967.

Truax, Maude: b. Chicago, IL, 7 Nov 1884; d. Los Angeles, CA, 6 Sep 1939.

Truax, Sarah: b. Cincinnati, OH, 12 Feb 1877; d. Seattle, WA, 25 Apr 1958.

True, Bess: b. 1899; d. New York, NY, 9 Jul 1947.

Truesdell, Fred C.: b. Coldwater, MI, 1874; d. Qunicy, MI, 9 May 1929.

Truesdell, George Frederick: b. Montclair, NJ, 1873; d. New York, NY, 3 May 1937.

Truesdell, Howard: b. Crawford County, PA, 3 Jan 1861; d. Los Angeles, CA, 8 Dec 1941.

Truex, Ernest: b. Kansas City, MO, 19 Sep 1889; d. Fallbrook, CA, 27 Jun 1973.

Trunnelle, Mabel: b. Dwight, IL, 8 Nov 1879; d. Glendale, CA, 29 Apr 1981.

Tryon, Glenn: b. Julietta, ID, 14 Sep 1899; d. Los Angeles, CA, 18 Apr 1970.

Tschechowa, Olga (Olga Chekova): b. Alexandropol, Russ, 26 Apr 1897; d. Munich, Ger, 9 Mar 1980.

Tucker, Cy: b. England, 3 Jun 1890; d. Los Angeles, CA, 4 Jul 1952.

Tucker, Ethel: b. 18??; d. 14 May 1926.

Tucker, George Loane: b. Chicago, IL, 12 Jun 1872; d. Los Angeles, CA, 20 Jun 1921.

Tucker, Harland: b. Ohio, 8 Dec 1893; d. Los Angeles Co, CA, 22 Mar 1949.

Tucker, John: b. 1860; d. New York, NY, ? Aug 1922.

Tucker, Richard: b. Brooklyn, NY, 4 Jun 1883; d, Los Angeles, CA, 5 Dec 1942.

Tully, Ethel: b. Brooklyn, NY, 1898; d. San Antonio, TX, 1 Oct 1968.

Tully, George F.: b. Co. Mayo, Ire, 22 Nov 1876; d. London, Eng, 2 Jul 1930.

Tummel, William F.: b. Kansas City, MO, 5 Mar 1892; d. Los Angeles, CA, 16 Nov 1977.

Tunis, Fay: b. 1890; d. Atlantic City, NJ, 4 Dec 1967.

Tunney, Gene: b. New York, NY, 25 May 1898; d. Greenwich, CT, 7 Nov 1978.

Turbett, Ben: b. Salem, MA, 1874; d. Atlanta, GA, 6 Mar 1936.

Turin, Viktor: b. Leningrad, Russ, 1895; d. 1945.

Turnbull, Stanley, b. Whitby, Yorks, Eng, 1881; d. London, Eng, 8 May 1924.

Turner, Bowd M.: b. Cumberland, MD, 1878; d. Los Angeles, CA, 12 Sep 1933.

Turner, D. H.: b. New York, NY, 12 Jan 1883; d. 19??.

Turner, Eardley: b. 18??; d. 23 Jan 1929.

Turner, Emanuel: b. 1885; d. Los Angeles, CA, 13 Dec 1941.

Turner, Florence: b. New York, NY, 6 Jan 1887; d. Los Angeles, CA, 28 Aug 1946.

Turner, Frank D.: b. 1881; d. Los Angeles Co, CA, 27 Oct 1957.

Turner, Fred A.: b. New York, 12 Oct 1858; d. 13 Feb 1923.

Turner, George: b. Findon Manor, Eng, 19 Feb 1902; d. New York, NY, 27 Jul 1968.

Turner, Maidel: b. Sherman, TX, 12 May 1888; d. Ocean Springs, MS, 12 Apr 1953.

Turner, Martin: b. Texas, 20 Dec 1882; d. Los Angeles Co, CA, 14 May 1957.

Turner, Otis: b. Fairfield, IN, 29 Nov 1862; d. Los Angeles, CA, 28 Mar 1918.

Turner, Raymond: b. New Mexico, 28 Oct 1895; d. Los Angeles Co, CA, 18 Aug 1981.

Turner, William H.: b. Ireland, 1861; d. Philadelphia, PA, 27 Sep 1942.

Turpin, Ben: b. New Orleans, LA, 19 Sep 1869; d. Los Angeles, CA, 1 Jul 1940.

Turpin, Carrie Lemieux: b. Quebec, Can, 1882; d. Los Angeles, CA, 1 Oct 1925.

Tyke, John: b. Oregon, 20 Oct 1894; d. Los Angeles, CA, 23 Feb 1940.

Tyler, Dallas: b. 1878; d. Holmesburg, PA, 25 Jul 1953.

Tyler, Odette: b. Savannah, GA, 26 Sep 1869; d. Los Angeles, CA, 8 Dec 1936.

Tyler, Tom: b. Port Henry, NY, 8 Aug 1903; d. Hamtramck, MI, 1 May 1954.

Tynan, Brandon: b. Dublin, Ire, 11 Apr 1875; d. New York, NY, 19 Mar 1967.

Tyndale, Kate: b. 18??; d. London, Eng, ? Aug 1919.

Tyroler, William X.: b. 1884; d. Torrence, CA, 4 Jan 1959.

U

Uhlig, Max E.: b. 1896; d. North Tarrytown, NY, 28 May 1958.

Ulmer, Anna: b. 1853; d. Peak's Island, ME, 28 Oct 1928.

Ulric, Lenore: b. New Ulm, MN, 21 July 1892; d. Orangeburg, NY, 30 Dec 1970.

Underhill, John G.: b. New York, NY, 26 Apr 1870; d. Los Angeles Co, CA, 26 May 1941.

Underwood, Franklin: b. Denver, CO, 1877; d. New York, NY, 22 Dec 1940.

Underwood, Lawrence: b. Albion, IA, 1871; d. Los Angeles, CA, 2 Feb 1939.

Underwood, Loyal: b. Rockford, IL, 6 Aug 1893; d. Los Angeles Co, CA, 30 Sep 1966.

Unterkircher, Hans: b. Germany, 1895; d. ? May 1971.

Upcher, Peter: b. Halesworth, Eng, 1892; d. London, Eng, ? Dec 1962.

Uraneff, Vadim: b. Russia, 6 Feb 1895; d. Duarte, CA, 5 Apr 1952.

Urban, Dorothy Karroll: b. 1869; d. Los Angeles, CA, 29 Oct 1961.

Urbont, Harry: b. Kipin, Russ, 1902; d. New York, NY, 29 Sep 1987.

Urson, Frank B.: b. Chicago, IL, 1887; d, Niles, MI, 16 Aug 1928.

Uttal, Fred: b. 1908; d. New York, NY, 28 Nov 1963.

Uzzell, Corene: b. Houston, TX, c. 1890; d. 19??.

V

Vaccaro, Frank A.: b. 1884; d. Derby, CT, 6 Jul 1948.

Vachon, Jean: b. ????; d. 2 Feb 1989.

Vale, Louise: b. New York, NY, 18??; d. Madison, WI, 28 Oct 1918.

Vale, Travers: b. Liverpool, Eng, 31 Jan 1865; d. Los Angeles, CA, 10 Jan 1927.

Valentine, Grace: b. Springfield, OH, 14 Feb 1884; d. New York, NY, 12 Nov 1964.

Valentino, Alberto: b. Castellaneta, Italy, 1892; d. Los Angeles, CA, 4 Jun 1981.

Valentino, Rudolph: b. Castellaneta, Italy, 6 May 1895; d. New York, NY, 23 Aug 1926.

Valerie, Olive: b. 1893; d. New York, NY, 27 Oct 1951.

Valerio, Albano: b. San Jose, CA, 1889; d. Los Angeles, CA, 2 Feb 1961.

Valkyrian, Valda: b. Denmark, 30 Sep 1895; d. Los Angeles, CA, 22 Oct 1956.

Vallentin, Hermann: b. 1870; d. Germany, ? Nov 1945.

Valli, Valli: b. Berlin, Ger, 11 Feb 1882; d. London, Eng, 3 Nov 1927.

Valli, Virginia: b. Chicago, IL, 10 Jun 1898; d. Palm Springs, CA, 24 Sep 1968.

Vallis, Robert: b. England, 1876; d. Brighton, Eng, 19 Dec 1932.

Valsted, Myrtle: b. 1910; d. Los Angeles, CA, 19 Sep 1928.

Van, Billy B.: b. Pottstown, PA, 3 Aug 1878; d. Newport, NH, 16 Nov 1950.

Van, Wally: b. Hyde Park, NY, 27 Sep 1885; d. Englewood, NJ, 9 May 1974.

Van Antwerp, Albert: b. Denver, CO, 1898; d. Mendocino Co, CA, 30 Oct 1946.

Van Auker, Cecil K.: b. Youngstown, OH, 18??; d. Frescott, AZ, 18 Feb 18 1938.

Vam Biene, Auguste: b. Holland, 16 May 1850; d. Brighton, Eng, 23 Jan 1913.

Vanburgh, Irene: b. Exeter, Devon, Eng, 2 Dec 1872; d. London, Eng, 30 Nov 1949.

Vanburgh, Violet: b. Exeter, Devon, Eng, 11 Jun 1867; d. London, Eng, 10 Nov 1982.

Van Buren, A. H.: b. Gloucester, NJ, 9 Apr 1879; d. Los Angeles, CA, 1 Aug 1965.

Van Buren, Mabel: b. Chicago, IL, 17 Jul 1878; d. Los Angeles, CA, 4 Nov 1947.

Vance, Clarice: b. Louisville, KY, 14 Mar 1871; d. Napa, CA, 24 Aug 1961.

Vance, Virginia: b. 1901; d. Los Angeles, CA, 13 Oct 1942,

Van Cortlandt, Jan: b. Holland, 1870; d. New York, NY, 21 Jul 1928.

Van Court, De Witt: b. 1860; d. Los Angeles, CA, 5 Oct 1937.

Vanderveer, Ellinor: b. 5 Aug 1886; d. Loma Linda, CA, 27 May 1976.

Van Dommelen, Garoline: b. 1874; d. 1957.

Van Dommelen, Jan: b. Amsterdam, Holland, 28 Apr 1878; d. 26 Oct 1942.

Van Dyke, Truman: b. Natchez, MS, 15 Nov 1897; d. Los Angeles, CA, 6 May 1984.

Van Dyke, W. S.: b. San Diego, CA, 21 Mar 1890; d. Brentwood, CA, 5 Feb 1943.

Vane, Denton: b. Brooklyn, NY, 1886; d. Union Hill, NJ, 17 Sep 1940.

Vane, Dorothy: b. England, 1871; d. 4 Mar 1947.

Vane, Myrtle: b. 1868; d. San Diego, CA, 17 Feb 1932.

Vanel, Charles: b. Rennes, Fr, 21 Aug 1892; d. Cannes, Fr, 14 Apr 1989.

Van Epps, John DeLacy: b. 1879; d. Teaneck, NJ, 15 Sep 1960.

Van Heusen, Dorothea: b. 1901; d. ? May 1989.

Van Horn, James: b. South Dakota, 24 Sep 1917; d. Los Angeles, CA, 20 Apr 1966.

Van Leer, Arnold: b. London, Eng, 1895; d. Boston, MA, 3 Jun 1975.

Van Loan, Philip: b. Amsterdam, Holland, 1884; d. 19??.

Van Meter, Harry (Harry Von Meter): b. Malta Bend, MO, 29 Mar 1871; d. Sawtelle, CA, 2 June 1956.

Van Meter, Joseph: b. Missouri, 3 Aug 1876; d. Los Angeles, CA, 22 Nov 1961.

Vann, Polly: b. Scranton, PA, 29 Jul 1882; d. Los Angeles, CA, 25 Aug 1952.

Vann, W. T.: b. 18??; d. 15 Sep 1927.

Van Name, Elsie: b. Staten Island, NY, 1890; d. 4 Nov 1934.

Van Sickle, Raymond: b. 1885; d. Kobe, Japan, 10 Jul 1964.

Van Sloan, Edward: b. San Francisco, CA, 1 Nov 1882; d. San Francisco, CA, 8 Mar 1964.

Van Tassell, Marie: b. Little Falls, NY, 6 Apr 1874; d. Oakland, CA, ? Jan 1946.

Van Tress, Mabel: b. San Bernardino, CA, 6 Oct 1872; d. Pasadena, CA, 16 Mar 1962.

Vam Trump, Jessalyn: b. St. Johns, OH, 16 Jan 1887; d. Los Angeles, CA, 2 May 1939.

Van Upp, Virginia: b. Chicago, IL, 1901; d. Los Angeles, CA, 25 Mar 1970.

Van Vleck, William: b. San Antonio, TX, 20 Jun 1886; d. Los Angeles Co, CA, 19 May 1966.

Varconi, Victor: b. Kisvard, Hungary, 31 Mar 1891; d. Santa Barbara, CA, 16 Jun 1976.

Vaser, Ernesto: b. Italy, 1876; d. 1934.

Vaughn, Ada Mae: b. Ashland, KY, 8 Nov 1905; d. Los Angeles, CA, 11 Sep 1943.

Vaughn, Alberta: b. Ashlard, KY, 27 Jun 1904; d. Studio City, CA, 26 Apr 1992.

Vaughn, Robert: b. St. Jouis, MO, 1877; d. 19??.

Vaughn, Vivian (Gypsy Gould): b.1901; d. Los Angeles, CA, 1 Feb 1966.

Vaulthier, Georges: b. France, ????; d. Paris, Fr, ? Apr 1926,

Vaverka, Anton: b. Czechoslovakia, 18??; d. Prague, Czech, 2 Jul 1937.

Vavitch, Michael: b. Odessa, Russ, 1885; d. Los Angeles, CA, 5 Oct 1930.

Veidt, Conrad: b. Berlin, Ger, 22 Jan 1893; d. Los Angeles, CA, 3 Apr 1943.

Vejar, Harry: b. Los Angeles, CA, 24 Apr 1889; d. Sawtelle, CA, 1 Mar 1968.

Vekroff, Perry N.: b. Alexandria, Egypt, 3 Jun 1880; d. Los Angeles, CA, 4 Jan 1937.

Velez, Lupe: b. San Luis Potosi, Mex, 18 Jul 1908; d. Beverly Hills, CA, 14 Dec 1944.

Veloise, Harry: b. 1877; d. Oklahoma City, OK, 16 Jan 1936.

Veness, Amy: b. England, 1876; d. Saltdean, Sussex, Eng, 22 Sep 1960,

Vanning, Una: b. Bedford, Eng, 12 Nov 1893; d. 9 Mar 1985.

Vensen, Florence: b. 1896; d. Los Angeles, CA, 30 Oct 1964.

Verly, Michele: b. 1911; d. Nice, Fr, 3 Mar 1952.

Vermilyea, Harold: b. New York, NY, 10 Oct 1889; d. New York, NY, 8 Jan 1958.

Vermoyal, Paul: b. France, 18??; d. Neuilly, Fr, ? Oct 1925.

Verner, Charles (Charles Vernon): b. 1848; d. Bosten, MA, 19 Mar 1926.

Vernon, Bobbie: b. Chicago, IL, 9 Mar 1897; d. Los Angeles, CA, 28 Jun 1939.

Vernon, Dorothy: b. Germany, 11 Nov 1875; d. Granada Hills, CA, 28 Oct 1970.

Vernon, Isabel: b. 1874; d. New York, NY, 21 Apr 1930.

Vernon, Percy: b. Kettering, Eng, 29 Dec 1857; d. London, Eng, 25 Dec 1926.

Vespermann, Kurt: b. Kulmsee, Prussia, 1887; d. Berlin, Ger, 13 Jul 1957.

Vibart, Herry: b. Musselburgh, Scot, 25 Dec 1863; d. 1939.

Victor Emmanuel III: b. Naples, Italy, 11 Nov 1869; d. Alexandria, Egypt, 28 Dec 1947.

Victor, Henry: b. London, Eng, 2 Oct 1892; d. Los Angeles, CA, 15 May 1945.

Victoria, Vesta: b. Leeds, Yorks, Eng, 26 Nov 1873; d. London, Eng, 7 Apr 1951.

Vidor, Florence: b. Houston, TX, 23 Jul 1895; d. Pacific Palisades, CA, 3 Nov 1977.

Vidor, King Wallis: b. Galveston, TX, 8 Feb 1894; d. Paso Robles, CA, 1 Nov 1982.

Vie, Florence: b. 1876; d. 12 Apr 1939.

Vigna, Grace: b. 1891; d. Cincinnati, OH, 9 Dec 1926.

Vignola, Robert G.: b. Albany, NY, 5 Aug 1882; d. Los Angeles, CA, 25 Oct 1953.

Viking, Vonceil: b. 1902; d. Banning, CA, 2 Dec 1929.

Vila, Sabra DeShon: b. Roxbury, MA, 1850; d. Brooklyn, NY, 20 Sep 1917.

Villares, Jessie: b. ????; d. ? Feb 1929.

Villiers, Mavis: b. Sydney, Austral, 18 Jan 1915; d. ? Mar 1976.

Vincent, Clive: b. England, ????; d. 11 Apr 1943.

Vincent, James: b. Springfield, MA, 19 Jul 1882; d. New York, NY, 12 Jul 1957.

Vinton, Horace: b. 1854; d. New York, NY, 26 Nov 1930.

Viotti, Gino: b. Torino, Italy, 1875; d. ? Dec 1951.

Visaroff, Michael: b. Russia, 18 Nov 1892; d. Los Angeles, CA, 27 Feb 1951.

Vivian, Ed: b. 18??; d. Redondo Beach, CA, 1911.

Vivian, Robert: b. London, Eng, 1859; d. New York, NY, 31 Jan 1944.

Voegtlin, Arthur: b. Chicago, IL, 1858; d. Los Angeles, CA, 18 Jan 1948.

Vogeding, Fredrik: b. Nymegen, Holland, 28 Mar 1887; d. Van Nuys, CA, 18 Apr 1942.

Vogel, Henry: b. 1865; d. New York, NY, 17 Jun 1925.

Voinoff, Anatole: b. Russia, 1895; d. New York, NY, 9 Feb 1965.

Vokes, Harry: b. Quincy, IL, 1867; d. Boston, MA, 15 Apr 1922.

Vokes, May: b. 1882; d. Stamford, CT, 13 Sep 1957.

Volnys, Jacques: b. 18??; d. Paris, Fr, ? May 1925.

Volotskoy, Vladimir: b. Russia, 1853; d. Los Angeles, CA, 7 Nov 1927.

Volpe, Frederick: b. Liverpool, Eng, 31 Jul 1865; d. London, Eng, 6 Mar 1932.

Von Alten, Ferdinand: b. Petrograd, Russ, 13 Apr 1885; d. Dessau, Ger, 17 Mar 1933.

Von Block, Bela: b. Moscow, Russ, 1889; d. Culver City, CA, 23 Mar 1962,

Von Bolvary, Geza: b. Hungary, 27 Dec 1897; d. Munich, Ger, 10 Aug 1961.

Von Brincken, William (William Vaughn, Roger Beckwith): b. Flensberg, Ger, 27 May 1881; d. Los Angeles, CA, 18 Jun 1946.

Von Diossy, Arthur: b. Austria, 1869; d. 29 Sep 1940.

Von Eltz, Theodore: b. New Haven, CT, 5 Nov 1893; d. Woodland Hills, CA, 6 Oct 1964.

Von Goth, Rolf: b. South Africa, 5 Nov 1906; d. 9 Nov 1961.

Von Nagy, Kathe: b. Szatnar, Hungary, 4 Apr 1904; d. 20 Dec 1973.

Vonnegut, Marjorie: b. Indianapolis, IN, 1892; d. New York, NY, 25 Oct 1936.

Von Ritgau, Erik: b. Copenhagen, Den, 6 Jul 1877; d. 28 Feb 1936.

Von Rue, Greta: b. ????; d. Los Angeles Co, CA, 2 Jun 1991.

Von Schiller, Carl (Jerome Sheldon): b. Columbus, OH, 13 Aug 1890; d. Los Angeles, CA, 15 Apr 1962.

Von Schlettow, Hans A.: b. Frankfurt, Ger, 11 Jun 1888; d. Berlin, Ger, ? Jun 1945.

Von Seyffertitz, Gustav: b. Tyrol, Austria, 4 Aug 1863; d. Los Angeles, CA, 25 Dec 1943.

Von Stroheim, Erich: b. Vienna, Austria, 22 Sep 1885; d. Paris, Fr, 12 May 1957.

Von Stroheim, Erich, Jr.: b. Los Angeles, CA, 25 Aug 1916; d. Woodland Hills, CA, 26 Oct 1968.

Von Twardowski, Hans H.: b. Germany, 1898; d. New York, NY, 19 Nov 1958.

Von Walther, Haertha: b. Hildesheim, Ger, 12 Jun 1903; d. Munich, Ger, 12 Apr 1987.

Von Wangenheim, Gustav: b. Wiesbaden, Ger, 18 Feb 1895; d. Munich, Ger, 5 Aug 1975.

Von Winterstein, Eduard: b. Vienna, Austria, 1 Aug 1871; d. Berlin, Ger, 22 Jul 1961.

Von Wolowski, Curt: b. 1879; d. 1985.

Vosburgh, Alfred (Alfred Whitman and Gayne Whitman): b. Chicago, IL, 19 Mar 1890; d. Los Angeles, CA, 31 Aug 1958.

Vosburgh, Harold: b. Penetanguishene, Ont, Can, 1870; d. New Orleans, LA, 17 Nov 1926.

Vosburgh, Jack (Jack Vosper): b. Chicago, IL, 3 Jul 1894; d. Los Angeles, CA, 6 Apr 1954.

Voshell, John M.: b. Smyrna, DE, 1882; d. Los Angeles, CA, 22 May 1952.

Voskoviec, George: b. Sazava, Czech, 19 Jun 1905; d. Pearlblossom, CA, 1 Jul 1981.

Voss, Frank (Fatty): b. Illinois, 12 Oct 1888; d. Los Angeles, CA, 22 Apr 1917.

Vroom, Frederick W.: b. Clements, Nova Scotia, Can, 11 Nov 1857; d. Los Angeles, CA, 24 Jun 1942.

W

Waddington, Patrick: b. York, Eng, 19 Aug 1901; d. York, Eng, 4 Feb 1987.

Wade, Bessie: b. 1885; d. Dallas, TX, 19 Oct 1966.

Wade, John P.: b. Indiana, 30 June 1876; d. Los Angeles, CA, 13 Jul 1949.

Wadhams, Golden: b. 1869; d. Los Angeles, CA, 26 Jun 1929.

Wadsworth, William: b. Pigeon Cove, MA, 7 Jun 1874; d. Brooklyn, NY, 6 Jun 1950.

Wagar, Duane: b. 1879; d. Ocean Park, CA, 2 Sep 1933.

Waggner, George: b. New York, NY, 7 Sep 1894; d. Woodland Hills, CA, 11 Dec 1984.

Wagner, Elsa: b. Reval, Estonia, 1881; d. ? Sep 1975.

Wagner, Emmett (Kid): b. 1892; d. Woodland Hills, CA, 25 Apr 1977.

Wagner, Jack: b. Ohio, 5 Jan 1897; d. Los Angeles, CA, 6 Feb 1965.

Wagner, Max: b. Mexico, 28 Nov 1901; d. Los Angeles, CA, 16 Nov 1975.

Wagner, William: b. New York, 7 Nov 1883; d. Los Angeles, CA, 11 Mar 1964.

Wahbi, Youssef: b. 14 Jul 1898; d. Cairo, Egypt, ? Dec 1982.

Wainwright, Godfrey: b. 1879; d. Woodland Hills, CA, 19 May 1956.

Wainwright, Marie: b. Philadelphia, PA, 8 May 1853; d. Scranton, PA, 17 Aug 1923.

Waite, James R.: b. 18??; d. New York, NY, 9 Nov 1913.

Waite, Malcolm: b. Menomonee, WI, 7 May 1892; d. Van Nuys, CA, 25 Apr 1949.

Wakefield, Frances: b. 1891; d. Batavia, NY, 26 Mar 1943.

Walbrook, Anton; b, Vienna, Austria, 19 Nov 1900; d. Starnberg, Ger, 9 Aug 1967.

Walburn, Raymond: b. Plymouth, IN, 9 Sep 1887; d. New York, NY, 26 Jul 1969.

Walcamp, Marie: b. Dennison, OH, 27 Jul 1894; d. Los Angeles, CA, 17 Nov 1936.

Walck, Ezra C.: b. 18??; d. Detroit, MI, ? Sep 1927.

Walcott, Julia: b. 1845; d. Chicago, IL, 25 May 1915.

Walden, Harold: b. 1889; d. 2 Dec 1955.

Walden, Harry: b. 22 Oct 1875; d. 4 Jun 1921.

Walden, Martha: b, 1891; d. Bussu, Holland, 21 Oct 1988.

Waldridge, Harold: b. New Orleans, LA, 1905; d. New York, NY, 26 Jun 1957.

Waldron, Andy: b. London, Eng, 20 Sep 1947; d. 1 Mar 1932.

Waldron, Charles D.: b. Waterford, NY, 23 Dec 1877; d. Los Angeles, CA, 4 Mar 1946.

Wales, Ethel: b. Passaic, NJ, 4 Apr 1878; d. Los Angeles, CA, 15 Feb 1952.

Wales, Wally (Hal Taliaferro): b. Sheridan, WY, 13 Nov 1895; d. Sheridan, WY, 12 Feb 1980.

Walker, Antoinette: b. 1874; d. Topsfield, MA, 14 Jul 1970.

Walker, Ben: b. 18??; d. Everett, MA, 3 Jan 1924.

Walker, Charlotte: b. Galveston, TX, 29 Dec 1878; d. Kerville, TX, 23 Mar 1958.

Walker, Christy, b. 1896; d. New York, NY, 29 Oct 1918.

Walker, David: b. ????; d. 28 Jul 1976.

Walker, Johnny: b. New York, NY, 1894; d. New York, NY, 5 Dec 1949.

Walker, June: b. Chicago, IL, 14 Jun 1900; d. Sherman Oaks, CA, 3 Feb 1966.

Walker, Laura: b. 1894; d. 17 May 1951.

Walker, Lillian (Dimples): b. Brooklyn, NY, 21 Apr 1887; d. Trindad, W. Indies, 10 Oct 1975.

Walker, Robert D.: b. Bethlehem, PA, 18 Jun 1888; d. Los Angeles Co, CA, 4 Mar 1954.

Walker, Syd: b. Manchester, Eng, 22 Mar 1887; d. Hove, Eng, 13 Jan 1945.

Walker, Thomas (Whimsical): b. Hull, Eng, 1850; d. Gorleston, Norfolk, Eng, 5 Nov 1934.

Walker, Wally: b. 1901; d. Woodland Hills, CA, 7 Aug 1975.

Walker, Walter: b. 1864; d. Honolulu, HI, 4 Dec 1947.

Wall, David V.: b. Coburg, Can, 1870; d. New York, NY, 1 Jun 1938.

Wallace, Ethel Lee: b. Springfield, MO, 1888; d. Springfield, MO, 7 Sep 1956.

Wallace, Inez: b. ????; d. Cleveland, OH, 28 Jun 1966.

Wallace, John: b. England, 24 Aug 1869; d. Los Angeles Co, CA, 16 Jul 1946.

Wallace, May: b. Russiaville, IN, 23 Aug 1877; d. Los Angeles, CA, 11 Dec 1938.

Wallace, Morgan: b. Lompoc, CA, 26 Jul 1881; d. Tarzana, CA, 12 Dec 1953.

Wallace, Nellie: b. Glasgow, Scot, 18 Mar 1882; d. Bowdoinham, ME, 24 Nov 1948.

Wallace, Thomas H.: b. 1872; d. 18 Mar 1932.

Waller, Lewis: b. Bilbao, Spain, 3 Nov 1860; d. London, Eng, 1 Nov 1915.

Waller, Wallet: b. 1882; d. 19 Mar 1951.

Wallerstein, Pearl Avnet: b. 1895; d. Burbank, CA, 2 Mar 1987.

Walling, Effie B.: b. California, 12 Apr 1879; d. Berkeley, CA, 9 Jun 1961.

Walling, Roy: b. Oregon, 1889; d. Stanfordville, NY, 7 May 1964.

Walling, Will R.: b. Sacramento City, IA, 2 Jun 1872; d. 5 Mar 1932.

Wallis, Bertram: b. London, Eng, 22 Feb 1874; d. 11 Apr 1952.

Wallock, Edwin L.: b. Council Bluffs, IA, 6 Nov 1877; d. Los Angeles Co, CA, 4 Feb 1951.

Walpole, Stanley: b. Melbourne, Austral, 1886; d. 19??.

Walsh, Billy: b. 18??; d. Brooklyn, NY, 16 Jun 1952.

Walsh, Blanche: b. New York, NY, 4 Jan 1873; d. Cleveland, OH, 31 Oct 1915.

Walsh, Frank: b. 1860; d. New York, NY, 18 Jul 1932.

Walsh, George: b. New York, NY, 16 Mar 1889; d. Pomona, CA, 13 Jun 1981.

Walsh, Raoul: b. New York, NY, 11 Mar 1887; d. Simi Valley, CA, 31 Dec 1980.

Walsh, Thomas H.: b. 9 Jan 1863; d. New York, NY, 25 Apr 1925.

Walsh, William J.: b. 1879; d. Mamaroneck, NY, 8 Nov 1921.

Walska, Ganna: b. Poland 24 Jun 1887; d. Santa Barbara, CA, 2 Mar 1984.

Waltemeyer, Jack K.: b. Salida, CO, 10 Jun 1883; d. Los Angeles, CA, 12 Jan 1959.

Walter, Eugene: b. Cleveland, OH, 27 Nov 1874; d. Los Angeles, CA, 26 Sep 1941.

Walter, Wilmer: b. 1884; d. New York, NY, 23 Aug 1941.

Walters, Dorothy: b. 1877; d. New York, NY, 17 Apr 1934.

Walters, Mrs. George W.: b. England, 18??; d. New York, NY, 21 Feb 1916.

Walters, Jack: b. Sylvia, KS, 5 May 1884; d. Los Angeles, CA, 23 Jan 1944.

Walters, Laura: b. 1894; d. Toledo, OH, 10 Apr 1934.

Walthall, Anna Mae: b. Alabama, 3 Oct 1894; d. Van Nuys, CA, 17 Apr 1950.

Walthall, Henry B.: b. Shelby County, AL, 16 Mar 1878; d. Monrovia, CA, 17 Jun 1936.

Walton, Charles: b. Sharpsburg, PA, 1884; d. New York, NY, 18 Nov 1955.

Walton, Florence: b. Wilmington, DE, 1890; d. New York, NY, 7 Jan 1981.

Walton, Fred: b. Paisley, Scot, 29 Aug 1866; d. Los Angeles, CA, 27 Dec 1936.

Walton, Gladys: b. Boston, MA, 14 Apr 1904; d. Morro Bay, CA, 15 Nov 1993.

Wang, James: b. 1853; d. Los Angeles, CA, 20 Apr 1935.

Wangel, Hedwig: b. Berlin, Ger, 23 Sep 1875; d. Rendsburg, Ger, 12 Mar 1961.

Ward, Albert: b. England. 1870; d. 9 Dec 1956.

Ward, Beatrice: b. 1890; d. Los Angeles, CA, 11 Dec 1964.

Ward, Carrie Clark: b. Virginia City, NV, 9 Jan 1862; d. Los Angeles, CA, 6 Feb 1926.

Ward, Chance E.: b. Dayton, OH, 16 Sep 1877; d. Los Angeles Co, CA, 2 Sep 1949.

Ward, David: b. 1891; d. Los Angeles, CA, 31 Dec 1946.

Ward, Fannie: b. St. Louis, MO, 22 Jun 1872; d. New York, NY, 27 Jan 1952.

Ward, Fleming: b. Lock Haven, PA, 28 Oct 1886; d. New York, NY, 2 Aug 1962.

Ward, Hap (John O'Donnell): b. Cameron, PA, 1868; d. New York, NY, 3 Jan 1944.

Ward, Katherine Clare: b. Bradford. MA, 31 Mar 1871; d. Los Angeles, CA, 14 Oct 1938.

Ward, Leon: b. Parowan, UT, 1906; d. Los Angeles, CA, 28 May 1927.

Ward, Lucille: b. Dayton, OH, 25 Feb 1880; d. McLean Township, OH, 8 Aug 1952.

Ward, May: b. 1886; d. Far Rockaway, NY, 5 Jul 1936.

Ward, Peggy: b. Pennsylvania, 10 Feb 1879; d. Los Angeles CA, 8 Mar 1960.

Ward, Roscoe (Tiny): b. 1893; d. Los Angeles, CA, 12 Sep 1956.

Ward, Sam: b. 1889; d. Sawtelle, CA, 1 May 1952.

Ward, Wawick: b. St. Ives, Eng, 1891; d. 9 Dec 1967.

Warde, Ernest C.: b. Liverpool, Eng, 1874; d. Los Angeles, CA, 9 Sep 1923.

Warde, Frederick: b. Deddington, Eng, 23 Feb 1851; d. Brooklyn, NY, 7 Feb 1935.

Wardwell, Geoffrey: b. York, Eng, 30 Jul 1900; d. 9 Aug 1955.

Ware, Helen: b. San Francisco, CA, 15 Oct 1877; d. Carmel, CA, 25 Jan 1939.

Ware, Walter: b. Boston, MA, 1880; d. Los Angeles, CA, 3 Jan 1936.

Warfield. Irene: b. 1896; d. New York, NY, 10 Apr 1961.

Warfield. Marjoric: b. Philadelphia, PA, 1902; d. Los Angeles, CA, 15 Apr 1991.

Waring, Mary: b. 1891; d. Washington, DC, 10 Jan 1964.

Warmington, Stanley J.: b. Herts, Eng, 16 Dec 1884; d. London, Eng, 10 May 1941.

Warner, H. B.: b. London, Eng, 26 Oct 1875; d. Woodland Hills, CA, 21 Dec 1958.

Warner, Jack L.: b. London, Ont, Can, 2 Aug 1892; d. Los Angeles, CA, 9 Sep 1978.

Warner, James B.: b. Nebraska, 1895; d. Los Angeles, CA, 9 Nov 1924.

Warren, E. Alyn: b. Richmond, VA, 2 Jun 1874; d. Los Angeles, CA, 22 Jan 1940.

Warren, Edward: b. Boston, MA, 1857; d. Los Angeles, CA, 3 Apr 1930.

Warren, Eleanor Stewart: b. Canada, 8 Jul 1892; d. Jamaica, NY, 6 Apr 1927.

Warren, Eliza: b. 1865; d. Cleveland. OH, 20 Jan 1935.

Warren, Fred H.: b. Rock Island, IL, 16 Sep 1880; d. Los Angeles, CA, 5 Dec 1940.

Warrenton, Lule: b. Flint, MI, 22 Jun 1862; d. San Diego, CA, 14 May 1932.

Warrington, Ann: b. Hillsboro, WI, 26 Sep 1864; d. Philadelphia, PA, 14 Nov 1934.

Warrington, Charles: b. 1877; d. Los Angeles, CA, 17 Aug 1926.

Warters, William E.: b. New Bern, NC, 1883; d. Los Angeles, CA, 29 Aug 1953.

Warwick, Robert: b. Sacramento, CA, 9 Oct 1878; d. Los Angeles, CA, 6 Jun 1964.

Washburn, Alice: b. Oshkosh, WI, 12 Sep 1861; d. Oshkosh, WI, 28 Nov 1929.

Washburn, Bryant: b. Chicago, IL, 28 Apr 1889; d. Woodland Hills, CA, 30 Apr 1963.

Washburn, John H.: b. 18??; d. New York, NY, 11 Dec 1917.

Washington, Edgar (Blue): b. Los Angeles, CA, 12 Feb 1898; d. Los Angeles Co, CA, 15 Sep 1970.

Washington, Jesse: b. ????; d. Newport, RI, 4 Sep 1919.

Waterman, Ida: b. 10 Mar 1852; d. Cincinnati, OH, 22 May 1941.

Waters, Tom: b. 1872; d. Harrisburg, PA, 10 Jul 1953.

Waters, Mrs. Tom b. 1880; d. New York, NY, 16 Sep 1928.

Watson, Adele: b. Minnesota, 31 Jan 1890; d. Los Angeles, CA, 27 Mar 1933.

Watson, Billy (Beef Trust): b. New York, NY, 1867; d. Asbury Park, NJ, 14 Jan 1945.

Watson, Bobby: b. Springfield, IL, 28 Nov 1887; d. Los Angeles, CA, 22 May 1965.

Watson, Coy (James Coy, Sr.): b. 1890; d. Edendale, CA, 22 May 1968.

Watson, Harry B.: b. Philadelphia, PA, 1876; d. Monrovia, CA, 23 Sep 1930.

Watson, Lucile: b. Quebec, Can, 27 May 1879; d. New York, NY, 24 Jun 1962.

Watson, Margaret: b. 1875; d. 31 Oct 1940.

Watson, Minor: b. Marianna, AR, 22 Dec 1889; d. Alton, IL, 28 Jul 1965.

Watson, Roy: b. Richmond. VA, 1876; d. Los Angeles, CA, 7 Jun 1937.

Watson, William (Sliding Billy): b. 18??; d. New York, NY, 4 Jun 1939.

Watts, Dodo: b. London, Eng, 27 Dec 1910; d. Teddington, Eng, 25 Dec 1990.

Watts, James A.: b. Australia, 1881; d. London, Eng, 5 Oct 1961.

Waxman, M. D. (Morris): b. 1876; d. 10 Nov 1931.

Wayburn, Ned: b. Pittsburgh, PA, 30 Mar 1874; d. New York, NY, 2 Sep 1942.

Wayne, John: b. Winterset, IA, 26 May 1907; d. Los Angeles, CA, 11 Jun 1979.

Wayne, Justina: b. Oakland. CA, ????; d. Freeport, NY, 2 Dec 1951.

Wayne, Maude: b. Beatrice, NE, 26 Mar 1895; d. Los Angeles, CA, 10 Oct 1983.

Wayne, Richard: b. Beatrice, NE, 18??; d. Los Angeles, CA, 15 Mar 1958.

Wayne, Robert: b. Pittsburgh, PA, 28 Oct 1864; d. Los Angeles, CA, 26 Sep 1946.

Weatherford. Tazwell: b. Indiana, 1889; d. Los Angeles, CA, 22 Jul 1917.

Weathersby, Jennie: b. England. 10 Jul 1855; d. New York, NY, 17 Mar 1931.

Weatherwax, Walter S.: b. Fort Scott, KS, 31 May 1867; d. Los Angeles Co. CA, 19 Jan 1943.

Weaver, Henry: b. Pittsburgh, PA, 21 Jun 1858; d. Sea Bright, NJ, 9 May 1922.

Webb. Austin: b. Guysville, OH, 1879; d. Los Angeles, CA, 8 Dec 1937.

Webb, Beth: b. 1897; d. Studio City, CA, 25 Jul 1986.

Webb, Clifton: b. Indianapolis, IN, 19 Nov 1889; d. Los Angeles, CA, 13 Oct 1966.

Webb, George: b. Indianapolis, IN, 3 Oct 1887; d. Los Angeles, CA, 24 May 1943.

Webb, Harry: b. 1887; d. Burbank, CA, 16 Jul 1984.

Webb, Millard: b. Clay City, KY, 6 Dec 1893; d. Los Angeles, CA, 21 Apr 1935.

Webber, Frederick: b. 18??; d. Cleveland. OH, 21 Jul 1925.

Weber, Christine: b. ????; d. Los Angeles, CA, 8 Oct 1936.

Weber, Joseph M.: b. New York, NY, 11 Aug 1867; d. Los Angeles, CA, 10 May 1942.

Weber, Lois: b. Pittsburgh, PA, 13 Jun 1879; d. Los Angeles, CA, 13 Nov 1939.

Weber, Rex: b. Lexington, KY, 1889; d. Chicago, IL, 8 Dec 1918.

Webster, Ben: b. London, Eng, 2 Jun 1864; d. Los Angeles, CA, 26 Feb 1947.

Webster, Lillian: b. ????; d. Los Angeles, CA, 6 Jul 1920.

Weeks, Marion: b. 1887; d. New York, NY, 20 Apr 1968.

Wegener, Paul: b. Bischdorf, Ger, 11 Dec 1874; d. Berlin, Ger, 13 Sep 1948.

Wehlen, Emmy: b. Mannheim, Ger, 1887; d. 19??.

Wehn, Josephine: b. 1880; d. Bronx, NY, 18 Jul 1939.

Weidman, Charles: b. 1902; d. 15 Jul 1975.

Weigel, Paul: b. Halle, Ger, 18 Feb 1867; d. Los Angeles Co, CA, 25 May 1951.

Weil, Harry: b. 1878; d. Los Angeles, CA, 23 Jan 1943.

Weinberg, Gus: b. Milwaukee, WI, 1865; d. Portland. ME, 11 Aug 1952.

Weingarten, Lawrence: b. Chicago, IL, 1898; d. Los Angeles, CA, 5 Feb 1975.

Weisse, Hanni: b. Chemnitz, Ger, 16 Oct 1892; d. Bad Liebenzell, Ger, 13 Dec 1967.

Weixler, Dorrit: b. 1892; d. Berlin, Ger, 30 Nov 1916.

Welch, James: b. Liverpool, Eng, 6 Nov 1865; d. London, Eng, 10 Apr 1917.

Welch, James T.: b. New York, NY, 14 Mar 1869; d. Los Angeles, CA, 6 Apr 1949.

Welch, Joseph: b. New York, NY, 1869; d. Green Farms, CT, 15 Jul 1918.

Welch, Lew: b. 1885; d. Miami, FL, 22 Jun 1952.

Welch, Niles: b. Hartford. CT, 29 Jul 1888; d. Laguna Nigel, CA, 21 Nov 1976.

Welch, Scott: b. 18??; d. New York, NY, 19 Apr 1931.

Welchman, Harry: b. Barnstable, Devon, Eng, 24 Feb 1886; d. Penzance, Eng, 3 Jan 1966.

Weldon, Francis (Bunny): b. Los Angeles, CA, 14 Jun 1896; d. Santa Cruz, CA, 28 Oct 1959.

Weldon, Jessie: b. Kleine Valley, NY, ????; d. Los Angeles, CA, ? Sep 1925.

Welford. Dallas: b. Liverpool, Eng, 23 May 1872; d. Santa Monica, CA, 28 Sep 1946.

Wellesley, Charles: b. Dublin, Ire, 17 Nov 1873; d. Amityville, NY, 24 Jul 1946.

Wellesley, Marie: b. 18??; d. Englewood. NJ, 24 Sep 1927.

Wellington, Babe: b. 1897; d. New York, NY, 28 Dec 1951.

Wellman, William: b. Brookline, MA, 29 Feb 1896; d. Brentwood. CA, 9 Dec 1975.

Wells, Billy: b. London, Eng, 31 Aug 1887; d. London, Eng, 11 Jun 1967.

Wells, Charles B.: b. 1851; d. Bayside, NY, 14 Oct 1924.

Wellas H. G.: b. Bromley, Kent, Eng, 21 Sep 1866; d. London, Eng, 13 Aug 1946.

Wells, L. M.: b. Cincinnati, OH, 5 Feb 1862; d. 1 Jan 1923.

Wells, Mai: b. San Francisco, CA, 1862; d. Los Angeles, CA, 1 Aug 1941.

Wells, Raymond: b. Anna, IL, 14 Oct 1880; d. Los Angeles Co, CA, 9 Aug 1941.

Wells, Ted (Pawnee Bill, Jr.): b. Midland. TX, 11 Jul 1899; d. Wickenburg, AZ, 7 Jun 1948.

Wells, William K.: b. New York, NY, 1884; d. New York, NY, 17 Apr 1956.

Welsh, William J: b. Philadelphia, PA, 9 Feb 1870; d. Los Angeles, CA, 16 Jul 1946.

Wenkhaus, Rolf: b. Germany, 9 Sep 1917; d. 1942.

Wenman, Henry: b. Leeds, Eng, 7 Sep 1875; d. 6 Nov 1953.

Wentworth, Stephen: b. England, 18??; d. 20 Mar 1935.

Werkmeister, Lotte: b. Germany, 24 May 1886; d. Bergholz-Rehbrueck, Ger, ? Jul 1970.

Werner-Kahle, Hugo: b. Aachen, Ger, 5 Aug 1882; d. Berlin, Ger, 1 May 1961.

Wernicke, Otto: b. Osterode/Harz, Ger, 30 Sep 1893; d. Munich, Ger, 7 Nov 1965.

Wertz, Clarence P.: b. Bloomfield, NJ, 3 Mar 1891; d. Los Angeles, CA, 2 Dec 1935.

Wesner, A. Burt: b. 1866; d. Boulder City, CO, 3 Jan 1920.

Wessell, Vivian: b. 1893; d. ? Oct 1965.

West, Billie: b. Kentucky, 5 Aug 1891; d. Plainfield. NJ, 7 Jun 1967.

West, Billy: b. Russia, 22 Sep 1892; d. Los Angeles, CA, 21 Jul 1975.

West, Buster: b. Philadelphia, PA, 1902; d. Los Angeles, CA, 18 Mar 1966.

West, Charles H.: b. Pittsburgh, PA, 30 Nov 1885; d. Los Angeles, CA, 10 Oct 1943.

West, Ford: b. Dallas, TX, 27 Mar 1873; d. 3 Jan 1936.

West, George: b. 1890; d. Glasgow, Scot, 27 Oct 1963.

West, Henry: b. 1868; d. Norwalk, CT, 29 Jan 1936.

West, Isabelle: b. 1858; d. Brentwood, NY, 21 Jul 1942.

West, Col. J. A.: b. 1841; d. Wilmington, OH, 10 Jul 1928.

West, Lillian Mildred: b. New York, NY, 8 Feb 1890; d. 19??.

West, Neva: b. California, 10 Sep 1883; d. Glendale, CA, 5 Oct 1965.

West, Olive: b. San Francisco, CA, 1858; d. Los Angeles, CA, 29 May 1943.

West, Thomas: b. Philadelphia, PA, 1859; d. Philadelphia, PA, 28 Jul 1932.

West, Tony: b. Chicago, IL, 18??; d. Los Angeles, CA, 25 Jun 1923.

West, William: b. c. 1886; d. New York, NY, 23 Sep 1918.

West, William Herman: b. Newport, RI, 26 Jul 1860; d. Los Angeles, CA, 20 Aug 1915.

West, Willie: b. England. 22 Sep 1867; d. London, Eng, 5 Feb 1922.

Westbrooke, Virginia: b. 1844; d. Eatontown, NJ, 28 Dec 1923.

Westcott, Netta, b. London, Eng, 1893; d. 9 Aug 1953.

Westerton, Frank H.: b. London, Eng, 1871; d. New York, NY, 25 Aug 1923.

Westman, Theodore: b. 1903; d. New York, NY, 22 Nov 1927.

Weston, Charles: b. 18??; d. 1917.

Weston, George: b. 18??; d. New York, NY, 7 Apr 1923.

Weston, Maggie: b. 18??; d. New York, NY, 3 Nov 1926.

Westover, Winifred: b. San Francisco, CA, 9 Nov 1899; d. Los Angeles, CA, 18 Mar 1978.

Westwood, Martin F.: b. 1883; d. Glendale, CA, 19 Dec 1928.

Wetherall, Frances: b. Greenwich, Kent, Eng, 18??; d. London, Eng, 13 Nov 1923.

Wetherell, M. A.: b. Leeds, Eng, 1884; d. Johannesburg, So Africa, 25 Feb 1939.

Weyher, Ruth: b. Nowinjasta, Poland, 28 May 1901; d. ? Jan 1983.

Wheat, Lawrence: b. Wheeling, WV, 20 Oct 1876; d. Los Angeles Co, CA, 7 Aug 1963.

Wheatcroft, Stanhope: b. New York, NY, 11 May 1888; d. Woodland Hills, CA, 13 Feb 1966.

Wheeler, Bert: b. Paterson, NJ, 7 Apr 1895; d. New York, NY, 18 Jan 1968.

Wheeler, Teresa (Cabaret Tess): b. ????; d. Los Angeles Co, CA, 26 Dec 1975.

Wheelock, Charles: b. Boston, MA, 1875; d. Los Angeles, CA, 25 May 1948.

Whelan, Hazel: b. ????; d. East Orange, NJ, 22 Jun 1937.

Whelan, Lee M.: b. Bridgeport, CT, 1876; d. Arlington, NJ, 15 Oct 1952.

Whelan, Tim: b. Cannelton, IN, 2 Nov 1893; d. Beverly Hills, CA, 12 Aug 1957.

Whelar, Lanois Mardi: b. 1898; d. France, 17 Oct 1918.

Whiffen, Mrs. Thomas: b. London, Eng, 12 Mar 1845; d. Montvale, VA, 25 Nov 1936.

Whipper, Leigh: b. Charleston, SC. 29 Oct 1876; d. New York, NY, 26 Jul 1975.

Whistler, Edna: b. 1886; d. New York, NY, 11 Jul 1934.

Whistler, Margaret: b. Louisville, KY, 1886; d. Los Angeles, CA, 23 Aug 1939.

Whitaker, Charles (Slim): b. Kansas City, MO, 29 Jul 1893; d. Los Angeles Co, CA, 27 Jun 1960.

Whitby, Arthur: b. Ottery St. Mary, Eng, 1869; d. London, Eng, 29 Nov 1922.

Whitcomb. Barry: b. Australia, 1872; d. 25 Oct 1928.

White, Alice: b. Paterson, NJ, 28 Aug 1907; d. Los Angeles, CA, 19 Feb 1983.

White, Archibald: b. 1887; d. Santa Rosa, CA, 28 Sep 1924.

White, Arthur: b. 1882; d. Blackpool, Eng, ? Jul 1957.

White, Bill: b. Sacramento, CA, 26 Apr 1856; d. Los Angeles, CA, 21 Apr 1933.

White, Carolina: b. Boston, MA, 1886; d. Rome, Italy, 5 Oct 1961.

White, Chrissie: b. London, Eng, 23 May 1895; d. Chobham, Surrey, Eng, 18 Aug 1989.

White, Frances: b. Seattle, WA, 1898; d. Los Angeles, CA, 24 Feb 1969.

White, George: b. Toronto, Can, 1890; d. Los Angeles, CA, 10 Oct 1968.

White, J. Fisher: b. Bristol, Eng, 1 May 1865; d. London, Eng, 14 Jan 1945.

White, J. Irving: b. 1865; d. Los Angeles, CA, 17 Apr 1944.

White, Jack: b. Budapest, Hungary, 2 Mar 1897; d. North Hollywood, CA, 10 Apr 1984.

White, Jules J.: b. Budapest, Hungary, 17 Sep 1900; d. Van Nuys, CA, 30 Apr 1985.

White, Leo: b. Graudenz, Ger, 10 Nov 1882; d. Los Angeles, CA, 20 Sep 1948.

White, Madge: b. England. ????; d. 1978.

White, Pearl: b. Greenridge, MO, 4 Mar 1889; d. Paris, Fr, 4 Aug 1938.

White, Raymond: b. 1901; d. Los Angeles, CA, 31 Jan 1934.

White Eagle, Chief (Louis Scott): b. 5 May 1892; d. Los Angeles Co, CA, 4 Apr 1984.

White Eagle, Chief: b. 1892; d. Los Angeles, CA, 28 Feb 1926.

Whiteford. John (Blackie): b. New York, NY, 27 Apr 1889; d. Los Angeles, CA, 21 Mar 1962.

Whitelaw, Barrett: b. Cape Girardeau, MO, 25 May 1890; d. Los Angeles, CA, 2 Oct 1947.

Whiteman, Paul: b. Denver, CO, 28 Mar 1890; d. Doylestown, PA, 29 Dec 1967.

Whiteside, Walker: b. Logansport, IN, 16 Mar 1869; d. Hastings-on-Hudson, NY, 17 Aug 1942.

Whitespear, Greg: b. Oklahoma, 18 Apr 1897; d. Los Angeles Co, CA, 20 Feb 1956.

Whitford, Annabelle: b. 1878; d. Chicago, IL, 30 Nov 1961.

Whitlock, T. Lloyd: b. Springfield. MO, 2 Jan 1891; d. Los Angeles, CA, 8 Jan 1966.

Whitman, Fred J.: b. Findley, OH, 6 Dec 1887; d. South Pasadena, CA, 11 Oct 1945.

Whitman, Velma: b. Richmond, VA, c. 1890; d. 19??.

Whitman, Walt: b. Lyon, NY, 1859; d. Santa Monica, CA, 27 Mar 1928.

Whitney, Claire: b. New York, NY, 6 May 1890; d. Los Angeles, CA, 27 Aug 1969.

Whitney, Ralph: b. 1874; d. Los Angeles, CA, 14 Jun 1928.

Whitson, Frank L.: b. New York, NY, 22 Mar 1877; d. Los Angeles Co, CA, 19 Mar 1946.

Whittell, Josephine: b. Arizona, 30 Nov 1883; d. Los Angeles, CA, 1 Jun 1961.

Whittington, Margery: b. 1904; d. New York, NY, 23 Oct 1957.

Whittle, W. E.: b. 1862; d. Bloomfield, NJ, 4 Jul 1924.

Whitty, Dame May: b. Liverpool, Eng, 19 Jun 1865; d. Los Angeles, CA, 29 May 1948.

Whytal, Mrs. Adelaide: b. New York, NY, 8 Nov 1863; d. Los Angeles Co, CA, 13 Jul 1946.

Whytall, Russ: b. Boston, MA, 20 Jun 1860; d. New York, NY, 24 Jun 1930.

Wickland, Larry: b. Kansas City, MO, 28 Jun 1898; d. Los Angeles, CA, 18 Apr 1938.

Widdecomb. Wallace: b. 1869; d. 12 Jul 1969.

Wieck, Dorothea: b. Davos, Switz, Jan 1908; d. Berlin, Ger, 20 Feb 1986.

Wieman, Mathias: b. Osnabruck, Ger, 23 Jun 1902; d. Zurich, Switz, 3 Dec 1969.

Wirgin, Con W.: b. 18??; d. Winnipeg, Man, Can, 21 Nov 1917.

Wilber, Robert: b. Louisville, KY, 6 May 1896; d. 21 Jun 1980.

Wilbur, Crane: b. Athens, NY, 17 Nov 1886; d. North Hollywood, CA, 18 Oct 1973.

Wilcox, Silas: b. Ohio, 8 Feb 1863; d. Los Angeles, CA, 11 Feb 1945.

Wild. John P.: b. Apponang, RI, 18??; d. Venice, CA, 2 May 1921.

Wilder, Marshall P.: b. Geneva, NY, 19 Sep 1859; d. St. Paul, MN, 10 Jan 1915.

Wiley, John A.: b. 1884; d. San Antonio, TX, 30 Sep 1962.

Wilk, Jake: b. 1886; d. New York, NY, 12 Nov 1956.

Wilke, Hubert: b. Stettin, Ger, 1882; d. Yonkers, NY, 22 Oct 1940.

Wilkes, Lillian: b. 28 Apr 1892; d. Los Angeles, CA, 16 Dec 1976.

Wilkes, Mattie: b. 1885; d. Montclair, NJ, 9 Jul 1927.

Wilkes, Winona: b. 1904; d. Long Beach, CA, 11 Jun 1926.

Willa, Suzanne: b. Los Angeles, CA, 1893; d. New York, NY, 24 Mar 1951.

Willard. Mrs. Charles: b. 1863: d. New York, NY, 12 Jan 1945.

Willard. Jess: b. Pottawotamie, KS, 29 Dec 1881; d. Los Angeles, CA, 15 Dec 1968.

Willard. John: b. San Francisco, CA, 28 Nov 1885; d. Los Angeles Co, CA, 30 Aug 1942.

Willat, Irvin V.: b. Stamford. CT, 18 Nov 1890; d. Santa Monica, CA, 17 Apr 1976.

William, Joseph (Ranger Bill): b. 1878; d. 12 Nov 1939.

Willlam, Warren (Warren Krech): b. Aitken, MN, 2 Dec 1894; d. Los Angeles, CA, 24 Sep 1948.

Williams, Arnold: b. 1875; d. 1927.

Williams, Bert: b. New Providence, Nassau, 12 Nov 1874; d. New York, NY, 4 Mar 1922.

Williams, Bransby: b. London, Eng, 14 Aug 1870; d. London, Eng, 3 Dec 1961.

Williams, C. Jay: b. New York, NY, 1859; d. New York, NY, 26 Jan 1945.

Williams, Charles B.: b. Albany, NY, 27 Sep 1898; d. Los Angeles, CA, 4 Jan 1958.

Williams, Clara: b. Seattle, WA, 3 May 1888; d. Los Angeles, CA, 8 May 1928.

Williams, Cora: b. Chelsea, MA, 6 Dec 1870; d. Los Angeles, CA, 1 Dec 1927.

Williams, Craig: b. Germany, 1877; d. New York, NY, 5 Jul 1941.

Williams, Earle: b. Sacramento, CA, 28 Feb 1880; d. Los Angeles, CA, 25 Apr 1927.

Williams, Elaine: b. ????; d. Los Angeles, CA, 9 May 1947.

Williams, Eric Bransby: b. London, Eng, 1900; d. 19??.

Williams, Fred G.: b. New York, 1849; d. Coney Island, NY, 4 Aug 1924.

Williams, Fred J.: b. Chicago, IL, 2 Jul 1874; d. Los Angeles, CA, 29 May 1942.

Williams, George A.: b. Kinnikinnick, WI, 11 Aug 1854; d. Los Angeles, CA, 21 Feb 1936.

Williams, George B.: b. Vermont, 1866; d. Santa Monica, CA, 17 Nov 1931.

Williams, Guinn (Big Boy): b. Decatur, TX, 26 Apr 1899; d. Van Nuys, CA, 6 Jun 1962.

Williams, Gwen: b. ????; d. Worthing, Sussex, Eng, 27 May 1962.

Williams, Hattie: b. Boston, MA, 17 Mar 1870; d. New York, NY, 17 Aug 1942.

Williams, Horace: b. Dallas, TX, 1879; d. 19??.

Williams, Jeffrey: b. 1860; d. Los Angeles, CA, 27 Dec 1938.

Williams, John J.: b. Lynn, MA, 1856; d. New York, NY, 5 Oct 1918.

Williams, Josephine: b. Liverpool, Eng, 1855; d. New York, NY, 14 Jun 1937.

Williams, Julia: b. 1879; d. New York, NY, 7 Feb 1936.

Williams, Kathlyn: b. Butte, MT, 31 May 1888; d. Los Angeles, CA, 23 Sep 1960.

Williams, Lottie: b. Indianapolis, IN, 20 Jan 1874; d. Los Angeles Co, CA, 16 Nov 1962.

Williams, Malcolm: b. Spring Valley, MN, 16 Jul 1870; d. New York, NY, 10 Jun 1937.

Williams, Marie: b. 1921; d. Encino, CA, 5 Jul 1967.

Williams, Spencer: b. Vadalia, LA, 14 Jul 1893; d. West Los Angeles, CA, 13 Dec 1969.

Williams, Walter: b. 15 Oct 1887; d. New York, NY, 29 Oct 1940.

Williams, William A.: b. 1870; d. Los Angeles, CA, 4 May 1942.

Williams, Zack: b. Louisiana, 6 Oct 1884; d. Los Angeles Co, CA, 25 May 1958.

Williamson, Alan J.: b. Kent, Eng, 3 Feb 1886; d. Sydney, Austral, 3 May 1952.

Williamson, George M.: b. 1885; d. Denver, CO, 23 May 1956.

Williamson, James A.: b. Scotland. 1855; d. 1933.

Williamson, Melvin E.: b. Memphis, TN, 1900; d. Scott Air Force Base, IL, 15 Feb 1959.

Williamson, Robert: b. Glasgow, Scot, 1885; d. Amityville, NY, 13 Mar 1949.

Williamson, Robin E.: b. Denver, CO, 30 Jun 1889; d. Los Angeles, CA, 21 Feb 1935.

Willingham, Harry: b. 1881; d. North Hollywood, CA, 17 Nov 1943.

Willis, Hubert: b. Reading, York, Eng, 18??; d. Suffolk, Eng, 29 Sep 1984.
Willis, Leo: b. Oklahoma, 5 Jan 1890; d. Monterey Co, CA, 10 Apr 1952.
Willis, Louise: b. 1880; d. Chicago, IL, 2 Jan 1929.
Willis, Richard: b. London, Eng, 15 Oct 1876; d. Los Angeles, CA, 8 Apr 1945.
Willoughby, Lewis: b. 10 Jul 1876; d. Clearwater, FL, 12 Sep 1968.
Wills, Drusilla: b. London, Eng, 14 Nov 1884; d. London, Eng, 6 Aug 1951.
Wills, Nat M.: b. Fredericksburg, VA, 11 Jul 1873; d. Woodcliff, NJ, 9 Dec 1917.
Wills, Walter: b. New York, NY, 22 Aug 1881; d. Los Angeles, CA, 18 Jan 1967.
Wilmer-Brown, Maisie: b. 1892; d. London, Eng, 13 Feb 1973.
Wilsey, Jay (Buffalo Bill Jr.): b. Hillsdale, MO, 6 Feb 1896; d. Los Angeles, CA, 25 Oct 1961.
Wilshin, Sunday: b. London, Eng, 26 Feb 1905; d. Chelmsford, Essex, Eng, 19 Mar 1991.
Wilson, Al: b. 18??; d. Cleveland. OH, 5 Sep 1932.
Wilson, Alice (Alice Rae): b. Offalan, MO, 14 Jun 1887; d. Los Angeles, CA, 12 May 1944.
Wilson, Ben: b. Corning, IA, 7 Jul 1876; d. Glendale, CA, 25 Aug 1930.
Wilson, Burton S.: b. 1871; d. Los Angeles Co, CA, 14 Oct 1956.
Wilson, Charles Cahill: b. New York, NY, 29 Jul 1894; d. 7 Jan 1948.
Wilson, Clarence H. (Wilson Hummel): b. Cincinnati, OH, 17 Nov 1876; d. Los Angeles, CA, 5 Oct 1941.
Wilson, Constance (Connie Lewis): b. 1905; d. Philadelphia, PA, 4 Jan 1968.
Wilson, Edward L.: b. 1916; d. 6 Feb 1975.
Wilson, Elsie Jane: b. New Zealand, 7 Nov 1890; d. Los Angeles, CA, 16 Jan 1965.
Wilson, Francis: b. Philadelphia, PA, 7 Feb 1854; d. New York, NY, 7 Oct 1935.
Wilson, Frederick: b. 18??; d. London, Eng, 2 Oct 1920.
Wilson, Hal: b. New York, NY, 2 Oct 1861; d. Los Angeles, CA, 22 May 1933.
Wilson, Helene: b. 1888; d. Woodland Hills, CA, 29 Jul 1981.
Wilson, Janice: b. Illinois, 28 Oct 1900; d. Encino, CA, 5 Nov 1982.
Wilson, Jay: b. La Crosse, WI, 1871; d. New York, NY, 27 Jul 1940.
Wilson, Lois: b. Pittsburgh, PA, 28 Jun 1894; d. Reno, NV, 3 Mar 1988.
Wilson, Margery: b. Gracey, KY, 31 Oct 1897; d. Arcadia, CA, 21 Jan 1986.
Wilson, Millard K.: b. Louisville, KY, 1890; d. Long Beach, CA, 5 Oct 1933.
Wilson, Olivia McBride: b. 1896; d. 24 Aug 1976.
Wilson, Roberta: b. Texas, 11 Jun 1905; d. Los Angeles, CA, 2 Feb 1972.
Wilson, Roy: b. 1902; d. Dry Lake, CA, 25 Jun 1932.
Wilson, Tom: b. Helena, MT, 27 Aug 1880; d. Los Angeles Co, CA, 19 Feb 1965.
Wilson, W. Cronin: b. ????; d. London, Eng, 16 Feb 1934.

Wilson, Wendell C.: b. 1889; d. Vancouver, Can, 9 Jan 1927.

Wilson, William F.: b. 1894; d. Woodland Hills, CA, 10 May 1956.

Wiltsie, Simeon: b. New York, NY, 1853; d. Englewood. NJ, 12 Jan 1918.

Wimen, Dwight Deere: b. Moline, IL, 8 Aug 1895; d. Hudson, NY, 20 Jan 1951.

Winant, Forrest: b. New York, NY, 21 Feb 1888; d. Alameda, CA, 30 Jan 1928.

Winar, Ernst: b. Holland, 1894; d. 28 Jun 1978.

Wincott, Rosalie Avolo: b. 1873; d. Los Angeles, CA, 3 Nov 1951.

Windermere, Fred C.: b. Muscatine, IA, 15 Apr 1892; d. Newport Beach, CA, 18 Mar 1970,

Window, Muriel: b. ????; d. Pompano Beach, FL, 19 Sep 1965.

Windsor, Claire: b. Coffee City, KS, 14 Apr 1897; d. Los Angeles, CA, 23 Oct 1972.

Wing, Ah: b. China, 23 Jul 1851; d. Weimar, CA, 27 Feb 1941.

Wing, Ward: b. Springfield, MO, 18 Feb 1893; d. Los Angeles, CA, 4 Jun 1945.

Wingfield. H. Conway: b. Borg, Ire, 1872; d. New York, NY, 9 Feb 1948.

Winn, Godfrey: b. Birmingham, Warwick, Eng, 15 Oct 1906; d. England, 19 Jun 1971.

Winninger, Charles: b. Athens, WI, 26 May 1884; d. Palm Springs, CA, 27 Jan 1969.

Winslow, Dick: b. Jennings, LA, 25 Mar 1915; d. North Hollywood, CA, 7 Feb 1991.

Winslow, Herbert Lippincott: b. 1895; d. 1918.

Winston, Bruce: b. Liverpool, Eng, 4 Mar 1879; d. At sea, 27 Sep 1946.

Winston Laura: b. 18??; d. Los Angeles Co, CA, 10 Apr 1951.

Winter, Jessie: b. London, Eng, 1887; d. London, Eng, 8 Aug 1971.

Winter, Laska: b. St. Louis, MO, 25 Aug 1905; d. South Pasadena, CA, 8 Aug 1980.

Winter, Percy: b. Toronto, Can, 16 Nov 1861; d. Boonton, NJ, 4 May 1928.

Winter, Winona: b. Huntsville, AL, 1888; d. Los Angeles, CA, 27 Apr 1940.

Winthrop, Barbara: b. 1890; d. New York, NY, 5 Sep 1927.

Winthrop, Joy: b. 1864; d. Los Angeles, CA, 1 Apr 1950.

Winton, Jane: b. Philadelphia, PA, 10 Oct 1905; d. New York, NY, 22 Sep 1959.

Wirth, Leo: b. New York, NY, 7 Nov 1887; d. 19??.

Wise, Harry: b. New York, 1871; d. New York, NY, 26 Dec 1947.

Wise, Jack: b. Pennsylvania, 2 Jan 1888; d. Los Angeles, CA, 7 Mar 1954.

Wise, Thomas A.: b. Faversham, Kent, Eng, 23 Mar 1865; d. New York, NY, 21 Mar 1928.

Withee, Mabel: b. ????; d. Bayside, NY, 3 Nov 1952.

Withers, Grant: b. Pueblo, CO, 17 Jan 1904; d. North Hollywood, CA, 27 Mar 1959.

Withers, Isabel: b. Frankton, TN, 20 Jan 1896; d. Los Angeles, CA, 3 Sep 1968.

Withey, Chester: b. Park City, UT, 8 Nov 1887; d. 6 Oct 1939.

Wittels, Toni: b. Vienna, Austria, 10 July 1870; d. Munich, Ger, 15 Aug 1930.

Witting, Arthur E,: b. Michigan, 21 Oct 1868; d. San Diego Co, CA, 1 Feb 1941.

Witting, Mattie Davis: b. Palla, IA, 9 Mar 1863; d. San Diego Co, CA, 30 Jan 1945.

Witwer, Harry Charles: b. Athena, PA, 1889; d. Los Angeles, CA, 9 Aug 1929.

Wix, Florence: b. England. 1883; d. Woodland Hills, CA, 23 Nov 1956.

Wolbert, Dorothea: b. Philadelphia, PA, 12 Apr 1874; d. Los Angeles, CA, 15 Sep 1958.

Wolbert, William: b. Petersburg, VA, 1883; d. Los Angeles, CA, 12 Dec 1918.

Wolcott, Julia: b. 1845; d. Chicago, IL, 25 May 1915.

Wolf, Bill: b. New York, NY, 14 Aug 1894; d. Los Angeles Co, CA, 16 Feb 1975.

Wolfe, Edwin R.: b. 1893; d. Holmes, NY, 22 Sep 1983.

Wolfe, Jane: b. St. Petersburg, PA, 21 Mar 1875; d. Glendale, CA, 29 Mar 1958.

Wolgast, Ad: b. Cadillac, MI, 8 Jan 1888; d. Camarillo, CA, 14 Apr 1955.

Wolheim, Louis: b. Russia, 28 Mar 1880; d. Los Angeles, CA, 18 Feb 1931.

Wong, Anna May: b. Los Angeles, CA, 3 Jan 1905; d. Santa Monica, CA, 3 Feb 1961.

Wonn, Edward: b. 1872; d. Baltimore, MD. 5 Jan 1927.

Wonter, Arthur: b. London, Eng, 21 Jan 1875; d. London, Eng, 10 Jul 1960.

Wood, Ernest: b. Atchison, KS, 17 Apr 1887; d. Los Angeles, CA, 13 Jul 1942.

Wood, Freeman: b. Denver, CO, 1 Jul 1896; d. Los Angeles, CA, 19 Feb 1956.

Wood, Baby Gloria (K. T. Stevens): b. Los Angeles, CA, 20 Jul 1919; d. Brentwood, CA, 13 Jun 1994.

Wood, Grace: b. Fort Lyon, MO, 1884; d. 30 May 1952.

Wood, Marjorie: b. London, Eng, 5 Sep 1882; d. Los Angeles, CA, 9 Nov 1955.

Wood, Peggy: b. Brooklyn, NY, 9 Feb 1892; d. Stamford, CT, 18 Mar 1978.

Wood, Rose: b. England. 1850; d. Tenafly, NJ, 7 Mar 1932.

Wood, Sam: b. Philadelphia, PA, 10 Jul 1883; d. Los Angeles, CA, 22 Sep 1949.

Wood, Tommy (Fatty): b. Eau Claire, WI, ? May 1894; d. Minneapolis, MN, 28 Dec 1932.

Woodford, John: b. Austin, TX, 1862; d. Saranac Lake, NY, 17 Apr 1927.

Woodruff, Bert: b. Peoria, IL, 29 Apr 1856; d. Los Angeles, CA, 14 Jun 1934.

Woodruff, Eleanor: b. Towanda, PA, 12 Sep 1891; d. Princeton, NJ, 7 Oct 1980.

Woodruff, Eunice Elenor: b. 1910; d. Los Angeles, CA, 15 Jul 1921.

Woodruff, Henry: b. Hartford, CT, 1 Jun 1869; d. New York, NY, 6 Oct 1916.

Woods, Adelaide: b. 18??; d. ? Mar 1917.

Woods, Al: b. 1895; d. Pasadena, CA, 3 Jun 1946.

Woods, Daddy: b. 18??; d. 1916.

Woods, Harry Lewis: b. Cleveland. OH, 5 May 1889; d. Los Angeles, CA, 28 Dec 1968.

Woods, Joseph A.: b. 1860; d. New York, NY, 13 Feb 1926.

Woods, Nick: b. Germany, 1857; d. New Rochelle, NY, 21 Mar 1936.

Woodthrope, Mrs. Georgia: b. 11 Oct 1859; d. Glendale, CA, 24 Aug 1927.

Woodward, Mrs. Eugenie: b. Cincinnati, OH, 1859; d. White Plains, NY, 29 Mar 1947.

Woodward, H. Guy: b. Minneapolis, MN, 1868; d. Detroit, MI, 20 Aug 1919.

Woodward, Henry F.: b. Charleston, WV, 11 Dec 1891; d. 19??.

Wooldridge, Doris: b. California, 2 Apr 1892; d. Los Angeles, CA, 17 Jul 1921,

Woolnough, James: b. Cambridgeport, MA, 1870; d. Los Angeles, CA, 21 May 1937.

Worne, Howard B. (Duke): b. Philadelphia, PA, 14 Dec 1888; d. Los Angeles, CA, 13 Oct 1933.

Worsley, Wallace A.: b. Wappingers Falls, NY, 8 Dec 1878; d. Los Angeles, CA, 26 Mar 1944.

Worth, Peggy: b. 1891; d. New York, NY, 23 Mar 1956.

Worthing, Helen Lee: b. Louisville, KY, 31 Jan 1905; d. Los Angeles, CA, 25 Apr 1948.

Worthington, William J.: b. Troy, NY, 8 Apr 1872; d. Beverly Hills, CA, 9 Apr 1941.

Wright, Cowley: b. Anerley, Eng, 6 Oct 1889; d. London, Eng, 18 Jan 1923.

Wright, Fanny: b. London, Eng, 1872; d. 29 Dec 1954.

Wright, Fred: b. Dover, Kent, Eng, 8 Mar 1871; d. New York, NY, 12 Dec 1928.

Wright, George A.: b. 18??; d. Norwalk, CT, 14 Mar 1937.

Wright, Haidee: b. London, Eng, 13 Jan 1868; d. London, Eng, 29 Jan 1943.

Wright, Hugh E.: b. Cannes, Fr, 13 Apr 1879; d. Eton, Bucks, Eng, 12 Feb 1940.

Wright, Huntley: b. London, Eng, 7 Aug 1869; d. Bangor, Wales, 10 Jul 1941.

Wright, Mack V.: b. Princeton, IN, 1895; d. Boulder City, NV, 14 Aug 1965.

Wright, Marie: b. England, 1862; d. London, Eng, 1 May 1949.

Wright, Tenny: b. Brooklyn, NY, 18 Nov 1885; d. Los Angeles, CA, 13 Sep 1971.

Wuest, Ida: b. Wiesbaden, Ger, 3 Jan 1884; d. Berlin, Ger, 2 Nov 1958.

Wunderlee, Frank: b. St. Louis, MO, 12 Mar 1875; d. New York, NY, 11 Dec 1925.

Wycherly, Margaret: b. London, Eng, 26 Oct 1881; d. New York, NY, 6 Jun 1956.

Wyndham, Sir Charles: b. Liverpool, Eng, 23 Mar 1837; d. London, Eng, 12 Jan 1919.

Wyndham, Poppy: b. Simla, India, 1893; d. At sea, 14 Mar 1928.

Wynn, Bessie: b. 1876; d. Towaco, NJ, 8 Jul 1968.

Wynn, Doris: b. 1910; d. Los Angeles, CA, 14 Jul 1925.

Wynn, Ed: b. Philadelphia, PA, 9 Nov 1886; d. Los Angeles, CA, 19 Jun 1966.

Wynne, Gladys: b. 1886; d. Paris, Fr, 10 Nov 1964.

Wynne, Hugh: b. New York, NY, 1866; d. Huntington, NY, 10 Feb 1949.

Y

Yacorelli, Frank: b. Italy, 2 Oct 1898; d. Los Angeles, CA, 19 Nov 1965.

Yamamoto, Kajiro: b. Japan, 1902; d. Japan, 28 Sep 1974.

Yanner, Joseph: b. 1879; d. Kansas City, MO, 12 Dec 1949.

Yantis, Fanny: b. ????; d. Glendale, CA, 19 Jul 1929.

Yapp, Cecil: b. Montreal, Que, Can, 4 Apr 1879; d. St. Paul, MN, 4 Feb 1959.

Yarde, Margaret: b. Dartmouth, Devon, Eng, 2 Apr 1878; d. London, Eng, 11 Mar 1944.

Yearance, William: b. 1853; d. Boston, MA, 19 Dec 1917.

Yearsley, Relph: b. London, Eng, 6 Oct 1896; d. Los Angeles, CA, 4 Dec 1928.

Yohe, May: b. Bethlehem, PA, 6 Apr 1869; d. Boston, MA, 28 Aug 1938.

Yorke, Alice: b. 1886; d. Flushing, NY, 22 Oct 1938.

Yorke, Augustus: b. 1860; d. 27 Dec 1939.

Yorke, Edith: b. Derby, Eng, 23 Dec 1867; d. Southgate, CA, 28 Jul 1934.

Yorke, Oswald: b. London, Eng, 24 Nov 1966; d. New York, NY, 25 Jan 1943.

Yorkney, John C.: b. Argentina, 1871; d. Fort Lee, NJ, 20 Aug 1941.

Yost, Herbert A. (Barry O'Moore): b. Harrison, OH, 1880; d. New York, NY, 23 Oct 1945.

Young, Clara Kimball: b. Chicago, IL, 6 Sep 1890; d. Woodland Hills, CA, 15 Oct 1960.

Young, Clifton (Bonedust): b. 1917; d. Los Angeles, CA, 10 Sep 1951.

Young, J. Arthur: b. Chicago, IL, 1880; d. Kew Gardens, NY, 14 Sep 1943.

Young, James: b. Baltimore, MD, 1 Jan 1875; d. 19??.

Young, John (Bull): b. ????; d. Los Angeles, CA, 2 Aug 1913.

Young, Marvin: b. 1903; d. Los Angeles, CA, 26 May 1993.

Young, Mary H.: b. 1857; d. Los Angeles, CA, 13 Nov 1934.

Young, Noah: b. Nevada, CO, 2 Feb 1887; d. Los Angeles, CA, 18 Apr 1958.

Young, Roland: b. London, Eng, 11 Nov 1887; d. New York, NY, 5 Jun 1953.

Young, Tammany: b. New York, NY, 1887; d. Los Angeles, CA, 26 Apr 1936.

Young, Walter: b. 1878; d. New York, NY, 18 Apr 1957.

Young Deer, James: b. Dakota City, NE, ????; d. New York, NY, ? Apr 1946.

Younge, Lucille: b. Lyons, Fr, 1892; d. Los Angeles, CA, 2 Aug 1934.

Yowlachie, Chief Daniel: b. Washington, 15 Aug 1891; d. Los Angeles, CA, 7 Mar 1966.

Yurka, Blanche: b. St. Paul, MN, 18 Jun 1887; d. New York, NY, 6 Jun 1974.

Yvoneck (Arthur Julian): b. 1873; d. Paris, Fr, 23 Apr 1929.

Z

Zabelle, Flora: b. Constantinople, Turkey, 1 Apr 1880; d. New York, NY, 7 Oct 1968.

Zacconi, Ermete: b. Italy, 14 Sep 1857; d. Viareggio, Italy, 14 Oct 1948.

Zampi, Mario: b. Rome, Italy, 1 Nov 1903; d. London, Eng, 2 Dec 1963.

Zany, King (Charles W. Dill): b. Ohio, 11 Jun 1889; d. Mojave, CA, 19 Feb 1939.

Zears, Marjorie: b. 1911; d. Los Angeles, CA, 9 Mar 1952.

Zecca, Ferdinand: b. Paris, Fr, 1864; d. Paris, Fr, 26 Mar 1947.

Zagel, Ferdinand: b. New Jersey, 1 Jan 1895; d. Los Angeles, CA, 16 Jun 1973.

Zeliff, Seymour: b. New Jersey, 16 May 1886; d. Los Angeles, CA, 17 Jan 1953.

Zellman, Tollie: b. Stockholm, Sweden, 31 Aug 1887; d. Stockholm, Sweden, 9 Oct 1964.

Ziegfeld Florenz: b. Chicago, IL, 21 Mar 1869; d. Los Angeles, CA, 22 Jul 1932.

Zilzer, Max: b. Hungary, 1868; d. 19??.

Zimina, Valentine: b. Bordeaux, Fr, 1899; d. Los Angeles, CA, 3 Dec 1928.

Zimmerly, Arline: b. ????; d. Venice, CA, ? Mar 1923.

Zirato, Bruno: b. Italy, 28 Sep 1884; d. New York, NY, 28 Nov 1972.

Zuber, Byrdine: b. Illinois, 18 Nov 1886; d. Glendale, CA, 5 Sep 1968.

Bibliography

Books

Briscoe, Johnson, *The Actor's Birthday Book.* New York: Moffat, Yard and Company, 1907.

Fox, Charles D. and Silver, Milton L., *Who's Who on the Screen.* New York: Ross Publishing Company, 1920.

Hanson, Patricia King, ed., *American Film Institute Catalog: Feature Films 1911-1920.* Berkeley: University of California Press, 1988.

Munden, Kenneth W., ed. *American Film Institute Catalog: Feature Films 1921-1930.* New York and London: R. R. Bowker Company, 1971.

Stewart, William, Jones, Ken D. and McClure, Arthur F. *International Film Necrology.* New York: Garland Publishing, 1981.

Truitt, Evelyn Mack, *Who Was Who on Screen.* New York: R. R. Bowker Company, 1983.

Directories

Motion Picture Studio Directory and Trade Annual. New York: Motion Picture News, 1918-1924.

New York Times Directory of the Film. New York: Arno Press, 1953.

The Picturegoer's Who's Who and Encyclopaedia. London: Odhams Press, 1933.

Standard Casting Directory, May 1923.

Who's Who in Filmland. London: Chapman and Hall, 1931.

Who's Who in the Film World. Los Angeles: Film World Publishing Company, 1914.

Periodicals

The Billboard
Classic Film Collector
Classic Images
Courier Journal (Louisville, KY)
Films in Review
The Hollywood Reporter
Los Angeles Times
Motion Picture
Motion Picture Classic
The New York Times
Photoplay
The Picturegoer
Picture Play
Screen Actor
Variety (Weekly & Daily)

Addendum

Alt, Al (Alexander): b. New York State, 8 Oct 1897; d. Santa Monica, CA, 8 Feb 1992.

Basquette, Lina: b. San Mateo, CA, 19 Apr 1907; d. Wheeling, WV, 30 Sep 1994.

Belle, Tula: b. Norway, 28 Jul 1906; d. Newport Beach, CA, 13 Oct 1992.

Concord, Lillian: b. Omaha, NE, 19 Jul 1884; d. Highland Park, CA, 6 Aug 1973.

Daniels, Eleanor: b. 1887; d. 18 Mar 1994.

Fernandez, Escamille: b. Connecticut, 6 Sep 1879; d. Los Angeles, CA, 31 Mar 1952.

Freeman, Helen: b. St. Louis, MO, 3 Aug 1886; d. Los Angeles, CA, 25 Dec 1960.

Heilman, Vada Lee: b. Illinois, 25 Dec 1907; d. Inglewood, CA, 13 Oct 1953.

Jowitt, Anthony: b. Leeds, Eng, 14 Sep 1900; d. Great Barrington, MA, 21 Nov 1977.

Lawrence, Wingold: b. London, Eng, 1874; d. London, Eng, 13 Mar 1938.

Lewis, Katherine: b. Newark, NJ, 7 Nov 1906; d. Van Nuys, CA, 25 Aug 1949.

Luxford, Nola: b. Hastings, N.Z., 1895; d. Pasadena, CA, 10 Oct 1994.

Lyle, Edith: b. 18??; d. Los Angeles, CA, 8 Jan 1982.

Marton, Alatia: b. Texas, 15 Sep 1894; d. Dallas, TX, 4 Jun 1972.

Miller, Winston: b. St. Louis, MO, 22 Jun 1910; d. Los Angeles, CA, 21 Jun 1994.

Neff, Pauline: b. Altoona, PA, 17 Apr 1885; d. Los Angeles, CA, 3 Jul 1951.

Renaud, Madeline: b. Paris, Fr, 21 Feb 1900; d. Paris, Fr, 23 Sep 1994.

Shipman, Barry: b. South Pasadena, CA, 24 Feb 1912; d. San Bernardino, CA, 12 Aug 1994.

Skavlan, Olaf: b. Oslo, Norway, 1885; d. San Francisco, CA, 2 Jun 1949.

About the Author

BILLY H. DOYLE is a graduate of Western University, Bowling Green, Kentucky. His graduate studies were completed at the University of Louisville in the field of elementary education. Mr. Doyle was a teacher in the Jefferson County (KY) Public Schools until his retirement. Since then his time has been devoted to film research and writing for several film publications.